CONTEMPORARY
FINANCIAL MANAGEMENT

Second Edition

CONTEMPORARY FINANCIAL MANAGEMENT

Second Edition

R. Charles Moyer
TEXAS TECH UNIVERSITY

James R. McGuigan
JRM INVESTMENTS

William J. Kretlow
UNIVERSITY OF HOUSTON

West Publishing Company
ST. PAUL ● NEW YORK ● LOS ANGELES ● SAN FRANCISCO

COPYEDITOR Mary Berry,
Naples Editing Service
ARTWORK Taly Design Group
COMPOSITION The Clarinda Company
COVER PHOTOGRAPH © Tom Tracy
COVER LAYOUT Taly Design Group

Immediately following p. R–22 a $5.00 rebate coupon for the Texas Instruments Professional Business Analysts Calculator (BA-55) is provided. The use of this calculator is illustrated in special sections throughout the book.

A study guide has been written to assist you in mastering concepts presented in this text. The study guide reinforces your understanding of these concepts by presenting them in condensed and concise form. Additional illustrations, examples, and problems are also included. The study guide is available from your local bookstore under the title *Study Guide to Accompany Contemporary Financial Management, Second Edition*, prepared by John D. Stowe and Edward L. Schrems.

COPYRIGHT © 1980 By WEST PUBLISHING CO.
COPYRIGHT © 1984 By WEST PUBLISHING CO.
50 West Kellogg Boulevard
P.O. Box 3526
St. Paul, Minnesota 55164

Printed in the United States of America

Library of Congress Cataloging in Publication Data

Moyer, R. Charles, 1945–
Contemporary financial management.

Includes bibliographies and index.
1. Corporations—Finance. 2. Business enterprises—
Finance. 1. McGuigan, James R. II. Kretlow, William.
III. Title.
HG4026.M68 1984   658.1'5   83-14767
IBSN 0-314-77931-0
2nd Reprint—1985

To Laura, Craig, and Sally
RCM

To the memory of my mother and father
JRM

To Wilbur, John, and James
WJK

TABLE OF CONTENTS

PREFACE

The managerial finance field has witnessed a number of significant changes during the 1970s and 1980s. Inflation has caused the firm's cost of funds (capital) to increase rather sharply. This, in turn, has forced firms to be more careful in the allocation of their resources. Also, corporate and other financial practioners are increasingly employing newer financial management techniques and sophisticated computer resources to aid in their decision making. At the same time, financial researchers have been making important theoretical strides. *Contemporary Financial Management, Second Edition,* incorporates these changes into a text designed primarily for an introductory course in managerial finance. The book also will be useful for management development programs and as a reference aid to practicing finance professionals.

Although we recognize that students will enter this course with a wide variety of backgrounds in mathematics, economics, accounting, and statistics, the only presumption we make regarding prior preparation is that all students will have had at least one course in accounting.

DISTINCTIVE FEATURES

The financial management text market has become increasingly crowded with competitive texts. Many of these texts are well written and provide adequate coverage of the important topics in financial management.

In writing this text, we, too, were concerned with providing a complete and well-written introduction to the field of financial management. In addition, we have created a text that is a unique improvement over current texts in three areas: organizational design, pedagogical aids to learning, and readability.

ORGANIZATIONAL DESIGN

Contemporary Financial Management (CFM) is organized around the objective of maximizing the value of the firm for its shareholders. This objective is introduced early in the book, and each major financial decision is linked to the impact it has on the value of the firm.

CFM also emphasizes the importance of risk-return tradeoffs, which must be made as a part of most financial decisions. The analysis of risk-return relationships is developed early in the book (Chapter 5) and is illustrated and emphasized throughout the text.

Other distinctive content features include the following:

1. **Extensive treatment of working capital management.** For many small and medium-sized companies, the management of working capital can present more challenges than any other area of financial management. To provide a more complete exposure to this area than is generally available in competitive texts, a thorough and up-to-date five-chapter section on working capital management is included.

2. **Emphasis on the impact of inflation.** During the 1970s and 1980s, finance practitioners were forced to learn how to operate in an inflationary environment. Inflation has had an impact on most areas of financial management. Therefore, this text contains frequent discussions on the impact of inflation.

3. **Introductory coverage of investment topics.** The majority of students taking a managerial finance course will not take a separate investments course. Yet these students are interested in and need to have an understanding of investment topics. Therefore, sections on understanding the financial pages, the operation of security markets, financial futures, and options are included.

4. **Attention to the special problems of financial management in public and not-for-profit organizations.** Many business school students take positions outside the private sector. Although many of the principles and techniques of financial management are equally applicable in the public and not-for-profit sectors, financial decision making in these areas does pose some special problems of analysis. These problems are addressed in Chapter 25.

5. **Attention to problems of international financial management.** In an economy that is increasingly affected by international trade, it is important that finance students be aware of some of the most important dimensions of international finance. The inclusion of this material (primarily in Chapter 25) is consistent with the emphasis of the business school accrediting group (AACSB) on internationalizing the business school curriculum.

6. **Extensive development of the cash flow estimation process in capital budgeting.** Perhaps the most important step in the capital budgeting process is the estimation of cash flows for potential projects. Whereas this topic often is given only a casual treatment in competing texts, *CFM* devotes an entire chapter to this important area, with a detailed discussion of the impact of recent tax law changes that affect the capital budgeting decision.

PEDAGOGICAL AIDS

Contemporary Financial Management has been carefully designed to assist student learning and to stimulate student interest. Accordingly, the following distinctive pedagogical features are included:

1. **Financial Dilemmas.** Each chapter begins with an illustration of a financial management problem faced by a firm or individual. The majority of these lead-ins come from real-firm situations—including Penn Central, Washington Public Power System, W. T. Grant, Chrysler, Franklin National Bank,

Lockheed, Bendix, Braniff International, Pan American, International Harvester, Billie Sol Estes, and other recognizable firms or institutions. These examples tend to focus on financial problems in the topic area discussed in the chapter in order to highlight the importance of learning sound financial management principles. They have been extensively revised and updated since the first edition.

2. Focus on Corporate Practice Examples. Throughout the text we have included sections detailing how specific firms approach particular problems. Many of these have been written by senior financial executives. These are designed to bridge the gap between textbook theory and actual practice. They show the book's readers that the tools and techniques discussed in *CFM* are actually being used in day-to-day financial decision making. In this edition we have revised and updated many of the "Focus on Corporate Practice" examples from the first edition and added ten new examples.

3. Integrative Problems Cases. Each major part in the book includes one or more integrative minicases that illustrate and apply the most important concepts of the preceding chapters. These minicases have been pretested and were found to be an extremely useful tool to the help the book's users assimilate the material in the chapters. They have been revised from the first edition to retain their classroom integrity.

4. Chapter Glossaries. Each chapter begins with a glossary of important new terms that are discussed in the chapter. This placement of the glossary in the beginning of the chapter insures that students will not be frustrated by encountering concepts before they have been defined. An index to the glossary is provided at the end of the text.

5. Extensive Use of Examples. A large number of examples to illustrate important concepts and techniques is contained in each chapter. The majority of the examples come from actual firm situations. These examples have been revised and updated for this new edition. The extensive use of examples clearly shows students how financial principles are used in everyday business practice.

6. Problems and Questions. Each chapter includes a complete set of problems and questions keyed to the most important issues and techniques in that chapter. Because we feel that end-of-chapter problems are an extremely important teaching and learning device, this text has one of the largest end-of-chapter problem sets available. Most concepts are illustrated with more than one problem to provide additional flexibility for the instructor and in-depth learning opportunities for the students. Answers to selected end-of-chapter problems are provided at the end of the book. The end-of-chapter questions and problem sets have been increased in number by over 50 percent compared with the first edition.

7. End-of-Chapter References. A list of selected references that cover major pieces of theoretical and applications-oriented literature in the area is included in each chapter. These references form a basis for extended reading or research by students. They have been updated to include the results of much recent financial research.

8. Calculator Applications. At the ends of Chapters 3, 4, 5, 8, and 10 we have provided "Calculator Applications" sections, which describe how to use the Texas Instruments Professional Business Analyst (BA-55) calculator to solve many of the problems encountered in the text. This calculator is representative of other financial calculators which are available. Since it is not feasible to illustrate the use of all available calculators in the text, the BA-55 calculator was chosen because of its extensive capabilities and relatively low price. A coupon good for a $5 rebate on the BA-55 calculator is provided at the end of the book. The "Calculator Applications" sections give professors the *option* to do much of the teaching for the course with the aid of a sophisticated financial calculator. Even if the course is not taught with a student calculator requirement, many students will find these sections to be of great value in learning to use calculators they have purchased on their own.

9. **Complete Set of Ancillary Materials.** A complete set of ancillary materials is available to supplement the text, including the following:

- The Instructor's Manual contains solutions to the end-of-chapter questions and problems

- A Test Bank containing nearly 1,000 multiple choice questions and additional problems is available to adopters.

- A set of Transparency Masters of the most important tables and graphs in the book is available to adopters.

- A set of Demonstration Problems in transparency master form is available to adopters. The problems parallel each major example developed in the text.

- A pull-out set of abbreviated interest tables is included in each book for test purposes.

- *Cases in Financial Management* (2nd edition) by Vincent P. Apilado, Jerry B. Poe, Ronald J. Kudla, George W. Gallinger, and Glenn V. Henderson, Jr., is available from West Publishing and includes an Instructor's Manual.

10. **Student Study Guide.** Professors John D. Stowe of the University of Missouri–Columbia and Edward L. Schrems of the University of Oklahoma have written an excellent student study guide containing a detailed chapter outline, solved true-false questions, and a large number of solved numerical problems.

11. **Two-Color Presentation.** The use of two colors in this edition enhances the student's learning of important concepts. Key equations are printed in color. Problems containing check answers at the end of the book are numbered in color. In addition, the figures and other artwork in the book are highlighted with the effective use of color.

READABILITY

One of the major achievements of the first edition of *CFM* was the creation of a uniformly readable text. Both professors and students have found the text presentation to be easy to follow, even when difficult concepts are presented. The frequent use of real-world examples maintains student interest and enhances learning. We have worked hard to be sure that the second edition of *CFM* retains the reputation of being the most readable text available.

MAJOR CHANGES IN THIS EDITION

This edition has been extensively updated and revised along the lines suggested by first edition users. The *major* changes in this edition are:

1. A new chapter (Chapter 5) dealing with an analysis of risk and return concepts has been added to complement and more fully develop the valuation concepts introduced in Chapter 4.

2. Separate chapters dealing with mergers and acquisitions (Chapter 23) and business failure and reorganization (Chapter 24) have been developed. These chapters have been extensively updated to include a description of the impact of the Bankruptcy Reform Act of 1978 on the bankruptcy process.

3. A new appendix (Appendix 12A) that introduces the concept of interest rate futures and illustrates their use by financial managers who wish to control interest rate risk has been added at the end of the cost of capital chapter (Chapter 12).

4. A new appendix (Appendix 13A) that summarizes some of the major theoretical work in the area of capital structure analysis has been added at the end of the capital structure chapter (Chapter 13).

5. An appendix (Appendix 18A) that introduces key determinants of the term structure of interest rates is included following the first working capital management chapter (Chapter 18).

6. The material formerly contained in Chapter 11 of the first edition ("Raising Funds in the Capital Markets") has been integrated into Chapters 2, 16, and 17 of this edition.

7. Appendix 2A has been updated to fully reflect the tax law changes brought about by the Economic Recovery Tax Act (ERTA) of 1981 and the Tax Equity and Fiscal Responsibility Act (TEFRA) of 1982.

8. "Calculator Applications" sections have been added at the ends of Chapters 3, 4, 5, 8, and 10.

9. Funds flow analysis concepts are now contained exclusively in Chapter 8. Chapter 8 has been completely revised to emphasize the financial planning process, pro forma financial statements, and the tools of financial planning.

10. The effects of the ERTA (1981) and TEFRA (1982) have been incorporated into the chapters dealing with capital budgeting (Chapters 9, 10, and 11). For teaching flexibility, many of the problems at the ends of the capital budgeting chapters offer the choice of solving them using Accelerated Cost Recovery System (ACRS) depreciation or straight line depreciation.

11. The equivalent annual annuity approach to handling the unequal lives problem for mutually exclusive investments has been added to Appendix 10A.

12. The certainty equivalent approach to capital budgeting risk analysis has been added to Chapter 11. The discussion of sensitivity analysis in capital budgeting has been expanded and now includes a discussion of the use of sensitivity curves and electronic worksheets such as VISICALC®.

13. The determinants of break points in the marginal cost of capital schedule have been more fully developed.

14. The effects of ERTA and TEFRA are fully incorporated in the leasing chapter, and the lease-buy analysis example has been modified to include these tax effects. Safe harbor leases and finance leases also are discussed.

15. The cash management chapter (Chapter 19) has been updated to reflect new developments in this area, including wire deposits, depository transfer checks, preauthorized checks, and bank-offered money market accounts.

16. In the chapter dealing with accounts receivable management (Chapter 20), the opportunity cost treatment of an additional investment in receivables has been changed to reflect the full amount of the receivables increase.

17. The international financial management material in Chapter 25 has been expanded to incorporate the risks associated with both foreign trade and foreign investment.

18. Interest tables have been expanded to cover 60 years. This will allow instructors to work with monthly compounding (such as 1 percent per month) for reasonably long periods of time. An abbreviated pull out set of interest tables is provided with each book for test purposes.

19. Ten new "Focus on Corporate Practice" examples have been added to this edition, and those that carry over from the first edition have been updated where necessary.

20. "Financial Dilemmas" have been revised and updated.

21. There has been over a 50 percent increase in the number of end-of-chapter problems and questions in this edition.

22. All problems have been revised to use a 40 percent marginal ordinary tax rate. This enhances the students's understanding of the tax effects of various financial decisions and simplifies many of the required calculations.

23. Each major part of the book begins with a schematic diagram and a summary description of how the chapters contained in that part contribute to the overall firm goal of shareholder wealth maximization. This reinforces the importance of the wealth maximization objective as it relates to various financial decisions made in the firm.

In addition to these major changes and additions, there have been literally hundreds of other small changes and an updating of the material from the first edition. Many of these changes were based on the excellent suggestions of first edition users.

ORGANIZATION AND INTENDED USE

CFM is organized into eight major parts. Part 1 defines the finance function and discusses the institutional environment facing financial decision makers. Part 2 develops the theory of valuation, risk-return analysis, and the tools of financial mathematics. Part 3 consists of three chapter that deal with financial analysis. Part 4 presents the capital investment decision, emphasizing both the theoretical and the practical aspects of capital budgeting. Part 5 deals with the determinants of an optimal capital structure, the cost of capital, and the firm's dividend policy. Part 6 describes the sources of intermediate- and long-term funds. Part 7 consists of a five-chapter sequence covering the important area of working capital management. Finally, Part 8 includes chapters dealing with mergers, bankruptcy, international financial management, and financial decision making in the public and not-for-profit sectors.

Those instructors who wish to cover topics in an order other than that provided in the text will find it quite easy to make adjustments. For example, many instructors prefer to cover working capital management early in the course. They should find no difficulty in moving all or a portion of Chapters 18 through 22 to a position following Chapters 3, 4, or 5. Similarly, some instructors may prefer to cover the area of financial analysis later in the course. Accordingly, Chapters 6 through 8 can be moved easily to another location that is more consistent with the instructor's teaching style and objectives.

This book is designed for use in a typical 3–semester hour (or the equivalent in the quarter system) course in financial management. Typically, within the constraints of this time limit, it is not possible to fully cover the material in Chapters 23 through 25. This material is usually left for a second financial management course—often with a case orientation. Also, some instructors may wish to defer the dividend policy chapter (Chapter 14), the capital structure chapter (Chapter 13), and/or the leasing material in Chapter 15 until a later course. Finally, some schools cover inventory policy in a production (or similar) course. In these cases, Chapter 21 either can be omitted or covered only briefly.

Even though the entire book may not be used in any 1–semester course, we believe it is important for students to have easy access to a comprehensive finance text—both for current and future course work and for later reference in their business careers. Fortunately, the cost differential between a text like *CFM* and other abbreviated texts is very small.

ACKNOWLEDGMENTS

The authors wish to acknowledge the helpful comments provided by many of our first edition users. We are particularly grateful for the careful reviews and suggestions made by the following individuals:

Don Bowlin	Kamal Haddad	Keith B. Johnson
Dorothy Cassetta	Charles Harper	Charles P. Jones
Robert Chatfield	Delbert Hastings	Kee Kim
John Crockett	Pat Hays	Thomas Klaasen
Bill Dukes	Shantaram P. Hedge	Donita Koval
Fred Ebeid	Robert Hehre	Keith Laycock
Mike Ferri	George Hettenhouse	David Lindsley
Jane Finley	L. Dean Hiebert	Charles Linke
Richard Gendreau	K. P. Hill	Wayne M. Marr
Jim Gentry	Shalom Hochman	Z. Lew Melynk
Michael Gombola	Thomas Howe	Richard Meyer

Robert A. Olsen	William J. Regan	David Upton
Susan M. Phillips	Charles T. Rini	Howard E. Van Anken
Mario Picconi	Richard Sapp	John M. Wachowicz, Jr.
Ralph Pope	Bernard A. Shinkel	Charlie Wade
Dwight Porter	Phil Sisneros	J. Daniel Williams
Robert Porter	Richard J. Teweles	Richard Zock
Kelly Price	George Ulseth	J. Kenton Zumwalt

In addition, we wish to acknowledge the assistance of the many business professionals who have reviewed various aspects of the text material and/or supplied us with the material for our "Financial Dilemma" and "Focus on Corporate Practice" examples:

Richard H. Brock	Carl J. Lange	Thomas R. Mongan
Roy V. Campbell	Martin H. Lange	Robert B. Morris III
Norman Dmuchowski	Lewis Lehr	M. W. Ramsey
Stephen H. Grace	C. Londa	William J. Regan
Samuel C. Hadaway	Paul MacAvoy	Julie Salamon
R. Lee Haney	Frank Mastrapasqua	Kenneth Schwartz
Raymond A. Hay	John H. Maxheim	Terry J. Winders
Lawrence Ingrassia		

We are also indebted to Wayne State University, the University of Houston, Lehigh University, the University of New Mexico, and Texas Tech University for the considerable support they provided. We thank Betty Heisser, Pat Burns, and Tanya Terry for their typing assistance. We also owe thanks to our fellow faculty members at these universities for the encouragement and assistance they provided on a continuing basis during the preparation of the manuscript. We appreciate the support provided by Texas Instruments, and especially Elaine Kaufman in the preparation of the "Calculator Applications" sections of the book. We thank Mary Berry for her careful and thorough copy editing of the manuscript.

Finally, we wish to express our thanks to the members of the West Publishing Company staff. We are particularly appreciative of the total project support provided by Ken Zeigler and the marketing support provided by Kristen McCarthy. Lenore Franzen, our production editor, did a superb job of designing and supervising the production of a most attractive and technically precise text. She was a delight to work with. Most of all we would like to thank our editor, Mary Schiller, who has provided a continual flow of excellent ideas for this project. Her high performance standards and in-depth knowledge of publishing have been invaluable in the development of this text.

PART ONE

Introduction

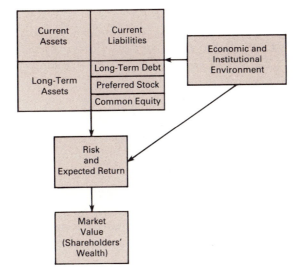

Part I of the text provides an overview introduction to the field of financial management. Chapter 1 discusses the relationship between finance and other business disciplines, the organization of the financial management function in a firm, and the history of the financial management field. This chapter also introduces the overall objective of the firm—shareholder wealth maximization. Chapter 2 looks at the relationship between the firm and the economic/institutional environment. Economic and institutional factors have a major impact on the expected returns and the risk of these returns generated by the firm. Risk and expected return are two of the key determinants of the value of a firm and its securities. Appendix 2A highlights some aspects of Federal income tax law that are relevant to many financial management decisions.

CHAPTER 1

The Finance Function: An Overview

A FINANCIAL DILEMMA

Problems in Financial Management

- In 1978 the Coronado Credit Union, a relatively small institution, lost over $400,000 while investing in "risk-free" securities.

- In 1978 National Airlines stock increased from $15 per share to over $40 per share in a little over 6 months.

- In the mid-1970s New York City experienced a severe financial crisis, which necessitated a substantial Federal loan guarantee to that city.

- During the 1960s Lockheed decided to go ahead with its L-1011 jet transport project in spite of unfavorable cash flow projections.

- In 1970 Penn Central Railway went bankrupt.

- During the late 1950s Billie Sol Estes managed to swindle some of this country's largest financial institutions out of more than $25 million in "secured" loans.

- In 1973 Scientific Resources, an actively merging, growth-oriented conglomerate, failed only 5 years after having embarked on what appeared to be a reasonable and sensible growth strategy.

- In 1982 Braniff Airlines crash landed in financial failure, shortly after embarking on an aggressive expansion program.

- In October 1979 underwriters of IBM's $1 billion debt issue lost an estimated $15 million on the issue they had earlier fought hard to get control of.

Each of these situations was the direct result of financial decision making. Financial management is not an abstract field of study. Financial decisions made within various enterprises—whether large or small; international, national, or local; profit seeking or not for profit—help to determine the kinds of products and services we consume, their price, availability, and quality. In short, financial decision making has results that are felt throughout our entire economy.

The situations described above pose a number of questions in financial management which are examined in this text.

GLOSSARY OF NEW TERMS

Capital expenditure   the amount of money spent to purchase a long-term asset, such as a piece of equipment. This cash outlay is generally expected to result in a flow of future cash benefits extending beyond 1 year in time. (Also called *capital investment*.)

Capital structure   the relative amount of permanent debt, preferred stock, and common equity used to finance a firm.

Cost of capital   the cost of funds which are supplied to a firm. (Also called the *investor's required rate of return*.) It provides a basis for choosing among various capital investment projects.

Dividend   the amount of earnings that a firm pays to its stockholders. Dividends may be paid in the form of cash or as securities.

Inflation   a generalized increase in the overall price level for goods and services.

Wealth maximization   the primary objective used to guide financial management decision making. *Shareholder wealth* is measured as the market value of the shareholders' common stock holdings.

Working capital   the investment a firm makes in short-term assets, primarily cash, marketable securities, accounts receivable, and inventories.

INTRODUCTION

The field of financial management is an exciting and challenging one. Students who choose to major in finance will find a wide range of rewarding job opportunities open in the fields of corporate financial management, investments analysis and management, banking, real estate, insurance, and the public sector—to name only a few broad areas of potential career opportunities. Students who do not choose to major in finance still will be confronted with important financial decisions—both in their career and in their personal life—on a nearly daily basis.

The importance and relevance of the skills that can be learned in this finance course are apparent from the results of a recent survey of graduates of business schools. *By a wide margin, these executives indicated that the courses taken in financial management were the most useful courses in their business school curriculum.*[1]

---

[1]John A. Pollock, J. R. Bartol, B. C. Sherony, and G. R. Carnaham, "Executives' Perceptions of Future MBA Programs." *Collegiate News and Views* (Spring 1983): 23–25.

Any business—whether large or small, profit seeking or not for profit—is a financial concern, and as such its success or failure depends in a large part on the quality of its financial decisions. Thus, financial management is an exciting area of business administration. Nearly every key decision made by a firm's managers has important financial implications, and managers daily face questions like the following:

- Will a particular investment be profitable?
- Where will the funds come from to finance the investment?
- Does the firm have adequate cash or access to cash—through bank borrowing agreements, for example—to meet its daily operating needs?
- What kind of credit should be granted the firm's customers, and which customers should be given credit privileges?
- How much inventory should be held?
- Is a merger or acquisition advisable?
- How should profits be used or distributed? That is, what is the optimal dividend policy?
- In trying to arrive at the best financial management decisions, how should risk and return be balanced?

This text presents an introduction to the theory, institutional background, and analytical tools essential for proper decision making in these and related areas.

Chapter 1 explores the following basic questions in the field of financial management:

- How does the financial management function draw upon other disciplines—specifically, economics and accounting—to provide a framework for analysis, a set of tools, and usable data?
- What goals and objectives guide financial decision making? That is, what should the financial manager try to achieve for the firm and its owners?
- How is the financial management function organized in a typical firm?

The remaining sections of this chapter present a brief history of the financial management field, discuss current topics of concern in financial management, and outline the organization of the text as a whole.

FINANCIAL MANAGEMENT AND OTHER DISCIPLINES

Financial management is not a totally independent area in business administration. Instead, it draws heavily on related disciplines and fields of study. The most important of these are *accounting* and *economics*; in the latter discipline, *macroeconomics* and *microeconomics* are of special significance. *Marketing, production,* and the study of *quantitative methods* also have an impact on the financial management field. Each of these is discussed in the following sections.

ACCOUNTING

Financial managers often turn to accounting data to assist them in making decisions. Generally a company's accountants are responsible for developing financial reports and measures that assist its managers in assessing the past performance and future direction of the firm and in meeting certain legal obligations, such as the payment of taxes. The accountant's role includes the development of financial statements such as the *balance sheet,* the *income statement,* and the *sources and uses of funds statement* (also called the *statement of changes in financial position*).

In contrast, financial managers are primarily concerned with a firm's *cash flows,* since they often determine the feasibility of certain investment and financing decisions. The financial manager refers to accounting data when making future resource allocation decisions concerning long-term investments, when managing current investments in working capital, and when making a number of other financial decisions, for example, determining the most appropriate capital structure and identifying the best and most timely sources of funds needed to support the firm's investment programs.

In many small and medium-sized firms the accounting function and the financial management function may be handled by the same person or group of persons. In such cases the distinctions identified above may become blurred.

ECONOMICS

There are two areas of economics with which the financial manager must be familiar: *microeconomics* and *macroeconomics.* Microeconomics deals with the economic decisions of individuals, households, and firms, while macroeconomics looks at the economy as a whole.

The typical firm is heavily influenced by the overall performance of the economy and is dependent upon the money and capital markets for investment funds. Thus, financial managers should recognize and understand how monetary policies affect the cost of funds and the availability of credit. Financial managers also should be versed in fiscal policy and how it affects the economy. What the economy can be expected to do in the future is a crucial factor in generating sales forecasts as well as other types of forecasts.

The financial manager uses microeconomics when developing decision models that are likely to lead to the most efficient and successful modes of operation within the firm. Specifically, the financial manager may utilize the basic economic notion from microeconomic theory of setting marginal cost equal to marginal revenue when making long-term investment decisions *(capital budgeting)* and when managing cash, inventories, and accounts receivable *(working capital management).*

MARKETING, PRODUCTION, AND QUANTITATIVE METHODS

Figure 1–1 depicts the relationship between financial management and its primary supportive disciplines. Marketing, production, and quantitative

FIGURE 1–1   **Impact of Other Disciplines on Financial Management**

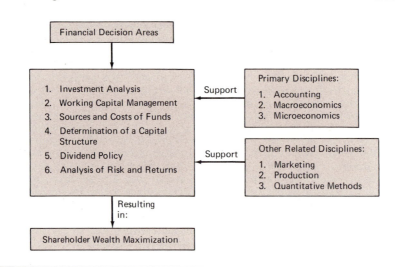

methods are indirectly related to the key day-to-day decisions made by financial managers.

For example, financial managers should consider the impact of new product development and promotion plans made in the marketing area, since these plans will require capital outlays and have an impact on the firm's projected cash flows. Similarly, changes in the production process may necessitate capital expenditures, which the firm's financial managers must evaluate and finance. And, finally, the tools of analysis developed in the quantitative methods area frequently are helpful in analyzing complex financial management problems.

FINANCIAL MANAGEMENT OBJECTIVES

Decision making in the financial management area requires an understanding of the objectives of the firm. This section defines a set of workable objectives that have been widely applied in making financial decisions.

PROFIT MAXIMIZATION

It is easy to assume that profit maximization is a primary objective of financial management. After all, it is the predominant objective of microeconomic models, and the marginal decision-making rules implied by this objective can be very useful to the financial manager in handling certain specific problems. Unfortunately, however, this objective has a number of limitations.

First, the standard microeconomic model of profit maximization is *static*; that is, it lacks a time dimension. Specifically, the profit maximization objective provides no explicit basis for comparing long-term and short-term profits. Major decisions made by financial managers, however, *must* reflect the time dimension. For example, capital expenditure decisions, which are central to the finance function, have a long-term impact on the performance of the firm. Financial managers must constantly make tradeoffs between short-run and long-run profits in conjunction with these long-term decisions.

The second limitation has to do with the definition of profits. Should a firm attempt to maximize the *dollar amount* of profits or the *rate* of profit? If the latter is chosen, what specific rate should be emphasized—profit in relation to sales, total assets, or shareholders' equity? What measure of profits should be used—the readily available measure of accounting profits or the economist's broader definition of profits, which includes (among other things) the opportunity cost of funds committed by the owners of an enterprise as a business expense? (This definition is an important concept, but it is very difficult to calculate.)

The third problem associated with this objective is that it provides no real way for the financial manager to consider the risk associated with alternative decisions. For example, two projects generating identical future expected revenues and requiring identical outlays may be vastly different with respect to their *degree of risk*. The financial manager should attempt to incorporate risk considerations into any analysis of the advisability of certain resource allocations.

These three flaws in the profit maximization objective make it necessary for the financial manager to consider other objectives as well. Some of these are discussed in the following sections.

SHAREHOLDER WEALTH MAXIMIZATION

The objective of shareholder wealth maximization stresses the maximization of the *present value* of all future benefits the owners (that is, shareholders) of a firm can expect to receive. *Present value* is defined as the value *today* of some future benefit or stream of payments. It takes into account the returns that are available from alternative investment opportunities during a specific time period.[2]

Shareholder wealth is measured by the market value of the shareholders' common stock holdings. *Market value* is defined as the price at which the stock trades in the marketplace, such as on the New York Stock Exchange. Thus, total shareholder wealth equals the number of shares outstanding times the market price per share.

The objective of shareholder wealth maximization has a number of distinct advantages. First, it is conceptually possible to determine whether a particular financial decision is consistent with this objective. If a decision made by a firm has the effect of increasing the market price of the firm's stock, it is a good decision. If it appears that a certain action will not achieve this result, the action should not be taken (at least not voluntarily).

Second, shareholder wealth maximization is an *impersonal* objective. Stockholders who may be offended by a firm's policies are free to sell their shares *under more favorable terms* (that is, at a higher price) *than are available under any other strategy* and invest their funds elsewhere.

---

[2]Present value concepts are discussed in detail in Chapter 3.

Third, this objective allows the financial manager to consider the elements of both timing and risk when making various decisions. (This advantage will become more apparent later during the discussion of capital expenditure analysis.)

For the reasons cited, the shareholder wealth maximization objective has become the preferred objective in financial management. Nevertheless, in the process of making decisions that are designed to maximize shareholder wealth, financial managers often use the marginal decision rules from microeconomics.

SOCIAL OBJECTIVES

Today's firms are often required to exercise a sense of social responsibility in dealing with a number of constituent groups, including employees, suppliers, customers, and community neighbors. In many cases these social responsibilities take on almost as much importance as laws and other formal obligations. The shareholder wealth maximization objective does not deny the existence of these obligations, and financial managers should attempt to allocate resources efficiently for these purposes. The "Focus on Corporate Practice" example at the end of this chapter presents the businessperson's perspective on social responsibility.

ORGANIZATION OF THE
FINANCIAL MANAGEMENT FUNCTION

Most firms distribute the financial management function among a number of different groups, each of which is responsible for some aspect of the firm's financial activity. The financial management area is typically headed by the *financial vice-president*, who reports directly to the president of the firm. Large corporations may have several financial vice-presidents, and one of them is normally designated the *chief financial officer* to whom the other financial vice-presidents report. Various sections within the finance department are headed by managers or supervisors, with other personnel bearing such broad titles as *financial analyst* and *credit analyst*. Some companies also use the titles *budget analyst* and *planning analyst*.

The departments, or *sections*, usually found in the financial management area of a firm include the following:

- **The operating budget section.** This group is responsible for preparing and updating the firm's operating budgets, and its personnel work closely with the accounting department. In companies having a number of plants and divisions, this section can serve an important coordinating function.

- **The capital budgeting section.** This section is responsible for preparing capital expenditure analyses. Depending on the company, this group also can be responsible for linking engineering and purchasing personnel with top financial and general management.

- **The financial planning section.** Most companies have a group of persons (or at least one person) responsible for analyzing financing alternatives. This group or person may be involved with analyzing financial market conditions and interest coverages and coordinating with investment bankers.

• The short-term financing section. This group is usually responsible for managing the company's short-term finances and normally reports to the company treasurer. Its personnel are involved in working closely with the company's bankers and may be concerned with short-term investments in the money market.

• The credit section. Most companies have a group or department responsible for determining the extent and type of credit the firm will extend to its customers. Whereas this group may be responsible for performing financial analyses, it is often located in the marketing area of the firm because of its close relationship with sales.

• The financial relations section. Many large companies have on their staff a person who is at least partially responsible for working with institutional investors, bond rating agencies, stockholders, and the general financial community.

Figure 1–2 depicts the organization of the financial management function in the typical firm.

FIGURE 1–2   Organization of the Financial Management Function

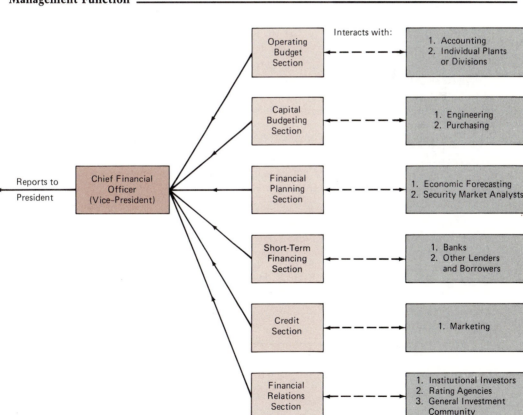

A BRIEF HISTORY OF THE
FINANCIAL MANAGEMENT FIELD

Prior to the 1930s the field of financial management basically was confined to descriptive discussions of the various financial markets and the securities traded in those markets.[3] Thus, finance as a field of study traditionally focused on the liabilities and stockholders' equity side of the balance sheet and on fund raising.

The field underwent a number of significant changes during the Great Depression, when it became more involved with legal matters of bankruptcy, reorganization, and government regulation. Finance texts written during the 1930s and 1940s often devoted many chapters to bankruptcy-related matters, such as reorganization and liquidation.

Through the 1940s and into the 1950s the teaching of financial management continued to be basically qualitative and descriptive. During the 1950s, however, a number of significant changes took place in the field. First, financial management was expanded to include the asset side of the balance sheet, or the uses of a firm's funds. In addition, the application of discounted cash flow techniques to the problems of capital expenditure analysis was being refined and perfected. Also, financial researchers were making significant breakthroughs in developing techniques for measuring the cost of capital and valuing financial assets. Progress in both the capital budgeting and the cost of capital areas has continued to the present day.

During the 1960s mathematical models using statistical and optimization techniques were applied to the allocation of current assets, such as cash, accounts receivable and inventories, and fixed assets. Throughout the 1960s and 1970s the trend continued toward a more quantitative and precise concept of financial management. Another important emphasis of the last two

TABLE 1–1   **Evolution of Financial Management**

Period	Focus
Pre-1930	Descriptive emphasis on financial markets and securities. Little attention to asset management.
1930s and 1940s	Focus on legal matters dealing with bankruptcy and reorganization and the effects of newly emerging government regulation.
1950s	Increasing emphasis on asset management. Significant theoretical developments in valuation theory.
1960s	Application of mathematical models to allocation of current and fixed assets. Additional theoretical developments in valuation theory, cost of capital, dividend policy, and risk analysis.
1970s	Development of more precise theories and measures of risk. Application of these theories to investment analysis and valuation.
1980s	Increasing application of computer technology to assist in financial decision making.

---

[3]The terms *financial management, managerial finance, corporate finance,* and *business finance* are virtually equivalent and are used interchangeably. Most financial managers, however, seem to prefer either *financial management* or *managerial finance.*

decades has been the integration of specific finance topics with a risk-adjusted model in an attempt to maximize the value of the firm and achieve shareholder wealth maximization.

During the decade of the 1980s there will be an increasing emphasis on applying computer (and computer-related) technology to assist in financial decision making. In addition, financial managers will become more aggressive in managing the assets of the firm in response to an environment characterized by high interest rates.

Over the past 50 years financial management has developed into a more rigorous discipline, and today's employers expect business and finance graduates to possess a solid working knowledge of modern finance techniques. Table 1–1 summarizes the most significant developments in the evolution of financial management.

CURRENT TOPICS IN
FINANCIAL MANAGEMENT

Virtually every current issue of the professional journals devoted to finance contains at least one, and often several, articles dealing with some aspect of *risk*. This has become a major topic of concern for finance professionals. In a broad sense, risk is related to the *potential deviation from expectations* and is closely tied to *uncertainty*. In fact, most financial analysts use the terms *risk* and *uncertainty* interchangeably. This text emphasizes the analysis of risk in financial decision making. Consequently, the text includes a discussion of modern portfolio theory and the capital asset pricing model as applied to corporate finance.

One aspect of risk that is especially important today is *inflation*. During the 1950s and early 1960s the United States experienced only mild inflation, but in the mid-1970s and early 1980s inflation rates reached double-digit proportions (for example, 11 percent in 1974 and over 12 percent in 1980). Figure 1–3 shows the changes in the Consumer Price Index since 1967.

Inflation has serious effects on financial management decision making. For example, suppose a manufacturing company is considering investing in a new plant. The investment is expected to earn a 10 percent return; that is, for each $1,000 invested, the company expects to receive $100 per year from the plant. The decision to invest in the new plant depends on a number of factors, and one that is of particular importance is concerned with how much of the $100 per year in benefits will be required to pay for the $1,000 in funds used. In other words, how much of the benefits will have to be used to pay the cost of capital? If inflation is low (and this is reflected in low interest rates) and the company can acquire its funds for 6 percent, it might consider the investment. But if inflation is high and the company has to pay over 10 percent for the funds it needs to make the initial investment, the new plant may not be profitable. Thus, inflation increases the cost of the firm's capital, thereby potentially limiting investment and growth.

In a broader sense, inflation has a profound effect on nearly all economic decisions. For example, it can cause severe problems with the reliability

11

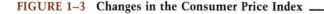

FIGURE 1–3   **Changes in the Consumer Price Index**

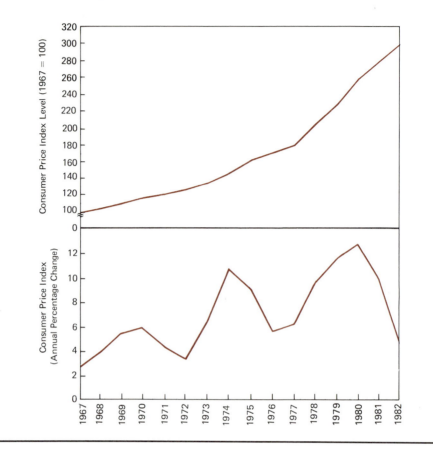

of accounting data that finance professionals use and on which taxes are based.

ORGANIZATION OF THE TEXT

This text provides an introduction to both analytical tools and descriptive materials that are useful in financial management. Because this is an introductory-level text, however, it does *not* attempt to make the reader an expert in every aspect of financial decision making. Instead, it is intended to do the following:

▪ Acquaint the reader with the types of decisions faced by financial managers.

▪ Develop a framework for analyzing these decisions in a systematic manner.

▪ Provide the reader with the background necessary to pursue more advanced readings and courses in financial management.

Although the subject matter in this text is divided into a series of parts, it should be noted that the various types of financial decisions are interrelated and should not be considered in isolation from one another.

Part I Introduction   Chapter 1 examines the financial goals of the firm and the role of the financial manager in the decision-making process. Chapter 2 provides an overview of the business environment in the United States and discusses the various forms of business organization, the role of financial institutions in the economy, and the impact of government regulations and taxes. Chapter 2 also introduces the general problem of the risk and return tradeoffs that financial managers face.

Part II Determinants of valuation   Chapter 3 develops the concepts of discounting, compounding, and present value. These concepts are used in the valuation of securities and in the evaluation of capital expenditure projects that are expected to provide benefits over a number of years. Chapter 4 considers the determinants of the valuation of a firm's shares of common stock and other long-term securities it may issue. The chapter builds explicit valuation models for each major type of security issued by a firm and relates these models to the key financial decisions made in the firm. The valuation concept is a central theme that is carried throughout the text and related to all key financial decisions. Chapter 5 provides a comprehensive introduction to the concept of risk in finance and the relationship between risk, required returns, and the shareholder wealth maximization goal of the firm.

Part III Financial analysis   Chapters 6 through 8 present some basic tools that are useful in financial analysis. Chapter 6 considers various ratios that can be used in evaluating the financial performance of a firm. Chapter 7 develops the concepts of operating and financial leverage and analyzes their effects on the firm's risk, and Chapter 8 examines the use of various types of financial planning methods, including the cash budget and the funds flow statement.

Part IV The capital investment decision   This portion of the text focuses on capital expenditures, that is, investments in long-term assets. Chapters 9 and 10 present the fundamentals of capital budgeting, namely, the process of investing in long-term assets. Chapter 9 deals with the measurement of the cash flows (benefits and costs) associated with long-term investment projects; Chapter 10 considers various decision-making criteria that can be used when choosing projects that will maximize the value of the firm. Chapter 11 extends the concepts developed in Chapter 10 by considering some of the decision-making techniques that attempt to deal with the problem of the risk associated with a specific project's cash flow.

Part V The cost of capital, capital structure, and dividend policy   Chapter 12 illustrates the principles of measuring a firm's cost of capital. The cost of funds to a firm is an important input in the capital budgeting process. Chapter 13 addresses the relationship of the cost of capital to the firm's capital structure. Chapter 14 discusses the factors that influence the choice of a dividend policy and the impact of various dividend policies on the value of a firm.

Part VI Sources of intermediate and long-term funds   This part of the text describes the characteristics of the major sources of intermediate and long-term funds. Specifically, Chapter 15 deals with term loans and leases; Chapter 16 with long-term debt, preferred stock, and common stock; and Chapter 17 with various types of convertible securities and warrants.

Part VII The management of working capital   Chapters 18 through 22 examine the management of a firm's current asset and liability accounts (that is, working capital). Chapter 18 provides an overview of working capital management, with emphasis on the risk-return tradeoffs involved in working capital decision making. Chapters 19 through 21 examine the factors that must be considered in managing a firm's investments in various types of current assets. Specifically, Chapter 19 deals with cash and marketable securities, Chapter 20 with accounts receivable, and Chapter 21 with inventories. Finally, Chapter 22 discusses the various sources (and associated costs) of secured and unsecured short-term credit.

Part VIII Selected topics in contemporary financial management   Chapter 23 examines the merger and acquisition alternative, which many firms choose as a way of expanding, diversifying, or both. Chapter 24 describes the alternatives available to a failing firm. The final chapter of this text, Chapter 25, discusses international financial management and financial decision making in not for profit enterprises.

SUMMARY

- Financial management is closely related to other areas of business decision making, particularly accounting and economics.
- The primary objective of financial management decision making is the *maximization of shareholder wealth* as measured by the price of the firm's stock. This objective permits decision makers explicitly to make the needed tradeoffs between risk and return and between long-run versus short-run profits.
- The financial management function is organized into a number of different tasks. The departments usually found in the financial management area of a firm include the operating budget section, the capital budgeting section, the financial planning section, the short-term financing section, the credit section, and the financial relations section.
- *Risk* and *inflation* are major topics of concern for today's financial managers.

Corporate Social Responsibility *

LEWIS W. LEHR
CHAIRMAN AND CEO, 3M

While serving society, primarily as a generator of economic good, corporations by virtue of the talents and resources at their disposal are often able to reach out and help society in additional ways. Maintaining public confidence is possible, however, only if we perform our major economic role well, harnessing resources in a productive and profitable way.

More corporate philanthropy is certainly desirable at a time when private sector leadership is being sought to fill gaps in support for existing social programs. But the broad base of corporate responsibility must remain a pervasive social consciousness in all of our dealings, respecting the legitimate interests of customers, suppliers, employees, stockholders and neighbors. Only when the bills are paid, the payroll met, the customer served and our owners fairly rewarded can we add in any responsible way the "frosting on the cake."

My view is that the needs and interests of society are *not* in opposition to those of business. Public interest and private profit are compatible. Our challenge is to find innovative ways in which self-interest *and* the common good can be served.

For a company to be especially conscious of its responsibility to the communities in which it operates is more than altruism. It is good business, and good for business.

A fleet of vans for more than a thousand commuting employees may strike some as an expensive fringe benefit and others as a worthy conservation initiative. In fact, the program is largely a self-funded one which saves our company what it would otherwise have spent on parking lots and ramps.

Pollution prevention is more than an obligation which business owes to society. It is rather an obligation we owe to ourselves and our communities. And pollution prevention can pay off in our bottom line.

Carefully focused and well-leveraged corporate philanthropy can likewise serve as a channel for enlightened self-interest. My own company's interest is clear in the millions given each year to education. We expect to benefit from a well-educated citizenry.

Whether the giving is in time or money, expertise or judgment, it can surely be in the stockholders' interest . . . if the result is a society more conducive to the long-range survival and success of corporate endeavor. Anything less than an innovative response by corporations to the current challenge may well put future profits at risk.

DR. PAUL MACAVOY
PROFESSOR OF ECONOMICS, YALE UNIVERSITY

In recent years, there have been mounting pressures on the corporation to serve social interests as well as private investors. These pressures intensify as the Reagan Administration cuts back on government social programs and calls on corporations to fill the void. But at the same time, increased domestic and international competitiveness makes it more necessary than ever for the corporation to accelerate investment so as to provide better and cheaper goods and services which consumers are willing to buy, rather than those of competitors. The corporation cannot use the same cash flow to benefit social interest groups and make investments.

How can such social and efficiency objectives be reconciled? Certainly not by the example of how well the government has traded one off against the other. The difficult choices of "how much more" that confounded government social programs have been passed on to the corporation without any indication of how to make them.

There are even more basic problems than just finding the limits of conflicting responsibility. The corporation as now constituted cannot, given its legal obligations, pursue charitable enterprises. It is set up so that if management deviates substantially from the pursuit of investor returns to pursue social policy objectives, it becomes a takeover target by other companies and even dissatisfied stockholders. Furthermore, antitrust and regulatory policies in this country are designed to achieve maximum investment, and deviations such as price fixing are not condoned on grounds that they are in the public service, as defined by charitable groups. What the company can do as a matter of business strategy is to make investments and conduct operations so as to produce the highest possible returns to stockholders. In a competitive economy, such as we now have, this enhances investment, which increases productivity, innovation and the total volume of goods and services for all consumers.

When the corporation invites various social or political constituencies to share in the basic returns from investment, this system breaks down. Sooner or later, these socially responsible constituencies require obsolete plants to be kept in operation, or employment to be maintained in a recession. Doing these things resolves social conflicts, but destroys the corporation as an investment institution.

Furthermore, to practice social policy consistently, the corporation would have to be "democratized" to make it responsive to these other constituencies. This would require that community and labor leaders, and church members be added to the board of directors to represent such interests. After all, present board members have no expertise in representing such interests. But a board elected by such constituencies would undermine the pursuit of economic objectives which the corporation does better than any other institution.

KENNETH SCHWARTZ
VICE PRESIDENT, OPINION RESEARCH CORPORATION

In today's society, the corporation is viewed as more than an economic institution; it must also meet certain social responsibilities.

This is the principal finding of a nationwide survey of 500 opinion leaders in business, media, academics, labor, government, and public interest groups. The interviews were performed by the Opinion Research Corporation on behalf of the LTV Corporation.

The vast majority of those in every subgroup polled believed that the corporation *does* have certain social responsibilities. Labor union leaders were nearly unanimous (97%) in this belief, and most other groups concurred. The one exception is academic leaders—almost a quarter of this group, 23%, felt that a corporation is solely an economic institution.

To what degree should business be responsible for the social, cultural and educational programs formerly provided by the Federal government? Overall, 57% feel that business has at least a fair amount of responsibility. Public interest group leaders are most firm in this belief—88% consider business responsible for such programs, while less than half of the academic leaders (41%) feel this way. Business executives are divided on this issue: 47% believe they have a great deal or fair amount of responsibility, 45% think they have little or no responsibility.

Areas of responsibility Opinion leaders who say business should assume some responsibility were given a chance to react to the importance of business support in a number of areas. Ninety percent of this group overall consider providing more employment opportunities and job training programs for the unemployed and minorities as very or somewhat important. Other areas evaluated as important were expanded services/benefits for employees, such as day care, van pooling, or health services; support of educational institutions; additional support of established community services and charities; support of scientific research outside the company; increased support for cultural activities and development of new social service programs for the community.

Whether business actually will assume financial responsibility in these areas is another matter. A majority of opinion leaders overall think business will do so in supporting educational institutions (61%), employee benefits (59%), funding community services and charities (56%) and providing jobs for unemployed (54%). But leaders are divided on how business will support science and the arts—and almost two-thirds (64%) think business will *not* assume the financial responsibility of developing new social service programs for communities.

Consistently, business executives seem more confident than other opinion leaders that corporations actually will assume financial responsibility in areas considered most important.

RAYMOND A. HAY
CHAIRMAN OF THE BOARD AND CHIEF EXECUTIVE
OFFICER, LTV CORPORATION

The relationship between the American public and American business has had, like any other long-term relationship, its definite ups and downs. Sometimes, business has been viewed as the darkest villain, interested only in profits; at other times, business has been applauded as the engine which moves the nation to marvelous economic and technological feats.

And out of these ups and downs, our relationship is changing to one in which the public acknowledges a business's need for efficiency and profitability, while corporations understand social needs and their role in them.

Clearly, the corporation cannot be a dispassionate bystander. The evolutionary process which has made business such a force in American society also heaps a great deal of social responsibility on business. By and large, I believe America's businesses have risen quite effectively to meet those challenges.

Interrelated responsibilities   The first and foremost responsibility of business remains its function as employer, supplier of goods, and profit maker. This must be uppermost in the minds of business decision-makers as they set policies and make strategic decisions.

But the corporation's economic responsibilities are so closely related to overall social responsibility that they cannot be ignored.

It takes people to work factories, it takes natural resources to produce goods—and people and resources and communities must remain healthy for business to be healthy. They must be enriched in order for business to be enriched.

The argument that contributions to worthy social programs and causes deprive stockholders of the profits they deserve is no longer really a valid one. Those who invest in our corporations also enjoy the fruits of a better society. I feel that our willingness to share some of our profits to serve our communities is a move that stockholders understand, expect, and endorse.

I am confident that in the ever-evolving relationship of corporation and public, the many aspects of our society can and will benefit.

*Reprinted with permission. The LTV Corporation.

QUESTIONS AND TOPICS FOR DISCUSSION

1. What are the differences between shareholder wealth maximization and profit maximization? If a firm chooses to pursue the objective of shareholder wealth maximization, does this preclude the use of profit maximization decision-making rules? Explain.

2. Which type of corporation is more likely to be a shareholder wealth maximizer—one with wide ownership and no owners directly involved in the firm's management, or one that is closely held?

3. What are some of the most important financial problems that face financial decision makers today?

4. How does financial management in the 1970s and 1980s differ from financial management in the 1920s and 1930s—both as a profession and as a field of study?

ADDITIONAL READINGS AND REFERENCES

Anthony, Robert N. "The Trouble with Profit Maximization." *Harvard Business Review* 38 (Nov.–Dec. 1960): 126–134.

DeAlessi, Louis. "Private Property and Dispersion of Ownership in Large Corporations." *Journal of Finance* 28 (Sept. 1973): 839–851.

Findlay, Chapman M., and Whitmore, G. A. "Beyond Shareholder Wealth Maximization." *Financial Management* 3 (Winter 1974): 25–35.

Haley, Charles W., and Schall, Lawrence D. *The Theory of Financial Decisions*, 2nd ed. New York: McGraw-Hill, 1979.

Hill, Lawrence W. "The Growth of the Corporate Finance Function." *Financial Executive* 44 (July 1976): 38–43.

Lewellen, Wilbur G. "Management and Ownership in the Large Firm." *Journal of Finance* 24 (May 1969): 299–322.

McGuigan, James R., and Moyer, R. Charles. *Managerial Economics*, 3rd ed. St. Paul, Minn.: West, 1983, chap. 1.

Scanlon, John J. "Bell System Financial Policies." *Financial Management* 1 (Summer 1972): 16–26.

CHAPTER 2

The Corporation and the Institutional Environment

A FINANCIAL DILEMMA

A Look at the Yield Curve

Interest rates were relatively low during 1977. In the first quarter of that year, for example, the interest rate for a 90-day U.S. Treasury Bill was about 4.6 percent, and the yield on 20-year U.S. Government bonds was about 7.62 percent. The relationship between short-term and long-term interest rates having the same level of default risk often is portrayed as a *yield curve,* as in the figure here.

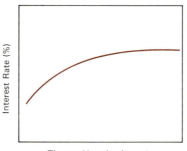

In 1977 Coronado Credit Union had assets slightly in excess of $5 million and a surplus of liquid funds. This led to its considering a number of investment possibilities, and it eventually decided to try to exploit the relationship between short- and long-term interest rates. The Credit Union purchased $2.5

million in U.S. Government guaranteed securities on 5 percent margin; that is, only 5 percent of the needed funds were provided by the credit union. The remaining 95 percent was borrowed through a securities firm at a rate determined on a monthly basis. The borrowing agreement called for this rate to increase or decrease (on the basis of a predetermined formula) as short-term interest rates rose or fell.

What seemed to be a good financial decision turned out to be a disastrous one. By late 1978 Coronado Credit Union's position was precarious. Interest rates rose, and the market value of the government bonds declined. With each successive decline in the bonds' value, the credit union was called upon to make additional payments to meet its 5 percent margin obligations. In addition, the short-term interest rate rose to a higher level than the long-term bond rate. As a result, the credit union ended up paying out more in monthly interest expense than it was receiving in interest income from the government securities. In the end, this small financial institution lost over $400,000. This situation might have been avoided if the credit union's decision makers had had a solid understanding of the functioning of the money and capital markets and the determinants of interest costs. These issues are introduced in this chapter.

GLOSSARY OF NEW TERMS

Capital markets   financial markets in which long-term securities are bought and sold.

Common stock   shares in the ownership of a company. Common stock represents a residual form of ownership in that dividends are paid out only after more senior financial obligations are fulfilled, such as interest on debt.

Corporation   a business organization that is created as a "legal person" separate and distinct from the individual or individuals who own the firm's stock. The primary characteristics of and advantages of incorporating include limited liability for the firm's owners, permanency, and flexibility with respect to making changes in ownership.

Expected value   the average of individual possible outcomes from an event, such as an investment, weighted by the probability of each possible outcome.

Investment banker   a financial institution that underwrites and sells new securities. In general, investment bankers assist firms in obtaining new financing.

Money markets   financial markets in which short-term debt securities are bought and sold.

Partnership   a business organization in which two or more persons form a business with the intention of making a profit. In a *general partnership* each partner has unlimited liability for the debts of the firm. *Limited partnerships* allow one or more partners to have limited liability.

Preferred stock   a form of equity that has a senior claim on earnings—in the form of a (normally) fixed periodic dividend payment—and assets of a firm. This is in contrast to the claims of common stockholders.

Primary markets   financial markets in which *new* securities are bought and sold for the first time. Investment bankers are active in the primary markets.

Risk   the possibility that actual future returns will deviate from expected returns.

Risk premium   the difference between the required rate of return on a risky investment and the rate of return on a risk-free asset (for example, U.S. Government Treasury Bills) having the same maturity.

Secondary markets   financial markets in which *existing* securities are offered for resale. The New York Stock Exchange is a secondary market.

Sole proprietorship   a business owned by one person. The owner of a sole proprietorship has unlimited liability for debts incurred by the firm.

Term structure of interest rates   the pattern of interest rate yields for debt securities that are similar in all respects except for their length of time to maturity. The term structure of interest rates is usually represented by a graphic plot called a *yield curve.*

Underwriting   a process whereby a group of investment bankers agrees to purchase a new security issue at a set price and then offer it for sale to the general public.

INTRODUCTION

The way a firm's finance function operates is strongly influenced by current conditions in the firm's industry and in the economy as a whole. This chapter provides background for understanding the finance function by looking closely at the corporation and its institutional environment.

The chapter begins by examining the three basic forms of business organization. Next, an overview of the U.S. financial system is presented. Finally, the chapter discusses interest rate variability and the risk-return tradeoff concept.

FORMS OF BUSINESS ORGANIZATION

Most businesses are organized into either a *sole proprietorship,* a *partnership,* or a *corporation.*

SOLE PROPRIETORSHIP

A sole proprietorship is a business owned by one person. For example, Larry Jackson decides to go into the construction and remodeling business. He acquires some tools, solicits customers, and his business is on its way. He discovers one of the major advantages to a sole proprietorship: *ease of entry.*

There is also a major disadvantage to this type of business organization, however: *unlimited liability* on the part of the owners. Suppose that Jackson's venture begins to lose money, and he incurs some business debts. In order to pay those debts, Jackson may have to dip into his personal savings. If his business continues to lose money, he even may have to sell some of his personal belongings to pay his creditors.

Sole proprietorships have another disadvantage in that their owners often have difficulty raising funds to finance growth. Thus, sole proprietorships are generally small. While approximately 80 percent of all businesses in the United States are of this type, their dollar volume of business activity amounts to only 10 percent of the total business activity in the country. Sole proprietorships are especially important in the retail trade and service industries.

PARTNERSHIP

A partnership is a business organization in which two or more co-owners form a business, normally with the intention of making a profit. Each partner agrees to provide a certain percentage of the funds necessary to run the business and also agrees to do some portion of the necessary work. In return the partners share in the profits (or losses) of the business.

Partnerships may be either *general* or *limited*. In a *general partnership* each partner has unlimited liability for all of the obligations of the business. Thus, general partnerships have the same major disadvantage as sole proprietorships. Even so, approximately 90 percent of all partnerships in the United States are of this type.

A *limited partnership* usually involves one or more general partners and one or more limited partners. While the limited partners may limit their liability, the extent of this liability can vary, and the terms should be set forth in the partnership agreement. Limited partnerships are common in real estate ventures.

Although a partnership of either type is a relatively easy way to form a business, there are disadvantages to this type of organization. If one partner leaves (or dies) or another enters, the existing partnership must be dissolved and another formed. This can be especially inconvenient in a larger business. Thus, only about 5 percent of the dollar volume of business activity in the U.S. economy is represented by partnerships. Partnerships are most common in the professional areas of law, medicine, consulting, and accounting.

CORPORATION

A corporation is a "legal person" composed of one or more actual individuals or legal entities. It is considered to be separate and distinct from those individuals or entities. Money contributed to start a corporation is called *capital stock* and is divided into *shares;* the owners of the corporation are called *stockholders* or *shareholders*.

The corporate form of business organization has three major advantages over both sole proprietorships and partnerships including the following:

▪ **Limited liability.**   Once stockholders have paid for their shares, they are not liable for any obligations or debts the corporation may incur. They are liable only to the extent of their investment in the shares.

- **Permanency.** The legal existence of a corporation is not affected by whether or not stockholders sell their shares. Thus, it is a more permanent form of business organization.

- **Flexibility.** It is relatively easy to effect a change of ownership within a corporation; one individual can merely sell shares to another. Even when shares of stock are sold, the corporation continues to exist in its original form.

As a "legal person," a corporation can purchase and own assets, borrow money, sue, and be sued. Its officers are considered to be *agents* of the corporation and are authorized to act on the corporation's behalf. For example, only an officer, such as the treasurer, can sign an agreement to repay a bank loan for the corporation.

Corporate organization In most corporations the stockholders elect a *board of directors,* which, in theory, is responsible for managing the corporation. In practice, however, the board of directors usually deals only with broad policy matters, leaving the day-to-day operations of the business to the *officers,* who are elected by the board. Corporate officers normally include a *president, vice-president(s), treasurer,* and *secretary.* In some corporations one person holds more than one office; many small corporations have a person who serves as secretary-treasurer. In most corporations the president and various other officers are also members of the board of directors. These officers are called "inside" board members, whereas other board members, such as the company's attorney or banker, are called "outside" board members. A corporation's board of directors usually contains at least three members. Figure 2–1 is a typical corporate organizational chart.

Corporate securities In return for the use of their funds, investors in a corporation are issued certificates, or *securities.* Corporate securities represent claims against the assets and future earnings of the firm.

FIGURE 2–1 Simplified Corporate Organizational Chart _____

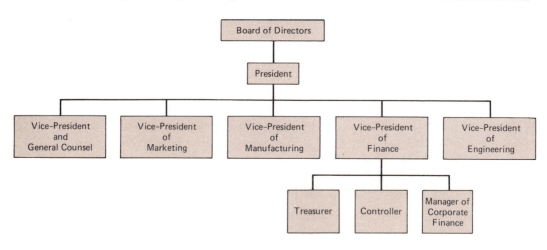

There are two types of corporate securities. Investors who lend money to the corporation are issued *debt securities;* these investors expect periodic interest payments, as well as the eventual return of their principal. Owners of the corporation are issued *equity securities.* Equity securities take the form of either *common stock* or *preferred stock.* Common stock is a residual form of ownership; that is, the claims of common stockholders on the firm's earnings and assets are considered only after all other claims—such as those of the government, debtholders, and preferred stockholders—have been met. Common stockholders are considered to be the true owners of the corporation.

Preferred stockholders have priority over common stockholders with regard to the firm's earnings and assets. They are paid cash dividends before common stockholders. In addition, if the corporation goes bankrupt, is reorganized, or is dissolved, preferred stockholders have priority over common stockholders in the distribution of the corporation's assets. However, preferred stockholders are second in line behind the firm's creditors.

Stockholder rights   Corporate stockholders possess certain rights, or claims, including the following:[1]

- **Dividend rights.**   Stockholders have the right to share equally on a per-share basis in any distribution of corporate earnings in the form of dividends.[2]

- **Asset rights.**   In the event of a liquidation, stockholders have the right to assets that remain after the obligations to the government (taxes), employees, and debtholders have been satisfied.

- **Voting rights.**   Stockholders have the right to vote on stockholder matters, such as the selection of the board of directors.

- **Preemptive rights.**   Stockholders may have the right to share proportionately in any new stock sold. For example, a stockholder who owns 20 percent of a corporation's stock may be entitled to purchase 20 percent of any new issue.

Because of the advantages of limited liability, permanency, and flexibility, and because ownership shares in corporations tend to be more liquid (and hence relatively more valuable) than ownership interests in proprietorships and partnerships, it is easy to see why the majority of business conducted in the United States is done under the corporate form of organization. This book stresses the corporate form of organization in the analysis it presents, although most of the techniques and principles discussed are equally applicable to proprietorships and partnerships.

Since all firms must operate in the confines of the macroeconomic and financial institutional environment, the following sections provide an introductory discussion of these factors. The final section of the chapter discusses risk and return tradeoffs, which must be made by all firms in all phases of financial planning and decision making.

---

[1]Stockholder rights are discussed in greater detail in Chapter 16, Appendix A.
[2]The terms *earnings, income,* and *profits* are used interchangeably throughout this text.

THE U.S. FINANCIAL SYSTEM:
AN OVERVIEW

In considering any economy as a whole, the actual savings for a given period of time must equal the actual investments. This phenomenon is called the *saving-investment cycle.*

Table 2–1 presents a summary of the saving-investment cycle in the United States for 1981. Total gross savings for that year equaled $454.1 billion—$107.3 billion from personal savings by individuals, $372.7 billion from business, and a government deficit of $25.9 billion. (This latter figure is a combination of Federal, state, and local deficits, and it may be viewed as dissavings. Gross investment also totaled $454.1 billion—$450.7 billion in gross private domestic investments plus $3.4 billion in net foreign investments.

The saving-investment cycle depends on net savers, or *surplus spending units,* and net investors, or *deficit spending units.* The cycle is completed when the surplus spending units transfer funds to the deficit spending units. The main purpose of the U.S. financial system—including the financial markets and all financial institutions—is to facilitate this transfer of funds. Figure 2–2 graphically depicts this continual flow.

Funds flow from surplus spending units, such as households, to deficit spending units, such as businesses, through *financial middlemen* or *financial intermediaries. Financial middlemen* include *brokers,* who buy securities for investors; *dealers,* who sell securities to investors out of an inventory they carry; and *investment bankers,* who assist corporations in selling their securities. These securities are called *primary claims,* since they are sold directly by the borrower and bought directly by the saver (lender).

Financial intermediaries include commercial banks and savings institutions. They differ from financial middlemen in that they issue *secondary claims* to the lender instead of primary claims. (A bank savings account is an example of a secondary claim.) A financial intermediary may lend money to a corporation even though there is a small chance that the corporation will default on its loan. In general, individuals or households are unwilling to lend

TABLE 2–1   U.S. Gross Savings and Investment, 1981 (in Billions of Dollars)

Personal savings		$ 107.3
Gross business savings;		
Undistributed profits	$ 78.6	
Inventory valuation adjustment	− 27.5	
Depreciation allowances	321.6	372.7
Government surplus or deficit (−)		− 25.9
Gross savings		$ 454.1
Gross private domestic investment:		
Fixed investment	$ 433.7	
Net change in business inventories	17.0	$ 450.7
Net foreign investment		3.4
Gross investment		$ 454.1

SOURCE: *Federal Reserve Bulletin* (March 1982).

FIGURE 2–2 Flow-of-Funds Diagram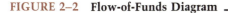

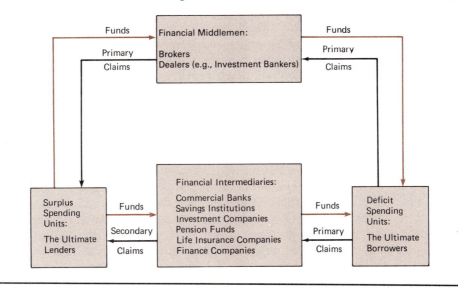

funds to a corporation under these circumstances, but they will allow a commercial bank to use their funds, because the bank can guarantee them both liquidity and safety.

Thus, financial intermediaries facilitate the transfer of funds. They are compensated for their services by an *interest rate spread.* For example, a bank might loan money to a business at an average of 11 percent interest, pay depositors an average of 8 percent interest, and use the 3 percent difference to pay employee salaries and other expenses, as well as to provide a return to their stockholders.

FINANCIAL ASSETS

Whereas *money* is the most obvious financial asset, there are others as well, including *debt securities* and *equity securities.* Debt securities are certificates issued to persons who loan money to a corporation by purchasing a bond or some other form of security. The investor is normally paid interest every 6 months until the loan comes due, or *matures,* and receives the entire principal on the *maturity date.* Equity securities are issued to co-owners or stockholders. Both debt and equity securities represent claims against the assets and future earnings of the corporation.

Debt and equity securities are financial *assets* of the investors who own them, and at the same time, these securities appear on the *liabilities* and stockholders' equity side of the issuing company's balance sheet.

FINANCIAL MARKETS

Financial markets are the vehicles through which financial assets are bought, sold, or traded. They generally are classified as *money* or *capital markets* and *primary* or *secondary markets.*

Money and capital markets   *Money markets* deal in *short-term* securities having maturities of 1 year or less. *Capital markets* deal in *long-term* securities having maturities greater than 1 year. (In both cases the 1-year breaking point is somewhat arbitrary.)

Most large corporations participate in the money markets, especially when they have more cash on hand than is needed to run their businesses. For example, Browning-Ferris Industries, a waste collection company, had $30 million in short-term investments at the end of 1982—approximately 17 percent of its current assets. By participating in the money market, the company earned interest, rather than leaving its funds in a noninterest-bearing commercial bank checking account.

Corporations enter the capital markets to obtain long-term funds, either debt or equity. Most large U.S. corporations are unable to generate enough funds *internally* to satisfy their needs, so they raise additional funds *externally* in the capital markets. For example, the El Paso Company, a diversified energy company, used $677 million during 1982 for capital expenditures (new fixed assets), but it generated only $333 million from internal sources. The company acquired additional funds needed for capital expenditures by selling new common stock ($23 million), new preferred stock ($75 million), and long-term debt ($442 million) to investors. (During 1982 the company had various other miscellaneous sources and uses of funds, which accounts for the discrepancies among the figures cited here.)

Primary and secondary markets   An investor who purchases *new* securities is participating in a *primary* financial market. Net proceeds from the sale of new securities go directly to the issuing company. On virtually any given business day the *Wall Street Journal* contains announcements about the issuance of new debt and equity securities. (These are called *tombstones* because of their resemblance to epitaphs.) Figure 2–3 is an example of such an announcement.

An investor who resells existing securities is participating in a *secondary* financial market. Secondary markets are well established in the United States, where stocks can be traded on the "floor" of a security exchange, such as the New York Stock Exchange (NYSE) or the American Stock Exchange (ASE or AMEX). (Some debt securities, such as bonds, also are traded on these exchanges.) Both the New York and the American stock exchanges are located in the Wall Street financial district of New York City. In addition, there are various regional security exchanges around the country, including the Midwest Exchange in Chicago and the Pacific Stock Exchange in San Francisco and Los Angeles.

Most individuals who invest in stocks are involved with secondary financial markets. Participation in these markets is relatively easy. Suppose, for example, that Susan Jones desires to purchase a stock that is traded, or "listed," on the NYSE. She telephones a security or brokerage firm that is a member of (that is, owns a "seat" on) that exchange. The firm wires Jones's order to its representative on the exchange floor, who purchases the stock for her.

Stocks that are not traded on security exchange floors are said to be traded "over the counter." The over-the-counter market is normally conducted by

FIGURE 2–3   Announcement of a New Security Issue

This announcement is neither an offer to sell nor a solicitation of offers to buy any of these securities.
The offering is made only by the Prospectus.

<u>NEW ISSUE</u>   March 29, 1983

$75,000,000

Long Island Lighting Company

General and Refunding Bonds, 12⅝% Series Due 1992

Price 98.82%
plus accrued interest from April 1, 1983

Copies of the Prospectus may be obtained in any State in
which this announcement is circulated only from such of the
undersigned as may legally offer these securities in such State.

The First Boston Corporation

Blyth Eastman Paine Webber
Incorporated

Lehman Brothers Kuhn Loeb
Incorporated

Merrill Lynch White Weld Capital Markets Group
Merrill Lynch, Pierce, Fenner & Smith Incorporated

Salomon Brothers Inc

Shearson/American Express Inc.

Basle Securities Corporation	**A. G. Edwards & Sons, Inc.**	**Ladenburg, Thalmann & Co. Inc.**
Oppenheimer & Co., Inc.	**Dominion Securities Ames Inc.**	**McDonald & Company**
Nomura Securities International, Inc.		**Wood Gundy Incorporated**
Howard, Weil, Labouisse, Friedrichs Incorporated		**Dorsey & Company** Incorporated

Reprinted with permission Long Island Lighting Company.

telephone and computer reporting of price quotations between brokerage firms that "make a market," that is, agree to buy and sell a particular security.

FINANCIAL INSTITUTIONS

Almost any market contains a number of middlemen—companies or individuals who transfer and distribute goods from the producer to the ultimate consumer. Grocery stores and food processing companies, for example, are considered middlemen because they distribute farm products to consumers.

The finance field also contains middlemen, or intermediaries, including *investment bankers* and *commercial banks.*

Investment bankers   Investment bankers bring together suppliers and users of funds in the capital markets. For example, if Company A wished to raise capital by selling a new security issue, it would probably enlist the services of an investment banker. Since even the largest U.S. corporations rarely sell new security issues more than two or three times a year, investment bankers provide the necessary expertise.

For large, secure corporations, investment bankers often *underwrite* an entire security issue by guaranteeing to purchase the issue at a set price. Thus, investment bankers often are called *underwriters.* For small, risky corporations, however, investment bankers will agree to sell the new security issue on a "best efforts" basis, which does not involve a guarantee.

Investment bankers sell securities through their own specialized marketing organizations. Most large issues are sold through syndicates, or groups of investment bankers. Most brokerage firms active in the secondary markets also serve as investment bankers in the primary markets. In March 1983, for example, Chrysler sold 26 million new shares of common stock through a syndicate of underwriters. If you had had an account with one of these underwriters at the time, you might have received a telephone call from your broker asking whether you were interested in investing in the new shares.

Some companies elect to make *private placements* of debt or preferred stock issues by selling them directly to large investors (such as an insurance company) rather than selling the securities to the public through investment bankers. This is a common corporate practice.

Commercial banks   Commercial banks provide a variety of services to businesses. In particular, they are an important source of short-term loans. Seasonal businesses, such as retailers, certain manufacturers (for example, those who deal in leisure products), some food processors, and builders often require short-term financing to help them through peak periods. Many other types of businesses have a more or less continuing need for short-term financing and make prior arrangements with their banks to borrow on short notice. Thus, banks provide significant amounts of both temporary and "permanent" short-term financing.

Banks are also a major source of *term loans,* or those that have maturities greater than 1 year. The proceeds from term loans can be used to finance current assets, such as inventory or accounts receivable, and to finance the purchase of fixed plant facilities and equipment, as well as to repay other debts.

In addition to making loans, banks advise their business clients on investments, new projects, and credit-granting decisions.

30

VARIABILITY OF INTEREST RATES

The interest rates that a firm pays for funds obtained in the money or capital markets are determined by supply and demand considerations. Interest rates on different securities may vary because of differences in *maturity, risk of default, tax status,* and *liquidity.*

TERM STRUCTURE OF INTEREST RATES

The *term structure of interest rates* is the pattern of interest rate yields for debt securities that are similar in all respects except for their length of time to maturity. Graphically plotting interest rates against time to maturity results in a *yield curve.*

Table 2–2 shows the interest rates on U.S. Treasury securities of different maturities. The interest rates increase as the time to maturity increases. If these data were plotted on a graph, the yield curve would be upward sloping, which is often indicative of expected rising future interest rates. Figure 2–4 is an example of an upward-sloping yield curve.

At times the yield curve also can be *downward sloping.* For example, in early 1980, short-term rates were about 14 percent, and long-term rates were in the 12 percent range. A downward-sloping yield curve indicates that future declines in interest rates are anticipated. (Appendix 18A has a more complete discussion of the term structure of interest rates.)

RISK STRUCTURE OF INTEREST RATES

The *risk structure of interest rates* is the pattern of interest rate yields for debt securities that are similar in all respects except for their default risk. As the default risk increases, so do the interest rate yields (expected return).

In March 1983, for example, long-term corporate issues rated Aaa (the highest possible rating) by Moody's rating service were yielding approximately 11.7 percent, whereas long-term debt issues rated Baa (a lower rating) were yielding approximately 13.7 percent.[3] The 2 percent difference can be attrib-

TABLE 2–2 Term Structure of Interest Rates*

Security	Interest Rate Yield (%) (February 25, 1983)
3-month Treasury bills	7.91
1-year Treasury bills	8.06
5-year Treasury securities	9.95
Long-term Treasury securities	10.59

*All interest rates are normally stated as annual rates.
SOURCE: *U.S. Financial Data,* Federal Reserve Bank of St. Louis (March 4, 1983).

[3] *U.S. Financial Data,* Federal Reserve Bank of St. Louis (March 11, 1983).

FIGURE 2–4   Upward-Sloping Yield Curve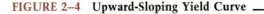

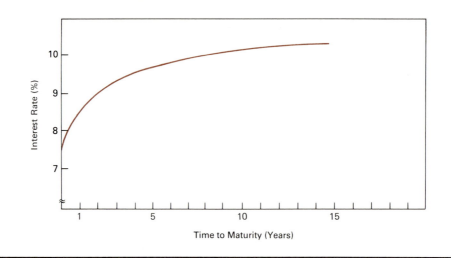

uted to differences in the default risk.[4] High-rated companies usually employ a lower relative amount of debt to finance their assets than low-rated companies. High-rated companies also usually have a higher ratio of times interest earned, that is, operating income divided by total interest payments.

TAX AND LIQUIDITY CONSIDERATIONS

Differences in tax rates and liquidity also can affect interest rates. For example, the debt securities of local and state governments, commonly called "municipals," are usually exempt from Federal income taxes, and they are offered at lower interest rates than taxable debt issues.

The liquidity of an asset is the ease with which it can be bought and sold without incurring substantial losses or transactions costs. In general, the more liquid a debt security, the lower its interest rate.

VARIABILITY OF INTEREST RATES OVER TIME

Whereas maturity, risk of default, tax status, and liquidity all determine interest rates at a *point in time*, interest rates also can vary substantially *over time*. For example, during the inflationary period following the 1973 Arab oil embargo, short-term interest rates in the United States reached 12 percent during the summer of 1974. They fell back into the 6 percent range by 1977, rose into the 20 percent range by 1980, and fell back into the 8 percent range by the spring of 1983.

---

[4]Differences, or changes, in the interest rates often are expressed in terms of *basis points* by finance professionals. Each 1 percent difference in interest rates is divided into 100 basis points. Therefore, if the interest rate difference between two securities is 0.4 percent, this difference could be referred to as a difference of 40 basis points.

Long-term interest rates fluctuate less sharply than short-term ones, but they nevertheless vary over a wide range with time. For example, the American Telephone and Telegraph Company (AT&T) has a number of presently outstanding long-term debt issues. One issue maturing in 1986 sold in 1946 at an interest rate of 2⅝ percent. Another issue maturing in 2007 sold in 1975 at an interest rate of 8⅝ percent, and in 1981 the company issued debt maturing in 1991 at an interest rate of 13¼ percent. This upward trend in interest rates has affected most U.S. companies since the 1930s.

When inflation causes interest rates to rise, companies have to pay higher interest costs to acquire new capital and, as a result, have to earn higher returns on new projects in order to cover the cost of funds. Thus, inflation can affect both a company's decisions about financing and its decisions about investments.

RELATIONSHIP BETWEEN RISK AND EXPECTED RETURN

Understanding the tradeoffs that have to be made between risk and expected return is integral to financial decision making. For example, investors who purchase shares of common stock hope to receive returns that will exceed those that might be earned from some alternative investment, such as a regular savings account, U.S. Government bonds, or corporate bonds. Investors recognize that the expected return from common stocks over the long run tends to be higher than the expected return from less risky investments. To receive this higher return, however, investors must be prepared to accept a higher level of risk.

Figure 2–5 illustrates the conceptual tradeoff between risk and expected return. Note that the expected returns and risk for some common stocks overlap the expected returns and risk for some corporate bonds. Examples of low-risk common stocks include AT&T and General Foods; examples of high-risk bonds include International Harvester and Pan Am.

Before continuing the discussion of the risk–expected return tradeoff, it is necessary to define some important terms and concepts. The return from holding a security can be defined by the following equation:

$$\text{Percentage rate of return} = \frac{\text{Ending price} - \text{Beginning price} + \text{Distributions}}{\text{Beginning price}} \times 100\%. \quad \textbf{(2.1)}$$

Distributions are the interest on debt or the dividends on stock.

To illustrate, suppose Tom Johnson purchased shares of Shasta Company common stock 1 year ago for $20 per share, sold them now for $22 each, and received dividends of $1 per share. His return would be calculated as follows:

$$\text{Percentage rate of return} = \frac{22 - 20 + 1}{20} \times 100\%$$

$$= 15\%.$$

33

**FIGURE 2–5   Conceptual Risk–Expected Return
Relationship**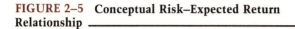

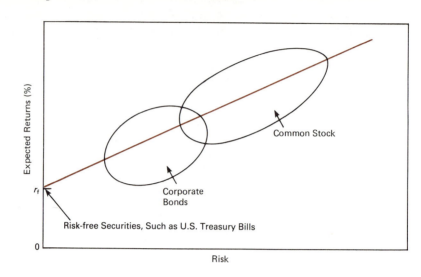

Returns are expressed as a percentage or fraction and usually are quoted on an annual basis.

The return Johnson received is called a *realized*, or *ex post* (after-the-fact), return. Realized returns differ from *expected*, or *ex ante* (before-the-fact), returns. Although they are calculated in the same manner, ending prices and distributions for expected returns are estimated, whereas ending prices and distributions for realized returns are actual values.

The term *risk* is used in a broad sense to refer to deviations from expectations. In finance, risk often is measured in terms of the variability of returns. Suppose, for example, that you decided to deposit a sum of money in a passbook savings account at a commercial bank, expecting to earn an annual return of 5.5 percent. Because bank failures occur infrequently and most bank deposits are insured by an agency of the government, deviations from your expected 5.5 percent return would most probably be zero. Thus, the risk associated with a passbook account is considered to be nearly zero.

Now suppose you decided to put your money into common stock. You hope or expect that the price of your stock will increase, but you also recognize that the price may decrease. Deviations from your expectation of an increased price are likely to be high. Thus, the risk associated with common stock investments is considered to be high.

The relationship between risk and expected return can be defined by the following equation:

$$\text{Expected return} = \text{Risk-free return} + \text{Risk premium.} \qquad (2.2)$$

A *risk premium* is a potential "reward" that an investor can expect to receive from making a risky investment.

To illustrate, suppose a group of investors has the opportunity to purchase stock in a new oil company that plans to drill wells in a region where no previous commercial discoveries have been made. If the risk-free return is equal to 6 percent and the forecast, or expected, return is estimated to be fairly low—say, 12 percent—it is unlikely that many investors will purchase the new stock. If the forecast return is estimated to be fairly high, however— say, 30 percent—more investors will be willing to invest in the stock. While many investors would consider a 6 percent premium insufficient compensation for the risk, they might consider a 24 percent premium enough of a reward.

The risk-return tradeoff concept is one of the most important principles in finance. It has a significant impact on the determinants of value of individual securities. It plays a major role in capital budgeting decision making, working capital management decision making, the determination of the cost of capital, and capital structure decision making. In short, there are few financial management decisions that can be made without some consideration of the risk and expected return tradeoffs involved.

SUMMARY

- The three principal forms of business organization are the *sole proprietorship*, the *partnership*, and the *corporation*. Corporations have certain advantages over the other two forms of business organization, especially for large businesses; as a result, corporations account for about 85 percent of the dollar volume of business activity in the United States.

- A corporation is defined as a "legal person" composed of one or more actual individuals or legal entities. The owners of a corporation are called *stockholders* or *shareholders*. The stockholders elect a *board of directors* that usually deals with broad policy matters, while the day-to-day operations are supervised by the *officers*.

- Corporations issue *debt securities* to investors who lend money to the corporation and *equity securities* to investors who become owners.

- The main purpose of an economy's financial system is to facilitate the transfer of funds from *surplus spending units* to *deficit spending units*. *Financial middlemen*, such as investment bankers, bring together the surplus and deficit spending units in the capital markets so that funds can be transferred. *Financial intermediaries*, such as commercial banks, receive *primary claims* from their borrowers and issue *secondary claims* to their lenders. Secondary claims have different risk and liquidity characteristics than primary claims.

- *Financial assets* consist of *money*, *debt securities*, and *equity securities*.

- *Financial markets* are the vehicles through which financial assets are bought and sold. They include *money* or *capital markets* and *primary* or *secondary markets*. Money markets deal in securities with maturities of approximately 1 year or less, while capital markets deal in securities with maturities greater than 1 year. Primary markets are those in which *new* securities are issued; secondary markets are those in which *existing* securities are

35

traded. Interest rates on securities vary at any point in time for several reasons, including maturity differences (the *term structure of interest rates*), differences in default risk (the *risk structure of interest rates*), differences in *taxability*, and differences in *liquidity*.

▪ Tradeoffs between *risk* and *expected return exist* in nearly all areas of finanoial decision making. Generally, the higher the risk associated with a security, investment project, and so on, the higher the return expected by investors.

QUESTIONS AND TOPICS FOR DISCUSSION

1. Name and discuss some advantages that the corporate form of organization has over the sole proprietorship and the partnership.
2. How are corporations organized?
3. Describe and discuss the saving-investment cycle.
4. What roles do financial middlemen and financial intermediaries play in the operation of the U.S. financial system? How do the two differ?
5. How do money and capital markets differ? How do primary and secondary markets differ? Discuss each type.
6. What is the term structure of interest rates?
7. What is the risk structure of interest rates?
8. How is *risk* defined in a financial sense?
9. Discuss the general relationship between risk and expected return.

PROBLEMS *

1. An investor bought 100 shares of Apollo Corporation common stock 1 year ago for $30 per share. She just sold the shares for $33 each, and during the year she received four quarterly dividend checks for $35 each. Calculate the investor's percentage rate of return.
2. An investor bought ten Cohen Industries, Inc. long-term bonds 1 year ago, when they were first issued by the company. He paid $1,000 each for the bonds, and today the bonds are selling at $970 each (long-term interest rates have increased slightly over the past year). The bonds have a stated interest rate of 12 percent per year. The investor received an interest payment equaling $60 per bond 6 months ago and has just received another $60 interest payment per bond. Calculate the investor's percentage rate of return for the 1 year he has held the bonds.
3. Three months ago an investor bought some 3-month Treasury Bills that were *expected* to pay her interest equal to an 8 percent annual return. She has just received the exact amount of interest she was expecting, as well as the return of her principal. One year ago she bought the common stock of Hill Data Products, a new small computer company, for $10 a share. Prior to her purchase, she had read a report that stated that Hill Data Products had an *expected* annual rate of return equal to 30 percent. However, since her purchase of the stock, the Hill Data Products common stock price has fallen to $8 a share. Hill Data Products does not pay a dividend on its common stock.

*Problems in color have check answers provided at the end of the book.

a. Calculate the investor's *realized* percentage rate of return on the Hill Data Products common stock.

b. What is the *realized* percentage rate of return on her Treasury Bill purchase?

c. What can be said about the level of risk associated with the investor's two security purchases?

d. Would your answer to Part c of this question be any different if Hill Data Products stock had risen to $20 a share over the past year? Why?

ADDITIONAL READINGS AND REFERENCES

Carr, J. L., Halpern, P. J., and McCallum, J. S. "Correcting the Yield Curve: A Re-Interpretation of the Duration Problem." *Journal of Finance* 29 (Sept. 1974): 1287–1294.

Elliott, J. W., and Baier, J. R. "Econometric Models and Current Interest Rates: How Well Do They Predict Future Rates?" *Journal of Finance* 34 (Sept. 1979): 975–986.

Friedman, Milton. "Factors Affecting the Level of Interest Rates," in *Savings and Residential Financing.* Chicago: U.S. Savings and Loan League, 1968:10–27.

Grossman, Herschel I. "The Term Structure of Interest Rates." *Journal of Finance* 22 (Dec. 1967): 611–622.

Ibbotson, R. R. "Price Performance of Common Stock New Issues." *Journal of Financial Economics* 2 (Sept. 1975): 235–272.

Malkiel, Burton G. *The Term Structure of Interest Rates: Theory, Empirical Evidence and Applications.* New York: McCaleb-Seiler, 1970.

Mancuso, Joseph R. *How to Start, Finance and Manage Your Own Small Business.* Englewood Cliffs, N.J.: Prentice-Hall, 1978.

Norgaard, Richard L. "An Examination of the Yields of Corporate Bonds and Stocks." *Journal of Finance* 29 (Sept. 1974): 1275–1286.

Van Horne, James C. *Financial Market Rates and Flows.* Englewood Cliffs, N.J.: Prentice-Hall, 1978.

Walker, Ernest W., and Petty, J. William. *Financial Management of the Small Firm.* Englewood Cliffs, N.J.: Prentice-Hall, 1978.

Federal Income Taxes

GLOSSARY OF NEW TERMS

Capital gains (long term)   profits on the sale of capital assets held longer than 1 year.

Capital losses (long term)   losses on the sale of capital assets held longer than 1 year.

Investment tax credit (ITC)   a credit that eligible businesses are permitted to take against their tax liabilities. It is generally equal to 6 or 10 percent of the cost of certain qualified assets the business acquires during the tax year, and it is intended to encourage business investment.

Marginal tax rate   the tax rate on the last dollar of taxable income earned by an individual or firm.

S corporation   a small business that takes advantage of the corporate form of organization while having its income taxed directly to the stockholders at their individual personal income tax rates. Also called a subchapter S corporation.

Tax credit   a direct subtraction from the tax bill. Thus, a $100 tax credit reduces the tax bill by $100.

Tax deduction   an amount subtracted from taxable income. For a corporation with a 46 percent marginal tax rate, a $100 tax deduction reduces taxable income by $100 and reduces taxes owed by $46.

INTRODUCTION

Because so many financial decisions are based on after-tax cash flows, finance and business professionals must have a basic understanding of tax matters. Tax knowledge is essential in making a wide variety of business decisions, including what form of business organization to select, what type of securities to issue, whether to lease or buy business equipment, and whether to expense or capitalize a $7,500 piece of equipment in a small business.

CORPORATE INCOME TAXES

In general, the taxable income of a corporation is calculated by subtracting business expenses from revenues. Tax-deductible business expenses normally include the cost of goods sold, selling and administrative expenses, depreciation allowances, and interest expenses.[1] Federal income taxes are computed on the resulting taxable income.

As of 1983, the tax rates imposed on a corporation were as follows:

- 15 percent of the first $25,000 of taxable income.
- 18 percent of the next $25,000.
- 30 percent of the next $25,000.
- 40 percent of the next $25,000.
- 46 percent of any taxable income over $100,000.

Suppose a corporation has taxable income of $110,000 in 19X1. Given these rates, its total tax would be computed as follows:

$$
\begin{aligned}
\text{Total tax} &= (15\% \times \$25,000) + (18\% \times \$25,000) + (30\% \times \$25,000) \\
&\quad + (40\% \times \$25,000) + (46\% \times \$10,000) \\
&= \$3,750 + \$4,500 + \$7,500 + \$10,000 + \$4,600 \\
&= \$30,350.
\end{aligned}
$$

The *average tax rate* of a corporation is calculated by dividing the total tax by the taxable income. In this example the average tax rate would be as follows:

$$
\frac{\$30,350}{\$110,000} = 0.276, \text{ or } 27.6\%.
$$

The *marginal tax rate* of a corporation is defined as the tax rate on the last dollar of taxable income—in this example, 46 percent. The marginal tax rate is more important than the average tax rate for financial planning purposes. All but the smallest corporations (or firms operating at a loss) are taxed at the 46 percent rate on *new* income.

Taxable income that is taxed at the 46 percent rate is called *operating* or *ordinary* income. Ordinary income is often contrasted with *capital gains income* and *dividend income*, which are both taxed at lower rates.

CAPITAL GAINS INCOME

As a general rule, whenever a corporate asset is held for longer than 1 year and then sold, the resulting gain or loss is classified as a *long-term capital gain or loss*. The maximum capital gains tax rate for most large U.S. corpo-

[1] Chapter 9 contains a detailed discussion of depreciation methods.

rations in 1983 was 28 percent. *Short-term capital gains* on assets held for 1 year or less are taxed at the same marginal tax rate as ordinary income.

To illustrate the capital gains tax, suppose a large corporation purchased a factory site. The corporation later changed its plan and recently sold the land for $3 million, realizing a $1 million long-term capital gain. Assuming an effective capital gains tax rate of 28 percent, the company would owe $280,000 in Federal income taxes on the capital gain.

DIVIDEND INCOME

Intercompany dividends, or dividends paid by one corporation to another, are normally entitled to an 85 percent exclusion from Federal income taxes. To illustrate, suppose that the Hastings Corporation owns stock in the Fremont Corporation and that Fremont pays $100,000 in dividends to Hastings during this year. Hastings has to pay taxes on only 15 percent of the $100,000, or $15,000. (The other 85 percent, or $85,000, is excluded, that is, received tax-free. However, Fremont has to pay taxes on its income before paying the $100,000 to Hastings, because dividends are *not* considered tax-deductible expenses.) The $15,000 of taxable dividend income is taxed at ordinary income tax rates.[2] Assuming that Hastings is large enough to have a marginal tax rate of 46 percent, the tax on the dividends is calculated as follows:

$$\$15,000 \times 0.46 = \$6,900.$$

For corporations having a marginal tax rate of 46 percent, intercompany dividends are taxed at an effective rate of 6.9 percent; that is, $(1 - 0.85)46\%$.

INVESTMENT TAX CREDIT (ITC)

As a fiscal policy measure designed to encourage economic expansion, the Federal government permits businesses to take a *credit* against their taxes amounting to either 6 percent or 10 percent of their qualifying investments (capital expenditures). The Economic Recovery Tax Act of 1981 significantly changed the depreciation rules for Federal income tax purposes. Generally, only three different asset lives are allowed for tax purposes—3 years for automobiles, light-duty trucks, and research and development equipment; 5 years for most other equipment; and 15 years for real estate. The investment tax credit (ITC) is 6 percent for 3-year assets and 10 percent for 5-year assets. Real estate is not eligible for the ITC.[3] For tax purposes most companies take the credit in the year during which a new investment is made. However, for financial reporting purposes a company can either take the entire credit in the year of the investment (the *flow-through method*) or amortize the credit over the life of the asset (the *normalization method*).

To illustrate the ITC, suppose a corporation expands its plant in 19X1 and

---

[2]This example assumes that the two companies are not affiliated. If they were—that is, if they had a *parent-subsidiary relationship* and the parent owned at least 80 percent of the subsidiary— 100 percent of the intercompany dividends would be excluded.

[3]The investment tax credit is discussed in detail in Chapter 9.

makes capital expenditures on new equipment totaling $10 million. Given a taxable income of $25 million, the new investment effectively reduces taxes by $1 million (see Table 2A–1).

A corporation may take ITCs up to approximately 90 percent of its taxable income in any one year. Thus, companies that are losing money or earning only small amounts cannot take full advantage of the ITC. This situation has existed in the airline industry at various times. As a result, some airlines lease their aircraft from other companies that are in a position to receive the ITC. Presumably, the airlines then benefit from lower rentals than they would be charged if the leasing companies did not receive the ITC.

Loss carrybacks and carryforwards

Corporations that sustain net operating losses during a particular year are permitted by tax laws to apply the losses against any taxable income in other years, thereby lowering the taxes owed in those years. If such a loss is applied against a previous year, it is called a *loss carryback*; if it is applied against a succeeding year, it is called a *loss carryforward*.

The tax laws specify that a corporation's net operating loss may be carried back 3 years and forward 15 years to offset taxable income in those years. For example, suppose the NOL Corporation incurs a net operating loss totaling $200,000 in 19X6. This loss may be carried back 3 years to 19X3. If the NOL Corporation had 19X3 taxable income of $125,000, for example, it could receive a tax refund equal to the taxes it paid for that year. The remaining $75,000 portion of the 19X6 net operating loss next could be carried back to 19X4.

Deferred federal income taxes

Companies may opt to *defer* payment of some portion of their Federal income taxes for a number of legal reasons. For example, many corporations use the straight-line depreciation method to calculate the income they report to their stockholders and an accelerated depreciation method to calculate taxable income. As shown in Table 2A–2, this usually results in the taxes currently owed being less than they would be if the company used straight-line depreciation methods for tax purposes. Using straight-line depreciation, the company's income before taxes is $20 million; using accelerated depreciation, its income before taxes is $18 million. Taxes of $9.2 million are calculated on the taxable income figure of $20 million, but only $8.28 million in taxes is

TABLE 2A–1 Sample Tax Computation

Taxable income		$25.0 million
Taxes:		
Tax (assume a 46% rate)	$11.5 million	
Less: Investment tax credit		
(10% × $10 million)	1.0 million	10.5 million
Net income		$14.5 million

TABLE 2A–2   Simplified Income Statements Illustrating Deferred Federal Income Taxes

(A) CALCULATION OF TAXES FOR FINANCIAL REPORTING AND TAX PURPOSES (IN MILLIONS OF DOLLARS)

	Financial Reporting Purposes	Tax Purposes
Sales	$100.00	$100.00
Expenses, excluding depreciation	70.00	70.00
Depreciation:		
Straight-line	10.00	
Accelerated		12.00
Income before taxes	$ 20.00	$ 18.00
Taxes (46%)	9.20	8.28
Net income	$ 10.80	$ 9.72

(B) PARTIAL INCOME STATEMENT REPORTED TO STOCKHOLDERS (IN MILLIONS OF DOLLARS)

Income before taxes	$ 20.00
Federal income taxes:	
Current	$ 8.28
Deferred	0.92
Total Federal income tax	$ 9.20
Net income	$ 10.80

currently owed. The result is that $0.92 million in taxes is deferred. The company effectively can continue to defer payment of these taxes as long as it continues to purchase a sufficient amount of new fixed assets. When it ceases purchasing such assets or purchases fewer of them, it will have to pay the deferred taxes.

Deferred taxes also can result from other timing differences, such as differences in the timing of the recognition of income on long-term contracts.

S CORPORATIONS

The Internal Revenue Code allows certain small businesses to take advantage of the corporate form of organization while having their business income taxed directly to their shareholders at individual income tax rates. These businesses were previously called *Subchapter S corporations* and were renamed *S corporations* in the Subchapter S Revision Act of 1982. To qualify for S corporation status, a firm may not have more than 35 shareholders.

Gains or losses of S corporations are not taxed as corporate income. Rather, they are taxed as individual income to the shareholders regardless of whether the shareholders actually receive any income. For new businesses that incur losses, the S corporation form of organization can be advantageous if the shareholders have other taxable income with which to offset the losses. In addition, S corporations avoid the *double taxation of dividends* (discussed in the following section), since the corporate income is taxed only once.

INDIVIDUAL INCOME TAXES

Individuals are required to pay Federal income taxes on earnings from wages, interest, dividends, and rents. In 1983 the first $3,400 of taxable income for married taxpayers filing jointly was not taxed, while the next $2,100 of taxable income was taxed at a rate of 11 percent. The marginal rate increased gradually up to 50 percent for taxable incomes over $109,400 for married couples.

Due to persistent inflation in recent years, many individuals find that their effective purchasing power in terms of after-tax dollars is decreasing. Suppose, for example, that Emily Wilson receives an 8 percent salary increase in a year in which inflation is also 8 percent. On a pretax basis she is "keeping up with inflation." However, since her salary increase is likely to be taxed at a higher marginal tax rate than her previous earnings, her actual purchasing power is *less* than it was during the previous year.

For most individuals, long-term capital gains are taxed at 40 percent of their marginal tax rate. Suppose, for example, that Robert Bloomfield sold stock in 1983 for $3,000 more than its original purchase price. Assuming that he is in a 50 percent tax bracket (that is, his income is taxed at a 50 percent marginal rate) and that he had held the stock for longer than 1 year, the $3,000 is a long-term capital gain and is effectively taxed at a 20 percent (40 percent of the 50 percent) marginal tax rate.

Single taxpayers may exclude from their taxable income $100 in dividends received from domestic corporations. (The dividend exclusion is $200 on a joint return.) For example, if a single taxpayer in a 30 percent tax bracket receives $500 in dividends during a particular year, the tax owed is $400 × 0.30 = $120. Interest income is fully taxable.

Dividends are paid by corporations out of their after-tax earnings. Thus, dividends are in effect taxed *twice,* since individuals receiving them also pay taxes on them. This *double taxation* of *dividends* has been the subject of much controversy in recent years. Although many economists claim that it hinders capital formation, the government has been reluctant to relinquish this source of revenue.

Since long-term capital gains are taxed at lower rates than dividends, most individuals prefer to receive capital gains, all other things being equal. The effects of this tax treatment are evident in the types of stocks that have been traditionally held. As a *very* general rule, retired persons in lower tax brackets who need current income to live on have owned stocks that pay good dividends. Working people in higher tax brackets who have money to invest have tended to own stocks in companies that reinvest a large portion of their earnings back into the company. These "growth" companies usually pay smaller dividends, but their investors hope to receive capital gains, which will be taxed later at lower rates.

QUESTIONS AND TOPICS FOR DISCUSSION

1. What are the differences between the operating income, capital gains income, and dividend income of a corporation? At approximately what rates are these different types of income taxed?

2. What is the investment tax credit (ITC)?

3. What are deferred Federal income taxes?

4. What is an S corporation?

5. How do corporate and individual tax rates differ?

6. What is meant by the "double taxation of dividends"?

7. Imagine that a wealthy family has investments that yield dividends that put them in a 50 percent tax bracket. They would like to incorporate in order to reduce their taxes, but an aspect of the tax laws prevents them from doing this. Discuss.

8. Suppose that someone running for public office in your area has begun criticizing one of the prominent local corporations because its income tax rate is only 35 percent instead of the statutory 46 percent. What are some of the possible reasons why the corporation can operate well within the law and still have an income tax rate less than the statutory 46 percent.?

PROBLEMS *

1. Last year, the Connersville Corporation had taxable ordinary income of $2 million and capital gains income of $500,000. The company also had $50,000 in dividend income and paid its stockholders $150,000 in dividends. Assuming that all ordinary income is taxed at 46 percent and capital gains are taxed at 28 percent, calculate the Connersville Corporation's tax bill.

2. Last year the Muncie Corporation had earnings before interest and taxes (operating income) equal to $1 million. It paid $200,000 in dividends to its stockholders and $100,000 in interest to its creditors. During the year the company also repaid a bank loan of $150,000. In addition, it had capital expenditures of $500,000, all of which qualified for a 10 percent investment tax credit. Assuming a corporate tax rate of 46 percent on all taxable income, calculate the Muncie Corporation's tax bill.

3. Calculate the income tax that a single individual in a 30 percent tax bracket would pay on the following items:

    a. A $600 gain on the sale of stock held for 3 months.
    b. A $600 gain on the sale of stock held for 3 years.
    c. Dividend income of $600.
    d. Interest income of $600.

*Problems in color have check answers provided at the end of the book.

PART TWO

Determinants of Valuation

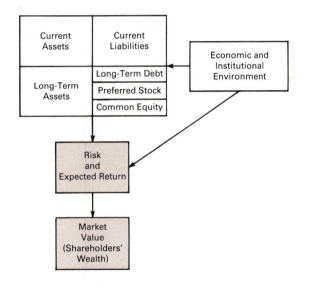

The primary objective of financial management is to maximize the value of the stock of the firm's shareholders. This section discusses the valuation process in detail. Chapter 3 develops the tools of financial mathematics essential for any serious analysis of important financial decisions that have an impact on the firm over a number of years. Chapter 4 builds valuation models for a firm's securities. This is a most important chapter since valuation is the dominant theme that is carried throughout the text and related to all financial decisions. Chapter 5 explores the determinants of risk and relates risk to the valuation process.

CHAPTER 3

Financial
Mathematics

A FINANCIAL DILEMMA

Prepaying Your Mortgage Loan

In June 1982 interest rates were near their historical highs. Home mortgage rates of 16 to 18 percent were not uncommon for conventional new home mortgages. Savings and loan institutions were paying very high costs to attract and retain funds. At the same time, these institutions were burdened with many older mortgages written at low, fixed rates of interest.

In an attempt to free up some funds invested in low interest rate mortgages, a number of savings and loans offered various plans designed to encourage people to pay off their low rate mortgages more rapidly. First Federal Savings and Loan Association offered Natalie Mayer the opportunity to increase her monthly principal and interest mortgage payments from $852.39 to $1,691.49. In return, First Federal agreed to reduce the interest rate on the loan from 10.875 percent per annum to 10.00 percent. With the new payment plan, the loan would be paid off in 5 years and 10 months, compared with 27 years and 10 months under the original loan terms. First Federal computed the total (undiscounted) interest savings over the life of the loan to be $166,577.47. The current loan balance is $89,435.61.

If Mayer believes she will have opportunities to invest the funds needed for the early payment plan at a 15 percent annual rate of return over the life of the mortgage, should she accept the First Federal offer?

This type of problem illustrates the value of having a working knowledge of financial mathematics. As we shall see later in the chapter, the difference between the two alternatives is dramatic.

GLOSSARY OF NEW TERMS

Annuity the payment or receipt of a series of equal amounts of money per period for a specified amount of time. In an *ordinary annuity*, payments are made at the end of each period; in an *annuity due*, payments are made at the beginning.

Capital recovery problem   an annuity amount necessary to recover a capital investment.

Compound interest   interest that is paid not only on the principal, but also on any interest earned but not withdrawn during earlier periods.

Discount rate   the rate of interest used in the process of finding present values (discounting).

Effective interest rate   the actual rate of interest paid by the borrower or earned by the lender.

Future value (or terminal value)   the value at some future point in time of a present amount of money, or a series of payments, evaluated at the appropriate interest (growth) rate.

Interest   the return earned by or the amount paid to an individual who foregoes current consumption or alternative investments and "rents" money to a business, bank, the government, some other form of institution, or another individual.

Nominal interest rate   the periodic rate of interest that is stated in a loan agreement or security. Frequently the *effective interest rate* is greater than the nominal rate because of factors like the frequency of compounding and the deduction of interest in advance.

Present value   the value today of a future amount of money or a series of future payments evaluated at the appropriate discount rate.

Principal   an amount of money that has been borrowed or invested.

Sinking fund problem   an annuity amount that must be invested each period (year) to produce a future value.

INTRODUCTION

Understanding the concept of compound interest is crucial to effective financial management. In fact, anyone who is involved with money should have some comprehension of compound interest. Consider the following:

- A banker who makes loans and other investments.

- A financial officer whose job includes the consideration of various alternative sources of funds in terms of their cost.

- A corporate planner who must choose among various alternative investment projects.

- A securities analyst who evaluates the securities that the firm sells to investors.

- An individual who is confronted with a host of daily financial problems ranging from personal credit account management to deciding whether to make certain purchases for the home.

Each of these individuals makes frequent use of some form of financial mathematics. However, many people fear that a working knowledge of compound interest might be too difficult to master. Instead, the availability of interest tables and calculators make the subject readily accessible.

While an understanding of compound interest factors is useful in and of itself, it is also a necessary prelude to topics including the following:

- Capital budgeting (the analysis of investment projects).
- Working capital (short-term asset and liability) management.
- Lease analysis.
- Valuation.
- The cost of capital.

This chapter introduces the concepts and skills necessary to understand compound interest and its applications. The analysis in this chapter assumes that the student will use the interest tables (Tables I through IV) at the end of the book. The "Calculator Applications" section that follows the "Problems" in this chapter illustrates the use of a popular financial calculator to solve the types of problems discussed in the chapter.

INTEREST

Money can be thought of as having a time value. In other words, money received today is worth more than the same dollar amount would be if it were received a year from now. (This holds true even if risk and inflation are not considerations.) Suppose, for example, that you had $100 and decided to put it into a savings account for a year. By doing this, you would temporarily give up, or forego, spending the $100 however you wished, or you might forego the return that the $100 might earn from some alternative investment, such as U.S. Treasury bonds. Or you might forego paying an additional $100 on your mortgage. Similarly, a bank that loans money to a firm foregoes the opportunity to earn a return on some alternative investment.

Interest is the return earned by or the amount paid to someone who has foregone current consumption or alternative investment opportunities and "rented" money in a creditor relationship.[1] The *principal* is the amount of money borrowed or invested. The *term* of a loan is the length of time or number of time periods during which the borrower can use the principal. The *rate of interest* is the percentage on the principal that the borrower pays the lender per time period as compensation for foregoing other investment or consumption opportunities.

SIMPLE INTEREST

Simple interest is the interest paid (in the case of borrowed money) or earned (in the case of invested money) on the principal sum only. The amount of

---

[1]Although there are other forms of returns, and these are dealt with throughout the text, this discussion is limited to borrowing/lending situations.

simple interest is equal to the product of the principal times the rate per time period times the number of time periods:

$$I = PV_0 \times i \times n , \tag{3.1}$$

where I = the simple interest in dollars; PV_0 = the principal amount at time 0, or the present value; i = the interest rate per time period; and n = the number of time periods. The following problems illustrate the use of Equation 3.1.

1. *What is the simple interest on $100 at 10 percent per annum for 6 months?* Substituting $100 for PV_0, 10% (0.10) for i, and $\%_{12}$ (0.5) for n yields the following:

$$I = \$100 \times 0.10 \times 0.5$$
$$= \$5 .$$

2. *If Gene Smith bought a house and borrowed $30,000 at a 10 percent annual interest rate, what would be his first month's interest payment?* Substituting $30,000 for PV_0, 10 percent (0.10) for i, and $\frac{1}{12}$ for n yields the following:

$$I = \$30,000 \times 0.10 \times {}^1/_{12}$$
$$= \$250 .$$

3. *Mary Schiller receives $30 every 3 months from a bank account that pays a 6 percent annual interest rate. How much is invested in the account?* Because PV_0 is the unknown in this example, Equation 3.1 is rearranged:

$$PV_0 = \frac{I}{i \times n} . \tag{3.2}$$

Substituting $30 for I, 0.06 for i, and $\frac{1}{4}$ (0.25) for n yields the following:

$$PV_0 = \frac{\$30}{0.06 \times 0.25}$$
$$= \$2,000 .$$

It is also useful to be able to calculate the amount of funds a person can expect to receive at some point in the future. In financial mathematics, the *terminal*, or future value of an investment is called FV_n and denotes the principal plus interest accumulated at the end of n years. It is written as follows:

$$FV_n = PV_0 + I . \tag{3.3}$$

4. *Mr. E. Z. Go borrows $1,000 for 9 months at a rate of 8 percent per annum. How much will he have to repay at the end of the 9-month period?*

49

Combining Equations 3.1 and 3.3 to solve for FV_n results in the following new equation:

$$FV_n = PV_0 + (PV_0 \times i \times n),$$

or

$$FV_n = PV_0[1 + (i \times n)] . \tag{3.4}$$

Substituting $1,000 for PV_0, 0.08 for i, and ¾ (9 months = ¾ of 1 year) for n yields the following:

$$FV_{3/4} = \$1,000[1 + (0.08 \times {}^3/_4)]$$
$$= \$1,000(1 + 0.06)$$
$$= \$1,060 .$$

This problem can be illustrated using the following time line:

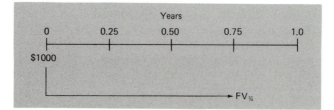

5. *Ms. E. Z. Come agrees to invest $1,000 in a venture that promises to pay 10 percent simple interest each year for 2 years. How much money will she have at the end of the second year?* Using Equation 3.4 and assuming two 10 percent simple interest payments, the future value of Ms. E. Z. Come's investment at the end of 2 years is computed as follows:

$$FV_2 = PV_0 + (PV_0 \times i \times 2)$$
$$= \$1,000 + (\$1,000 \times 0.10 \times 2)$$
$$= \$1,000 + \$200$$
$$= \$1,200 .$$

This problem can be illustrated using the following time line:

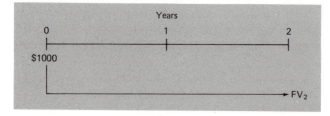

In general, in the case of *simple interest*, the future, or terminal, value FV_n at the end of n years is given by Equation 3.4.

50

COMPOUND INTEREST AND FUTURE VALUE

Compound interest is interest that is paid not only on the principal, but also on any interest earned but not withdrawn during earlier periods. For example, if Jerry Jones deposits $1,000 in a savings account paying 6 percent interest compounded annually, the future (compound) value of his account at the end of 1 year (FV$_1$) is calculated as follows:

$$FV_1 = PV_0(1 + i) \tag{3.5}$$
$$= \$1,000(1 + 0.06)$$
$$= \$1,060 \, .$$

This problem can be illustrated using the following time line:

If Jones leaves the $1,000 *plus* the accumulated interest in the account for another year, its worth at the end of the second year is calculated as follows:

$$FV_2 = FV_1(1 + i) \tag{3.6}$$
$$= \$1,060(1 + 0.06)$$
$$= \$1,123.60 \, .$$

This problem can be illustrated using the following time line:

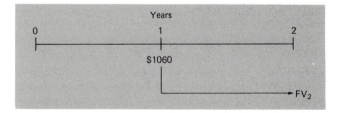

Recall that in the case of compound interest, interest in each period is earned not only on the principal, but also on any interest accumulated during previous periods and not withdrawn. Note that if Jones's account paid simple interest instead of compound interest, its value at the end of 2 years would be $1,120 instead of $1,123.60. The $3.60 difference is the interest on the first period's interest, 0.06 × $60.

If Jones makes no withdrawals from the account for another year, it will total the following at the end of the third year:

$$FV_3 = FV_2(1 + i) \tag{3.7}$$
$$= \$1,123.60(1 + 0.06)$$
$$= \$1,191.02 .$$

This problem can be illustrated using the following time line:

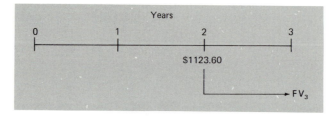

If the account paid only simple interest, it would be worth only $1,180 at the end of 3 years.

A general formula for computing compound values can be developed by combining Equations 3.5, 3.6, and 3.7. Substituting Equation 3.6 into Equation 3.7 yields the following equation:

$$FV_3 = FV_1(1 + i)(1 + i) ,$$

or

$$FV_3 = FV_1(1 + i)^2 . \tag{3.8}$$

Substituting Equation 3.5 into Equation 3.8 yields the following:

$$FV_3 = PV_0(1 + i)(1 + i)^2 ,$$

or

$$FV_3 = PV_0(1 + i)^3 . \tag{3.9}$$

This equation can be further generalized to calculate the future value at the end of year n for any sum compounded at interest rate i:

$$FV_n = PV_0(1 + i)^n . \tag{3.10}$$

Although Equation 3.10 is useful for solving compound value problems involving 1, 2, 3, or even 4 years into the future, it is rather tedious to use this equation for problems involving longer time periods. For example, solving for 20 years into the future would require calculating $(1 + i)^{20}$. *Compound value interest factors* (CVIFs) are commonly used to simplify such computations. Table I at the end of the book provides a listing of compound value interest factors for interest rates up to 60 years. Since each compound value interest factor is defined as $(1 + i)^n$, Equation 3.10 may be rewritten as follows:

$$FV_n = PV_0(CVIF_{i,n}) , \qquad\qquad (3.11)$$

where i = the nominal interest rate per annum, and n = the number of years.

To better understand Table I, it is helpful to think of each factor as the result of investing or lending $1 for a given number of time periods, n at interest rate i. The solution for any amount other than $1 is the product of that principal amount times the factor for a $1 principal amount.

A portion of Table I is reproduced here as Table 3–1. Table 3–1 can be used to determine the value of $1,000 compounded at 6 percent for 20 years:

$$FV_{20} = PV_0(CVIF_{0.06,20})$$
$$= \$1,000(3.207)$$
$$= \$3,207 .$$

The 3.207 figure is arrived at by reading the 6 percent or 0.06, column down and the 20 row under the "Year" heading across to where they meet.

As another example, $1,000 compounded at 10 percent for 20 years yields the following:

$$FV_{20} = PV_0(CVIF_{0.10,20})$$
$$= \$1,000(6.728)$$
$$= \$6,728 .$$

The compound value interest factor tables also can be used to solve for interest rates and the number of years. For example, to determine how long it would take for $1,000 invested at 8 percent to double, search the 8 percent column to locate a compound value interest factor of 2.000. The closest value to this figure is 1.999. Reading to the left of this figure, it can be seen that the original $1,000 would be worth nearly $2,000 in 9 years.

TABLE 3–1   Compound (Future) Value Interest Factors (CVIFs) for $1 at Interest Rate i for n Years*

			INTEREST RATE (i)		
Year (n)	1%	5%	6%	8%	10%
1	1.010	1.050	1.060	1.080	1.100
2	1.020	1.102	1.124	1.166	1.210
3	1.030	1.158	1.191	1.260	1.331
4	1.041	1.216	1.262	1.360	1.464
5	1.051	1.276	1.338	1.469	1.611
8	1.083	1.477	1.594	1.851	2.144
9	1.094	1.551	1.689	1.999	2.358
10	1.105	1.629	1.791	2.159	2.594
20	1.220	2.653	3.207	4.661	6.728
25	1.282	3.386	4.292	6.848	10.835

*The values in this and similar tables in this text have been rounded off to three places. When large sums of money are involved, more accurate tables or financial calculators should be used.

This problem also can be solved algebraically:

$$FV_n = PV_0(CVIF_{0.08,n})$$

$$CVIF_{0.08,n} = \frac{FV_n}{PV_0}$$

$$= \frac{\$2,000}{\$1,000}$$

$$= 2.000 .$$

Referring to Table 3–1, the closest value to CVIF = 2.000 under the 8 percent column is 1.999, which occurs at approximately 9 years.[2]

It is also useful to be able to solve compound value problems for i. For example, the compound value interest factor for an investment requiring an initial outlay of $1,000 and promising a $1,629 return after 10 years is as follows:

$$CVIF_{i,10} = \frac{FV_{10}}{PV_0}$$

$$= \frac{\$1,629}{\$1,000}$$

$$= 1.629 .$$

Reading across the 10-year row in Table 3–1, 1.629 is found in the 5 percent column. Thus, the investment yields a 5 percent compound rate of return. For values that fall between those found in the interest tables in this book, interpolation can be used. Examples of interpolation are provided in Chapter 10. Financial calculators can provide accurate answers to all the problems discussed in this chapter. Interpolation is not required when calculators are used. (See the "Calculator Applications" section at the end of this chapter.)

Compounding also can be illustrated graphically. Figure 3–1 shows the effects of time, n, and interest rate, i, on the growth of a $100 investment. As the figure shows, the higher the compound interest rate, the faster the growth rate of the value of the initial principal. The notion that an interest rate may be thought of as a *growth rate* will be useful during later discussions of valuation and cost of capital.

PRESENT VALUE

The compound, or future, value calculations answer the question, What will be the future value of X dollars invested today, compounded at some rate of interest, i? The financial decision maker, however, often is faced with an-

[2]In a shortcut solution to this type of problem known as the "Rule of 72," the number 72 is divided by the interest rate to determine the number of years it would take for a sum of money to double. In this case, 72/8% = 9. The Rule of 72 also can be used to determine the interest rate required for a sum of money to double in a given number of years: 72/9 = 8%. The Rule of 72 does not yield exact figures, but it can be used to calculate very good approximations.

FIGURE 3–1   **Growth of a $100 Investment at Various Compound Interest Rates** _____

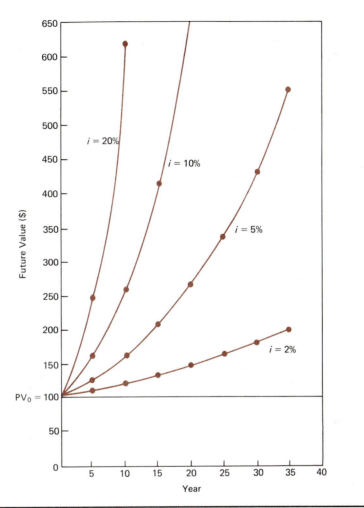

other type of problem: Given some future value, FV_n, what is its equivalent value today? That is, what is its present value, PV_0? The solution requires *present value* calculations, which are used to determine the dollar amount today, PV_0, that is equivalent to some promised *future* dollar amount, FV_n. The equivalence depends upon the rate of interest (return) that can be earned on investments during the time period under consideration.

The relationship between compound value and present value can be shown by rewriting Equation 3.10 to solve for PV_0:

$$FV_n = PV_0(1 + i)^n ,$$ (3.10)

or

$$PV_0 = FV_n \left[\frac{1}{(1 + i)^n} \right] ,$$ (3.12)

where $1/(1+i)^n$ is the reciprocal of the compound value factor. The process of finding present values is frequently called *discounting*. Equation 3.12 is the basic discounting formula.

To illustrate the use of Equation 3.12, suppose your banker offers to pay you $255.20 in 5 years if you deposit X dollars today at an annual 5 percent interest rate. Whether the investment would be worthwhile depends on how much money you must deposit, or the *present value* of the X dollars. Table 3–1 can be used to solve the problem as follows:

$$PV_0 = FV_5\left(\frac{1}{CVIF_{0.05,5}}\right)$$

$$= \$255.20\left(\frac{1}{1.276}\right)$$

$$= \$200 .$$

This problem can be illustrated with the following time line:

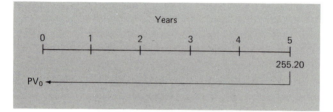

Thus, an investment of $200 today would yield a return of $55.20 in 5 years.

Because determining the reciprocals of the compound value interest factors, $1/(1 + i)^n$, can be a tedious process, *present value interest factors* (PVIFs) are commonly used to simplify such computations. Accordingly, Equation 3.12 can be written in the following form:

$$PV_0 = FV_n(PVIF_{i,n}) . \tag{3.13}$$

Table II at the end of the book provides a number of present value interest factors. A portion of Table II is reproduced here as Table 3–2.

For example, Table 3–2 can be used to determine the present value of $1,000 received 20 years in the future discounted at 10 percent:

$$PV_0 = FV_{20}(PVIF_{0.10,20})$$

$$= \$1,000(0.149)$$

$$= \$149 .$$

Thus, $149 invested today at 10 percent interest compounded annually for 20 years would be worth $1,000 at the end of the period. Conversely, the promise of $1,000 in 20 years is worth $149 today, given a 10 percent interest rate.

Present value interest factors also can be used to solve for interest rates. For example, suppose you wish to borrow $5,000 today from an associate.

TABLE 3–2   Present Value Interest Factors (PVIFs) for $1 at Interest Rate _i_ for _n_ Years

Year (n)	INTEREST RATE, (i)					
	1%	5%	6%	8%	10%	13%
1	0.990	0.952	0.943	0.926	0.909	0.885
2	0.980	0.907	0.890	0.857	0.826	0.783
3	0.971	0.864	0.840	0.794	0.751	0.693
4	0.961	0.823	0.792	0.735	0.683	0.613
5	0.951	0.784	0.747	0.681	0.621	0.543
8	0.923	0.677	0.627	0.540	0.467	0.376
10	0.905	0.614	0.558	0.463	0.386	0.295
20	0.820	0.377	0.312	0.215	0.149	0.087
25	0.780	0.295	0.233	0.146	0.092	0.047

The associate is willing to loan you the money if you promise to pay back $6,802 in 4 years from today. The compound interest rate your associate is charging can be determined as follows:

$$PV_0 = FV_4(PVIF_{i,4})$$

$$\$5,000 = \$6,802(PVIF_{i,4}).$$

$$PVIF_{i,4} = \frac{5,000}{6,802}$$

$$= 0.735.$$

Reading across the 4-year row in Table 3–2, 0.735 is found in the 8 percent column. Thus, the effective interest rate on the loan is 8 percent per year, compounded annually.

Another common example of the use of present value tables is the calculation of the compound rate of growth of an earnings or dividend stream. Suppose the Gamma Machine Corporation had earnings of $3.50 per share in 19X1. These earnings grew to $6.45 at the end of 19X6. Over this 5-year period, what was the compound annual rate of growth in Gamma's earnings? The answer to this problem can be obtained by solving for the present value interest factor over the 5-year period as follows:

$$\$3.50 = \$6.45(PVIF_{i,5})$$

$$PVIF_{i,5} = 0.543.$$

From Table II or Table 3–2 we find this present value interest factor in the 5-year row under the 13 percent interest, or growth rate, column. Hence the compound annual rate of growth in Gamma's earnings per share is 13 percent.

The discounting process also can be illustrated graphically. Figure 3–2 shows the effects of time, _n_, and interest rate, _i_, on the present value of a $100 investment. As the figure shows, the higher the discount rate, the lower the present value of the $100.

57

FIGURE 3–2   Present Value of $100 at Various Discount Rates

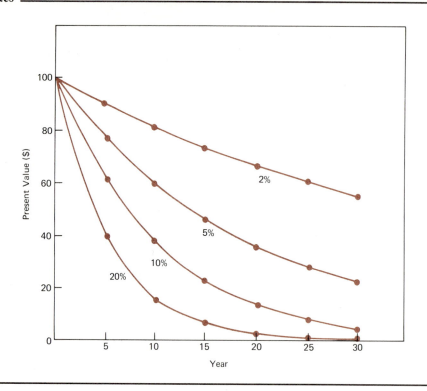

ANNUITIES

An *annuity* is the payment or receipt of equal amounts of money per period for a specified amount of time.[3] An *ordinary annuity* is one in which the payments or receipts occur at the *end* of each period, as shown in Figure 3–3. An *annuity due* is one in which payments or receipts occur at the *beginning* of each period, as shown in Figure 3–4. Most lease payments, such as apartment rentals, as well as life insurance premiums, are annuities due.

In a 4-year ordinary annuity the last payment is made at the end of the fourth year. In a 4-year annuity due, the last payment is made at the end of the third year (the beginning of the fourth year).[4]

COMPOUND SUM (FUTURE VALUE)
OF AN ANNUITY

Compound sum of annuity (CSAN) problems ask the question, If *R* dollars are deposited in an account at the end of each year for *n* years, and if the deposits earn interest rate *i* compounded annually, what will be the value of

---

[3]This discussion focuses primarily on periods of 1 year.

[4]This discussion emphasizes ordinary annuities. The procedure for adjusting ordinary annuity interest factors to accommodate annuity due calculations is found in Appendix 3A to this chapter.

FIGURE 3–3   Time Line of an Ordinary Annuity of $100 per Period for 4 Periods _____

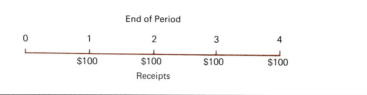

the account at the end of n years? To illustrate, suppose Ms. Jefferson receives a 3-year annuity of $1,000 per year and deposits the money in a savings account at the end of each year. The account earns interest at a rate of 6 percent compounded annually. How much will her account be worth at the end of the 3-year period?

The problem involves the calculation of future values. The last deposit, R_3, made at the end of year 3, will earn no interest. Thus, its future value follows:

$$FV_{3rd} = R_3(1 + 0.06)^0$$
$$= \$1,000(1)$$
$$= \$1,000 .$$

The second deposit, R_2, made at the end of year 2, will be in the account for one full year before the end of the 3-year period, and it will earn interest. Thus, its future value is as follows:

$$FV_{2nd} = R_2(1 + 1.06)^1$$
$$= \$1,000(1.06)$$
$$= \$1,060 .$$

The first deposit, R_1, made at the end of year 1, will be in the account earning interest for two full years before the end of the 3-year period. Thus, its future value is the following:

$$FV_{1st} = R_1(1 + 0.06)^2$$
$$= \$1,000(1.124)$$
$$= \$1,124 .$$

FIGURE 3–4   Time Line of an Annuity Due of $100 per Period for 4 Periods _____

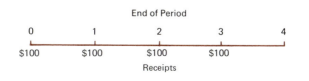

The sum of the three figures is the compound sum of the annuity:

$$\begin{aligned} \text{CSAN} &= \text{FV}_{3\text{rd}} + \text{FV}_{2\text{nd}} + \text{FV}_{1\text{st}} \\ &= \$1{,}000 + \$1{,}060 + \$1{,}124 \\ &= \$3{,}184 \; . \end{aligned}$$

The compound sum of an annuity interest factor (CVIFA) is the sum of the compound value interest factors from Table I. In this example the compound sum of an annuity interest factor is calculated as:

$$\begin{aligned} \text{CVIFA}_{0.06,3} &= \text{CVIF}_{0.06,2} + \text{CVIF}_{0.06,1} + \text{CVIF}_{0.06,0} \\ &= 1.124 + 1.060 + 1.000 \\ &= 3.184 \; . \end{aligned}$$

Figure 3–5 illustrates this concept.

Tables of the compound sum of an ordinary annuity interest factors are available to simplify such computations. Table III at the end of the book provides a number of compound sum of an annuity interest factors. A portion of Table III is reproduced here as Table 3–3.

The compound sum of an ordinary annuity (CSAN) may be calculated by multiplying the annuity amount, R, by the appropriate interest factor, $\text{CVIFA}_{i,n}$:[5]

$$\text{CSAN} = R(\text{CVIFA}_{i,n}) \; . \tag{3.14}$$

Table 3–3 can be used to solve the problem involving Ms. Jefferson's annuity. Since $R = \$1{,}000$, the interest factor for $n = 3$ years, and $i = 6\%$ is

FIGURE 3–5   Time Line of a Compound Sum of an Ordinary Annuity ($R = \$1{,}000; i = 6\%; n = 3$) _____

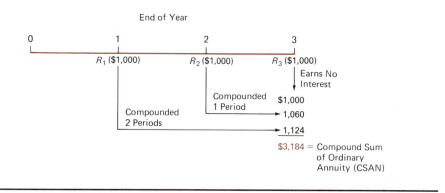

_____

[5]The formula for computing CVIFAs other than those shown in Table III is $\text{CVIFA}_{i,n} = [(1+i)^n - 1]/i$

TABLE 3–3   Compound Sum of an Ordinary Annuity Interest Factors (CVIFA) for $1 per Year at Interest Rate _i_ for _n_ Years

End of year, (n)	INTEREST RATE, (i)			
	1%	5%	6%	10%
1	1.000	1.000	1.000	1.000
2	2.010	2.050	2.060	2.100
3	3.030	3.152	3.184	3.310
4	4.060	4.310	4.375	4.641
5	5.101	5.526	5.637	6.105
10	10.462	12.578	13.181	15.937
20	22.019	33.066	36.786	57.275
25	28.243	47.727	54.865	98.347

3.184, the compound sum of an ordinary annuity can be calculated as follows:

$$CSAN = R(CVIFA_{0.06,3})$$
$$= \$1,000(3.184)$$
$$= \$3,184 .$$

Sinking fund problem   Compound sum of an annuity interest factors also can be used to find the annuity amount that must be invested each year to produce a future value. This is sometimes called a _sinking fund problem_. Suppose the Omega Graphics Company wishes to set aside an equal, annual, end-of-year amount in a "sinking fund account" earning 10 percent per annum over the next 5 years. The firm wants to have $5 million in the account at the end of 5 years in order to retire (pay off) $5 million in outstanding bonds. How much must be deposited in the account at the end of each year?

We know that the future value (CSAN) is $5 million, and that the appropriate interest factor (CVIFA) from Table 3–3 or Table III is 6.105 (10 percent for 5 years). Using Equation 3.14, we can solve for the annuity amount (that is, the sinking fund deposit) as follows:

$$CSAN = R(CVIFA_{0.10,5})$$
$$\$5,000,000 = R(6.105)$$
$$R = \$819,001 .$$

By depositing $819,001 at the end of each of the next 5 years in the account earning 10 percent per annum, Omega will accumulate the $5 million needed to retire the bonds.

PRESENT VALUE OF AN ANNUITY

The present value of an annuity (PVAN) is the sum of the present value of a series of equal periodic payments.[6] For example, to find the present value of

[6]This text focuses primarily on annual payments.

a $1,000 annuity received at the end of each year for 5 years discounted at a 6 percent rate, the sum of the individual present values would be determined as follows:

$$PVAN = \$1,000\left[\frac{1}{(1 + 0.06)^1}\right] + \$1,000\left[\frac{1}{(1 + 0.06)^2}\right]$$
$$+ \$1,000\left[\frac{1}{(1 + 0.06)^3}\right] + \$1,000\left[\frac{1}{(1 + 0.06)^4}\right]$$
$$+ \$1,000\left[\frac{1}{(1 + 0.06)^5}\right].$$

Referring to the interest factors in Table 3–2 yields the following:

$$
\begin{aligned}
PVAN &= \$1,000(PVIF_{0.06,1}) + \$1,000(PVIF_{0.06,2}) + \$1,000(PVIF_{0.06,3}) \\
&\quad + \$1,000(PVIF_{0.06,4}) + \$1,000(PVIF_{0.06,5}) \\
&= \$1,000(0.943) + \$1,000(0.890) + \$1,000(0.840) \\
&\quad + \$1,000(0.792) + \$1,000(0.747) \\
&= \$1,000(0.943 + 0.890 + 0.840 + 0.792 + 0.747) \\
&= \$4,212 .
\end{aligned}
$$

Figure 3–6 illustrates this concept.

Tables of the present value of an ordinary annuity interest factors (PVIFA) are available to simplify such computations.[7] Table IV at the end of the book provides a number of present value of an annuity interest factors. A portion of Table IV is reproduced here as Table 3–4.

The present value of an annuity can be determined by multiplying the annuity amount by the appropriate interest factor:

FIGURE 3–6   Time Line of a Present Value of an Ordinary Annuity ($R = \$1,000$; $i = 6\%$; $n = 5$)

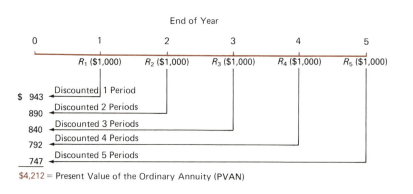

$4,212 = Present Value of the Ordinary Annuity (PVAN)

[7] The formula for computing PVIFAs other than those shown in Table IV is $PVIFA_{i,n} = [1 - 1/(1 + i)^n]/i$.

TABLE 3–4   Present Value of an Ordinary Annuity Interest Factors (PVIFA) for $1 per Year at Interest Rate *i* for *n* Years

End of year, (n)	INTEREST RATE, (i)			
	1%	5%	6%	10%
1	0.990	0.952	0.943	0.909
2	1.970	1.859	1.833	1.736
3	2.941	2.723	2.673	2.487
4	3.902	3.546	3.465	3.170
5	4.853	4.329	4.212	3.791
10	9.471	7.722	7.360	6.145
20	18.046	12.462	11.470	8.514
25	22.023	14.094	12.783	9.077

$$PVAN = R(PVIFA_{i,n}) . \qquad (3.15)$$

Referring to Table 3–4 to determine the interest factor for $i = 6\%$ and $n = 5$, the present value of an annuity in the previous problem can be calculated as follows:

$$PVAN = R(PVIFA_{0.06,5})$$
$$= \$1,000(4.212)$$
$$= \$4,212 .$$

Present value of an annuity interest factors also can be used to solve for the rate of return expected from an investment. Suppose the Big Spring Tool Company purchases a machine for $100,000. This machine is expected to generate annual cash flows of $23,742 to the firm over the next 5 years. What is the expected rate of return from this investment?

Using Equation 3.15, we can determine the expected rate of return in this example as follows:

$$PVAN = R(PVIFA_{i,5})$$
$$\$100,000 = \$23,742(PVIFA_{i,5})$$
$$PVIFA_{i,5} = 4.212 .$$

From the 5-year row in Table 3–4 or Table IV, we see that a PVIFA of 4.212 occurs in the 6 percent column. Hence, this investment offers a 6 percent expected rate of return.

Capital recovery problem and loan amortization   Present value of an annuity interest factors also can be used to find the annuity amount necessary to recover a capital investment, given a required rate of return on that investment. This is called a *capital recovery problem*. Similarly, present value of an annuity interest factors can be used to find the payments necessary to pay off a loan.

Suppose you borrowed $10,000 from the Whisperwood Bank. The loan is for a period of 3 years at an interest rate of 10 percent. It requires that you make three equal, annual, end-of-year payments that include both principal and interest on the outstanding balance. Equation 3.15 and either Table 3–4 or Table IV can be used to solve this problem as follows:

$$PVAN = R(PVIFA_{0.10,3})$$
$$\$10,000 = R(2.487)$$
$$R = \$4,020.91 \ .$$

By making three annual, end-of-year payments to the bank of $4,020.91 each, you will completely pay off your loan, plus provide the bank with its 10 percent interest return. This can be seen in the following loan amortization table:

End of Year	Payment	Interest (10%)	Principal Reduction	Remaining Balance
0	—	—	—	$10,000.00
1	$4,020.91	$1,000.00	$3,020.91	6,979.09
2	4,020.91	697.91	3,323.00	3,656.09
3	4,020.91	365.61	3,656.09*	0*

*Due to rounding, the remaining balance is not exactly zero. The use of a calculator or more accurate interest tables would eliminate this rounding error. (See the "Calculator Applications" section of this chapter for the calculator solution to this problem.)

At the end of each year, you pay the bank $4,020.91. During the first year, $1,000 of this payment is interest ($0.10 \times \$10,000$ remaining balance), and the rest ($3,020.91) is applied against the principal balance owed at the beginning of the year. Hence, after the first payment, you owe $6,979.09 ($10,000 − $3020.91). Similar calculations are done for years 2 and 3.

SOLVING THE FINANCIAL DILEMMA

Recall from the "Financial Dilemma" at the beginning of this chapter that Natalie Mayer has been offered the option of continuing her present mortgage payments of $852.39 over the next 27 years and 10 months to pay off her 10.875 percent home mortgage, or to increase the monthly payments to $1,691.49, receive a reduction in the interest rate to 10 percent, and pay off the loan in 5 years and 10 months. If Mayer has investment opportunities expected to yield a 15 percent rate of return over the life of the mortgage, should she accept the early payoff offer?

This problem can be treated as a present value of an annuity problem.[8] What Mayer wishes to determine is which alternative has the lower present value cost. For simplicity, she will ignore the effects of the tax deductibility of interest in this example. Including the tax effect does not alter the final

---

[8]The solution to this problem requires either a more complete set of tables than those provided in your text or, preferably, a financial calculator. We have simply set up the problem and indicated the final answer here. The calculations were done on a Texas Instruments Professional Business Analyst (BA-55) calculator. See the "Calculator Applications" section following "Problems" in this chapter.

decision. Under the original mortgage, Mayer would make 334 payments of $852.39 each month. The monthly discount rate is 1.25 percent (15%/12 months per year). The following is the present value of this annuity:

$$PVAN = \$852.39(PVIFA_{0.0125,334})$$
$$= \$67,115 .$$

Under the First Federal option, Mayer would make seventy payments of $1,691.49 each month. The monthly discount rate is 1.25 percent. The present value of this annuity follows:

$$PVAN = \$1,691.49(PVIFA_{0.0125,70})$$
$$= \$78,603 .$$

Thus, given a 15 percent investment opportunity rate for Mayer, the early payment plan is not worth accepting, since its present value cost is more than $11,000 higher than the present value cost of the original alternative.

COMPOUNDING PERIODS

Thus far it has been assumed that compounding (and discounting) occur annually. Recall the general compound interest equation:

$$FV_n = PV_0(1 + i)^n , \tag{3.10}$$

where PV_0 is the initial deposit, i the annual interest rate, n the number of years, and FV_n the future value that will accumulate from the annual compounding of PV_0. An interest rate of i percent per year for n years is assumed.

In some circumstances, interest on an account is compounded *semiannually* instead of annually; that is, half of the nominal annual interest rate, $i/2$, is earned at the end of 6 months. The investor earns additional interest on the interest earned *before* the end of the year, or $(i/2)PV_0$. In calculating interest compounded semiannually, Equation 3.10 is rewritten as follows:

$$FV_n = PV_0\left(1 + \frac{i}{2}\right)^{2n} .$$

The same logic applies to interest compounded *quarterly:*

$$FV_n = PV_0\left(1 + \frac{i}{4}\right)^{4n} .$$

In general, the compound interest for any number of periods during a year may be computed by means of the following equation:

$$FV_n = PV_0\left(1 + \frac{i}{m}\right)^{mn} , \tag{3.16}$$

TABLE 3–5 Effects of Different Compounding Frequencies on Future Values of $1,000 at a 10 Percent Interest Rate*

Initial Amount	Compounding Frequency	Future Value, FV_1 (End of Year 1)
$1,000	Yearly	$1,100.00
1,000	Semiannually	1,102.50
1,000	Quarterly	1,103.81
1,000	Monthly	1,104.71
1,000	Daily	1,105.16
1,000	Continuously*	1,105.17

*For advanced applications, it is useful to know that continuous compounding is obtained by letting m approach infinity in $FV_n = PV_0(1 + i/m)^{mn}$. In this case, $\lim_{m \to \infty}(1 + i/m)^m = e^i$, and the compound value expression becomes $FV_n = PV_0(e)^{in}$, where e is the exponential number having the approximate value of 2.71828.

where i is the *annual nominal interest rate,* or the yearly rate of interest stated in the security or loan agreement; m is the number of times during the year the interest is compounded; and n is the number of years.

Table 3–5 contains a number of future values, FV_1, for $1,000 earning a nominal interest of 10 percent with several different compounding frequencies. It can be seen that the more frequent the compounding, the greater the future value of the deposit, and the greater the *effective* interest rate. Effective interest, in contrast to *nominal* interest, is the *actual* rate of interest earned by the lender.

The relationship between present values and compound values suggests that present values also will be affected by the frequency of compounding. In general, the present value of a sum to be received at the end of year n, discounted at the rate of i percent and compounded m times per year, is as follows:

$$PV_0 = \frac{FV_n}{(1 + i/m)^{mn}}. \tag{3.17}$$

Table 3–6 contains a number of present values, PV_0, for $1,000 received one year in the future discounted at a nominal interest rate of 10 percent with several different compounding frequencies. It can be seen that the more frequent the compounding, the smaller the present value of a future amount.

TABLE 3–6 Effects of Different Compounding Frequencies on Present Values of $1,000 at a 10 Percent Interest Rate

Amount	Compounding Frequency	Present Value, PV_0
$1,000	Yearly	$909.09
1,000	Semiannually	907.03
1,000	Quarterly	905.95
1,000	Monthly	905.21
1,000	Daily	904.85
1,000	Continuously	904.84

Throughout the text, discussion focuses on annual compounding instead of compounding for more frequent periods, because it simplifies matters and because the differences between the two are small. Similarly, unless otherwise stated, cash flows from a security or investment project are assumed to be received in a lump sum at the beginning or end of each period. More frequent compounding periods require more extensive tables or the use of a business calculator programmed to solve financial mathematics problems.

PRESENT VALUE OF UNEVEN CASH FLOWS

Many problems in finance—particularly in the area of capital budgeting—cannot be solved according to the simplified format of the present value of an annuity, because the periodic cash flows are not equal. Consider, for example, the following stream of cash flows from an investment in a piece of machinery:

End of Year	Cash Flow
0	− $1,000
1	+ 500
2	+ 1,500
3	+ 2,000

The present value of this or any other stream of unequal cash flows (whether positive or negative) is equal to the sum of the present values. Assuming an interest rate of 10 percent, the present value of this investment above is calculated as follows:

$$
\begin{aligned}
PV_0 &= -\$1,000(PVIF_{0.10,0}) + \$500(PVIF_{0.10,1}) \\
&\quad + \$1,500(PVIF_{0.10,2}) + \$2,000(PVIF_{0.10,3}) \\
&= -\$1,000(1.000) + \$500(0.909) + \$1,500(0.826) + \$2,000(0.751) \\
&= \$2,195.50 \, .
\end{aligned}
$$

An individual who invests the initial $1,000 and requires a 10 percent return will earn $2,195.50 in present value cash flows *in addition* to the required 10 percent. This is shown in Figure 3–7.

As can be seen later in the text, during the discussion of capital budgeting, calculations of this type are extremely important when making project evaluations.

DETERMINANTS OF DISCOUNTING AND COMPOUNDING RATES

This chapter has assumed values for the compounding and discounting rates that were used in the various problems. What factors determine the appropriate rate to use in a specific situation?

67

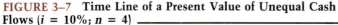

FIGURE 3–7   Time Line of a Present Value of Unequal Cash Flows ($i = 10\%$; $n = 4$)

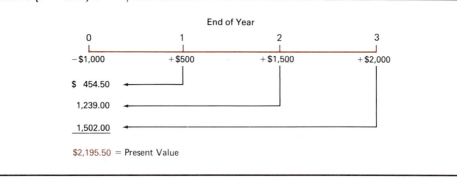

One important factor is the general level of interest rates in the economy. Interest rates are set by the forces of supply and demand for funds in the economy. An important factor that influences the general level of interest rates is the current and expected future level of inflation. When the inflation rate is high, interest rates also tend to be high.

The time frame over which an investment is being considered also influences the choice of a discounting or compounding rate. In general, interest rates tend to be higher on securities having a longer maturity than on securities having a shorter maturity.

Finally, the risk of the investment that is being considered also determines the appropriate compounding or discounting rate. At any point in time an array of interest rates are available in the market. For example, investors in low risk U.S. Government securities might require a 10 percent annual return. Investors in somewhat riskier corporate bonds might require a 13 percent annual return. Finally, investors in common stock might require a 17 percent rate of return. Generally, the higher the risk, the greater the required return on a security or investment project. The nature of risk and its impact on required returns is discussed in more detail in Chapters 5 and 12.

SUMMARY

- Financial mathematics plays an important role in many areas of financial decision making.

- An understanding of the concept of *interest* is crucial to sound financial management. *Simple interest* is interest that is either paid or earned on the principal sum only. The basic simple interest formula follows:

$$I = PV_0 \times i \times n .$$

- *Compound interest* is interest that is paid not only on principal, but also on any interest earned but not withdrawn during earlier periods. The basic compound (future) value formula is as follows:

$$FV_n = PV_0(1 + i)^n .$$

Compound value interest factors, like those provided in Table I at the end of the book, simplify compound value calculations.

- The *present value* of a sum of money to be received at some point of time in the future is determined by the number of years the investment extends into the future and the interest rate earned during that period. The following is the basic present value formula:

$$PV_0 = \frac{FV_n}{(1 + i)^n} .$$

Present value interest factors are found in Table II at the end of the book.

- An *annuity* is the payment or receipt of a series of equal sums per period for a specified number of periods. In an *ordinary annuity* the payments or receipts occur at the *end* of each period. In an *annuity due* the payments or receipts occur at the *beginning* of each period. Tables III and IV at the end of the book contain interest factors for the *compound sum of an ordinary annuity* and for the *present value of an ordinary annuity*.

- *Sinking fund problems* determine the annuity amount that must be invested each year to produce a future value.

- *Capital recovery problems* determine the annuity amount necessary to recover some initial investment.

- The more frequently compounding occurs during a given period, the higher the *effective* interest rate on an investment. More frequent compounding results in higher future values and lower present values than less frequent compounding at the same interest rate.

- In solving financial mathematics problems it is necessary to answer two questions:
1. Do we need a future value or a present value?
2. Are we dealing with a single amount or an annuity?
Once these questions have been successfully answered, the following table can be used to select the appropriate table of interest factors:

	Future Value	Present Value
Single Sum	Table I	Table II
Annuity	Table III	Table IV

- The appropriate compounding or discount rate to use in a particular problem depends upon the general level of interest rates in the economy, the time frame used for analysis, and the risk of the investment being considered.

QUESTIONS AND TOPICS FOR DISCUSSION

1. Which would you rather receive—the proceeds from a 2-year investment paying 5 percent simple interest per year, or from one paying 5 percent compound interest? Why?

2. Which is greater—the compound value interest factor (CVIF) for 10 percent and 2 years or the present value interest factor (PVIF) for 10 percent and 2 years?

3. What happens to the present value of an annuity as the interest rate increases? What happens to the compound sum of an annuity as the interest rate increases?

4. Which would you prefer to invest in—a savings account paying 6 percent compounded annually, or a savings account paying 6 percent compounded daily? Why?

5. What type of contract might require the use of annuity due computations?

6. What effect does more frequent compounding have on present values?

7. Why should each of the following be familiar with compounding and present value concepts?
   a. A marketing manager.
   b. A personnel manager.

8. Explain what is meant by the "Rule of 72." How can it be used in finance applications? (See Footnote 2.)

9. What is the relationship between present value and future value?

10. What is the difference between an ordinary annuity and an annuity due? Give examples of each.

11. If the required rate of return increases, what is the impact on the following?
    a. A present value of an annuity.
    b. A future value (compound sum) of an annuity.

12. Explain how compound sum of an annuity interest factors can be used to solve a sinking fund problem.

13. Describe how to set up a loan amortization schedule.

14. November 21, 1980, was the day of the tragic fire in the MGM Grand Hotel in Las Vegas. At the time of the fire, the hotel had only $30 million of liability insurance. One month after the fire, the hotel bought an extra $170 million of liability coverage for a premium of $37.5 million, retroactive to November 1, 1980 (before the fire). Based on your knowledge of present value concepts, why would insurers be willing to issue insurance to MGM under these conditions?

PROBLEMS*

1. How much will $1,000 deposited in a savings account earning a compound annual interest rate of 6 percent be worth at the end of the following number of years?
   a. 3 years.
   b. 5 years.
   c. 10 years.

2. If you require a 9 percent return on your investments, which would you prefer?
   a. $5,000 today.
   b. $15,000 5 years from today.
   c. $1,000 per year for 15 years.

*Problems in color have check answers provided at the end of the book.

3. A leading broker has advertised money multiplier certificates that will triple your money in 9 years; that is, if you buy one for $333.33 today, it will pay you $1,000 at the end of 9 years. What rate of return will you earn on these money multiplier certificates?

4. You have $10,000 to invest. Assuming annual compounding, how long will it take for the $10,000 to double if it is invested at the following rates?
   a. 5 percent.
   b. 10 percent.
   c. 15 percent.
   d. 20 percent.

5. The Tried and True Corporation had earnings of $0.20 per share in 1967. By 1984, a period of 17 years, they had grown to earnings of $1.01 per share. What has been the compound annual rate of growth in the company's earnings?

6. What is the present value of $600 to be received at the end of 8 years, assuming the following annual interest rate?
   a. 4 percent.
   b. 8 percent.
   c. 20 percent.
   d. 0 percent.

7. Mr. Jones bought a building for $50,000 payable on the following terms: a $10,000 down payment and twenty-five equal annual installment payments to include principal and interest of 10 percent per annum. Calculate the amount of the installment payments. How much of the first year's payment goes toward reducing the principal amount?

8. A firm purchases 100 acres of land for $200,000 and agrees to remit twenty equal annual installments of $41,067 each. What is the true annual interest rate on this loan?

9. Thirty years ago, Jesse Jones bought ten acres of land for $500 per acre in what is now downtown Houston. If this land grew in value at a 10 percent per annum rate, what is it worth today?

10. Susan Robinson is planning for her retirement. She is 30 years old today and would like to have $500,000 when she turns 55. She estimates that she will be able to earn an 8 percent rate of return on her retirement investments over time; she wants to set aside a constant amount of money every year (at the end of the year) to help achieve her objective. How much money must Robinson invest at the end of each of the next 25 years to realize her goal of $500,000 at the end of that time?

11. What would you be willing to pay for a $1,000 bond paying $80 interest each year and maturing in 25 years if you wanted the bond to yield the following rates of return?
   a. 5 percent.
   b. 8 percent.
   c. 12 percent.
   (NOTE: At maturity, the bond will be retired and the holder will receive $1,000 in cash. Bonds typically are issued with $1,000 face, or par, values. The actual market value at any point in time will tend to rise as interest rates fall and fall as interest rates rise.)

12. James Street's son, Harold, is 10 years old today. Harold is already making plans to go to college on his eighteenth birthday, and his father wants to start putting money away now for that purpose. Street estimates that Harold will need $15,000, $16,000, $17,000, and $18,000 for his freshman, sophomore, junior, and senior

years, respectively. He plans on making these amounts available to Harold at the beginning of each of these years.

Street would like to make eight annual deposits (the first of which would be made on Harold's eleventh birthday, 1 year from now, and the last on his eighteenth birthday, the day he leaves for college) in an account earning 10 percent. He wants the account to eventually be worth enough to *just* pay for Harold's college expenses. Any balances remaining in the account will continue to earn the 10 percent.

How much will Street have to deposit in this "planning" account each year to provide for Harold's education?

13. There are two investment opportunities open to you: Investment 1 and Investment 2. Each has an initial cost of $10,000. Assuming that you desire a 12 percent return on your initial investment, compute the present value of the two alternatives and evaluate their relative attractiveness:

INVESTMENT 1		INVESTMENT 2	
Cash flows	Year	Cash flows	Year
$5,000	1	$8,000	1
6,000	2	7,000	2
7,000	3	6,000	3
8,000	4	5,000	4

14. Your great-uncle Claude is 82 years old. Over the years he has accumulated savings of $70,000. He estimates that he will live another 10 years at the most and wants to spend his savings by then. (If he lives longer than that, he figures that you will be happy to take care of him.)

Uncle Claude places his $70,000 into an account earning 9% percent annually and sets it up in such a way that he will be making ten equal annual withdrawals—the first one occurring 1 year from now—such that his account balance will be zero at the end of 10 years. How much will he be able to withdraw each year?

15. You decide to purchase a building for $30,000 by paying $5,000 down and assumming a mortgage of $25,000. The bank offers you a 15-year mortgage requiring annual end-of-year payments of $3,188 each. The bank also requires you to pay a 3 percent loan origination fee, which will reduce the effective amount the bank lends to you. Compute the annual percentage rate of interest on this loan.

16. You purchase a 5-acre vacation property for $10,000. Five years from now you expect to sell the property for $22,550. Your anticipated annual end-of-year tax payments will be $500 for each of the next 5 years. Compute the annual rate of return on this investment.

HINT: Try 14 percent.

17. An investment promises to pay $5,000 at the end of each year for the next 5 years and $4,000 at the end of each year for years 6 through 10.

a. If you require a 10 percent rate of return on an investment of this sort, what is the maximum amount you would pay for this investment?

b. Assuming that the payments are received at the *beginning* of each year, what is the maximum amount you would pay for this investment?

18. You are considering investing in a bond that matures 20 years from now. It pays an annual end-of-year coupon rate of interest of 8.75 percent, or $87.50 per year. The bond currently sells for $915. Your marginal income tax rate (applied to in-

terest payments) is 50 percent. Your capital gains tax rate is 25 percent. Capital gains taxes are paid when the bond matures 20 years from now; they are computed based on the difference between the bond's current price and its maturity value of $1,000. What is your *after-tax* rate of return if you buy this bond today and hold it until maturity?

HINT Try 5 percent.

19. Your parents have discovered a $500 bond at the bottom of their safe deposit box. The bond was given to you by your late great-aunt Hilda on your second birthday. The bond pays interest at a rate of 4 percent per annum, compounded annually. Interest accumulates and is paid at the time the bond is redeemed. You are now 27 years old. What is the present worth of the bond (principal plus interest)?

20. Suppose that a local savings and loan association advertises a 6 percent annual rate of interest on regular accounts, compounded monthly. What is the effective annual percentage rate of interest paid by the savings and loan association?

21. Your mother is planning to retire this year. Her firm has offered her a lump sum retirement payment of $40,000 or a $5,000 lifetime annuity—whichever she chooses. Your mother is in reasonably good health and expects to live for at least 15 more years. Which option should she choose, assuming that a 7 percent interest rate is appropriate to evaluate the annuity?

22. A life insurance company has offered you a policy that will be fully paid up when you turn 45. At that time it will have a cash surrender value of $13,000. When you turn 65 the policy will have a cash surrender value of $41,675. What rate of interest is the insurance company promising you on your investment?

23. Your aunt would like to help you set up your new medical practice when you complete your medical training in 6 years. She wishes to have $150,000 available for your use at that time. How much must she invest in an account at the end of each of the next 6 years in order to reach her goal, if the account offers a 10 percent annual rate of return?

24. Strikler, Inc., has issued a $10 million, 10-year bond issue. The bonds require Strikler to establish a sinking fund and make ten equal, end-of-year deposits into the fund. These deposits will earn 9 percent annually, and the sinking fund should have enough accumulated in it at the end of 10 years to retire the bonds. What are the annual sinking fund payments?

25. Construct a loan amortization schedule for a 3-year, 9 percent loan of $30,000. The loan requires three equal, end-of-year payments.

26. You have just had your thirtieth birthday. You have two children. One will go to college 10 years from now and require four beginning-of-year payments for college expenses of $10,000, $11,000, $12,000, and $13,000. The second child will go to college 15 years from now and require four beginning-of-year payments for college expenses of $15,000, $16,000, $17,000, and $18,000. In addition, you plan to retire in 30 years. You want to be able to withdraw $50,000 per year (at the end of each year) from an account throughout your retirement. You expect to live 20 years beyond retirement. The first withdrawal will occur on your sixty-first birthday.

What equal, annual, end-of-year amount must you save for each of the next 30 years to meet these goals, if all savings earn a 15 percent annual rate of return?

27. If you deposit $1,000 a year (at the end of each of the next 5 years) in an account paying 12 percent per year, compounded semiannually, how much will you have in the account at the end of 10 years?

28. Shyster Investments has offered you the following investment opportunity:

- $5,000 at the end of each year for the first 5 years, plus

- $2,000 at the end of each year from years 6 through 10, plus
- $1,000 at the end of each year from years 11 through 20.

    a. How much would you be willing to pay for this investment if you required a 12 percent rate of return?

    b. If the payments were received at the beginning of each year, what would you be willing to pay for this investment?

29. Upon retirement your goal is to spend 5 years traveling around the world. To travel in the style to which you are accustomed will require $150,000 per year at the beginning of each year. If you plan to retire in 30 years, what are the equal, annual, end-of-year payments necessary to achieve this goal? The funds in the retirement account will compound at 10 percent annually.

CALCULATOR APPLICATIONS

Over the past decade there have been major technological advances in the area of calculators and microcomputers. These developments have brought dramatic increases in the computational power available to students and businesspeople at very low costs. Today, preprogrammed financial calculators have come down in price from initial levels of $500 and more to $25 to $60 for some of the most popular models now available. We are likely to witness a similar revolution in the price and general availability of microcomputers over the next 5 years.

    Because of the increasing availability of financial calculators at reasonable costs, "Calculator Applications" sections have been included throughout the book. These illustrate the use of the Texas Instruments (TI) Professional Business Analyst (BA-55) calculator. This calculator is widely used and relatively inexpensive. It has a broad range of capabilities that will serve you in nearly all business courses and in your future career. Other financial calculators also are available that have similar capabilities and operate in a similar manner. Owners of these calculators should refer to their user's manual for detailed instructions regarding the capabilities and operation of these devices.

FUTURE VALUE (COMPOUND INTEREST) PROBLEMS

Suppose you wish to know to how much $1,000 deposited in an account earning 8.85 percent interest, compounded quarterly, will grow over 5 years. This problem could not be handled very easily with generally available financial tables, because the interest rate is carried to two decimal places and because the problem assumes quarterly compounding.

1. First, turn on the calculator and clear the calculator and mode registers. Press [on/c] [2nd] **CL mode.**

2. Press the sequence [2nd] **Mode** until the display indicates you are in the FIN mode.

3. Press [2nd] **Fix** 2. This sets the display to two decimal places.

These first three steps are done each time you turn on the calculator to begin a new set of calculations.

4. Enter the initial deposit, that is, the present value: 1000 $\boxed{PV}$.
   The display will read *1000.00.*

5. Compute the rate of interest per quarter: 8.85 $\boxed{\div}$ 4 $\boxed{=}$.
   The display will read *2.21.*

6. Enter this quarterly interest rate by pushing $\boxed{\%i}$.
   The display will read *2.21.*

7. Enter the number of periods (quarters): 20 $\boxed{N}$.
   The display will read *20.00.*

8. To compute the future value, press $\boxed{CPT}$ $\boxed{FV}$.
   The answer is **$1549.10.**

Hence, at the end of 5 years the initial $1,000 deposit will grow to $1,549.10. It should be noted that in this and all the following financial mathematics calculations, the interest rate $\boxed{\%i}$, the number of periods $\boxed{N}$, the present value $\boxed{PV}$, the future value $\boxed{FV}$, and the periodic payment $\boxed{PMT}$ can be entered in any order on the TI-Professional Business Analyst calculator. The variable being solved for is always entered last and is preceded by the $\boxed{CPT}$ command.

PRESENT VALUE PROBLEMS

What is the present value of $175,300 received 6 years from today if the discount rate is 11.6 percent?

1. Clear the calculator and mode registers, set Mode to FIN, and fix the decimal places to two.
2. Enter the future value: 175300 $\boxed{FV}$.
3. Enter the discount rate per year: 11.6 $\boxed{\%i}$.
4. Enter the number of periods (years): 6 $\boxed{N}$.
5. Compute the present value: $\boxed{CPT}$ $\boxed{PV}$.

The answer is **$90,739.58.**

   The financial function keys also can be used to solve for the interest or growth rate. Tucson Electric Power Company had earnings per share of $1.70 in 1975 and $3.00 in 1982. What has been the compound annual rate of growth in earnings per share for Tucson?

1. Clear the calculator and mode registers, set Mode to FIN, and fix the decimal places to two.
2. Enter the future (ending) value: 3.00 $\boxed{FV}$.
3. Enter the number of years: 7 $\boxed{N}$.
4. Enter the present (beginning) value: 1.70 $\boxed{PV}$.
5. Compute the compound annual growth rate: $\boxed{CPT}$ $\boxed{\%i}$.

The answer is **8.45 percent.**

COMPOUND SUM (FUTURE VALUE) OF AN ANNUITY

Suppose you wish to know to how much $10,000 deposited into an account at the end of each of the next 10 years will grow assuming the account earns a 12.6 percent annual rate of return.

1. Clear the calculator and mode registers, set Mode to FIN, and fix the decimal places to two.
2. Enter the number of periods (years): 10 [N].
3. Enter the periodic (annual) rate of interest: 12.6 [%i.].
4. Enter the annual annuity amount (payment) as a negative amount (indicating an outlay): 10000 [+/−] [PMT].
5. Compute the future value (compound sum) of the annuity: [CPT] [FV].

The answer is **$180,658.88.**
   This problem also can be solved assuming that the payments are made at the beginning of each year, that is, an annuity due. To solve this problem as an annuity due, substitute the following step in place of Step 5: [2nd] **Due** [FV].
The answer is **$203,421.89.**
   Of course, the calculator can be used to solve for the payment [PMT] if you know the future value (CSAN) [FV], the interest rate per period [%i], and the number of periods [N]. Similarly, it can solve for the interest rate or the number of periods if the other input variables are known.

PRESENT VALUE OF AN ANNUITY

Assume that you plan to borrow $10,000 and intend to repay it over the next 3 years with three equal, annual, end-of-year payments of principal and interest. The annual rate of interest is 10 percent. What payment must be made at the end of each year?

1. Clear the calculator and mode registers, set Mode to FIN, and fix the decimal places to two.
2. Enter the present value: 10000 [PV].
3. Enter the annual interest rate: 10 [%i].
4. Enter the number of periods (years): 3 [N].
5. Compute the payment: [CPT] [PMT].

The answer is **$4021.15.** Note that this is slightly different from the answer found in the "Present Value of an Annuity" section in the main body of the chapter because of the rounding that occurs in the tables used in the book.
   If you wish to set up a loan amortization schedule for the loan, your calculator can be very helpful:

6. Compute the principal paid the first year: 1 [CPT] [2nd] **P/I.**
   Answer: **$3,021.15.**
7. Compute the first year's interest: [x⤢y].   Answer: **$1,000.00.**

8. Compute the principal paid the second year: 2 $\boxed{\text{CPT}}$ $\boxed{\text{2nd}}$ **P/I**. Answer: **$3,323.26.**

9. Compute the second year's interest: $\boxed{\text{x}\blacktriangleright\text{y}}$.   Answer: **$697.89.**

10. Compute the balance owed at the end of two periods: 2 $\boxed{\text{CPT}}$ $\boxed{\text{2nd}}$ **Bal.**   Answer: **$3,655.59.**

11. Compute the principal paid the third year: 3 $\boxed{\text{CPT}}$ $\boxed{\text{2nd}}$ **P/I**. Answer: **$3,655.59.**

12. Compute the third year's interest: $\boxed{\text{x}\blacktriangleright\text{y}}$.   Answer: **$365.56.**

13. Compute the total interest paid over 3 years: 3 $\boxed{\text{CPT}}$ $\boxed{\text{2nd}}$ **Acc.** Answer: **$2,063.44.**

14. Compute the balance owed at the end of 3 years: $\boxed{\text{x}\blacktriangleright\text{y}}$. Answer: **$0.00.**

This illustration demonstrates the power of preprogrammed financial calculators. The user's manual for this calculator illustrates the full range of capabilities of the calculator. Other illustrations of the financial applications of the calculator are provided in later chapters.

Calculators are excellent tools for taking the drudgery out of financial calculations. However, they are not a substitute for careful reasoning. You must still identify what kind of problem you are dealing with, and you need to set up the problem logically before beginning to work on your calculator. It is important that you double-check all work done on a calculator to be sure you have not pushed the wrong button during your calculations. You should also look at your answer to see that it is reasonable. You will get a feeling of the reasonability of various answers by examining Tables I through IV at the back of the text and working through a number of problems by hand, as well as with the aid of your calculator.

Adjusting Tables for Annuity Due Calculations

COMPOUND SUM OF AN ANNUITY DUE

Chapter 3 notes that Table III at the end of the book (compound sum of an annuity interest factor) assumes *ordinary* (end-of-year) annuities. For an *annuity due*, in which payments are made at the *beginning* of each year, the interest factors in Table III must be modified.

Consider the case of Ms. Jefferson cited in the chapter. If she deposits $1,000 in a savings account at the *beginning* of each year for the next 3 years and the account earns 6 percent interest, compounded annually, how much will be in the account at the end of 3 years? (Recall that when the deposits were made at the *end* of each year the account totaled $3,184 at the end of 3 years.)

Figure 3A–1 illustrates this problem as an *annuity due*. R_1 is compounded for 3 periods, R_2 for 2 periods, and R_3 for 1 period. The correct *annuity due* interest factor may be obtained from Table III by multiplying the CVIFA for 3 years and 6 percent (3.184) by 1 plus the interest rate (1 + 0.06). This yields

FIGURE 3A–1 Time Line of a Compound Sum of an Annuity Due (R = $1,000; i = 6%; n = 3) ⸻

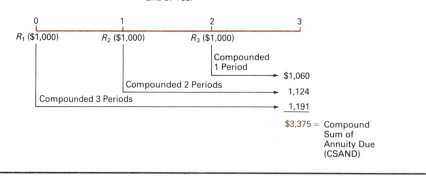

a CVIFA for an annuity due of 3.375, and the compound sum of the annuity due (CSAND) is calculated as follows:

$$\text{CSAND} = R[\text{CVIFA}_{i,n}(1 + i)] , \qquad (3A.1)$$

and

$$\text{CSAND} = \$1,000(3.375)$$
$$= \$3,375 .$$

Note that this amount is larger than the $3,184 obtained in the ordinary annuity example given in the chapter.

PRESENT VALUE OF AN ANNUITY DUE

Annuity due calculations are also important when dealing with the present value of an annuity problem. In these cases the interest factors in Table IV must be modified.

Consider the case of a 5-year annuity of $1,000 each year, discounted at 6 percent. What is the present value of this annuity if each payment is received at the *beginning* of each year? (Recall the example presented in Chapter 3, illustrating the concept of the present value of an annuity, in which each payment was received at the *end* of each year and the present value was $4,212.) Figure 3A–2 illustrates this problem.

The first payment received at the beginning of year 1 (end of year 0) is already in its present value form and therefore requires no discounting. R_2 is discounted for 1 period, R_3 is discounted for 2 periods, R_4 is discounted for 3 periods, and R_5 is discounted for 4 periods.

The correct *annuity due* interest factor for this problem may be obtained from Table IV by multiplying the present value of an ordinary annuity interest factor for 5 years and 6 percent (4.212) by 1 plus the interest rate (1 +

FIGURE 3A–2 Time Line of a Present Value of an Annuity Due ($R = \$1,000; i = 6\%; n = 5$)

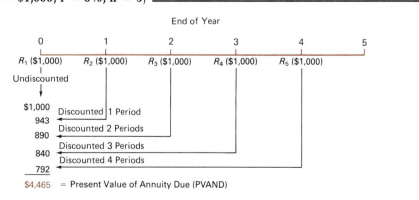

0.06). This yields a PVIFA for an annuity due of 4.465, and the present value of this annuity due (PVAND) is calculated as follows:

$$\text{PVAND} = R[\text{PVIFA}_{i,n}(1 + i)] , \qquad\qquad \textbf{(3A.2)}$$

and

$$\begin{aligned}\text{PVAND} &= \$1,000(4.465) \\ &= \$4,465 .\end{aligned}$$

Note that this amount is larger than the $4,212 obtained in the ordinary annuity example given in the chapter.

Annuity due calculations are especially important when dealing with rental or lease contracts, since it is common for these contracts to require that payments be made at the beginning of each period.

PROBLEMS*

1. The Lancer Leasing Company has agreed to lease a hydraulic trencher to the Chavez Excavation Company for $20,000 a year over the next 7 years. Lease payments are to be made at the beginning of each year.

    Assuming that Lancer invests these payments at an annual rate of 8 percent, how much will it have accumulated by the end of the seventh year?

2. The Mutual Assurance and Life Company is offering an insurance policy under either of the following two terms:
    a. Make a series of twelve $1,500 payments at the beginning of each of the next 12 years (the first payment being made today).
    b. Make a single lump sum payment today of $11,000 and receive coverage for the next 12 years.

    If you had investment opportunities offering a 9 percent annual return, which alternative would you prefer?

---

*Problems in color have check answers provided at the end of the book.

Chapter 4

The Valuation of Long-Term Securities

A FINANCIAL DILEMMA

National Airlines

The value of a security is determined by a number of different factors, in particular the expected returns from holding that security and the degree of risk involved. As the following example shows, the value of a security can change dramatically over time to reflect changes in expectations and demand.

On June 1, 1978, National Airlines stock traded for $15.75 per share on the New York Stock Exchange. During the previous year, it had traded for as much as $18.75 and as little as $10.12. Earnings were about $1.30 per share, and the stock was paying $0.50 in annual dividends.

On July 11, 1978, Texas International Airlines announced that it had acquired 9.2 percent of the shares of National Airlines stock and was considering making an attempt to gain control. On August 24, Pan American announced a plan to acquire National at a price of $35 per share, amended to $41 per share as of September 1. Subsequently, Eastern Airlines offered a $50 proposal of its own. Meanwhile, Texas International came back with an offer of $49.50 per share with an option to increase that amount.

To resolve this conflict, National proposed a five-round bidding procedure between Texas International, Pan American, and Eastern. Pan American was the successful bidder, paying $50 per share for National's stock.

Postscript: In spite of Pan American's high hopes for the merger, it has had a great deal of difficulty putting the two airlines together profitably. Since the merger, Pan American has experienced an almost continual stream of red ink—losing over $485 million in 1982 alone. Perhaps the market assessment of a $15.75 price for National was correct!

This chapter develops basic concepts and specific models of valuation for assets and securities. Since the maximization of the value of the enterprise is the primary objective of financial management, a full understanding of the valuation process is central to the study of financial management.

GLOSSARY OF NEW TERMS

Bond a long-term debt instrument that promises to pay the lender a series of periodic interest payments in addition to returning the principal at maturity. Most corporate bonds are offered in $1,000 principal amounts.

Book value the accounting value of an asset or a corporation. The book value per share of common stock is equal to the total book value of the company (that is, net worth) divided by the total number of shares of common stock outstanding.

Capitalization of income a method of determining the present value of an asset that is expected to produce a stream of future benefits. This involves *discounting* the stream of expected future benefits at an appropriate rate.

Coupon rate of interest the interest rate stated on a bond. The coupon rate of interest times the *par*, or principal, value of a bond determines the periodic dollar interest payments received by the bondholder.

Debenture a bond that is *not* secured by a mortgage on any specific asset but instead by the general credit and earning power of the issuing firm.

Going-concern value the value of a firm, assuming that the firm's organization and assets remain intact and are used to generate future income and cash flows.

Interest rate risk the variation in the market price (and hence in the realized rate of return, or yield) of a security that arises from changes in interest rates.

Liquidation value the value of a firm, assuming that it sells all its assets and stops using them to generate future income and cash flows.

Mortgage bond a bond that is secured by a pledge of a specific asset or group of assets.

Perpetual bond a bond that has no maturity date.

Required rate of return the rate used to value a stream of future benefits from an asset (also called the *discount rate*). The riskier the return from the asset, the higher the required rate of return.

Yield to maturity the discount rate that equates the present value of all expected payments and the repayment of principal from a bond with the present bond price.

INTRODUCTION

Firms issue various types of long-term securities to help meet their needs for funds. These include long-term debt, preferred stock, and common stock. The valuation of long-term securities is important to a firm's financial managers, as well as current owners, prospective investors, and security analysts.

For example, financial managers should understand how the price or value of the firm's securities (particularly common stock) is affected by investment, financing, and dividend decisions. Similarly, both current owners and prospective investors should be able to compare their own valuations of a firm's securities with actual market prices in order to make rational security purchase and sale decisions. Likewise, security analysts use valuation techniques in evaluating long-term corporate securities when making investment recommendations.

The chapter begins with a discussion of the general concept of valuation. It continues by developing valuation models for bonds, preferred stock, and common stock.

It is assumed throughout the chapter that the firms under discussion are *going concerns;* that is, their organization and assets will remain intact and be used to generate future income and cash flows. Techniques other than the ones described here must be used to value long-term securities of firms faced with the possibility of bankruptcy. In such cases the *liquidation value* of the firm's assets is the primary determinant of the value of the various types of long-term securities.[1]

VALUATION OF ASSETS

The value of any asset is based on the *expected future benefits* the owner will receive over the life of the asset. For example, the value of a *physical asset,* such as a new piece of equipment or production plant, is based on the expected cash inflows the asset will generate for the firm over its useful life. These cash inflows take the forms of increased revenues and/or reduced costs plus any salvage value received from the sale of the asset.[2]

Similarly, the value of a *financial asset,* such as a stock or bond, is based on the expected cash returns the asset will generate for the owner during the *holding period.* These returns take the form of interest or dividend payments over the holding period plus the amount the owner receives when the asset is sold.

One way of determining the value of an asset is to calculate the present value of the stream of expected future benefits discounted at an appropriate *required rate of return.* This is known as the *capitalization-of-income* method of valuation and is represented algebraically as follows:

$$V_0 = \frac{R_1}{(1 + i)^1} + \frac{R_2}{(1 + i)^2} + \ldots + \frac{R_n}{(1 + i)^n}, \tag{4.1}$$

or, using summation notation, as follows:

$$V_0 = \sum_{t=1}^{n} \frac{R_t}{(1 + i)^t}, \tag{4.2}$$

where V_0 is the value of the asset at time zero, R_t the expected cash return in period t, i the required rate of return, or discount rate, and n the length of the holding period.

[1]This topic is discussed in Chapter 24.
[2]Chapter 9 contains a more lengthy discussion of capital budgeting.

For example, assume that the cash returns, R_t, on a long-term security are expected to be an annuity of $1,000 per year for $n = 6$ years, and the required rate of return, i, is 8 percent. Using the capitalization-of-income method, the value of this security is computed as follows:

$$V_0 = \sum_{t=1}^{6} \frac{\$1,000}{(1 + 0.08)^t}$$
$$= \$1,000(\text{PVIFA}_{0.08,6})$$
$$= \$1,000(4.623)$$
$$= \$4,623 \ .$$

The *required rate of return, i,* on an asset is a function of the uncertainty, or risk, associated with the returns from the asset.[3] The risk-return relationship is illustrated in Figure 4–1. Note that the function slopes upward, indicating that the higher the risk, the higher the investor's required rate of return. The risk-free rate (r_f in Figure 4–1) represents the investor's required rate of return on an asset whose returns are known with certainty, that is, an asset with which no risk of default (that is, failure to pay principal and interest when due) is associated. The measurement of risk and the development of the risk-return tradeoff function is discussed further in the next chapter.

FIGURE 4–1   **Required Rate of Return on an Asset as a Function of Risk**

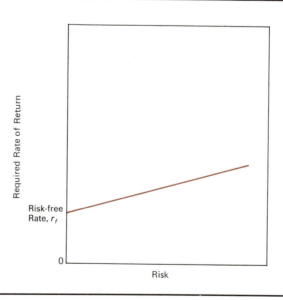

[3]Recall that risk was defined in Chapter 2 as the possibility that actual future returns will deviate from expected returns.

MARKET VALUE OF ASSETS AND
MARKET EQUILIBRIUM

From Equation 4.1 it can be seen that the value of an asset depends on both the expected cash returns, R_t, and the owner's (or prospective buyer's) required rate of return, i. However, potential buyers and sellers can have different opinions of an asset's value based on their individual assessments of the potential cash returns from the asset and individual required rates of return.

The *market price*, or *market value*, of an asset is determined in much the same way as the price of most goods and services in a market-oriented economy—namely, by the interaction of supply and demand. This is shown in Figure 4–2. Potential buyers are represented by a *demand* schedule showing the maximum prices they are willing to pay for given quantities of an asset, and potential sellers are represented by a *supply* schedule showing the minimum prices at which they are willing to sell given quantities of the asset. The transaction price, the price at which an asset is sold, occurs at the intersection of the demand and supply schedules. The intersection represents the *market value*, or *market price*, of the asset, P_m, in Figure 4–2.

The market price of an asset is the value placed on the asset by the *marginally satisfied buyer and seller* who exchange assets in the marketplace. A marginally satisfied buyer is one who paid his or her maximum acceptable price for the asset, and a marginally satisfied seller is one who received his or her minimum acceptable price for the asset. Clearly, many owners (potential sellers) will place a higher value on the asset than the current market

FIGURE 4–2   Market Price of an Asset

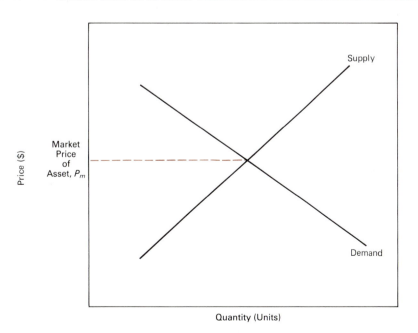

price; likewise, many investors (potential buyers) will place a lower value on the asset than the current market price.

Market equilibrium exists whenever there is no tendency for the price of the asset to move higher or lower. At this point the *expected* rate of return on the asset is equal to the marginal investor's *required* rate of return. *Market disequilibrium* occurs when investors' required rates of return, i, and/or the expected returns, R_t, from the asset change. The market price adjusts over time—that is, it moves upward or downward—to reflect changing conditions, and a new market equilibrium is established.

Most financial assets are bought and sold in organized markets. The bonds, preferred stock, and common stock of many small, as well as most medium and large, firms are traded in one or more national or regional exchanges or in the over-the-counter market. Since large numbers of competing buyers and sellers operate in the markets, the market price of a security represents a *consensus* judgment as to the security's value or worth. While no such market-determined measure of value exists for securities of firms that are not publicly traded, their market values can be approximated using the market price of publicly traded securities of firms having similar operating and financial characteristics.

Book value of an asset

The book value of an asset represents the *accounting* value, or the historical acquisition cost minus any accumulated depreciation or other write-offs. Since market value is normally related to expected future returns, and book value is based on historical cost, the market value of an asset does not necessarily bear any relationship to the book value. In fact, the market value may be either greater or less than the book value, depending on the changes over time in the market capitalization rate and the asset's expected future returns. For example, in the early 1980s, AT&T's stock was selling at a price nearly $10 below its book value. When *new* shares of stock are sold at a price below book value, the effect is a dilution in earnings and book values per share to *existing* stockholders.

BOND VALUATION

The valuation of bonds is a relatively straightforward process, since future cash returns to the bondholder are always specified ahead of time in a contract. The firm issuing the bonds must meet the interest and principal payments as they come due, or the bonds will go into default. Defaulting on bond payments can have disastrous consequences for the firm and its stockholders, such as possible bankruptcy, reorganization, or both.

Due to default risk, investors normally require a higher rate of return than the risk-free rate before agreeing to hold a firm's bonds. The required rate of return varies among bond issues of different firms, depending on their relative risks of default. All other things being equal, the greater the default risk on a given bond issue, the higher the required rate of return.

BONDS HAVING FINITE MATURITY DATES

Bonds that mature within finite periods of time pay the investor two types of returns: interest payments $(I_1, I_2, \ldots, I_n)$ during each of the next n periods and a principal payment (M) in period n. Period n is defined as the bond's *maturity date*, or the time at which the principal must be repaid and the bond issue retired.

The value of a bond can be computed by applying the capitalization-of-income method to the series of cash returns:

$$P_0 = \frac{I_1}{(1 + k_d)^1} + \frac{I_2}{(1 + k_d)^2} + \cdots + \frac{I_{n-1}}{(1 + k_d)^{n-1}} + \frac{I_n + M}{(1 + k_d)^n}, \quad (4.3)$$

where P_0 is the present value of the bond at time zero, or its purchase date, and k_d is the investor's required rate of return on this particular bond issue.

Since all of the interest payments on a bond are normally equal (that is, $I_1 = I_2 = \ldots = I_{n-1} = I_n = I$), Equation 4.3 can be simplified as follows:

$$P_0 = \sum_{t=1}^{n} \frac{I}{(1 + k_d)^t} + \frac{M}{(1 + k_d)^n}. \quad (4.4)$$

The first term in Equation 4.4, $\sum_{t=1}^{n} I/(1 + k_d)^t$, represents the present value of an *annuity* of I per period for n periods; the second term, $M/(1 + k_d)^n$, represents the present value of a *single payment* of M in period n. Equation 4.4 can be further simplified as follows:

$$P_0 = I(\text{PVIFA}_{k_d,n}) + M(\text{PVIF}_{k_d,n}). \quad (4.5)$$

To illustrate the use of Equation 4.5, consider the following example. Standard Oil of California issued 7 percent *debentures* (that is, bonds that are not secured by any specific asset) maturing in 1996. The bonds were issued in $1,000 denominations. For the purpose of simplifying this example, assume that the bonds mature at the *end* of 1996 and that interest is paid annually at the *end* of each year.[4]

An investor who wishes to purchase one of these bonds on December 31, 1984, and requires an 8 percent rate of return on this particular bond issue would compute the value of the bond as will be shown.[5] These calculations assume that the investor will hold the bond until maturity and receive

---

[4]This particular bond issue actually matures on April 1, 1996, and pays interest *semiannually* on April 1 and October 1 each year.

[5]A question often arises as to why investors would require an 8 percent rate of return on bonds that pay only 7 percent interest. The answer is that the required rate of return has increased since the bonds were originally issued. At the time of issue, the prevailing rate of interest (that is, the required rate of return) on bonds of this maturity and quality was approximately 7 percent. Hence, the coupon rate was set at 7 percent. Because of such factors as tight credit market conditions, higher inflation, increased firm risk, and so on, investors now require a higher rate of return to induce them to purchase these bonds.

FIGURE 4–3   **Illustration of the Cash Returns from a Standard Oil of California Bond**

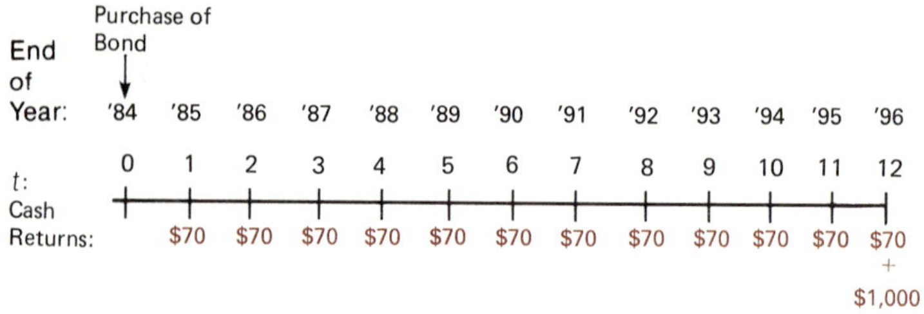

twelve annual interest payments of $70 each ($I$ = $1,000 × 0.07) plus a principal payment, M, of $1,000 at the end of the twelfth year, 1996. The cash returns from this bond are shown in Figure 4–3. Substituting these values along with k_d = 8% (0.08) into Equation 4.4 gives the following value for the bond:[6]

$$P_0 = \sum_{t=1}^{12} \frac{\$70}{(1 + 0.08)^t} + \frac{\$1,000}{(1 + 0.08)^{12}}$$

$$= \$70(\text{PVIFA}_{0.08,12}) + \$1,000(\text{PVIF}_{0.08,12})$$

$$= \$70(7.536) + \$1,000(0.397)$$

$$= \$527.52 + \$397$$

$$= \$924.52 \ (\text{or } \$925) \ .$$

In other words, an investor requiring an 8 percent return on this bond would be willing to pay $925 for it at the end of 1984.

An investor who desires more than an 8 percent rate of return on this bond would value it at a price less than $925. Similarly, an investor who requires less than 8 percent rate of return would value it at a price greater than $925. This *inverse relationship* between the required rate of return and the corre-

---

[6]Bond interest is normally paid *semiannually*. With semiannual interest and compounding, the value of this Standard Oil bond would actually be the following:

$$P_0 = \sum_{t=1}^{24} \frac{\$35}{(1 + 0.04)^t} + \frac{\$1,000}{(1 + 0.04)^{24}}$$

$$= \$35(\text{PVIFA}_{0.04,24}) + \$1,000(\text{PVIF}_{0.04,24})$$

$$= \$35(15.247) + \$1,000(0.390)$$

$$= \$533.65 + \$390$$

$$= \$923.65 \ (\text{or } \$924) \ .$$

This value differs only slightly from the value determined in the example in the text. Note that in the case of semiannual compounding, the annual interest rate is divided by 2 (0.08/2 = 0.04), and the number of periods is multiplied by 2 (12 × 2 = 24).

TABLE 4–1 Value of 7 Percent Coupon Rate Bonds at Various Required Rates of Return

Required Rate of Return, k_d	Value of 12-Year Bond	Value of 3-Year Bond
3%	$1,398	$1,113
5	1,177	1,055
6	1,084	1,027
7	1,000	1,000
8	925	974
9	857	949
11	740	902

sponding value of a bond to the investor is illustrated in Table 4–1 and Figure 4–4.

The relationship between a bond's value and the investor's required rate of return depends on the time remaining before maturity. All other things being equal, the value of a longer-term bond is affected more by changes in required rates of return than the value of a shorter-term bond. As Table 4–1 and Figure 4–4 show, the variation in the value of the 12-year bond is considerably greater than the variation of the 3-year bond over the range of required rates of return (3 to 11 percent).

Investors who purchase a bond at the price determined by Equation 4.4 and *hold it until maturity* will realize their required rate of return, regardless of

FIGURE 4–4 Value of 3-Year and 12-Year 7 Percent Coupon Rate Bonds

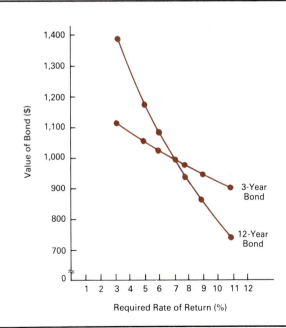

any changes in the market price of the bond.[7] However, if the market price of the bond declines due to a rise in prevailing interest rates (required rates of return), and if the bond is sold *prior to maturity*, the investors will earn less than their required rate of return and may even incur a loss on the bond. This variation in the market price (and hence in the realized rate of return) of a bond (or any fixed income security) is known as *interest rate risk*.

PERPETUAL BONDS

A *perpetual bond*, or perpetuity, is a bond issued without a finite maturity date.[8] Perpetual bonds promise to pay interest indefinitely, and there is no contractual obligation to repay the principal—that is, $M = 0$.

The valuation of a perpetual bond is simpler than the valuation of a bond having a finite maturity date. Assuming that the bond pays a fixed amount of interest, I, per period forever, the value is as follows:

$$P_0 = \sum_{t=1}^{\infty} \frac{I}{(1 + k_d)^t} \tag{4.6}$$

where k_d is the required rate of return. Equation 4.6 can be simplified in this way:[9]

---

[7]This assumes that the investor reinvests all interest received from the bond at a rate equal to the required rate of return on the bond. Otherwise the realized return will differ slightly from the required return.

[8]Perpetual bonds, also referred to as "consuls," are rare. Some countries, such as Great Britain, and some railroads, such as the Canadian Pacific and the Canadian National, have issued perpetual bonds.

[9]Equation 4.6 is the present value of an infinite series and can be simplified to Equation 4.7 by means of the following calculations:

Rewrite Equation 4.6 as follows:

$$P_0 = I \left[\frac{1}{(1 + k_d)^1} + \frac{1}{(1 + k_d)^2} + \frac{1}{(1 + k_d)^3} + \dots + \frac{1}{(1 + k_d)^n} \right]. \tag{a}$$

Multiply both sides of Equation a by $(1 + k_d)$:

$$P_0(1 + k_d) = I \left[1 + \frac{1}{(1 + k_d)^1} + \frac{1}{(1 + k_d)^2} + \frac{1}{(1 + k_d)^3} + \dots + \frac{1}{(1 + k_d)^{n-1}} \right]. \tag{b}$$

Subtract Equation a from Equation b:

$$P_0(1 + k_d - 1) = I \left[1 - \frac{1}{(1 + k_d)^n} \right]. \tag{c}$$

As $n \to \infty$ then $1/(1 + k_d)^n \to 0$ and Equation c approaches the following:

$$P_0(k_d) = I, \tag{d}$$

or

$$P_0 = \frac{I}{k_d} \text{ (Equation 4.7)}.$$

$$P_0 = \frac{I}{k_d} \, . \tag{4.7}$$

Consider, for example, the Canadian Pacific Limited Railroad's perpetual 4 percent debentures. What is the value of a $1,000 bond to an investor who requires an 8 percent rate of return on these Canadian Pacific bonds? Since I = 0.04 × $1,000, or $40, and k_d = 8%, Equation 4.7 can be used to compute the answer as follows:

$$P_0 = \frac{\$40}{0.08}$$

$$= \$500 \, .$$

Thus, the investor would be willing to pay up to $500 for this bond.

YIELD TO MATURITY OF A BOND

The *yield to maturity* of a bond is the rate of return earned on a bond purchased at a given price and held until maturity.[10] If the current price of a bond, P_0, the uniform annual interest payments, I, and the maturity value, or principal, M, are known, the yield to maturity of a bond having a finite maturity date can be calculated by solving the following equation for r:

$$P_0 = \sum_{t=1}^{n} \frac{I}{(1 + r)^t} + \frac{M}{(1 + r)^n} \, . \tag{4.8}$$

Note that Equation 4.8 is very similar to Equation 4.4, except that k_d, the required rate of return, has been replaced by r, the yield to maturity. Equation 4.4 is used to determine the value of a bond P_0 to the investor when I, M, and k_d are known, whereas Equation 4.8 is used to determine the yield to maturity r, when I, M, and P_0 are known. The yield to maturity can be used to compare the risk of two or more bonds that are similar *in all other respects*, including time to maturity. The bond with the higher yield to maturity is the one perceived to be the riskier by investors. Also, the yield to maturity on existing bonds can be used as an estimate of the required returns of investors on any new (and similar) bonds the firm may issue.

There are a number of ways to compute the yield to maturity for a bond. First, special bond tables can be used to directly identify the yield to maturity for any particular bond. Also, many financial calculators currently available are capable of computing yields to maturity. (The "Calculator Applications" section at the end of this chapter illustrates this type of calculation.) In the absence of these aids it is necessary to use the "trial-and-error" approach in

---

[10]In contrast, *current yield* on a bond having a finite maturity date is defined as the annual interest payment, I, divided by the current price, P_0. The yield to maturity calculation assumes that cash flows from the bond occurring prior to maturity are reinvested at a rate equal to the yield to maturity.

conjunction with the present value tables found at the end of the text.[11]

Suppose, for example, that the Tanoan Development Corporation has a bond outstanding with 20 years remaining to maturity. The bond pays annual coupon interest at the rate of 8 percent, or $80 per year. The bond is currently selling for $761. What is its yield to maturity?

Since the bond is selling at a discount—that is, less than its $1,000 par value—the rate of return required by investors (the yield to maturity) is greater than the 8 percent coupon rate. First try 10 percent:

$$P_0 = \$80(\text{PVIFA}_{0.10,20}) + \$1,000(\text{PVIF}_{0.10,20})$$
$$= \$80(8.514) + \$1,000(0.149)$$
$$= \$830 .$$

Since this value is higher than the current bond price, it is necessary to try an even higher discount rate. Using 12 percent,

$$P_0 = \$80(\text{PVIFA}_{0.12,20}) + \$1,000(\text{PVIF}_{0.12,20})$$
$$= \$80(7.469) + \$1,000(0.104)$$
$$= \$702 .$$

Since this value is below the current bond price, it is necessary to try a lower rate, such as 11 percent:

$$P_0 = \$80(\text{PVIFA}_{0.11,20}) + \$1,000(\text{PVIF}_{0.11,20})$$
$$= \$80(7.963) + \$1,000(0.124)$$
$$= \$761 .$$

Thus, the yield to maturity on this bond is 11 percent.[12]

The rate of return, or yield to maturity, on a *perpetual* bond can be found by solving the following bond valuation equation for *r*:

$$P_0 = \frac{I}{r} , \qquad\qquad (4.9)$$

---

[11]An *approximate* yield to maturity can be calculated by using the following expression:

$$\text{Approximate yield to maturity} = \frac{\text{Annual interest} + \dfrac{\text{Bond discount or premium}}{\text{Years to maturity}}}{\text{Average investment}}$$

$$= \frac{I + (M - P_0)/n}{(P_0 + M)/2} .$$

If the bond is selling at a discount (premium), then the term $M - P_0$ is positive (negative). (Problems 5 and 6 at the end of the chapter contain examples of the application of this expression.)

[12]The yield to maturity equation implicitly assumes that the annual interest payments are reinvested over the remaining life of the bond at the calculated rate, *r*.

which gives

$$r = \frac{I}{P_0}. \tag{4.10}$$

It is not necessary to employ the trial-and-error method to determine the yield for a perpetual bond.

For example, recall the 4 percent Canadian Pacific Limited Railroad debentures described earlier. If the current price of a bond is $640, what is the yield on the bond? Substituting $P_0 = \$640$ and $I = \$40$ (or 4 percent of $1,000) into Equation 4.10 gives the following:

$$r = \frac{\$40}{\$640}$$

$$= 0.0625 \text{ (or 6.25 percent)}.$$

VALUATION OF PREFERRED STOCK

Most preferred stock pays regular, fixed dividends. Preferred dividends per share are normally not increased when the earnings of a firm increase, nor are they cut or suspended unless the firm faces serious financial problems. If preferred stock dividends are cut or suspended for a period of time for whatever reason, the firm is usually required to make up the past due payments before paying any common stock dividends.[13] Thus, the investor's expected cash return from holding most preferred stocks can be treated as a fixed, constant amount per period.

The investor's required rate of return on a preferred stock issue is a function of the risk that the firm will be unable to meet its dividend payments. The higher the risk, the higher the required rate of return. Since bondholders have a prior claim over preferred stockholders on the income and assets of a firm, it is more risky to hold a firm's preferred stock than to hold its bonds. As a result, investors normally require a higher rate of return on preferred stock than on bonds.

Since many preferred stock issues do not have maturity dates, the cash returns (dividend payments) from holding no-maturity preferred stock can be treated as a perpetual stream of payments, or a *perpetuity*. Capitalizing the perpetual stream of dividend payments gives the following valuation expression:

$$P_0 = \sum_{t=1}^{\infty} \frac{D_p}{(1 + k_p)^t}, \tag{4.11}$$

---

[13]This feature of preferred stock is called the *cumulative dividend feature*.

where D_p is the dividend per period, and k_p is the investor's required rate of return.[14]

Equation 4.11 can be simplified into the following valuation model:

$$P_0 = \frac{D_p}{k_p} . \qquad (4.12)$$

To illustrate the use of Equation 4.12, assume that Gulf and Western pays annual end-of-year dividends on a $5.75 cumulative preferred stock issue. What is the value of this stock to an investor who requires a 9 percent rate of return on the investment? Substituting $5.75 for D_p and 0.09 for k_p yields the following:

$$P_0 = \frac{\$5.75}{0.09}$$

$$= \$63.89 .$$

GENERAL MODEL
FOR THE VALUATION OF COMMON STOCK

In principle, the valuation of common stock is no different from the valuation of other types of securities such as bonds and preferred stock. The basic procedure involves capitalizing (that is, discounting) the expected stream of returns received from holding the common stock. This is complicated by several factors, however.

First, the returns from holding a common stock take two forms: the cash dividend payments made during the holding period and/or changes in the price of the stock (capital gains or losses) over the holding period. All the returns paid to the common stockholder are derived from the firm's earnings and can either be paid to shareholders in the current period as cash dividends or reinvested in the firm to (it is hoped) provide higher future dividends and a higher stock price.

Second, because common stock dividends are normally expected to grow rather than remain constant, the relatively simple annuity and perpetuity formulas used in the valuation of bonds and preferred stock generally are not applicable, and more complicated models must be used.

Finally, the future returns from common stock usually are much more uncertain than the returns from bonds and preferred stock. Common stock dividend payments are related to the firm's earnings in some manner, and it can be very difficult to forecast future long-term earnings and dividend payments with a high degree of accuracy.

---

[14]Some preferred stock issues have a *call provision* that allows the firm to call in the stock for redemption under certain conditions that are spelled out when the preferred stock is issued. If an investor is considering purchasing a preferred stock issue that is expected to be called in the future, its value is calculated by capitalizing (that is, discounting) the call price plus the dividend payments to be received before the issue is called.

To better understand the application of the capitalization-of-income valuation method to common stock, it is best to begin by considering the *one*-period dividend valuation model and then move on to consider multiple-period valuation models.

ONE-PERIOD DIVIDEND VALUATION MODEL

Assume that an investor plans to purchase a common stock and hold it for *one* period. At the end of that period, the investor expects to receive a cash dividend, D_1, and sell the stock for a price, P_1. What is the value of this stock to the investor *today* (time 0), given a required rate of return on the investment, k_e?

In the capitalization-of-income valuation method the discounted present value of the returns on the stock is calculated as follows:

$$P_0 = \frac{D_1}{1 + k_e} + \frac{P_1}{1 + k_e}. \tag{4.13}$$

For example, if Ohio Engineering Company common stock is expected to pay a $1.00 dividend and sell for $27.50 at the end of 1 period, what is the value of this stock to an investor who requires a 14 percent rate of return? The answer is computed like this

$$
\begin{aligned}
P_0 &= \frac{\$1.00}{(1 + 0.14)} + \frac{\$27.50}{(1 + 0.14)} \\
&= \$1.00(\text{PVIF}_{0.14,1}) + 27.50(\text{PVIF}_{0.14,1}) \\
&= \$1.00(0.877) + 27.50(0.877) \\
&= \$24.99 \text{ (or } \$25\text{)} .
\end{aligned}
$$

Thus, the investor who purchases the stock for $25.00, collects the $1.00 dividend, and sells the stock for $27.50 at the end of 1 period will receive the 14 percent required rate of return.

TWO-PERIOD DIVIDEND VALUATION MODEL

Next, consider an investor who plans to purchase a common stock and hold it for *two* periods. The cash returns to the investor consist of cash dividends—D_1 at the end of the first period and D_2 at the end of the second period—and an amount, P_2, from the sale of the stock at the end of the second period. Capitalizing the returns at the investor's required rate of return, k_e, gives the following valuation equation:

$$P_0 = \frac{D_1}{(1 + k_e)^1} + \frac{D_2}{(1 + k_e)^2} + \frac{P_2}{(1 + k_e)^2}. \tag{4.14}$$

Returning to the example of the Ohio Engineering Company, assume that the company is expected to pay common stock dividends of $1.00 at the end of next year and $1.00 at the end of the second year, and that the market price of the stock is expected to be $30.35 two years from now. What is the current value of the stock if the investor requires a 14 percent rate of return? Substituting $1.00 for D_1, $1.00 for D_2, $30.35 for P_2, and 14 percent, or 0.14, for k_e into Equation 4.14 gives the following value for the stock:

$$P_0 = \frac{\$1.00}{(1 + 0.14)^1} + \frac{\$1.00}{(1 + 0.14)^2} + \frac{\$30.35}{(1 + 0.14)^2}$$

$$= \$1.00(PVIF_{0.14,1}) + \$1.00(PVIF_{0.14,2}) + \$30.35(PVIF_{0.14,2})$$

$$= \$1.00(0.877) + \$1.00(0.769) + \$30.35(0.769)$$

$$= \$24.98 \text{ (or } \$25 \text{)}.$$

n-PERIOD DIVIDEND VALUATION MODEL

The dividend valuation process just described can be generalized to the n-period case. The returns to the investor who purchases a share of common stock and holds it for n periods consist of dividend payments during each of the next n periods—D_1, D_2, . . ., D_n—plus an amount, P_n, from the sale of the stock at the end of the nth period. Capitalizing the returns at the investor's required rate of return, k_e, gives the following valuation equation:

$$P_0 = \frac{D_1}{(1 + k_e)^1} + \frac{D_2}{(1 + k_e)^2} + \dots + \frac{D_n}{(1 + k_e)^n} + \frac{P_n}{(1 + k_e)^n}, \quad (4.15)$$

which can be summarized as:

$$P_0 = \sum_{t=1}^{n} \frac{D_t}{(1 + k_e)^t} + \frac{P_n}{(1 + k_e)^n}. \quad (4.16)$$

Consider again the Ohio Engineering Company common stock. Suppose that the investor is considering purchasing a share of this stock and holding it for 5 years. Assume that the investor's required rate of return is still 14 percent. Dividends from the stock are expected to be $1.00 in the first year, $1.00 in the second year, $1.00 in the third year, $1.25 in the fourth year, and $1.25 in the fifth year. The expected selling price of the stock at the end of 5 years is $41.00.

Using Equation 4.16, the value of the stock to the investor is computed as follows:

$$P_0 = \frac{\$1.00}{(1 + 0.14)^1} + \frac{\$1.00}{(1 + 0.14)^2} + \frac{\$1.00}{(1 + 0.14)^3}$$

$$+ \frac{\$1.25}{(1 + 0.14)^4} + \frac{\$1.25}{(1 + 0.14)^5} + \frac{\$41.00}{(1 + 0.14)^5}$$

$$= \$1.00(PVIF_{0.14,1}) + \$1.00(PVIF_{0.14,2}) + \$1.00(PVIF_{0.14,3})$$

$$+ \$1.25(PVIF_{0.14,4}) + \$1.25(PVIF_{0.14,5}) + \$41.00(PVIF_{0.14,5})$$

$$= \$1.00(0.877) + \$1.00(0.769) + \$1.00(0.675)$$
$$+ \$1.25(0.592) + \$1.25(0.519) + \$41.00(0.519)$$
$$= \$24.99 \text{ (or } \$25) .$$

Note that the *current* value of a share of Ohio Engineering common stock is the same (that is, $P_0 = \$25.00$) regardless of whether the investor plans to hold it for 1, 2, or 5 years.[15]

A GENERAL MODEL
FOR THE VALUATION OF DIVIDENDS

In each of the valuation models described, the current value of the stock, P_0, is dependent upon the expected price of the stock at the end of the expected holding period—P_1 in the 1-period case, P_2 in the 2-period case, and P_n in the n-period case. Although this seems straightforward, providing accurate forecasts of stock prices when applying the models to specific stocks can be difficult, if not impossible. A final generalization permits the elimination of P_n from the model while at the same time showing that the dividend valuation models that have been discussed are consistent with one another.

First, the value of the stock at the end of the nth period, P_n, must be redefined. Using the capitalization-of-income approach, it can be shown that P_n is a function of all expected *future* dividends that the investor will receive in periods $n + 1$, $n + 2$, and so on. Discounting the stream of dividends at the required rate of return, k_e, gives the value of the stock at the end of the nth period:

$$P_n = \sum_{t=n+1}^{\infty} \frac{D_t}{(1 + k_e)^{t-n}} . \tag{4.17}$$

Substituting Equation 4.17 into Equation 4.16 yields the following:

$$P_0 = \sum_{t=1}^{n} \frac{D_t}{(1 + k_e)^t} + \sum_{t=n+1}^{\infty} \frac{D_t}{(1 + k_e)^t} ,$$

which can be further simplified into the following *general dividend valuation model:*

$$P_0 = \sum_{t=1}^{\infty} \frac{D_t}{(1 + k_e)^t} . \tag{4.18}$$

Thus, *the value of a firm's common stock to the investor is equal to the discounted present value of the expected future dividend stream.* As was shown, the valuation of a firm's common stock given by the n-period model

---

[15]The value of a stock at *any* point in time is simply the present value of all dividends expected to be paid from that time forward. Hence, the price, P_5, of $41 reflects the present value of dividends expected in years 6 through infinity.

(Equation 4.16) is equivalent to the valuation given by the general model (Equation 4.18). In addition, the 1- and 2-period valuation models (Equations 4.13 and 4.14) are equivalent to the general model (Equation 4.18).[16] The general dividend valuation model is applicable regardless of whether the stream of dividends over time is fluctuating or constant, increasing or decreasing.

Note that the general dividend valuation model treats the stream of dividends as a *perpetuity* having no finite termination date. Whereas this assumption is reasonable for firms that are going concerns, shorter time horizons must be used when considering firms that might be either acquired by other firms or liquidated in the foreseeable future.

There are some profitable firms (such as Digital Equipment and Teledyne) that reinvest all their earnings and do not pay current cash dividends. In fact, some profitable firms have *never* paid cash dividends for as long as they have been in existence and are not expected to do so in the near future. How can the general dividend valuation model be applied to the common stock of a firm such as this? It must be assumed that the firm will be able to start making regular, periodic cash dividend payments to its shareholders *at some time in the future*. Or, these returns could consist of the *proceeds from the sale of the firm's outstanding common stock* should the firm be acquired by another company. The value of such a firm's stock according to the general dividend valuation model (Equation 4.18) would be zero only if the firm were *never* expected to pay a cash dividend *of any type* to its shareholders.

As stated in Chapter 1, the primary goal of most firms is the *maximization of shareholder wealth*. The general dividend valuation model (Equation 4.18) indicates that shareholder wealth, as measured by the value of the firm's common stock, P_0, is a function of the expected stream of future dividend payments and the investor's required rate of return. Thus, when making financial decisions that are consistent with the goal of maximizing shareholder wealth, management should be concerned with how these decisions affect both the expected future dividend stream and the discount rate that investors apply to the dividend stream. The relationship between financial decision

FIGURE 4–5   Relationship between Financial Decisions and Shareholder Wealth

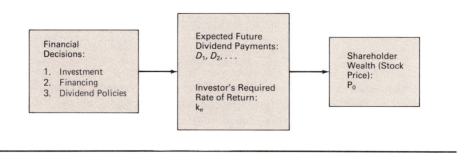

[16]You will be asked to demonstrate these relationships in Problem 15 at the end of this chapter.

98

making and shareholder wealth is illustrated in Figure 4–5. A primary emphasis of the financial management function is attempting to define and measure this relationship.

GROWTH MODELS FOR THE VALUATION OF COMMON STOCK

The general dividend valuation model can be simplified if a firm's dividend payments over time are expected to follow one of several fairly straightforward patterns, including *constant growth, zero growth,* and *above-normal growth.*

CONSTANT GROWTH DIVIDEND VALUATION MODEL

If a firm's future dividend payments per share are expected to grow at a *constant* rate, g, per period forever, then the dividend at any future time period t can be forecasted as follows:

$$D_t = D_0(1 + g)^t , \qquad (4.19)$$

where D_0 is the dividend in the current period $(t = 0)$. The expected dividend in period 1 is $D_1 = D_0(1 + g)^1$, whereas the expected dividend in period 2 is $D_2 = D_0(1 + g)^2$, and so on. The constant-growth curve in the center of Figure 4–6 illustrates such a dividend pattern.

FIGURE 4–6 **Dividend Growth Patterns**

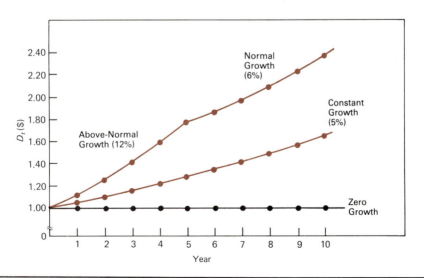

Substituting Equation 4.19 for D_t in the general dividend valuation model (Equation 4.18) yields the following:

$$P_0 = \sum_{t=1}^{\infty} \frac{D_0(1 + g)^t}{(1 + k_e)^t} . \tag{4.20}$$

Assuming that the required rate of return, k_e, is greater than the dividend growth rate, g, Equation 4.20 can be transformed algebraically to obtain the following simplified common stock valuation model:[17]

$$P_0 = \frac{D_1}{k_e - g} . \tag{4.21}$$

To apply this valuation model to a specific common stock issue, it is necessary to estimate the expected future dividend growth rate, g, per period for the firm. If the firm's historical dividend growth pattern is expected to continue into the foreseeable future, the growth rate in dividends per share for the past several years can be used to estimate the future compound annual expected dividend growth rate.

The constant growth dividend valuation model can be used to illustrate the two forms of returns an investor can expect to receive from holding a common stock. Solving Equation 4.21 for k_e yields the following:

$$k_e = \frac{D_1}{P_0} + g . \tag{4.22}$$

The investor's required rate of return is equal to the expected dividend yield, D_1/P_0, plus the capital gains yield, g—the expected increase in dividends and, ultimately, in the price of the stock.

For example, consider the Pennsylvania Manufacturing Company, which has estimated its common stock dividend for *next* year to be $0.90 per share. Earnings and dividends have been increasing at a compound annual rate of 5 percent for the past several years, and this growth rate is expected to continue into the foreseeable future. What is the value of a share of this stock to an investor who requires an 11 percent rate of return? Substituting $0.90 for D_1, 5 percent (0.05) for g, and 11 percent (0.11) for k_e in Equation 4.21 yields the following value for the Pennsylvania Manufacturing common stock:

$$P_0 = \frac{\$0.90}{0.11 - 0.05}$$

$$= \frac{\$0.90}{0.06}$$

$$= \$15 .$$

---

[17]Equation 4.21 is often referred to in finance literature as the *Gordon model*, for Myron J. Gordon, who pioneered its use. See Myron J. Gordon. *The Investment, Financing, and Valuation of the Corporation.* Homewood, Ill.: Irwin, 1962.

Thus, the investor's 11 percent required rate of return consists of a 6 percent dividend yield $(D_1/P_0 = \$0.90/\$15)$ plus a 5 percent capital gains yield.

ZERO GROWTH DIVIDEND VALUATION MODEL

If a firm's future dividend payments per share are not expected to grow over time—that is, if they are expected to remain constant *forever*—then D_t in Equation 4.18, the general dividend valuation model, can be replaced by a constant value D to yield the following:

$$P_0 = \sum_{t=1}^{\infty} \frac{D}{(1 + k_e)^t} . \qquad (4.23)$$

Equation 4.23 is analogous to those used for valuing a perpetual bond (Equation 4.6) and a preferred stock (Equation 4.11), and it can be simplified to obtain this:

$$P_0 = \frac{D}{k_e} . \qquad (4.24)$$

Equation 4.24 is really a special case of the constant growth model in which the dividend growth rate, g, is zero. Substituting 0 for g and D for D_1 in the constant growth dividend valuation formula gives the zero growth dividend valuation expression. Again, this model is valid only when a firm's dividend payments are expected to remain constant *forever*. Although there are few, if any, common stocks that strictly satisfy these conditions, the model still can be used to approximate the value of a stock for which dividend payments are expected to remain constant for a relatively long period into the future. Figure 4–6 also illustrates a zero growth dividend payment pattern.

To illustrate the zero growth dividend valuation model, assume that the Mountaineer Railroad common stock pays an annual dividend of $1.50 per share, which is expected to remain constant for the foreseeable future. What is the value of the stock to an investor who requires a 12 percent rate of return? Substituting $1.50 for D and 12 percent (0.12) for k_e in Equation 4.24 yields the following:

$$P_0 = \frac{\$1.50}{0.12}$$
$$= \$12.50 .$$

ABOVE-NORMAL GROWTH DIVIDEND VALUATION MODEL

Many firms experience growth rates in sales, earnings, and dividends that are *not* constant. Typically, a firm will have a period of above-normal growth as it exploits new technologies, new markets, or both; this generally occurs relatively early in the firm's life cycle. Following this period of rapid growth,

101

earnings and dividends tend to stabilize, or grow at a more normal rate comparable to the overall average rate of growth in the economy. The reduction in the growth rate occurs as the firm reaches maturity and has fewer sizable growth opportunities. Figure 4–6 also illustrates an above-normal growth pattern.[18]

A relatively simple model can be developed to determine the value of a common stock having the dividend pattern just described. If g_1 is defined as the above-normal growth rate over the first m years, and g_2 is the normal growth rate beginning in year $m + 1$ and continuing indefinitely, the current value of the common stock can be computed as follows:

$$P_0 = \sum_{t=1}^{m} \frac{D_0(1 + g_1)^t}{(1 + k_e)^t} + \frac{P_m}{(1 + k_e)^m} , \qquad (4.25)$$

or

$$P_0 = \sum_{t=1}^{m} \frac{D_0(1 + g_1)^t}{(1 + k_e)^t} + \frac{1}{(1 + k_e)^m} \left(\frac{D_{m+1}}{k_e - g_2} \right) , \qquad (4.26)$$

where k_e is the investor's required rate of return and D_0 and D_{m+1} are the dividend payments in years 0 and $m + 1$, respectively. Equation 4.25 indicates that the value of a firm's common stock is equal to the discounted present value of the stream of dividends received during the above-normal growth period plus the discounted present value of the stock price at the end of the above-normal growth period.

Because dividends are expected to grow at a constant rate, g_2, beginning in year $m + 1$, the constant growth model, $D_{m+1}/(k_e - g_2)$, can be used to find the value of the stock in year m, P_m.

For example, consider the Jackson Manufacturing Company, which expects earnings and common stock dividends to grow at a rate of 12 percent per annum for the next 5 years. Following the period of above-normal growth, dividends are expected to grow at the slower rate of 6 percent for the foreseeable future. The firm currently pays a dividend D_0 of $2.00 per share. What is the value of Jackson's common stock to an investor who requires a 15 percent rate of return?

Table 4–2 illustrates the solution to this problem. The present values of the dividends received during the above-normal growth period total $9.25. Based on the constant growth model, the value of the Jackson Manufacturing Company common stock at the end of year 5, P_5, is $41.56. Adding the present value of P_5, $20.66, to the present value of the dividends received during the first 5 years gives a total value of the common stock of $29.91 per share.

---

[18]The transition between the periods of above-normal and normal, or average, growth is usually not as pronounced as Figure 4–6 indicates. Typically, a firm's growth rate *declines gradually* over time from the above-normal rate to the normal rate. Growth models similar to Equation 4.26 can be developed to handle cases like this. As an illustration, see the Focus on Corporate Practice example at the end of this chapter.

TABLE 4–2 Value of the Jackson Manufacturing Company Common Stock

Year, t	Dividend, $D_t = \$2.00(1 + 0.12)^t$	Present Value Interest Factor, $PVIF_{0.15,t}$	Present Value, D_t
Present Value of First 5 Years' Dividends, $\sum\limits_{t=1}^{5} \dfrac{D_0(1 + g_1)^t}{(1 + k_e)^t}$			
1	$\$2.00(1 + 0.12)^1 = \$2.24$	0.870	$\$1.95$
2	$2.00(1 + 0.12)^2 = 2.51$	0.756	1.90
3	$2.00(1 + 0.12)^3 = 2.81$	0.658	1.85
4	$2.00(1 + 0.12)^4 = 3.15$	0.572	1.80
5	$2.00(1 + 0.12)^5 = 3.52$	0.497	1.75
			$\$9.25$

Value of Stock at End of Year 5, $P_5 = \dfrac{D_6}{k_e - g_2}$

$$P_5 = \frac{D_6}{0.15 - 0.06}.$$
$$D_6 = D_5(1 + g_2)$$
$$= \$3.53(1 + 0.06)$$
$$= \$3.74.$$
$$P_5 = \frac{\$3.74}{0.15 - 0.06}$$
$$= \$41.56.$$

Present Value of P_5, $PV(P_5) = \dfrac{P_5}{(1 + k_e)^5}$

$$PV(P_5) = \frac{\$41.56}{(1 + 0.15)^5}$$
$$= \$41.56(PVIF_{0.15,5})$$
$$= \$41.56(0.497)$$
$$= \$20.66.$$

Value of Common Stock, $P_0 = PV$ (First 5 Years' Dividends) $+ PV(P_5)$

$$P_0 = \$9.25 + \$20.66$$
$$= \$29.91.$$

SUMMARY

- The value of a long-term security is based on the *expected future returns* the owner will receive in the period during which the asset is held.
- The *capitalization-of-income* method of valuation can be used to determine the value of a security to an investor. This involves calculating the present value of the stream of expected future returns discounted at the investor's required rate of return. The required rate of return is a function of the *risk* associated with the returns from the asset.

103

- The *market price* of a security represents the value placed on it by marginally satisfied buyers and sellers.

- The value of a *bond having a finite maturity date* is equal to the present value of the stream of interest and principal payments discounted at the investor's required rate of return.

- The value of a *perpetual bond* is equal to the interest payment divided by the investor's required rate of return.

- The *yield to maturity* on a bond is the percentage rate of return the investor will earn if the bond is purchased at a given price and held until maturity.

- The returns from most *preferred stocks* can be treated as perpetuities. Thus, the value of a preferred stock is equal to the annual preferred dividend divided by the investor's required rate of return.

- The valuation of *common stocks* is considerably more complicated than the valuation of either bonds or preferred stocks for the following reasons:

1. The returns can take two forms: cash dividend payments and capital gains.

2. Common stock dividends are normally expected to grow and not remain constant.

3. The returns from common stocks are generally more uncertain than the returns from other types of securities.

- In the *general dividend valuation model* the value of a common stock is equal to the present value of all the expected future dividends discounted at the investor's required rate of return. Simpler common stock valuation models can be derived from assumptions concerning the expected growth of future dividend payments.

- Assuming that dividends continue to grow at a *constant* rate, g, indefinitely, the value of a common stock is equal to the next year's dividend, D_1, divided by the difference between the investor's required rate of return, k_e, and the growth rate, g.

Common Stock Evaluation Techniques Used by Wells Fargo Investment Advisors

Robert B. Morris III
Vice-President
Wells Fargo Investment Advisors (WFIA)
A Division of Wells Fargo Bank, N.A.

Wells Fargo Investment Advisors (WFIA), a large investment advisory firm, is somewhat unique in that it applies, in a disciplined manner, the dividend valuation model to the problem of security valuation. The model maintains that the price of a share of stock is equal to the present value of all future dividends discounted at an appropriate rate. WFIA employs a dividend valuation model that extends into perpetuity. The time horizon requires that several factors be considered, including long-term industry and company developments regarding the industry structure, the pricing environment, and technological developments, as well as returns on equity. Given the discount rate and the risk associated with a particular stock, WFIA is able to identify overpriced or underpriced equity securities.

To effectively apply this model to a particular firm under consideration, WFIA security analysts make four distinct types of forecasts:

- Estimates of the firm's earnings and dividends for a 5-year period.
- An estimate of a fifth-year normalized earnings growth rate and dividend payout rate.
- An estimate of a maturity date and earnings growth decay rate.
- An estimate of a maturity earnings growth rate and dividend payout rate.

After having studied the latest actual earnings and dividends of the firm, the WFIA analyst estimates earnings and dividends for each of the next 5 years. Following this, the analyst estimates a normalized earnings growth rate between years 5 and 6, assuming that earning conditions are normal (that is, devoid of cyclical peaks or troughs). The analyst also estimates a normalized payout ratio based upon the same assumptions. Normalized growth and earnings projections are made within the context of "real" Gross National Product (GNP) and inflation assumptions developed within Wells Fargo Bank, which are used as a basis for evaluation by all of WFIA's security analysts.

Because a company's revenues cannot increase forever at a rate faster than the nominal GNP rate, the analyst must also estimate when earnings gains will decline *below* the nominal GNP rate: The estimate is defined as the *maturity date*. The analyst must also forecast how rapidly corporate earnings growth is expected to decay toward maturity growth. The decay rate can be either *slow*, *medium*, or *fast*. A slow rate implies that earnings advance in line with the fifth-year normalized rate for a number of years and then decay very quickly as the maturity date approaches. A medium rate implies that earnings growth slows by an equal amount between the sixth year and the maturity date. A fast rate implies that earnings move very quickly from the fifth-year earnings rate to the maturity rate.

The final component of the model requires the analyst to estimate the dividend payout ratio and earnings growth rate of the firm from the date of maturity into perpetuity. The maturity phase is not considered to be a period of zero revenue growth. On the contrary, it is simply a point when earnings advances are no greater than the nominal GNP rate.

Figure 4–7 illustrates the nature of the forecasts made in this valuation procedure.

Once these parameters have been specified, the expected return for the security can be solved for. Through an *iterative*, or repetitive, process the expected return can be found by solving for the discount rate that equates the present value of the forecasted future dividend stream with the current price of the stock. WFIA then compares the expected return for the security being analyzed with the expected return of other stocks having similar risk characteristics in order to identify overpriced and underpriced stocks.[19]

Based on their observations of overpriced and underpriced stocks, portfolio managers attempt to maximize the expected return of a portfolio (that is, a collection of stocks) for a given level of risk. The maximization process is accomplished through the use of a portfolio optimization program. The optimal, or best, portfolio is then selected from among the underpriced stocks.

FIGURE 4–7   Dividend Payout Ratio and Earnings Growth Assumptions

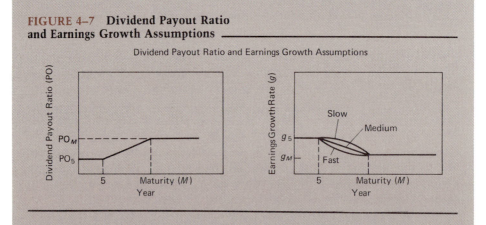

[19]To determine the expected returns for other securities of similar risk, WFIA uses the concept of a security's *beta*, a measure of risk, and the security market line from the theory of the capital asset pricing model. This theory is explained in Chapter 5. Basically it provides a basis for assessing the tradeoffs required by investors between risk and required return.

QUESTIONS AND TOPICS FOR DISCUSSION

1. What variables must be known (or estimated) in applying the capitalization-of-income method of valuation to a physical or financial asset?

2. Define the following:
   a. The market value of an asset.
   b. Market equilibrium.

3. What is the primary difference between the book value and the market value of an asset?

4. How does the yield to maturity on a bond differ from the coupon yield or current yield?

5. What factor or factors make the valuation of common stocks more complicated than the valuation of bonds and preferred stocks?

6. According to the general dividend valuation model, a firm that reinvests all its earnings and pays no cash dividends can still have a common stock value greater than zero. How is this possible?

7. Explain the relationship between financial decisions and shareholder wealth.

8. Explain how *each* of the following factors would affect the valuation of a firm's common stock, assuming that all other factors remain constant:
   a. The general level of interest rates shifts upward, causing investors to require a higher rate of return on securities in general.
   b. Increased foreign competition reduces the future growth potential of the firm's earnings and dividends.
   c. Investors reevaluate upward their assessment of the risk of the firm's common stock as the result of increased South American investments by the firm.

9. Rank in ascending order the rates of return a typical investor would require on an investment in the following of a given firm:
   a. Common stock.
   b. Preferred stock.
   c. Bonds.
   Justify your rankings.

10. Explain why the valuation models for a perpetual bond, preferred stock, and common stock with constant dividend payments (zero growth) are virtually identical.

PROBLEMS*

1. Give the value of a $1,000 Canadian Pacific Limited perpetual 4 percent debenture (bond) at the following required rates of return:
   a. 4 percent.
   b. 5 percent.
   c. 6 percent.

2. Canadian Pacific Limited's debentures (see Problem 1) are traded on the New York Exchange. During 1982 the high and low market prices of these bonds were $360 and $335, respectively. Give the yield to maturity of one of these debentures if it was purchased under the following conditions:
   a. At the high 1982 market price.
   b. At the low 1982 market price.

*Problems in color have check answers provided at the end of the book.

3. Consider DuPont's 8 percent bonds that mature at the end of 1986 (that is, on December 31). Assume that the interest on these bonds is paid and compounded annually. What is the value of a $1,000 denomination bond of this nature as of the end of 1982 to an investor who holds the bond until maturity and whose required rate of return is the following?
    a. 6 percent.
    b. 8 percent.
    c. 10 percent.

4. Public Service Electric and Gas has issued 12 percent bonds that mature at the end of 2004. Assume that interest is paid and compounded annually. Determine the *exact* yield to maturity (to the nearest whole percent) by the trial-and-error method if an investor purchases a $1,000 denomination bond for $1,080 at the end of 1984.

5. Determine the *approximate* yield to maturity on the Public Service Electric and Gas bonds (see Problem 4) using the method described in Footnote 11 of this chapter. How does the approximate yield compare with the exact yield?

6. General Telephone & Electronics has issued 5 percent bonds that will mature at the end of 1992. Assume that interest is paid and compounded annually. If an investor purchases a $1,000 denomination bond for $743 at the end of 1982, determine the following:
    a. The bond's *exact* yield to maturity (to the nearest whole percent) using the trial-and-error method.
    b. The bond's *approximate* yield to maturity using the method described in Footnote 11 of this chapter.

7. What would be the value of the DuPont bonds (see Problem 3) at a 6 percent required rate of return if the interest were paid and compounded semiannually?

8. What is the value of a share of Litton Industries Series B $2.00 cumulative preferred stock to an investor who requires the following rates of return?
    a. 9 percent.
    b. 10 percent.
    c. 12 percent.

9. The Seagram Company's earnings and common stock dividends have been growing at an annual rate of 6 percent over the past 10 years and are expected to continue growing at this rate for the foreseeable future. The firm currently (that is, as of year 0) pays an annual dividend of $2.50 per share. Determine the current value of a share of Seagram's common stock to investors with each of the following required rates of return:
    a. 12 percent.
    b. 14 percent.
    c. 16 percent.
    d. 6 percent.
    e. 4 percent.

10. General Grain's common stock dividends have been growing at an annual rate of 7 percent per year over the past 10 years. Current dividends are $0.85 per share. What is the current value of a share of this stock to an investor who requires a 12 percent rate of return if the following conditions exist?
    a. Dividends are expected to continue growing at the historical rate for the foreseeable future.
    b. The dividend growth rate is expected to *increase* to 9 percent per year.
    c. The dividend growth rate is expected to *decrease* to 6.5 percent per year.

11. The Superior Maintenance Company currently (that is, as of year 0) pays a com-

mon stock dividend of $0.50 per share. Dividends are expected to grow at a rate of 11 percent per year for the next 4 years and then to continue growing thereafter at a rate of 5 percent per year. What is the current value of a share of Superior's common stock to an investor who requires a 14 percent rate of return?

12. During the previous 4 years Wilson Company's common dividends have grown from $2.00 (year 0) to $2.72 (year 4) per share.
    a. Determine the compound annual dividend growth rate over the 4-year period. HINT: Refer to the compound value techniques developed in Chapter 3, especially Equation 3.10.
    b. Forecast Wilson's dividends for the next 5 years, assuming that dividends continue to grow at the rate determined in Part a.
    c. Determine the current value of a share of Wilson's common stock to an investor who plans to hold it for 5 years, assuming that the stock price *increases at the same rate* as the dividends. The investor's required rate of return is 12 percent.

13. Bailey Mining Company expects its earnings and dividends to increase by 7 percent per year over the next 6 years and then to remain relatively constant thereafter. The firm currently (that is, as of year 0) pays a dividend of $4.00 per share. Determine the value of a share of Bailey stock to an investor with a 12 percent required rate of return.

14. The chairman of Mission Industries told a meeting of financial analysts that he expects the firm's earnings and dividends to double over the next 6 years. The firm's current (that is, as of year 0) earnings and dividends per share are $5.00 and $1.00, respectively.
    a. Estimate the compound annual dividend growth rate over the 6-year period (to the nearest whole percent).
    b. Forecast Mission's earnings and dividends per share for each of the next 6 years, assuming that they grow at the rate determined in Part a.
    c. Based on the constant growth dividend valuation model, determine the current value of a share of Mission Industries common stock to an investor who requires an 18 percent rate of return.
    d. Why might the stock price calculated in Part c not represent an accurate valuation to an investor with an 18 percent required rate of return?
    e. Determine the current value of a share of Mission Industries common stock to an investor (with an 18 percent required rate of return) who plans to hold it for 6 years, assuming that earnings and dividends per share grow at the rate determined in Part (a) for the next 6 years and then at 6 percent thereafter.

15. Show that the 1-period and 2-period valuation models (Equations 4.13 and 4.14) are equivalent to the general dividend valuation model (Equation 4.18).

16. Ten years ago Video Magic began manufacturing and selling coin-operated arcade games. Dividends are currently $0.50 per share, having grown at a 15 percent compound annual rate over the past 5 years. This growth rate is expected to be maintained for the next 3 years, after which dividends are expected to grow at half that rate for 3 years. Beyond that time, Video Magic's dividends are expected to grow at 5 percent per year. What is the current value of a share of Video Magic's common stock if your required rate of return is 18 percent?

17. Creative Financing, Inc., is planning to offer a $1000 par value 15-year maturity bond with a coupon interest rate that changes every 5 years. The coupon rate for the first 5 years is 10 percent, 10.75 percent for the next 5 years, and 11.50 percent for the final 5 years. If you require an 11 percent rate of return on a bond of this quality and maturity, what is the maximum price you would pay for the bond? (Assume interest is paid annually at the end of each year.)

This section illustrates the use of the Texas Instruments Professional Business Analyst (BA-55) calculator to compute the value of a bond and of a stock (using the above-normal growth dividend valuation model).

VALUE OF A BOND

Consider again the Standard Oil of California 7 percent debentures that mature on December 31, 1996. We wish to compute the value of one of these bonds to an investor who is considering the purchase of it on December 31, 1984, and requires an 8 percent rate of return on this bond. The calculations that follow initially assume annual interest payments of $70. They are then modified to account for semiannual payments of interest.

Procedure	Press	Display
1. Clear calculator and mode registers; select two decimal places.	on/c 2nd **CLmode** 2nd **Fix** 2	0.00
2. Press 2nd **Mode** until the FIN indicator is displayed.	2nd **Mode**	0.00
3. Enter the annual interest payments (an annuity).	70 PMT	70.00
4. Enter the required rate of return per year.	8 %i	8.00
5. Enter the maturity value of the bond.	1000 FV	1000.00
6. Enter the number of payments until the bond matures.	12 N	12.00
7. Calculate the present value of the bond.	CPT PV	**924.64**

Note that this answer differs slightly from the one computed in the chapter because of rounding in the interest tables at the end of the book.

In the case of semiannual payment of interest, the procedure just outlined must be modified by changing the payment to $35, changing the number of payments to 24, and changing the required rate of return to 4 percent per payment period (per half year in this case). If this is done, the value of the bond is **$923.77,** slightly higher than the $923.65 computed in Footnote 6 using the tables at the end of the book.

These calculations have assumed that the bond is purchased on one of the interest payment dates. If a bond is purchased between payment dates, which is the most common situation, the calculations are a bit more complex. The user's manual for your calculator provides instructions for making this type of calculation.

To compute the yield to maturity of a bond purchased on an interest payment date, the steps previously outlined must be modified slightly. Consider the bonds of the Tanoan Development Corporation discussed in the chapter. They pay 8 percent interest per year ($80), and they mature in 20 years. The current price of the bond is $761. Calculate the yield to maturity of the bond.

Procedure	Press	Display
1. Repeat Steps 1 and 2 previously given.		0.00
2. Enter the annual interest payments.	80 PMT	80.00
3. Enter the number of payments until the bond matures.	20 N	20.00
4. Enter the maturity value of the bond.	1000 FV	1000.00
5. Enter the current value of the bond.	761 PV	761.00
6. Calculate the yield to maturity.	CPT %i	**11.00**

The yield to maturity on the bond is 11 percent, the same as was calculated in the chapter using the interest tables at the end of the book.

VALUE OF A COMMON STOCK (ABOVE-NORMAL GROWTH DIVIDEND VALUATION MODEL)

The value of the stock of the Jackson Manufacturing Company (discussed in the chapter) can be calculated easily with the aid of your calculator. Recall that the current dividend is $2 per share. For the next 5 years investors expect this dividend to grow at a rate of 12 percent per annum and then to grow at a slower rate of 6 percent for the foreseeable future. What is the value of Jackson's common stock to an investor who requires a 15 percent rate of return?

Procedure	Press	Display
1. Clear calculator and mode registers; select two decimal places.	on/c 2nd CLmode 2nd Fix 2	0.00

2. Press 2nd **Mode** until the CF indicator is displayed.

2nd **Mode**

0.00

3. Calculate and enter the first year's expected dividend.

2 X 1.12 = STO 1

2.24

4. Calculate and enter the second year's expected dividend.

X 1.12 = STO 2

2.51

5. Calculate and enter the third year's expected dividend.

X 1.12 = STO 3

2.81

6. Calculate and enter the fourth year's expected dividend.

X 1.12 = STO 4

3.15

7. Calculate and enter the fifth year's expected dividend.

X 1.12 = STO 5

3.52

8. Calculate the sixth year's expected dividend.

3.52 X 1.06 =

3.74

9. Calculate the expected stock price at the end 5 years. (Recall that the divisor, 0.09 in this case, is equal to the required return, 0.15, minus the expected long-run growth rate, 0.06.)

÷ .09 =

41.51

10. Add this value to the amount stored in Register 5.

RCL 5 + 41.51 =

45.03

11. Store this in Register 5.

STO 5

45.03

12. Enter the required rate of return.	15 %i	15.00
13. Compute the current value of the stock.	CPT 2nd **NPV**	**29.88**

This value differs slightly from the $29.91 computed in the chapter because of rounding differences in the use of the interest tables.

ADDITIONAL READINGS AND REFERENCES

Brigham, Eugene F., and Pappas, James L. "Duration of Growth, Changes in Growth Rates, and Corporate Share Prices." *Financial Analysts Journal* 24 (May–June 1966): 157–162.

Copeland, Thomas E., and Weston, J. Fred. *Financial Theory and Corporate Policy.* 2nd ed. Reading, Mass.: Addison-Wesley, 1983.

Elton, Edwin J., and Gruber, Martin J. "Earnings Estimates and the Accuracy of Expectational Data." *Management Science* 18 (April 1972): 409–424.

————. "Valuation and the Cost of Capital for Regulated Industries." *Journal of Finance* 26 (June 1971): 661–670.

Fisher, Lawrence. "Determinants of Risk Premiums on Corporate Bonds." *Journal of Political Economy* 67 (June 1959): 217–237.

Keenan, Michael. "Models of Equity Valuation: The Great Serm Bubble." *Journal of Finance* 25 (May 1970): 243–273.

Mao, James C. T. "The Valuation of Growth Stocks: The Investment Opportunities Approach." *Journal of Finance* 21 (March 1966): 95–102.

Margoshes, S. L. "Present Value Techniques of Stock Valuation." *Financial Analysts Journal* 17 (March–April 1961): 37–42.

Olsen, I. J. "Valuation of a Closely Held Corporation." *Journal of Accountancy* 128 (August 1969): 35–47.

Reilly, Frank K. *Investment Analysis and Portfolio Management.* Hinsdale, Ill.: Dryden Press, 1979, Chapters 9–14.

CHAPTER 5

Analysis of
Risk and Return

A FINANCIAL DILEMMA

Risk and Return in the Securities Markets

In early 1983 International Harvester had a series of bonds due to mature in 2002 that were selling to yield investors a 25 percent annual return if held until their scheduled maturity. At the same time, AT&T had a series of bonds with a similar scheduled maturity that offered investors a yield to maturity of only 10.6 percent per annum. The dramatic difference between the computed yields on these two bonds reflects the differences in the risk of the two firms. The securities of AT&T have come to be known as some of the least risky available to investors. In contrast, International Harvester was in the midst of a severe financial crisis at that time—one that threatened its long-term existence. Because of this risk of imminent failure, International Harvester investors demanded much higher returns on its bonds than was being demanded on the AT&T bonds.

The same relationship can be observed in the market for common stocks. For example, Boeing has long dominated the commercial airplane market. In addition, it is a major military contractor. In contrast, Lockheed ran into serious financial difficulty when it attempted to enter the commercial market with its L-1011 plane. The project was a financial disaster, and Lockheed was forced to acquire government loan guarantees to remain afloat. Although Lockheed has terminated the L-1011 project, the effects have lingered. In early 1983 investors were willing to pay a stock price equal to 12 times the earnings for Boeing, but only 9 times the earnings for Lockheed. Although some of this difference may be due to the different earnings growth prospects of the two firms, much of it is undoubtedly due to the higher risk of Lockheed as perceived by investors relative to that of Boeing.

This chapter develops the relationship between risk and required returns. This relationship is one of the dominant themes in finance; that is, higher returns are normally achieved by assuming greater risk. In finance there is no free lunch.

GLOSSARY OF NEW TERMS

Beta a measure of systematic risk. It is a measure of the volatility of a security's returns relative to the returns of a broad-based market portfolio of securities.

Characteristic line a regression line relating the periodic returns for a specific security to the periodic returns on the market portfolio. The slope of this regression line is an estimate of the *beta* of the security—a measure of its systematic risk.

Coefficient of variation the ratio of the *standard deviation* to the *expected value*. It provides a *relative* measure of risk.

Correlation a relative statistical measure of the degree to which two series of numbers, such as the returns from two securities, tend to move or vary together.

Covariance an absolute statistical measure of how closely two variables (such as securities' returns) move together. It measures the degree to which increases (decreases) in the level of one variable tend to be associated with increases (decreases) in the level of another variable over time.

Diversification the act of investing in a set of securities or assets having different risk-return characteristics.

Portfolio a collection of two or more assets or securities.

Security market line (SML) the relationship between systematic risk and required rates of return for individual securities.

Standard deviation a statistical measure of the dispersion, or variability, of a set of observations around its arithmetic average, or mean. Operationally it is defined as the square root of the weighted average squared deviations of individual observations from the expected value. The standard deviation provides an *absolute* measure of risk.

Systematic risk that portion of the variability of an individual security's returns that is caused by factors affecting the market as a whole. This is also called *nondiversifiable risk*.

Unsystematic risk risk that is unique to a firm; this is also called *diversifiable risk*.

INTRODUCTION

Chapter 4 talked about the investor's *required rate of return* on a bond, preferred stock, and common stock. These required rates of return were used to discount the expected cash flows from each of these securities to determine the value of that security. In Chapter 4 the required rate of return from a security (or other asset) was represented as an increasing function of that security's *risk*; that is, the greater the risk, the greater the required rate of return.

This chapter defines risk in more precise terms; looks at a number of alternative techniques for measuring risk; and then considers the relationships between risk, required return, and security values.

THE MEANING OF RISK

Risk is defined by *Webster's Dictionary* as the "possibility of loss or injury; hazard; peril; danger." Hence, risk implies that there is a chance for some unfavorable event to occur. From the perspective of security analysis or the analysis of an investment in some project (such as the development of a new product line), risk is the *possibility that actual cash flows (returns) will be less than forecasted cash flows (returns).*

An investment is said to be *risk-free* if the dollar returns from the initial investment are known with certainty. Some of the best examples of risk-free investments are United States Treasury securities. There is virtually no chance that the Treasury will fail to redeem these securities at maturity or that the Treasury will default on any interest payments owed. As a last resort, the Treasury can always print more money.[1]

In contrast, New York City bonds constitute a *risky* investment because it is possible that New York City will default on one or more interest payments and will lack sufficient funds to redeem the bonds at face value at maturity. In other words, the possible returns from this investment are *variable*, and each potential outcome can be assigned a *probability*.

If, for example, you were considering investing in New York City bonds, you might assign the following probabilities to the three possible outcomes of this investment:

Outcome	Probability
No default, bonds redeemed at maturity	0.80
Default on interest for one or more periods	0.15
No interest default, but bonds not redeemed at maturity	0.05
	1.00

These probabilities are interpreted to mean that an 80 percent chance exists that the bonds will not be in default over their life and will be redeemed at maturity, a 15 percent chance of interest default during the life of the bonds, and a 5 percent chance that the bonds will not be redeemed at maturity.

Hence, from an investment perspective, risk refers to the chance that returns from an investment will be less than expected. We can define risk more precisely, however, by introducing some probability concepts.

PROBABILITY DISTRIBUTIONS

The *probability* that a particular event will occur is defined as the *percentage chance* of its outcome. Probabilities may be either objectively or subjectively

---

[1] Note that this discussion of risk deals with *dollar returns* and ignores other considerations, such as potential losses in purchasing power. In addition, it assumes that securities are held until maturity, which is not always the case. Sometimes a security must be sold prior to maturity for less than face value because of changes in the level of interest rates.

determined. An objective determination is based on past outcomes of similar events, whereas a subjective one is merely an opinion made by an individual about the likelihood that a given event will occur. In the case of projects that are frequently repeated—such as the drilling of developmental oil wells in an established oil field—reasonably good objective estimates can be made about the success of a new well. Similarly, good objective estimates can often be made about the expected returns of an AT&T bond. However, the expected returns from securities of new, small firms are often much more difficult to estimate objectively. Hence, highly subjective estimates regarding the likelihood of various returns are necessary. *The fact that many probability estimates in business are at least partially subjective does not diminish their usefulness.*

Let us consider the concept of probability and risk with a sample probability distribution of the returns available from an investment of $100,000 in the stock of either Consolidated Properties, Inc. (CPI), a public utility firm, or International Farm Products (IFP), a maker of farm machinery. By investing in the stock of either of these firms, an investor expects to receive dividend payments plus stock price appreciation. We will assume that the investor plans to hold the stock for 1 year and then sell it. Over the year, the investor feels there is a 20 percent chance for an economic *boom*, a 60 percent chance for a *normal* economic environment, and a 20 percent chance for a *recession*. Given this assessment of the economic environment over the next year, the investor estimates the probability distribution of returns from the investment in CPI and IFP, as Table 5–1 shows.

EXPECTED VALUES

From this information the *expected value* of returns from investing in the stock of CPI and IFP can be calculated. It is the weighted average of the possible returns from each stock, with the weights being the probability of occurrence.

Algebraically the expected value of the returns from a security or project may be defined as follows:

$$\hat{R} = \sum_{j=1}^{n} R_j P_j , \qquad (5.1)$$

TABLE 5–1   Probability Distribution of Returns from CPI and IFP

State of the Economy	Probability	Rate of Return Anticipated Under Each State of the Economy*	
		CPI	IFP
Recession	0.2	10%	−4%
Normal year	0.6	18	18
Boom	0.2	26	40
	1.0		

*For example, a 10 percent rate of return for CPI means that the stock value plus dividends total $110,000 at the end of 1 year. Working with a *discrete* probability distribution, as this example does, indicates that there is no probability of a loss by investing in CPI. This is, of course, unrealistic. In the following discussion of continuous distributions this assumption is relaxed.

117

TABLE 5–2   Expected Return Calculation for Investment in CPI and IFP

CPI			IFP		
R_j	P_j	$R_j \times P_j$	R_j	P_j	$R_j \times P_j$
10%	0.2	2.0%	−4%	0.2	−0.8%
18	0.6	10.8	18	0.6	10.8
26	0.2	5.2	40	0.2	8.0
	Expected return = $\hat{R}$ = 18.0%			Expected return = $\hat{R}$ = 18.0%	

where $\hat{R}$ is the expected return; R_j is the outcome for the *j*th case, where there are *n* possible outcomes; and P_j is the probability that the *j*th outcome will occur. The expected return for CPI and IFP is computed in Table 5–2. It is 18 percent for both CPI and IFP.

STANDARD DEVIATION:
AN ABSOLUTE MEASURE OF RISK

The standard deviation is a statistical measure of the dispersion of a variable about the mean. It is defined as the *square root of the weighted average squared deviations of individual observations from the mean:*

$$\sigma = \sqrt{\sum_{j=1}^{n} (R_j - \hat{R})^2 P_j} \, , \tag{5.2}$$

where σ is the standard deviation.

The standard deviation can be used to measure the variability of returns from an investment. As such, it gives an indication of the *risk* involved in the asset or security. The larger the standard deviation, the more variable an investment's returns and the riskier the investment. A standard deviation of zero indicates no variability and thus no risk. Table 5–3 shows the calculation of the standard deviations for the investments in CPI and IFP.

From the calculations in Table 5–3, it can be seen that IFP appears riskier than CPI, because possible returns from IFP are more variable, measured by its standard deviation of 13.91 percent, than those from CPI, which have a standard deviation of only 5.06 percent.

This example dealt with a *discrete* probability distribution of outcomes (returns) for each firm; that is, a *limited* number of possible outcomes were identified, and probabilities were assigned to them. In reality, however, many different outcomes are possible for the investment in the stock of each firm— ranging from losses during the year to returns in excess of IFP's 40 percent return. To indicate the probability of *all* possible outcomes for these investments, it is necessary to construct a *continuous* probability distribution. This is done by developing a table similar to Table 5–1, except that it would have many more possible outcomes and their associated probabilities. That detailed table of outcomes and probabilities can be used to develop the expected value of returns from both IFP and CPI, and a continuous curve would be

118

TABLE 5–3   Computation of Standard Deviations of Returns—CPI and IFP

	j	R_j	$\hat{R}$	$R_j - \hat{R}$	$(R_j - \hat{R})^2$	P_j	$(R_j - \hat{R})^2 P_j$
CPI	1 (Recession)	10%	18%	−8%	64	0.2	12.8
	2 (Normal)	18	18	0	0	0.6	0
	3 (Boom)	26	18	+8	64	0.2	12.8

$$\sum_{j=1}^{3} (R_j - \hat{R})^2 P_j = 25.6$$

$$\sigma = \sqrt{\sum_{j=1}^{n} (R_j - \hat{R})^2 P_j} = \sqrt{25.6} = 5.06\%$$

	j	R_j	$\hat{R}$	$R_j - \hat{R}$	$(R_j - \hat{R})^2$	P_j	$(R_j - \hat{R})^2 P_j$
IFP	1 (Recession)	−4%	18%	−22%	484	0.2	96.8
	2 (Normal)	18	18	0	0	0.6	0
	3 (Boom)	40	18	+22	484	0.2	96.8

$$\sum_{j=1}^{3} (R_j - \hat{R})^2 P_j = 193.6$$

$$\sigma = \sqrt{\sum_{j=1}^{n} (R_j - \hat{R})^2 P_j} = \sqrt{193.6} = 13.91\%$$

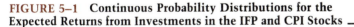

constructed to approximate the probabilities associated with each outcome. Figure 5–1 illustrates continuous probability distributions of returns for investments in the stock of IFP and CPI.

From this figure it can be seen that the CPI expected return has a tighter probability distribution, indicating a lower variability of returns, whereas the IFP expected return has a flatter distribution, indicating higher variability and, by extension, more risk.

The expected returns from many investments can be estimated by assuming that they follow the *normal* probability distribution. The normal proba-

FIGURE 5–1   Continuous Probability Distributions for the Expected Returns from Investments in the IFP and CPI Stocks

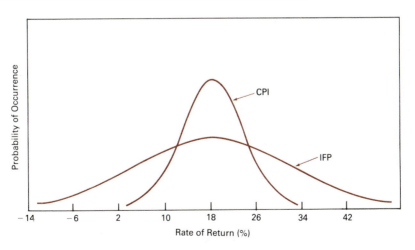

FIGURE 5–2   Sample Illustration of Areas under the Normal Probability Distribution Curve

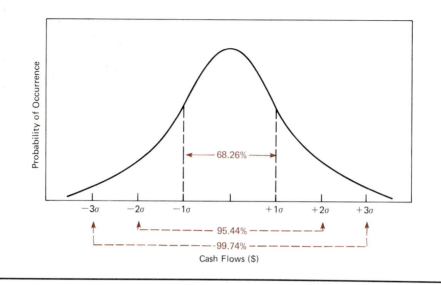

bility distribution is characterized by a symmetrical, bell-like curve. If the expected continuous probability distribution of returns is approximately normal, a table of the *standard normal probability function* (Table V at the end of this text) can be used to compute the probability of occurrence of any particular outcome. From this table, for example, it is apparent that the actual outcome should be between plus or minus 1 standard deviation from the expected value 68.26 percent of the time,[2] between plus or minus 2 standard deviations 95.44 percent of the time, and between plus or minus 3 standard deviations 99.74 percent of the time. This is illustrated in Figure 5–2.

The number of standard deviations, z, that a particular value of R is from the expected value, $\hat{R}$, can be computed as follows:

$$z = \frac{R - \hat{R}}{\sigma}. \tag{5.3}$$

Table V and Equation 5.3 can be used to compute the probability of a return for an investment in IFP being less than some value R—for example, 0 percent return. First, the number of standard deviations that 0 percent is from the expected return (18 percent) must be calculated. Substituting the expected return and the standard deviation from Tables 5–2 and 5–3 into Equation 5.3 yields the following:

[2]For example, Table V indicates that there is a probability of 0.1587 of a value occurring that is greater than $+1\sigma$ from the mean *and* a probability of 0.1587 of a value occurring that is less than -1σ from the mean. Hence, the probability of a value *between* $+1\sigma$ and -1σ is 68.26 percent—that is, $1.00 - (2 \times 0.1587)$.

$$z = \frac{0\% - 18\%}{13.91\%}$$

$$= -1.29 \ .$$

In other words, the return of 0 percent is 1.29 standard deviations *below* the mean. The nearest value in Table V is the probability associated with 1.30 standard deviations, or 9.68 percent (0.0968). Thus, there is a slightly greater chance (because the actual value is 1.29 standard deviations below the mean) than 9.68 percent that IFP will have returns below 0 percent.[3] Conversely, there is nearly a 90.32 percent chance that the return will be greater than 0 percent.

COEFFICIENT OF VARIATION: A RELATIVE MEASURE OF RISK

The standard deviation is an appropriate measure of risk when the investments being compared are approximately equal in size and the returns are estimated to have symmetrical probability distributions. Because the standard deviation is an *absolute* measure of variability, it is generally *not* suitable for comparing investments with different expected returns. In these cases the *coefficient of variation* provides a better measure of risk.

Consider, for example, two assets, T and S. Asset T has expected annual returns of 25 percent and a standard deviation of 20 percent, whereas Asset S has expected annual returns of 10 percent and a standard deviation of 18 percent. Intuition tells us that Asset T is less risky, since its *relative* variation is smaller.

The coefficient of variation, v, considers relative variation and thus is well suited for use when a comparison is being made between two investments with different expected returns. It is defined as the ratio of the standard deviation, σ, to the expected value, $\hat{R}$:

$$v = \frac{\sigma}{\hat{R}} \ . \tag{5.4}$$

As the coefficient of variation increases, so does the relative risk of an asset. The coefficients of variation for Assets T and S are computed as follows:

Asset T:

$$v = \frac{\sigma}{\hat{R}}$$

$$= \frac{20\%}{25\%}$$

$$= 0.8 \ .$$

[3] By interpolation, the chance of having a value less than 1.29 standard deviations below the mean is 0.0986, or $0.1056 - 0.8(0.1056 - 0.0968)$.

121

Asset S:

$$V = \frac{\sigma}{\hat{R}}$$
$$= \frac{18\%}{10\%}$$
$$= 1.8 \ .$$

Asset S's returns have a larger coefficient of variation than Asset T's, and therefore Asset S is the more risky of the two investments.

In general, when comparing two equal-sized investments, the standard deviation is an appropriate measure of risk. When comparing two investments with different expected returns, the coefficient of variation is the more appropriate measure of risk.

RISK AS AN INCREASING
FUNCTION OF TIME

Most investment decisions require that returns be *forecasted* several years into the future. The riskiness of these forecasted returns may be thought of as an *increasing function of time.* Returns that are generated early can generally be predicted with more certainty than those that are anticipated farther out into the future.

Consider the risk facing a firm that plans to begin producing and marketing a new home computer system. This project is expected to generate cash flows to the firm of $2 million per year over the 7-year life of the project. Even though the expected annual cash flows are equal for each year, it is reasonable to assume that the riskiness of these flows increases over time as more and more presently unknown variables have a chance to affect the project's cash flows. Figure 5–3 illustrates this situation.

The distribution is relatively tight in year 1, since the market conditions affecting that year's cash flows are reasonably well known. By year 7, however, the distribution has become flat, indicating a considerable increase in the standard deviation, caused by increased uncertainty in market conditions.

Some types of cash flows are not subject to increasing variability. These include, for example, contractual arrangements, such as lease payments, in which the expected cash flows remain constant (or change at some predefined rate) over the life of the contract. In spite of the exceptions, it is reasonable to conclude that the riskiness of the cash flows from most investment projects gradually increases over time. Similarly, the riskiness of returns from most securities increases the farther into the future these returns are being considered. For instance, the return from the purchase of Ford Motor Company bonds is nearly guaranteed for the next year. However, projecting the returns to be received 10 years in the future is much more difficult due to the potential impact of competition, new technology, and other factors.

FIGURE 5–3   Sample Illustration of the Risk of a Project over Time

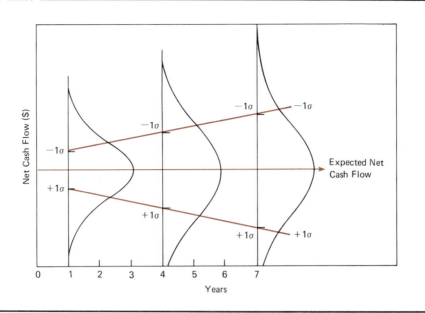

PORTFOLIO RISK ANALYSIS

Up to now the risk associated with single investments (physical assets or securities) has been considered. But firms hold portfolios of many different assets, and individuals generally hold many different securities. *Portfolio risk,* the risk associated with collections of assets or securities, is considered in the following sections. Generally we can conclude that a security or a physical asset held as part of a portfolio is *less* risky than if it were held alone.

The nature of portfolio risk will be considered. We also develop procedures to measure the risk of assets held in a portfolio. Next, a model of the relationship between risk and return in a portfolio of assets or securities is developed. This model, the *Capital Asset Pricing Model* (CAPM), provides a strong analytical basis for evaluating risk-return relationships—both in the context of financial management and investment decisions.

INVESTMENT DIVERSIFICATION AND RISK

Most physical assets and financial assets are held as parts of portfolios. Banks hold many different loans and many different bonds; individuals hold many different bonds and stocks; and corporations hold many different physical assets. Consequently, it is important to know how the returns from portfolios of investments behave over time—not only how the returns from any indi-

123

vidual asset in the portfolio behave. The questions of importance are as follows:

- What return can be expected to be earned from the portfolio?
- What is the risk of the portfolio?

For example, assume that the Kreiser Aluminum Company is considering diversifying into gold mining and refining. During economic boom periods, aluminum sales tend to be brisk; gold, on the other hand, tends to be most in demand during economic downturns.[4] Thus, the returns from the aluminum business and the gold mining business are inversely, or *negatively*, related. If Kreiser expands into gold mining and refining, its overall return will tend to be less variable than individual returns from these projects. This is illustrated in Figure 5–4. Graph a shows the variation of rates of return in the aluminum industry over time, Graph b shows the corresponding variation of returns from gold mining over the same time frame, and Graph c shows the combined rate of return for both lines of business.

As can be seen from this figure, when the return from aluminum operations is high, the return from gold mining tends to be low, and vice versa. The *combined* returns are more stable, and thus less risky.

This *portfolio effect* of reduced variability results because a *negative correlation* exists between the returns from aluminum operations and the returns from gold mining. The *correlation* between any two variables—such as rates of return or net cash flows—is a relative statistical measure of the degree to which these variables tend to move together. The *correlation coefficient* measure is the extent to which high (or low) values of one variable are associated with high (or low) values of another. Values of the correlation coefficient can range from +1.0 for *perfectly positively correlated* variables to −1.0 for *perfectly negatively correlated* variables. Figure 5–5 illustrates per-

FIGURE 5–4 Sample Illustration of Diversification and Risk Reduction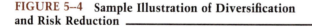

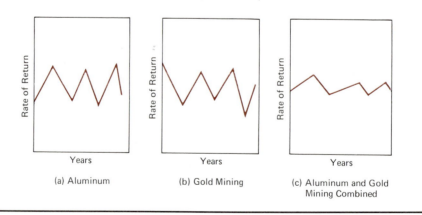

(a) Aluminum   (b) Gold Mining   (c) Aluminum and Gold Mining Combined

[4]As investors lose confidence in the economy's performance, many of them turn to gold as an investment. This drives the price of gold up and increases returns to gold mining firms, whose costs of operation are not directly related to the demand for gold.

FIGURE 5–5 **Perfect Positive and Perfect Negative Correlation for Two Projects**

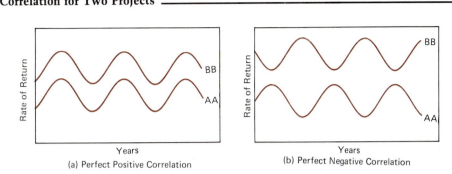

(a) Perfect Positive Correlation

(b) Perfect Negative Correlation

fect positive and negative correlations for two investments, AA and BB.

For perfect positive correlation (Graph a), high rates of return from AA are always associated with high rates of return from BB; conversely, low rates of return from AA are always associated with low rates of return from BB. For perfect negative correlation (Graph b), however, the opposite is true; high rates of return from AA are associated with low rates of return from BB, and vice versa. If two variables are unrelated, the correlation coefficient between these two variables will be 0.

When two investments are perfectly negatively correlated, the maximum benefits of risk reduction are achieved by diversification. When two investments are perfectly positively correlated, adopting both of them does not result in any risk reduction. When the correlation coefficient between two projects is between +1 and −1, some risk reduction is achieved by diversification. The less positively correlated the returns from two investments are, the greater the portfolio effects of risk reduction will be if the firm or individual diversifies by investing in both.

In practice, the returns from most investments a firm or individual considers are positively correlated with other investments held by the firm or individual. For example, returns from projects that are closely related to the firm's primary line of business have a high positive correlation with returns from projects already being carried out, and thus provide limited opportunity to reduce risk. In the Kreiser example, if Kreiser were to build a new smelter, it would not realize the risk reduction possibilities that investing in gold mining and refining would produce. Similarly, the returns from most common stocks are positively correlated, because these returns are influenced by such common factors as the general state of the economy, the level of interest rates, and so on.

EXPECTED RETURNS FROM A PORTFOLIO

When two or more securities are combined into a portfolio, the expected return of the portfolio is equal to the weighted average of the expected returns from the individual securities. For example, assume a portfolio contains Acme Corporation (A) securities and Babbo Corporation (B) securities, which

125

have expected returns of 12 percent and 8 percent, respectively. If a portion W_A of the available funds (wealth) is invested in Security A, and the remaining funds W_B is invested in Security B, the expected return of the portfolio $\hat{R}_p$ is as follows:

$$\hat{R}_p = W_A\hat{R}_A + W_B\hat{R}_B , \qquad (5.5)$$

where $\hat{R}_A$ and $\hat{R}_B$ are the expected returns for Securities A and B, respectively. Furthermore, $W_A + W_B = 1$, indicating that all funds are invested in either Security A or Security B.

The range of possible expected returns for a portfolio consisting of Securities A and B is 12 percent (if 100 percent of the portfolio is invested in Security A and 0 percent is invested in Security B) to 8 percent (if 100 percent is invested in Security B and 0 percent is invested in Security A). In addition, any linear weighted combination of returns for Securities A and B between 8 and 12 percent is also possible. For example, assume that 30 percent of this portfolio consists of Security A, and Security B constitutes the remaining 70 percent. In this case the expected return on the portfolio is computed as follows:

$$\hat{R}_p = 0.3(12\%) + 0.7(8\%)$$
$$= 9.2\%.$$

In general, the expected return from any portfolio of n securities or assets is equal to the sum of the expected returns from each security times the proportion of the total portfolio invested in that security:

$$\hat{R}_p = \sum_{i=1}^{n} W_i\hat{R}_i , \qquad (5.6)$$

where $\Sigma W_i = 1$ and $0 \le W_i \le 1$.

PORTFOLIO RISK

Although the expected returns from a portfolio of two or more securities can be computed as a weighted average of the expected returns from the individual securities, it is not sufficient merely to calculate a weighted average of the risk of each individual security to arrive at a measure of the portfolio's risk. Whenever the returns from the individual securities are not perfectly positively correlated, the risk of any portfolio of these securities may be reduced through the effects of diversification. Thus, diversification can be achieved by investing in a diverse set of securities that have different risk-return characteristics. The amount of risk reduction achieved through diversification depends on the degree of correlation between the returns of the individual securities in the portfolio. The lower the correlations among the individual securities, the greater the possibilities for risk reduction.

The risk for a two-security portfolio, measured by the standard deviation of portfolio returns, is computed as follows:

$$\sigma_p = \sqrt{W_A^2\sigma_A^2 + W_B^2\sigma_B^2 + 2W_AW_B\rho_{AB}\sigma_A\sigma_B}\,, \qquad (5.7)$$

where W_A is the proportion of funds invested in Security A, W_B is the proportion of funds invested in Security B, $W_A + W_B = 1$, σ_A^2 is the variance of returns from Security A (or the square of the standard deviation for Security A, σ_A), σ_B^2 is the variance of returns from Security B (or the square of the standard deviation for Security B, σ_B), and ρ_{AB} is the correlation coefficient of returns between Securities A and B.

For example, consider a portfolio containing Securities A and B as described here:

	Acme (A)	Babbo (B)
Expected return	0.12	0.08
Standard deviation of returns	0.09	0.09
Proportion invested in each security	0.5	0.5

Given various values for the correlation between the securities' returns, the risk of a portfolio containing equal proportions of the two securities can be computed.

First, consider the case where $\rho_{AB} = +1.0$ (that is, perfect *positive* correlation). The portfolio's risk is calculated as follows:

$$\sigma_p = \sqrt{(0.5)^2(0.09)^2 + (0.5)^2(0.09)^2 + 2(0.5)(0.5)(+1)(0.09)(0.09)}$$
$$= \sqrt{0.002025 + 0.002025 + 0.00405}$$
$$= \sqrt{0.0081}$$
$$= 0.09.$$

When the returns from the two securities are perfectly positively correlated, the risk of the portfolio is equal to the weighted average of the risk of the individual securities (9 percent in this example). *Thus, no risk reduction is achieved when perfectly positively correlated assets are combined in a portfolio.*

Fortunately, most assets are not perfectly positively correlated, and this allows for risk reduction through diversification. For example, consider next the case of a low positive correlation of returns, such as $\rho_{AB} = +0.1$. The portfolio risk in this example follows:

$$\sigma_p = \sqrt{(0.5)^2(0.09)^2 + (0.5)^2(0.09)^2 + 2(0.5)(0.5)(+0.1)(0.09)(0.09)}$$
$$= \sqrt{0.002025 + 0.002025 + 0.000405}$$
$$= \sqrt{0.004455}$$
$$= 0.067.$$

In this case diversification reduces the portfolio risk from 9 percent (the weighted average of the individual security risks) to 6.70 percent.

Finally, consider the case of a perfect *negative* correlation, $\rho_{AB} = -1.0$. In this example the portfolio risk is completely eliminated.

TABLE 5–4   Portfolio Risk and Security Correlations in the Two-Security Case

Correlation Coefficient, ρ_{AB}	Portfolio Risk, σ_p *
+1.0	0.090
+0.5	0.078
+0.1	0.067
0.0	0.064
−0.5	0.045
−1.0	0.000

NOTE: *The standard deviation of returns for Securities A and B equals 0.09 and 0.09, respectively. Each possible portfolio contains equal proportions of both securities.

Table 5-4 summarizes the effects of different degrees of correlation on portfolio risk, assuming that the portfolio contains equal proportions of two securities.

The preceding calculations illustrate possibilities for portfolio risk reduction when two or more securities are combined to form a portfolio. Unfortunately, when more than two securities are involved—as is usually the case—the number of calculations required to compute the portfolio risk increases geometrically. For example, while 45 correlation coefficients are needed for a portfolio containing 10 securities, 4,950 correlation coefficients must be computed for a portfolio containing 100 securities. In other words, a 10-fold increase in securities causes a greater than 100-fold increase in the required calculations.[5] In addition, a substantial computational undertaking is required to find the particular portfolio of securities that minimizes portfolio risk for a given level of return or maximizes return for a given level of risk, even for a portfolio that contains only a few securities. Obviously a more workable method is needed to assess the effects of diversification on a portfolio of assets; this problem is discussed in the following sections.

RISK REDUCTION THROUGH DIVERSIFICATION

Whenever the individual securities in a portfolio are less than perfectly positively correlated, diversification can reduce the portfolio's risk below the weighted average of the total risk (measured by the standard deviation) of the individual securities. Since most securities are positively correlated with returns in the securities market in general, it is usually not possible to totally eliminate risk in a portfolio of securities. As the economic outlook improves, returns on most individual securities tend to increase; as the economic outlook deteriorates, individual security returns tend to decline. In spite of this positive "comovement" among the returns of individual securities, each security experiences some "unique" variation in its returns that is unrelated to

[5]The number of correlation coefficients needed to evaluate an n-security portfolio is computed as $(n^2 - n)/2$.

the underlying economic factors that influence all securities. In other words, there are two types of risk inherent in all securities:

- *Systematic*, or *nondiversifiable*, risk.
- *Unsystematic*, or *diversifiable*, risk.

SYSTEMATIC RISK

Systematic risk refers to that portion of the variability of an individual security's returns caused by factors affecting the market as a whole; as such, it can be thought of as being nondiversifiable. Systematic risk accounts for 25 to 50 percent of the total risk of any security. Some of the sources of systematic risk, which cause the returns from all securities to vary more or less together, include the following:

- Interest rate changes.
- Changes in purchasing power.
- Changes in investor expectations about the overall performance of the economy.

Since diversification cannot eliminate systematic risk, it is this type of risk that is the predominant determinant of individual security risk premiums.

UNSYSTEMATIC RISK

Unsystematic risk is risk that is unique to the firm. It is the variability in a security's returns that is caused by factors such as the following:

- Management capabilities and decisions.
- Strikes.
- The availability of raw materials.
- The unique effects of such government regulation as pollution control.
- The effects of foreign competition.
- The particular levels of financial and operating leverage the firm employs.

Because unsystematic risk is unique to each firm, an efficiently diversified portfolio of securities can successfully eliminate most of the unsystematic risk inherent in individual securities, as is shown in Figure 5-6.

To eliminate effectively the unsystematic risk inherent in a portfolio's individual securities, it is not necessary for the portfolio to include a large number of securities. In fact, randomly constructed portfolios of as few as ten to fifteen securities can successfully diversify away a large portion of the unsystematic risk of the individual securities.[6] The risk remaining *after* diversification is market-related risk, often called *systematic risk*, and it cannot be eliminated through diversification. Since unsystematic risk commonly accounts for 50 percent or more of the total risk of most individual securities,

---

[6]W. H. Wagner and S. C. Lau. "The Effect of Diversification on Risk." *Financial Analysts Journal* (Nov.–Dec 1971):48–53.

FIGURE 5–6   Unsystematic Risk and Portfolio Diversification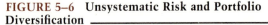

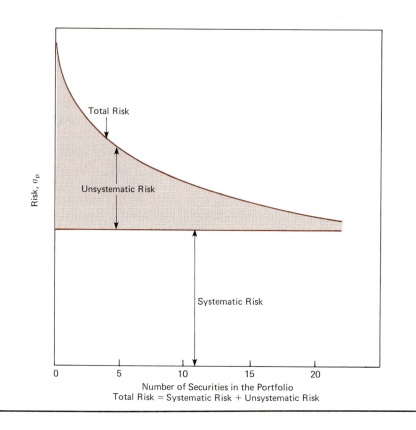

it should be obvious that the risk-reducing benefits of efficient diversification are well worth the effort.

Given the small number of securities required for efficient diversification by an individual investor, as well as the dominance of the securities markets by many large institutional investors who hold widely diversified portfolios, it is safe to conclude that the relevant risk that must be considered for any widely traded individual security is its systematic risk. The unsystematic portion of total risk is relatively easy to diversify away.

SECURITY MARKET LINE (SML)

The return required of any risky asset is determined by the prevailing level of risk-free interest rates plus a risk premium. The greater the level of risk an investor perceives about a security's return, the greater the required risk premium will be. In other words, investors require returns that are commensurate with the risk level they perceive. In algebraic terms, the required return, from any Security j, k_j, is equal to the following:

FIGURE 5–7   The Security Market Line (SML)

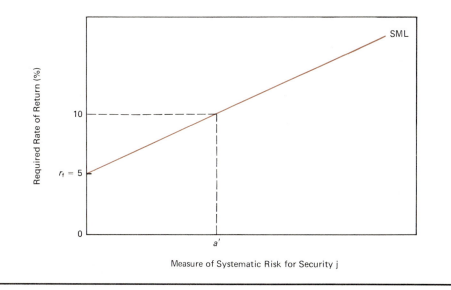

Measure of Systematic Risk for Security j

$$k_j = r_f + \theta_j , \qquad\qquad (5.8)$$

where r_f is the risk-free rate and θ_j, the risk premium required by investors.

The security market line (SML) indicates the "going" required rate of return in the market for a given amount of systematic risk, and it is illustrated in Figure 5-7. The SML intersects the vertical axis at the risk-free rate, r_f, indicating that any security with an expected risk premium equal to zero should be required to earn a return equal to the risk-free rate. As risk increases, so do the risk premium and the required rate of return. According to Figure 5-7, for example, a security having a risk level of a' should be required to earn a 10 percent rate of return.

INFLATION AND THE SECURITY MARKET LINE

The risk-free rate of return, r_f, can be thought of as consisting of the following two components:

- A *real* rate of return that is free from the effects of any inflationary expectations.

- A *premium* that is equal to the effects of expected inflation.

Historically the real rate of return on risk-free securities, such as U.S. Government bonds, has averaged 2 to 5 percent per annum. The inflation premium is normally equal to investors' expectations about future purchasing power changes. If, for example, inflation is expected to average 2 percent over some future period, the risk-free rate of return on government securities (assuming a real rate of return of 3 percent) should be approximately the following:

131

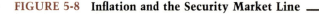

FIGURE 5-8   **Inflation and the Security Market Line**

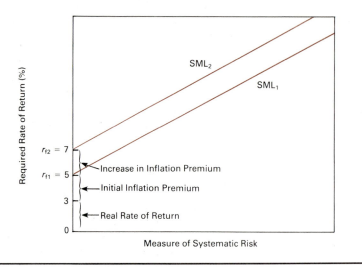

$$r_f = \text{Real return} + \text{Inflation premium} \qquad (5.9)$$
$$= 3\% + 2\%$$
$$= 5\%.$$

By extension, if inflation expectations suddenly increased from 2 to 4 percent, the risk-free rate should increase from 5 to 7 percent (3 percent real return plus 4 percent inflation premium).

Since the required return on any risky security, k_j, is equal to the risk-free rate plus the risk premium, an increase in inflationary expectations effectively increases the required return on all securities. This is shown in Figure 5-8. In the figure, SML_2 represents the returns required on all securities following a change in the expected future inflation rate. The required returns of all securities increase by 2 percent—the change in expected inflation. When investors increase their required returns, they become unwilling to purchase securities at existing prices, causing prices to decline. It should come as no surprise, then, that securities analysts and investors take a dim view of increased inflation.

BETA: A MEASURE OF SECURITY RISK

Thus far we have not addressed the question of the appropriate risk measure to use when considering the risk-return tradeoffs illustrated by the SML. The previous discussion of risk in a portfolio context suggests that some measure of systematic risk is an appropriate starting point.

The systematic risk of a security is determined by the standard deviation of the security's returns, the standard deviation of the returns from the market portfolio, and the correlation of the security's returns with those of all other securities in the market. A broad-based security market index, such as

132

the *Standard and Poor's 500 Market Index* or the *New York Stock Exchange Index*, is normally used as a measure of total market returns.

One useful measure of the systematic risk of a Security j is the value called *beta*. Beta is a measure of the volatility of a security's returns relative to the returns of a broad-based Market Portfolio m. It is defined as the ratio of the covariance (or comovement) of returns on Security j and Market Portfolio m to the variance of returns on the market portfolio:

$$\text{Beta}_j = \frac{\text{Covariance}_{j,m}}{\text{Variance}_m}.$$

$$\text{Beta}_j = \frac{\rho_{jm}\sigma_j\sigma_m}{\sigma_m^2}, \tag{5.10}$$

where beta$_j$ is the measure of systematic risk for Security j, σ_j is the standard deviation of returns for Security j, σ_m is the standard deviation of returns for Market Portfolio m, σ_m^2 is the variance of returns for Market Portfolio m, and ρ_{jm} is the correlation coefficient between returns for Security j and Market Portfolio m.

In practice, beta may be computed as the slope of a regression line between the periodic (usually yearly, quarterly, or monthly) returns on the market portfolio (as measured by a market index, such as the *Standard and Poor's 500 Market Index*) and the periodic returns for Security j, as follows:

$$R_j = a_j + b_j R_m + e_j, \tag{5.11}$$

where R_j is the periodic return for Security j, a_j is a constant term determined by the regression, b_j is the computed historical beta for Security j, R_m is the periodic return for the market index, and e_j is a random error term.

This equation describes a line called Security j's *characteristic line*. Figure 5-9 shows the characteristic line for General Motors. The slope of this line is 0.97, indicating that the systematic returns from General Motors common stock are slightly less variable than the returns for the market as a whole. A beta of 1.0 for any security indicates that the security is of average systematic risk; that is, a security with a beta of 1.0 has the same risk characteristics as the market as a whole when only systematic risk is considered. When beta = 1.0, a 1 percent increase (decline) in market returns indicates that the *systematic* returns for the individual security should increase (decline) by 1 percent.[7] A beta of 1.5, for example, indicates that when market returns increase (decline) by 1 percent, the security's systematic returns can be expected to increase (decline) by 1.5 percent. A beta of less than 1—for example, 0.5—is indicative of a security of less than average systematic risk. In this case a 1 percent increase (decline) in market returns implies a 0.5 percent increase (decline) in the security's systematic returns. Table 5-5 summarizes the interpretation of betas.

The beta for the market portfolio as measured by a broad-based market

---

[7]Of course, there will also be *unsystematic* components to a security's returns at any point in time. We assume these are diversified away in the portfolio.

FIGURE 5–9   The Characteristic Line for General Motors

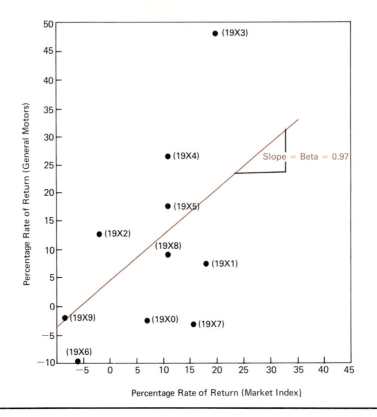

index equals 1.0. This can be seen in Equation 5.10. Since the correlation of the market with itself is 1.0, the beta of the market portfolio must also be 1.0.

Finally, the beta of any portfolio of n securities or assets is simply the weighted average of the individual security betas:

TABLE 5–5   Interpretation of Beta Coefficients

Beta Value	Direction of Movement in Returns	Interpretation
2.0	Same as market	Twice as risky (responsive) as market
1.0	Same as market	Risk equal to that of market
0.5	Same as market	Half as risky as market
0	Uncorrelated with market movements	No market-related risk
−0.5	Opposite of market	Half as responsive as market, but in the opposite direction

TABLE 5–6 **Betas for Selected Stocks**

Company Name	Value Line Beta
RCA	1.05
Digital Equipment	1.20
IBM	0.95
Union Pacific	1.30
DuPont	1.10
Gibralter Financial	1.45
De Beers Consolidated Mines, Ltd.	0.45
Alcoa	1.00
U.S. Steel	1.00
Bethlehem Steel	1.20
Deere and Company	0.95
International Harvester	1.00
Campbell Soup	0.65
Hershey Foods	0.75
Coca Cola	0.85
K Mart	1.00
Public Service of Colorado	0.70
Walt Disney Productions	0.95
Dow Jones and Company	0.95
Reading and Bates	1.75
Wells Fargo and Company	1.00
Chrysler	1.00
Atlantic Richfield	1.20
Lockheed	1.50

SOURCE: *Value Line Investment Survey* (New York: Arnold Bernhard and Co., Inc), various issues, 1982 and 1983.

$$\text{Beta}_p = \sum_{j=1}^{n} W_j \text{beta}_j .\qquad (5.12)$$

This concept is particularly useful when evaluating the effects of capital investment projects or mergers on a firm's systematic risk.

Fortunately for financial managers, it is not necessary to compute the beta for each security every time a security's systematic risk measure is needed. Several investment advisory services, including the *Value Line Investment Survey* and Merrill Lynch, regularly compute and publish individual security beta estimates, and these are readily available. Table 5-6 lists the Value Line computed betas for selected stocks.

SECURITY MARKET LINE AND BETA

Given the information presented thus far, it is possible to compute risk premiums, θ, that are applicable to individual securities. The SML also may be defined in terms of beta. The risk premium for any Security j is equal to the difference between the required returns of investors, k_j, and the risk-free rate, r_f:

$$\theta_j = k_j - r_f .\qquad (5.13)$$

135

For example, if the expected return on the overall market portfolio, $\hat{k}_m$, is 10 percent, and the expected risk-free rate, $\hat{r}_f$, is 5 percent, the market risk premium is equal to the following:

$$\hat{\theta}_m = \hat{k}_m - \hat{r}_f$$
$$= 10\% - 5\%$$
$$= 5\%.$$

For a security with average risk (beta$_j$ = 1.0), the risk premium should be equal to the market risk premium. A security whose beta is 2.0, however, is twice as risky as the average security, so its risk premium should be twice the market risk premium:

$$\theta_j = b_j(\hat{k}_m - \hat{r}_f)$$
$$= 2.0(10\% - 5\%)$$
$$= 10\%.$$

The required return for any security may be defined in terms of its systematic risk (beta), the expected market return, $\hat{k}_m$, and the expected risk-free rate, as follows:

$$k_j = \hat{r}_f + \hat{\theta}_j ,$$

or

$$k_j = \hat{r}_f + b_j(\hat{k}_m - \hat{r}_f) . \tag{5.14}$$

For example, if the risk-free rate is 7 percent and $\hat{k}_m$ is 12 percent, the required return for a security having a beta of 1.3 is computed as follows:

$$k_j = 7\% + 1.3 (12\% - 7\%)$$
$$= 7\% + 6.5\%$$
$$= 13.5\%.$$

Equation 5.14 provides an explicit definition of the SML in terms of the systematic risk of individual securities. Figure 5–10 illustrates the SML from Equation 5.14. Assuming a risk-free rate of 7 percent and a market return of 12 percent, the return required on a low risk stock (for example, beta = 0.5) is 9.5 percent. The return required on a high risk stock (for example, beta = 2.0) is 17 percent, and the return required on a stock of average risk (for example, beta = 1.0) is 12 percent, the same as the market required return.

The slope of the SML is shown as being constant throughout. When mea-

FIGURE 5–10   The Security Market Line in Terms of Beta

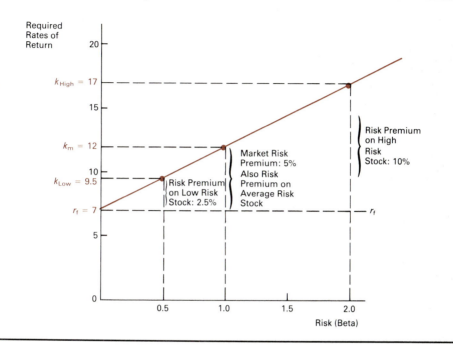

sured between beta $= 0$ and beta $= 1.0$, it is equal to $(k_m - r_f)/(1 - 0)$, or simply $k_m - r_f$. This slope represents the risk premium on an average risk security.

If the average risk premium (measured by the slope of the SML) increases because of an increase in uncertainty regarding the future economic outlook, or because investors as a group have tended to become more averse to risk and thus require a higher rate of return for any level of risk, the slope of the SML will increase. This, in turn, will increase the risk premium on stocks with greater than average risk (beta > 1.0) more than on stocks with less than average risk (beta < 1.0). For example, if the market risk premium increases from 5 to 6 percent, the required risk premium on a security with a beta of 0.5 increases by only 0.5 percent, or $0.5 \times (6.0\% - 5.0\%)$. In contrast, the risk premium on a security with a beta of 2.0 experiences a rise in its required risk premium of 2 percent $(2.0 \times 1.0\%)$.

USES OF THE CAPM
AND PORTFOLIO RISK CONCEPTS

The notion of portfolio risk and the CAPM as previously developed are powerful pedagogical tools to explain the nature of risk and its relationship to required returns on securities and physical assets. In Chapter 12 the CAPM is discussed as one technique that can be used to estimate the cost of equity capital. That chapter considers where the necessary data may be obtained to

137

apply the model. Also, Chapter 11 considers the use of CAPM-determined required rates of return as a technique to adjust for risk in the capital budgeting process.

ASSUMPTIONS AND LIMITATIONS OF THE CAPITAL ASSET PRICING MODEL (CAPM)

The theoretical CAPM and its applications are based upon a number of crucial assumptions about the securities markets and investors' attitudes, including the following:

- Securities are actively traded in a competitive market, where information about a given firm and its future prospects is freely available.
- Investors can borrow and lend at the risk-free rate, which remains constant over time.
- There are no brokerage charges for buying and selling securities.
- There are no taxes.
- All investors prefer the security that provides the highest return for a given level of risk, or the lowest amount of risk for a given level of return.
- All investors have common (homogeneous) expectations regarding the expected returns, variances, and correlations of returns among all securities.

Whereas these assumptions may seem fairly limiting at first glance, extensions of the basic theory presented in this chapter, which relax the assumptions, generally have yielded results consistent with the fundamental theory. In addition, statistical tests of observed behavior in securities markets tend to support the results implied by the model presented here. In spite of these restrictive assumptions, this basic model has been extensively used, both practically and conceptually, to consider the risk-return tradeoff required by investors in the securities market. For example, the CAPM (or a modification thereof) has been increasingly used in regulated public utility rate case testimony aimed at determining a reasonable allowed rate of return for the utility's investors.

However, users of this approach also should be aware of some of the major problems encountered in practical applications. These include the following:

- Estimating expected future market returns.
- Determining the most appropriate estimate of the risk-free rate.
- Determining the best estimate of an asset's *future* beta.
- Reconciling the fact that some empirical tests have shown that investors do not totally ignore unsystematic risk, as the theory suggests.

OTHER DIMENSIONS OF RISK

This chapter has focused on various measures of variability in returns—either total variability, measured by the *standard deviation* and the *coefficient of variation*, or systematic variability, measured by *beta*. Although variability of returns is very important, it does not adequately consider another important risk dimension—that is, the risk of failure. In the case of an individual investment project, failure is a situation in which a project generates a *negative* rate of return. In the case of a total firm, failure is the situation in which a firm loses money and is ultimately forced into bankruptcy.

For risk-averse investors, the risk of failure may play a large role in determining the types of investments undertaken. For example, the management of a firm is not likely to be eager to invest in a project that has a high risk of failure and that ultimately may cause the firm to fail if it proves to be unsuccessful. After all, the continued survival of the firm is closely tied to the economic well-being of management.

From a shareholder wealth maximization perspective, failure is a particularly undesirable occurence. The direct and indirect costs of bankruptcy can be very high. Consequently, this failure risk is often an important determinant of investment risk. The risk and cost of failure can explain, in large part, the desire of many firms to diversify. In addition to reducing the overall risk of a firm, diversification can result in a lower probability of bankruptcy and thus lower *expected* costs incurred during bankruptcy. These costs include the following:

- The loss of funds that occurs when assets are sold at distressed prices during liquidation.

- The legal fees and selling costs incurred when a firm enters bankruptcy proceedings.

- The opportunity costs of the funds that are unavailable to investors during the bankrupcty proceedings (for example, it took over 8 years to settle the Penn-Central bankruptcy).

If, through diversification, a firm can decrease the probability of bankruptcy, it can reduce its *expected* bankruptcy costs. Lower expected bankruptcy costs should increase shareholder wealth, all other things being equal.

Diversification also may reduce a firm's cost of capital. By reducing the overall risk of the firm, diversification will lower the default risk of the firm's debt securities, and the firm's bonds will receive higher ratings and require lower interest payments. In addition, the firm may be able to increase the proportion of low cost debt relative to equity in its optimal capital structure, further reducing the cost of capital and increasing shareholder wealth.[8]

Although we will focus primarily on return variability as our measure of risk in this book, the risk and cost of failure also should be kept in mind.

SUMMARY

- The *risk* of a security or an investment project is defined in terms of the potential *variability* of its returns. When only one return is possible—for example, as with U.S. Government securities held to maturity—there is no

---

[8]The concept of optimal capital structure is discussed in Chapter 13.

risk. When more than one return is possible for a particular project, it is risky.

- The *standard deviation, σ,* of the expected return from an investment is an *absolute* measure of risk. It is computed as the square root of the weighted average squared deviations of individual observations from the expected value.

- When projects of unequal size (or investments with unequal expected returns) are being compared, the *coefficient of variation, v,* is a more appropriate measure of risk. The coefficient of variation is the ratio of the standard deviation to the expected value.

- Because cash flow projections and expected returns can be estimated with less certainty farther into the future, risk is generally thought to *increase over time.*

- Risk is also influenced by the possibility of investment *diversification.* For example, if a proposed project's returns are not *perfectly correlated* with the returns from the firm's other investments, the total risk of the firm may be reduced by accepting the proposed project. This is known as the *portfolio effect.*

- The *expected return from a portfolio* of two or more securities is equal to the weighted average of the expected returns from the individual securities.

- The *risk of a portfolio* is a function of both the risk of the individual securities in the portfolio and the correlation among the individual securities' returns.

- The *unsystematic* portion of the total risk in a security's return is that portion of return variability unique to the firm. Efficient diversification of a portfolio of securities can eliminate most unsystematic risk.

- *Systematic* risk refers to the portion of total risk in a security's return caused by overall market forces. This risk cannot be diversified away in a portfolio. Systematic risk forms the basis for the risk premium required by investors in any risky security.

- The *security market line* (SML) provides an algebraic or graphic representation of the risk-return tradeoff required in the marketplace for risky securities. It measures risk in terms of systematic risk.

- An index of systematic risk for a security is the security's *beta.* Beta is determined from the slope of a regression line, the *characteristic line,* between the market return and the individual security's return. It is a measure of the volatility of a security's returns relative to the returns of the market as a whole.

- The required return on common stock consists of the risk-free rate plus a risk premium. This risk premium is equal to a security's beta times the market risk premium, and the market risk premium is equal to the difference between the expected market return and the risk-free rate.

QUESTIONS AND TOPICS FOR DISCUSSION

1. Define the following terms:
   a. Risk.
   b. Probability distribution.

140

c. Standard deviation.
d. Required rate of return.
e. Coefficient of variation.
f. Beta coefficient.
g. CAPM.
h. Correlation coefficient.

i. Portfolio.
j. Characteristic line.
k. Security market line.
l. Covariance.
m. Systematic risk.
n. Unsystematic risk.

2. If the returns from a security were known with certainty, what shape would the probability distribution of returns graph have?

3. What is the nature of the risk associated with "risk-free" U.S. Government bonds?

4. If inflation expectations increase, what would you expect to happen to the returns required by investors in bonds? What would happen to bond prices?

5. Under what circumstances will the coefficient of variation of a security's returns and the standard deviation of that security's returns give the same relative measure of risk when compared with the risk of another security?

6. Explain how diversification can reduce the risk of a portfolio of assets to below the weighted average of the risk of the individual assets.

7. What are the primary variables that influence the risk of a portfolio of assets?

8. Distinguish between unsystematic and systematic risk. Under what circumstances are investors likely to ignore the unsystematic risk characteristics of a security?

9. What effect do increasing inflation expectations have on the required returns of investors in common stock?

10. The stock of Amrep Corporation has a *beta* value estimated to be 1.4. How would you interpret this beta value? How would you evaluate the firm's systematic risk?

11. How is a security's beta value computed?

12. Under what circumstances can the beta concept be used to estimate the rate of return required by investors in a stock? What problems are encountered when using the CAPM?

PROBLEMS *

1. You have estimated the following probability distributions of expected future returns for Stocks X and Y:

STOCK X		STOCK Y	
Probability	Return	Probability	Return
0.1	−10%	0.2	2%
0.2	10	0.2	7
0.4	15	0.3	12
0.2	20	0.2	15
0.1	40	0.1	16

a. What is the expected rate of return for Stock X? Stock Y?
b. What is the standard deviation of expected returns for Stock X? For Stock Y?
c. Which stock would you consider to be riskier? Why?

2. The return expected from Project number 542 is 22 percent. The standard deviation of this expected return is 11 percent. If expected returns from the project are

* Problems in color have check answers provided at the end of the book.

normally distributed, what is the chance that the project will result in a rate of return above 33 percent? What is the risk that the project will result in losses (negative rates of return)?

3. The expected rate of return for the stock of Cornhusker Enterprises is 20 percent, with a standard deviation of 15 percent. The expected rate of return for the stock of Mustang Associates is 10 percent, with a standard deviation of 9 percent.
   a. Which stock would you consider to be riskier? Why?
   b. If you knew that the beta coefficient of Cornhusker stock is 1.5 and the beta of Mustang is 0.9, how would your answer to Part a change?

4. The current dividend, D_0, of the stock of Sun Devil Corporation is $3 per share. Under present conditions this dividend is expected to grow at a rate of 6 percent annually for the foreseeable future. The beta of Sun Devil's stock is 1.2. The risk-free rate of return is 8 percent, and the expected market rate of return is 13 percent.
   a. At what price would you expect Sun Devil's common stock to sell?
   b. If the risk-free rate of return declines to 7 percent, what will happen to Sun Devil's stock price? (Assume the expected market rate of return remains at 13 percent).
   c. Sun Devil's management is considering acquisitions in the machine tool industry. They expect the firm's beta to increase to 1.3 as a result of these acquisitions. The dividend growth rate is expected to increase to 7 percent annually. Would you recommend this acquisition program to management? (Assume the same initial conditions that existed in Part a.)

5. You are considering purchasing a portfolio of securities. The securities available to you have the following expected returns:

SECURITY	EXPECTED RETURN (%)
A	12
B	8
C	14
D	10

   a. If you invest 20 percent of your funds in Security A, 40 percent in B, 20 percent in C, and 20 percent in D, what is the expected return of the portfolio?
   b. How does the expected return of the portfolio change if you invest 40 percent in A, 10 percent in B, 40 percent in C, and 10 percent in D?
   c. In addition to the portfolio in Part b having a different expected return than the portfolio in Part a, how would you expect the two portfolios to differ with respect to risk?

6. You are considering investing in two securities, X and Y. The following data are available for the two securities:

	SECURITY X	SECURITY Y
Expected return	0.10	0.07
Standard deviation of returns	0.08	0.04

   a. If you invest 40 percent of your funds in Security X and 60 percent in Security Y, and if the correlation of returns between X and Y is $+0.5$, compute the following:
      i. The expected return from the portfolio.
      ii. The standard deviation of returns from the portfolio.

b. What happens to the expected return and standard deviation of returns of the portfolio in Part a if 70 percent of your funds are invested in Security X and 30 percent of your funds are invested in Security Y?

c. What happens to the expected return and standard deviation of returns of the portfolio in Part a if the following conditions exist?

    i. The correlation of returns between Securities X and Y is $+1.0$.

    ii. The correlation of returns between Securities X and Y is 0.

    iii. The correlation of returns between Securities X and Y is -0.7.

7. The SML has been estimated as follows:

$$k_i = 0.06 + 0.05 \text{ beta} .$$

This estimate assumes an expected rate of inflation of 4 percent. If inflation expectations increase from 4 to 6 percent, what will be the equation of the new SML?

8. The stock of Pizza Hot, Inc., a Mexican pizza chain, has an estimated beta of 1.5. Give the required rate of return on Pizza Hot's stock if the SML in Problem 7 is appropriate, assuming the following:

a. The original inflation expectation of 4 percent.

b. The new inflation expectation of 6 percent.

9. Caledonia Minerals has an estimated beta of 1.6. The company is considering the acquisition of another firm that has a beta of 1.2. Both companies are exactly the same size.

a. What is the expected new beta value for the combined firm?

b. The risk-free rate of return is estimated at 7 percent, and the market return is estimated as 12 percent. What is your estimate of the required return of investors in Caledonia before and after the merger?

10. Caledonia Minerals (see Problem 9) is expected to pay a $1 dividend next year ($D_1 = \$1$). This dividend is expected to grow at a rate of 6 percent per year for the forseeable future if the merger is not completed. The merger is not expected to change the current dividend rate, but future dividends are expected to grow at a 7 percent rate as a result of the merger.

a. What is the value of a share of stock in Caledonia Minerals prior to the merger?

HINT: Use the required equity return computed in Problem 9.

b. What is the new value of a share of stock, assuming that the merger is completed?

c. Would you recommend that Caledonia go ahead with the merger?

11. Globe Steel has decided to diversify into the home improvement field. As a result of this expansion, Globe's beta value drops from 1.3 to 1.0, and the expected future growth rate in the firm's dividends drops from 8 to 6 percent. The expected market return, k_m, is 13 percent; the risk-free rate, r_f, is 7 percent; and current dividends per share, D_0, are $3. Should Globe undertake the planned diversification?

12. Tucker Manufacturing Company has a beta estimated at 1.0. The risk-free rate is 6 percent, and the expected market return is 12 percent. Tucker expects to pay a $4 dividend next year ($D_1 = \$4$). This dividend is expected to grow at 3 percent per year for the foreseeable future. The current market price for Tucker is $40.

a. Is the current stock price an equilibrium price, based upon the SML calculation of k_e for Tucker?

b. What do you think the appropriate equilibrium price is? How will that price be achieved?

13. Using Equation 5.14, you have computed the *required* rate of return for the stock of Bulldog Trucking to be 19.6 percent. Given the current stock price, the current dividend rate, and analysts' projections for future dividend growth, you *expect* to earn a rate of return of 20.8 percent.
    a. Would you recommend buying or selling this stock? Why?
    b. If your *expected* rate of return from the stock of Bulldog is 18 percent, what would you expect to happen to Bulldog's stock price?

14. You want to construct a portfolio with a 20 percent expected return. The portfolio is to consist of some combination of Security A and Security B:

Security	Expected Return	Beta
A	15%	0.82
B	28	1.75

a. What percentage of your portfolio should consist of Security A? Of Security B?
b. What is the beta of the portfolio?

15. Equation 5.7 can be modified to compute the risk of a three-security portfolio as follows:

$$\sigma_p = \sqrt{\begin{array}{l} W_A{}^2\sigma_A{}^2 + W_B{}^2\sigma_B{}^2 + W_C{}^2\sigma_C{}^2 + 2W_AW_B\rho_{AB}\sigma_A\sigma_B + 2W_AW_C\rho_{AC}\sigma_A\sigma_C \\ + 2W_BW_C\rho_{BC}\sigma_B\sigma_C \end{array}}$$

You have decided to invest 40 percent of your wealth in Security A, 30 percent in Security B, and 30 percent in Security C. The following information is available about the possible returns from the three securities:

SECURITY A		SECURITY B		SECURITY C	
Return (%)	Probability	Return (%)	Probability	Return (%)	Probability
10	0.25	13	0.30	14	0.40
12	0.50	16	0.35	18	0.30
14	0.25	19	0.35	22	0.30

Compute the expected return of the portfolio and the risk of the portfolio if the correlations between returns from the three securities are $\rho_{AB} = 0.70$; $\rho_{AC} = 0.60$; and $\rho_{BC} = 0.85$.

CALCULATOR APPLICATIONS

This section illustrates the use of the Texas Instruments Professional Business Analyst (BA-55) calculator to compute the expected value, standard deviation, coefficient of variation, and variance of a distribution of returns using discrete probabilities. It also illustrates the calculation of correlation coefficients and beta values.

EXPECTED VALUE, STANDARD DEVIATION, VARIANCE, AND COEFFICIENT OF VARIATION

Consider the example developed in the chapter illustrating the returns available from investing in the stock of International Farm Products (IFP).

Return	Probability of Occurrence
−4%	0.2
18	0.6
40	0.2

Procedure	Press	Display
1. Clear calculator and mode registers; select two decimal places.	on/c 2nd **CLmode** 2nd **Fix** 2	0.00
2. Press 2nd **Mode** until the STAT indicator is displayed.	2nd **Mode**	0.00
3. Enter the first return.	4 +/−	−4
4. Enter the probability in percentage form.	2nd **Frq** 20	Fr 020
5. Enter the values.	Σ +	20.00
6. Repeat Steps 3, 4, and 5 for each set of the values: **a.** Second set.	18 2nd **Frq** 60 Σ +	80.00
b. Third set.	40 2nd **Frq** 20 Σ +	100.00
7. Calculate the expected value.	ȳ	**18.00**
8. Calculate the standard deviation.	σ_n	**13.91**
9. Calculate the variance.	2nd x^2	**193.60**

10. Calculate the coefficient of variation.	13.91 ÷ 18.00	**0.77**

CALCULATING CORRELATION COEFFICIENTS

In analyzing the risk of several assets combined into a portfolio, it is important to know the correlation between the returns of all pairs of assets in the portfolio. Consider the following set of returns from investing in the stock of ABC Corporation and XYZ Corporation over the past 10 years:

Year	Annual Holding Period Returns from ABC(y)	Annual Holding Period Returns from XYZ (x)
19X1	15%	13%
19X2	7	8
19X3	−2	9
19X4	8	5
19X5	16	18
19X6	20	17
19X7	4	10
19X8	22	15
19X9	9	4
19Y0	11	12

The correlation between the returns from the stock of ABC and the returns from the stock of XYZ can be computed as follows:

Procedure	Press	Display
1. Clear calculator and mode registers; select two decimal places.	on/c 2nd **CLmode** 2nd **Fix** 2	0.00
2. Press 2nd **Mode** until the STAT indicator is displayed.	2nd **Mode**	0.00
3. Enter the data (The calculator displays the current number of data entries):		
a. Enter the first x value.	13 x◄y	0.00
Enter the first y value.	15 Σ +	1.00
b. Enter the second pair of data points.	8 x◄y 7 Σ +	2.00

Procedure	Press	Display

c. Continue to enter the remaining eight pairs of data points.

4. Compute the correlation coefficient. | 2nd **Corr** | **0.69**

This is the correlation between the returns from ABC and XYZ over the past 10 years.

CALCULATING THE BETA COEFFICIENT OF A STOCK

As was discussed in the chapter, the beta coefficient of a stock is simply the slope of a regression line between the returns from some Stock j and the returns from the Market Portfolio m as measured by a broad-based market index such as the *Standard and Poor's 500 Market Index*.

To illustrate the calculation of beta coefficients, consider the returns from Stock ABC and Stock XYZ previously listed. Now, instead of the returns from XYZ representing the returns for an individual stock, assume they are really the returns from a broad-based market index. Using this data set, with ABC representing the returns for Stock ABC and XYZ representing the market return series, the parameters of Equation 5.11 can be estimated on your calculator:

Procedure	Press	Display
1. Perform the first three steps in the correlation example. Remember that the returns from ABC are the dependent variable, *y*, and the market returns are the independent variable, *x*.		
2. Calculate the intercept term in Equation 5.10.	2nd **Intcp**	−0.81
3. Calculate the beta (slope) coefficient.	2nd **Slope**	**1.06**

Thus, on the basis of these calculations, the beta of ABC is 1.06, indicating that it is slightly more risky than the average stock in the marketplace.

ADDITIONAL READINGS AND REFERENCES

Blume, Marshall E., and Friend, Irwin. "A New Look at the Capital-Asset Pricing Model." *Journal of Finance* 28 (March 1973): 19–34.

Bowman, R. G. "The Theoretical Relationship between Systematic Risk and Financial (Accounting) Variables." *Journal of Finance* (June 1979): 617–630.

Ibbotson, Roger G., and Sinquefield, Rex A. *Stocks, Bonds, Bills, and Inflation: The Past and the Future.* Charlottesville, Va.: Financial Analysts Research Foundation, 1982.

Litzenberger, Robert H., and Rao, C. U. "Portfolio Theory and Industry Cost-of-Capital Estimates." *Journal of Financial and Quantitative Analysis* 7 (March 1972): 1443–1462.

Modigliani, Franco, and Pogue, Gerald A. "An Introduction to Risk and Return: Concepts and Evidence, Part I." *Financial Analysts Journal* 30 (March–April 1974): 68–80.

Myers, S. C., and Pogue, G. A. "An Evaluation of the Risk of Comsat's Common Stock." (Aug. 1973). Submitted to the FCC in connection with Comsat's rate case.

Pettit, R. Richardson, and Westerfield, Randolph. "Using the Capital Asset Pricing Model and the Market Model to Predict Security Returns." *Journal of Financial and Quantitative Analysis* 9 (Sept. 1974): 579–605.

Roll, Richard. "A Critique of the Asset Pricing Theory's Tests." *Journal of Financial Economics* (March 1977): 129–176.

Rubinstein, M. E. "A Mean-Variance Synthesis of Corporate Financial Theory." *Journal of Finance* 28 (March 1973): 167–181.

Sharpe, William F. *Portfolio Analysis and Capital Markets.* New York: McGraw-Hill, 1970.

Wagner, W. H., and Lau, S. C. "The Effect of Diversification on Risk." *Financial Analysts Journal* (Nov.–Dec. 1971): 48–53.

Weston, J. Fred. "Investment Decisions Using the Capital Asset Pricing Model." *Financial Management* 2 (Spring 1973): 25–33.

PART THREE

Financial Analysis

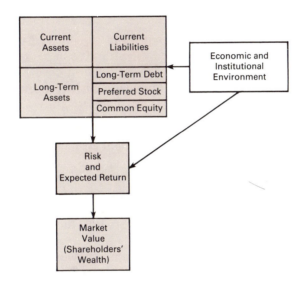

In assessing the financial condition and the risk of a firm, the tools of financial statement analysis can be very helpful. These are discussed in Chapter 6. Chapter 7 develops the concepts of operating and financial leverage and analyzes their effects on a firm's risk. Finally, Chapter 8 looks at the financial planning process for a firm. If the objective of shareholder wealth maximization is to be achieved, the firm must make long-term financial plans. Effective financial planning also can alert management to potential problem areas well in advance. By carefully evaluating current financial strengths and weaknesses and by planning for the future, risk and return can be effectively controlled to maximize the value of the firm.

CHAPTER 6

The Analysis of Financial Statements

A FINANCIAL DILEMMA

Accounting Income: A Question of Interpretation

> Remember: There are only two items in a balance sheet that are for real—cash, which can be counted, and all liabilities.[*]

Financial analysts are professionals who evaluate the financial condition of firms. In the process, a financial analyst often compares the performance of a firm under consideration with that of competitive firms or an industry standard. The analysis can provide useful insights into the direction and relative strength of the firm.

The financial analyst should keep in mind, however, that generally accepted accounting principles give firms considerable latitude in reporting their financial positions. Two very similar firms may come up with very different statements of their positions. This can severely limit the value and validity of standard financial analysis techniques—unless the analyst considers the specific procedures used by the firms being analyzed.

For example, in determining the cost of goods sold, some firms value inventory based on a first-in, first-out (FIFO) system. Other firms use a last-in, first-out (LIFO) system, and still others use an actual cost system. Similarly, some firms report depreciation using straight line procedures; others use the sum-of-the-years'-digits method, the double declining balance method, the units of production method, or the new Accelerated Cost Recovery System (discussed in Chapter 9). Firms also have considerable latitude in the areas of sales recognition (determining when a sale becomes a sale for accounting purposes); the treatment of research and development costs, as well as pension costs; and the handling of extraordinary sources of income.

---

[*]Heinz H Biel, (Vice-president of the NYSE firm of Janney, Montgomery and Scott). "Beware of Shibboleths" *Forbes* (May 10, 1982): 318.

Given the latitude permitted by generally accepted accounting principles, there are literally thousands of accounting definitions of the net income, assets, liabilities, and equity a firm may report on its financial statements. Consequently, a good financial analyst must use great caution when attempting to reach conclusions about the financial condition of a firm based solely on reported accounting data.

In this chapter we develop some of the tools that can be used to assist the financial analyst. Financial ratio analysis is developed in considerable detail as one of the techniques that is a most valuable first step in the financial analysis of a firm.

GLOSSARY OF NEW TERMS

Activity ratios   financial ratios that indicate how efficiently a firm is utilizing its assets to generate sales.

Balance sheet   a financial statement that lists a firm's assets, liabilities, and owners' equity at a point in time.

Comparative analysis   an examination of a firm's performance based on one or more financial ratios, which are compared with the financial ratios of competitive firms or with an industry standard.

Discriminant analysis   a statistical technique designed to classify observations (firms) into two or more predetermined groups based on certain characteristics (such as financial ratios) of the observations.

EAT   the abbreviation for *earnings after taxes.*

EBIT   the abbreviation for *earnings before interest and taxes* (also called *operating earnings*).

EPS   the abbreviation for *earnings per share.*

FIFO   the abbreviation for the *first-in, first-out* inventory valuation method. The method assumes that a firm uses the oldest items in the inventory first. Thus, they are *priced out* of the inventory based on the oldest inventory acquisition costs rather than the most recent.

Financial analysis   the utilization of a group of analytical techniques, including financial ratio analysis, to detemine the strengths, weaknesses, and direction of a company's performance.

Financial leverage ratios   financial ratios that measure the degree to which a firm is financing its assets with fixed charge sources of funds such as debt, preferred stock, or leases.

Financial ratio   a statistical yardstick that relates two numbers generally taken from a firm's income statement, balance sheet, or both at a specific point in time.

Income statement   a financial statement that indicates how a firm performed during a period of time.

LIFO   the abbreviation for the *last-in, first-out* inventory valuation method. The method assumes that a firm uses the most recently acquired items in

151

the inventory first. Thus they are *priced out* of the inventory based on the most recent inventory acquisition costs rather than the oldest.

Liquidity ratios   financial ratios that indicate a firm's ability to meet short-term financial obligations.

Profitability ratios   financial ratios that measure the total effectiveness of a firm's management in generating profits.

Stockholders' equity   the total of a firm's common stock at par, contributed capital in excess of par, and retained earnings accounts from the balance sheet. It is sometimes called the *book value* of the firm, *owners' equity*, or *net worth*.

Trend analysis   an examination of a firm's performance over time. It is frequently based on one or more financial ratios.

INTRODUCTION

Chapters 6 through 8 develop the tools of financial analysis and financial forecasting. This chapter deals with the analysis of financial statements. A carefully executed financial statement analysis can assist the financial manager in assessing the current financial condition of the firm. Chapter 7 looks at the risk dimension of a firm's current financial position. The concepts of operating and financial leverage are developed as measures of a firm's risk.

Once the current financial condition of the firm and the firm's risk profile have been assessed, the financial manager is in a position to plan for the future direction of the firm, given the constraints imposed by, and the strengths of, the current financial condition. Financial managers plan for the acquisition and management of both long- and short-term assets (the capital budgeting decision and the working capital management decision). In addition, the financial manager must plan how the assets of the firm are to be funded (the capital structure decision). The impact of these plans on the future financial condition of the firm is projected by the use of pro forma financial statements and budgets. These tools are developed in Chapter 8.

USES OF FINANCIAL ANALYSIS

A *financial analysis* assists in identifying the major strengths and weaknesses of a business enterprise. It indicates whether a firm has enough cash to meet obligations; a reasonable accounts receivable collection period; an efficient inventory management policy; sufficient plant, property, and equipment; and an adequate capital structure—all of which are necessary if the firm is to achieve the goal of maximizing shareholder wealth. Financial analysis also can be used to assess a firm's viability as an ongoing enterprise and to determine whether a satisfactory return is being earned for the risks taken.

When performing a financial analysis, the analyst may discover specific problem areas in time for remedial action. Or, the analyst may find that the firm has unused borrowing power that could finance additional income-producing assets. The results of a financial analysis can indicate certain facts and trends that can aid the financial manager in planning and implementing a course of action consistent with the goal of maximizing shareholder wealth.

Financial analyses also are used by persons other than financial managers. For example, credit managers may examine some basic financial ratios concerning a prospective customer when deciding whether or not to extend credit. Security analysts use financial analysis to assess the investment worth of different securities. Bankers use the tools of financial analysis when deciding whether to grant loans. Financial ratios have been used successfully to forecast such financial events as impending bankruptcy. Unions refer to them when evaluating the bargaining positions of certain employers. Finally, students and other job hunters may perform financial analyses of potential employers to determine career opportunities.

INTERPRETING FINANCIAL RATIOS

A *financial ratio* is a relationship that indicates something about a firm's activities, such as the ratio between the firm's assets and liabilities, or between its accounts receivable and its annual sales. Financial ratios enable an analyst to make a comparison of a firm's financial condition over time or in relation to that of other firms. Ratios essentially standardize various elements of financial data for differences in the size of a series of financial data when making comparisons over time or between firms. For example, the total profits of IBM are many times those of Apple Computer, because IBM is a much larger firm than Apple. By computing a ratio such as net profits divided by total assets, the relative performance of the two firms can be more accurately assessed.

Successful financial ratio analysis requires that the analyst keep in mind the following key points:

- Any discussion of financial ratios is likely to include only a representative sample of possible ratios. Many other ratios can be developed to provide additional insights. In some industries, such as banking, the analyst will use special ratios unique to the activities of the firms in those industries.

- Financial ratios are only "flags" indicating potential areas of strength or weakness. A thorough analysis requires the examination of other data as well.

- Frequently a financial ratio must be dissected to discover its true meaning. For example, a low ratio may be caused by either a low numerator or a high denominator. A good financial analyst will examine both the numerator and the denominator before drawing any conclusions.

- A financial ratio is meaningful only when it is compared with some standard, such as an industry ratio trend, a ratio trend for the specific firm being analyzed, or a stated management objective.

- When financial ratios are used to compare one firm with another, it is important to remember that differences in accounting techniques may result in substantial differences in financial ratios. Failure to keep this in mind can lead to incorrect conclusions.

BASIC CLASSIFICATIONS OF FINANCIAL RATIOS

Because different groups in- and outside the firm have varying objectives and expectations, they approach financial analysis from different perspectives. For example, suppliers and short-term creditors are likely to be most concerned with a firm's current liquidity and near-term cash-generating capacity. Bondholders and holders of preferred stock, who have long-term claims on a firm's earnings and assets, focus on the firm's cash-generating ability over the long run and on the claims other investors have on the firm's cash flows. Owners (common stockholders) and potential investors are especially interested in measures of profitability and risk, since common stock prices are dependent on the amount and stability of a firm's future earnings and dividends. Management is concerned with all aspects of financial analysis on both a short- and a long-term basis, since it is responsible for conducting the firm's day-to-day operations and earning a competitive rate of return for risks taken.

No single financial ratio could begin to answer all these analytical needs. Thus, four different groups of ratios have been developed:

- *Liquidity ratios* indicate a firm's ability to meet short-term financial obligations.

- *Activity ratios* indicate how efficiently a firm is using its assets to generate sales.

- *Financial leverage ratios* indicate a firm's capacity to meet short- and long-term debt obligations.

- *Profitability ratios* measure how effectively a firm's management generates profits on sales, assets, and owners' investments.

Each type is discussed in detail in this chapter.[1] The financial statements of the Sandia Manufacturing Company, a medium-sized firm that produces various replacement components for the lawn equipment industry, will be examined to illustrate how ratios are used in financial analysis. Data will be used from Sandia's *balance sheet* for the years ending December 31, 19X6 and 19X5 and from its *income statement* for the year 19X6.

The balance sheet shown in Table 6–1 contains information on Sandia's *assets, liabilities,* and *owners' equity.* The figures provide a "snapshot" view of the firm's financial health on December 31, 19X6, and December 31, 19X5. Sandia's assets are recorded on the balance sheet at the price the company paid for them (that is, at historical cost). The liabilities are amounts the firm

---

[1]The ratios discussed in this chapter are only a representative sample of the total number of financial ratios that may be analyzed.

TABLE 6–1   Sandia Manufacturing Company Balance Sheet (in Thousands of Dollars)

		December 31, 19X6		December 31, 19X5
Assets				
Cash		$ 2,540		$ 2,750
Marketable securities		1,800		1,625
Accounts receivable, net		18,320		16,850
Inventories		27,530		26,470
Total current assets		$50,190		$47,695
Plant and equipment	$43,100		$39,500	
Less: Accumulated depreciation	11,400		9,500	
Net plant and equipment		$31,700		$30,000
Total assets		$81,890		$77,695
Liabilities and Owners' Equity				
Accounts payable		$ 9,721		$ 8,340
Notes payable—bank (10%)		8,500		5,635
Accrued taxes payable		3,200		3,150
Other current liabilities		2,102		1,750
Current portion of long-term debt		2,000		2,000
Total current liabilities		$25,523		$20,875
Long-term debt (9⅝% mortgage bonds)*		$22,000		$24,000
Common stock ($10 par)	$13,000		$13,000	
Contributed capital in excess of par	10,000		10,000	
Retained earnings	11,367		9,820	
Total stockholders' equity		$34,367		$32,820
Total liabilities and stockholders' equity		$81,890		$77,695

*Mortgage bonds require a $2,000(000) annual payment to a sinking fund.

owes its creditors, and the owners' equity (also termed *net worth* or *stockholders' equity*) is the difference between total assets and total liabilities.

The income statement in Table 6–2 indicates Sandia's performance during the year ending December 31, 19X6. The *cost of goods sold, other operating expenses, interest expenses,* and *taxes* are deducted from the revenues generated, or *net sales,* to arrive at the firm's *net income,* or *earnings after taxes (EAT).* The income statement also shows how the firm's earnings are distributed between dividend payments (payments to stockholders) and earnings retained (reinvested in the firm).

The *sources and uses of funds statement* is also useful in financial analysis. (This statement is also called the *statement of changes in financial position* or the *funds flow statement.*) It indicates how a firm obtained and invested funds during a specific time period. The sources and uses of funds statement is discussed in Chapter 8.

LIQUIDITY RATIOS

If a firm intends to remain a viable business entity, it must have enough cash on hand to pay bills on time. One way to determine whether this is the case is to examine the relationship between a firm's current assets and approach-

TABLE 6–2   Sandia Manufacturing Company Income Statement (in Thousands of Dollars)

For the Year Ending December 31, 19X6

Net sales		$112,760
Cost of goods sold		85,300
Gross margin		$ 27,460
Operating expenses:		
Selling	$6,540	
General and administrative*	9,400	
Total operating expenses		15,940
Earnings before interest and taxes (EBIT)		$ 11,520
Interest charges:		
Interest on bank notes	$ 850	
Interest on mortgage bonds	2,310	
Total interest charges		3,160
Earnings before taxes (EBT)		$ 8,360
Federal and state income taxes at a		
combined 48% rate		4,013
Earnings after taxes (EAT) and available for		
common stockholders		$ 4,347
Dividends paid on common stock		2,800
Earnings retained in the firm		$ 1,547

*Includes $150(000) in annual lease payments.

ing obligations. Liquidity ratios are quick measures of a firm's ability to provide sufficient cash to conduct business over the next few months.[2]

This section discusses two different liquidity ratios—the *current ratio* and the *quick ratio*.

Current ratio   The current ratio is defined as follows:

$$\text{Current ratio} = \frac{\text{Current assets}}{\text{Current liabilities}}. \qquad (6.1)$$

Current assets include the cash a firm already has on hand and in the bank, plus any assets that can be converted into cash within a "normal" operating period of 12 months, such as marketable securities held as short-term investments, accounts receivable, inventories, and prepayments. Current liabilities include any financial obligations expected to fall due within the next year, such as accounts payable, notes payable, the current portion of long-term debt due, other payables, and various accruals such as taxes and wages due.

Using data from Table 6–1, Sandia's current ratio at year-end 19X6 can be calculated as $50,190/$25,523 = 1.97, or about 2:1. Or, it can be said that Sandia's current assets *cover* its current liabilities about 2 times.

The ratio is interpreted to mean that to satisfy the claims of short-term creditors exclusively from existing current assets, Sandia must be able to convert each dollar of current assets into at least $0.51 of cash ($1.00/1.97 =

---

[2]*Cash budgets* provide the best assessment of a firm's liquidity position. They are discussed in Chapter 8.

$0.507, or $0.51). The *industry average* for the current ratio is 2.40 times,[3] meaning that the average firm in the industry must convert only $0.42 ($1.00/2.40 = $0.416, or $0.42) of each dollar of current assets into cash to meet short-term obligations.

The fact that Sandia's current ratio is below the industry average does *not* mean that the firm would consider closing its doors voluntarily to meet the demands of short-term creditors. Nor does it mean that Sandia's creditors are any less well protected than the creditors of competing firms, since no two firms—even those in the same industry—are identical. In fact, ratios that suggest the presence of a problem in one firm may be quite satisfactory for another firm.[4] Sandia's current ratio provides only *one* standard for measuring liquidity. The financial analyst must dissect, or "go behind," the ratio to discover why it differs from the industry average and determine whether a serious problem exists.

Quick ratio   The quick ratio is defined as follows:

$$\text{Quick ratio} = \frac{\text{Current assets} - \text{Inventories}}{\text{Current liabilities}}. \qquad (6.2)$$

This ratio, sometimes called the "acid test," is a more stringent measure of liquidity than the current ratio. Referring to the figures on Sandia's balance sheet (Table 6–1), the firm's quick ratio at year-end 19X6 is calculated as follows:

$$\frac{\$50,190 - \$27,530}{\$25,523} = \frac{\$22,660}{\$25,523} = 0.89 \text{ times.}$$

The industry average is 0.92 times; Sandia's quick ratio is nearly equal to that.

The quick ratio is interpreted to mean that Sandia's cash and other current assets one step removed from cash—that is, marketable securities and accounts receivable—are equal to 89 percent of the current liabilities.[5] The crucial assumption behind the quick ratio is that a firm's accounts receivable may be converted into cash within the "normal" collection period (and with little "shrinkage"), or within the period of time for which credit was initially granted.

The analyst who doubts the liquidity of a firm's receivables may wish to

---

[3]Industry averages are obtained from various sources. The "Sources of Comparative Financial Data" section later in this chapter discusses a number of such sources.

[4]Many practitioners view a current ratio of 2 times (2.0) as satisfactory for industrial firms. Public utilities, on the other hand, typically function with considerably lower ratios. However, the financial analyst must be very cautious when using any of these "rules of thumb." The safe level of a current ratio is a function of how fast the firm's current assets and liabilities turn over. In the case of a public utility, the accounts receivable turn over on a monthly basis—much faster than in the typical industrial firm. Thus, public utilities are able to safely sustain lower current ratios than industrial firms.

[5]A quick ratio of 1 times (1.0) is considered satisfactory for most industrial firms.

prepare an *aging schedule.* The following one lists Sandia's accounts receivable as of December 31, 19X6:

Days Outstanding	Amount Outstanding (in Thousands of Dollars)	Percentage of Total
Less than 30	$ 9,450	51.6%
30–59	5,161	28.2
60–89	2,750	15.0
Over 90	959	5.2
Total accounts receivable	$18,320	100.0%

Unfortunately, the data required to prepare an aging schedule are normally not available to outside analysts. Hence, the aging schedule is useful primarily for internal analysis.

To evaluate the figures contained in an aging schedule, the analyst would need to consider Sandia's selling terms. If, for example, Sandia's customers are expected to pay within 40 days (which, in fact, they are), then the aging schedule indicates that many accounts are past due. However, since only 5.2 percent of the firm's receivables have been outstanding over 90 days, the major problem appears to be with slow-paying rather than uncollectible accounts. Some analysts adjust the quick ratio *downward* if a significant percentage of a firm's receivables are long past due and have not been written off as losses. Adjusting Sandia's quick ratio downward involves the following calculation:

$$\frac{\begin{array}{c}(\text{Current assets } - \text{ Inventories})\\ - \text{Accounts outstanding over 90 days}\end{array}}{\text{Current liabilities}} = \frac{\$22,660 - \$959}{\$25,523} = 0.85 \text{ times.}$$

The 0.04 difference between the quick ratio, 0.89 times, and the adjusted ratio, 0.85 times, is probably insignificant. Thus, even if Sandia's accounts over 90 days old were considered uncollectible, this alone would not indicate any real problem for the firm.

ACTIVITY RATIOS

One objective of financial management is to determine how a firm's resources can best be distributed among the various asset accounts. If a proper mix of cash, receivables, inventories, plant, property, and equipment can be achieved, the firm's asset structure will be more effective in generating sales revenue.

Activity ratios indicate how much a firm has invested in a particular type of asset (or group of assets) relative to the revenue the asset is producing. By comparing activity ratios for the various asset accounts of a firm with established industry norms, the analyst can determine how efficiently the firm is allocating its resources.

This section discusses several types of activity ratios, including the *average collection period*, the *inventory turnover ratio*, the *fixed asset turnover ratio*, and the *total asset turnover ratio*.

Average collection period   The average collection period is the average number of days an account receivable remains outstanding. It is usually determined by dividing a firm's year-end receivables balance by the average daily credit sales (based on a 360-day year):[6]

$$\text{Average collection period} = \frac{\text{Accounts receivable}}{\text{Annual credit sales}/360} . \qquad (6.3)$$

Using figures from both Sandia's balance sheet (Table 6–1) and the income statement (Table 6–2), the average collection period ratio at year-end 19X6 can be calculated as $18,320/($112,760/360) = $18,320/$313.22 = 58.5 days. Since the industry average for this ratio is 47 days, Sandia's ratio is substantially above the average.

Sandia's credit terms call for payment within 40 days. The ratio calculations show that 58.5 days of sales are tied up in receivables, meaning that a significant portion of Sandia's customers are not paying bills on time. (This is also indicated by the aging schedule of the firm's accounts receivable.) The analyst would interpret this ratio to mean that Sandia has allocated a greater proportion of total resources to receivables than the average firm in the industry. If Sandia implemented a more vigorous collection program and reduced the collection period to the industry norm of 47 days, some of these funds would be released for investment elsewhere. The released funds of (58.5 days − 47 days) × $313.22 per day = $3,602 could be invested in other assets that might contribute more significantly to profitability.[7]

An average collection period substantially above the industry norm is usually not desirable and may indicate too liberal a credit policy. Ultimately the firm must determine if the liberal credit policy generates enough sales and profits to justify the cost.[8] In contrast, an average collection period far *below* the industry norm may indicate that the firm's credit terms are too stringent and are hurting sales by restricting credit only to the very best customers. Although moderate-to-slow paying customers may seem troublesome individually, they can be profitable as a group, and a credit policy that is too tight may drive them to competitor firms.

---

[6]When credit sales figures are not available (which is frequently the case), total sales figures are customarily used in calculating the ratio. This results in an *overstatement* of the average daily sales and an *understatement* of the average collection period.

For firms with seasonal sales, the analyst should calculate an average of the end-of-month receivables balances. When comparing average collection period ratios with industry norms, the analyst must make sure the industry ratios have been computed in the same manner as the particular firm's ratios.

[7]Recall that the analysis for Sandia is being done in terms of thousands of dollars. Hence, the actual released funds total $3,602,000.

[8]Chapter 20 contains an example of this type of analysis.

Inventory turnover ratio The inventory turnover ratio is defined as follows:

$$\text{Inventory turnover} = \frac{\text{Costs of goods sold}}{\text{Average inventory}}. \qquad (6.4)$$

Whereas the cost of goods sold is usually listed on a firm's income statement, the average inventory has to be calculated. This can be done in a number of ways. For example, if a firm has been experiencing a significant and continuing rate of growth in sales, the average inventory may be computed by adding the figures for the beginning and ending inventories for the year and dividing by 2. If sales are seasonal or otherwise subject to wide fluctuations, however, it would be better to add the month-end inventory balances for the entire year and divide by 12.

Some analysts calculate inventory turnover as simply the ratio of annual sales to ending inventory. Although the *sales-to-inventory ratio* is technically inferior and gives different results than more commonly used ratios, it may be satisfactory if used consistently when making comparisons between one firm and the industry as a whole. However, there is a problem with this ratio in that it tends to differ from one firm to another, depending on policies regarding markups on the cost of goods sold.

Since Sandia's sales are spread evenly over the year and its growth rate has been fairly moderate, the average inventory can be calculated by taking the average of the beginning and ending inventory balances, ($27,530 + $26,470)/2 = $27,000. Dividing the cost of goods sold by this figure, $85,300/$27,000, gives the inventory turnover ratio of 3.16 times. This is considerably below the industry norm of 3.9 times, indicating that Sandia has a larger investment in inventory relative to the sales being generated than the average firm.

Two factors may be responsible for Sandia's allocating an excessive amount of resources to inventory:

- The firm may be attempting to carry all possible types of replacement parts so that every order can be filled immediately. Sandia should carefully examine this policy to determine whether the cost of carrying excessive stocks is justified by the profits earned on additional sales.[9]

- Some of Sandia's inventory may be damaged, obsolete, or slow moving. Stock falling into these categories has questionable liquidity and should be recorded at a value more reflective of the realizable market value.

If a firm's inventory turnover ratio is too high, it may mean the firm is frequently running out of certain items in stock and losing sales to competitors. For inventory to contribute fully to profitability, the firm has to maintain a reasonable balance of inventory levels.

Fixed asset turnover ratio The fixed asset turnover ratio is defined as follows:

$$\text{Fixed asset turnover} = \frac{\text{Sales}}{\text{Net fixed assets}}. \qquad (6.5)$$

---

[9]The determination of optimal inventory levels is discussed in Chapter 21.

It indicates the extent to which a firm is utilizing existing property, plant, and equipment to generate sales.

The balance sheet figures that indicate how much a firm has invested in property, plant, and equipment are affected by several factors, including the following:

- The cost of the assets when acquired.
- The length of time since acquisition.
- The depreciation policies adopted by the firm.
- The extent to which fixed assets are leased rather than owned.

Because of these factors it is possible for firms with virtually identical plants to have significantly different fixed asset turnover ratios. Thus, the ratio should be used primarily for year-to-year comparisons within the same company rather than for intercompany comparisons.

Sandia's fixed asset turnover ratio is $112,760/$31,700 = 3.56 times—considerably below the industry average of 4.6 times. However, the financial analyst should acknowledge the shortcomings of the ratio and perform further analyses before concluding that Sandia makes inefficient use of property, plant, and equipment.

Total asset turnover ratio   The total asset turnover ratio is defined as follows:

$$\text{Total asset turnover} = \frac{\text{Sales}}{\text{Total assets}}. \qquad (6.6)$$

It indicates how effectively a firm uses total resources to generate sales and is a summary measure that is influenced by each of the activity ratios previously discussed.

Sandia's total asset turnover ratio is $112,760/$81,890 = 1.38 times, while the industry average is 1.82 times. In view of Sandia's other asset turnover ratios, the firm's relatively poor showing with regard to this ratio is not surprising. Each of Sandia's major asset investment programs—accounts receivable; inventory; and property, plant, and equipment—has been found apparently lacking. The analyst could look at these various ratios and conclude that Sandia is not generating the same level of sales from its assets relative to other firms in the industry.

FINANCIAL LEVERAGE RATIOS

Whenever a firm finances a portion of assets with any type of fixed-charge financing—such as debt, preferred stock, or leases—the firm is said to be using financial leverage. Financial leverage ratios measure the degree to which a firm is employing financial leverage, and as such are of interest to creditors and owners alike.

Both long- and short-term creditors are concerned with the amount of leverage a firm employs, since it indicates the firm's risk exposure in meeting debt service charges (that is, interest and principal repayment). A firm that is heavily debt financed offers creditors less protection in the event of bankruptcy. For example, if a firm's assets are financed with 85 percent debt, the value of the assets can decline by only 15 percent before creditors' funds are endangered. In contrast, if only 15 percent of a firm's assets are debt financed, asset values can drop by 85 percent before jeopardizing the creditors.

Owners are interested in financial leverage because it influences the rate of return they can expect to realize on investment and the degree of risk involved. For example, if a firm is able to borrow funds at 9 percent and employ them at 12 percent, the owners earn the 3 percent difference and are likely to view financial leverage favorably. On the other hand, if the firm can only earn 3 percent on the borrowed funds, the -6 percent difference $(3\% - 9\%)$ will result in a lower rate of return to the owners.[10]

Either balance sheet or income statement data can be used to measure a firm's use of financial leverage. The balance sheet approach gives a *static* measure of financial leverage at a specific point in time and emphasizes *total* amounts of debt, whereas the income statement approach provides a more *dynamic* measure and relates required interest payments on debt to the firm's ability to pay. Both approaches are widely employed in practice.

There are several types of financial leverage ratios, including the *debt ratio*, the *debt-to-equity ratio*, the *times interest earned ratio*, and the *fixed charge coverage ratio*.

Debt ratio   The debt ratio is defined as follows:

$$\text{Debt ratio} = \frac{\text{Total debt}}{\text{Total assets}}. \tag{6.7}$$

It measures the proportion of a firm's total assets that is financed with creditors' funds. As used here, the term *debt* encompasses all short-term liabilities and long-term borrowings.

Bondholders and other long-term creditors are among those who are likely to be interested in a firm's debt ratio. They tend to prefer a low debt ratio, since it provides more protection in the event of liquidation or some other major financial problem. As the debt ratio increases, so do a firm's fixed interest charges. If the debt ratio becomes too high, the cash flows a firm generates during economic recessions may not be sufficient to meet interest payments. Thus, a firm's ability to market new debt obligations when it needs to raise new funds is crucially affected by the size of the debt ratio and by investors' perceptions about the risk implied by the level of the ratio.

Debt ratios are stated in terms of percentages. Sandia's debt ratio as of year-end 19X6 is ($25,523 + $22,000)/$81,890 = $47,523/$81,890 = 0.58, or 58 percent. The ratio is interpreted to mean that Sandia's creditors are financing

---

[10]The tradeoff between risk and return resulting from the use of financial leverage is discussed in Chapter 7.

58 percent of the firm's total assets. This figure is considerably higher than the 47 percent industry average, indicating that Sandia has less unused borrowing capacity than the average firm in the industry.

A high debt ratio implies a low *proportionate equity base,* that is, the percentage of assets financed with equity funds. As the proportionate equity base declines, investors are more hesitant to acquire a firm's debt obligations. Whether Sandia can continue to finance its assets with 58 percent of "outsiders'" money largely depends on the growth and stability of future earnings and cash flows.

Debt-to-equity ratio   The debt-to-equity ratio is defined as follows:

$$\text{Debt-to-equity} = \frac{\text{Total debt}}{\text{Total equity}} . \tag{6.8}$$

It is similar to the debt ratio and relates the amount of a firm's debt financing to the amount of owner financing.

Since most interest costs are incurred on long-term borrowed funds—that is, those having maturities greater than 1 year—some analysts prefer to use a *long-term debt-to-equity ratio.* Many analysts also include a firm's preferred stock with its debt when computing the debt-to-equity ratio, because preferred stock dividends, like interest requirements, are usually fixed.

The debt-to-equity ratio also is stated as a percentage. Sandia's debt-to-equity ratio at year-end 19X6 is $47,523/$34,367 = 1.383, or 138.3 percent. Since the industry average is 88.7 percent, Sandia's ratio indicates that the firm uses more than the usual amount of borrowed funds to finance its activities. Specifically, Sandia raises nearly $1.38 from creditors for each dollar invested by owners. This is interpreted to mean that the firm's debt suppliers have a lower margin of safety than is common in the industry. In addition, Sandia has a greater potential for financial distress if earnings do not exceed the cost of borrowed funds.

Times interest earned ratio   The times interest earned ratio is defined as follows:

$$\text{Times interest earned} = \frac{\text{Earnings before interest and taxes (EBIT)}}{\text{Interest charges}} . \tag{6.9}$$

Often referred to as simply "interest coverage," this ratio employs income statement data to measure a firm's use of financial leverage. It tells the analyst the extent to which the firm's current earnings are able to meet current interest payments. The EBIT figures are used because the firm makes interest payments out of operating income, or EBIT.

Sandia's times interest earned ratio is $11,520/$3,160 = 3.65 times. In other words, Sandia covers annual interest payments 3.65 times; this figure is considerably below the industry norm of 6.7 times. This is further evidence that Sandia makes extensive use of creditors' funds to finance operations.

Fixed charge coverage ratio   The fixed charge coverage ratio is defined as follows:

$$\text{Fixed charge coverage} = \frac{\text{EBIT} + \text{Lease payments}}{\begin{array}{c}\text{Interest} + \text{Lease payments} + \text{Preferred}\\ \text{dividends before tax} + \text{Before}\\ \text{tax sinking fund}\end{array}} \quad (6.10)$$

It measures the number of times a firm is able to cover total *fixed charges*, which include (in addition to interest payments) preferred dividends and payments required under long-term lease contracts. Many industrial corporations also are required to make *sinking fund* payments on bond issues, which are annual payments aimed at either retiring a portion of the bond obligation each year or providing for the ultimate redemption of bonds at maturity.[11]

In calculating the fixed charge coverage ratio, the analyst must consider each of the firm's obligations on a *before-tax* basis. However, since sinking fund payments and preferred stock dividends are not tax deductible and therefore must be paid out of after-tax earnings, a mathematical adjustment has to be made. After-tax payments must be divided by $(1 - t)$, where t is the marginal tax rate. This effectively converts such payments to a before-tax basis, or one that is comparable to the EBIT.[12] And, since lease payments are deducted in arriving at the EBIT, they must be added back into the numerator of the ratio, because the fixed charges (in the denominator) also include lease payments.

The fixed charge coverage ratio is a more severe measure of a firm's ability to meet fixed financial obligations. Using figures from Sandia's income statement for 19X6,[13] the fixed charge coverage ratio can be calculated as follows:

$$\frac{\$11,520 + \$150}{\$3,160 + \$150 + \$2,000/(1 - 0.48)} = \frac{\$11,670}{\$7,156} = 1.63 \text{ times.}$$

Since the industry average is 4.5 times, it is once again apparent that Sandia provides creditors with a smaller margin of safety—that is, a higher level of risk—than the average firm in the industry. As a result, Sandia is probably

---

[11]Under most sinking fund provisions the firm either may make these payments to the bondholders' representative (the *trustee*), who determines by lot which of the outstanding bonds will be retired, or deliver to the trustee the required number of bonds purchased by the firm in the open market. Either way, the firm's outstanding indebtedness is reduced.

[12]The rationale for this computation follows:

$$\text{After-tax earnings} = \text{Before-tax earnings} - \text{Tax}$$
$$= (\text{Before-tax earnings}) - (\text{Before-tax earnings}) \times t$$
$$= \text{Before-tax earnings}(1 - t).$$
$$\frac{\text{After-tax earnings}}{1 - t} = \text{Before-tax earnings.}$$

[13]Some analysts exclude preferred dividend payments when computing the fixed charge coverage ratio. In the calculation that follows, the $150 represents annual long-term lease payments, and the $2,000 represents sinking fund obligations.

straining its relations with creditors. If a "tight money" situation developed in the economy, Sandia's high debt and low coverage ratios would probably limit the firm's access to new credit sources, and Sandia might be forced to curtail operations or borrow on prohibitively expensive and restrictive terms.

PROFITABILITY RATIOS

More than anything else, a firm's *profits*[14] demonstrate how well the firm is making investment and financing decisions. If a firm is unable to provide adequate returns in the form of dividends and share price appreciation to investors, it may be unable to maintain, let alone increase, its asset base. Profitability ratios measure how effectively a firm's management is generating profits on sales; total assets; and, most importantly, stockholders' investment. Thus, anyone whose economic interests are tied to the long-run survival of a firm will be interested in profitability ratios.

There are several types of profitability ratios, including the *gross profit margin ratio*, the *net profit margin ratio*, the *return on investment ratio*, and the *return on stockholders' equity ratio*.

Gross profit margin ratio   The gross profit margin ratio is defined as follows:

$$\text{Gross profit margin} = \frac{\text{Sales} - \text{Cost of goods sold}}{\text{Sales}}. \qquad \textbf{(6.11)}$$

It measures the relative profitability of a firm's sales after the cost of goods sold has been deducted, thus revealing how effectively the firm's management is making decisions regarding pricing and the control of production costs.

Sandia's gross profit margin ratio is $27,460/$112,760 = 24.4%. This is just slightly below the industry average of 25.6 percent, indicating that either Sandia's pricing policies or production methods are not quite as effective as those of the average firm in the industry. Differences in inventory accounting methods (and, to a lesser extent, depreciation methods) used by Sandia and the firms included in the industry average also influence the cost of goods sold and, by extension, the gross profit margin.

Net profit margin ratio   The net profit margin ratio is defined as follows:

$$\text{Net profit margin} = \frac{\text{Earnings after taxes (EAT)}}{\text{Sales}}. \qquad \textbf{(6.12)}$$

It measures how profitable a firm's sales are after all expenses, including taxes and interest have been deducted.[15]

---

[14]The terms *profits, earnings,* and *net income* are used interchangeably in the discussion.

[15]Some analysts also compute an *operating profit margin ratio*, defined as EBIT/sales, which measures the profitability of a firm's operations before considering the effects of financing decisions.

Sandia's net profit margin ratio is $4,347/$112,760 = 3.85%. This is below the industry average of 4.50 percent and is interpreted to mean that Sandia is earning 0.65 percent less on each dollar of sales than the average firm in the industry. This indicates that Sandia may be having difficulty controlling either total expenses (including interest, operating expenses, and the cost of goods sold) or the prices of its products. In this case the former is probably more accurate, since Sandia's financial structure contains a greater proportion of debt, resulting in more interest charges.

Return on investment (total assets) ratio The return on investment ratio is defined as follows:

$$\text{Return on investment} = \frac{\text{Earnings after taxes (EAT)}}{\text{Total assets}}. \qquad \textbf{(6.13)}$$

It measures a firm's net income in relation to the total asset investment.

Sandia's return on investment ratio $4,347/$81,890, is 5.31 percent—considerably below the industry average of 8.19 percent. This is a direct result of the firm's low activity ratios and low profit margins.

Return on stockholders' equity ratio The return on stockholders' equity ratio is defined as follows:

$$\text{Return on stockholders' equity} = \frac{\text{Earnings after taxes (EAT)}}{\text{Stockholders' equity}}. \qquad \textbf{(6.14)}$$

It measures the rate of return that the firm's owners—that is, the common stockholders—realize on their investment. Since only the stockholders' equity appears in the denominator, the ratio is directly influenced by the amount of debt a firm is using to finance assets.

Sandia's return on stockholder's equity ratio is $4,347/$34,367 = 12.65%. Again, Sandia's ratio is below the industry average of 15.45 percent. The firm's low activity ratios and low profit margins result in its profitability ratios being inferior to the industry norms, even after the effects of debt financing (financial leverage) are considered.

SUMMARY OF FINANCIAL RATIO ANALYSIS

Table 6–3 on pp. 168–169 lists all the financial ratios calculated for the Sandia Manufacturing Company, summarizing the comparative financial ratio analysis undertaken for the firm.

The assessment column to the right of the table contains an evaluation of each of Sandia's ratios in comparison with the industry averages. For example, the firm's liquidity position is rated fair to satisfactory. Whereas its current ratio is somewhat below the industry norm, its quick ratio is satisfactory, indicating that Sandia probably has sufficient liquidity to meet maturing obligations. The firm's asset structure is not generating sufficient sales revenues, however. Sandia's activity ratios indicate that the firm is investing too much in receivables and inventories, as well as property, plant, and equipment, relative to the sales volume being generated. Thus, Sandia should consider implementing more stringent credit and collection policies as well as better inventory controls. The firm should also evaluate its investment in property, plant, and equipment to determine whether reductions could be made without impairing operations.

Sandia's financial leverage ratios indicate that the firm is using significantly more debt to finance operations than the average firm in the industry. Because of its poor coverage ratios, the company will likely have difficulty obtaining debt financing for further asset additions. In the event of an economic slowdown, Sandia's creditors would probably reevaluate the firm's borrowing capacity and make less funds available to it. If Sandia wants to restore its borrowing capacity, it should take steps to increase its equity base.

TREND ANALYSIS

Thus far the analysis of the Sandia Manufacturing Company has focused solely on the year 19X6. This has provided a fairly complete, if rather static, picture of the company's situation at that particular point in time in comparison with industry standards. To gain insight into the direction the company is moving, however, a trend analysis should be performed. A trend analysis indicates a firm's performance *over time* and reveals whether its position is improving or deteriorating relative to other companies in the industry.

A trend analysis requires that a number of different ratios be calculated over several years and charted to yield a graphic representation of the company's performance. Figure 6–1 depicts a trend analysis for the Sandia Company for the years 19X0 to 19X6 and indicates the direction the firm has been taking for the last several years. Each of the four different categories of financial ratios is represented in the figure. For example, it is evident that the firm's liquidity position—as measured by the quick ratio—has gradually declined over the 7-year period, falling to slightly below the industry average in 19X6. Unless this downward trend continues, however, liquidity should not be a major problem for the firm.

The trend analysis tells another story about the firm's leverage and profitability. Sandia's use of debt has exceeded the industry average since 19X2. The activity ratios—the total asset turnover ratio and the average collection period ratio—indicate that the company has used much of this new debt to finance additional assets, including a buildup in receivables. Unfortunately, the new assets have not produced offsetting increases in profits. As a result, returns on investment have dropped below the industry standards by increasing amounts over the past 7 years.

In summary, the comparative financial ratio analysis and the trend analysis combined provide the financial analyst with a fairly clear picture of Sandia's performance. It is evident that the firm has employed excessive debt to finance asset additions, which have not been sufficiently productive in generating sales revenues. This has resulted in returns on investment and stockholders' equity that are significantly lower than average. If the firm intends

TABLE 6–3   Ratio Analysis Summary for the Sandia Manufacturing Company ⸻⸻⸻⸻⸻⸻⸻⸻

RATIO	DEFINITION
Liquidity	
1. Current ratio	$\dfrac{\text{Current assets}}{\text{Current liabilities}}$
2. Quick ratio (acid test)	$\dfrac{\text{Current assets} - \text{Inventories}}{\text{Current liabilities}}$
Activity	
3. Average collection period	$\dfrac{\text{Accounts receivable}}{\text{Credit sales}/360}$
4. Inventory turnover	$\dfrac{\text{Cost of goods sold}}{\text{Average inventory}}$
5. Fixed asset turnover	$\dfrac{\text{Sales}}{\text{Fixed assets}}$
6. Total asset turnover	$\dfrac{\text{Sales}}{\text{Total assets}}$
Financial leverage	
7. Debt ratio	$\dfrac{\text{Total debt}}{\text{Total assets}}$
8. Debt-to-equity	$\dfrac{\text{Total debt}}{\text{Total equity}}$
9. Times interest earned	$\dfrac{\text{Earnings before interest and taxes (EBIT)}}{\text{Interest charges}}$
10. Times fixed charges earned	$\dfrac{\text{EBIT} + \text{Lease payments}}{\text{Interest} + \text{Lease payments} + \text{Before-tax sinking fund} + \text{Preferred stock dividends before tax}}$
Profitability	
11. Gross profit margin	$\dfrac{\text{Sales} - \text{Cost of goods sold}}{\text{Sales}}$
12. Net profit margin	$\dfrac{\text{Earnings after taxes (EAT)}}{\text{Sales}}$
13. Return on investment	$\dfrac{\text{Earnings after taxes (EAT)}}{\text{Total assets}}$
14. Return on stockholders' equity	$\dfrac{\text{Earnings after taxes (EAT)}}{\text{Stockholders' equity}}$

to reverse these trends, it will have to make more effective use of assets and reduce the use of creditors' funds. This will enable the firm to improve relations with creditors and potentially increase profitability and reduce risk for its owners.

RETURN ON INVESTMENT

The preceding discussion on ratios indicates that a firm's return on investment (ROI) is defined as the ratio of earnings after taxes (EAT) to total assets.

CALCULATION	INDUSTRY AVERAGE	ASSESSMENT
$\dfrac{\$50,190}{25,523} = 1.97$ times	2.40 times	Fair
$\dfrac{\$22,660}{\$25,523} = 0.89$ times	0.92 times	Satisfactory
$\dfrac{\$18,320}{\$112,760/360} = 58.5$ days	47 days	Unsatisfactory
$\dfrac{\$85,300}{(\$27,530 + \$26,470)/2} = 3.16$ times	3.9 times	Unsatisfactory
$\dfrac{\$112,760}{\$31,700} = 3.56$ times	4.6 times	Poor
$\dfrac{\$112,760}{\$81,890} = 1.38$ times	1.82 times	Poor
$\dfrac{\$47,523}{\$81,890} = 58$ percent	47 percent	Poor
$\dfrac{\$47,523}{\$34,367} = 138.3$ percent	88.7 percent	Poor
$\dfrac{\$11,520}{\$3,160} = 3.65$ times	6.7 times	Poor
$\dfrac{\$11,520 + \$150}{\$3,160 + \$150 + \$2,000/(1 - 0.48)} = 1.63$ times	4.5 times	Poor
$\dfrac{\$27,460}{\$112,760} = 24.4$ percent	25.6 percent	Fair
$\dfrac{\$4,347}{\$112,760} = 3.85$ percent	4.50 percent	Unsatisfactory
$\dfrac{\$4,347}{\$81,890} = 5.31$ percent	8.19 percent	Poor
$\dfrac{\$4,347}{\$34,367} = 12.65$ percent	15.45 percent	Poor

The ROI ratio can be examined more closely to provide additional insights into its significance.

The ROI also can be viewed as a function of the net profit margin times the total asset turnover, since the net profit margin ratio = EAT/sales, and the total asset turnover ratio = sales/total assets:

$$\frac{EAT}{Total\ assets} = \frac{EAT}{Sales} \times \frac{Sales}{Total\ assets}. \qquad (6.15)$$

It is important to examine a firm's ROI in terms of "margin" and "turn-

FIGURE 6–1   Trend Analysis of the Financial Ratios for the Sandia Manufacturing Company from 19X0 to 19X6

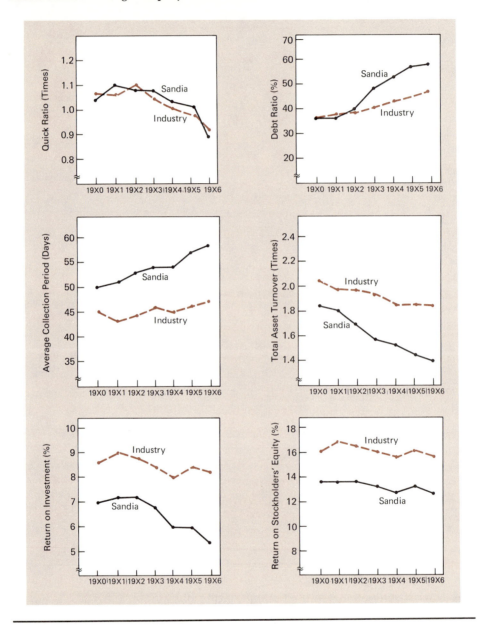

over," since each plays a major role in contributing to profitability. "Margin" measures the profit earned per dollar of sales but ignores the amount of assets used to generate sales. The ROI relationship brings these two components together and shows that a deficiency in either one will lower a firm's return on investment.

Using the figures from the net profit margin ratio and total asset turnover

FIGURE 6–2   Determinants of Return on Investment for the Sandia Manufacturing Company, 19X6

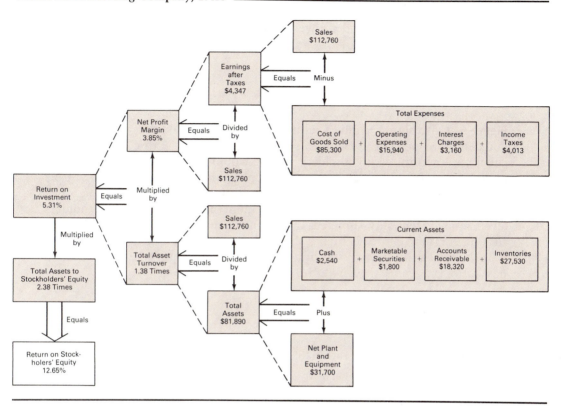

ratio calculated previously for the Sandia Company, the firm's ROI for 19X6 can be computed as 3.85% × 1.38 = 5.31%. Figure 6–2, called a *DuPont chart* because it was developed and is used by the DuPont Corporation, illustrates this relationship. For purposes of comparison, the industry average ROI = 4.50% × 1.82 = 8.19%. The ROI relationship shows Sandia to be deficient in both margin and turnover relative to the industry average. Improvement in either area would increase the firm's ROI. To improve its *margin*, for example, Sandia must either increase sales revenues more than costs or decrease costs more than sales revenues. To improve its *turnover*, the firm must either increase sales revenue or reduce the asset level required to support the current sales volume.

The relative contributions of the net profit margin and the asset turnover ratio in the ROI relationship differ from industry to industry. Specifically, the turnover ratio is largely dependent on a firm's investment in property, plant, and equipment. Firms with large investments in fixed assets tend to have low turnover ratios; public utilities, railroads, and large industrial firms fall into this category. If these companies are to succeed, their relatively low turnover ratios must be offset by correspondingly high margins to produce competitive ROIs. For example, electric and gas utilities typically have net profit margins of 10 to 15 percent. In contrast, other industries require much lower investments in fixed assets, resulting in higher turnover ratios. A typical example is the retail grocery chain industry, which has margins of only 1 or 2 percent. Firms in this industry often achieve turnovers of 10 times or more. If a grocery chain had a lower turnover, its ROI probably would not be sufficient to attract investors.

RETURN ON STOCKHOLDERS' EQUITY

Figure 6–2 also shows Sandia's return on stockholders' equity, which is computed as 12.65 percent. If the firm were financed solely with common equity (stock), the return on stockholders' equity would equal the return on investment. Sandia's stockholders have only supplied about 42 percent of the firm's total capital, whereas creditors have supplied the remaining 58 percent. Since the entire 5.31 percent return on investment belongs to the stockholders (even though they only supplied 42 percent of the total capital), Sandia's return on common equity is higher than its return on investment.

To better clarify how the return on stockholders' equity is determined, a new ratio, the *equity multiplier ratio*, is defined:

$$\text{Equity multiplier} = \frac{\text{Total assets}}{\text{Stockholders' equity}}. \tag{6.16}$$

Sandia's equity multiplier ratio is computed from figures found in Table 6–1 as $81,890/$34,367 = 2.38 times. The industry average for the ratio is 1.89 times. Once again it can be seen that Sandia has financed a greater proportion of assets with debt than the average firm in the industry.

The equity multiplier ratio may be used to show how a firm's use of debt to finance assets affects the return on equity, as follows:

$$\begin{aligned}
\text{Return on stockholders' equity} &= \frac{\text{Net profit}}{\text{margin}} \times \frac{\text{Total asset}}{\text{turnover}} \times \frac{\text{Equity}}{\text{multiplier}} \\[6pt]
&= \frac{\text{Earnings after taxes}}{\text{Sales}} \times \frac{\text{Sales}}{\text{Total assets}} \\[6pt]
&\quad \times \frac{\text{Total assets}}{\text{Stockholders' equity}}.
\end{aligned} \tag{6.17}$$

In Sandia's case the return on stockholders' equity is 3.85% × 1.38 × 2.38 = 12.65%.

Although this figure is the same as the return on equity that was computed directly by dividing earnings after tax by stockholders' equity, the calculations shown illustrate more clearly how Sandia managed to magnify a 5.31 percent return on total investment into a 12.65 percent return on stockholders' equity by making more extensive use of debt financing than did the average firm in the industry. This increased use of debt has improved Sandia's return on equity but has also increased its risk—most likely resulting in a decline in Sandia's stock price relative to other, similar firms.

SOURCES OF
COMPARATIVE FINANCIAL DATA

The analyst may refer to a number of sources of financial data when preparing a comparative financial analysis, including the following:

- **Dun and Bradstreet.** Dun and Bradstreet (D&B) prepares a series of fourteen key business ratios for eight hundred different lines of business. These ratios are based on the financial statements of some 400,000 companies. The ratios are divided into three size categories by annual sales of the firms in the sample. D&B reports three values for each ratio—the *median*, the *upper quartile*, and the *lower quartile*. Table 6–4 contains a representative sample of ratios. The median is the figure that falls in the middle when individual ratios of sampled firms are arranged by size. The figure halfway between the median and the ratio with the highest value is the upper quartile, and the figure halfway between the median and the ratio with the lowest value is the lower quartile. By reporting three values for each ratio, D&B enables the analyst to compare a particular firm with the "average" (median) firm, as well as with the "typical" firms in the top and bottom halves of the sample. The complete D&B data are reported in *Key Business Ratios*. Summary data are reported annually in *Dun's Business Month* magazine.

- **Robert Morris Associates.** This national association of bank loan and credit officers uses information provided by loan applications to compile sixteen ratios for over 250 lines of business. Like D&B, Robert Morris Associates reports the median, upper quartile, and lower quartile for each ratio. Data are presented for four categories of firm size. This source is especially useful to the analyst gathering information about smaller firms. The Robert Morris publication containing the data is titled *Statement Studies*.

- *Quarterly Financial Reports for Manufacturing Companies.* The Federal Trade Commission (FTC) and the Securities and Exchange Commission (SEC) cooperate in jointly publishing quarterly reports on balance sheet and income statement data of various manufacturing companies. These include analyses of the firms by industry and asset size, along with presentations of financial statements in ratio form.

- **Prentice-Hall's** *Almanac of Business and Industrial Financial Ratios.* This annual almanac of business and industrial financial ratios reports twenty-two ratios for 162 separate industries. It also includes the number of establishments in the sampled industry, the number without net income, and the total dollar receipts for each of the eleven size groups into which firms in each industry are classified.

- *Financial Studies of Small Business.* This annual publication of Financial Research Associates is particularly valuable for the evaluation of small firms.

173

TABLE 6–4 Dun and Bradstreet Quartile Ratios for Selected Business Lines, 1982* _____

LINE OF BUSINESS AND NUMBER OF CONCERNS REPORTING	QUICK RATIO	CURRENT RATIO	CURRENT LIABILITIES TO NET WORTH	CURRENT LIABILITIES TO INVENTORY	TOTAL LIABILITIES TO NET WORTH	FIXED ASSETS TO NET WORTH
	Times	Times	Percent	Percent	Percent	Percent
Mining, Agriculture, and Construction						
1211	1.6	2.5	20.2	283.2	31.1	58.6
Bituminous Coal &	**0.9**	**1.5**	**52.2**	**447.8**	**113.0**	**109.3**
Lignite (164)	0.5	0.9	138.7	999.9	237.8	193.5
1381	1.7	2.3	18.3	237.1	42.9	53.3
Drilling Oil & Gas	**1.0**	**1.3**	**60.5**	**512.9**	**128.2**	**132.7**
Wells (123)	0.6	0.9	107.1	999.9	249.3	222.2
1521	2.6	4.3	8.8	75.0	27.2	28.2
General	**1.1**	**2.1**	**33.2**	**169.5**	**62.9**	**70.0**
Contractors—	0.3	1.3	86.5	587.9	132.9	104.8
Houses (119)						
0241	1.4	4.0	6.2	58.4	24.3	51.3
Dairy Farms (124)	**0.4**	**1.5**	**15.6**	**121.0**	**43.9**	**87.8**
	0.2	0.6	40.7	515.7	118.3	121.1
Communication, Transportation, and Utilities						
4911	1.2	2.6	13.7	180.6	137.3	163.3
Electric Services	**0.8**	**1.7**	**23.0**	**269.7**	**211.3**	**234.9**
(112)	0.4	1.0	33.2	438.1	384.1	334.0
4212	2.7	3.3	12.4	242.2	25.4	45.7
Local Trucking	**1.3**	**1.8**	**33.1**	**437.3**	**59.0**	**76.4**
Without Storage	0.6	0.9	61.0	999.9	135.4	129.4
(104)						
4811	1.4	2.2	15.1	351.5	119.0	163.1
Telephone	**0.8**	**1.4**	**26.3**	**846.9**	**182.7**	**248.7**
Communication	0.4	0.7	46.6	999.9	385.0	337.1
(Wire or Radio)						
(111)						
Manufacturing						
2911–2999	1.5	2.3	41.0	113.0	52.1	24.4
Petroleum Refining	**1.0**	**1.7**	**65.9**	**176.4**	**123.5**	**51.4**
(99)	0.6	1.3	117.4	322.5	215.6	127.9
3312–3317	1.4	2.8	31.4	86.9	55.4	51.8
Blast Furnaces &	**0.9**	**1.9**	**57.8**	**124.8**	**102.5**	**80.3**
Steel Mills (146)	0.7	1.4	117.8	177.6	192.2	117.1
Retailing						
5611	2.0	4.9	17.4	39.5	21.5	6.6
Clothing &	**0.8**	**2.5**	**37.8**	**56.5**	**49.1**	**15.3**
Furnishings, Men's	0.3	1.9	73.9	88.2	91.1	51.0
& Boys' (108)						
5311	2.2	5.7	13.0	27.7	16.0	6.4
Department Stores	**1.3**	**3.0**	**44.1**	**58.8**	**65.8**	**24.6**
(108)	0.6	2.0	76.8	88.6	149.6	50.8
Services						
7011	1.5	2.5	9.6	441.4	56.2	103.7
Hotels, Motels &	**0.6**	**1.0**	**29.5**	**999.9**	**151.5**	**160.5**
Tourist Courts (100)	0.2	0.4	60.9	999.9	508.2	348.5
7372–7374	2.2	3.1	31.0	165.2	45.2	23.1
Computer & Data	**1.2**	**1.8**	**65.1**	**358.2**	**89.5**	**46.1**
Processing Services	0.8	1.3	112.7	921.3	160.9	91.9
(116)						
Financial Institutions						

	EQUITY TO ASSETS	EQUITY TO LOANS	LOANS TO DEPOSITS	LOANS TO ASSETS	NET INTEREST MARGIN	FEE INCOME
Commercial Banks	9.6	21.7	48.6	42.5	6.3	0.9
	8.3	**16.7**	**57.7**	**50.6**	**5.3**	**0.6**
	7.2	13.3	66.1	57.7	4.6	0.4
Savings and Loans	6.2	7.2	94.9	83.8	0.8	0.8
	4.6	**5.3**	**101.1**	**87.7**	**0.3**	**0.5**
	3.2	3.7	109.1	90.2	(0.3)	0.3

*Ratios shown are for the upper quartile, median, and lower quartile. Boldface numbers indicate median value.
SOURCE: Reprinted with special permission of *Dun's Business Month* (formerly *Dun's Review*), February 1983, Copyright 1983, The Dun and Bradstreet Publications Corporation.

COLLECTION PERIOD	NET SALES TO INVENTORY	TOTAL ASSETS TO NET SALES	NET SALES TO NET WORKING CAPITAL	ACCOUNTS PAYABLE TO NET SALES	RETURN ON NET SALES	RETURN ON TOTAL ASSETS	RETURN ON NET WORTH
Days	Times	Percent	Times	Percent	Percent	Percent	Percent
23.3	71.1	44.6	4.0	3.2	11.6	15.3	36.4
39.7	**29.8**	**70.1**	**9.9**	**6.2**	**5.7**	**5.1**	**18.4**
55.6	14.5	104.6	19.6	9.1	0.6	0.9	2.5
31.3	70.5	48.3	4.1	3.1	21.9	24.2	56.9
68.6	**27.8**	**91.8**	**7.8**	**5.7**	**15.0**	**10.6**	**28.2**
100.3	9.9	189.8	12.7	13.4	8.5	5.7	15.0
5.8	99.2	42.2	2.9	1.3	13.1	17.9	25.5
18.9	**17.9**	**76.7**	**5.3**	**3.4**	**5.1**	**8.9**	**14.4**
48.9	4.5	152.8	11.8	6.7	2.1	4.6	7.8
9.4	25.9	148.5	1.9	2.5	17.8	6.7	10.4
18.6	**5.8**	**241.9**	**4.0**	**3.5**	**6.9**	**2.4**	**4.1**
35.7	2.8	425.9	9.1	6.3	2.4	1.3	1.9
23.7	35.3	167.9	5.4	5.8	10.9	4.6	12.6
32.4	**20.1**	**207.1**	**8.3**	**7.0**	**6.3**	**3.2**	**10.4**
39.4	10.9	258.3	13.8	8.8	3.0	1.7	5.0
18.9	319.9	33.7	4.8	1.7	11.2	21.8	31.2
33.2	**79.4**	**46.7**	**9.3**	**3.3**	**6.7**	**8.0**	**18.0**
45.9	57.9	86.4	19.3	5.2	1.9	2.7	3.7
27.7	48.8	236.9	2.7	4.2	15.5	5.5	16.9
45.2	**26.6**	**313.6**	**4.6**	**6.8**	**12.7**	**4.4**	**12.5**
58.7	16.3	417.6	10.9	11.9	8.7	2.5	8.7
21.9	23.8	26.2	5.2	3.5	4.9	9.9	23.4
34.6	**14.8**	**41.8**	**9.6**	**6.7**	**2.9**	**4.9**	**13.0**
52.5	9.8	59.6	20.4	10.9	0.8	2.2	6.6
35.0	11.4	41.7	4.8	4.2	6.0	10.4	23.8
43.5	**7.7**	**60.2**	**6.6**	**6.3**	**4.2**	**6.1**	**12.9**
54.1	5.5	75.4	11.8	9.2	1.8	2.9	7.6
6.5	5.6	40.6	2.4	3.1	10.0	15.5	24.1
22.6	**4.0**	**55.3**	**3.6**	**5.4**	**5.0**	**9.8**	**15.1**
43.4	2.8	94.4	6.0	9.4	1.7	2.3	5.4
5.9	6.1	36.9	3.3	4.1	2.0	5.0	9.5
29.2	**4.8**	**50.5**	**4.7**	**6.4**	**0.8**	**2.2**	**4.7**
66.4	3.8	71.6	7.1	9.1	0.1	0.1	0.2
4.7	111.3	103.7	4.2	2.2	16.0	10.0	25.0
10.9	**65.5**	**192.6**	**7.2**	**3.4**	**9.2**	**6.3**	**13.4**
15.3	38.2	321.8	39.2	4.8	3.4	2.2	3.3
30.6	84.2	32.2	3.2	2.5	13.1	18.3	33.4
42.3	**37.5**	**57.2**	**7.3**	**5.1**	**7.5**	**10.1**	**17.0**
59.8	17.1	82.1	16.5	8.2	2.5	2.1	4.8

OVERHEAD	OPERATING EFFICIENCY	NET CHARGE-OFFS TO LOANS	PROVISION FOR LOSS TO LOANS	ALLOWANCE FOR LOSS TO LOANS	RETURN ON ASSETS	RETURN ON EQUITY	DIVIDEND PAYOUT
2.6	46.7	0.2	0.2	1.2	1.6	17.4	14.3
3.3	**56.1**	**0.3**	**0.4**	**1.0**	**1.1**	**13.6**	**26.5**
4.2	65.6	0.7	0.8	0.8	0.8	9.9	43.7
1.3	83.6	—	0.1	0.3	(0.2)	(1.6)	—
1.5	**130.1**	—	**0.1**	**0.1**	**(0.6)**	**(11.2)**	—
1.8	238.7	—	0.3	0.1	(1.0)	(25.2)	—

- **Moody's or Standard and Poor's Industrial, Financial, Transportation, and Over-the-Counter Manuals.** These contain a large amount of balance sheet and income statement data, as well as other relevant background information about a firm.

- **Annual reports.** Most corporations publish an annual report containing income statement and balance sheet data along with other information of interest.

- **10K Reports.** Every widely held firm is required to annually file a 10K report with the SEC. These reports contain income statement and balance sheet data, plus a wide range of other relevant information dealing with the firm's past and current performance and expected future prospects.

- **Trade journals.** These are published by trade associations and contain a great deal of financial and other types of information on member firms.

- **Commercial banks.** Frequently banks compile financial reports on selected industries. One example is First Chicago's semiannual financial survey of sales finance and consumer finance companies.

A WORD OF CAUTION ABOUT FINANCIAL RATIO ANALYSIS

Throughout the analysis of the Sandia Manufacturing Company performed in this chapter, it has been emphasized that the analyst must exercise caution when evaluating a firm's financial ratios. Although ratios can provide valuable information, they also can be misleading for a number of reasons.

First, ratios are only as reliable as the accounting data on which they are based. Different firms follow different accounting procedures for inventory valuation, depreciation, reporting of long-term leases, pension fund contributions, and mergers and acquisitions, to name just a few. These, in turn, affect reported earnings, assets, and owners' investments. Unless the analyst makes adjustments for accounting reporting differences, ratio comparisons between individual companies and with various industry norms can never be viewed as definitive.

Second, with the exception of disclosing upper and lower quartile values, firms that compile industry norms often do not report information about the *dispersion*, or distribution, of the individual values around the mean ratio. If the reported ratios are widely dispersed, the industry average will be of questionable value, since it may not reflect the "typical" firm in the industry. Furthermore, the standard of comparison probably should not be the "typical" firm, but rather the better performing firms in the industry. Without some measure of dispersion, however, ratios for these better performing firms cannot be determined.

Third, valid comparative analysis depends on the availability of data for appropriately defined industries. Some industry classifications are either too broad or too narrow to be reliable sources of comparative data when an analyst is evaluating a particular firm. Most firms operate in more than one industry, and this makes analysis more difficult.

Fourth, it is important to remember that financial ratios provide a *histori-*

cal record of the performance and financial condition of a firm. Further analysis is required before this historical record can be used as a basis for future projections.

Finally, comparisons of a firm's ratios with industry norms may not always be what they seem. Ratios comparing unfavorably with industry norms should be construed as "red flags" indicating the need for further investigation—not as signals of impending doom. On the other hand, even if a firm's ratios compare favorably with those of the better performing firms in the industry, it does not necessarily mean the firm is performing adequately. If, for example, the industry itself is experiencing a declining demand for its goods and services, favorable ratio comparisons may simply indicate that a firm is not decaying as rapidly as the typical firm in the industry. Thus, comparisons of selected ratios—particularly those relating to profitability—must be made with *national* industry averages in order to determine whether a particular firm in a particular industry is justified in making further investments.

In summary, ratios should not be viewed as substitutes for sound business judgment. Instead, they are simply tools that can help management make better decisions.

USING FINANCIAL RATIOS TO FORECAST FUTURE FINANCIAL PERFORMANCE

One of the primary limitations of traditional financial ratio analysis is that it looks at only one ratio at a time and then relies on the analyst to form a judgment about the overall financial profile of the firm. Recently, more powerful statistical techniques have been applied to assist the analyst in making judgments about the financial condition of the firm.

Discriminant analysis is a statistical technique that helps the analyst classify observations (firms) into two or more predetermined groups based on certain characteristics of the observation. In the context of financial statement analysis, the characteristics are typically financial ratios.

One early application of discriminant analysis in finance was a model developed by Edward Altman to predict bankruptcy of firms.[16] Altman identified five financial ratios that contributed significantly to the predictive accuracy of his model. The basic model was developed from a sample of sixty-six manufacturing firms—half of which went bankrupt. The following is the final discriminant function derived by Altman:

$$Z = 0.012X_1 + 0.014X_2 + 0.033X_3 + 0.006X_4 + 0.999X_5 , \qquad \textbf{(6.18)}$$

where

Z = The discriminant function score of a firm.

[16]Edward I. Altman. "Financial Ratios, Discriminant Analysis, and the Prediction of Corporate Bankruptcy." *Journal of Finance* (Sept. 1968): 589–609.

X_1 = Net working capital/Total assets (percentage).

X_2 = Retained earnings/Total assets (percentage).

X_3 = EBIT/Total assets (percentage).

X_4 = Market value of total equity (common and preferred)/Book value of total debt (percentage).

X_5 = Sales/Total assets (number of times).

On the basis of his analysis, Altman established a guideline Z score, which can be used to classify firms as either financially sound (a score above 2.675) or headed toward bankruptcy (a score below 2.675). The lower the score, the greater the probability of bankruptcy; the higher the score, the lesser the probability of bankruptcy.

The Altman model can be applied to the Sandia Manufacturing Company data in 19X6 to help assess its long-term financial condition. The market price of Sandia's common stock is $20 per share:

$$X_1 = \frac{\text{Current assets} - \text{Current liabilities}}{\text{Total assets}} = \frac{\$50,190 - \$25,523}{\$81,890}$$

$$= 30.12\%.$$

$$X_2 = \frac{\text{Retained earnings}}{\text{Total assets}} = \frac{\$11,367}{\$81,890} = 13.88\%.$$

$$X_3 = \frac{\text{EBIT}}{\text{Total assets}} = \frac{\$11,520}{\$81,890} = 14.07\%.$$

$$X_4 = \frac{\text{Market value of total equity}}{\text{Book value of total debt}} = \frac{\$20/\text{share} \times 1,300 \text{ shares}}{\$25,523 + \$22,000}$$

$$= 54.71\%.$$

$$X_5 = \frac{\text{Sales}}{\text{Total assets}} = \frac{\$112,760}{\$81,890} = 1.38 \text{ times.}$$

By substituting these values into the Altman Z score equation we get the following:

$$Z = 0.012(30.12) + 0.014(13.88) + 0.033(14.07)$$
$$+ 0.006(54.71) + 0.999(1.38)$$
$$= 2.73.$$

This score is slightly above the 2.675 cutoff score and indicates that even though Sandia is not in the best financial condition, failure is not expected—at least over the next year or two (the forecasting horizon used by Altman with the best predictive accuracy).

Recent refinements of Altman's bankruptcy forecasting model have broadened the spectrum of firms to which it can be applied to include retailing as well as manufacturing firms.[17] The new model is about 70 percent accurate as much as 5 years prior to bankruptcy.

INFLATION AND
FINANCIAL STATEMENT ANALYSIS

Inflation can cause a number of problems for the financial analyst who is trying to assess the performance of a firm over time and in comparison with other firms in the industry. In particular, *inventory profits*, or short-lived increased profits that occur as a result of the timing of price increases, can make a significant difference in a firm's reported earnings from year to year.

For example, consider a supply company that buys equipment parts wholesale from the manufacturer for $4.00 each and sells them at a retail price of $5.00 each, realizing a profit of $1.00 per unit. Suppose the manufacturer announces a price increase of $0.50 per unit to $4.50, effective on the first of next month. If the supply company passes the increase on to customers and announces a price increase of its own to $5.50, also effective on the first of next month, it will realize a gross profit of $1.50 on every unit sold, which originally cost $4.00. In other words, the company will make additional profit on the units already in inventory *prior to the price increase.* Once it begins purchasing parts from the manufacturer at the new price of $4.50 per unit, it will revert to its original $1.00 profit. In the meantime, however, the timing of the price increase will allow the company to enjoy short-lived increased profits, or inventory profits.

Most companies do not want to pay income taxes on inventory profits, preferring to use these funds to replenish inventories—especially in inflationary times. Fortunately, there is a way of avoiding or deferring the necessity of reporting these higher profits. The *last-in, first-out* (LIFO) inventory valuation method assumes that the items a firm uses from inventory are those that were acquired most recently. Thus, they can be *priced out* of the inventory based on the most recent inventory acquisition costs. In contrast, the *first-in, first out (FIFO)* method of inventory valuation, which assumes that the items a firm uses from inventory are the oldest items in inventory, results in the firm's having to show a higher profit and therefore pay higher income taxes.

During the 1960s, most large U.S. corporations were using the FIFO method. Inflation at that time was low to moderate, and the majority of companies thought it desirable to report their net income as high as possible. By 1974, however, inflation rates had risen to about 12 percent, and companies that were experiencing increasing inventory profits began switching to the LIFO method in an attempt to conserve cash by paying less income taxes.

The accounting method used for inventory will affect a firm's profits and its balance sheet. Hence, any financial ratio that contains balance sheet in-

---

[17]Edward I. Altman, R. G. Haldeman, and P. Narayanan. "Zeta Analysis: A New Model to Identify Bankruptcy Risk of Corporations." *Journal of Banking and Finance* (June 1977): 29–54.

ventory figures (for example, the total asset turnover ratio) or net income will vary from one firm to another, depending on the firm's accounting treatment of inventory. Another effect of inflation on financial statements is the tendency for the value of fixed assets to be understated. Also, to the extent that inflation causes a rise in interest rates, the value of long-term debt outstanding will decline. Thus, a firm will appear to be more financially levered in an inflationary period than is actually the case.

In an attempt to provide users of financial data with a better indication of the effects of inflation, the Financial Accounting Standards Board (FASB) issued *Statement of Accounting Standards No. 33*, which requires companies to supply additional information to indicate the effects of inflation on their performance over time. FASB *Statement No. 33* requires that a firm restate its "income from continuing operations" as if depreciation were based on assets all purchased with the same purchasing power. This requirement eliminates the distortion caused by a $1 million asset purchase in 1970 being treated the same as a $1 million asset purchased in 1984. Clearly, the purchasing power of a dollar was much greater in 1970 than in 1984.

FASB *Statement No. 33* also requires that a firm present a 5-year comparison of such financial data as operating revenues, cash dividends, and market price per share. These financial data must be stated in terms of constant purchasing power. All inflation adjustments under FASB *Statement No. 33* are made using the Consumer Price Index for All Urban Consumers. At this point it is not clear whether the inflation reporting requirements under FASB *Statement No. 33* will be of any great value in assisting financial analysts. Nevertheless, these inflation-adjusted statements do provide a rough indication of the effects of inflation on a firm's performance over time.

Inventory profits and inflation are only two factors that can affect a firm's reported earnings. Differences in the reporting of earnings, the recognition of sales, and other factors also can make comparisons between firms somewhat misleading. Again, the good financial analyst will always "go behind" the figures stated on a firm's income statement or balance sheet to find out what is actually occurring within a company. It should be obvious at this point that financial analysis is no simple matter. At first, it may appear as if all it involves is the evaluation of a certain number of apparently clear-cut ratios. As is evident from this chapter, however, it involves a great deal more.

SUMMARY

- *Financial ratios* are statistical yardsticks that relate two numbers generally taken from a firm's income statements and balance sheets.

- Financial ratios fall into four categories:

1. *Liquidity ratios*, which measure a firm's ability to meet its maturing obligations.

2. *Activity ratios*, which measure how efficiently a firm is using resources to generate sales.

3. *Leverage ratios*, which measure how much debt the firm is employing to finance assets.

4. *Profitability ratios,* which measure the firm's ability to generate profits on sales, assets, and owners' investment.

▪ *Trend analysis* introduces the element of time into financial ratio analysis. It gives the analyst a more dynamic view of a company's situation than does a pure comparative financial ratio analysis alone.

▪ The relationship of the return on investments (ROI) to "margin" and "turnover" can be used to determine if one or both of the two is deficient in contributing to the profitability of a firm.

▪ To gain further insight into the relative financial position of a firm, the analyst must compare the financial ratios with *industry averages.* The more diversified the firm, the more difficult it will be to make such a comparison. Two major sources of industry ratios are Dun and Bradstreet and Robert Morris Associates.

▪ Financial ratios have been used in conjunction with sophisticated statistical techniques to forecast events such as bankruptcy of a firm.

▪ *Inflation* can have a significant impact on a firm's reported earnings. For example, it can influence the firm to choose a different inventory valuation method and cost accounting system. When comparing the performance of two or more firms, the financial analyst should recognize that the firms may use different accounting methods to calculate net income.

Union Carbide's Paper Boom·

If the sheer magnitude of numbers makes news, then the effect of three accounting changes announced Jan. 24 by Union Carbide Corp. qualifies at once. Those changes will add $129 million to Carbide's regular earnings for 1980, pushing reported profits some 25% higher than analysts initially had projected. When a related, but extraordinary, one-time credit of $214 million is added in, Carbide's final net income may soar 70% over earlier estimates.

The impact, however, will be reflected only in the earnings the company reports to shareholders. How Carbide computes income and actual taxes for the Internal Revenue Service will not change, and thus its cash flow will not be affected by the accounting switch.

Even as analysts argue whether the accounting shift at Carbide provides more realistic or less useful numbers, or simply confuses investors, it could be a portent of similar moves by other industrial companies as they begin to wrestle with inflation accounting and changing notions of what depreciation allowances should reflect. As in other areas of change, analysts are sure to demand more data on corporate depreciation policies to help track what is afoot.

TAKING TAX CREDITS

To be sure, not all of the accounting changes were made at Carbide's choice. The Financial Accounting Standards Board (FASB) recently mandated that certain interest costs associated with new construction projects be capitalized, thus deferring those costs to later years, after the plant goes on stream. That rule applies to all major companies. For Carbide, the change will add an extra $20 million to this year's reported earnings.

The move bringing most impact for 1980 earnings, however, was at the company's discretion. From here on, Carbide says that it will recognize on its shareholder books the full amount of any investment tax credit (ITC) allowed by the government on new plant and equipment in the year that those investments are made—just as it does for IRS purposes. Previously, for financial reporting, the company reflected those credits in book earnings year by year over the life of the asset. That shift to the flow-through method will add $17 million to Carbide's regular 1980 earnings.

But Carbide also has considerable ITC amounts on the books that it had deferred from previous years. So, in addition, during the first quarter of 1980, it will take a one-time $214 million extraordinary credit to income in order to make the balance sheet reflect the shift to flow-through accounting.

How Union Carbide's Accounting Changes Will Boost its 1980 Earnings

	NET INCOME (MILLIONS OF DOLLARS)
Estimated income before changes*	$481
Additions from accounting changes	
Longer 'life' for equipment lowers depreciation charge	92
Capitalizing construction financing defers some interest cost to future	20
1980 investment tax credit flow-through cuts income tax	17
Income before extraordinary gain	610
Flow-through of unamortized prior year tax credits produces one-time gain	214
Estimated income after changes	824

*Based on mid-range of analysts' projections.
Data: Lynch, Jones & Ryan Institutional Brokers Estimate System, Union Carbide, BW estimate

Louis G. Peloubet, Carbide's controller, argues that if the ITC is deferred, its impact on earnings is blunted by inflation. Rather than providing an immediate boost to reported profits, the ITC is taken in bit by bit over 10 or more years, while costs rise and the dollar's value shrinks. With flow-through treatment, he asserts, earnings better reflect the current impact of investment decisions and are more consistent with cash flow. Studies made by Price Waterhouse & Co. and the American Institute of Certified Public Accountants conclude that more than 75% of the companies in the chemical industry and nearly 90% of all big industrial corporations now use ITC flow-through accounting. Carbide's switch, Peloubet contends, now makes his company's results more comparable with most of its competitors.

A COST REDUCTION?

Among the five largest chemical companies, only Du Pont Co. continues to defer and amortize investment tax credits. Outside the industry, companies such as General Electric, General Motors, and AT&T follow similar policies. "It's a difference in philosophy," explains John J. Quindlen, Du Pont's controller. "We look upon the investment tax credit as a reduction in the cost of the related asset."

Along with rival Dow Chemical Co., Du Pont also differs from the other big chemical companies in the use of accelerated depreciation for both tax and investor accounting. Under that method, depreciation charges are higher during the early life of new plant and equipment; both taxes and net income are lower, and the tax break boosts cash flow.

In contrast, a majority of companies, including Union Carbide, use accelerated depreciation only for IRS purposes. That nails down the tax benefit. But for shareholder reports, these companies employ a straight-line accounting method that recognizes depreciation charges in equal annual amounts over the life of the asset. Since these initial depreciation charges are lower than those using accelerated methods, reported earnings for most such companies are higher.

A WELCOME CUSHION

Many analysts like the conservative cushion that ITC deferral and accelerated depreciation provide. Since rapid inflation has rendered present depreciation charges woefully inadequate to cover the eventual replacement of plant and equipment, they argue that such an approach puts reported earnings more in line with current economic reality. "Accelerated depreciation gets you closer to today's world," says a Dow spokesman. "For us, it does a better job." Adds Du Pont's Quindlen: "In the chemical industry, there's a high exposure to technological obsolescence. We're satisfied that our present accounting is appropriate and prudent."

A few skeptics call such adjustments a half measure at best. And other observers argue that they may be unnecessary in light of the FASB's new inflation disclosure requirements. Beginning with 1979 annual reports, due later this spring, investors for the first time will be able to compare operating earnings based on traditional historical costs with earnings adjusted for inflation.

Up to now, Union Carbide had its own way of at least partially adjusting reported earnings for inflation. It used relatively short IRS guideline lives of machinery and equipment to calculate depreciation charges for both tax and investor reporting. Most companies in the chemical industry use somewhat longer lives for shareholder reports—lives more akin to the length of time they actually plan to use the assets. Carbide concluded that its policy gave it higher depreciation charges than many of its competitors and left it with too many assets that were fully depreciated on the books but still in use. So for future investor reporting, Carbide will lengthen by about 35% the asset lives for most machinery and equipment.

A FORERUNNER

Over the long term, that change is likely to bring the biggest boost to Carbide's reported earnings. For 1980, the company figures it will add $92 million. The shift to longer asset lives also will mean that Carbide will show up a bit better when historical-cost earnings are compared with inflation-adjusted earnings. Even so, the gap between those figures will remain larger than similar comparisons for Du Pont and Dow, its closest competitors.

Bookkeeping changes may lift Carbide's net 70%. A sign of things to come?

Carbide's move to longer asset lives could be a forerunner of similar changes at other companies. For one thing, if Congress approves legislation for even shorter depreciation lives for tax purposes, such as the proposed 10/5/3 scheme, the already tenuous link between tax and actual service lives of assets will vanish. More corporations may then revamp their shareholder calculations.

As more investors compare historical cost and inflation-adjusted earnings, U.S. companies may be tempted to follow their counterparts in Britain. Martin Gibbs, partner at the British brokerage firm of Phillps Drew, notes that when companies there started to compute inflation-adusted earnings, they found that earnings were coming out too low, so they started to spread depreciation over a longer period.

THE BRITISH EXPERIENCE

The experience of the British giant, Imperial Chemical Industries Ltd., is a case in point. "In the past, we had partially accounted for inflation by shortening asset lives," explains Harry E. Smith, ICI's assistant controller. In the early 1970s, for example, the company reduced the usable life for a basic petrochemical plant from 12 or 13 years to 10 years, and it still uses a 10-year life in historical-cost accounts.

But Smith adds that that policy now has been overstating inflation for several years. In calculating its current costs for inflation-adjusted earnings, he says, "we've added about 50% to the remaining asset lives."

If that trend develops in the U.S., it opens the door to wide swings in reported earnings, as the Union Carbide experience proves. And since those changes now are not always revealed, analysts are sure to demand more disclosure on corporate depreciation policies and the lives of existing assets so that they may better evaluate the overall effect.

QUESTIONS AND TOPICS FOR DISCUSSION

1. What are the primary limitations of ratio analysis as a technique of financial statement analysis?
2. What is the major limitation of the current ratio as a measure of a firm's liquidity? How may this limitation be overcome?
3. What problems may be indicated by an average collection period that is substantially above or below the industry average?
4. What problems may be indicated by an inventory turnover ratio that is substantially above or below the industry average?
5. What factors limit the use of the fixed asset turnover ratio in comparative analyses?
6. What are the three most important determinants of a firm's return on stockholders' equity?
7. What specific effects can the use of alternative accounting procedures have on the validity of comparative financial analyses?
8. How can inflation affect the comparability of financial ratios between firms?

PROBLEMS*

1. Vanity Press, Inc., has annual credit sales of $1,400,000 and a gross profit margin of 30 percent.
   a. If the firm wishes to maintain an average collection period of 50 days, what level of accounts receivable should it carry? (Assume a 360-day year.)
   b. The inventory turnover for this industry averages 6 times. If all of Vanity's sales are on credit, what level of inventory should the firm maintain in order to achieve the same inventory turnover figure as the industry?

2. Using the data in the following table for a number of firms in the same industry, do the following:
   a. Compute the total asset turnover, the net profit margin, the equity multiplier, and the return on equity for each firm.
   b. Evaluate each firm's performance by comparing the firms with one another and with the industry averages. Which firm or firms appear to be having problems? What corrective action would you suggest the submarginal firms take? Finally, what additional data would you want to have on hand when conducting your analyses?

	Firm			
	A	B	C	D
Sales (in millions of dollars)	20	10	15	25
Net income after tax (in millions of dollars)	3	0.5	2.25	3
Total assets (in millions of dollars)	15	7.5	15	24
Stockholders' equity (in millions of dollars)	10	5.0	14	10

Industry Averages	
Total asset turnover	1.4 times
Net profit margin	0.12
Equity multiplier	1.5 times
Return on equity	0.25

3. Pacific Fixtures lists the following accounts as part of its balance sheet.

Total assets	$10,000,000
Accounts payable	$ 2,000,000
Notes payable (8%)	1,000,000
Bonds (10%)	3,000,000
Common stock at par	1,000,000
Contributed capital in excess of par	500,000
Retained earnings	2,500,000
Total liabilities and stockholders' equity	$10,000,000

Compute the return on stockholders' equity if the company has sales of $20 million and the following net profit margin:
   a. 3 percent.
   b. 5 percent.

*Problems in color have check answers provided at the end of the book.

The following data for the Van Horne Tuba Company should be used to answer Problems 4 through 9.

VAN HORNE TUBA COMPANY'S BALANCE SHEET
DECEMBER 31, 19X1

Cash and securities	$ 120,000	Accounts payable	$ 190,000
Accounts receivable	160,000	Notes payable (9%)	210,000
Inventory	520,000	Other current liabilities	25,000
Total current assets	$ 800,000	Total current liabilities	$ 425,000
Net plant and equipment	400,000	Long-term debt (10%)	400,000
Total assets	$1,200,000	Stockholder's equity	375,000
		Total liabilities and stockholders' equity	$1,200,000

INCOME STATEMENT
FOR THE YEAR ENDED DECEMBER 31, 19X1

Net sales (all on credit)		$1,500,000
Cost of goods sold		900,000
Gross margin		$ 600,000
Operating expenses:		
Selling	$150,000	
General and administrative	280,000	
Total operating expenses		430,000
Earnings before interest and taxes		$ 170,000
Interest:		
Notes	$ 18,900	
Long-term debt	40,000	
Total interest charges		58,900
Earnings before taxes		$ 111,100
Federal income tax (40%)		44,440
Earnings after taxes		$ 66,660

INDUSTRY AVERAGES

Current ratio	2.5 times
Quick ratio	1.1 times
Average collection period (360-day year)	35 days
Inventory turnover ratio	2.4 times
Total asset turnover ratio	1.4 times
Times interest earned ratio	3.5 times
Net profit margin ratio	4.0 percent
Return on investment ratio	5.6 percent
Total assets/stockholders' equity (equity multiplier) ratio	3.0 times
Return on stockholders' equity ratio	16.8 percent

4. Evaluate the liquidity position of Van Horne relative to that of the average firm in the industry. Consider the current ratio, the quick ratio, and the net working capital for Van Horne. What problems, if any, are suggested by this analysis?

5. Evaluate Van Horne's performance by looking at key activity ratios. Are any problems apparent from this analysis?

6. Evaluate the financial risk of Van Horne by examining its times interest earned ratio and its equity multiplier ratio relative to the same industry average ratios.

7. Evaluate the profitability of Van Horne relative to that of the average firm in its industry.

8. Give an overall evaluation of the performance of Van Horne relative to other firms in its industry.

9. Construct a Du Pont chart analysis for Van Horne. What areas appear to have the greatest need for improvement?

10. Tarheel Furniture Company is planning to establish a wholly owned subsidiary to manufacture upholstery fabrics. Tarheel expects to earn $1 million after tax on the venture during the first year. The president of Tarheel wants to know what the subsidiary's balance sheet would look like. The president believes that it would be advisable to begin the new venture with ratios that are similar to the industry average.

   Tarheel plans to make all sales on credit. All calculations assume a 360-day year. In your computations you should round all numbers to the nearest $1,000.

   Based upon the industry average financial ratios presented here: complete the projected balance sheet for Tarheel's upholstery subsidiary.

	Industry Averages
Current ratio	2:1
Quick ratio	1:1
Net profit margin ratio	5 percent
Average collection period ratio	5 days
Debt ratio	50 percent
Total asset turnover ratio	4 times
Current debt/net worth ratio	20 percent

Forecasted Upholstery Subsidiary Balance Sheet

Cash	—	Accounts payable	—
Accounts receivable	—	Total current liabilities	—
Inventory	—	Long-term debt	—
Total current assets	—	Total debt	—
Fixed assets	—	Stockholders' equity	—
Total assets	—	Total liabilities and stockholders' equity	—

11. Using one (or more) of the sources of comparative financial data mentioned in this chapter, evaluate the performance of Bethlehem Steel Corporation versus the performance of Armco Steel. In particular, evaluate the total asset turnover, the fixed asset turnover, the net profit margin, the return on investment, and the return on stockholders' equity for each firm. Then do the following:
    a. Determine which firm seems to be performing better. What criterion did you use in reaching this conclusion?
    b. Point out some problems Bethlehem Steel seems to be having.
    c. Using the latest 5 years of data, perform a financial trend analysis on Bethlehem Steel Corporation. Consider such ratios as the current, quick, inventory turnover, average collection period, total asset turnover, net profit margin, return on investment, and return on stockholders' equity ratios. What can you say about the trend in the financial health of Bethlehem Steel?

12. The Jamesway Printing Corporation has current assets of $3.0 million. Of this total, $1.0 million is inventory, $0.5 million is cash, $1.0 million is accounts

receivable, and the balance is marketable securities. Jamesway has $1.5 million in current liabilities.

a. What are the current and the quick ratios for Jamesway?

b. If Jamesway takes $0.25 million in cash and pays off $0.25 million of current liabilities, what happens to its current and quick ratios? What happens to its real liquidity?

c. If Jamesway sells $0.5 million of its accounts receivable to a bank and uses the proceeds to pay off short-term debt obligations, what happens to its current and quick ratios?

d. If Jamesway sells $1.0 million in new stock and places the proceeds in marketable securities, what happens to its current and quick ratios?

e. What do these examples illustrate about the current and quick ratios?

13. Red Raider Corporation had sales in 19X1 of $36 million, 40 percent of which were cash. If Red Raider normally carries 50 days of credit sales in accounts receivable, what are its average accounts receivable balances? (Assume a 360-day year.)

14. Mustang Oil Company had a return on stockholders' equity of 30 percent during 19X1. Its total asset turnover was 2 times, and its equity multiplier was 1.5 times. Calculate Mustang's net profit margin.

15. The Sooner Pigskin Company has total assets of $100 million. Of this total, $40 million was financed with common equity and $60 million with debt (both long and short term). Its average accounts receivable balance is $20 million, and this represents an 80-day average collection period. Sooner believes it can reduce its average collection period from 80 days to 60 days without affecting sales or the dollar amount of net income after tax (currently $5 million). What will be the effect of this action on Sooner's return on investment and its return on stockholders' equity if the funds received by reducing the average collection period are used to buy back its common stock at book value? What impact will this action have on Sooner's debt ratio?

16. Pacific Tours has a net profit margin of 10 percent and earnings after taxes of $500,000. Its current balance sheet follows:

Current assets	$1,800,000	Current liabilities	$ 600,000
Fixed assets	3,200,000	Long-term debt	2,000,000
Total assets	$5,000,000	Common stock (at par)	500,000
		Retained earnings	1,900,000
		Total liabilities and stockholders' equity	$5,000,000

a. Calculate Pacific's return on equity.

b. The industry average ratios are as follows:

Net profit margin	6 percent
Total asset turnover	2.5 times
Equity multiplier	1.4 times

Compare Pacific Tours with the average firm in the industry. What is the source of the major differences between Pacific and the industry average ratios?

17. Given the following data for Profiteers, Inc., and the corresponding industry averages, perform a trend analysis of the return on investment and the return on

stockholders' equity. Plot the data and discuss any trends that are apparent. Also, discuss the underlying causes of these trends.

	YEARS				
	19X1	19X2	19X3	19X4	19X5
Profiteers, Inc.					
Net profit margin	14%	12%	11%	9%	10%
Asset turnover	1.26×	1.22×	1.20×	1.19×	1.21×
Equity multiplier	1.34×	1.40×	1.61×	1.65×	1.63×
Industry Averages					
Net profit margin	12%	11%	11%	10%	10%
Asset turnover	1.25×	1.27×	1.30×	1.31×	1.34×
Equity multiplier	1.42×	1.45×	1.47×	1.51×	1.53×

ADDITIONAL READINGS AND REFERENCES

Altman, Edward I. "Financial Ratios, Discriminant Analysis, and the Prediction of Corporate Bankruptcy." *Journal of Finance* (Sept. 1968): 589–609.

Altman, Edward I., Haldeman, R. G., and Narayanan P. "Zeta Analysis: A New Model to Identify Bankruptcy Risk of Corporations." *Journal of Banking and Finance* (June 1977): 29–54.

Benishay, H. "Economic Information in Financial Ratio Analysis." *Accounting and Business Research* (Spring 1971): 174–179.

Chen, Kung H., and Shimerda, Thomas A. "An Empirical Analysis of Useful Financial Ratios." *Financial Management* (Spring, 1981): 51–60.

Davidson, S., and Weil, R. L. "Inflation Accounting and 1974 Earnings." *Financial Analysts Journal* 31 (Sept.–Oct. 1975): 42–54.

——. "Predicting Inflation-Adjusted Results." *Financial Analysts' Journal* 31 (Jan.–Feb. 1975): 27–31.

Eiteman, David K. "A Computer Program for Financial Statement Analysis." *Financial Analysts Journal* 20 (Nov.–Dec. 1964): 61–68.

Foster, George. *Financial Statement Analysis.* Englewood Cliffs, N.J.: Prentice-Hall, 1978.

Helfert, Erich A. *Techniques of Financial Analysis.*, 3rd ed. Homewood, Ill.: Irwin, 1972.

Horrigan, James C. "A Short History of Financial Ratio Analysis." *Accounting Review* (April, 1968): 284–294.

Lev, Baruch. *Financial Statement Analysis: A New Approach.* Englewood Cliffs, N.J.: Prentice-Hall, 1974.

Murray, Roger F. "The Penn Central Debacle: Lessons for Financial Analysis." *Journal of Finance* (May 1971): 327–332.

Packer, Stephen B. "Flow of Funds Analysis: Its Uses and Limitations." *Financial Analysts Journal* 20 (July–Aug. 1964): 117–123.

Reiling, Henry B., and Burton, John C. "Financial Statements: Signposts as Well as Milestones." *Harvard Business Review* (Nov.–Dec. 1972): 45–54.

Searby, Frederick W. "Return to Return on Investment." *Harvard Business Review* 53 (March–April 1975): 113–119.

Smith, Jay M., and Skousen, Fred K. *Intermediate Accounting.* Cincinnati: Southwestern Publishing, 1981.

Weston, Frank T. "Adjust Your Accounting for Inflation." *Harvard Business Review* 53 (Jan.–Feb. 1975): 22–29.

CHAPTER 7

The Analysis of Operating and Financial Leverage

A FINANCIAL DILEMMA

The Airline Industry

The airline industry is subject to a great deal of cyclical variability. During recessions, for example, airline profits usually decline substantially. The high level of fixed costs airlines incur is one cause of this high degree of profit variability. It costs very little less to fly a plane that is 60 percent full than to fly one that is 80 percent full. Hence, when airline passenger traffic diminishes during a recession, airline profits tend to drop at a much more rapid rate.

Any firm whose production processes require the payment of substantial fixed costs relative to total costs is said to use a high level of operating leverage. Because this tends to increase the variability of a firm's earnings over the business cycle, investors associate high levels of operating leverage with high levels of business (operating) risk.

Firms exposed to high levels of operating risk often try to offset this risk by using relatively low amounts of debt financing, that is, by using low levels of financial leverage. When a firm uses high levels of debt financing (and incurs the additional high fixed financing charges, namely, interest), this further increases the variability of its earnings per share as sales and operating income vary over the business cycle. The increased use of debt also increases the potential for bankruptcy.

Thus, it might be expected that firms in the airline industry would tend to employ low levels of financial leverage to offset their high levels of operating risk. Delta Airlines, for example, had a long-term debt to net worth ratio of about 20 percent in 1982. Delta has been one of the most stable performers in the airline industry, reporting profits for all but one year from 1973 to 1982.

In contrast, Eastern Airlines has not effectively balanced its operating risk with low levels of financial risk. Its debt to net worth ratio was 476 percent in 1982. Eastern has reported losses during five of the years between 1973 and 1982, and its earnings have been far more volatile than Delta's. From 1979 to 1982, Eastern lost $158.2 million.

Risk is an important factor affecting the value of a firm's securities. Accordingly, both the firm's managers and outside analysts need to develop a complete understanding of the components of risk. This chapter considers important measures of operating and financial risk that can be used to assess the total risk of a firm.

GLOSSARY OF NEW TERMS

Breakeven analysis   a technique used to examine the relationship between a firm's sales, costs, and profits at various levels of output. It is sometimes termed *cost-volume-profit analysis.*

Business risk   the inherent variability or uncertainty of a firm's operating earnings (EBIT). In general, the greater the degree of operating leverage a firm uses, the greater its business risk.

Contribution margin   the difference between price and variable cost per unit in breakeven analysis.

Degree of combined leverage (DCL)   the percentage change in a firm's earnings per share (EPS) resulting from a 1 percent change in sales or output. This is also equal to the degree of operating leverage times the degree of financial leverage used by the firm.

Degree of financial leverage (DFL)   the percentage change in a firm's EPS resulting from a 1 percent change in EBIT.

Degree of operating leverage (DOL)   the percentage change in a firm's EBIT resulting from a 1 percent change in sales or output.

Financial leverage   the extent to which a firm is financed by securities having fixed costs or charges, such as debt and preferred stock.

Financial risk   the variability of the returns to a firm's shareholders. In general, the more financial leverage a firm uses, the greater its financial risk.

Fixed costs   costs that do not vary as the level of a firm's output varies.

Operating leverage   the extent to which a firm uses assets having fixed costs.

Variable costs   costs that vary in close relationship with changes in a firm's level of output.

INTRODUCTION

The concepts of operating and financial leverage are useful to financial analysis, planning, and control. In finance, *leverage* is defined as a firm's use of assets and liabilities having fixed costs in an attempt to increase potential returns to stockholders. Specifically, operating leverage involves the use of *assets* having fixed costs, whereas financial leverage involves the use of *sources of funds* having fixed costs.

A firm utilizes operating and financial leverage in the hope of earning returns in excess of the fixed costs of the assets and sources of funds, thereby increasing the returns to common stockholders. Leverage is a two-edged sword, however, since it also increases the *variability* (or risk) of these returns. If, for example, a firm earns returns that are *less* than the fixed costs of assets and sources of funds, then the use of leverage can actually *decrease* the returns to common stockholders. Thus, leverage magnifies shareholders' potential losses as well as potential gains. Leverage concepts are particularly revealing to the financial analyst in that they highlight the *risk-return tradeoffs* of various types of financial decisions.

This chapter begins by discussing the relationship between a firm's use of leverage and the income statement. It then moves to the concept of break-even analysis. Next, the measurement of operating leverage and its relationship to risk is illustrated. This is followed by an examination of financial leverage and its relationship to risk. And, finally, the chapter concludes with a discussion of the combined effects of operating and financial leverage on a firm's overall level of risk and returns.

LEVERAGE AND
THE INCOME STATEMENT

Financial statements of the Allegan Manufacturing Company are referred to throughout this chapter for purposes of illustration. Table 7–1 contains two types of income statements for the firm, a traditional format and a revised format. The traditional format shows various categories of costs as separate entries. *Operating costs* include such items as the cost of goods sold and general, administrative, and selling expenses. Interest charges and preferred dividends, which represent *capital costs*, are listed separately, as are income taxes.

The revised format is more useful in leverage analysis, since it divides the firm's operating costs into two categories, *variable* and *fixed*.

FIXED AND VARIABLE COSTS

Over the short run, certain operating costs within a firm vary directly with the level of sales while other costs remain constant, regardless of changes in this level. Costs that move in close relationship to changes in sales are called *variable costs.* They are tied to the number of units produced and sold by the firm rather than to the passage of time. They include raw material and direct labor costs, as well as sales commissions.

Over the short run, certain other operating costs are independent of sales or output levels. These are termed *fixed costs* and are primarily related to the passage of time. Depreciation on property, plant, and equipment; rent; insurance; lighting and heating bills; property taxes; and the salaries of management are all usually considered fixed costs. If a firm expects to keep functioning, it must continue to pay these costs, regardless of the sales level.

TABLE 7-1   Traditional and Revised Income Statements

ALLEGAN MANUFACTURING COMPANY

YEAR ENDING DECEMBER 31, 19X1

Traditional Income Statement Format

	Sales		$5,000,000
Operating leverage	*Less:* Cost of goods sold	$2,500,000	
	Selling, administrative, and general expenses	1,500,000	
	Total operating costs		4,000,000
	Earnings before interest and taxes (EBIT)		1,000,000
	Less: Interest expense		250,000
	Earnings before taxes (EBT)		750,000
Financial leverage	*Less:* Income taxes (40% rate)		300,000
	Earnings after taxes (EAT)		450,000
	Less: Preferred stock dividends		150,000
	Earnings available to common stockholders		$ 300,000
	Earnings per share (EPS)—100,000 shares		$3.00

Revised Income Statement Format

	Sales		$5,000,000
Operating leverage	*Less: Variable* operating costs	$3,000,000	
	Fixed operating costs	1,000,000	
	Total operating costs		4,000,000
	Earnings before interest and taxes (EBIT)		1,000,000
Financial leverage	*Less: Fixed* capital costs (interest)		250,000
	Earnings before taxes (EBT)		750,000
	Less: Income taxes *(variable)*, 40% rate		300,000
	Earnings after taxes (EAT)		450,000
	Less: Fixed capital costs (Preferred stock dividends)		150,000
	Earnings available to common stockholders		$ 300,000
	Earnings per share (EPS)—100,000 shares		$3.00

A third category, *semivariable costs,* can also be considered. Semivariable costs are costs that increase in a *stepwise* manner as output is increased. One cost that sometimes behaves in a stepwise manner is management salaries. Whereas these costs are generally considered fixed, this assumption is not always strictly valid. For example, U.S. Steel, faced with continuing low levels of output during 1982 to 1983, reduced the salaries of its administrative personnel by 5 percent in July 1982 and again in January 1983.

Panels a, b, and c of Figure 7-1 show the behavior of variable, fixed, and semivariable costs, respectively, over the firm's output range.

Over the *long run,* all costs are variable. In time, a firm can change the size of its physical facilities and number of management personnel in response to changes in the level of sales. Not all costs can be classified as either completely fixed or variable; some have both fixed and variable components. Costs for utilities such as water and electricity frequently fall into this category. Whereas part of a firm's utility costs (such as electricity) are fixed and must be paid regardless of the level of sales or output, another part is variable in that it is directly tied to sales or production levels. In the revised format of Allegan's income statement, these are divided into their fixed and variable

FIGURE 7–1   Behavior of (a) Variable, (b) Fixed, and (c) Semivariable Costs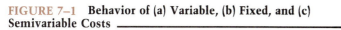

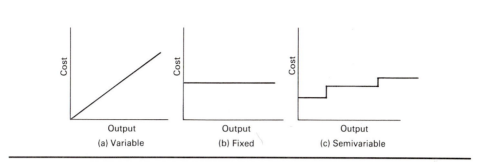

components and included in their respective categories of operating costs.

Note that in the revised income statement format, both interest charges and preferred dividends represent fixed capital costs. These costs are contractual in nature and thus are independent of a firm's level of sales or earnings. Also, note that income taxes represent a variable cost that is a function of earnings before taxes.

OPERATING AND FINANCIAL LEVERAGE

Whenever a firm incurs either fixed operating costs or fixed capital costs, it is said to be using *leverage.* Fixed obligations allow the firm to magnify small changes into larger ones—just as a small push on one end of an actual lever results in a large "lift" at the other end.

Operating leverage has fixed operating costs for its "fulcrum." When a firm incurs fixed operating costs, a change in sales revenue is magnified into a relatively larger change in earnings before interest and taxes (EBIT). The multiplier effect resulting from the use of fixed operating costs is known as the *degree of operating leverage.*

Financial leverage has fixed capital costs for its "fulcrum." When a firm incurs fixed capital costs, a change in EBIT is magnified into a larger change in earnings per share (EPS). The multiplier effect resulting from the use of fixed capital costs is known as the *degree of financial leverage.* (Both the degree of operating leverage and the degree of financial leverage are discussed in detail later in this chapter.)

BREAKEVEN ANALYSIS

Many of the planning activities that take place within a firm are based on anticipated levels of output. The study of the interrelationships among a firm's sales, operating costs, and EBIT at various output levels is known as *cost-volume-profit analysis,* or *breakeven analysis.*

The term *breakeven analysis* is somewhat misleading, since this type of analysis is typically used to answer many other questions besides those dealing with the breakeven output level of a firm. For example, breakeven analysis is also used to evaluate the financial profitability of new firms and new product lines. In addition, it is a valuable analytical tool for measuring the effects of changes in selling prices, fixed costs, and variable costs on the output level that must be achieved before the firm can realize operating profits.

A breakeven analysis of a firm can be developed either graphically or algebraically (or as a combination of the two).

GRAPHIC METHOD

Figure 7–2 is an example of a basic linear breakeven analysis chart. Costs and revenues (measured in dollars) are plotted on the vertical axis, while output (measured in units) is plotted on the horizontal axis. The *total revenue* function, TR, represents the total revenue the firm will realize at each output level, given that the firm charges a constant selling price, P, per unit of output. Similarly, the *total (operating) cost* function, TC, represents the total cost the firm will incur at each output level. Total cost is computed as the sum of the firm's fixed costs, F, which are independent of the output level, plus the variable costs, which increase at a constant rate, V, per unit of output.

The assumptions of a constant selling price per unit, P, and a constant variable cost per unit, V, yield *linear* relationships for the total revenue and total cost functions. These linear relationships are only valid, however, over some *relevant range* of output values, such as from Q_1 to Q_2 in Figure 7–2. (The concept of relevant range is discussed later in this chapter.)

The breakeven point occurs at point Q_b in Figure 7–2, where the total revenue and the total cost functions intersect. If a firm's output level is below this breakeven point—that is, if TR < TC—it incurs *operating losses*, defined as a *negative EBIT*. If the firm's output level is above this breakeven point—that is, if TR > TC—it realizes *operating profits*, defined as a *positive EBIT*.

FIGURE 7–2   Linear Breakeven Analysis Chart _____

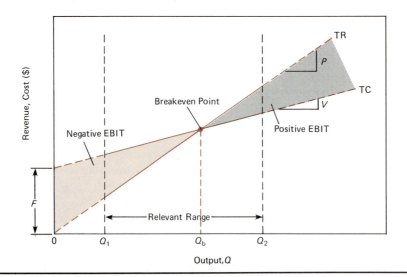

Determining a firm's breakeven point graphically involves three steps:

1. Drawing a line through the origin with a slope of P to represent the TR function.

2. Drawing a line that intersects the vertical axis at F and has a slope of V to represent the TC function.

3. Determining the point where the TR and TC lines intersect, dropping a perpendicular line to the horizontal axis, and noting the resulting value of Q_b.

ALGEBRAIC METHOD

To determine a firm's breakeven point algebraically, it is necessary to set the total revenue and total (operating) cost functions equal to each other and solve the resulting equation for the breakeven volume.

Total revenue is equal to the selling price per unit times the output quantity:

$$TR = P \times Q .\qquad (7.1)$$

Total (operating) cost is equal to fixed plus variable costs, where the variable cost is the product of the variable cost per unit times the output quantity:

$$TC = F + (V \times Q) .\qquad (7.2)$$

Setting the total revenue and total cost expressions equal to each other (that is, setting EBIT = TR − TC = 0) and substituting the breakeven output Q_b for Q results in the following:

$$TR = TC ,$$

or

$$PQ_b = F + VQ_b .\qquad (7.3)$$

Finally, solving Equation 7.3 for the breakeven output Q_b yields the following:

$$PQ_b - VQ_b = F .$$
$$(P - V)Q_b = F .$$
$$Q_b = \frac{F}{P - V} .\qquad (7.4)$$

The *difference* between the selling price per unit and the variable cost per unit, $P - V$, is sometimes referred to as the *contribution margin per unit*. It measures how much each unit of output contributes to meeting fixed costs and operating profits. Thus, it can also be said that the breakeven output is equal to the fixed costs divided by the contribution margin per unit.

197

Breakeven analysis can also be performed in terms of dollar *sales* rather than units of output. The breakeven dollar sales volume, S_b, can be determined by the following expression:

$$S_b = \frac{F}{1 - (V/P)},$$ (7.5)

where V/P is the variable cost ratio (that is, the variable cost per dollar of sales).

Occasionally the analyst is interested in determining the output quantity at which a *target profit* (expressed in dollars) is achieved. An expression similar to Equation 7.4 can be used to find such a quantity:

$$\text{Target volume} = \frac{\text{Fixed cost + Target profit}}{\text{Contribution margin per unit}}.$$ (7.6)

EXAMPLES OF BREAKEVEN ANALYSIS

The equations defined in the preceding section can be used to perform a breakeven analysis for the Allegan Manufacturing Company for the year ending December 31, 19X1. Assume that the firm manufactures one product, which it sells for $250 per unit. The current output, Q, is obtained by dividing total dollar sales ($5,000,000) by the selling price per unit ($250) to obtain 20,000 units per year. Its variable (operating) costs per unit, V, are determined by dividing total variable costs ($3,000,000) by current output (20,000) to obtain $150 per unit.

The firm's fixed costs, F, are given in Table 7–1 as $1,000,000. Substituting these figures into Equation 7.4 yields the following breakeven output:

$$Q_b = \frac{\$1,000,000}{\$250 - \$150}$$
$$= 10,000 \text{ units .}$$

Allegan's breakeven output can also be determined graphically, as shown in Figure 7–3.

Since a firm's breakeven output is dependent upon a number of variables—in particular, the price per unit and variable (operating) costs per unit—the firm may wish to analyze the effects of changes in any one of the variables on the breakeven output. For example, it may wish to consider either of the following: (1) Changing the selling price, or (2) Substituting fixed costs for variable costs.

Assume that Allegan increased the selling price per unit by $25 to $275, P'. Substituting this figure into Equation 7.4 gives a new breakeven output:

$$Q'_b = \frac{\$1,000,000}{\$275 - \$150}$$
$$= 8,000 \text{ units .}$$

198

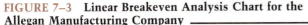

FIGURE 7–3   Linear Breakeven Analysis Chart for the Allegan Manufacturing Company ────────

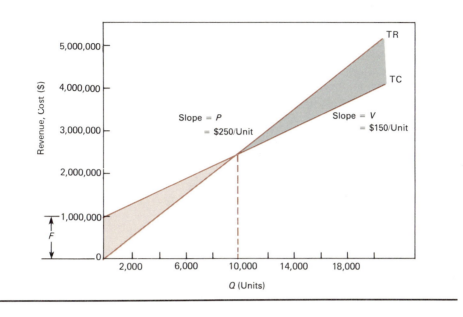

This can also be seen in Figure 7–4, in which an increase in the price per unit increases the slope of the total revenue function, TR', and reduces the breakeven output.

Rather than increasing the selling price per unit, Allegan's management may decide to substitute fixed costs for variable costs in some aspect of the company's operations. For example, as labor wage rates increase over time, many firms seek to reduce operating costs through automation, which in effect represents the substitution of fixed-cost capital equipment for variable-cost labor. Suppose that Allegan determines it can reduce labor costs by $25 per unit by purchasing $1,000,000 in additional equipment. Assume that the new equipment is depreciated over a 10-year life using the straight line method. Under these conditions, annual depreciation of the new equipment would be $1,000,000/10 = $100,000, and the firm's new level of fixed costs, F', would be $1,000,000 + $100,000 = $1,100,000. Variable costs per unit, V', would be $150 − $25 = $125. Substituting $P = $250 per unit, $V' = $125 per unit, and $F' = $1,100,000 into Equation 7.4 yields a new breakeven output:

$$Q'_b = \frac{\$1,100,000}{\$250 - \$125}$$
$$= 8,800 \text{ units .}$$

As can be seen in Figure 7–5, the effect of this change in operations is to raise the intercept on the vertical axis; decrease the slope of the total cost function, TC'; and reduce the breakeven output.

199

FIGURE 7–4 **Linear Breakeven Analysis Chart for the Allegan Manufacturing Company Showing the Effects of a Price Increase**

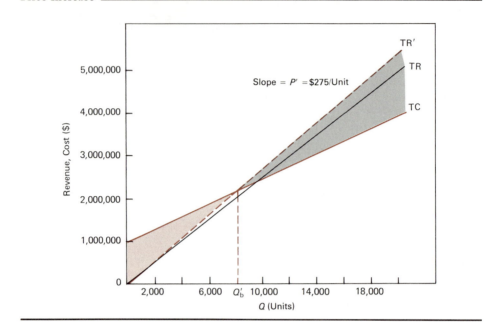

FIGURE 7–5 **Linear Breakeven Analysis Chart for the Allegan Manufacturing Company Showing the Effects of Substituting Fixed Costs for Variable Costs**

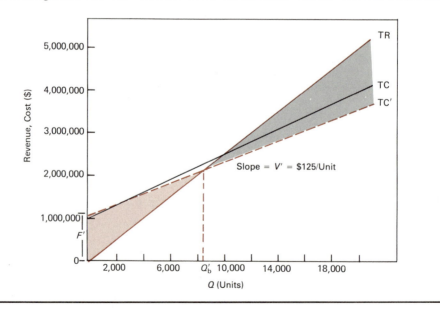

200

CASH BREAKEVEN ANALYSIS

Another concept that is sometimes useful in financial planning is *cash breakeven analysis*. Some of the firm's fixed operating costs, particularly depreciation, may represent *noncash outlays*. The cash breakeven point is calculated by deducting these noncash charges, N, from fixed costs, F, in the numerator of the breakeven equation (Equation 7.4):

$$\text{Cash breakeven output} = \frac{F - N}{P - V}. \tag{7.7}$$

It measures the volume of output (units) required to cover the firm's fixed cash operating outlays, such as management salaries, rent, and utilities.

Cash breakeven analysis also can be performed in terms of dollar sales. The cash breakeven dollar sales volume can be determined with the following expression:

$$\text{Cash breakeven sales} = \frac{F - N}{1 - (V/P)}. \tag{7.8}$$

All other things being equal, a firm with a larger proportion of its fixed costs in the form of noncash outlays will have a lower cash breakeven point and be better able to survive during a business downturn than will a firm whose fixed costs consist mainly of cash outlays.

In the Allegan Manufacturing Company example described earlier in the chapter, if $300,000 of the firm's $1,000,000 fixed costs, F, are noncash outlays, N, then Allegan's cash breakeven point can be found as follows using Equation 7.7:

$$\text{Cash breakeven output} = \frac{\$1,000,000 - \$300,000}{\$250 - \$150}$$
$$= 7,000 \text{ units}.$$

It should be emphasized that the calculation of a firm's cash breakeven output does not constitute a comprehensive method of cash flow analysis. A complete cash flow analysis, which takes account of the timing of all the firm's cash receipts and disbursements, requires the preparation of a detailed cash budget. The development and analysis of cash budgets are discussed in the following chapter.

SOME LIMITATIONS OF BREAKEVEN ANALYSIS

Breakeven analysis as it was just developed has a number of limitations. These arise from the *assumptions* that are made in constructing the model and developing the relevant data. The application of breakeven analysis is of value only to the extent that these assumptions are valid.

Constant selling price and variable cost per unit   Recall that in the graphic breakeven analysis model, the assumptions of a constant selling price and

FIGURE 7–6   **Nonlinear Breakeven Analysis Chart**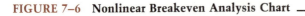

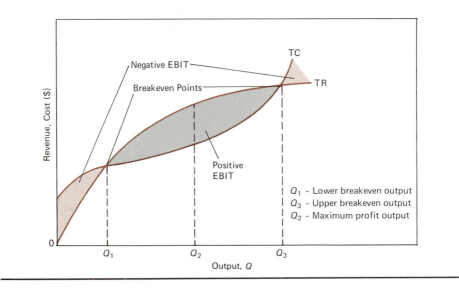

variable cost per unit yield *linear* relationships for the total revenue and total cost functions. In practice these functions tend to be nonlinear. In many cases a firm can sell additional units of output only by lowering the price per unit. This results in a curvilinear total revenue function, as shown in Figure 7–6, instead of a straight line.

In addition, a firm's total cost function may be nonlinear as variable costs per unit initially decrease and then increase. This is also shown in Figure 7–6. Decreasing variable costs per unit can occur if, for example, labor specialization results in increased output per labor hour. Increasing variable costs per unit can occur if, for example, a firm uses more costly overtime labor as output approaches production capacity.

Nonlinear TC and TR functions can result in a firm's having more than one breakeven output point. This is shown in Figure 7–6, where a breakeven situation occurs at both Point Q_1 and Point Q_3. This is interpreted to mean that the firm will incur operating losses *below* an output level of Q_1 and *above* an output level of Q_3. The firm's total operating profits are maximized within the range of $Q_1 - Q_3$ at the point where the vertical distance between the TR and TC curves is greatest, that is, at output level Q_2.

In summary, the assumption of a constant selling price and variable cost per unit is probably valid over some "relevant range" of output levels. However, consideration of output levels outside this range will normally require modifications in the breakeven chart.

Composition of operating costs   Another assumption of breakeven analysis is that costs can be classified as either fixed or variable. In fact, fixed and variable costs are dependent on both the time period involved and the output range under consideration. As mentioned earlier, all costs are variable in the long run. In addition, some costs are partly fixed and partly variable. Furthermore, some costs increase in a stepwise manner as output is increased (that is, *semivariable costs*) and are constant only over relatively narrow ranges of output.

Multiple products   The breakeven model also assumes that a firm is producing and selling either a *single* product or a *constant mix* of different products. In many cases the product mix changes over time, and problems can arise in allocating fixed costs among the various products.

Uncertainty   Still another assumption of breakeven analysis is that the selling price and variable cost per unit, as well as fixed costs, are known at each level of output. In practice these parameters are subject to uncertainty. Thus, the usefulness of the results of breakeven analysis depends on how accurate the estimates of these parameters are.

Short-term planning horizon   Finally, breakeven analysis is normally performed for a planning period of 1 year or less. However, the benefits received from some costs may not be realized until subsequent periods. For example, research and development costs incurred during a specific period may not result in new products for several years. For breakeven analysis to be a dependable decision-making tool, a firm's operating costs must be matched with resulting revenues for the planning period under consideration.

OPERATING LEVERAGE AND BUSINESS RISK

As mentioned earlier in this chapter, the more operating leverage a firm uses, the greater its risk tends to be. Thus, the *degree of operating leverage* utilized by a firm can have a significant effect on the degree of risk perceived by stockholders.

DEGREE OF OPERATING LEVERAGE

A firm's degree of operating leverage (DOL) is defined as the multiplier effect resulting from the firm's use of fixed operating costs. More specifically, DOL can be defined as the *percentage change* in earnings before interest and taxes (EBIT) resulting from a given *percentage change* in sales (output):

$$\text{DOL at } X = \frac{\text{Percentage change in EBIT}}{\text{Percentage change in sales}}.$$

This can be rewritten as follows:

$$\text{DOL at } X = \frac{\dfrac{\Delta \text{EBIT}}{\text{EBIT}}}{\dfrac{\Delta \text{Sales}}{\text{Sales}}}, \qquad (7.9)$$

where ΔEBIT and ΔSales are the changes in the firm's EBIT and sales, respectively. Since a firm's DOL differs at each sales (output) level, it is necessary to indicate the sales (units of output) point X, at which operating leverage is measured. The degree of operating leverage is analogous to the elasticity concept of economics (for example, price and income elasticity) in that it relates percentage changes in one variable (output) to percentage changes in another variable (EBIT).

The calculation of the DOL can be illustrated using the Allegan Manufacturing Company example discussed earlier. From Table 7–1, recall that Allegan's variable operating costs were $3,000,000 at the current sales level of $5,000,000. Thus, the firm's variable operating cost ratio is $3,000,000/ $5,000,000 = 0.60, or 60 percent.

Suppose the firm increased sales by 10 percent to $5,500,000 while keeping fixed operating costs constant at $1,000,000 and the variable (operating) cost ratio at 60 percent. As can be seen in Table 7–2, this would increase the firm's earnings before interest and taxes (EBIT) to $1,200,000. Substituting the two sales figures ($5,000,000 and $5,500,000) and associated EBIT figures ($1,000,000 and $1,200,000) into Equation 7.9 yields the following:

$$\text{DOL at } \$5,000,000 = \frac{\dfrac{\$1,200,000 - \$1,000,000}{\$1,000,000}}{\dfrac{\$5,500,000 - \$5,000,000}{\$5,000,000}}$$

$$= \frac{\$200,000}{\$1,000,000} \times \frac{\$5,000,000}{\$500,000}$$

$$= 2.0 .$$

A DOL of 2.0 is interpreted to mean that each 1 percent change in sales from a base sales level of $5,000,000 results in a 2 percent change in EBIT *in the same direction as the sales change*. In other words, a sales *increase* of 10 percent results in a $10\% \times 2.0 = 20\%$ *increase* in EBIT. Similarly, a 10 percent *decrease* in sales produces a $10\% \times 2.0 = 20\%$ *decrease* in EBIT. The greater a firm's DOL, the greater the magnification of sales changes into EBIT changes.

Equation 7.9 requires the use of two different values of sales and EBIT. Another equation that can be used to compute a firm's DOL more easily is as follows:[1]

$$\text{DOL at } X = \frac{\text{Sales } - \text{ Variable costs}}{\text{EBIT}} \tag{7.10}$$

Inserting data from Table 7–1 on the Allegan Manufacturing Company into Equation 7.10 gives the following:

---

[1]Equation 7.10 is derived from Equation 7.9. Problem 13 at the end of this chapter asks for an explanation of how this is done.

TABLE 7–2   **Effect on Earnings per Share of a 10 Percent Increase in Sales**

ALLEGAN MANUFACTURING COMPANY
YEAR ENDING DECEMBER 31, 19X1

		(1)		(2)	% Change [(2) − (1)] ÷ (1)
Sales		$5,000,000		$5,500,000	+10%
Less: Variable operating costs (0.60 × Sales)	$3,000,000		$3,300,000		+10%
Fixed operating costs	1,000,000		1,000,000		0%
Total operating costs		4,000,000		4,300,000	+ 8%
Earnings before interest and taxes		1,000,000		1,200,000	+20%
Less: Interest payments (fixed capital cost)		250,000		250,000	0%
Earnings before taxes		750,000		950,000	+27%
Less: Income taxes (variable), 40%		300,000		380,000	+27%
Earnings after taxes		450,000		570,000	+27%
Less: Preferred dividends (fixed capital cost)		150,000		150,000	0%
Earnings available to common stockholders		$ 300,000		$ 420,000	+40%
Earnings per share (100,000 shares)		$3.00		$4.20	+40%

$$\text{DOL at } \$5,000,000 = \frac{\$5,000,000 - \$3,000,000}{\$1,000,000}$$

$$= 2.0 \ .$$

This result is the same as that obtained using the more complex Equation 7.9.

A firm's DOL is a function of the nature of the production process. If the firm employs large amounts of labor-saving equipment in its operations, it tends to have relatively high fixed operating costs and relatively low variable operating costs. Such a cost structure yields a high DOL, which results in large operating profits (positive EBIT) if sales are high and large operating losses (negative EBIT) if sales are depressed.

DOL AND BREAKEVEN ANALYSIS

The variables defined in the preceding section on breakeven analysis can also be used to develop a formula for determining a firm's DOL at any given output level. Since sales are equivalent to TR, or $P \times Q$, variable cost is equal to $V \times Q$, and EBIT is equal to total revenue, TR, less total (operating) cost, or $(P \times Q) - F - (V \times Q)$, these values can be substituted into Equation 7.10 to obtain the following:

$$\text{DOL at } Q = \frac{(P \times Q) - (V \times Q)}{(P \times Q) - F - (V \times Q)},$$

205

or

$$\text{DOL at } Q = \frac{(P - V)Q}{(P - V)Q - F}. \tag{7.11}$$

In the earlier discussion of breakeven analysis for the Allegan Manufacturing Company, the parameters of the breakeven model were determined as $P = \$250/\text{unit}$, $V = \$150/\text{unit}$, and $F = \$1,000,000$. Substituting these values into Equation 7.11 along with the respective output values yields the DOL values shown in Table 7–3.

Note that Allegan's DOL is largest (in absolute value terms) when the firm is operating near the breakeven point (that is, where $Q_b = 10,000$ units). Note also that the firm's DOL is negative below the breakeven output level. A negative DOL indicates the percentage *reduction* in operating *losses* that occurs as a result of a 1 percent *increase* in output. For example, the DOL of -1.50 at an output level of 6,000 units indicates that, from a base output level of 6,000 units, the firm's operating *losses* are *reduced* by 1.5 percent for each 1 percent *increase* in output.

BUSINESS RISK

Business risk refers to the inherent variability or uncertainty of a firm's EBIT. It is a function of several factors, one of which is the firm's DOL. The DOL is a measure of how sensitive a firm's EBIT is to changes in sales. The greater a firm's DOL, the larger the change in EBIT will be for a given change in sales. Thus, *all other things being equal,* the higher a firm's DOL, the greater the degree of business risk.

Other factors can also affect a firm's business risk, including the variability or uncertainty of sales. A firm with high fixed costs and very stable sales will have a high DOL, but it will also have stable EBIT and, therefore, low busi-

TABLE 7–3   Allegan Manufacturing Company: DOL at Various Output Levels _____

Output, Q	Degree of Operating Leverage, DOL
0	0
2,000	−0.25
4,000	−0.67
6,000	−1.50
8,000	−4.00
10,000	(Undefined)
12,000	+6.00
14,000	+3.50
16,000	+2.67
18,000	+2.25
20,000	+2.00

ness risk. Public utilities and pipeline transportation companies are examples of firms having these operating characteristics.

Another factor that may affect a firm's business risk is uncertainty concerning selling prices and variable costs. A firm having a low DOL can still have high business risk if selling prices and variable costs are subject to considerable variability over time.

In summary, a firm's DOL is only one of several factors that determine the firm's business risk.

FINANCIAL LEVERAGE AND FINANCIAL RISK

As mentioned earlier, financial leverage occurs whenever a firm employs funds having fixed costs. The main reason a firm employs fixed-cost funds is to increase the earnings available to common stockholders. The basic source of these funds is debt. Another source is preferred stock.[2] Fixed capital costs represent contractual obligations the company must meet regardless of EBIT.[3]

A firm's financial leverage represents the change in earnings per share (EPS) that occurs as a result of a given change in EBIT. Figure 7–7 illustrates the concept of financial leverage. Line A represents the financial leverage used by a firm financed *entirely with common stock*. A given percentage change in EBIT results in the *same* percentage change in EPS.

Line B represents a firm that uses debt (or other sources of fixed cost funds). This increases the *slope* of the EPS − EBIT line, thus increasing the responsiveness of EPS to changes in EBIT. As can be seen in Figure 7–7, a given change in EBIT yields a larger change in EPS if the firm is using debt financing (ΔEPS_B) than if the firm is financed entirely with common stock (ΔEPS_A).

It is also clear from Figure 7–7 that the use of financial leverage magnifies the returns—both positive and negative—to the shareholder. When EBIT is at a relatively high level, such as $EBIT_2$, Firm B's use of financial leverage *increases* EPS above the level attained by Firm A, which is not using financial leverage. On the other hand, when EBIT is relatively low—for example, at $EBIT_0$—the use of financial leverage *decreases* EPS below the level that would be obtained otherwise; that is, $EPS'_0 < EPS_0$. At $EBIT_0$ the use of financial leverage results in negative EPS for Firm B.

For example, the Allegan Manufacturing Company employs financial leverage, since it incurs both fixed interest and preferred stock dividend payments. Table 7–4 illustrates Allegan's EPS for various alternative levels of EBIT.

A 20 percent increase in Allegan's EBIT from $1,000,000 to $1,200,000 results in a 40 percent increase in EPS, since ($4.20 − $3.00)/$3.00 = 0.4. Similarly, a 20 percent decrease in EBIT from $1,000,000 to $800,000 yields a 40 percent decrease in EPS. Figure 7–8 is an EPS-EBIT graph for Allegan.

---

[2]Although leases also represent a significant source of fixed cost financing for many firms, they are not discussed here in order to simplify the analysis.

[3]In financial emergencies, firms are usually able to omit preferred dividends. This can have undesirable consequences for a firm, however. Thus, the payment of preferred dividends is treated here as if it were a contractual obligation.

FIGURE 7–7   **Illustration of Financial Leverage**

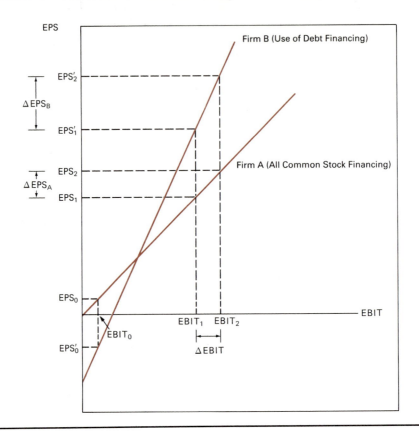

TABLE 7–4   **Earnings per Share for Alternative Levels of EBIT**

	ALLEGAN MANUFACTURING COMPANY				
	YEAR ENDING DECEMBER 31, 19X1				
EBIT	$400,000	$800,000	$1,000,000	$1,200,000	$1,600,000
Less: Interest expenses	250,000	250,000	250,000	250,000	250,000
Earnings before taxes	$150,000	$550,000	$ 750,000	$ 950,000	$1,350,000
Less: Income taxes	60,000	220,000	300,000	380,000	540,000
Earnings after taxes	$ 90,000	$330,000	$ 450,000	$ 570,000	$ 810,000
Less: Preferred dividends	150,000	150,000	150,000	150,000	150,000
Earnings available to common stockholders	−$60,000	$180,000	$300,000	$420,000	$660,000
Earnings per share (EPS)	−$0.60	$1.80	$3.00	$4.20	$6.60

FIGURE 7–8   EPS-EBIT Graph for the Allegan Manufacturing Company

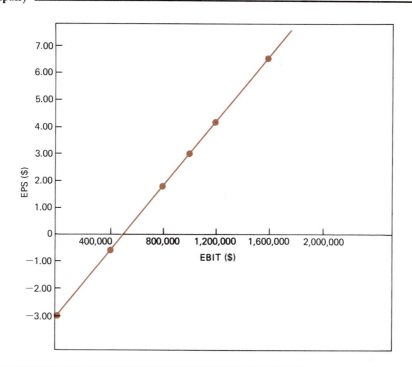

DEGREE OF FINANCIAL LEVERAGE

A firm's degree of financial leverage (DFL) is defined as the *percentage change* in earnings per share (EPS) resulting from a given *percentage change* in earnings before interest and taxes (EBIT):

$$\text{DFL at } X = \frac{\text{Percentage change in EPS}}{\text{Percentage change in EBIT}}.$$

This can also be written as follows:

$$\text{DFL at } X = \frac{\dfrac{\Delta \text{EPS}}{\text{EPS}}}{\dfrac{\Delta \text{EBIT}}{\text{EBIT}}}, \tag{7.12}$$

where ΔEPS and ΔEBIT are the changes in EPS and EBIT, respectively. Since a firm's DFL is different at each EBIT level, it is necessary to indicate the EBIT point, X, at which financial leverage is being measured.

Using the information contained in Table 7–4, the degree of financial leverage used by the Allegan Manufacturing Company can be calculated. The firm's EPS level is $3.00 at an EBIT level of $1,000,000. At an EBIT level of

209

$1,200,000, EPS equals $4.20. Substituting these quantities into Equation 7.12 yields the following:

$$\text{DFL at } \$1,000,000 = \frac{\dfrac{\$4.20 - \$3.00}{\$3.00}}{\dfrac{\$1,200,000 - \$1,000,000}{\$1,000,000}}$$

$$= \frac{\$1.20}{\$3.00} \times \frac{\$1,000,000}{\$200,000}$$

$$= 2.0 \ .$$

A DFL of 2.0 indicates that each 1 percent change in EBIT from a base EBIT level of $1,000,000 results in a 2 percent change in EPS *in the same direction as the EBIT change.* In other words, a 10 percent *increase* in EBIT results in a 10% × 2.0 = 20% *increase* in EPS. Similarly, a 10 percent *decrease* in EBIT produces a 20 percent *decrease* in EPS. The larger the firm's DFL, the greater the magnification of EBIT changes into EPS changes.

Measuring a firm's DFL using Equation 7.12 is somewhat cumbersome, since it necessitates using two EBIT and EPS projections. Computation is simplified when Equation 7.12 is rewritten as follows:[4]

$$\text{DFL at } X = \frac{\text{EBIT}}{\text{EBIT} - I - D_p/(1 - t)} \ , \tag{7.13}$$

where I is the firm's interest payments, D_p the firm's preferred dividend payments, t the firm's marginal income tax rate, and X the level of EBIT at which the firm's DFL is being measured.

Unlike interest payments, preferred dividend payments are not tax deductible. Thus, on a comparable tax basis, a dollar of preferred dividends costs the firm more than a dollar of interest payments. Dividing preferred dividends in Equation 7.13 by $(1 - t)$ puts interest and preferred dividends on an equivalent, *pretax* basis.

Consider again the data presented in Table 7–1 on the Allegan Manufacturing Company. According to that table, EBIT = $1,000,000, I = $250,000, D_p = $150,000, and t = 40%, or 0.40. Substituting these values into Equation 7.13 yields the following:

$$\text{DFL at } \$1,000,000 = \frac{\$1,000,000}{\$1,000,000 - \$250,000 - \$150,000/(1 - 0.40)}$$
$$= 2.0 \ .$$

[4]For the firm with no preferred stock, Equation 7.13 becomes the following:

$$\text{DFL at } X = \frac{\text{EBIT}}{\text{EBIT} - I}$$

$$= \frac{\text{EBIT}}{\text{EBT}} \ ,$$

where EBT represents earnings before taxes.

210

This result is the same as that obtained using Equation 7.12.

Just as a firm can change its DOL by raising or lowering fixed operating costs, it can also change its DFL by increasing or decreasing fixed capital costs. The amount of fixed capital costs incurred by a firm depends primarily on the mix between debt and common stock equity in the firm's *capital structure*. Capital structure is defined as all *permanent sources of capital* available to a firm, including permanent debt, preferred stock, and common stock equity. Thus, a firm that has a relatively large proportion of debt and preferred stock in its capital structure will have relatively large fixed capital costs and a high DFL.

FINANCIAL RISK

Financial risk refers to the variability of a firm's returns to shareholders. Financial leverage is one of several factors that affect financial risk. The use of increasing amounts of financial leverage raises the firm's fixed financial costs; this, in turn, increases the level of EBIT that the firm must earn in order to meet its financial obligations and remain in business. The use of financial leverage increases the variability of a firm's EPS returns to common stockholders. It also increases the firm's risk of insolvency. (Insolvency occurs when a firm is unable to meet contractual financial obligations—such as interest and principal payments, accounts payable, and income taxes—as they come due.) Thus, *all other things being equal*, the higher a firm's DFL, the greater its financial risk.

Various financial ratios can be used to measure the financial risk associated with a firm's use of leverage in its capital structure. These include the total debt-to-total assets ratio, the debt-to-equity ratio, the times interest earned ratio, and the fixed charge coverage ratio.[5] In particular, the times interest earned ratio and the fixed charge coverage ratio can help the analyst measure the extent to which a firm will be able to meet fixed capital costs out of EBIT.

COMBINED LEVERAGE AND OVERALL RISK

Combined leverage occurs whenever a firm employs *both* operating leverage and financial leverage in an effort to increase the returns to common stockholders. It represents the magnification of sales increases (or decreases) into relatively larger earnings per share increases (or decreases), which result from the firm's use of both types of leverage. The joint multiplier effect is known as the *degree of combined leverage.*

DEGREE OF COMBINED LEVERAGE

A firm's degree of combined leverage (DCL) is defined as the percentage change in earnings per share resulting from a given percentage change in sales (output):

[5]Chapter 6 contains detailed explanations of these ratios.

$$\text{DCL at } X = \frac{\text{Percentage change in EPS}}{\text{Percentage change in sales}}.$$

This can be rewritten as follows:

$$\text{DCL at } X = \frac{\dfrac{\Delta \text{EPS}}{\text{EPS}}}{\dfrac{\Delta \text{Sales}}{\text{Sales}}}, \qquad (7.14)$$

where ΔEPS and ΔSales are the changes in a firm's EPS and sales, respectively, and X represents the level of sales at which the firm's combined leverage is measured. The degree of combined leverage is also equal to the product of the degree of operating leverage and the degree of financial leverage:[6]

$$\text{DCL at } X = \text{DOL} \times \text{DFL}. \qquad (7.15)$$

To simplify matters, Equations 7.10 and 7.13 can be substituted into Equation 7.15 to obtain a new formula for determining the DCL in terms of basic income statement quantities:

$$\text{DCL at } X = \frac{\text{Sales} - \text{Variable cost}}{\text{EBIT}} \times \frac{\text{EBIT}}{\text{EBIT} - I - D_p/(1 - t)},$$

or

$$\text{DCL at } X = \frac{\text{Sales} - \text{Variable costs}}{\text{EBIT} - I - D_p/(1 - t)}. \qquad (7.16)$$

These three formulas for calculating DCL can be illustrated using the Allegan Manufacturing Company example developed earlier in the chapter. Equation 7.14 can be used to calculate Allegan's DCL with the data from Tables 7–1 and 7–2. The EPS level was $3.00 at a sales level of $5,000,000 and $4.20 at a sales level of $5,500,000. Substituting these values into Equation 7.14 yields the following:

$$\text{DCL at } \$5,000,000 = \frac{\dfrac{\$4.20 - \$3.00}{\$3.00}}{\dfrac{\$5,500,000 - \$5,000,000}{\$5,000,000}}$$

[6]This follows logically from the definitions of DOL, DFL, and DCL:

$$\frac{\text{Percentage change in EPS}}{\text{Percentage change in sales}} = \frac{\text{Percentage change in EBIT}}{\text{Percentage change in sales}} \times \frac{\text{Percentage change in EPS}}{\text{Percentage change in EBIT}}$$

$$= \frac{\$1.20}{\$3.00} \times \frac{\$5,000,000}{\$500,000}$$

$$= 4.0 .$$

Substituting Sales = \$5,000,000, Variable costs = \$3,000,000, EBIT = \$1,000,000, I = \$250,000, D_p = \$150,000, and t = 40% (0.40) into Equation 7.16 gives the same value for Allegan's DCL:

$$\text{DCL at } \$5,000,000 = \frac{\$5,000,000 - \$3,000,000}{\$1,000,000 - \$250,000 - \$150,000/(1 - 0.40)}$$

$$= 4.0 .$$

Also, recall from the earlier discussions of operating and financial leverage for Allegan that DOL = 2.0, and DFL = 2.0. Substituting these values into Equation 7.15 yields a DCL value identical to that just calculated:

$$\text{DCL at } \$5,000,000 = 2.0 \times 2.0$$

$$= 4.0 .$$

This DCL is interpreted to mean that each 1 percent change in sales from a base sales level of \$5,000,000 results in a 4 percent change in Allegan's EPS.

OVERALL RISK

The degree of combined leverage used by a firm is a measure of the overall variability of EPS due to fixed operating and capital costs. These costs can be combined in many different ways to achieve a desired DCL. In other words, there are a number of possible tradeoffs that can be made between operating and financial leverage.

Equation 7.15 shows that DCL is a function of DOL and DFL. If a firm has a relatively high DOL, for example, and wishes to achieve a certain DCL, it can offset this high DOL with a lower DFL. Or it may have a high DFL, in which case it would aim for a lower DOL. To illustrate, assume that a firm is considering purchasing assets that will increase fixed operating costs. To offset this high DOL, the firm may want to decrease the proportion of debt (and/or preferred stock) in its capital structure, thereby reducing fixed financial costs and the DFL.

The firm is limited in the amount of operating and financial leverage it can use in seeking to increase EPS. As the firm's use of leverage increases, so does its degree of risk, and investors who supply funds to the firm in the form of preferred and common equity and debt will consider this degree of risk when determining their required rates of return. The greater the firm's overall risk, the higher the rates of return investors will require. In other words, a firm that uses "excessive" amounts of leverage will have to pay higher costs for debt and preferred stock. These higher costs will tend to offset the returns gained from the use of leverage. Finally, "excessive" use of leverage will cause the market price of the firm's common stock to decline.

SUMMARY

- *Leverage* refers to a firm's use of assets and liabilities having fixed costs. A firm uses leverage in an attempt to earn returns in excess of the fixed costs of these assets and liabilities, thus increasing the returns to common stockholders.

- *Breakeven analysis* is used to examine the relationship among a firm's revenues, costs, and operating profits (EBIT) at various output levels. Frequently the analyst constructs a breakeven chart based on linear cost-output and revenue-output relationships to determine the operating characteristics of a firm over a limited output range.

- The *breakeven point* is defined as the output level at which total revenues equal total (operating) costs. In the linear breakeven model, the breakeven point is found by dividing fixed (operating) costs by the difference between price and variable cost per unit.

- *Operating leverage* occurs when a firm uses assets having fixed operating costs. The *degree of operating leverage* (DOL) measures the percentage change in a firm's EBIT resulting from a 1 percent change in sales (or units of output). As a firm's fixed operating costs rise, its DOL increases.

- *Business risk* refers to the variability of a firm's EBIT. It is a function of several factors, including the firm's DOL and the variability of sales. All other things being equal, the higher a firm's DOL, the greater its business risk.

- *Financial leverage* occurs when a firm makes use of funds (primarily from debt and preferred stock) having fixed capital costs. The *degree of financial leverage* (DFL) measures the percentage change in the firm's EPS resulting from a 1 percent change in EBIT. As a firm's fixed capital costs rise, its DFL increases.

- *Financial risk* refers to the variability of a firm's EPS that results from the use of financial leverage.

- The *combined leverage* of a firm is equal to the *product* of the degrees of operating and financial leverage. These two types of leverage can be combined in many different ways to achieve a given degree of combined leverage (DCL). The total variability of the firm's EPS is a combination of business risk and financial risk.

QUESTIONS AND TOPICS FOR DISCUSSION

1. Define *leverage* as it is used in finance.
2. Define and give examples of the following:
   a. Fixed costs.
   b. Variable costs.
3. Explain how a linear breakeven chart is constructed when a firm's selling price, variable costs per unit, and fixed costs are known.
4. Define *contribution margin*. What is its relationship to linear breakeven analysis?
5. What are some of the limitations of breakeven analysis? How can these limitations affect actual financial decision making?

6. Define the following:
   a. Operating leverage.
   b. Business risk.

7. What other factors besides operating leverage can affect a firm's business risk?

8. Define the following:
   a. Financial leverage.
   b. Financial risk.

9. How is a firm's degree of combined leverage (DCL) related to its degree of operating and financial leverage?

10. Assuming that all other factors remain unchanged, determine how a firm's break-even point is affected by each of the following:
    a. The firm finds it necessary to reduce the price per unit because of competitive conditions in the market.
    b. The firm's direct labor costs increase as a result of a new labor contract.
    c. The Occupational Safety and Health Administration (OSHA) requires the firm to install new ventilating equipment in its plant. (Assume that this action has no effect on worker productivity.)

PROBLEMS*

Refer to the following data when working Problems 1 through 6:

The Bedford Company forecasts that next year's sales will be $3,000,000. Fixed operating costs are estimated to be $500,000, and the variable cost ratio (that is, variable costs as a fraction of sales) is estimated to be 0.75. The firm has a $500,000 loan at 10 percent interest. It has 10,000 shares of $3 preferred stock and 50,000 shares of common stock outstanding. Bedford is in the 40 percent corporate income tax bracket.

1. Forecast Bedford's earnings per share (EPS) for next year. Develop a complete income statement using the revised format illustrated in Table 7–1 of this chapter. Then determine what Bedford's EPS would be if sales were 10 percent above the projected $3,000,000 level.

2. Calculate Bedford's degree of operating leverage (DOL) at a sales level of $3,000,000 using the following:
   a. The definitional formula (Equation 7.9).
   b. The simpler, computational formula (Equation 7.10).
   c. What is the economic interpretation of this value?

3. Calculate Bedford's degree of financial leverage (DFL) at the EBIT level corresponding to sales of $3,000,000 using the following:
   a. The definitional formula (Equation 7.12).
   b. The simpler, computational formula (Equation 7.13).
   c. What is the economic interpretation of this value?

4. Calculate Bedford's degree of combined leverage (DCL) using the following:
   a. The definitional formula (Equation 7.14).
   b. The simpler, computational formula (Equation 7.16).
   c. The degrees of operating and financial leverage calculated in Problems 2 and 3.
   d. What is the economic interpretation of this value?

5. Calculate Bedford's breakeven dollar sales volume.

*Problems in color have check answers printed at the end of the book.

6. Construct an EPS-EBIT graph for the Bedford Company.

Refer to the following data when working Problems 7 through 9:

East Publishing Company is doing an analysis of a proposed new finance text. The following data have been obtained:

Fixed costs (per edition):	
Development (reviews, class testing, and so on)	$ 9,000
Copy editing	2,500
Selling and promotion	3,500
Typesetting	20,000
Total	$35,000
Variable costs (per copy):	
Printing and binding	$ 2.10
Administrative costs	0.80
Salespeople's commission (2% of selling price)	0.30
Author's royalties (12% of selling price)	1.80
Bookstore discounts (20% of selling price)	3.00
Total	$ 8.00
Projected selling price	$15.00

7. Using the above data, do the following:
   a. Determine the company's breakeven volume for this book:
      i. In units.
      ii. In dollar sales.
   b. Develop a breakeven chart for the text.
   c. Determine the number of copies East must sell in order to earn an (operating) profit of $21,000 on this text.
   d. Determine total (operating) profits at the following sales levels:
      i. 3,000 units.
      ii. 5,000 units.
      iii. 10,000 units.

8. a. Determine the degree of operating leverage (DOL) at the following sales levels:
      i. 3,000 units.
      ii. 7,000 units.
   b. What is the economic interpretation of the DOL value at 3,000 units?

9. Suppose East feels that $15.00 is too high a price to charge for the new finance text. It has examined the competitive market and determined that $12.00 would be a better selling price. What would the breakeven volume be at this new selling price?

Refer to the following data when working Problems 10 and 11:

The Alexander Company reported the following income statement for 19X1:

Sales		$15,000,000
Less: Operating expenses		
Wages, salaries, benefits	$6,000,000	
Raw materials	3,000,000	
Depreciation	1,500,000	
General, administrative, and selling expenses	1,500,000	
Total operating expenses		12,000,000

216

Earnings before interest and taxes (EBIT)	$ 3,000,000
Less: Interest expense	750,000
Earnings before taxes	$ 2,250,000
Less: Income taxes	1,000,000
Earnings after taxes	$ 1,250,000
Less: Preferred dividends	250,000
Earnings available to common stockholders	$ 1,000,000
Earnings per share—250,000 shares outstanding	$4.00

Assume that all depreciation and 75 percent of the firm's general, administrative, and selling expenses are *fixed costs* and that the remainder of the firm's operating expenses are *variable costs.*

10. a. Determine Alexander's fixed costs, variable costs, and variable cost ratio.
  b. Based on its 19X1 sales, calculate the following:
   i. The firm's DOL.
   ii. The firm's DFL.
   iii. The firm's DCL.
  c. Assuming that next year's sales increase by 15 percent, fixed operating and financial costs remain constant, and the variable cost ratio and tax rate also remain constant, use the leverage figures just calculated to forecast next year's EPS.
  d. Show the validity of this forecast by constructing Alexander's income statement for next year according to the revised format.
  e. Determine Alexander's breakeven dollar sales volume.
  f. Construct an EPS-EBIT graph based on Alexander's 19X1 income statement.

11. Suppose that depreciation represents a *noncash* outlay.
  a. Compute Alexander's cash breakeven dollar sales volume.
  b. How does the cash breakeven sales volume compare with the ordinary breakeven sales volume computed in Problem 10?

12. Gibson Company sales for the year 19X1 were $2,500,000. The firm's variable operating cost ratio was 0.50, and fixed costs (that is, overhead and depreciation) were $750,000. Its average (and marginal) income tax rate is 40 percent. Currently, the firm has $2,000,000 of long-term bank loans outstanding at an average interest rate of 12.5 percent. The remainder of the firm's capital structure consists of common stock (100,000 shares outstanding at the present time).
  a. Calculate Gibson's degree of combined leverage for 19X1.
  b. Gibson is forecasting a 10 percent increase in sales for next year (19X2). Furthermore, the firm is planning to purchase additional labor-saving equipment, which will increase fixed costs by $150,000 and reduce the variable cost ratio to 0.475. Financing this equipment with debt will require additional bank loans of $500,000 at an interest rate of 12.5 percent. Calculate Gibson's expected degree of combined leverage for 19X2.
  c. Determine how much Gibson must reduce its debt in 19X2 (for example, through the sale of common stock) to maintain its DCL at the 19X1 level of 5.0.

13. Show algebraically that Equation 7.10,

$$\text{DOL at } X = \frac{\text{Sales} - \text{Variable costs}}{\text{EBIT}},$$

is equivalent to Equation 7.9,

$$\text{DOL at } X = \frac{\Delta EBIT/EBIT}{\Delta Sales/Sales}.$$

14. Albatross Airlines' fixed operating costs are $5,800,000, and its variable cost ratio is 0.20. The firm has $2,000,000 in bonds outstanding with a coupon interest rate of 8 percent. Albatross has 30,000 shares of preferred stock outstanding, which pays a $2.00 annual dividend. There are 100,000 shares of common stock outstanding. Revenues for the firm are $8,000,000, and the firm is in the 40 percent corporate income tax bracket.
    a. Compute Albatross's degree of operating leverage.
    b. Compute its degree of financial leverage.
    c. Compute its degree of combined leverage, and interpret this value.

15. Using the data on Albatross in Problem 14, compute the firm's breakeven dollar sales volume.

16. Given the following information for Computech, compute the firm's degree of combined leverage (dollars are in thousands except EPS):

	19X1	19X2
Sales	$500,000	$570,000
Fixed costs	120,000	120,000
Variable costs	300,000	342,000
Earnings before interest and taxes	80,000	108,000
Interest	30,000	30,000
Earnings per share (EPS)	$1.00	$1.56

ADDITIONAL READINGS AND REFERENCES

Ghandhi, J. K. S. "On the Measurement of Leverage." *Journal of Finance* 21 (Dec. 1966): 715–726.

Gritta, Richard D. "The Effect of Leverage on Air Carrier Earnings: A Breakeven Analysis." *Financial Management* 8 (Summer 1979): 53–60.

Haslem, John A. "Leverage Effects on Corporate Earnings." *Arizona Review* 19 (March 1970): 7–11.

Hunt, Pearson. "A Proposal for Precise Definitions of 'Trading on the Equity' and 'Leverage'." *Journal of Finance* 16 (Sept. 1961): 377–386.

Jaedicke, Robert K., and Robichek, Alexander A. "Cost-Volume-Profit Analysis under Conditions of Uncertainty." *Accounting Review* 39 (Oct. 1964): 917–926.

Kelvie, William E., and Sinclair, John M. "New Techniques for Breakeven Charts." *Financial Executive* 36 (June 1968): 31–43.

Krainer, Robert E. "Interest Rates, Leverage , and Investor Rationality." *Journal of Financial and Quantitative Analysis* 12 (March 1977): 1–16.

Morrison, Thomas A., and Kaczka, Eugene. "A New Application of Calculus and Risk Analysis to Cost-Volume-Profit Changes." *Accounting Review* 44 (April 1969): 330–343.

Percival, John R. "Operating Leverage and Risk." *Journal of Business Research* 2 (April 1974): 223–227.

Raun, D. L. "The Limitations of Profit Graphs, Break-even Analysis, and Budgets." *Accounting Review* 39 (Oct. 1964): 927–945.

Reinhardt, U. E. "Break-Even Analysis for Lockheed's Tri Star: An Application of Financial Theory," *Journal of Finance* 28 (Sept. 1973): 821–838.

Shalit, Sol S. "On the Mathematics of Financial Leverage." *Financial Management* 4 (Spring 1975): 57–66.

CHAPTER 8

Financial Planning

A FINANCIAL DILEMMA

Chrysler's Financial Planning

In 1979 Chrysler Corporation, the third largest U.S. auto maker, was near bankruptcy. The company suffered huge losses in 1979 and 1980. By 1981 Chrysler managed to post a small profit, much of it coming from the sale of its tank division. By early 1983 the company appeared to have returned to profitable operations. During the near-bankrupt period and the period of increased sales that followed, the financial planners at Chrysler had the enormous task of managing the company's finances.

Profitable firms are at least partially able to satisfy their financing needs internally. In the case of Chrysler, the company had to rely entirely on external financing to stay in business. Chrysler worked with its suppliers to extend the payment periods on accounts payable. This meant the company had to raise less money from other sources. The company also worked with its bankers, borrowing as much as it could and extending the repayment periods. In addition, Chrysler borrowed large amounts of longer-term debt, including $1.2 billion in loans guaranteed by the U.S. government. By 1983 Chrysler's common stock price had increased to a level at which the company and its financial advisors felt the sale of common stock could be used as an external financing source.

Throughout this difficult period for Chrysler, the company's financial planners had to continually estimate the amount of external financing the company would need and determine the best sources to raise the needed funds. This chapter deals with the financial planning process and focuses on pro forma financial statements, which are an integral part of any financial plan.

GLOSSARY OF NEW TERMS

Capital budget   a projection of the capital investment projects the firm plans to place in service during some future period.

Cash budget   a projection of a company's cash receipts and disbursements over some future period of time.

Deterministic model   a financial planning model that projects single number estimates of a financial variable or variables without specifying their probability of occurrence.

Financial forecasting   the projection and estimation of a firm's future financial statements.

Financial planning model   a computerized representation of some aspect of a firm's financial planning process.

Operating budget   a collection of individual budgets that combine to form a part of a firm's integrated business plan, usually for the next year. It is normally composed of a *sales budget* and a *production budget.*

Optimization model   a financial planning model that projects an output figure for a firm representing the "best" level the firm can obtain using available inputs or resources.

Percentage of sales forecasting method   a method of estimating the additional financing that will be needed to support a given future sales level.

Probabilistic model   a financial planning model that uses probability distributions as inputs and generates a probability distribution for financial variables as output.

Pro forma financial statements   financial statements that project the results of some *assumed* event rather than an *actual* event.

Sensitivity analysis   a method of analysis that, when used with deterministic models, enables the financial decision maker to rerun the model to determine how much one or more of a firm's financial variables will change for given changes in certain inputs.

Trend analysis   a method of analysis that estimates the future value of a financial variable on the basis of past actual data.

INTRODUCTION

Any firm that hopes to operate successfully within the competitive environment of the 1980s will have to make detailed corporate plans stating its objectives and how it intends to achieve them. A firm's financial managers normally play important roles in setting objectives and formulating plans. In addition, they are responsible for acquiring the funds necessary to run the company. Since the various types of funds available—long term versus short term, internal versus external, and debt versus equity—have different costs and can place different limitations and obligations on the company, it is also necessary to draw up detailed *financial plans* for the orderly acquisition and expenditure of funds.

Pro forma financial statements, which show the results of some *assumed* event rather than an *actual* event, are usually an integral part of any financial plan. For example, an operating budget that shows the level of net income that can be expected if sales and expenses are at a given assumed level next year is a pro forma income statement. Short-term plans—those that deal with 1 year or less—tend to be rather detailed, whereas long-term plans are more general.

This chapter presents an overview of the financial planning process, with an emphasis on the important role of pro forma financial statements. The chapter is organized as follows:

- The first section shows how financial forecasting methods can be used to estimate financing needs and develop pro forma statements.

- The next section considers the budgeting aspects of the financial planning process.

- The following section shows how pro forma funds flow statements can be used in the financial planning process.

- The final section discusses computer applications of the financial planning process and the development of pro forma statements.

FINANCIAL FORECASTING

Financial forecasting involves the projection and estimation of a firm's *future* financing needs and pro forma statements. This section specifically introduces the percentage of sales forecasting method and trend analysis.

PERCENTAGE OF SALES FORECASTING METHOD

The percentage of sales forecasting method permits a company to forecast the amount of financing it will need for a given increase in sales. The use of this method is illustrated with the following example of the Industrial Supply Company (ISC).

The present ISC balance sheet and income statement are shown in Table 8–1. At the present time, the company's management expects sales to reach

TABLE 8–1   Industrial Supply Company

BALANCE SHEET
AS OF DECEMBER 31, 19X4

Cash	$ 100,000	Accounts payable	$ 300,000
Accounts receivable	400,000	Notes payable	200,000
Inventories	800,000	Long-term debt	100,000
Fixed assets, net	200,000	Stockholders' equity	900,000
Total assets	$1,500,000	Total liabilities and equity	$1,500,000

INCOME STATEMENT
FOR THE YEAR ENDED DECEMBER 31, 19X4

Sales	$3,000,000
Expenses, including interest and taxes	$2,850,000
Net income	$ 150,000

the $4.5 million range within approximately 1 year. One of management's primary questions is the amount of funds that will be needed to finance this expected growth. Up to now, the company has financed its growth by using both *internal* and *external* funds. The company has reinvested its past earnings back into the company, primarily into additional inventory. The company has also used external financing in the form of short-term borrowings from its bank.

To determine the amount of additional financing necessary to reach and maintain the $4.5 million annual sales level, the ISC management has made the following observations about the company's various assets and liabilities:

1. Cash. Management feels the company's cash balances are generally adequate for the present sales level and would have to increase proportionately as sales increase.

2. Accounts receivable. The company's present average collection period is approximately 48 days. Management feels the company's present credit policies are appropriate for its type of business. As a result, they feel that the average collection period will remain approximately constant and that accounts receivable will increase proportionately as sales increase.

3. Inventory. Management feels the company's inventory is properly managed at present. Therefore, they feel inventory would have to increase proportionately for sales to increase.

4. Fixed assets. The company is a distributor with relatively few fixed assets (delivery trucks, forklifts, office equipment, storage racks, and so forth). Because the company's fixed assets are being utilized at nearly full capacity, management feels fixed assets will have to increase as sales grow. For financial planning purposes, management is willing to assume that the *net* fixed asset figure on the balance sheet will increase proportionately as sales increase.

5. Accounts payable. The company now maintains good relations with its suppliers. As the company purchases more inventory, its accounts payable balance will increase proportionately as sales increase.

6. Long-term debt. Long-term debt and notes payable do not necessarily have a direct relationship to sales level. For example, a portion of the company's future profits may be used to pay off the present debt.

In summary, as the company's sales increase, its assets will increase proportionately to support the new sales. In addition, the current liabilities that vary directly with sales will also increase. The difference between the forecasted asset increase and the forecasted current liability increase is equal to the total financing the company will need. This relationship can be expressed in equation form, as follows:

$$
\begin{aligned}
\text{Total financing needed} &= \text{Forecasted asset increase} - \text{Forecasted current liability increase} \\
&= \frac{A}{S}(\Delta S) - \frac{CL}{S}(\Delta S),
\end{aligned}
$$

(8.1)

where A is the company's present asset level, S is the company's present sales, CL is the company's present level of current liabilities that vary proportionately with sales, and ΔS is the forecasted sales increase.

A portion of the total financing needed can be generated internally. Specifically, the internal financing generated during the time period when sales increase from S to $S + \Delta S$ can be expressed in equation form as follows:[1]

$$\begin{array}{l}\text{Internal} \\ \text{financing} \\ \text{provided}\end{array} = \begin{array}{l}\text{Forecasted} \\ \text{net income } (NI) \\ \text{during time} \\ \text{period } S \text{ to} \\ S + \Delta S\end{array} - \text{Dividends } (D) \tag{8.2}$$

$$= NI - D \, .$$

The external financing needed can be calculated by subtracting the internal financing provided from the total financing needed:

$$\begin{array}{l}\text{External} \\ \text{financing} \\ \text{needed}\end{array} = \begin{array}{l}\text{Total} \\ \text{financing} \\ \text{needed}\end{array} - \begin{array}{l}\text{Internal} \\ \text{financing} \\ \text{provided}\end{array} \tag{8.3}$$

$$= \left[\frac{A}{S} (\Delta S) - \frac{CL}{S} (\Delta S) \right] - [NI - D] \, .$$

Referring back to the ISC example, the external financing needed to support a sales increase of $1,500,000 up to the $4,500,000 level can now be calculated. Assume that management forecasts net income to be $200,000 during the year the increased sales are occurring. Assume further that the company does not pay dividends at the present time:[2]

$$\begin{array}{l}\text{External} \\ \text{financing} \\ \text{needed}\end{array} = \left[\left(\frac{\$1,500,000}{\$3,000,000} (\$1,500,000) - \frac{\$300,000}{\$3,000,000} (\$1,500,000) \right) \right] -$$

$$[\$200,000 - \$0]$$

$$= \$400,000 \, .$$

The approximate amount of external financing that will be needed to finance ISC's forecasted growth from $3,000,000 to $4,500,000 in sales is $400,000.[3] Even though the financing will be needed gradually as sales increase, the ISC management has to decide whether to (1) borrow on a short-term basis, (2) borrow on a long-term basis, or (3) sell additional common stock. The factors that influence the debt versus equity decision are discussed

---

[1]This equation does not consider depreciation, because *net* fixed assets are assumed to increase proportionately with sales. If *gross* fixed assets are assumed to increase proportionately with sales, depreciation is treated as a source of internal financing.

[2]Typically, small growth companies pay little, if any, dividends. Dividend policy is discussed in Chapter 14.

[3]The $400,000 figure assumes that none of the present notes payable or long-term debt will have to be repaid during the next year.

TABLE 8–2   Industrial Supply Company

Pro Forma Balance Sheet
as of December 31, 19X5

Cash	$ 150,000	Accounts payable	$ 450,000
Accounts receivable	600,000	Notes payable	600,000
Inventories	1,200,000	Long-term debt	100,000
Fixed assets, net	300,000	Stockholders' equity	1,100,000
Total assets	$2,250,000	Total liabilities and equity	$2,250,000

in Chapter 13, and the factors that influence the short-term versus long-term debt decision are discussed in Chapter 18.

Table 8–2 shows ISC's pro forma balance sheet at the end of the next year, *assuming* that net income during the year is $200,000 and that all of the $400,000 in external financing is in the form of short-term notes payable.

By using the formula for calculating the external financing needed, the ISC management knows in advance approximately how much financing will be needed during the upcoming year. The results of this financial planning should aid management in arranging the financing.

The percentage of sales forecasting method for calculating external financing needs is a useful and convenient financial planning technique. However, as with all analytical techniques, the application of this method should be supplemented by any additional factors that are unique to the particular situation.

FIGURE 8–1   Linear Trend Analysis

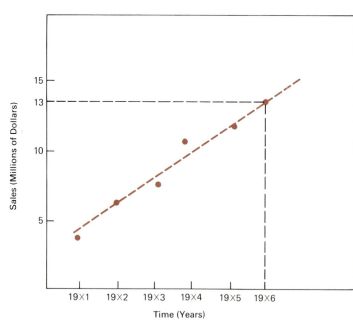

FIGURE 8–2   **Nonlinear Trend Analysis**

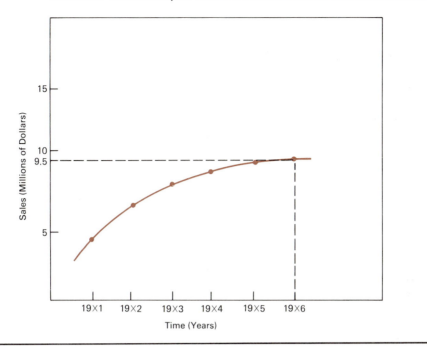

TREND ANALYSIS

Trend analysis is the process of estimating the future value of some financial variable on the basis of past actual data. It may be performed graphically and can be either *linear* or *nonlinear.*

To illustrate a linear trend analysis, consider a company that wishes to forecast its 19X6 sales based on known sales figures since 19X1. As shown in Figure 8–1, a simple analysis can be performed by visually estimating the "best" straight line passing through the plotted past actual data and *extrapolating* the line forward to 19X6. This visual analysis results in a 19X6 sales forecast of $13 million.[4] (Least squares trend analysis, a technique for statistically fitting the trend line, is illustrated in the "Calculator Applications" section at the end of this chapter.)

In some cases a nonlinear trend analysis is more representative than a linear one. This is especially true for maturing growth companies, or those whose past sales have been growing at a decreasing rate. Assume that one such company wishes to forecast 19X6 sales based on past actual sales figures since 19X1. As Figure 8–2 shows, this can be accomplished by plotting the past actual data and, instead of estimating the "best" straight line passing through these points, fitting a smooth curve and extending it until 19X6. The

---

[4]A more sophisticated type of trend analysis involves the use of *least squares* estimation procedures. (See J. R. McGuigan and R. C. Moyer. *Managerial Economics,* 3rd ed. St. Paul: West, 1983, chap. 5.)

visual curve–fitting technique results in an estimate of $9.5 million in sales for the year.

Although trend analysis can be a useful financial forecasting technique, it has limitations. Specifically, it assumes that future trends will simply be a continuation of past trends, and this is not always the case. Thus, the analyst must exercise caution when performing a trend analysis and take into account current information about industry and economic cycles.

AN OVERVIEW OF BUDGETING

Budgets are simply pro forma financial statements that detail a firm's financial plans. They detail how the company's funds will be spent on labor, materials, and capital goods and indicate how funds will be obtained.

Budgets are used to *plan, coordinate,* and *control* a firm's operations. They are essential to *planning* because they represent the company's objectives in numerical terms, such as dollars of sales, units of production, pounds of raw materials, and dollars of funds required from the capital markets. Once a firm has made financial plans, it refers to the budgets when *coordinating* its overall activities. For example, the purchasing department examines the budgets when deciding how best to integrate purchasing activities with monthly production requirements to insure the availability of sufficient raw materials. The production and marketing departments then work together to guarantee that sufficient finished goods inventories are on hand. Finally, the finance department coordinates the company's need for funds with the requirements of the purchasing, production, and marketing departments.

The projected figures in a firm's budgets are also used as a *control* device against which actual figures are compared. This insures that the various departments and divisions are functioning properly and working together toward the objectives developed in the planning phase.

A firm's budgets are based on the *assumption* of certain future sales and production levels. As pro forma financial statements, budgets predict what a company's financial statements will look like if specific plans are realized. A firm's budgets can also be combined with the current balance sheet to give a pro forma balance sheet showing what the financial status of the company will be at some point in the future if the budget forecasts prove true.

As a general rule, companies prepare and use three basic types of budgets: *operating budgets, cash budgets,* and *capital budgets.*

OPERATING BUDGETS

An operating budget, or operating plan, is basically a collection of individual budgets combined to form a part of an integrated *business plan,* usually for the next year. It is normally detailed enough to be used in coordinating a company's activities. In addition, it can function as a control device by serving as a basis for measuring performance.

The first step in the development of an operating budget involves the preparation of *sales budgets.* This is an important and difficult part of budgeting,

TABLE 8–3   Corporate Operating Budget

Midwestern Manufacturing Company
Corporate Summary Operating Budget, 19X6
Pro Forma Income Statement
(in Millions of Dollars)

Sales	$96.4
Expenses:	
Cost of goods sold (excluding depreciation)	$57.5
Depreciation	6.0
Selling and administrative expenses	18.8
Interest	1.6
Income before taxes	$12.5
Income taxes	6.0
Net income	$ 6.5

since it requires the consideration of a large number of factors, including the overall condition of the economy and the industry, the company's plant capacity, the prices it charges and those its competitors charge, and advertising expenditures made by the company and others within the industry.

Once a firm has completed and approved the sales budgets, it can then prepare *production budgets* for its products. Normally a firm has two production goals: meeting expected sales for the budget period and providing for the desired level of ending inventory. The production budgets detail the plans for achieving these goals. In addition, the production budgets detail the firm's expected future production costs.

The final step in the development of an operating budget involves combining the sales and production budgets to calculate the expected gross profit levels for the firm's products.

Depending on how a company is organized, it can combine the operating budgets for the various products and divisions to prepare an overall corporate operating budget. Table 8–3 is an example of a corporate operating budget. Note that this is a pro forma financial statement. It assumes that the company will continue to operate successfully during the coming year at the projected sales, price, and cost levels.

CASH BUDGETS

A cash budget is the projection of a company's cash receipts and disbursements over some future period of time. Typically, a cash budget is prepared on an annual basis and subdivided into months. However, more detailed and refined cash budgeting is done on a weekly or even daily basis by some companies that employ good ongoing cash management procedures.

Short-term borrowed funds are almost always easier to obtain when the need for them is anticipated. Thus, the cash budget is one of the most important short-range financial planning tools, because it can indicate potential cash shortages during the upcoming year. And, like operating budgets, cash budgets can also be useful for control and coordination purposes.

To explore actual cash budgeting procedures, the Midwestern Manufactur-

TABLE 8–4 Cash Budget Worksheet

MIDWESTERN MANUFACTURING COMPANY—CENTRAL DIVISION
CASH BUDGET WORKSHEET
FIRST QUARTER, 19X6

	December	January	February	March
Estimated sales	$540,000	$500,000	$550,000	$620,000
Estimated credit sales	486,000	450,000	495,000	558,000
Estimated receipts:				
Cash sales		50,000	55,000	62,000
Collections of accounts receivable:				
70% of last month's credit sales		340,200	315,000	346,500
30% of current month's credit				
sales		135,000	148,500	167,400
Total accounts receivable				
collections		$475,200	$463,500	$513,900
Estimated purchases*	$275,000	$302,500	$341,000	
Estimated payments of accounts				
payable†		$275,000	$302,500	$341,000

*Purchases are estimated at 55 percent of next month's sales.
†Payments are estimated to lag purchases by 1 month.

ing Company Central Division will be examined. Table 8–4 illustrates a cash budget worksheet for that division for the first quarter of 19X6. Table 8–5 is an actual cash budget for the time period.

The first step in cash budget preparation is the estimation of cash receipts, which results directly from the sales forecast. Midwestern has found that, on the average, about 10 percent of total sales in any given month are cash sales. The remaining 90 percent are credit sales.[5]

About 30 percent of the firm's credit sales are collected during the month in which the sale is made, while all of the remaining 70 percent are collected during the following month. Thus, the total accounts receivable the firm can expect to collect during January are equal to 70 percent of the forecasted December credit sales plus 30 percent of the forecasted January sales:

$$(0.70 \times \$486,000) + (0.30 \times \$450,000) = \$340,200 + \$135,000$$
$$= \$475,200 \ .$$

The forecasted cash receipts for February and March are calculated the same way.

The next step in cash budgeting is the scheduling of *disbursements*, or payments the firm must make to others. Many of these items remain relatively constant and thus are relatively easy to budget. Others, however, such as the payment of accounts payable for purchases of merchandise, raw materials, and supplies, are more complicated. The key determinants of a firm's schedule of payables are the level of purchases per period and the terms given by suppliers.

---

[5]Estimated December credit sales are 90 percent of estimated December sales; that is, 0.90 × $540,000 = $486,000.

TABLE 8–5 Cash Budget

MIDWESTERN MANUFACTURING COMPANY—CENTRAL DIVISION
CASH BUDGET*
FIRST QUARTER, 19X6

	December	January	February	March
Sales	$540,000	$500,000	$550,000	$620,000
Projected cash balance, beginning of month		61,000	50,700	50,000
Receipts:				
Cash sales		50,000	55,000	62,000
Collection of accounts receivable		475,200	463,500	513,900
Total cash available		$586,200	$569,200	$625,900
Disbursements:				
Payment of accounts payable		$275,000	$302,500	$341,000
Wages and salaries		158,000	154,500	145,500
Rent		17,000	17,000	17,000
Other expenses		4,500	7,000	8,000
Taxes		81,000	—	—
Dividends on common stock		—	—	30,000
Purchase of new equipment (capital budget)		—	70,000	—
Total disbursements		$535,500	$551,000	$541,500
Excess of available cash over disbursements		$ 50,700	$ 18,200	$ 84,400
Cash loans needed to maintain balance of $50,000		—	31,800	—
Loan repayment		—	—	(31,800)
Projected cash balance, end of month		$ 50,700	$ 50,000	$ 52,600

*Prepared December 15, 19X5.

Frequently, accounts payable become due before goods are sold and cash is received; this can lead to temporary cash shortages. In fact, many companies experience cash difficulties immediately after a good sales period. Inventories are depleted and must be replenished, but cash is low because collections from the good sales period have not yet been received. Midwestern's purchases are generally estimated to be 55 percent of next month's sales. This percentage is based on the company's past experience and can vary considerably among industries and companies.

After cash receipts and disbursements have been estimated, the next step in the cash budgeting process is the determination of a desired cash balance at the beginning of each month. This minimum cash balance figure is usually a function of several factors, including the nature of the business, tax laws, and bank requirements. Table 8–5 lists Midwestern's projected cash balances for the beginnings of January, February, and March. In this example, $50,000 is assumed to be the most appropriate minimum cash balance for the first quarter, 19X6.[6]

It can be seen from Table 8–5 that Midwestern expects to need a short-

[6]Cash management is discussed further in Chapter 19.

term loan of $31,800 in February to maintain a minimum cash balance of $50,000. This is due to the fact that the company expects a decrease in the collection of accounts receivable in February, brought about by slightly lower than normal sales expected in January. In addition, the company plans to purchase new equipment in February, which will cost $70,000; this also contributes to the expected need for a short-term loan.

If the company planned to spend much more money than this on new equipment, it might decide to secure longer-term financing at this time instead of the short-term loan. The proceeds from longer-term financing could be budgeted as a separate cash receipt in February, permitting the company to separate short-term and long-term cash needs.

After projecting the need for a short-term loan in February the cash budget in Table 8–5 shows that the loan can probably be paid at the end of March, because the available cash balance of $84,400 will still be above $50,000 after repayment of $31,800. The company has indicated the repayment on the cash budget by adding another side caption: loan repayment.

Most companies follow this same general format for cash budgeting, yet few companies use *exactly* the same format. A company's actual cash budgeting system will depend on its business and its accounting procedures.

CAPITAL BUDGETS

A company's capital budget is a listing of the capital projects it plans to place in service during some future period, usually the next year. A capital project is a planned addition to the company's fixed assets that has an economic life greater than 1 year. Table 8–6 shows the 19X6 capital budget for Midwestern Manufacturing Company's Central Division.

Usually only major projects having expected expenditures above some dol-

TABLE 8–6   **Capital Budget**

MIDWESTERN MANUFACTURING COMPANY—CENTRAL DIVISION
CAPITAL BUDGET, 19X6

	Amount spent in prior years	Amount to be spent in 19X6	Amount to be spent in later years
Danville, Illinois, plant:			
Numerically controlled lathe		$ 74,000	
General office expansion and remodeling		117,000	$ 25,000
Pollution equipment		57,000	
Total projects under $50,000		165,000	
Total, Danville plant	$—	$ 413,000	$ 25,000
Racine, Wisconsin, plant:			
Fabrication department expansion	$58,000	$ 112,000	
Fabrication equipment		85,000	
New warehouse		575,000	$125,000
Total projects under $50,000		250,000	
Total, Racine plant	$58,000	$1,022,000	$125,000
Division total	$58,000	$1,435,000	$150,000

lar amount—in this case, $50,000—are listed separately on the capital budget. Smaller projects having expenditures under that dollar amount are totaled and represented by one figure.

A firm's capital budget is a summary of the analyses conducted to determine which proposed projects the company will actually decide to undertake.[7]

FUNDS FLOW ANALYSIS

Funds flow analysis is an important analytical technique used in the financial planning process. In fact, the *funds flow statement*,[8] the income statement, and the balance sheet combined constitute the major portion of a company's financial statements.

The notion of *funds* is roughly equivalent to *liquid assets*; that is, a company's liquid assets are the funds it uses to conduct business. Funds are normally defined on either a *cash basis* or a *working capital basis*. This discussion considers it on a working capital basis and considers its usefulness as a forecasting tool.

Funds flow analysis compares the *sources* of a company's funds during a particular time period—usually a year—with their *uses*. From a working capital perspective, the principal *sources* of funds are a company's operations, borrowings, proceeds from the sale of stock, and proceeds from the sale of fixed assets.

The company's operations are an *internal* source of funds, whereas the other sources are *external*. The company's operations are the most important source of funds, since the repayment of borrowings and any dividends paid to the firm's owners ultimately have to come from continuing operations, or the business cannot keep functioning.

From a working capital perspective, the principal *uses* of funds are dividends, capital expenditures, and repayment of long-term debt.

FUNDS FLOW STATEMENT

The funds flow statement is compiled from information gathered primarily from successive year-end balance sheets.[9] These comparative balance sheets are placed side by side so that *changes* that occurred during the intervening year can be clearly seen. Table 8–7 shows the Midwestern Manufacturing Company's comparative balance sheets for the years ending December 31, 19X4, and December 31, 19X5. The changes, listed in the right-hand column, can be used along with the information given in the note at the bottom of Table 8–7 to construct a funds flow statement, as shown in Table 8–8.

---

[7]Techniques of capital budgeting, also termed *capital expenditure analysis*, are dicussed in detail in Chapters 9 through 11.

[8]This is also termed the *sources and uses of funds statement*. In corporate annual reports it is referred to as the *statement of changes in financial position*.

[9]Funds flow analysis is not limited to annual financial statements. Quarterly or semiannual funds flow statements also can be developed from quarterly or semiannual balance sheet data.

TABLE 8-7   Comparative Balance Sheets ─────────────────────────────

MIDWESTERN MANUFACTURING COMPANY
COMPARATIVE BALANCE SHEETS
(IN MILLIONS OF DOLLARS)*

	12/31/X4	12/31/X5	Change
Assets			
Current assets:			
Cash	$ 3.9	$ 3.3	−0.6
Accounts receivable	5.2	5.8	+0.6
Inventories	13.7	18.0	+4.3
Total current assets	$22.8	$27.1	+4.3
Property and equipment	$40.7	$55.7	+15.0
Less: Accumulated depreciation	6.3	10.8	4.5
Net property and equipment	$34.4	$44.9	+10.5
Total assets	$57.2	$72.0	+14.8
Liabilities and Stockholders' Equity			
Current liabilities:			
Accounts payable	$ 4.0	$ 4.5	+0.5
Other current liabilities	6.0	8.2	+2.2
Total current liabilities	$10.0	$12.7	+2.7
Long-term debt	$ 8.8	$17.8	+9.0
Deferred Federal income taxes	$ 1.1	$ 1.4	+0.3
Stockholders' equity:			
Common stock	$ 1.0	$ 1.0	
Additional paid-in capital	19.0	19.0	
Retained earnings	17.3	20.1	+2.8
Total stockholders' equity	$37.3	$40.1	+2.8
Total liabilities and stockholders' equity	$57.2	$72.0	+14.8

*Net income for the year ending December 31, 19X5 totaled $5.3 million; dividends paid during the same period totaled $2.5 million; $1.0 million of long-term debt was retired in 19X5; and no fixed assets were sold during 19X5.

An analysis of the funds flow statement reveals that Midwestern generated total funds of $20.1 million during 19X5. This consisted of $10.1 million from operations and $10.0 million of long-term debt. The funds from operations were calculated by adding the company's noncash expenditures, depreciation, and deferred Federal income taxes to the net income.[10] The funds generated during 19X5 were used to pay dividends on common stock ($2.5 million), make expenditures for property and equipment ($15.0 million), and repay long-term debt ($1.0 million).

Since Midwestern's sources of funds—$20.1 million—exceeded its uses of funds—$18.5 million—during 19X5 by $1.6 million, the company's funds increased. If Midwestern were to show this increase on the comparative balance sheets, it would be described as an increase in working capital as follows:

---

[10]Many firms use accelerated depreciation methods for tax purposes and straight line depreciation for financial accounting purposes. The actual taxes currently owed are less than the total taxes calculated using straight line depreciation. The difference is a noncash adjustment to net income, appropriately termed *deferred Federal income tax*. A company's accumulated deferred Federal income taxes are listed as a liability on the balance sheet.

TABLE 8–8   Funds Flow Statement

Midwestern Manufacturing Company
Funds Flow Statement for the Year Ending December 31, 19X5
(in Millions of Dollars)*

Sources of Funds	
Funds provided from operations:	
Net income	$ 5.3
Plus: Depreciation	4.5
Deferred Federal income tax	0.3
Total funds provided from operations	$10.1
Common stock sold	—
Long-term debt incurred	10.0
Disposal of properties	—
Total sources of funds	$20.1
Uses of Funds	
Dividends	$ 2.5
Capital expenditures	15.0
Retirement of long-term debt	1.0
Total uses of funds	$18.5
Total increase (decrease) in funds (working capital)	$ 1.6

*In this example the increase in funds is an increase in working capital. Current assets increased by $4.3 million, and current liabilities increased by $2.7 million. Therefore, since working capital is defined as current assets minus current liabilities, the increase is $4.3 million − $2.7 million = $1.6 million.

	12/31/X4	12/31/X5	Change
Current assets	$22.8	$27.1	+4.3
Less: Current liabilities	10.0	12.7	+2.7
Working capital	$12.8	$14.4	+1.6

FUNDS FLOW ANALYSIS AS A
FINANCIAL PLANNING TECHNIQUE

Funds flow analysis can also be used to determine how much external financing a company will need in some future period. Suppose Midwestern is preparing its budgets for 19X6. In the fall of 19X5 the company's financial managers receive acceptable capital expenditure requests from the various divisions and plants totaling $20 million. Referring back to Table 8–3, it is evident that at this point in the budgeting process, net income for 19X6 is expected to be about $6.5 million, and depreciation is expected to be about $6.0 million. Deferred taxes are expected to be about $0.5 million. The firm's management plans to hold dividends constant at $2.5 million. Long-term debt retirement is expected to be $1.5 million, and the management feels that working capital should be increased by about $2.0 million. With this information at hand, the company's financial managers are in a good position to determine roughly how much external financing Midwestern will require during 19X6. The pro forma funds flow statement shown in Table 8–9 indicates that the firm will need $13 million in external financing during that year.

TABLE 8–9   Pro Forma Funds Flow Statement

Midwestern Manufacturing Company
Pro Forma Funds Flow Statement For 19X6
(in Millions of Dollars)

Expected Sources of Funds	
Funds expected from operations:	
Net income	$ 6.5
Plus: Depreciation	6.0
Deferred Federal income taxes	0.5
Total funds expected from operations	$13.0
External financing	X
Total expected sources of funds	$13.0 + X$
Expected Uses of Funds	
Dividends	$ 2.5
Capital expenditure requests	20.0
Retirement of long-term debt	1.5
Increases in working capital	2.0
Total expected uses of funds	$26.0

External financing required = Expected uses − Total funds expected from operations
$$= \$26.0 \text{ million} - \$13.0 \text{ million}$$
$$= \$13 \text{ million} .$$

Faced with this figure, the firm's management must consider one of the following:

- Lowering capital expenditure requests (capital rationing).
- Securing external financing.
- Some combination of both alternatives.[11]

Before making any final decision, Midwestern's management will want to perform an assessment of what capital market conditions are likely to be next year. It will also probably want to examine a *pro forma balance sheet,* that reflects the assumed funds flow planning illustrated in Table 8–9. An example of a pro forma balance sheet for the year ending December 31, 19X6, is shown in Table 8–10. This analysis allows the firm's management to examine the effects of different-sized capital budgets and various financing schemes on the company's balance sheet.

COMPUTERIZED
FINANCIAL PLANNING MODELS

In the last 25 years or so, many companies have spent considerable amounts of time and money developing models to represent various aspects of their financial planning process. Today, these representations are usually computerized and are generally called *financial planning models.* A detailed discussion of these models is beyond the scope of this text, since it requires a familiarity with a number of quantitative techniques, such as regression

[11]In this situation, a firm's dividends are normally not cut. Dividend cuts are discussed in Chapter 14.

TABLE 8-10   Pro Forma Balance Sheet

MIDWESTERN MANUFACTURING COMPANY
PRO FORMA SUMMARY BALANCE SHEET FOR THE YEAR ENDING
DECEMBER 31, 19X6

	DECEMBER 31, 19X5		DECEMBER 31, 19X6
	Actual*	Changes†	Projected
Assets			
Current assets‡	$27.1	+2.0	$29.1
Property and equipment	$55.7	+20.0	$75.7
Less: Accumulated depreciation	10.8	6.0	16.8
Net property and equipment	$44.9	+14.0	$58.9
Total assets	$72.0	+16.0	$88.0
Liabilities and Stockholders' Equity			
Current liabilities‡	$12.7	—	$12.7
Long-term debt‖	$17.8	−1.5 + 6.5	$22.8
Deferred Federal income taxes	$ 1.4	+0.5	$ 1.9
Stockholders' equity‖			
Common stock	$ 1.0	+0.5	$ 1.5
Additional paid-in capital	19.0	+6.0	25.0
Retained earnings	20.1	+4.0	24.1
Total stockholders' equity	$40.1	+10.5	$50.6
Total liabilities and stockholders' equity	$72.0	+16.0	$88.0

*From Table 8–7.
†From Table 8–9.
‡This schedule assumes that the working capital increase is added to current assets.
‖This schedule assumes that one half of the projected external financing needs are raised by issuing long-term debt and the other half are raised by selling common stock.

analysis and linear programming—topics not covered here. A brief general introduction to the topic, though, can be useful for informational purposes.

Financial planning models often are classified according to whether they are *deterministic* or *probabilistic* and whether or not they attempt to *optimize* (that is, achieve the most desirable level of) the value of some objective function, such as net income or stock price.

A *deterministic model* gives a single-number forecast of a financial variable or variables without stating anything about its probability of occurrence. An example of a deterministic model is a computerized representation of a firm's operating budget, or a *budget simulator.* Companies that employ budget simulators enter estimated future revenues and expenses into the computer and receive as output an estimate of various financial variables, such as net income and earnings per share. The model tells the company nothing about the chances of achieving these estimates, nor does it indicate whether the company will be able to manage its resources in such a way as to attain higher levels of these variables.

The main advantage of deterministic models is that they allow the user to perform *sensitivity analyses* quickly and easily. A sensitivity analysis essentially consists of rerunning the computerized model to see how much the output will change for given changes in certain inputs. For example, a company may want to know *what* net income will be *if* it discontinues some product line. Thus, sensitivity analysis is also called "what if" analysis.

In recent years some companies have started preparing different budgets to reflect different assumptions about the type of year they expect to have. For instance, a company may compile three separate budgets to reflect *pessimistic, realistic,* and *optimistic* assumptions about the coming year. Whereas these scenario analysis models are essentially deterministic, they represent a first step toward the use of probabilistic models.

Probabilistic models are becoming increasingly popular, because they provide financial decision makers with more useful information than other models. Whereas deterministic models yield single-point estimates, probabilistic models yield more general probability distributions. To illustrate, suppose a company is planning to build a new plant. Instead of estimating a single sales figure, the company's planners might estimate that there is a 25 percent chance that the firm's sales will be $2 million, a 50 percent chance that they will be $3 million, and a 25 percent chance that they will be $4 million. The use of a probabilistic planning model yields output in the form of a probability distribution, which often gives the company's planners more useful information than a deterministic model would. In the case of complex probabilistic models, more input is necessary.[12]

Optimization models give an output figure that represents the *best* level that can be obtained using the resources available to the firm. For example, consider an oil refinery whose capacity and production costs are known. By combining these known figures with estimates of the sales prices for gasoline and heating fuel, it is possible, with the use of an optimization model, to specify what output product mix will achieve an optimal level of operating income. Optimization models are not widely used in finance, even though various applications have been proposed in the financial literature.

SUMMARY

- A firm's financial manager plays an important role in the financial planning process. Basically, the financial planning process involves the development of a set of financial plans for the orderly acquisition and expenditure of funds. Pro forma financial statements are usually an integral part of any financial plan. *Pro forma financial statements* show the results of some *assumed* rather than *actual* events.

- *Financial forecasting* involves the projection and estimation of a company's future financial statements. Both the percentage of sales method and trend analysis are used for these purposes. In the case of the percentage of sales method, the amount of additional financing that will be needed to support a given future sales level is estimated. In the case of trend analysis, the future value of a financial variable is estimated by extrapolating historical data. In general, the analyst should exercise caution when using either the percentage of sales method or trend analysis, since the techniques involved in these analytical methods assume that the future will simply be a continuation of the past.

[12]Additional examples of probabilistic models are discussed in Chapter 11.

- *Budgets* are pro forma financial statements that detail a company's future plans regarding the acquisition and spending of funds. Budgets are used for *planning, coordinating,* and *controlling* the operations of the firm. Companies generally prepare and use three types of budgets: operating budgets, cash budgets, and capital budgets.

- *Operating budgets* combine sales revenue forecasts with production cost estimates to obtain a budgeted income figure.

- *Cash budgets* are projections of cash receipts and disbursements over some future time period. The steps involved in preparing a cash budget include the following:

1. Estimating cash receipts based on historical information about the collection of receivables.

2. Scheduling disbursements.

3. Determining a minimum cash balance.

- *Capital budgets* are listings of the capital projects (planned additions to the company's fixed assets) a firm plans to place in service during some future period, usually the next year.

- The *funds flow technique* analyzes the *sources* and *uses* of a firm's funds during a particular time period (usually a year). The principal sources of funds from a working capital perspective are the company's operations, borrowings, the sale of stock, and the sale of fixed assets. The principal uses of funds are dividends, capital expenditures, and repayment of long-term debt. In addition to analyzing the actual flow of funds within a company, financial planners often prepare a pro forma funds flow statement in an attempt to determine how much external financing the firm will require.

- A *financial planning model* is a computerized representation of some aspect of a firm's financial planning process. Financial planning models are usually classified as *deterministic* or *probabilistic.*

Financial Planning Models at Public Service Company of New Mexico (PNM)

Martin H. Lange
Senior Financial Analyst

Public Service Company of New Mexico (PNM) is the largest investor-owned electric utility in New Mexico. It provides electric service to many residential, commercial, and industrial customers in New Mexico. The company also makes wholesale power sales outside the state and provides water service to the city of Santa Fe, New Mexico. Recently PNM has embarked on a strategy of diversification into coal mining, real estate development, and forest products. As a public utility, PNM is closely regulated by the New Mexico Public Service Commission and the Federal Energy Regulatory Commission.

Because of the long lead times involved in building a new electric plant, long- and short-range financial planning and forecasting is essential. The company's financial planning model allows PNM to forecast, integrate and evaluate the impact of projected revenues, operating and maintenance expenses, and capital-spending requirements on funding requirements, earnings, coverages, and other financial measures.

The development of financial model data includes six principal sources of input:

1. Revenue projections are based on sales and capacity use (load) forecasts and existing rate levels and structures.

2. a. Operating and maintenance costs not related to fuel are developed by the operating divisions on a once-a-year basis. These expenses do not change very significantly due to sales or load changes and consequently are not changed for most studies.

   b. Fuel and purchased power expenses are developed through the use of a production-costing program that uses a probabilistic approach to the economic dispatch of sources of power to meet a given load. Detailed estimates of fuel consumption, load-related maintenance costs, and unit usage for a generating system for a specified period of time are provided, as well as energy purchase requirements from other utilities with which PNM is interconnected.

3. Construction expenditures are based upon all known and projected construction activities with expected completion dates. The bulk of construction expenditures are related to the construction of generating and transmission facilities. These are planned based on an analysis of the long-range forecast of load and energy requirements, present system characteristics, and the most cost-efficient method of meeting future loads.

4. Existing permanent financing (that is, long-term debt and equity levels), embedded costs of debt and preferred stock, plus interest and cash dividend payment requirements and timing are input into the model.

5. Existing plant characteristics, including plant in service balances, book and tax depreciation rates, construction work in progress balances, allowable investment tax credit rates, property tax rates, and planned plant retirements are important model inputs.

6. Financial assumptions, including general guidelines for external financing requirements, the mix and timing of financings, short-term debt levels, projected short- and long-term interest rates, dividend policy, and income tax rates and methodology are also considered by the model. Included as inputs are beginning balances of certain income statement, balance sheet, and funds flow accounts necessary for creating projected financial statements.

The relative magnitude of PNM's construction program and the volatility of economic conditions in recent years have increased the importance of the use of financial models. Various "what if" scenarios can be constructed in a minimal amount of time in response to management's information needs and the mandates of the financial markets. Using these six sources of input, an optimal plan for any given set of conditions can be constructed. A most likely scenario is finally selected and used as the basis for the company's financial planning and communications to outside analysts, investors, and regulatory agencies.

Another important output of the financial models is information regarding future rate levels. Based on existing rates, fuel adjustment projections, and anticipated additional revenue requirements, a forecast of average rate levels by customer class is prepared. These projected rates summarize the impact on PNM's customers of a given capital expansion plan and provide important feedback to the load forecasting effort.

As a part of the financial planning process, PNM regularly prepares a 5-year financial forecast, which details the capital requirements on a yearly basis, the sources of internal cash generation, and the external financing that will be required. A copy of the 5-year forecast and some of the assumptions that went into that forecast follows on pp. 240–241.

QUESTIONS AND TOPICS FOR DISCUSSION

1. What are pro forma financial statements?

2. What is the percentage of sales forecasting method? What are some of the limitations financial analysts should be aware of in applying this method?

3. What is an operating budget? What are the usual steps involved in preparing an operating budget?

4. What is a cash budget? What are the usual steps involved in preparing a cash budget?

5. What is a capital budget?

6. Describe funds flow analysis. What are the principal sources and uses of funds within a firm?

7. Illustrate how funds flow analysis can be used as a financial planning technique.

8. What are financial planning models, and how can they be classified?

PUBLIC SERVICE COMPANY OF NEW MEXICO
CAPITAL REQUIREMENTS AND INTERNAL CASH
(Millions of Dollars)

	Actual			Forecast			Total Forecast
	1982	1983	1984	1985	1986	1987	1983-1987
CAPITAL REQUIREMENTS:							
Capital Expenditures	$336	$320	$277	$144	$123	$ 131	$ 995 [a]
Construction AFUDC	(65)	(53)	(41)	(23)	(22)	(12)	(151)
Cash Expenditures	$271	$267	$236	$121	$101	$119	$ 844
Debt Maturities, Sinking Funds, and Other Cash Requirements	9	4	138 [b]	55 [c]	8	11	216
TOTAL CAPITAL REQUIREMENTS	$280	$271	$374	$176	$109	$ 130	$1,060
INTERNAL CASH GENERATION:							
Depreciation and Amortization	$ 38	$ 47	$ 57	$ 68	$ 72	$ 79	$ 323
Deferred Income Tax – Net [d]	4	21	27	31	35	36	150
ITC – Net [e]	17	10	5	6	8	20	49
Other [f]	8	(13)	(7)	(15)	3	17	(15)
Total	$ 67	$ 65	$ 82	$ 90	$118	$ 152	$ 507
Construction AFUDC	(65)	(53)	(41)	(23)	(22)	(12)	(151)
Total Internal Cash Generation	$ 2	$ 12	$ 41	$ 67	$ 96	$ 140	$ 356
Percent of Total Capital Requirements	0.7	4.4	11.0	38.1	88.1	107.7	33.6
Temporary Investments Utilization	$ 0	$ 33	$ 26	$ 0	$ 0	$ 0	$ 59
Outside Financing Requirements	$278	$226	$307	$109	$ 13	$ (10)	$ 645
Total Sources of Capital	$280	$271	$374	$176	$109	$ 130	$1,060
FINANCING PROGRAM:							
Common Stock	$184	$ 39					$ 39
Preferred Stock	35	0					0
First Mortgage Bonds	60	110	**TYPE NOT DETERMINED**				110
Pollution Control Draws	44	41					41
Short-term Borrowing (Net)	(45)	36					36
Type Not Determined	0	0	307	109	13	(10)	419
TOTAL FINANCING PROGRAM	$278	$226	$307	$109	$ 13	$ (10)	$ 645

NOTES ON STATEMENTS

   (a) Includes $114 million of subsidiary expenditures.
   (b) Includes refunding of June 1981 Pollution Control Revenue Bonds ($130 million).
   (c) Includes refunding of September 1980 First Mortgage Bonds ($50 million).
   (d) Assumes ACRS tax lives where applicable.
   (e) Assumes ITC applied only to current portion of Federal income tax by order of the NMPSC and the FERC.
   (f) Other includes annual additions to retained earnings, miscellaneous timing differences, and subsidiary internal cash generation.

PROBLEMS*

1. Using the percentage of sales method, calculate the external financing needed for the Industrial Supply Company (Table 8–1) if the following sales levels are expected to be reached in 1 year:
   a. $6.0 million.
   b. $3.2 million.
   Assume the company continues its policy of not paying dividends. Show the pro

*Problems in color have check answers provided at the end of the book.

PNM OPERATIONS

	Actual	Forecast				
	1982	**1983**	**1984**	**1985**	**1986**	**1987**
SALES – GWh						
Residential	1,132	1,161	1,233	1,314	1,419	1,550
Commercial	1,547	1,628	1,674	1,806	1,984	2,219
Industrial	878	941	1,053	1,096	1,148	1,226
Other	207	199	203	210	221	235
Sales for Resale	2,033	2,024	1,940	911	927	956
Subtotal Firm Sales	5,798	5,953	6,103	5,338	5,698	6,185
Additional Sales[a]	831	961	1,741	3,802	3,518	3,423
Total (GWh)	6,629	6,914	7,844	9,140	9,216	9,608
Percent Change in Total Sales (Year to Year)	15.09	4.30	13.45	16.52	0.83	4.25
CUSTOMERS – Average (x000)						
Residential	198.2	204.1	214.4	224.0	234.2	244.8
Commercial	21.6	22.4	23.5	24.4	25.2	26.1
Other (Including Industrial, Sales for Resale, and other Miscellaneous Customers)	.7	.7	.7	.7	.7	.7
Total	220.5	227.2	238.6	249.1	260.1	271.6
Percent Change in Total Customers (Year to Year)	2.23	3.04	5.02	4.40	4.42	4.42
NET EFFECTIVE GENERATION – MW		(at time of system peak)				
Generating Capacity Existing – Net of Retirements and Deratings	1,043	1,473	1,471	1,601	1,731	1,731
New – Net Rating[b]	432	0	130	130	0	130
Purchase (Sales) Known[c]	(216)	(121)	(251)	(251)	(251)	(251)
Inventoried Capacity[d]	(105)	(105)	(99)	(323)	(268)	(301)
Total Capacity – MW	1,154	1,247	1,251	1,157	1,212	1,309
Unadjusted System Peak Load – MW (Summer)[e]	961	1,022	1,038	960	1,026	1,118
Load Management Peak Reductions	(4)	(16)	(23)	(36)	(47)	(61)
Adjusted Peak[f]	957	1,006	1,015	924	979	1,057
Annual Percent Increase in Peak	(3.5)	5.1	0.9	(9.0)	6.0	8.0
Reserve Margin:						
MW	197	241	236	233	233	252
Percent	20.6	24.0	23.3	25.2	23.8	23.8
PERCENT FUEL MIX – MMBtu						
Coal	88.99	95.63	88.16	82.59	80.22	73.92
Gas	9.99	3.35	3.02	1.05	1.90	0.93
Oil	1.02	0.84	0.76	0.65	0.67	0.64
Nuclear	0.00	0.18	8.06	15.71	17.21	24.51

NOTES ON OPERATIONS:

(a) Includes energy sales to LADWP during 1980 through 1982 period, contingent sales commencing in 1982 to SDG&E, and other energy sales for 1982 through 1987. Both capacity and energy deliveries to SDG&E are subject to certain constraints relating to the operation of the Palo Verde Nuclear Generating Station (PVNGS) and the San Juan Plant.

(b) Assumes PVNGS Units 1, 2, and 3 become dependable capacity for 1984, 1985, and 1987, respectively.

(c) Includes 1982 purchase of 20 MW from City of Farmington. For the period 1982 through April 1988, 236 MW of contingent base load capacity are to be sold to SDG&E (1983 sale reduced to 106 MW due to delay in PVNGS Unit 1). Commencing in 1983, 15 MW of contingent peaking capacity will be sold to Plains. Not included is 35 MW sale of interruptible power to California Municipals from 1983 to 1986, 50 MW intended sale to EPE 1983 through 1984 and 200 MW intended sale to SPS 1985 through 1990.

(d) Inventoried capacity represents the portion of new generating capacity which is not required by, nor committed to, the service of firm customers. This capacity is being inventoried until it is required by our firm customers. Energy sales associated with this capacity are included in "Additional Sales."

(e) Peak load declines in 1985 due to reductions in contract demand of Plains and TNP. Plains reduction occurs due to in-service addition of Plains Escalante Station.

(f) Actual 1982 summer peak occurred on July 15, 1982.

forma balance sheets as of December 31, 19X5, assuming these sales levels are reached. Assume next year's net income will be $200,000 in both cases.

2. Using the percentage of sales method, calculate the external financing needed over the next 2 years for the Industrial Supply Company (Table 8–1) if a sales level of $6.0 million is expected to be reached in 2 years. Assume that the company expects net income in the first year to be $200,000 and in the second year to be $225,000.

3. Using the percentage of sales method, calculate the external financing needed over the next year for the Baldwin Products Company if a sales level of $6.0 million is expected to be reached in 1 year. The company expects net income during the next year to equal $400,000. During the past several years the company has been paying $50,000 in dividends to its stockholders. The company expects to continue this policy for at least the next year. The actual balance sheet and income statement for Baldwin during 19X8 is provided below. Show the pro forma balance sheet for the company as of December 31, 19X9, assuming a sales level of $6.0 million is reached. Assume that the external financing needed is obtained in the form of additional notes payable.

BALDWIN PRODUCTS COMPANY
BALANCE SHEET
AS OF DECEMBER 31, 19X8

Cash	$ 200,000	Accounts payable	$ 600,000
Accounts receivable	400,000	Notes payable	500,000
Inventories	1,200,000	Long-term debt	200,000
Fixed assets, net	500,000	Stockholders' equity	1,000,000
Total assets	$2,300,000	Total liabilities and equity	$2,300,000

INCOME STATEMENT
FOR THE YEAR ENDED DECEMBER 31, 19X8

Sales	$4,000,000
Expenses,including interest and taxes	$3,700,000
Net income	$ 300,000

4. This problem is an extension of Problem 3. Suppose that the Baldwin Products' management feels that the average collection period on its additional sales—that is, sales over $4 million—will be 60 days instead of the current level. By what amount will this increase in the average collection period increase the external financing needed by the company over the next year?

5. This problem is an extension of Problem 3. Suppose that the Baldwin Products' banker requires the company to maintain a current ratio equal to 1.6 or greater. What is the maximum amount of additional external financing that can be in the form of bank borrowings (notes payable)? What other potential sources of financing are available to the company?

6. Prepare a cash budget for Atlas Products, Inc., for the first quarter of 19X2, based on the following information.

The budgeting section of the corporate finance department of Atlas Products, Inc., has received the following sales estimates from the marketing department:

	Total Sales	Credit Sales
December 19X1	$825,000	$770,000
January 19X2	730,000	690,000
February 19X2	840,000	780,000
March 19X2	920,000	855,000

The company has found that, on the average, about 25 percent of its credit sales are collected during the month when the sale is made, and the remaining 75 percent of credit sales are collected during the month following the sale. As a result, the company uses these figures for budgeting.

The company estimates its purchases at 60 percent of next month's sales, and payments for those purchases are budgeted to lag the purchases by 1 month.

Various disbursements have been estimated as follows:

	January	February	March
Wages and salaries	$250,000	$290,000	$290,000
Rent	27,000	27,000	27,000
Other expenses	10,000	12,000	14,000

In addition, a tax payment of $105,000 is due on January 15, and $40,000 in dividends will be declared in January and paid in March. Also, the company has ordered a $75,000 piece of equipment. Delivery is scheduled for early January, and payment will be due in February.

The company's projected cash balance at the beginning of January is $100,000, and the company desires to maintain a balance of $100,000 at the end of each month.

7. Prepare a funds flow statement (defined in terms of net working capital) for the Corting Manufacturing Corporation for the year ending December 19X2, based on the following comparative balance sheets.

CORTING MANUFACTURING CORPORATION
COMPARATIVE BALANCE SHEETS
(IN MILLIONS OF DOLLARS)*

	December 31, 19X1	December 31, 19X2
Assets		
Current assets:		
Cash	$ 4.9	$ 0.8
Accounts receivable	7.2	7.5
Inventories	13.8	14.5
Total current assets	$25.9	$ 22.8
Property and equipment	$80.7	$115.0
Less: Accumulated depreciation	16.3	25.8
Net property and equipment	$64.4	$ 89.2
Total assets	$90.3	$112.0
Liabilities and Stockholders' Equity		
Current liabilities:		
Accounts payable	$ 8.0	$ 9.5
Other current liabilities	6.0	8.2
Total current liabilities	$14.0	$ 17.7
Long term debt	$18.8	$ 31.8
Deferred Federal income taxes	$ 1.2	$ 1.4
Stockholders' equity:		
Common stock	$ 3.0	$ 3.0
Additional paid-in capital	29.0	29.0
Retained earnings	24.3	29.1
Total stockholders' equity	$56.3	$ 61.1
Total liabilities and stockholders' equity	$90.3	$112.0

*Net income for the year ended December 31, 19X2, totaled $8.3 million; dividends paid during the same period totaled $3.5 million; $2.0 million of long-term debt was retired in 19X2; and fixed assets were sold during 19X2 for $1.0 million.

8. The Norfolk Corporation is considering a $200 million expansion (capital expenditure) program next year. The company wants to know approximately how much, if any, external financing will be required if it decides to go through with the expansion program. Next year the company expects to earn $80 million after interest and taxes. The company also expects to maintain its present level of dividends, which is $15 million. If the expansion program is accepted, the company expects its working capital requirements to increase by approximately $20 million next year to a total of $230 million. Long-term debt retirement obligations total $10 million for next year, and depreciation is expected to be $80 million. The company does not expect to sell any fixed assets next year.

AN INTEGRATIVE CASE PROBLEM

Financial Analysis and Control

Last year (19X2) Midwest Chemicals, Inc. (MCI), undertook a $10 million plant expansion and modernization program. The firm had originally planned to finance the program partially from the sale of new common stock. However, due to depressed stock prices, a stock offering was not feasible at that time, Instead, the firm financed the entire $10 million with a 5-year term loan from a large insurance company. Because of tight money conditions in the economy and the relatively large amount of debt in its capital structure, MCI was required to pay 14 percent interest on the term loan. MCI also has a mortgage loan of $10 million outstanding, which is being repaid in annual installments of $1 million (due on December 30 each year) plus 10 percent interest. The balance sheet and income statement for the current year (19X3), along with some relevant industry ratios, are shown in the tables.

MIDWEST CHEMICALS, INC.
(A) BALANCE SHEETS AS OF DECEMBER 31, 19X3
(IN THOUSANDS OF DOLLARS)

Assets		
Cash	$ 2,000	
Accounts receivable	11,000	
Inventories	11,000	
Total current assets		$24,000
Plant and equipment	$35,000	
Less: Accumulated depreciation	15,000	
Net plant and equipment		20,000
Total assets		$44,000
Liabilities and Owners' Equity		
Accounts payable		$ 9,000
Current portion of motgage loan ($i = 10\%$)		1,000
Total current liabilities		$10,000
Mortgage loan ($i = 10\%$)		8,000
Term loan		10,000
Stockholders' equity (common stock and retained earnings)		16,000
Total liabilities and stockholders' equity		$44,000

(B) INCOME STATEMENT FOR THE YEAR ENDING
DECEMBER 31, 19X3
(IN THOUSANDS OF DOLLARS)

Sales		$74,000
Less: Raw materials	$38,000	
Labor	5,000	
Depreciation	3,000	
Cost of goods sold		46,000
Gross profit		$28,000
Less: Selling and administrative expenses		22,600
Earnings before interest and taxes		$ 5,400
Less: Interest expense		2,400
Net income before taxes		$ 3,000
Less: Federal and state income tax (40%)		1,200
Net income after taxes		$ 1,800
Less: Common stock dividends (1,000,000 × $1.00/ share)		1,000
Net additions to retained earnings		$ 800

Ratio	Industry Average
Current	2.7 times
Quick	1.7 times
Debt-to-equity	86%
Times interest earned (EBIT ÷ Interest charges)	5.4 times
Net profit margin on sales	3.77%
Return on stockholders' equity	13.5%

Conditions in the capital markets have improved considerably since last year (that is, the price of MCI common stock has risen and interest rates have fallen). The treasurer of MCI has decided that this would be an opportune time to float (that is, sell) an issue of common stock and use the proceeds to reduce the amount of high-cost debt in the firm's capital structure. Specifically, the firm plans to sell 200,000 shares of new common stock at a net price of $25 per share to yield the firm $5 million. The funds would be used to repay one-half of the term loan, thus reducing its interest expenses and improving its financial position.

The MCI economists have forecast a 10 percent increase in the firm's sales for next year (19X4). Raw material, labor, and selling and administrative expenses are also expected to increase by 10 percent next year. Depreciation expenses next year are anticipated to be $2 million. The firm's (combined) Federal and state income tax rate is expected to remain at 40 percent next year. The board of directors of the firm is expected to increase the dividend rate by 10 percent to $1.10 per share.

Receivables and inventories are expected to rise by 10 percent next year as a result of the forecasted sales increase. The treasurer feels that the firm's minimum cash needs can be met with the existing $2 million balance during the coming year. New additions to plant and equipment totaling $1 million are planned during the coming year. The firm has been paying many of its trade creditors beyond the due date and would like to avoid this situation in the future. To accomplish this, the firm wants to hold its accounts payable at $9 million during the coming year, even though its raw material purchases will increase.

1. Prepare a pro forma income statement for MCI for 19X4.

2. Prepare a pro forma balance sheet for MCI as of December 31, 19X4. Use "additional short-term debt" as the balancing account to reflect the need for additional financing. (HINT: First determine MCI's assets and then determine liabilities and net worth. Total assets should equal $45,200(000).)

3. How much additional financing (beyond that generated from operations) is required to meet the needs of the firm? What are some possible sources of these funds?

4. Prepare a pro forma funds flow statement for 19X4.

5. Using a ratio analysis of the firm's pro forma statements for 19X4, evaluate the impact of the proposed financing plan on the financial condition of the firm.

6. What are the reasons why the percentage of sales forecasting method cannot be used in this case?

■ CALCULATOR APPLICATIONS ■

This section illustrates the use of the Texas Instruments Professional Business Analyst (BA-55) calculator to do simple linear trend line forecasting. The statistical technique used is least squares trend analysis.

LINEAR TREND LINE ANALYSIS

The WKRP Corporation had the following sales levels over the past 7 years:

Year	Sales (in Millions of Dollars)
1977	5.0
1978	5.5
1979	5.8
1980	5.7
1981	6.8
1982	7.6
1983	8.2

You desire to predict the sales for WKRP in 1984 and 1985.

Procedure	Press	Display
1. Clear calculator and mode registers; choose two decimal places.	on/c 2nd CLmode 2nd Fix 2	0.00

2. Press ⌷2nd⌷ **Mode**   ⌷2nd⌷ **Mode**   0.00
until the STAT
indicator is
displayed.

3. Enter the data.   1977 ⌷x⇄y⌷ 5.0
The calculator   ⌷Σ+⌷   1.00
displays the   5.5 ⌷Σ+⌷   2.00
current number of   5.8 ⌷Σ+⌷   3.00
data entries.)   5.7 ⌷Σ+⌷   4.00
     6.8 ⌷Σ+⌷   5.00
     7.6 ⌷Σ+⌷   6.00
     8.2 ⌷Σ+⌷   7.00

4. Predict earnings   1984 ⌷2nd⌷ **Fcst Y**   **8.49**
for 1984 and 1985.   1985 ⌷2nd⌷ **Fcst Y**   **9.01**

5. Determine the   ⌷2nd⌷ **Corr**   **0.96**
correlation of time
to earnings growth
for WKRP. This
provides an
indication of the
past accuracy of
this trend line
forecasting model.

In this case, the model was extremely accurate, with a correlation of 0.96. If the conditions that influenced sales growth in the past do not change significantly in the future, this trend line forecasting model will be very accurate for making future forecasts.

ADDITIONAL READINGS AND REFERENCES

Bacon, Jeremy. *Managing the Budget Function.* Studies in Business Policy, Report 131. New York: National Industrial Conference Board, Inc., 1970.

Chambers, John C., Mullick, Satinder K., and Smith, Donald D. "How to Choose the Right Forecasting Technique." *Harvard Business Review* 49 (July–Aug. 1971): 45–74.

Dearden, John. "The Case Against ROI Control." *Harvard Business Review* 47 (May–June 1969): 124–35.

Gentry, James A., and Pyhrr, Stephen A. "Simulating an EPS Growth Model." *Financial Management* 2 (Summer 1973): 68–75.

Gershefski, George W. "Building a Corporate Financial Model." *Harvard Business Review* 47 (July–Aug. 1969): 61–72.

Gilmore, F. F. "Formulating Strategy in Smaller Companies." *Harvard Business Review* 49 (May 1971): 71–81.

Hamermesh, Richard G. "Responding to Divisional Profit Crises." *Harvard Business Review* 55 (March–April 1977): 124–130.

Hunt, Pearson. "Funds Position: Keystone in Financial Planning." *Harvard Business Review* 53 (May–June 1975): 106–115.

Judelson, David N. "Financial Controls That Work." *Fiancial Executive* 45 (Jan. 1977): 22–27.

Maier, Steven F., and Vander Weide, James H. "A Practical Approach to Short-Run Financial Planning." *Financial Management* (Winter 1978): 10–16.

Myers, Stewart C., and Pogue, Gerald A. "The Programming Approach to Corporate Financial Management." *Journal of Finance* 29 (May 1974): 579–699.

Smith, Gary, and Brainard, William. "The Value of A Priori Information in Estimating a Financial Model." *Journal of Finance* 31 (Dec. 1976): 1299–1322.

Warren, James M., and Shelton, John P. "A Simultaneous Equation Approach to Financial Planning." *Journal of Finance* 26 (Dec. 1971): 1123–1142.

Weston, J. Fred. "Forecasting Financial Requirements." *Accounting Review* 33 (July 1958): 427–440.

PART FOUR

The Capital Investment Decision

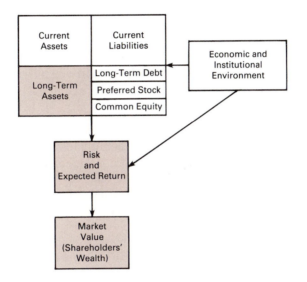

This part of the text looks at the financial management of the long-term asset portion of a firm's balance sheet. Investments in these assets (for example, property, plant, and equipment) have a major impact on a firm's future stream of earnings and the risk of those earnings. As such, the long-term investment (capital budgeting) decision has a significant effect on the value of the firm. Chapter 9 deals with the measurement of cash flows from long-term investments. Chapter 10 analyzes various investment decision criteria in light of the wealth maximization objective of the firm. Chapter 11 extends the analysis to consider techniques to account for differential levels of risk among projects.

Capital Budgeting and Cash Flow Analysis

The Results of Inadequate Cash Flow Analysis:
Lockheed's Tri-Star Project

In 1971 a series of Congressional hearings was held to discuss whether Lockheed should be given a $250 million guarantee for additional bank credit. The firm needed the loan to complete its Tri-Star program, which involved the production of its L-1011 wide-bodied commercial jet. At the time, Lockheed was experiencing a serious liquidity crisis caused primarily by cost overruns incurred on military projects and its stock price had dropped from $73 to $3 per share.

Lockheed argued that the Tri-Star program was basically sound. The firm estimated that in order to break even on the program, it would have to sell between 195 and 200 aircraft. At the time of the hearing, it had firm orders for, or options on, 178 aircraft. This made the firm confident that the project would be successful, and it was willing to commit as much as $2.5 billion to it over a 10-year period.

Unfortunately, Lockheed's analysis did not take into account the *opportunity cost* of the funds committed to the project. In other words, the firm did not consider the rate of return that could have been earned on the $2.5 billion had it been invested in some alternative program. If Lockheed had performed a correct analysis of the Tri-Star project, it would have been evident that the breakeven point was considerably higher than the number of aircraft the firm could reasonably expect to sell. In fact, the net present value of the project would have been negative at the 195 to 200 output level, and Lockheed would have been forced to drop it. (Lockheed actually produced about 240 of the planes.)

The firm received the loan guarantee, however, and continued to produce the L-1011 jets. The project has since proved unprofitable, resulting in $120 million in losses in 1977 alone. A more complete analysis of the project's *total* costs and expected revenues may have permitted Lockheed to avert some these losses. In late 1981 Lockheed announced the phasing out of the L-1011 program. In that year it recorded an additional $396 million loss on the program.

This chapter develops the principles of capital investment analysis—with emphasis being placed on the estimation of the cash flows from a project. Chapter 10 considers appropriate decision criteria in the capital budgeting process.

GLOSSARY OF NEW TERMS

ACRS depreciation   the Accelerated Cost Recovery System of depreciation, established in 1981.

Capital rationing   the process of limiting the number of capital expenditure projects because of insufficient funds to finance all projects that otherwise meet the firm's criteria for acceptability.

Contingent project   a project whose acceptance depends on the adoption of one or more other projects.

Depreciation   the systematic allocation of the cost of an asset over its expected economic life or some other period of time for financial reporting purposes, tax purposes, or both.

Independent project   a project whose acceptance or rejection does not directly result in the elimination of other projects from consideration.

Mutually exclusive project   a project whose acceptance precludes the acceptance of one or more alternative projects.

Net cash flow   cash inflow minus cash outflow. It is often measured as income after tax plus noncash expenses associated with a particular investment project.

Net investment   the net cash outlay required at the beginning of an investment project.

Normal project   a project whose cash flow stream requires an inital outlay of funds followed by a series of positive net cash inflows. This is also sometimes called a *conventional project.*

INTRODUCTION

This is the first of several chapters that explicitly deal with the financial management of the assets on a firm's balance sheet. In this and the following two chapters we consider the management of long-term assets, that is, the capital budgeting decision. Later in the book (Chapters 18 to 21) the emphasis shifts to the management of short-term assets, that is, the working capital decision.

A *capital expenditure* is a cash outlay that is expected to generate a flow

251

of future cash benefits lasting longer than 1 year. It is distinguished from a normal operating expenditure, which is expected to result in cash benefits during the coming 1-year period. (The choice of a 1-year period is arbitrary, but it does serve as a useful guideline.)

There are several different types of cash outlays that may be classified as capital expenditures and evaluated using the framework of capital budgeting models, including the following:

- The purchase of a new piece of equipment, real estate, or a building in order to expand an existing product or service line or enter a new line of business.

- The replacement of an existing capital asset, such as a drill press.

- Expenditures for an advertising campaign.

- Expenditures for a research and development program.

- Investments in permanent increases of target inventory levels or levels of accounts receivable.

- Investments in employee education and training.

- The refunding of an old bond issue with a new, lower interest issue.

- Lease-versus-buy analysis.

- Merger and acquisition evaluation.

Capital expenditures are important to a firm both because they require sizable cash outlays and because they have a long-range impact on the firm's performance. Table 9–1 summarizes the capital expenditures made by U.S. firms during 1980, 1981, and 1982. Total capital expenditures of all industries in the United States during 1982 exceeded $323 *billion* dollars. During 1982 Exxon earned about $3.9 billion after taxes and made outlays for new plant facilities and equipment in excess of $7.9 billion. U.S. Steel had 1982 losses of nearly $100 *million*, yet it made $1.7 *billion* in capital expenditures that year.

TABLE 9–1   Capital Expenditures Made by U.S. Firms

Industry	(in Billions of Dollars)		
	1980	1981	1982*
Total nonfarm business	$295.63	$321.49	$323.66
Manufacturing	115.81	126.79	124.23
Durable goods	58.91	61.84	59.50
Nondurable goods	56.90	64.95	64.74
Mining	13.51	16.86	16.48
Transportation	12.09	12.05	12.33
Railroad	4.25	4.24	4.51
Air	4.01	3.81	3.86
Other	3.82	4.00	3.95
Public utilities	35.44	38.40	40.90
Electric	28.12	29.74	32.29
Gas and other	7.32	8.65	8.61
Communication and other	36.99	41.06	42.33
Trade and services	81.79	86.33	87.40

NOTE: *Estimated.
SOURCE: *Survey of Current Business* (U.S. Department of Commerce), September 1982.

A firm's capital expenditures affect its future profitability and, when taken together, essentially plot the company's future direction by determining which products will be produced, which markets will be entered, where production facilities will be located, and what type of technology will be used. Capital expenditure decision making is important for another reason as well. Specifically, it is often difficult, if not impossible, to reverse a major capital expenditure without incurring considerable additional expense. For example, if a firm acquires highly specialized production facilities and equipment, it must recognize that there may be no ready used-equipment market in which to dispose of them if they do not generate the desired future cash flows. For these reasons, a firm's management should establish a number of definite procedures to follow when analyzing capital expenditure projects. Choosing from among such projects is the objective of capital budgeting models.

KEY TERMS AND CONCEPTS IN CAPITAL BUDGETING

Before proceeding with the discussion of the capital budgeting process, it is necessary to introduce a number of terms and concepts encountered in subsequent chapters.

COST OF CAPITAL

A firm's *cost of capital* is defined as the cost of the funds supplied to it. It is also termed the *required rate of return,* since it specifies the minimum necessary rate of return required by the firm's investors. In this context, the cost of capital provides the firm with a basis for choosing among various capital investment projects. In this and the following two chapters it is assumed that the cost of capital is a known value. Chapter 12 explores the methods used to determine the cost of capital.

HOW PROJECTS ARE CLASSIFIED

A firm usually encounters several different types of projects when making capital expenditure decisions, including *independent projects, mutually exclusive projects,* and *contingent projects.*

Independent projects   An independent project is one whose acceptance or rejection does not directly eliminate other projects from consideration. For example, a firm may want to install a new telephone communications system in its headquarters and replace a drill press during approximately the same time. In the absence of a constraint on the availability of funds, both projects could be adopted if they meet minimum investment criteria.

Mutually exclusive projects   A mutually exclusive project is one whose acceptance precludes the acceptance of one or more alternative proposals. Since two mutually exclusive projects have the capacity to perform the same function for a firm, only one should be chosen. For example, Volkswagen was faced with deciding whether it should locate its U.S. assembly plant in Cleveland, Ohio, or New Stanton, Pennsylvania. It ultimately chose the New Stanton site, and this precluded the Cleveland alternative.

Contingent projects   A contingent project is one whose acceptance is dependent on the adoption of one or more other projects. For example, the installation of pollution control equipment in a new plant is contingent upon the acceptance of that new plant as a desirable investment. When a firm is considering contingent projects, it is best to consider together all projects that are dependent on one another and treat them as a single project for purposes of evaluation.

AVAILABILITY OF FUNDS

When a firm has adequate funds to invest in all projects that meet some capital budgeting selection criterion, the firm is said to be operating without a *funds constraint.* Frequently, however, the total initial cost of the acceptable projects in the absence of a funds constraint is greater than the total funds the firm has chosen to invest in capital projects. This necessitates *capital rationing*, or the setting of limits on capital expenditures, and results in some special capital budgeting problems.[1]

BASIC FRAMEWORK FOR
CAPITAL BUDGETING

According to economic theory, a firm should operate at the point where the marginal cost of an additional unit of output just equals the marginal revenue derived from the output. Following this rule leads to *profit maximization.* This principle may also be applied to capital budgeting decisions. In this context, a firm's marginal revenue is the rates of return earned on succeeding investments, and marginal cost may be defined as the firm's *marginal cost of capital* (MCC), that is, the cost of successive increments of capital acquired by the firm.

Figure 9–1 illustrates a simplified capital budgeting model. The projects under consideration are indicated by lettered bars on the graph.

Project A requires an investment of $2 million and is expected to generate a 24 percent rate of return. Project B will cost $1 million ($3 million minus $2 million on the horizontal axis) and is expected to generate a 22 percent rate of return, and so on. The projects are arranged in descending order according to their expected rates of return, in recognition of the fact that no firm has an inexhaustible supply of projects offering high expected rates of return. Typically, a firm will invest in its best projects first—such as Project A—before moving on to less attractive alternatives.

The MCC schedule represents the marginal cost of capital to the firm. Note that the schedule increases as more funds are sought in the capital markets. The reasons for this include the following:

---

[1] These are treated in Chapter 10.

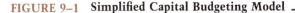

FIGURE 9–1 **Simplified Capital Budgeting Model**

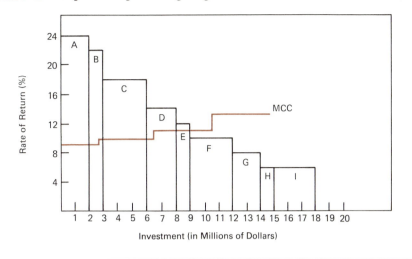

- Investors' expectations about the firm's ability to successfully undertake a large number of new projects.

- The business risk to which the firm is exposed because of its particular line of business.

- The firm's financial risk, which is due to its capital structure.

- The supply and demand for investment capital in the capital market.

- The cost of selling new stock, which is greater than the cost of retained earnings.

The basic capital budgeting model indicates that in principle, the firm should undertake Projects A, B, C, D, and E, since the expected returns from each project exceed the firm's marginal cost of capital. Unfortunately, however, financial decision making in practice is not this simple. Some practical problems are encountered in trying to apply this model, including the following:

- At any point in time a firm will probably not know all of the capital projects available to it. In most firms, capital expenditures are proposed continually, based on results of research and development programs, changing market conditions, new technologies, corporate planning efforts, and so on. Thus, a schedule of projects similar to Figure 9–1 will probably be incomplete at the time the firm makes its capital expenditure decisions.

- The shape of the MCC schedule itself may be difficult to determine.[2]

- In most cases a firm can make only uncertain estimates of a project's future costs and revenues (and, consequently, its rate of return). Some projects will be more risky than others.

_____
[2]The problems and techniques involved in estimating a firm's cost of capital are discussed in Chapter 12.

In spite of these and other problems, all firms make capital investment decisions. This chapter and the following two chapters provide tools that may be applied to the capital budgeting decision-making process.

Briefly, that process consists of four important steps:

1. Generating capital investment project proposals.
2. Estimating cash flows.
3. Evaluating alternatives and selecting projects to be implemented.
4. Reviewing, or postauditing, a project after it has been implemented.

The remainder of this chapter is devoted to a discussion of the first two steps.

GENERATING CAPITAL INVESTMENT PROJECT PROPOSALS

Ideas for new capital investments can come from many sources, both inside and ouside a firm. Proposals may originate at all levels of the organization—from factory workers up to the board of directors. Most large and medium-sized firms allocate the responsibility for identifying and analyzing capital expenditures to specific staff groups. These can include cost accounting, industrial engineering, marketing research, research and development, and corporate planning groups. In most firms, systematic procedures are established to assist in the search and analysis steps. For example, many firms provide detailed forms that the originator of a capital expenditure proposal must complete. These forms normally request information on the project's initial cost, the revenues it is expected to generate, and how it will affect the firm's overall operating expenses. An example of such a form is shown in Figure 9–2. These data are then channeled to a reviewer or group of reviewers at a higher level in the firm for analysis and possible acceptance or rejection.

Where a proposal goes for review often depends on how the particular project is *classified.*

CLASSIFYING INVESTMENT PROJECTS

As noted earlier, there are several types of capital expenditures. These can be grouped into *projects generated by growth opportunities, projects generated by cost reduction opportunities,* and *projects generated in order to meet legal requirements and health and safety standards.*

Projects generated by growth opportunities   Assume that a firm produces a particular product that is expected to be in increasing demand during the upcoming years. If the firm's existing facilities are inadequate to handle the demand, proposals should be developed for expanding the firm's capacity. These proposals may come from the corporate planning staff group, from a divisional staff group, or from some other source.

Since most existing products eventually become obsolete, a firm's growth is also dependent on the development and marketing of new products. This involves the generation of research and development investment proposals, marketing research investments, test marketing investments, and perhaps even investments in new plant, property, and equipment. For example, in order for the mineral extraction industries to keep growing, they must continually make investments in exploration and development. Similarly, firms in high technology industries—such as electronics and computers—must undertake continuing programs of research and development to compete successfully.

Projects generated by cost reduction opportunities Just as products become obsolete over time, so do plant, property, equipment, and production processes. Normal use makes older plants more expensive to operate because of the higher cost of maintenance and down time (idle time). In addition, new technological developments may render existing equipment economically obsolete. These factors create opportunities for cost reduction investments, which include replacing old, obsolete capital equipment with newer, more efficient equipment.

Projects generated in order to meet legal requirements and health and safety standards These projects include investment proposals for such things as pollution control, ventilation, and fire protection equipment. In terms of analysis, this group of projects is best considered as contingent upon other projects.

To illustrate, suppose a firm wishes to build a new steel plant in Cleveland, Ohio. The decision will be contingent upon the investment in the amount of pollution abatement equipment required by state and local laws. Thus, the decision to invest in the new plant must be based upon the *total* cost of the plant, including the pollution abatement equipment, and not just the operating equipment alone.

In the case of existing facilities, this type of decision making is sometimes more complex. For example, suppose a firm is told it must install new pollution abatement equipment in a plant that has been in operation for some time. The firm first needs to determine the lowest cost alternative that will meet these legal requirements. "Lowest cost" is normally measured by the smallest present value of net cash outflows from the project. Then management must decide whether the remaining stream of cash flows from the plant is sufficient to justify the expenditure. If it appears as though it will not be, the firm may consider building a new facility, or it may decide to simply close down the original plant. During 1981 all U.S. nonfarm industries made capital expenditures for air and water pollution abatement plant and equipment in excess of $8 *billion.*

Project size and the Decision-making process

Whereas the classification of a proposed project influences the capital investment decision-making process, there are other factors to consider—in particular, the size of the expenditure required to carry out the project.

Most firms *decentralize* the decision-making function. For example, whereas the approval of the president and the board of directors may be

FIGURE 9–2 **Sample Capital Budgeting Project Proposal Form**

ENGINEERING ECONOMY STUDY—New Product, Increased Capacity

DIVISION-WORKS	DEPARTMENT	PRODUCT LINE	PROJECT NO.
PROJECT DESCRIPTION	PREPARED BY DATE	INDUSTRIAL ENGINEERING MANAGER DATE	
PROJECT COMMITMENT	TOTAL APPROVED IN CAPITAL BUDGET	SALES OR MARKETING MGR.	ACCOUNTING MANAGER	WORKS MANAGER

1. PRODUCT ANALYSIS

DESCRIPTION AND APPLICATION

2. MARKET ANALYSIS

A. COMPETITIVE STATUS OF PRODUCT

B. IS THE REQUESTED EQUIPMENT NEEDED TO MEET CURRENT CONTRACT COMMITMENTS? YES ☐ NO ☐ IF YES, WITH WHOM? _____ WHAT IS FIRM BUSINESS IN HAND $_____ , LENGTH OF TIME ITEMS WILL BE USED ON FIRM BUSINESS _____ MO. IF NO, WHAT IS BASIS FOR INCREASED FACILITY REQUIREMENTS?

C. WILL THIS PRODUCT REPLACE OR COMPETE WITH EXISTING PRODUCTS? YES ☐ NO ☐ IF YES, DESCRIBE EFFECT ON EXISTING SALES.

D. FORECAST MARKET POTENTIAL

1. EST. TOTAL MARKET				2. EST. PENETRATION				3. ADDED SALES DUE TO FACILITIES EXPANSION	
YEAR	UNITS	DOLLARS		%	UNITS	DOLLARS		UNITS	DOLLARS

E. COMMENTS:

3. FORECAST ADDED SALES, INCOME, AND CASH FLOW

YEAR	FORECAST ADDED SALES	AFTER TAX INCOME	PERCENT TO SALES	INVESTMENT CREDIT	DEPRECIATION	AFTER TAX CASH FLOW	PRESENT VALUE FACTOR	PRESENT VALUE
	EST RESIDUAL VALUE							
TOTAL								

4. FORECAST RETURN ON INVESTMENT

A. TOTAL CAPITAL INVESTMENT REQUIRED $_____

D. DISCOUNTED CASH FLOW RATE OF RETURN ON INVESTMENT (AFTERTAX)   _____ %

B. ESTIMATED INCREASE IN WORKING CAPITAL $_____

E. NUMBER OF YEARS USED IN CALCULATION   _____ YRS.

TOTAL INVESTMENT $_____

F. PAYBACK PERIOD (AFTERTAX)   _____ YRS.

C. ESTIMATED RESIDUAL VALUE OF EQUIPMENT AND WORKING CAPITAL $_____ AFTER _____ YRS.

DEFINITION OF CAPITAL REQUIREMENTS			6. EFFECTS ON CURRENT OPERATIONS
NEW CAPITAL REQUIREMENTS	ESTIMATED CAPITAL COST	ASSOCIATED EXPENSE	A. BY WHEN DO YOU ANTICIPATE TO
	$		HAVE THE FACILITIES INSTALLED? _____
			BEGIN PRODUCTION? _____
			B. IS ANY OF THE WORK CURRENTLY SUBCONTRACTED?
			YES ☐ NO ☐ IF YES, AT WHAT COST $ _____
			GIVE BRIEF DESCRIPTION.
			C. IS ANY OF THE WORK CURRENTLY DONE ON OVERTIME THAT WILL BE ELIMINATED?
			☐ YES ☐ NO
TOTAL	$		IF YES, GIVE ASSOCIATED PREMIUM COST $_____ AND BRIEF DESCRIPTION.

7. FORECASTING OPERATING COSTS—BY YEAR

YEAR	PRESENT	19	19	19	19	19
A. FORECAST ADDITIONAL SALES						
B. STANDARD COST OF NET SALES						
MATERIAL						
DIRECT LABOR						
MANUFACTURING EXPENSE						
TOTAL STANDARD COST						
C. GROSS PROFIT AT STANDARD						
PERCENT TO SALES						
D. VARIANCES						
MATERIAL						
DIRECT LABOR						
OVERHEAD VARIABLE						
VOLUME						
SCRAP						
FREIGHT						
PRODUCT TOOLING						
SUBCONTRACTING						
INVENTORY ADJUSTMENT						
UNEXPENDED TOOLING AND SUPPLIES						
PREPRODUCTION EXPENSE						
OTHER						
TOTAL VARIANCES						
E. GROSS PROFIT						
PERCENT TO SALES						
F. DIVISION OPERATING EXPENSE						
G. DIVISION PROFIT (LOSS) BEFORE TAX						
PERCENT TO SALES						
H. STAFF ALLOCATIONS						
J. CORPORATE PROFIT (LOSS) BEFORE TAX						
K. NET INCOME (LOSS) AFTER TAX						
L. PERCENT TO SALES						

8. OTHER REMARKS

needed for especially large outlays, a divisional vice-president may be the final decision maker in the case of medium-sized outlays. A plant manager may have responsibility for deciding on smaller outlays, and a department head in a particular plant may be authorized to approve small outlays (of less than $2,000, for example). This "chain of command" varies with individual companies. In large firms, however, it is impossible for any one person to make every decision regarding proposed capital expenditures, and a decentralized system is usually employed.

<h2 style="text-align:center">PRINCIPLES OF
ESTIMATING CASH FLOWS</h2>

The capital budgeting process is primarily concerned with the estimation of the *cash flows* associated with a project, not just the project's contribution to accounting profits. Typically, a capital expenditure requires an initial *cash outflow*, termed the *net investment*. Thus, it is important to measure a project's performance in terms of the *net cash inflows* it is expected to generate over a number of future years.

Figure 9–3 shows the estimated cash flows for a particular project. After an initial net investment of $100,000, the project is expected to generate a stream of net cash inflows over its anticipated 5-year life of $50,000 in year 1, $40,000 in year 2, $30,000 in year 3, $25,000 in year 4, and $5,000 in year 5. This type of project is called a *normal* or *conventional project*.

Nonnormal or nonconventional projects have different cash flow patterns. Table 9–2 illustrates the cash flow patterns for four nonnormal projects. Project W, for example, might be a research and development effort for a new product, or perhaps a new construction project. The company has to make cash outlays for 3 years before the project is expected to generate any net benefits. This type of project poses few problems for analysis. Projects X, Y, and Z, in contrast, can cause some analytical problems, as we shall see. Project X might require that certain equipment be shut down and rebuilt in year 3, and Project Y could be an investment in a mining property, with the negative cash flow in year 5 representing abandonment costs associated with closing down the mine after its mineral wealth has been depleted. Finally, Project Z might represent the investment in some pollution control equipment.

Regardless of whether a project's cash flows are expected to be normal or

FIGURE 9–3   Illustration of Estimated Cash Flows for a Normal Capital Investment Project

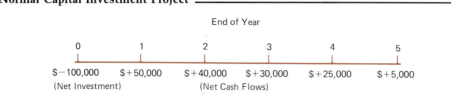

TABLE 9–2   Sample Cash Flow Patterns for Nonnormal Projects

Project				YEAR		
	0	1	2	3	4	5
W	– $100,000	– $30,000	– $20,000	+ $50,000	+ $150,000	+ $200,000
X	– 100,000	+ 80,000	+ 60,000	– 50,000	+ 75,000	+ 60,000
Y	– 200,000	+ 150,000	+ 50,000	+ 40,000	+ 30,000	– 20,000
Z	– 150,000	– 20,000	– 20,000	– 25,000	– 25,000	– 30,000

nonnormal, certain basic principles should be applied during their estimation, including the following:

▪ **Cash flows should be measured on an incremental basis.** In other words, the cash flow stream for a particular project should be estimated from the perspective of how the entire cash flow stream of the firm will be affected if the project is adopted as compared with how the stream will be affected if the project is not adopted. Thus, *all* changes in the firm's revenue stream, cost stream, and tax stream that would result from the acceptance of the project should be included in the analysis. In contrast, cash flows that would not be changed by the investment should be disregarded.

▪ **Cash flows should be measured on an after-tax basis.** Since the initial investment made on a project requires the outlay of after-tax cash dollars, the returns from the project should be measured in the same units—namely, after-tax cash flows.

▪ **All the indirect effects of a project should be included in the cash flow calculations.** For example, if a proposed plant expansion requires that working capital be increased for the firm as a whole—perhaps in the form of larger cash balances, inventories, or accounts receivable—the increase in working capital should be included in the *net investment* required for the project. As another example, assume that one division of a firm introduces a new product that competes directly with a product produced by another division. The first division may consider this product desirable, but when the impact on the second division's sales are considered, the project may be much less attractive.

These three principles of cash flow estimation may be applied to the specific problem of defining and calculating a project's *net investment* and *net cash flows*. Before discussing the mechanics of calculating the net investment and net cash flows for a project, we review some important tax considerations—namely, the investment tax credit and depreciation allowances.

INVESTMENT TAX CREDIT

The Investment Tax Credit (ITC) was initially established in 1962 as a fiscal policy tool for controlling the economy. The ITC has been modified many times since 1962. The most recent modifications have come about as a result of the Economic Recovery Tax Act (ERTA) of 1981 and the Tax Equity and

Fiscal Responsibility Act (TEFRA) of 1982. Many of the changes in the ITC were made to conform with the new Accelerated Cost Recovery System (ACRS) depreciation rules (see the section on depreciation that follows).

The ITC allows firms to receive a credit against their Federal income taxes for qualifying new property placed in service. Qualifying property generally includes depreciable property with an ACRS depreciation recovery period of 3 years or more. Buildings and their structural components are *not* eligible for the ITC. In addition to qualifying *new* property, the ITC is also available on $125,000 of *used* property before January 1, 1985, and increasing to $150,000 in used property on January 1, 1985. The amount of the credit is based on the ACRS recovery period as follows:

Recovery Period (Years)	Percentage of Credit
3	6%
5, 10, and 15	10%

The ITC cannot exceed a firm's tax liability in any year. It is further limited to 100 percent of a firm's first $25,000 of tax liability plus 85 percent of its tax liability in excess of $25,000. Tax credits that cannot be used in a given year are initially carried back 3 years (to the earliest year first). Any remaining unused credits are then carried forward a total of 15 years before they are lost.

If an asset is sold or disposed of prior to the end of the ACRS recovery period, all or a portion of the ITC is recaptured. The recaptured portion of the ITC is added to the taxpayer's regular tax liability for the year. Table 9-3 is a schedule of the percentage recapture for various assets. As we shall see, the ITC is an important determinant of the *net investment* portion of a project's cash flows.

DEPRECIATION

Depreciation is defined as the systematic allocation of the cost of an asset over more than 1 year. It allows a firm to spread the costs of fixed assets over a period of years to better match costs and revenues in each accounting period. The annual depreciation expense recorded for a particular asset is simply

TABLE 9–3 Investment Tax Credit Recapture Schedule

PROPERTY IS HELD FOR	RECAPTURE PERCENTAGE	
	5-, 10-, 15-Year property	3-Year property
Less than 1 year	100%	100%
1 year or more but less than 2 years	80	66
2 years or more but less than 3 years	60	33
3 years or more but less than 4 years	40	0
4 years or more but less than 5 years	20	0
5 years or more	0	0

an allocation of historical costs and does not necessarily indicate a declining market value. For example, a company that is depreciating an office building may find the building's market value *appreciating* each year.

There are a number of alternative methods of recording the depreciation of an asset for financial reporting purposes. These include straight line depreciation and various accelerated depreciation methods. Under the straight line depreciation method as defined in the ERTA, the annual amount of an asset's depreciation is calculated as follows:

$$\begin{array}{l} \text{Annual} \\ \text{depreciation} \\ \text{amount} \end{array} = \frac{\text{Installed cost}}{\text{Number of years over which the asset is depreciated}}.$$

For tax purposes, the depreciation rate a firm uses has a significant impact on the cash flows of the firm. This is so because depreciation represents a *noncash* expense that is deductible for tax purposes. Hence, the greater the amount of depreciation charged in a period, the lower will be the firm's taxable income. With a lower reported taxable income, the firm's tax obligation (a cash outflow) is reduced, and the cash inflows for the firm are increased. This can be seen in the following fundamental definition of cash flows:

Operating cash flow = Net income after tax + Noncash charges .

For example, if the Longhorn Tool Company has revenues of $1,000, cash operating expenses of $500, straight line depreciation of $100, and a marginal tax rate of 40 percent, its operating cash flow will be this:

Cash revenues		$1,000
Less: Cash operating expenses	$500	
Depreciation	100	
Total		600
Net income before taxes		$ 400
Less: Taxes (40%)		160
Net income after taxes		$ 240
Plus: Depreciation		100
Operating cash flow		$ 340

Now suppose Longhorn Tool opts to use an accelerated depreciation method for tax purposes rather than the straight line method. As a result, its depreciation expense is recorded as $150 instead of $100. Its new operating cash flow will be as follows:

Cash revenues		$1,000
Less: Cash operating expenses	$500	
Depreciation	150	
Total		650
Net income before taxes		$ 350
Less: Taxes (40%)		140
Net income after taxes		$ 210
Plus: Depreciation		150
Operating cash flow		$ 360

A comparison of the two cash flow statements shows that the use of accelerated depreciation reduces net income after taxes from $240 to $210 and reduces taxes from $160 to $140, but increases operating cash flow to $360 from $340. Since our concern is primarily with the cash flows of a firm and not its accounting income, the use of accelerated depreciation is desirable for the firm.

DEPRECIABLE LIFE OF AN ASSET

Prior to the 1981 tax act (ERTA) and the 1982 tax act (TEFRA), there was considerable controversy between taxpayers and the IRS over what constituted the appropriate period over which to depreciate an asset. The ERTA greatly simplified the determination of a period for depreciation by creating four property classes under the ACRS and assigning all depreciable assets to one of the classes. Table 9–4 summarizes the ACRS normal and the optional extended recovery period (depreciable life) for the four asset classes.

Under normal circumstances most firms will opt to use the ACRS normal recovery periods. Hence, we will only consider the ACRS normal recovery periods in the balance of the chapter.

DEPRECIATION RATE

In addition to establishing the depreciable life of an asset, the ACRS depreciation system also sets the depreciation rate to be applied to the depreciable basis of each asset. Under the ACRS, the *depreciable basis of an asset is equal to the purchase price plus installation and shipping charges less 50 percent of the amount of the ITC for which an asset is eligible.*[3] The estimated salvage value of an asset is *not* considered under the ARCS.

For example, assume the Longhorn Tool Company acquires a $10,000 piece of machinery (including shipping and installation costs). Under ACRS guidelines, this is a 5-year asset that is eligible for the full 10 percent ITC—or $1,000. The depreciable basis of this asset is as follows:

Asset cost (including shipping and installation)	$10,000
Less: 50% of 10% ITC	500
Depreciable basis	$ 9,500

Table 9–5 indicates the ACRS depreciation rates that are applied to the depreciable basis of all assets except real property. A separate recovery schedule is used for 15-year real property (buildings). In the case of real property, the depreciation that can be claimed in the first year depends on the month the

---

[3]As an alternative, the ACRS percentages can be applied to the full cost of the asset (including installation and shipping) without reducing this cost by 50 percent of the eligible ITC. In this case, the ITC is reduced by 2 percentage points, that is, from 6 percent to 4 percent for 3-year assets and from 10 percent to 8 percent for other assets. We do not consider this alternative in our future analysis, since it was included in the law only to assist firms that were precluded from taking advantage of the ITC because of such reasons as insufficient taxable income.

TABLE 9–4 ACRS Recovery Periods*

Property Class	ACRS Normal Recovery Period	Optional Extended Straight Line Recovery Period†
Autos, light-duty trucks, research and development equipment, and some special tools	3 years	3, 5, or 12 years
All other machinery and equipment except long-lived public utility property	5 years	5, 12, or 25 years
Certain public utility property, railroad tank cars, mobile homes, and theme park structures	10 years	10, 25, or 35 years
All other public utility property and real property (excluding land)	15 years	15, 35, or 45 years

*The ERTA allows a firm to expense, rather than to capitalize and depreciate, up to a total of $5,000 per year in 1982 and 1983, $7,500 per year in 1984 and 1985, and $10,000 per year in 1986 and later years. When this option is chosen, the ITC is forgone. We do not consider this alternative in our future analysis, since it has been shown to be generally disadvantageous to taxpayers.

†The optional extended straight line recovery period would only be used if a firm expected negative predepreciation net income over the near future. In this case, deferring depreciation until later years when predepreciation income is available would be advantageous.

The estimated salvage value is not considered when using the optional extended straight line recovery period.

TABLE 9–5 ACRS Depreciation Rates

Recovery Year	3-Year Property	5-Year Property	10-Year Property	15-Year Public Utility Property
1	25%	15%	8%	5%
2	38	22	14	10
3	37	21	12	9
4		21	10	8
5		21	10	7
6			10	7
7			9	6
8			9	6
9			9	6
10			9	6
11				6
12				6
13				6
14				6
15				6

property is placed in service. Table 9–6 provides the ACRS recovery percentages for 15-year real property.

Returning to the Longhorn Tool Company example, the annual ACRS depreciation would be the following:

Year	ACRS Depreciation Rate	Amount of Depreciation (ACRS Rate × $9,500)
1	15%	$1,425
2	22	2,090
3	21	1,995
4	21	1,995
5	21	1,995
	100%	$9,500

ACRS RECOVERY PERIODS AND ECONOMIC LIFE OF AN ASSET

With the adoption of the ACRS recovery periods for all assets, there is no longer any relationship between the period over which depreciation is taken on an asset and that asset's economic life. Consequently, when estimating the cash flows from a project, there normally will be several years beyond the ACRS recovery period when no depreciation expense will be recorded. It is important to remember that cash flows for all projects (assets) should be projected over the full economic life of the project, not just the ACRS recovery period.

NET INVESTMENT (NINV)

The *net investment* (NINV) in a project is defined as the project's initial net cash outlay. It is calculated using the following steps:

TABLE 9–6   ACRS Recovery Percentages for 15-Year Real Property (Other Than Low Income Housing)

YEAR	MONTH PLACED IN SERVICE											
	1	2	3	4	5	6	7	8	9	10	11	12
1	12%	11%	10%	9%	8%	7%	6%	5%	4%	3%	2%	1%
2	10	10	11	11	11	11	11	11	11	11	11	12
3	9	9	9	9	10	10	10	10	10	10	10	10
4	8	8	8	8	8	8	9	9	9	9	9	9
5	7	7	7	7	7	7	8	8	8	8	8	8
6	6	6	6	6	7	7	7	7	7	7	7	7
7	6	6	6	6	6	6	6	6	6	6	6	6
8	6	6	6	6	6	6	6	6	6	6	6	6
9	6	6	6	6	5	6	5	5	5	6	6	6
10	5	6	5	6	5	5	5	5	5	5	6	5
11	5	5	5	5	5	5	5	5	5	5	5	5
12	5	5	5	5	5	5	5	5	5	5	5	5
13	5	5	5	5	5	5	5	5	5	5	5	5
14	5	5	5	5	5	5	5	5	5	5	5	5
15	5	5	5	5	5	5	5	5	5	5	5	5
16	—	—	1	1	2	2	3	3	4	4	4	5

Step 1. The new project cost plus any installation and shipping costs associated with acquiring the asset and putting it into service[4]

PLUS

Step 2. Any increases in net working capital required as a result of the new investment[5]

MINUS

Step 3. The net proceeds from the sale of existing assets when the investment is a replacement decision[6]

PLUS or MINUS

Step 4. The taxes associated with the sale of the existing asset and/or the purchase of the new one[7]

EQUALS

The net investment (NINV).

The following example illustrates this four-step procedure. The Jones Equipment Company purchased an automated drill press 5 years ago that had an estimated economic life of 15 years. The drill press originally cost $150,000 and is being depreciated at the 5-year ACRS recovery rates. The current book value of the drill press is $0, since all 5 years' worth of depreciation have been utilized. The company is considering replacing the drill press with a new one costing $190,000. Shipping and installation charges will add an additional $10,000 to the cost. The new machine would be depreciated under the 5-year ACRS schedule. The new machine is expected to have a 10-year economic life, and its actual salvage value at the end of the 10-year period is estimated to be $20,000. The purchase of the new drill press qualifies for a 10 percent ITC. Jones' current marginal tax rate is 40 percent.

Steps 1 and 2 are easy to calculate; the new project cost plus shipping and installation is $200,000. In this case, no new net working capital is required.

Steps 3 and 4 pose some problems. The net proceeds received from the sale of the old drill press have to be adjusted for taxes; this is considered in Step 4.

To illustrate Step 4, consider the following four cases of what the tax treatment might be when an asset is disposed of.

---

[4]The asset cost plus installation and shipping costs form the basis upon which the ITC is computed.

[5]The increase in working capital (such as cash, inventories, and accounts receivable) should be calculated *net* of any automatic increases in current liabilities (such as accounts payable or wages and taxes payable) that occur because the project is adopted and that have no explicit (cash) cost to the firm. For replacement-type investments there is normally no net working capital increase. For expansion (new product or additional capacity) investments, additional net working capital would normally be required.

[6]This is normally computed as the actual salvage value of the asset being replaced less any costs associated with physically removing or selling it.

[7]These taxes include the effects of the ITC, as well as any taxes associated with the disposal of the old asset. The total tax effect may be either positive or negative; this is why it is either added to or subtracted from the new project cost.

Case 1. Sale of an asset for its book value[8]   (For ACRS purposes, tax book value equals the installed cost of the asset less one half of the ITC less accumulated ACRS depreciation. For assets acquired prior to January 1, 1983, tax book value equals the installed cost of the asset less accumulated tax depreciation.) If a company disposes of an asset for an amount exactly equal to that asset's tax book value, there is neither a gain nor a loss on the sale, and thus there are no tax consequences. For example, if the ABC Company sells for $50,000 an asset with a book value for tax purposes of $50,000, there are no taxes associated with this disposal.

Case 2. Sale of an asset for less than its book value   If the ABC Company sells for $20,000 an asset having a tax book value of $50,000, the firm incurs a $30,000 pretax loss. Assuming that this asset is used in business or trade (an essential criterion for this tax treatment), this loss may be treated as an operating loss or an offset to operating income. This operating loss effectively reduces the company's taxes by an amount equal to the loss times the company's marginal tax rate.

Assume that the company's income before taxes is $100,000 (before consideration of the operating loss from the disposal of the asset). Taxes on this income are $100,000 times the company's marginal (40 percent) tax rate, or $40,000. Because of the operating loss incurred by selling the asset for $20,000, the company's taxable income is reduced to $70,000, and the taxes decline to $28,000 (40 percent of $70,000). The $12,000 difference in taxes is equal to the tax loss on the sale of the old asset times the company's marginal tax rate ($30,000 × 40%).

Case 3. Sale of an asset for more than its book value but less than its original cost[9]   If the ABC Company sells the asset for $60,000—$10,000 more than the current tax book value—$50,000 of this amount constitutes a tax-free cash inflow, and the remaining $10,000 is taxed as operating income. As a result, the firm's taxes increase by $4,000, or the amount of the gain times the firm's marginal tax rate ($10,000 × 40%). (The IRS treats this gain as a recapture of depreciation.)

Case 4. Sale of an asset for more than its original cost   If the ABC Company sells the asset for $120,000 (assuming an original asset cost of $110,000), part of the gain from the sale is treated as ordinary income, and part is treated as a long-term *capital gain*. The gain receiving ordinary income treatment is equal to the difference between the original asset cost and the current tax book value, or $60,000 ($110,000 − $50,000). The capital gain portion is the amount in excess of the original asset cost, or $10,000.

[8]If there is a partial or full recapture of the ITC as a result of the sale of the asset before the full ITC has been earned, the basis from which a recapture of depreciation is computed is increased by 50 percent of the amount of the ITC to be recaptured.

[9]Even though ACRS depreciation is based on the installed cost of the asset less 50 percent of the ITC, recapture of depreciation (ordinary income) treatment is given to any amount that is more than the ACRS tax book value and less than or equal to the *full* installed cost; that is, the ITC reduction from installed cost, which determines the depreciable basis of an asset, does not affect depreciation recapture provisions.

TABLE 9–7   Net Investment Calculation for Jones Equipment Company

Cost of new drill press	$190,000
Plus: Shipping and installation charges	10,000
Equals: Installed cost	$200,000
Plus: Increase in net working capital	0
Less: Proceeds from sale of old drill press	40,000
Equals: Net investment before taxes	$160,000
Plus: Tax on gain from sale of old drill press (0.40 × $40,000)	16,000
Less: ITC on new drill press (10% × $200,000)	20,000
Equals: Net investment	$156,000

Taxes on long-term capital gains are computed at a lower rate (28 percent in 1983) than the normal tax rate. Assuming that the normal tax rate is 40 percent and the capital gains rate is 28 percent, the tax on the sale of the asset equals the taxes on the ordinary income plus the taxes on the capital gains, or

$$(\$60,000 \times 40\%) + (\$10,000 \times 28\%) = \$24,000 + \$2,800$$
$$= \$26,800 \, .$$

Returning to the Jones Equipment Company example, assume that the old drill press is sold for $40,000. The gain from this sale is treated as ordinary income, since it represents a recapture of depreciation. Table 9–7 summarizes the NINV calculation for Jones Equipment. As can be seen in this table, the NINV is equal to $156,000.

MULTIPERIOD NET INVESTMENTS

One final comment needs to be made concerning the computation of a project's NINV when a project such as W in Table 9–2 is considered. If a project requires outlays over more than 1 year before positive cash inflows are generated, the NINV for that project will be equal to the present value (at time 0) of this series of outlays, discounted at the firm's cost of capital. For example, the NINV of project W, assuming a cost of capital of 10 percent, equals $143,790, computed as follows:[10]

Year	Cash Outlay	$PVIF_{0.10,n}$	Present Value of NINV
0	$100,000	1.000	$100,000
1	30,000	0.909	27,270
2	20,000	0.826	16,520
			$143,790

[10]For tax purposes, the installed cost of this asset would be $150,000—the actual cash outlays required to put the plant or equipment in service. This example does not consider the ITC, which would further reduce the present value of NINV.

Having concluded a discussion of the calculation of the NINV, we next turn our attention to the determination of annual net cash flows from a project.

NET CASH FLOWS

Capital investment projects are expected to generate after-tax cash flow streams after the initial net investment has been made. The process of estimating project cash flows is an important part of the capital budgeting process.

In general, cash flows are defined as follows:

$$\text{Cash flow (CF)} = \text{Earnings after taxes (EAT)} + \text{Noncash charges} . \quad \textbf{(9.1)}$$

The most significant noncash charge normally found on a firm's income statement is depreciation.[11]

Capital budgeting is primarily concerned with the *incremental, after-tax net cash flows* (NCF) of a particular project, or cash inflows minus cash outflows. For any year during the life of a project, these may be defined as the change in earnings after taxes, ΔEAT, plus the change in depreciation, ΔD:

$$NCF = \Delta EAT + \Delta D . \quad \textbf{(9.2)}$$

ΔEAT is equal to the change in earnings before taxes (ΔEBT) times $(1 - t)$, where t is the marginal tax rate:

$$\Delta EAT = \Delta EBT(1 - t) . \quad \textbf{(9.3)}$$

ΔEBT is defined as the change in revenues, ΔR, minus the changes in cash operating costs, ΔO, and depreciation, ΔD:

$$\Delta EBT = \Delta R - \Delta O - \Delta D . \quad \textbf{(9.4)}$$

Substituting Equation 9.4 into Equation 9.3 yields the following:

$$\Delta EAT = (\Delta R - \Delta O - \Delta D)(1 - t) .$$

Substituting this equation into Equation 9.2 yields the following definition of net cash flow:

$$NCF = (\Delta R - \Delta O - \Delta D)(1 - t) + \Delta D . \quad \textbf{(9.5)}$$

This equation can be further extended into an *operational* definition of NCF by defining ΔR as $R_2 - R_1$, ΔO as $O_2 - O_1$, and ΔD as $D_2 - D_1$, where

---

[11]Depreciation *itself* if not a cash flow. Rather, it reduces earnings before taxes (EBT) and thus reduces income tax payments (a cash outflow). Equation 9.1 provides an easy procedure for reflecting the cash flow impact of depreciation.

R_1 = Revenues of the firm if it *does not* adopt the project.

R_2 = Revenues of the firm if it *adopts* the project.

O_1 = Cash operating costs for the firm *without* the project.

O_2 = Cash operating costs for the firm *with* the project.

D_1 = Depreciation charges for the firm *without* the project.

D_2 = Depreciation charges for the firm *with* the project.

The definition given in Equation 9.5 can be rewritten as follows:

$$NCF = [(R_2 - R_1) - (O_2 - O_1) - (D_2 - D_1)](1 - t) + (D_2 - D_1). \quad \textbf{(9.6)}$$

Consider again the Jones Equipment Company example and assume the company expects annual revenues to increase from $70,000 to $85,000 if the new drill press is purchased. (This might occur, because the new press is faster than the old one and can meet the increasing demands for more work.) Assume further that while the old drill press required two operators, the new drill press is more automated and needs only one, thereby reducing annual operating costs from $40,000 to $20,000. The old machine is fully depreciated, whereas the new machine will be depreciated over 5 years under ACRS depreciation rates. The marginal tax rate of 40 percent applies.

The net cash flows resulting from the purchase of the new drill press can be computed by substituting R_2 = $85,000, R_1 = $70,000, O_2 = $20,000, O_1 = $40,000, D_1 = $0, and t = 0.40 into Equation 9.6. The depreciation for the new machine, D_2, is according to ACRS rates as shown in Table 9–8.

Using the ACRS yearly depreciation from Table 9–8, annual net cash flows can be computed as follows:

$$NCF = [(R_2 - R_1) - (O_2 - O_1) - (D_2 - D_1)](1 - t) + (D_2 - D_1).$$

Year 1:

$$
\begin{aligned}
NCF_1 &= [(\$85,000 - \$70,000) - (\$20,000 - \$40,000) \\
&\quad - (\$28,500 - \$0)](1 - 0.4) + (\$28,500 - \$0) \\
&= \$32,400.
\end{aligned}
$$

Year 2:

$$
\begin{aligned}
NCF_2 &= [(\$85,000 - \$70,000) - (\$20,000 - \$40,000) \\
&\quad - (\$41,800 - \$0)](1 - 0.4) + (\$41,800 - \$0) \\
&= \$37,720.
\end{aligned}
$$

Years 3, 4, and 5:

$$
\begin{aligned}
NCF_{3-5} &= [(\$85,000 - \$70,000) - (\$20,000 - \$40,000) \\
&\quad - (\$39,900 - \$0)](1 - 0.4) + (\$39,900 - \$0) \\
&= \$36,960/\text{year}.
\end{aligned}
$$

TABLE 9–8   Computation of Annual Depreciation for Jones Equipment Company

Depreciable cost = $200,000 − 0.5 (0.10 ITC) ($200,000)

= $190,000 .

Year	ACRS Rate (%)	ACRS Depreciation, D_2 (ACRS Rate × Depreciable Cost)
1	15	$28,500
2	22	41,800
3	21	39,900
4	21	39,900
5	21	39,900
6	0	0
7	0	0
8	0	0
9	0	0
10	0	0

In years 6 through 9 there is no depreciation under either alternative; hence, net cash flows equal the following:

$$\begin{aligned} NCF_{6-9} &= [(\$85,000 - \$70,000) - (\$20,000 - \$40,000) \\ &\quad - (\$0 - \$0)](1 - 0.4) + (\$0 - \$0) \\ &= \$21,000/\text{year} . \end{aligned}$$

Net cash flows in year 10 will be the same as in years 6 through 9 except that the $20,000 estimated salvage from the new drill press must be added, along with its associated tax effects. This $20,000 salvage is treated as ordinary income, since it represents a recapture of depreciation for tax purposes.

$$\begin{aligned} NCF_{10} &= \$21,000 + \$20,000 \text{ salvage} - \text{Tax on salvage } (0.4 \times \$20,000) \\ &= \$21,000 + \$20,000 - \$8,000 \\ &= \$33,000 . \end{aligned}$$

Table 9–9 is a summary worksheet for computing the net cash flows for the Jones Company during the 10-year estimated economic life of the new drill press.

Table 9–10 summarizes the net cash flows for the entire project. This schedule of net cash flows plus the NINV computed in the preceding section form the basis for further analysis. In Chapter 10 several different capital budgeting decision models are applied to similar cash flow streams from other projects to determine the investment desirability of these projects. The cash flows developed in this chapter are an essential input in the capital budgeting decision process.

RECOVERY OF WORKING CAPITAL

In the last year of a project that has required net working capital as part of the initial net investment, this net working capital is assumed to be liquidated and returned to the firm as cash. Hence, the net working capital must

TABLE 9–9   Annual Net Cash Flow Worksheet for the Jones Equipment Company Drill Press Acquisition

	YEAR				
	1	2	3–5	6–9	10
Change in revenues ($R_2 - R_1$)*	$15,000	$15,000	$15,000	$15,000	$15,000
Less: Change in cash operating costs ($O_2 - O_1$)†	−20,000	−20,000	−20,000	−20,000	−20,000
Less: Change in depreciation ($D_2 - D_1$)‡	28,500	41,800	39,900	0	0
Equals: Change in earnings before taxes (EBT)	$ 6,500	$−6,800	$−4,900	$35,000	$35,000
Less: Tax (40%)‖	2,600	−2,720	−1,960	14,000	14,000
Equals: Change in earnings after taxes (EAT)	$ 3,900	$−4,080	$−2,940	$21,000	$21,000
Plus: Change in depreciation ($D_2 - D_1$)	28,500	41,800	39,900	0	0
Equals: Change in net cash flow before salvage	$32,400	$37,720	$36,960	$21,000	$21,000
Plus: Salvage	0	0	0	0	20,000
Less: Tax on salvage (0.4 × salvage)	0	0	0	0	8,000
Plus: Add-back of net working capital	0	0	0	0	0
Equals: Change in net cash flow	$32,400	$37,720	$36,960	$21,000	$33,000

NOTES: *The change in revenues from undertaking a project may be either positive or negative.
†The change in cash operating costs may be either positive or negative. In this case, the firm's cash operating costs *decline* by $20,000; that is, the change in cash operating costs is *negative*, indicating a cost saving. This cost saving is *added* to the change in revenues (subtracting a negative number is the same as adding a positive number). If, in another situation, operating costs were to *increase* as a result of a project, the increased costs would be *subtracted* from the change in revenues.
‡The change in depreciation may be either positive or negative. In this case, it is *positive* and has the effect of reducing the amount of taxable earnings, and thus reducing the amount of taxes paid. Hence, this *increases* the cash flow from the project. If the change in depreciation were *negative*, it would have the effect of increasing the taxable earnings, increasing taxes paid, and *reducing* the cash flows from the project.
‖In years 2 through 5 the tax figure is shown as a negative number. This is because the change in earnings before taxes is negative (indicating a reduction in taxable income). Because of this reduction in taxable income for the firm as a whole, taxes are reduced by an amount equal to the marginal tax rate (0.4) times the reduction in taxable income. This reduction in taxes is a benefit to the firm (subtracting a negative number is the same as adding a positive number).

be added to the net cash flows in the last year of the project. There are, of course, no tax consequences associated with this transaction. In the Jones Equipment Company example, there is no add-back of net working capital, since none was required to initiate the project.

PROBLEMS IN
CASH FLOW ESTIMATION

Since project cash flows occur in the future, there are varying degrees of *uncertainty* about the value of these flows. Thus, it is difficult to predict the

TABLE 9–10   **Summary Project Cash Flows for the Jones Equipment Company**

Year	Net Investment and Net Cash Flows
0	−$156,000
1	32,400
2	37,720
3	36,960
4	36,960
5	36,960
6	21,000
7	21,000
8	21,000
9	21,000
10	33,000

actual cash flows of a project. The capital budgeting process assumes the decision maker is able to estimate cash flows accurately enough that these estimates can be used in project evaluation and selection. For this assumption to be realistic, a project proposal should be based on inputs from marketing managers regarding revenue estimates and on inputs from the production and engineering staffs regarding costs and achievable levels of performance. Objective inputs from these sources can help reduce the uncertainty associated with cash flow estimation.

In addition, cash flow estimates for different projects may have varying degrees of uncertainty. For example, the returns from asset replacement projects are generally easier to forecast than the returns from new product introduction projects.[12]

Another difficulty in the practical application of capital budgeting arises because of the intentional or unintentional introduction of *bias* into cash flow estimates. Specifically, someone who has a vested interest in the adoption of a specific project may find it difficult to be completely objective when estimating the project's cash flows. For this reason it is a good idea to obtain an objective outside evaluation of a proposed project before the project is implemented. In addition, an aggressive project review and postaudit should be conducted once the project is under way. These procedures can indicate areas where bias has slipped into cash flow analysis and where corrective action may be needed.

INTEREST CHARGES

Often the purchase of a particular asset is closely tied to the creation of some debt obligation, such as the sale of mortgage bonds or a bank loan. Nevertheless, it is generally considered *incorrect* to deduct the interest charges asso-

---

[12]Chapter 11 discusses some of the techniques used to incorporate risk analysis into capital budgeting decision models.

ciated with a particular project from the estimated cash flows. This is true for two reasons.

First, the decision about how a firm should be financed can—and should—be made independently of the decision to accept or reject one or more projects. Instead, the firm should seek some combination of debt, equity (common stock), and preferred stock capital that is consistent with management's wishes concerning the tradeoff between financial risk and the cost of capital. In many cases this will result in a capital structure with the cost of capital at or near its minimum. Because investment and financing decisions normally should be made independently of one another, each new project can be viewed as being financed with the same proportions of the various sources of capital funds that are used to finance the firm as a whole.

Second, when a discounting framework is used for project evaluation, the discount rate, or cost of capital, already incorporates the cost of funds used to finance a project. Thus, including interest charges in cash flow calculations would essentially result in a double counting of costs.

SUMMARY

- Capital investments have a long-term impact on the performance of a firm. The proper forecasting of capital needs can help to insure that a firm's productive capacity will meet future requirements.

- Ideally a firm should invest in new projects up to the point at which the rate of return from the last project is equal to the marginal cost of capital.

- Projects may be classified as *independent, mutually exclusive,* or *contingent.* The acceptance of an independent project does not directly eliminate other projects from consideration; the acceptance of a mutually exclusive project precludes other alternatives; and the acceptance of a contingent project depends on the adoption of one or more other projects.

- The *cost of capital* is the cost of funds supplied to a firm. It is often used in conjunction with capital project evaluation techniques as a basis for choosing among various investment alternatives.

- There are four basic steps in the capital budgeting process: *the generation of proposals, the estimation of cash flows, the evaluation and selection of alternatives,* and *the postaudit/review.* The first two steps are detailed in this chapter.

- New projects may be generated by *growth opportunities, cost reduction opportunities,* or by *the need to meet legal requirements and health and safety standards.*

- Project cash flows should be measured on an *incremental after-tax* basis and should include all the indirect effects the project will have on the firm.

- The ACRS system of depreciation is now used to determine the depreciable lives of assets and the annual depreciation rates.

- The *net investment* (NINV) in a project is the net cash outlay required to place the project in service. It includes the project cost *plus* any necessary increases in working capital *minus* any proceeds from the sale of the old asset(s) (in the case of replacement decisions) *plus or minus* the taxes associated with the sale of the old asset(s) and/or the purchase of the new asset(s).

▪ The *net cash flows* (NCF) from a project are the incremental changes in a firm's cash flows that result from investing in the project. These flows include the changes in the firm's revenues, cash operating costs, and taxes with and without the project.

▪ Two problems that complicate the estimation of cash flows include the element of *uncertainty* associated with cash flows and the intentional or unintentional introduction of *bias* into the estimation procedure.

QUESTIONS AND TOPICS FOR DISCUSSION

1. Discuss how capital budgeting procedures might be used by each of the following:
   a. Personnel managers.
   b. Research and development staffs.
   c. Advertising executives.
2. What is a mutually exclusive investment project? An independent project? A contingent project? Give an example of each.
3. What effect does capital rationing have on a firm's ability to maximize shareholder wealth?
4. What are the primary types of capital investment projects? Does a project's type influence how it is analyzed?
5. Cash flows for a particular project should be measured on an incremental basis and should consider all the indirect effects of the project. What does this involve?
6. What factors should be considered when estimating a project's NINV?
7. Since depreciation is a noncash expense, why is it considered when estimating a project's net cash flows?
8. What are the potential tax consequences of selling an old asset in an asset replacement investment decision?
9. Why is it generally incorrect to consider interest charges when computing a project's net cash flows?
10. Under ACRS depreciation, does the ITC lower an asset's depreciable basis?
11. Under what conditions is the ITC recaptured when an asset is disposed of?
12. When would a firm choose to use optional extended straight line recovery periods instead of the ACRS recovery periods and rates?

PROBLEMS*

1. a. Calculate the annual ACRS depreciation for a machine in the 5-year ACRS recovery period group, assuming that the asset costs $20,000 and is eligible for a 10 percent ITC.
   b. If the firm uses optional extended straight line depreciation for 12 years, what is the annual depreciation?
   c. If you knew that this asset had an expected salvage value of $2,000 at the end of its 12-year economic life, would your answers to Parts a and b change?
2. The Longhorn Tube Company purchased an asset during 1983 for $100,000. The

*Problems in color have check answers provided at the end of the book.

asset was being depreciated over 5 years using ACRS depreciation rates. Longhorn claimed a 10 percent ITC at the time the asset was acquired. Two and one-half years later, Longhorn has decided to sell the asset for $80,000. Longhorn's marginal tax rate is 40 percent. What are the tax consequences of selling the asset at this time?

3. The Enid Company has sales of $100 million and total expenses (excluding depreciation) of $60 million. Straight line depreciation on the company's assets is $8 million and the maximum accelerated depreciation allowed by law is $12 million. Assume that all taxable income is taxed at 40 percent.

   a. Calculate the Enid Company's cash flow from operations using both straight line and accelerated depreciation.
   b. Assuming the company uses straight line depreciation for book purposes and accelerated depreciation for tax purposes, show the income statement reported to the stockholders. What is the cash flow from operations under these circumstances?

4. Calculate the annual depreciation of a new building acquired during March 1984. The cost of the building is $2 million.

5. Simonson Sewing Company has developed the following schedule of potential investment projects that may be undertaken during the next 6 months:

Project	Cost (in Millions of Dollars)	Expected Rate of Return (%)
A	3.0	20
B	1.5	22
C	7.0	7
D	14.0	10
E	50.0	12
F	12.0	9
G	1.0	44

   a. If Simonson requires a minimum rate of return of 10 percent on all investments, which projects should be adopted?
   b. In general, how would a capital budgeting constraint on the available amount of investment funds influence these decisions?
   c. How would differing levels of project risk influence these decisions?

6. A new machine costing $10,000 is expected to save the Parkman Company $2,000 per year for 12 years before depreciation and taxes. The machine will be depreciated on a straight line basis for a 12 year period to an estimated salvage value of $0. The firm's marginal tax rate is 40 percent. What are the annual net cash flows associated with the purchase of this machine?

7. Refer back to Problem 6. How would your answer change if the firm used ACRS depreciation rates over 5 years and claimed the ITC at the time the asset was acquired?

   HINT: Ignore the direct effect of the ITC on the first year's cash flows. The ITC does need to be considered when computing annual ACRS depreciation.

8. The Taylor Mountain Uranium Company currently has annual cash revenues of $1,200,000 and annual cash expenses of $700,000. Depreciation amounts to $200,000 per year. These figures are expected to remain constant for the foreseeable future (at least 15 years). The firm's marginal tax rate is 40 percent.

A new high-speed processing unit costing $1,200,000 is being considered as a potential investment designed to increase the firm's output capacity. This new piece of equipment will have an estimated usable life of 10 years and a $0 estimated salvage value. If the processing unit is bought, Taylor's annual cash revenues are expected to increase to $1,600,000, and annual cash expenses will increase to $900,000. Annual depreciation will increase to $320,000.

Compute the firm's annual net cash flows for the next 10 years, assuming that the new processing unit is purchased.

9. Refer back to Problem 8. How would your answer change if the new processing unit were depreciated over 5 years using ACRS depreciation rates and the firm claimed the ITC?

HINT: Ignore the direct effect of the ITC on the first year's cash flows. The ITC does need to be considered when computing annual ACRS depreciation.

10. A firm has an opportunity to invest in a new device that will replace two of the firm's older machines. The new device costs $570,000 and requires an additional outlay of $30,000 to cover installation and shipping. The new device will cause the firm to increase its net working capital by $20,000. Both the old machines can be sold—the first for $100,000 (book value equals $95,000) and the second for $150,000 (book value equals $75,000), and the original cost of the first machine was $200,000 and the original cost of the second machine was $140,000. The new device is eligible for a 10 percent ITC. There will be no ITC recapture on either of the two machines being replaced. Capital gains are taxed at 25 percent, and the firm's marginal tax bracket for ordinary income is 40 percent. Compute the net investment of this project.

11. Five years ago the Mori Foods Company acquired a bean processing machine. The machine cost $30,000 and was being depreciated using the straight line method over a 10-year period to an estimated salvage value of $0.

A new, improved processor is now available, and the firm is considering making a switch. The firm's marginal tax rate is 40 percent, and the appropriate capital gains rate is 28 percent. What are the after-tax cash flow effects of selling the old processing unit if it can be sold for the following prices?

a. $15,000.
b. $5,000.
c. $26,000.
d. $32,000.

12. Looking again at Problem 11, recompute the after-tax cash flow effects of selling the old processing unit, assuming that the firm was using ACRS depreciation and the old processing unit was sold for $5,000.

13. Looking again at Problem 11, assume that the new bean processor will cost $40,000 and will have an expected useful economic life of 10 years. The processor will be depreciated on a 5-year ACRS schedule. The new processor is eligible for the 10 percent ITC. In addition, installation and shipping costs for the new processor will be $2,000 (not included in the $40,000 purchase price). The new processor will not require any increases in working capital for the Mori Company.

Compute the net investment for the new processor, assuming that the old processor was being depreciated on a 5-year ACRS schedule and was sold for $5,000.

14. Returning to Problems 11 and 13, assume that the cash operating costs for the old bean processor are $15,000 per year. The old processor could continue to function for a maximum period of 10 more years, although operating costs for years 6 through 10 are expected to be $5,000 above current levels.

The new processor is expected to experience annual cash operating costs of

$12,000 over its anticipated economic life of 10 years, and it is expected to be worth $1,000 at the end of its 10-year life. The firm's marginal tax rate is 40 percent.

If both the new and the old processors are depreciated on a 5-year ACRS schedule, what will the net cash flows be over the next 10 years, assuming that Mori buys the new bean processor?

Note: The cost of the old processor was $30,000 and the cost of the new processor is $42,000, including installation and shipping charges. Also assume that both the new and the old processor were acquired at a time when ACRS depreciation rates were based on the installed asset cost less one half of the 10 percent ITC.

AN INTEGRATIVE CASE PROBLEM

Cash Flow Estimation in Capital Budgeting

Allied Interstate Banking is planning to offer a franchised network of its Rapid-Draw automatic teller machines (ATMs). Allied will supply the units to each of the franchise operators. The cost of each unit is estimated to be $100,000. Initially, a network of two hundred machines is planned. To set up the system, Allied also will have to purchase a $2 million computer system. Both the computer and the ATMs are expected to have a 7-year economic life. They will be depreciated over 5 years using ACRS depreciation rates. The actual salvage value of the ATMs and the computer at the end of 7 years is expected to be $1 million. Both the computer and the ATMs are eligible for the ITC.

Each ATM is expected to generate an average of 40,000 transactions per year. Allied will collect $0.75 per transaction from each of its franchise operators. Allied expects the operating cost of its system to be $1 million during the first year. It expects this cost to increase by 5 percent each year.

Allied pays taxes at a 40 percent marginal rate for ordinary income and at a 28 percent rate for capital gains.

1. Compute the net investment required for this franchised ATM system.

2. Compute the annual net cash flows associated with the investment in the complete ATM system.

We will continue this case at the end of Chapter 10. Using the information generated here and the techniques for project evaluation developed in Chapter 10, you will be able to assess the economic viability of this project.

ADDITIONAL READINGS AND REFERENCES

Bierman, Harold, Jr., and Smidt, Seymour. *The Capital Budgeting Decision*, 5th ed. New York: Macmillan Co., 1980.

Clark, John J., Hindelang, T. J., and Pritchard, R. D. *Capital Budgeting: Planning and Control of Capital Expenditures.* Englewood Cliffs, N. J.: Prentice-Hall, 1979.

Herbst, Anthony F. *Capital Budgeting.* New York: Harper & Row, 1982.

Levy, Haim, and Sarnat, Marshall. *Capital Investment and Financial Decisions,* 2nd ed. Englewood Cliffs, N. J.: Prentice-Hall International, 1982.

Quirin, G. David, and Wiginton, John C. *Analyzing Capital Expenditures.* Homewood, Ill.: Irwin, 1981.

Alternative Depreciation Methods

INTRODUCTION

Prior to the ACRS depreciation method developed in the ERTA (1981) and the TEFRA (1982), a number of alternative methods of depreciation were permitted by the IRS. These methods include straight line depreciation and various accelerated methods such as the sum-of-the-years'-digits and the declining balance methods.[1] Although the recent tax law changes have rendered these techniques out of date for tax purposes, it is still useful to understand them for the following reasons:

1. Most firms will continue to carry assets acquired before 1981 on their books for many years. These assets will be depreciated under the pre-ACRS rules.

2. Some firms may continue to use these methods for financial reporting purposes.

STRAIGHT LINE DEPRECIATION

Under the pre-ACRS straight line depreciation method, the annual amount of an asset's depreciation is calculated as follows:[2]

$$\text{Annual depreciation amount} = \frac{\text{Cost} - \text{Estimated salvage value}}{\text{Estimated economic life (years)}}. \qquad \textbf{(9A.1)}$$

---

[1] Occasionally an asset is depreciated according to its number of units of output or its number of hours of operation. Since these methods are not widely used, they are not discussed here.

[2] Note that under pre-ACRS depreciation rules, the annual depreciation amount was determined as the cost of the asset less its estimated salvage value divided by the estimated economic life. In comparison, under the optional extended straight line recovery periods in the ACRS system, no consideration is given to estimated salvage value in determining the annual depreciation amount.

For example, if a company purchases a machine that costs $12,000 and has an estimated salvage value of $2,000 at the end of a 5-year economic life, the annual depreciation amount is ($12,000 − $2,000)/5 = $2,000.

Straight line depreciation is an appropriate method to employ when an asset is being used up fairly evenly over its lifetime. Many companies use straight line depreciation for financial accounting purposes—that is, in their reports to stockholders, because it usually results in a greater reported net income—and an accelerated depreciation method for Federal income tax purposes, because accelerated depreciation can result in the deferment of tax payments.

ACCELERATED DEPRECIATION METHODS

Accelerated depreciation methods allow a firm to write off more of the cost of an asset during the early years of its life than would be possible with the use of straight line depreciation. The two most common pre-ACRS accelerated depreciation methods are the *declining balance method* and the *sum-of-the-years'-digits method.*

Declining balance method

The declining balance method allows a firm to take a percentage of the depreciation amount greater than the straight line amount during the first year of an asset's life. During subsequent years the book value, or undepreciated amount, of the asset is multiplied by this percentage to calculate annual depreciation costs.

Three commonly used variations of the declining balance method include the 200 percent declining balance, often termed *double declining balance*; the 150 percent declining balance; and the 125 percent declining balance. The pre-ACRS tax laws specified which variation could be used with different types of assets.

In the declining balance method, the annual depreciation amount of an asset is calculated by multiplying the straight line rate by the declining balance percentage figure to get an accelerated rate. The accelerated rate then is multiplied by the asset's book value at the end of each previous year. As each year's depreciation amount is subtracted from the cost of the asset, the resulting *balance* in the asset's book value *declines*. Thus, the depreciation amount *decreases* as the years pass.

Suppose the company mentioned earlier decides to depreciate its new $12,000 machine using the 200 percent declining balance method. Recall that the machine has a $2,000 salvage value and a 5-year expected life. Since the straight line depreciation rate is 20 percent ($2,000/$10,000), the 200 percent declining balance method results in a 40 percent depreciation rate. Table 9A–1 shows the depreciation calculations for this example.

The tax laws permitted businesses to switch from declining balance to straight line depreciation at the time when the declining balance depreciation

TABLE 9A–1 **Sample 200 Percent Declining Balance Depreciation Calculations**

Year (1)	Undepreciated Amount (Book Value, Beginning of Year) (2)	Depreciation Rate (3)	Depreciation Amount* (4) = (2) × (3)
1	$12,000	40%	$ 4,800
2	$12,000 − $4,800 = $7,200	40%	2,880
3	$7,200 − $2,880 = $4,320	40%	1,728
4	$4,320 − $1,728 = $2,592	40%	592
5	$2,592 − $592 = $2,000	—	0
			$10,000

NOTE *When using the declining balance method, the salvage value is not deducted from the cost of the asset. The asset may not be depreciated below its reasonable salvage value, however. Thus, in this example, the year 4 depreciation is only $592 (leaving a book value at the end of year 4 of $2,000—the estimated salvage value). No depreciation would be charged during year 5.

became less than the straight line amount. Most businesses followed this practice, since it allowed them to write off an asset more rapidly.

SUM-OF-THE-YEARS'-DIGITS METHOD

In the sum-of-the-years'-digits method, annual depreciation charges are computed by multiplying a decreasing fraction by the asset's original cost (less salvage value). The fraction's denominator is the sum of the digits that represent each year of the asset's expected economic life. For example, the sum-of-the-years'-digits for an asset with an expected 5-year lifetime is 5 + 4 + 3 + 2 + 1, or 15[3]. The numerator of the fraction for the first year is the highest digit—in this case, 5. The second year's numerator is the next highest digit—in this case, 4—and so on.

For example, suppose the company mentioned earlier decides to depreciate its $12,000 asset according to the sum-of-the-years'-digits method. Recall that the asset has a $2,000 expected salvage value and a 5-year expected useful life. The calculations are shown in Table 9A–2.

TABLE 9A–2 **Sample Sum-of-the-Years'-Digits Depreciation Calculations**

Year (1)	Depreciable Base (2)	Fraction (3)	Depreciation Amount (4) = (2) × (3)
1	$10,000	5/15	$ 3,333
2	10,000	4/15	2,667
3	10,000	3/15	2,000
4	10,000	2/15	1,333
5	10,000	1/15	667
			$10,000

[3]In general, the sum of the years' digits is equal to $n(n + 1)/2$, where n is the number of years.

PROBLEM

1. Using the following depreciation methods, calculate the depreciation schedule for an asset that has a $15,000 original cost, an expected useful life of 5 years, and no expected salvage value:
   a. Straight line depreciation.
   b. Sum-of-the-years'-digits depreciation.
   c. Double declining balance depreciation (200 percent).
   d. 150 percent declining balance depreciation.

CHAPTER 10

Capital Budgeting Decision Criteria

A FINANCIAL DILEMMA

Braniff International's Crash Landing*

During the 1960s and the mid-1970s, Braniff International prospered. It had a reputation for providing high-quality, innovative service to its airline passengers. During this period, Braniff was well respected by travelers in its traditional service area—the Southwest and the Southeast.

In 1978 airlines were deregulated, and Braniff sought to capitalize on the new deregulated environment. It immediately applied for 624 new routes—most of them outside its traditional service area. Routes were added nationwide and to Asia, Europe, and the Middle East. Within 6 months, Braniff snapped up 437 of the 1,300 routes that were offered by the Civil Aeronautics Board under deregulation. In contrast, the industry leader, United Airlines, added only one new route. To service the new routes, Braniff bought forty-one new airplanes, including eight 747s, at a cost of $925 million. Braniff's long-term debt surged to $733 million.

It is widely acknowledged that Braniff's new route system was very poorly conceived. Many routes could barely justify one flight a day. Service suffered, as did maintenance on this far-flung system. In 1979 Braniff lost $44.3 million. By 1981 this loss had increased to $160.6 million. In May 1982 Braniff declared bankruptcy.

The primary reason for Braniff's failure was incomplete and inadequate capital investment decisions. Over $900 million in aircraft was purchased to service routes with poor profit potential. This chapter considers a number of techniques that can be of value when analyzing the cash flows expected to be available from capital expenditures. The techniques developed are shown to be consistent with the firm's primary objective—the maximization of shareholder wealth.

---

*Based on "Braniff Makes a Crash Landing." *Business Week* (May 24, 1982): 62–65.

GLOSSARY OF NEW TERMS

Internal rate of return (IRR)   the discount rate that equates the present value of net cash flows from a project with the present value of the net investment. It is the discount rate that gives the project a net present value equal to zero. The IRR is used to evaluate, rank, and select from among various investment projects.

Multiple rates of return   two or more internal rates of return from the same project. This situation sometimes arises when the IRR method is being used for project selection. It occurs most frequently with nonnormal projects, or those whose cash flow patterns contain more than one sign change.

Net present value (NPV)   the present value of the stream of net cash flows resulting from a project, discounted at the firm's cost of capital, minus the project's net investment. It is used to evaluate, rank, and select from among various investment projects.

Opportunity cost   the rate of return that can be earned on funds if they are invested in the *next best* alternative investment.

Payback (PB) period   the period of time required for the cumulative cash inflows from a project to equal the initial cash outlay. It is used to evaluate, rank, and select from among various investment projects.

Profitability index (PI)   the ratio of the present value of net cash flows over the life of a project to the net investment. It is used to evaluate, rank, and select from among various investment projects. Frequently it is used in conjunction with resource allocation decisions in capital rationing situations.

Project postaudit   a review of a project that assesses its progress and evaluates its performance after termination.

Reinvestment rate   the rate of return at which cash flows from an investment project are assumed to be reinvested from year to year. The reinvestment rate may vary, depending on the investment opportunities available to the firm.

INTRODUCTION

This chapter looks at some widely used capital budgeting decision models, discussing and illustrating their relative strengths and weaknesses. When combined with the cash flow procedures developed in Chapter 9 and the discounting procedures developed in Chapter 3, these models provide the basis for making capital expenditure decisions.

This chapter also examines project review and postaudit procedures and concludes by tracing a sample project through the capital budgeting analysis process.

EVALUATING ALTERNATIVES: DECISION MODELS

As mentioned in Chapter 9, there are four basic steps in the capital budgeting process—the generation of proposals, the estimation of cash flows, the evaluation and selection of alternatives, and the project postaudit and review. This chapter discusses the final two steps in that process.

There are four commonly used criteria for evaluating and selecting investment projects,[1] including the following:

- Payback (PB) period.
- Net present value (NPV).
- Internal rate of return (IRR).
- Profitability index (PI).

PAYBACK (PB) PERIOD

The payback (PB) period of an investment is the period of time required for the cumulative cash inflows (net cash flows) from a project to equal the initial cash outlay (net investment).

To illustrate, assume a firm is considering two projects, A and B, having costs and cash flows as shown in Table 10–1.

If, as in Project A, the expected net cash inflows are *equal* in each year, the payback period is the ratio of the net investment to the annual net cash inflows:

$$PB = \frac{\text{Net investment}}{\text{Annual net cash inflows}} . \qquad (10.1)$$

TABLE 10–1   Sample Project Cash Flows

	PROJECT A		PROJECT B	
Year	Net cash flow after taxes	Cumulative net cash flow	Net cash flow after taxes	Cumulative net cash flow
1	$12,500	$12,500	$ 5,000	$ 5,000
2	12,500	25,000	10,000	15,000
3	12,500	37,500	15,000	30,000
4	12,500	50,000	15,000	45,000
5	12,500	62,500	25,000	70,000
6	12,500	75,000	30,000	100,000

Net investment for A = $50,000.
Net investment for B = $50,000.

[1]Another procedure sometimes used is the accounting rate of return (also called the average rate of return). It is computed as the ratio of average annual profits after taxes to the average investment in the project. Since this approach has been shown to be generally incorrect as a project selection criterion, it is not discussed here.

The payback (PB) period for Project A is computed as follows:

$$PB = \frac{\$50,000}{\$12,500}$$

$$= 4 \text{ years} .$$

When annual net cash inflows are *unequal*, as in Project B, the payback period is calculated by finding the point in time when cumulative net cash inflows *just equal* the net investment. As can be seen in Table 10–1, this occurs between years 4 and 5, since the cumulative net cash inflows for Project B are $45,000 after 4 years (less than the net investment) and $70,000 after 5 years (more than the net investment). The *exact* payback is computed by means of interpolation as follows:

$$PB = t + \frac{b - c}{d - c}, \tag{10.2}$$

where PB equals the payback period in years; t, the last full year in which cumulative net cash inflows are less than the net investment; b, the net investment; c, the cumulative cash inflow during the last full year when it is less than the net investment (year t); and d, the cumulative cash inflow in year $t + 1$. In this case the PB for Project B is as follows:

$$PB = 4 + \frac{\$50,000 - \$45,000}{\$70,000 - \$45,000}$$

$$= 4 + \frac{\$5,000}{\$25,000}$$

$$= 4.2 \text{ years} .$$

Decision rule   The payback period method is frequently used when a company is deciding whether to accept or reject an investment project. Specifically, the payback figure is compared with a *maximum acceptable payback figure*. The project is accepted if the calculated payback is less than this standard figure and rejected if it is greater. In this case, if the firm has a 5.5-year standard, both projects would be acceptable. If Projects A and B were *mutually exclusive*, however, A would be chosen over B because of its shorter payback period.

Advantages and disadvantages of the payback method   The payback method is widely used both because it is simple and because very long-term commitments tend to be viewed as undesirable. In spite of its widespread industry use, however, payback has a number of serious shortcomings.

First, it generally does not measure the profitability of investment projects and essentially ignores cash flows occurring after the payback period.[2] Thus, payback figures can be misleading.

For example, assume a firm is considering two projects, C and D, each costing $10,000. It is expected that Project C will generate net cash inflows of $5,000 per year for 3 years, and that Project D will generate net cash inflows of $4,500 per year forever. The payback period for Project C is 2 years ($10,000/$5,000), whereas the payback period for Project D is 2.2 years ($10,000/$4,500). If these projects were mutually exclusive, payback would favor C, because it has the lower payback period. Yet most people would prefer an investment yielding a cash flow stream of $4,500 per year forever to one yielding a cash flow stream of $5,000 per year for only 3 years. The payback approach does not adequately handle these types of situations.

Second, the payback method gives equal weight to all cash inflows within the payback period, regardless of when they occur during the period. In other words, the technique ignores the *time value of money.*

Assume, for example, that a firm is considering two projects, E and F, each costing $10,000. Project E is expected to yield cash flows over a 3-year period of $5,000 during the first year, $3,000 during the second year, and $2,000 during the third year. Project F is expected to yield cash flows of $2,000 during the first year, $3,000 during the second year, and $5,000 during the third year. Viewed from the payback perspective, these projects would appear to be equally attractive, yet present value concepts clearly indicate that Project E is the more desirable of the two.

Third, payback provides no *objective* criterion for decision making that is consistent with shareholder wealth maximization. The choice of an acceptable payback period is largely a *subjective* one, and different people using essentially identical data may make different accept-reject decisions about a project.

The payback method is sometimes justified on the basis that it provides a measure of the *risk* associated with a project. Although it is true that there may be less risk associated with a shorter payback period than with a longer one, risk is best thought of in terms of the *variability* of project returns. Since payback ignores this dimension, it is at best a crude tool for risk analysis.

A more valid justification for the use of the payback method is that it does give some indication of a project's desirability from a *liquidity* perspective, since it measures the time required for a firm to recover its initial investment in a project. A company that is very concerned about the early recovery of investment funds—such as one investing overseas in a politically unstable area, or one expecting a cash shortage in the future—might find this method useful.

Of course, many firms evaluate investment projects using more than one criterion. For instance, a firm might use the net present value or the internal

---

[2]There is no reason why a good analyst needs to ignore the cash flows occurring beyond the payback period when evaluating a specific project.

rate of return method—both of which are discussed later in this chapter—*in addition to* payback. The combination of these methods gives some indication of both a project's profitability and its liquidity. The use of payback in conjunction with other, more technically correct methods is quite common. One survey of the capital budgeting techniques used by over one hundred of the largest firms in the United States reported that only 9 percent used payback as their primary investment criterion, whereas 44 percent used it as a secondary technique for project evaluation.[3]

In summary, payback is not a satisfactory criterion for investment decision making, because it may lead to a selection of projects that do not make the largest possible contribution to a firm's value. It can, however, be useful as a supplementary decision-making tool.

NET PRESENT VALUE

The net present value (NPV) of an investment project is defined as the present value of the stream of net cash flows from the project minus the project's net investment. The cash flows are discounted at the firm's required rate of return, that is, its *cost of capital*. A firm's cost of capital is defined as its minimum acceptable rate of return for investment projects of average risk.

The net present value of a project may be expressed as follows:

$$NPV = PVNCF - NINV, \tag{10.3}$$

where NPV is the net present value; PVNCF, the present value of net cash flows; and NINV, the net investment.

Assuming a cost of capital, k, the net present value for a project with a 5-year expected life would be the following:

$$NPV = \frac{NCF_1}{(1 + k)^1} + \frac{NCF_2}{(1 + k)^2} + \frac{NCF_3}{(1 + k)^3}$$
$$+ \frac{NCF_4}{(1 + k)^4} + \frac{NCF_5}{(1 + k)^5} - NINV, \tag{10.4}$$

where $NCF_1 - NCF_5$ are the net cash flows occurring in years 1 through 5. NCF_5 may be assumed to include any salvage value remaining at the end of the project's life.

As mentioned in Chapter 9, the annual net cash flows for normal projects are usually positive after the initial net investment. Occasionally, however, one or more of the expected net cash flows over the life of a project may be negative. When this occurs, positive numbers are used for years having positive net cash flows (net inflows), and negative numbers are used for years having negative net cash flows (net outflows).

[3]See Lawrence J. Gittman and John R. Forrester, Jr. "A Survey of Capital Budgeting Techniques Used by Major U.S. Firms." *Financial Management* (Fall 1977): 66–71.

In general, the net present value of a project may be defined as follows:

$$NPV = \sum_{t=1}^{n} \frac{NCF_t}{(1 + k)^t} - NINV$$

$$= \left(\sum_{t=1}^{n} NCF_t \times PVIF_{k,t} \right) - NINV \,,$$

(10.5)

where n is the expected project life, and $\sum_{t=1}^{n} [NCF_t/(1 + k)^t]$ is the arithmetic sum of the discounted net cash flows for each year t over the life of the project (n years), that is, the present value of the net cash flows.

Table 10–2 shows the net present value computations for projects A and B introduced earlier in Table 10–1. These calculations assume a 14 percent cost of capital. The calculations in these tables also assume that cash flows are received at the end of each year rather than as a flow during the year. This assumption, although a normal one, tends to slightly understate a project's net present value or internal rate of return.

Decision rule In general, a project should be accepted if its net present value is greater than or equal to zero and rejected if its net present value is less than zero. This is so because a positive net present value in principle translates directly into increases in stock prices and increases in shareholders' wealth. In the previous example, Project A would be rejected because it has a negative net present value, and Project B would be accepted because it has a positive net present value.

If two or more *mutually exclusive* investments of approximately the same size all have positive net present values, the project having the largest net present value is the one selected. Assume, for example, that a firm has three mutually exclusive investment opportunities, G, H, and I, each requiring a net investment of about $10,000. Project G has a net present value of $2,000; H has a net present value of $4,000; and I has a net present value of $3,500.

TABLE 10–2 **Sample Net Present Value Calculations**

PROJECT A		PROJECT B		
	Year	NCF	$PVIF_{0.14,t}$*	PV of NCF
Present value of an annuity of $12,500 for 6 years at 14 percent:				
	1	$ 5,000	0.877	$ 4,385
PV of NCF = $12,500(PVIFA$_{0.14,6}$)	2	10,000	0.769	7,690
= $12,500(3.889)†	3	15,000	0.675	10,125
= $48,612.50	4	15,000	0.592	8,880
	5	25,000	0.519	12,975
Less: Net investment 50,000.00	6	30,000	0.456	13,680
Net present value $ – 1,387.50				$57,735
	Less: Net investment			50,000
	Net present value			$ 7,735

*From the PVIF table (Table II).
†From the PVIFA table (Table IV).

Of the three, H would be preferred to the other two, because it has the highest net present value and therefore is expected to make the largest contribution to the objective of shareholder wealth maximization.

Advantages and disadvantages of the net present value method   The net present value approach is superior to the payback method, because it considers both the magnitude and the timing of cash flows over a project's entire expected life. In a period of high inflation rates it is especially important to consider the time value of money in project analysis. Therefore, the net present value approach is favored over the payback approach, because the latter ignores the timing of cash flows.

The net present value approach also indicates whether a proposed project will yield the rate of return required by the firm's investors. The cost of capital (discount rate) represents this rate of return; when a project's net present value is greater than or equal to zero, the firm's investors can expect to earn at least their required rate of return.

The net present value criterion does have one weakness in that many people find it difficult to understand the exact meaning of the net present value dollars that are computed using this technique.[4] As a result, many firms use another present value–based method that is more easily interpreted, namely, the *internal rate of return* method.

INTERNAL RATE OF RETURN

The *internal rate of return* is defined as the discount rate that equates the present value of the net cash flows from a project with the present value of the net investment.[5] It is the discount rate that causes a project's net present value to equal zero.

A project's internal rate of return can be determined by means of the following equation:

$$\sum_{t=1}^{n} \frac{\text{NCF}_t}{(1 + r)^t} = \text{NINV} , \tag{10.6}$$

where $\text{NCF}_t/(1 + r)^t$ is the present value of net cash flows in period t discounted at the rate r, NINV is the net investment in the project, and r is the internal rate of return.

For a project having a 5-year life, this basic formula can be rewritten as follows:

$$\frac{\text{NCF}_1}{(1 + r)^1} + \frac{\text{NCF}_2}{(1 + r)^2} + \frac{\text{NCF}_3}{(1 + r)^3} + \frac{\text{NCF}_4}{(1 + r)^4} + \frac{\text{NCF}_5}{(1 + r)^5} = \text{NINV} . \tag{10.7}$$

[4]The net present value of a project may be thought of as the expected number of dollars the present value of the firm (that is, shareholders' wealth) is increased by as a result of adopting the project.

[5]This is also called the *discounted cash flow* (DCF) rate of return.

Subtracting the net investment, NINV, from both sides of Equation 10.7 yields the following:

$$\frac{NCF_1}{(1 + r)^1} + \frac{NCF_2}{(1 + r)^2} + \frac{NCF_3}{(1 + r)^3} + \frac{NCF_4}{(1 + r)^4} + \frac{NCF_5}{(1 + r)^5} - NINV = 0 . \quad \textbf{(10.8)}$$

This is essentially the same equation as that used in the net present value method. The only difference is that in the net present value approach a discount rate, k, is specified and the net present value is computed, whereas in the internal rate of return method the discount rate, r, which causes the project net present value to equal zero, is the unknown.

Figure 10–1 illustrates the relationship between net present value and internal rate of return. The figure plots the net present value of Project B (from Table 10–1) against the discount rate used to evaluate its cash flows. Note that at a 14 percent cost of capital, the net present value of B is $7,735—the same figure that resulted from the computations performed in Table 10–2.

FIGURE 10–1   **Relationship between the Net Present Value and the Internal Rate of Return for Projects A and B**

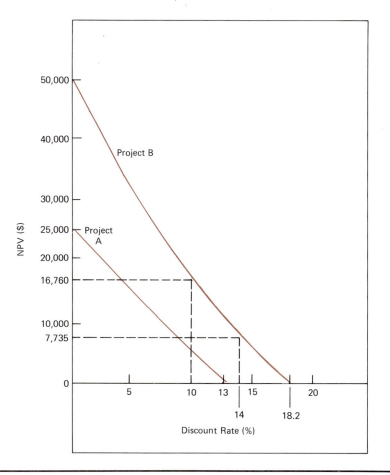

The internal rate of return of Project B is approximately equal to 18.2 percent. (The exact calculation will be illustrated algebraically.) Thus, the internal rate of return is a special case of the net present value computation.

The internal rates of return for Projects A and B now can be calculated. Since Project A is an annuity of $12,500 for 6 years requiring a net investment of $50,000, its internal rate of return may be computed directly with the aid of a PVIFA table such as Table IV.

In this case the present value of the annuity, PVAN, is $50,000, and the annuity, R, is $12,500 for $n = 6$ years. Equation 3.15 from Chapter 3,

$$PVAN = R(PVIFA_{i,n}) ,$$

can be rewritten to solve for the PVIFA as follows:

$$PVIFA_{i,n} = \frac{PVAN}{R} .$$

In this case, PVIFA = $50,000/$12,500 = 4.000. Referring to Table IV and reading across the table for $n = 6$, it can be seen that the interest factor of 4.000 occurs near 13 percent, where it is 3.998. Thus, the internal rate of return for Project A is about 13 percent.

The internal rate of return for Project B is more difficult to calculate, since the project is expected to yield uneven cash flows. In this case, the internal rate of return is computed by trial and error or with the help of a financial calculator. (See the "Calculator Applications" section at the end of the chapter.) The steps in this procedure are as follows:

Step 1. Make an approximate estimate of the internal rate of return.
Step 2. Use this rate to compute the project's net present value.
Step 3. Try a *higher* rate if a positive net present value results or a *lower* rate if a negative one results.
Step 4. Repeat the process (attempting to "bracket" the internal rate of return) until a rate is found at which the net present value is equal to zero.

Table 10–3 illustrates this procedure. First, an r of 15 percent is tried, resulting in a net present value of $5,745. Next, a higher discount rate, 19 percent, is chosen; in this case the net present value is $-$1,325. This indicates that the internal rate of return is between 15 and 19 percent. Trying 18 percent results in a net present value of $315, narrowing the range to between 18 and 19 percent.

A more exact internal rate of return can be computed by means of interpolation:

$$
\begin{aligned}
r &= 18\% + \frac{\$315}{\$315 + \$1,325}(19\% - 18\%) \\
&= 18\% + 0.19(1\%) \\
&= 18.19\% .
\end{aligned}
$$

TABLE 10–3 Trial-and-Error Computation of the Internal Rate of Return for Project B

YEAR (1)	NET CASH FLOW (2)	$PVIF_{0.15,t}$ (3)	PV CASH FLOWS (4) = (3) × (2)	$PVIF_{0.19,t}$ (5)	PV CASH FLOWS (6) = (5) × (2)	$PVIF_{0.18,t}$ (7)	PV CASH FLOWS (8) = (7) × (2)
1	$ 5,000	0.870	$ 4,350	0.840	$ 4,200	0.847	$ 4,235
2	10,000	0.756	7,560	0.706	7,060	0.718	7,180
3	15,000	0.658	9,870	0.593	8,895	0.609	9,135
4	15,000	0.572	8,580	0.499	7,485	0.516	7,740
5	25,000	0.497	12,425	0.419	10,475	0.437	10,925
6	30,000	0.432	12,960	0.352	10,560	0.370	11,100
			$55,745		$48,675		$50,315
		Less: NINV	50,000	*Less:* NINV	50,000	*Less:* NINV	50,000
			NPV = $ 5,745		NPV = $−1,325		NPV = $ 315

Decision rule Generally the internal rate of return method indicates that a project whose internal rate of return is greater than or equal to the firm's cost of capital should be accepted, whereas a project whose internal rate of return is less than the firm's cost of capital should be rejected. In the case of Projects A and B, if the cost of capital were 14 percent B would be acceptable and A would be unacceptable.

When two independent projects are considered under conditions of no capital rationing, the net present value and internal rate of return techniques result in the same accept-reject decision. This can be seen in Figure 10–1. For example, if the firm's cost of capital is 10 percent, Project B has a positive net present value ($16,760). Its internal rate of return is 18.19 percent, exceeding the cost of capital. When two mutually exclusive projects are being considered, it is *generally* preferable to accept the project having the highest internal rate of return as long as it is greater than or equal to the cost of capital. In this case, if A and B were mutually exclusive, B would be chosen over A, as can be seen in Figure 10–1. Exceptions to this general rule are considered later in the chapter.

Advantages and disadvantages of the internal rate of return method
The internal rate of return method is widely used in industry by firms that employ present value–based capital budgeting techniques. In fact, in a survey of over one hundred U.S. firms, nearly 54 percent reported the use of the internal rate of return as their *primary* capital budgeting technique.[6] This popularity may be due to the fact that many people feel more comfortable dealing with the concept of a project's rate of return than with its net present value.[7] Like the net present value approach, the internal rate of return technique takes into account both the magnitude and the timing of cash flows over the entire life of a project in measuring the project's economic desirability.

[6]Lawrence J. Gittman and John R. Forrester, Jr. *op. cit.*, pp. 66–71.
[7]It is also easy to program a computer to perform these calculations, thus eliminating the need for trial-and-error manipulations. Some financial calculators, such as the Texas Instruments Professional Business Analyst (illustrated in the "Calculator Applications" section of this chapter), can also solve internal rate of return problems when the periodic cash flows are uneven.

However, there are some potential problems involved in using the internal rate of return technique. The possible existence of *multiple internal rates of return* is one such problem. Whereas equating the net present value of a project to zero will yield only one internal rate of return, *r*, for *normal* investments, there are times when two or more rates may be obtained. Recall that a normal project has an initial cash outlay or outlays (net investment) followed by a stream of positive net cash flows. If for some reason—such as large abandonment costs at the end of a project's life or a major shutdown and rebuilding of a facility sometime during its life—the initial net investment is followed by one or more positive net cash flows (inflows) that then are followed by a negative cash flow,[8] it is possible to obtain more than one internal rate of return.

Whenever a project has multiple internal rates of return, the pattern of cash flows over the project's life contains more than one sign change, for example, − ↑ + + ↑ −. In this case there are two sign changes (indicated by the arrows)—from minus to plus, and again from plus to minus.

Consider the following investment, which has three internal rates of return—0, 100, and 200 percent:

Year	Net Cash Flows
0	− $ 1,000
1	+ $ 6,000
2	− $11,000
3	+ $ 6,000

Unfortunately, none of these rates can be compared to the firm's cost of capital to determine the project's acceptability.

Although several techniques have been proposed for dealing with the multiple internal rate of return problem, none provides a simple, complete, and generally satisfactory solution. The best approach is to use the net present value criterion. If a project's net present value is positive, it is acceptable; if it is negative, it is not acceptable. There are many computer software packages available that compute internal rates of return, and they will usually warn the user when a potential multiple internal rate of return problem exists. Whenever this is a possibility, the use of the net present value method is preferred.

PROFITABILITY INDEX

The profitability index (PI), or benefit-cost ratio, is the ratio of the present value of future net cash flows over the life of a project to the net investment. It is expressed as follows:

$$PI = \frac{\sum_{t=1}^{n} NCF_t/(1 + k)^t}{NINV}.$$ (10.9)

[8]Table 9–2 in Chapter 9 illustrates two such projects, X and Y.

Assuming a 14 percent cost of capital, k, and using the data from Table 10–2, the profitability index for Projects A and B can be calculated as follows:

$$PI_A = \frac{\$48,612.50}{\$50,000}$$

$$= 0.97 .$$

$$PI_B = \frac{\$57,735}{\$50,000}$$

$$= 1.15 .$$

The profitability index is interpreted as the present value return *for each dollar of initial investment.* In comparison, the net present value approach measures the total present value dollar return.

Decision rule   A project whose profitability index is greater than or equal to 1 is considered acceptable, while a project having a profitability index less than 1 is considered unacceptable.[9] In this case, Project B is acceptable, whereas Project A is not. When two or more *independent* projects with normal cash flows are considered, the profitability index, net present value, and internal rate of return approaches all will yield identical accept-reject signals; this is true, for example, with Projects A and B.

When dealing with mutually exclusive investments, conflicts may arise between the net present value and the profitability index criteria. This is most likely to occur if the alternative projects require significantly different net investments.

Consider, for example, the following information on Projects J and K. According to the net present value criterion, Project J would be preferred because of its larger net present value. According to the profitability index criterion, Project K would be preferred.

	Project J	Project K
Present value of net cash flows	$25,000	$14,000
Less: Net investment	−20,000	−10,000
Net present value	$ 5,000	$ 4,000
$PI = \dfrac{\text{Present value of net cash flows}}{\text{Net investment}}$	1.25	1.40

When a conflict arises, the final decision must be made on the basis of other factors. For example, if a firm has no constraint on the funds available to it for capital investment—that is, no capital rationing—the net present value approach is preferred, since it will select the projects that are expected

---

[9]When a project has a profitability index equal to 1, the present value of the net cash flows is exactly equal to the net investment. Thus, the project has a net present value of zero, meaning that it is expected to earn the investors' required rate of return and nothing more.

to generate the largest *total dollar* increase in the firm's wealth and, by extension, maximize shareholder wealth. If, however, the firm is in a capital rationing situation, and capital budgeting is being done for only 1 period,[10] the profitability index approach may be preferred, since it will indicate which projects will maximize the returns *per dollar of investment*—an appropriate objective when a funds constraint exists.

NET PRESENT VALUE VERSUS INTERNAL RATE OF RETURN: THE REINVESTMENT RATE ASSUMPTION

As was indicated, both the net present value and the internal rate of return methods result in identical decisions to either accept or reject an *independent* project. This is true because the net present value is greater than (less than) zero if and only if the internal rate of return is greater than (less than) the required rate of return, k. In the case of *mutually exclusive* projects, however, the two methods may yield contradictory results; one project may have a *higher* internal rate of return than another and, at the same time, a *lower* net present value.

Consider, for example, *mutually exclusive* Projects L and M described in the following table. Both require a net investment of $1,000. Using the internal rate of return approach, Project L is preferred, with an IRR of 21.5 percent compared with Project M's IRR of 18.3 percent. Using the net present value approach with a discount rate of 5 percent, Project M is preferred to Project L. Hence, it is necessary to determine which technique is the correct one to use in this situation.

	Project L	Project M
Net investment	$1,000	$1,000
Net cash flows:		
Year 1	$ 667	$ 0
Year 2	$ 667	$1,400
Net present value at 5%	$ 240	$ 270
Internal rate of return	21.5%	18.3%

The outcome depends on what *assumptions* the decision maker chooses to make about the *implied reinvestment rate* for the net cash flows generated from each project. This can be seen in Figure 10–2. For discount (reinvestment) rates below 10 percent, Project M has a higher net present value than Project L and is therefore preferred. For discount rates greater 10 percent, Project L is preferred using both the net present value and internal rate of return approaches. Hence, a conflict only occurs in this case for discount (cost-of-capital) rates below 10 percent. The net present value method assumes that cash flows are *reinvested at the firm's cost of capital*, whereas the internal rate of return method assumes that these flows are *reinvested at*

---

[10]If the firm makes capital budgeting decisions for more than 1 period in the future, it is usually necessary to use some kind of programming model. Footnote 14 lists a number of references for some of these techniques.

FIGURE 10–2   **Net Present Value versus Internal Rate of
Return for Mutually Exclusive Alternatives**

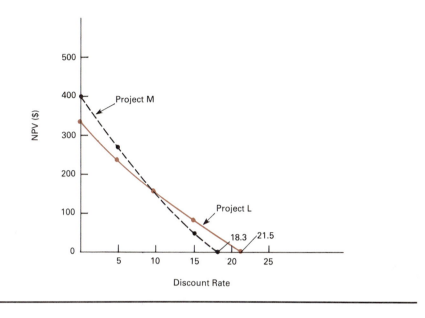

the computed internal rate of return.[11] Generally, the cost of capital is considered to be a more realistic reinvestment rate than the computed internal rate of return, because this is the rate the next (marginal) investment project can be assumed to earn. This can be seen in Figure 9–1 in Chapter 9. The last project invested in, Project E, offers a rate of return nearly equal to the firm's marginal cost of capital.

Consequently, in the absence of capital rationing, the net present value approach is normally superior to both the profitability index and the internal rate of return when choosing among mutually exclusive investments.

Table 10–4 presents a summary of the four capital budgeting decision models discussed in the chapter.

CAPITAL RATIONING AND
THE CAPITAL BUDGETING DECISION

For each of the selection criteria previously discussed, the decision rule is to undertake *all* independent investment projects that meet the acceptance standard. This rule places no restrictions on the total amount of acceptable capital projects a company may undertake in any particular period.

---

[11]A more complete discussion of this problem and the underlying assumptions is found in J. Hirshleifer. "On the Theory of the Optimal Investment Decision." *Journal of Political Economy* 66 (Aug. 1958): 95–103; and James H. Lorie and Leonard J. Savage. "Three Problems in Rationing Capital." *Journal of Business* 23 (Oct. 1955): 229–239.

TABLE 10–4   **Summary of the Capital Budgeting Decision Models**

Model	Project Acceptance Criterion	Strengths	Weaknesses
Payback (PB)	Accept project if PB period is less than the maximum acceptable PB.	Easy and inexpensive to use. Provides a crude measure of project risk. Provides a measure of project liquidity.	No objective decision criterion. Not a measure of profitability. Fails to consider timing of cash flows.
Net present value (NPV)	Accept project if project has a positive NPV, that is, if the present value of net cash flows, evaluated at the firm's cost of capital, exceeds the net investment required.	Considers the timing of cash flows. Provides an objective, return-based criterion for acceptance or rejection. Most conceptually correct approach.	Difficulty in interpreting the meaning of the NPV computation.
Internal rate of return (IRR)	Accept project if IRR exceeds the firm's cost of capital.	Same benefits as the NPV. Easy to interpret the meaning of IRR.	Multiple rates of return problem. Sometimes gives decision that conflicts with NPV.
Profitability index (PI)	Accept project if PI is greater than 1.0.	Same benefits as the NPV. Useful to guide decisions in capital rationing problems.	Sometimes gives decision that conflicts with NPV.

However, many firms do not have unlimited funds available for investment. Rather than letting the size of their capital budget be determined by the number of profitable investment opportunities available, many companies choose to place an upper limit, or *constraint*, on the amount of funds allocated to capital investments. This constraint may be either *self-imposed*—by the firm's management—or *externally imposed*—by conditions in the capital markets.

For example, a very conservative firm may be reluctant to use debt or external equity to finance capital expenditures. Instead, it would limit capital expenditures to cash flows from continuing operations minus any dividends paid. Another firm may feel that it lacks the managerial resources to successfully undertake all acceptable projects in a given year and choose to limit capital expenditures for this reason.

There are a number of externally imposed constraints that might limit a firm's capital expenditures. For example, a firm's loan agreements may contain restrictive covenants that limit future borrowing. The Ryder System, Inc., loan agreements contain a restrictive covenant that reads as follows:

Company may not permit total consolidated debt (which includes lease obligations) to exceed 400% of consolidated net worth.[12]

Some of U.S. Air's loan agreements are even more restrictive:

Company may not create any additional subordinated debt ranking on parity with the new debentures unless the total of such debt does not exceed the greater of $75,000,000 or 300% of the net worth of the company and all debt which it terms is subordinated to senior debt.[13]

Similarly, a weak financial position, conditions in the securities markets, or both may make the flotation of a new bond or stock issue by the firm impossible or prohibitively expensive. Examples of such market-imposed constraints include depressed stock market prices, unusually high interest rates due to a "tight money" policy on the part of the Federal Reserve, or a reluctance on the part of investors to purchase new securities if the firm has a large percentage of debt in its capital structure.

Several different methods can be used in making capital budgeting decisions under capital rationing. When the initial outlays occur in two (or more) periods, the methods are quite elaborate and require the use of linear, integer, or goal programming.[14] However, when the initial outlays are confined to 1 period, a relatively simple approach employing the profitability index can be used. Briefly, the approach consists of the following steps:

Step 1. Calculate the profitability index for each of a series of investment projects.
Step 2. Rank the projects according to their profitability indexes (from highest to lowest).
Step 3. Beginning with the project having the highest profitability index, proceed down through the list and accept projects having profitability indexes greater than or equal to 1 until the entire capital budget has been utilized.

At times a firm may not be able to utilize its entire capital budget because the next acceptable project on its list is too large, given the remaining available funds. In this case, the firm's management should choose among the following three alternatives:

[12]*Moody's Transportation Manual.* New York: Moody's Investors Service, 1978, p. 1160.
[13]*Ibid.*, p. 1005.
[14]The following references contain information on the use of these more advanced models: James R. McGuigan and R. Charles Moyer. *Managerial Economics*, 3rd ed. St. Paul: West Publishing, 1983, pp. 88–91; or H. Martin Weingartner. *Mathematical Programming and the Analysis of Capital Budgeting Problems.* Englewood Cliffs, N.J.: Prentice-Hall, 1963. See also Sang M. Lee and A. J. Lerro. "Capital Budgeting for Multiple Objectives." *Financial Management* 3 (Spring 1974): 58–66, and Richard H. Bernhard. "Mathematical Programming Models for Capital Budgeting: A Survey, Generalization, and Critique." *Journal of Financial and Quantitative Analysis* 4 (June 1969):111–158.

Alternative 1.   Search for another combination of projects, perhaps including some smaller, less profitable ones that will allow for a more complete utilization of available funds *and* increase the net present value of the combination of projects.

Alternative 2.   Attempt to relax the funds constraint so that sufficient resources are available to accept the last project for which funds were not fully available.

Alternative 3.   Accept as many projects as possible and either invest any excess funds in short-term securities until the next period,[15] pay out the excess funds to shareholders as dividends, use the funds to reduce outstanding debt, or do a combination of the above.

The following example illustrates how these alternatives can be applied to an actual capital budgeting decision. Suppose that management of the Old Mexico Tile Company has decided to limit next year's capital exenditures to $550,000. Eight capital exenditure projects have been proposed—P, R, S, U, T, V, Q, and W—and ranked according to their profitability indexes, as shown in Table 10–5. Given the $550,000 ceiling, the firm's management proceeds down the list of projects, selecting P, R, S, and U, in that order. Project T cannot be accepted, since this would require a capital outlay of $25,000 in excess of the $550,000 limit. Projects P, R, S, and U together yield a net present value of $114,750 but require a total investment outlay of $525,000, leaving $25,000 from the capital budget that is not invested in projects. Management is considering the following three alternatives:

Alternative 1.   It could attempt to find another combination of projects, perhaps including some smaller ones, that would allow for a more complete utilization of available funds and increase the cumulative net present value. In this case, a likely combination would be Projects P, R, S, T, and V. This combination would fully utilize the $550,000 available and create a net present value of $116,250—an increase of $1,500 over the net present value of $114,750 from projects P, R, S, and U.

Alternative 2.   It could attempt to increase the capital budget by another $25,000 to allow Project T to be added to the list of adopted projects.

Alternative 3.   It could merely accept the first four projects—P, R, S, and U—and invest the remaining $25,000 in a short-term security until the next period. This alternative is not especially desir-

---

[15]If a firm does not invest a portion of its available capital resources in projects earning a rate of return at least equal to the cost of capital, an implicit opportunity cost of lost earnings is incurred. For example, suppose a firm cannot invest a portion of its capital budget because the next acceptable project requires a larger net investment than is available in remaining funds. If the firm's after-tax cost of capital is 15 percent and the unutilized funds can only be invested in short-term securities earning 5 percent after taxes, the opportunity cost of this action is a 10 percent difference, representing a loss in potential earnings. Thus, as long as profitable investment alternatives exist, the firm should seek ways to fully utilize all available capital funds.

TABLE 10–5 Sample Ranking of Proposed Projects According to Their Profitability Indexes

Project (1)	Net Investment (2)	Net Present Value (3)	Present Value of Net Cash Flows (4)	PI = (4) ÷ (2)	Cumulative Net Investment	Cumulative Net Present Value
P	$100,000	$25,000	$125,000	1.25	$100,000	$ 25,000
R	150,000	33,000	183,000	1.22	250,000	58,000
S	175,000	36,750	211,750	1.21	425,000	94,750
U	100,000	20,000	120,000	1.20	525,000	114,750
T	50,000	9,000	59,000	1.18	575,000	123,750
V	75,000	12,500	87,500	1.17	650,000	136,250
Q	200,000	30,000	230,000	1.15	850,000	166,250
W	50,000	−10,000	40,000	0.80	900,000	156,250

able, however, since the return on the short-term investment would surely be less than the firm's cost of capital (required rate of return). Thus, the difference between the firm's cost of capital and the return on the short-term investment would constitute an *opportunity cost.*

In this case, *Alternative 1* seems to be the most desirable of the three. In rearranging the capital budget, however, the firm should never accept a project, such as W, that does not meet the minimum acceptance criterion of a positive net present value (a profitability index greater than 1).

REVIEWING AND POSTAUDITING AN ACCEPTED PROJECT

A final important step in the capital budgeting process is the review of investment projects after they have been implemented. This can provide useful information on the effectiveness of the company's selection process. The postaudit procedure consists of comparing *actual* cash flows from an accepted project with *projected* cash flows that were estimated when the project was adopted. Because projected flows contain an element of uncertainty, actual values would not be expected to exactly match estimated values. Instead, a project review should be concerned with identifying systematic biases or errors in cash flow estimation on the part of individuals, departments, plants, or divisions and attempting to determine *why* these biases or errors exist. This type of analysis, when properly performed, can help a company's decision makers better evaluate investment proposals submitted in the future.

Another objective of the project review process involves determining whether a project that has not lived up to expectations should be continued or abandoned. The decision to abandon a project requires the company to compare the cost of abandonment with any future cash flows that are expected over the project's remaining life. These estimates of future cash flows will usually be more accurate after the project has been in service for a period of time.[16]

A COMPREHENSIVE EXAMPLE OF CAPITAL BUDGETING: OPENING A NEW BANK BRANCH

The First National Bank and Trust Company has a single banking office located in the downtown business district of a medium-sized town. As the population has moved toward the suburbs, First National has seen its share of both local banking deposits and profits decline. One of the bank's vice-presidents has proposed that First National try to reverse this trend by building a branch in a new, affluent suburban community. He has presented the bank's executive committee with the following information.

The initial cost of the bank building and equipment is $1,100,000. This facility is expected to have a useful life of 20 years. The branch building and its equipment will be depreciated over their 20-year life using straight line depreciation to a $100,000 salvage value.[17] Consequently, annual depreciation will be ($1,100,000 − $100,000)/20 = $50,000. The bank building is to be constructed on land leased for $20,000 per year. In addition to the $1,100,000 investment for the building and equipment, the parent bank's net working capital must be increased by $100,000 to accommodate the new branch.

Based upon customer surveys, population trends, the location of competitor banks, and the experience other area banks have had with their branches, it is estimated that the annual revenues from the new branch will be $400,000. Of this $400,000 in revenues, $50,000 will be drawn away from the bank's main office. (Assume that the main office will not attempt to cut its expenses because of this loss in revenues.)

In addition to the $20,000 annual expense for the land lease, the new branch will incur about $130,000 per year in other expenses, including personnel costs, utilities, and interest paid on accounts. Both expenses and revenues are expected to remain approximately constant over the branch's 20-year life.

The bank's marginal tax rate is 40 percent. A 10 percent investment tax credit may be taken on the equipment installed in the new bank building. Of the combined building and equipment cost of $1,100,000, $200,000 represents equipment investments that are eligible for the investment tax credit.

The bank's cost of capital (required rate of return) is 9 percent after tax.

---

[16] A further discussion of the abandonment question may be found in Gordon Shillinglaw's two articles, "Profit Analysis for Abandonment Decision" and "Residual Values in Investment Analysis," reprinted in Ezra Solomon, ed. *The Management of Corporate Capital.* New York: Free Press, 1959, pp. 269–281 and 259–268, respectively. See also Alexander Robichek and James C. Van Horne. "Abandonment Value and Capital Budgeting." *Journal of Finance* 22 (Dec. 1967): 577–589.

[17] For simplicity, straight line depreciation has been assumed. As discussed in Chapter 9, the bank would most likely use a 15-year ACRS life on the building and a 5-year ACRS life on the equipment.

Step 1:   Computing the net investment.

New project cost	$1,100,000
Plus: Increase in working capital	100,000
Gross investment	$1,200,000
Less: Investment tax credit (10% × $200,000)	20,000
Net investment	$1,180,000

The net investment equals the new project cost ($1,100,000) plus the increase in working capital ($100,000) minus the investment tax credit that may be taken on $200,000 of the investment.

Step 2:   Computing net cash flows.

Net increase in revenues ($400,000 − $50,000)	$350,000
Less: Operating costs of branch ($130,000 + $20,000)	150,000
Less: Depreciation	50,000
Net income before taxes	$150,000
Less: Tax (40%)	60,000
Net income after taxes	$ 90,000
Plus: Depreciation	50,000
Net cash flow	$140,000

Net cash flows are calculated for years 1 through 19 by subtracting branch operating costs and depreciation from the incremental revenues of $350,000. This yields net income before taxes from which taxes (at the 40 percent rate) are deducted to arrive at net income after taxes. By adding back depreciation, the net cash flow equals $140,000 for each year from 1 through 19. Net cash flows in year 20 are computed by adding the $100,000 estimated salvage and the $100,000 return of working capital[18] to the annual net cash flow of $140,000 to equal $340,000.

Step 3.   Arraying project cash flows and evaluating alternatives.

Net investment	$1,180,000
Net cash flows:	
Years 1–19	$ 140,000
Year 20	$ 340,000

After the project cash flows have been computed and arrayed, the desirability of the project must be determined using one or more of the four decision criteria discussed in this chapter, namely, payback, net present value, internal rate of return, or profitability index. In this example the project is evaluated using all four approaches.

---

[18]The $100,000 working capital requirement is added back to the year 20 cash flows under the assumption that at the end of 20 years, when the project is terminated, there will no longer be a need for this incremental working capital, and thus the working capital of $100,000 can be liquidated and made available to the firm.

Criterion 1.   The payback period.

$$PB = \frac{\text{Net investment}}{\text{Annual net cash flow}}$$

$$= \frac{\$1,180,000}{\$140,000/\text{year}}$$

$$= 8.4 \text{ years .}$$

If the bank's cutoff payback period is greater than 8.4 years, the project would be accepted; if it is less than 8.4 years, the project would be rejected.

Criterion 2.   Net present value.

$$NPV = PVNCF - NINV$$

$$= \sum_{t=1}^{19} \frac{\$140,000}{(1 + 0.09)^t} + \frac{\$340,000}{(1 + 0.09)^{20}} - \$1,180,000$$

$$= (\$140,000 \times PVIFA_{0.09,19}) + (\$340,000 \times PVIF_{0.09,20}) - \$1,180,000 .$$

The first term in the net present value equation is the present value of an annuity of \$140,000 for 19 years at 9 percent, the bank's cost of capital. Using the present value of an annuity table (Table IV), an interest factor of 8.950 may be found. The second term is the present value of \$340,000 received in 20 years at 9 percent. From the present value table (Table II), an interest factor of 0.178 is found. Thus, the net present value of this project at a 9 percent cost of capital is as follows:

$$NPV = \$140,000(8.950) + \$340,000(0.178) - \$1,180,000$$

$$= \$1,253,000 + \$60,520 - \$1,180,000$$

$$= \$133,520 .$$

Using the net present value criterion and a cost of capital of 9 percent, this project would be acceptable, since it has a positive net present value.

Criterion 3.   Internal rate of return.

According to this method, a discount rate that makes the net present value of the project equal to zero must be found:

$$\text{Present value of net cash flows} - \text{Net investment} = 0 ,$$

or

$$\sum_{t=1}^{19} \frac{\$140,000}{(1 + r)^t} + \frac{\$340,000}{(1 + r)^{20}} - \$1,180,000 = 0 ,$$

were r is the internal rate of return.

Since the net present value was positive at an interest rate of 9 percent, only higher rates need be considered, because the higher the rate, the lower the net present value. Trying $r = 11\%$ yields the following:

$$\begin{aligned} \text{NPV} &= \$140,000(7.839) + \$340,000(0.124) - \$1,180,000 \\ &= \$1,097,460 + \$42,160 - \$1,180,000 \\ &= -\$40,380 . \end{aligned}$$

Because the net present value is negative, a lower r, such as $r = 10\%$, should be tried next:

$$\begin{aligned} \text{NPV} &= \$140,000(8.365) + \$340,000(0.149) - \$1,180,000 \\ &= \$1,171,100 + \$50,660 - \$1,180,000 \\ &= \$41,760 . \end{aligned}$$

Since this figure is positive, the actual internal rate of return falls somewhere between 10 and 11 percent. It is computed by interpolation as follows:

$$\begin{aligned} \text{IRR} &= 10\% + \frac{\$41,760}{\$41,760 + \$40,380}(1\%) \\ &= 10\% + 0.51(1\%) \\ &= 10.51\% . \end{aligned}$$

Since the internal rate of return equals 10.51 percent, which is greater than the cost of capital, the project is acceptable by this criterion.

Criterion 4.   Profitability index.

The profitability index is the ratio of the present value of future net cash flows to the net investment. From the previous net present value calculation, we know that the present value of net cash flows at a 9 percent cost of capital is $1,313,520 ($1,253,000 + $60,520). Thus, the profitability index is computed as follows:

$$\begin{aligned} \text{PI} &= \frac{\$1,313,520}{\$1,180,000} \\ &= 1.11 . \end{aligned}$$

Because the profitability index is greater than 1, the new branch bank project is acceptable according to this criterion.

Based on these calculations, it appears that the new branch proposal will increase shareholder wealth and therefore should be undertaken.[19] The only

---

[19]It is not normal to evaluate a project by all four criteria, as was done here. Often, however, when more than one approach is used, each is used to check a different aspect of the project. For example, the net present value might be used to check the project's profitability, and payback might be used to evaluate its risk and liquidity.

step remaining is to monitor the performance of the project to see if it meets, falls short of, or exceeds its projected cash flow estimates. Based upon the actual results of this project, the bank's management will be able to evaluate other new branch bank proposals in a more knowledgeable manner.

INFLATION AND CAPITAL EXPENDITURES

During inflationary periods the level of capital expenditures made by firms tends to decrease. For example, suppose the Apple Manufacturing Company has an investment opportunity that is expected to generate 10 years of cash inflows of $300 per year. The original cash outflow is $2,000. If the company's cost of capital is relatively low—say, 7 percent—the net present value is positive:

$$
\begin{aligned}
NPV &= PV \text{ cash inflows } - PV \text{ cash outflows} \\
&= \$300(PVIFA_{0.07,10}) - \$2,000 \\
&= \$300(7.024) - \$2,000 \\
&= \$107.2 \ .
\end{aligned}
$$

According to the net present value decision rule, this project is acceptable.

Suppose, however, that inflation expectations increase and the overall cost of the firm's capital rises to, say, 10 percent. The net present value of the project would then be negative:

$$
\begin{aligned}
NPV &= PV \text{ cash inflows } - PV \text{ cash outflows} \\
&= \$300(PVIFA_{0.10,10}) - \$2,000 \\
&= \$300(6.145) - \$2,000 \\
&= -\$156.5 \ .
\end{aligned}
$$

Under these conditions, the project would not be acceptable.

The example assumes that expected cash inflows are not affected by inflation. Admittedly, project revenues usually will increase with rising inflation, but so will expenses. As a result, it is somewhat difficult to generalize about net cash inflows. The experience of recent years, however, seems to indicate that cash flow increases are often not sufficient to offset the increased cost of capital. Thus, capital expenditure levels tend to be lower (in real terms) during periods of relatively high inflation than during low inflation times.

Fortunately, it is quite easy to adjust the capital budgeting procedure to take inflationary effects into account. The cost of capital already includes the effects of expected inflation.[20] As the expected future inflation rate increases, the cost of capital also tends to increase. Thus, the financial manager has to estimate future cash flows (revenues and expenses) that reflect the expected inflationary rate. For example, if prices are expected to increase at a rate of 5 percent per year over the life of a project, the revenue estimates made for the

---

[20]This is discussed in Chapter 12.

project should reflect this rising price trend. Cost or expense estimates also should be adjusted to reflect anticipated inflationary increases, such as labor wage rate increases and raw material price increases.

If these steps are taken, the capital budgeting procedure outlined in this and the preceding chapters will assist the financial manager even in an inflationary environment.

SUMMARY

- The *payback period* is the number of years required for the cumulative net cash flows from a project to equal the net investment. Although the payback method is widely used, it has serious weaknesses, including the failure to account for the time value of money or to consider cash flows after the payback period.

- The *net present value* is calculated by subtracting a project's net investment from the net cash flows discounted at the firm's cost of capital. The net present value method overcomes the major flaws in the payback method.

- The *internal rate of return* of a project is the discount rate that gives the project a net present value equal to zero. This approach also solves some of the problems of the payback method.

- The *profitability index* is the ratio of the present value of net cash flows to the net investment. It gives a measure of the relative present value return per dollar of initial investment. The profitability index is useful when choosing among projects in a *capital rationing* situation.

- The net present value and internal rate of return approaches normally yield the same accept-reject decisions for a particular project. However, conflicts may arise when dealing with *mutually exclusive* projects. The reinvestment rate assumption embodied in the net present value approach—namely, that cash flows from a project are reinvested at the cost of capital—is generally more realistic than that underlying the internal rate of return method. For this reason the net present value method is generally preferred to the internal rate of return method.

- Project postaudit reviews provide useful information regarding the effectiveness of a company's capital budgeting analysis and selection procedures. If a postaudit uncovers systematic biases in these procedures, corrective action should be taken. Project reviews may also identify whether a project should be abandoned prior to, at, or after its scheduled termination.

- In general, relatively high levels of inflation tend to reduce the level of capital expenditures in the economy. The general capital budgeting procedures discussed in this text can be applied with equal validity in an inflationary environment as long as the estimates of revenues and costs used in the capital budgeting process include expected price and cost increases.

Gulf Oil Corporation's Use of the Discounted Cash Flow Method in Evaluating Capital Projects

Adapted from M. W. Ramsey and C. Londa, "Use of the Discounted Cash Flow Method in the Evaluation of Capital Projects," Gulf Oil Corporation, July 30, 1968

The widespread use of discounted cash flow (DCF) techniques is a relatively recent phenomenon. This example illustrates the analysis that Gulf Oil Corporation undertook when deciding whether to adopt a DCF approach to evaluate its proposed capital expenditures.

Between 1963 and 1968 Gulf Oil averaged $770 million per year in capital investments. Prior to 1968 the primary methods used to analyze these capital investments were as follows:

- Payout (payback). The number of years it takes Gulf to recoup the initial capital outlay from the cash flows of a project.

- Return on gross investment (average rate of return). The average annual book net income during the project's economic life divided by the original capital outlay.

In 1968 a report was made by the corporate comptroller's department recommending that Gulf shift its evaluation methods from payout and return on gross investment to a DCF approach.

Why was this change proposed? The report cited a number of weaknesses of the two methods in use at that time. Regarding payout, it noted these points:

- Payout does not consider the earning power or profitability of an investment.

- Payout ignores the time value of money.

- It is difficult to set an objective cutoff goal for payout.

- Payout overemphasizes project liquidity as a goal of the capital expenditure program.

The primary disadvantage noted about the return on gross investment method was that it gives no consideration to the timing of cash flows.

As an alternative, it was proposed that Gulf adopt a DCF rate of return approach, which is similar to the internal rate of return approach. The report went on to note that the primary advantages of the DCF approach include the following:

- It makes allowances for the differences in the time at which investments generate their income.

- It considers the whole life of a project and produces a profitability measure based on lifetime earnings.

- The DCF rate of return can be directly compared with the company's cost of capital for decision-making purposes.

The report also noted that while the net present value approach is generally an acceptable yardstick for evaluating projects, it should be rejected in this case: "In our opinion the DCF is a more practical measure because it dramatizes a project's economic consequences in terms that have become familiar—that is, percent return rather than absolute dollars as does net present value."

Finally, the report recommended that the firm continue to use payout in conjunction with the DCF in order to retain a measure of a project's liquidity and to provide a measure of project risk.

QUESTIONS AND TOPICS FOR DISCUSSION

1. What are the primary strengths and weaknesses of the payback approach as a capital budgeting decision model?

2. How does the net present value model complement the objective of maximizing shareholder wealth?

3. When is it possible for the net present value and the internal rate of return approaches to give conflicting rankings of mutually exclusive investment projects?

4. When are multiple rates of return likely to occur in an internal rate of return computation? What should be done when a multiple rate of return problem arises?

5. Describe how the profitability index approach may be used by a firm faced with a capital rationing investment funds constraint.

6. What are the primary objectives of the investment project postaudit review?

7. What is the likely effect of inflation on the level of capital expenditures made by private firms? What must the financial manager do to insure that a firm's capital budgeting procedures will be effective in an inflationary environment?

8. What are the major problems you can foresee in applying capital budgeting techniques to investments made by public and not-for-profit sector enterprises or organizations?

9. Show that the internal rate of return of the following investment is 0, 100, and 200 percent:

Net investment	− $1,000	Year 0
Net cash flows	+ 6,000	Year 1
	− 11,000	Year 2
	+ 6,000	Year 3

10. What effect would you expect the use of ACRS depreciation rules to have on the acceptability of a project having a 10-year economic life but a 5-year ACRS classification?

PROBLEMS*

1. A firm wishes to bid on a contract that is expected to yield the following after-tax net cash flows at the end of each year:

Year	Net Cash Flow
1	$4,000
2	6,000
3	8,000
4	7,000
5	6,000
6	4,000
7	2,000
8	−2,000

To secure the contract, the firm must spend $25,000 to retool its plant. This retooling will have no salvage value at the end of the 8 years. Comparable investment alternatives are available to the firm that earn 10 percent compounded annually. The depreciation tax benefit from the retooling is reflected in the net cash flows in the table. Ignore the effects of the investment tax credit.
   a. Compute the project's payback period.
   b. Compute the project's net present value.
   c. Should the project be adopted?

2. A machine that costs $8,000 is expected to operate for 10 years. The estimated salvage value at the end of 10 years is $0. The machine is expected to save the company $1,554 per year before taxes and depreciation. The machine is eligible for the 10 percent investment tax credit. The company depreciates its assets on a straight line basis and has a marginal tax rate of 40 percent. What is the internal rate of return on this investment?

3. Recalculate the internal rate of return for the machine investment in Problem 2 assuming that the firm uses 5-year ACRS depreciation rates instead of straight line depreciation over 10 years. The economic life of the machine is still 10 years, and its estimated salvage value is $0.

4. An acre planted with walnut trees is estimated to be worth $4,000 in 25 years. If you want to realize a 12 percent rate of return on your investment, how much can you afford to invest per acre? (Ignore all taxes and assume that annual cash outlays to maintain your stand of walnut trees are nil.)

5. A company is planning to invest $50,000 (before tax) in a personnel training program. The $50,000 outlay will be charged off as an expense by the firm this year (year 0). The returns from the program, in the form of greater productivity and a reduction in employee turnover, are estimated as follows (on an after-tax basis):

Years 1–10:	$5,000 per year
Years 11–20:	$15,000 per year

The company has estimated its cost of capital to be 15 percent. Assume that the entire $50,000 is paid at time 0 (the beginning of the project). The marginal tax rate for the firm is 40 percent.

*Problems in color have check answers provided at the end of the book.

Should the firm undertake the training program? Why or why not?

6. Two mutually exclusive investment projects have the following forecasted cash flows:

Year	A	B
0	– $20,000	– $20,000
1	+ 10,000	0
2	+ 10,000	0
3	+ 10,000	0
4	+ 10,000	+ 60,000

a. Compute the internal rate of return for each project.
b. Compute the net present value for each project, if the firm has a 10 percent cost of capital.
c. Which project should be adopted? Why?

7. ABC Hydronics is considering replacing one of its larger control devices. A new unit sells for $30,000 (delivered). An additional $3,000 will be needed to install the device. A 10 percent investment tax credit is available to the firm. The new device has an estimated 20-year service life. The estimated salvage value at the end of 20 years will be $2,000. The new control device will be depreciated over 20 years on a straight line basis to its estimated salvage value. The existing control device has been in use for 22 years, and it has been fully depreciated (that is, the book value equals zero). Its scrap value is estimated to be $1,000. The existing device could be used indefinitely, assuming the firm is willing to pay for its very high maintenance costs. The firm's marginal tax rate is 40 percent. The new control device requires lower maintenance costs and frees up personnel who would normally have to monitor the system. Estimated annual cash savings from the new device will be $9,000. The firm's cost of capital is 12 percent.

Using this information, evaluate the relative merits of replacing the old control device using the net present value approach.

8. Recalculate the net present value of the control device investment in Problem 7, assuming that the new control device is depreciated over 5 years under the ACRS schedule. At the end of 20 years the estimated salvage value of the new device will continue to be $2,000.

Compare the answers you get to Problems 7 and 8. What effect does the use of ACRS depreciation have on the economic desirability of the project?

9. A $1,230 investment has the following expected cash returns:

Year	Net Cash Flow
1	$800
2	200
3	400

Compute the internal rate of return for this project.

10. Pinion Pot Company has $1 million available for capital investments during the current year. A list of possible investment projects, together with their net investments and net present values, is provided in the following table:

313

Project	Net Investment	Net Present Value
1	$200,000	$20,000
2	500,000	41,000
3	275,000	50,000
4	150,000	5,000
5	250,000	20,000
6	100,000	5,000
7	275,000	22,000
8	200,000	−18,000

a. Rank the various investment projects in terms of their profitability indexes (computed to three decimal places).

b. In the order of decreasing profitability index values and considering the capital constraints, which projects should be adopted? Are all capital funds expended?

c. Is there another combination that produces a higher aggregate net present value than the one developed in Part b?

d. If less than the entire amount of available funds is invested, what is the opportunity cost of the unused funds?

11. A junior executive is fed up with the operating policies of his boss. Before leaving the office of his angered superior, the young man suggests that a well-trained monkey could handle the trivia assigned to him. Pausing a moment to consider the import of this closing statement, the boss is seized by the thought that this must have been in the back of her own mind ever since she hired the junior executive. She decides to consider seriously replacing the executive with a bright young baboon. She figures that she could argue strongly to the board that such "capital deepening" is necessary for the cost-conscious firm. Two days later, a feasibility study is completed, and the following data are presented to the president:

- It would cost $12,000 to purchase and train a reasonably alert baboon with a life expectancy of 20 years.

- Annual expenses of feeding and housing the baboon would be $4,000.

- The junior executive's annual salary is $7,000 (a potential saving if the baboon is hired).

- The baboon will be depreciated on a straight line basis over 20 years to an estimated salvage value of $400.

- The baboon purchase is eligible for a 10 percent investment tax credit.

- The firm's marginal tax rate is 40 percent.

- The firm's current cost of capital is estimated to be 11 percent.

On the basis of the net present value criterion, should the monkey be hired (and the junior executive fired)?

12. The L-S Mining Company is planning to open a new strip mine in Western Pennsylvania. The net investment required to open the mine is $10 million. Net cash flows are expected to be +$20 million at the end of year 1 and +$5 million at the end of year 2. At the end of year 3 L-S will have a net cash *outflow* of $17 million to cover the cost of closing the mine and reclaiming the land.

a. Calculate the net present value of the strip mine if the cost of capital is 5, 10, 15, 30, 71, and 80 percent.

b. What is unique about this project?

c. Should the project be accepted if L-S's cost of capital is 10 percent? 20 percent?

13. Fred and Frieda have always wanted to enter the blueberry business. They locate a 50-acre piece of hillside in Maine that is covered with blueberry bushes. They figure that the annual yield from the bushes will be 200 crates. Each crate is estimated to sell for $400 for the next 10 years. This price is expected to rise to $500 per crate for all sales from years 11 through 20.

In order to get started, Fred and Frieda must pay $150,000 for the land plus $20,000 for packing equipment. The packing equipment will be depreciated on a straight line basis to a zero estimated salvage value at the end of 20 years. The packing equipment is eligible for a 10 percent investment tax credit. Fred and Frieda believe that at the end of 20 years they will want to retire to Florida and sell their property.

Annual cash operating expenses, including salaries to Fred and Frieda, are estimated to be $50,000 per year for the first 10 years and $60,000 thereafter. The land is expected to appreciate in value at a rate of 5 percent per year. The couple's marginal tax rate is 30 percent for ordinary income and 15 percent for capital gains and losses.

a. If the couple requires at least a 13 percent return on their investment, should they enter the blueberry business?

b. Assume that the land can be sold for only $50,000 at the end of 20 years (a capital loss of $100,000). Should the couple invest in the land and blueberry business? (Assume that the couple may claim the full amount of their capital loss in the year it occurs—year 20).

14. The Sisneros Company is considering building a chili processing plant in Hatch, New Mexico. The plant is expected to produce 50,000 pounds of processed chili peppers each year for the next 10 years. During the first year, Sisneros expects to sell the processed peppers for $2 per pound. This price is expected to increase at a 7 percent rate per year over the 10-year economic life of the plant. The cash costs of operating the plant, including the cost of fresh peppers, are estimated to be $50,000 during the first year. These costs are expected to increase at an 8 percent rate per year over the next 10 years.

The plant will cost $80,000 to build. It is eligible for the 10 percent investment tax credit and will be depreciated as a 5-year ACRS asset. The estimated salvage at the end of 10 years is zero. The firm's marginal tax rate is 40 percent.

a. Calculate the net investment required to build the plant.

b. Calculate the annual net cash flows from the project.

c. If Sisneros uses a 20 percent cost of capital to evaluate projects of this type, should the plant be built? (Use the net present value criterion.)

(Continued from Chapter 9)

Cash Flow Estimation in Capital Budgeting

In the integrative case problem at the end of Chapter 9, you were asked to compute the net investment and annual net cash flows for Allied Interstate Banking's proposed franchised network of Rapid-Draw automatic teller machines. Using this information, you are now in a position to evaluate the economic feasibility of this project. To do this, you should compute the following:

1. The payback period for the project. The payback period gives an indication of the time it will take for Allied to recover its initial investment. The payback period is often used as a crude risk-screening technique, especially when a project involves investments in an area characterized by rapid technological advance.

2. The net present value of this project. The firm requires a 15 percent rate of return on projects of this type. Should the project be accepted? Interpret the net present value as computed for this project.

3. The internal rate of return for this project. According to the internal rate of return criterion, should the project be accepted? (This problem can be solved most efficiently using a sophisticated financial calculator.)

CALCULATOR APPLICATIONS

This section illustrates the use of the Texas Instruments Professional Business Analyst (BA-55) calculator to compute the net present value of a project and the project's internal rate of return.

NET PRESENT VALUE

The Swazey Company is considering an investment that requires an initial outlay (NINV) of $50,000. The net cash flows from the project have been estimated as follows:

Year	Net Cash Flow
1	$ 5,000
2	8,000
3	25,000
4	20,000
5	20,000
6	10,000
7	10,000

The firm's cost of capital is 12 percent. Calculate the net present value of this project.

Procedure	Press	Display
1. Clear calculator and mode registers; select two decimal places.	on/c 2nd **CLmode** 2nd **Fix** 2	0.00
2. Press 2nd **Mode** until the CF indicator is displayed.	2nd **Mode**	0.00
3. Enter the cost of capital (discount rate) per period.	12 %i	12.00
4. Enter the net investment (initial outlay) as a negative number.	50000 +/− PV	− 50000.00
5. Enter all after-tax net cash flows:		
Period 1.	5000 STO 1	5000.00
Period 2.	8000 STO 2	8000.00
Period 3.	25000 STO 3	25000.00
Period 4.	20000 STO 4	20000.00
Period 5.	20000 STO 5	20000.00
Period 6.	10000 STO 6	10000.00
Period 7.	10000 STO 7	10000.00
6. Compute the net present value.	CPT 2nd **NPV**	**12285.05**

The net present value of this project is $12,285.05. Therefore, the project is acceptable.

INTERNAL RATE OF RETURN

To calculate the internal rate of return of the project presented in the previous section, only a few changes need to be made in the procedure outlined there.

First, Step 3 is omitted, since we are solving for the discount rate in this instance. In addition, Step 6 is modified to compute the internal rate of return as follows:

CPT 2nd **IRR**

The internal rate of return of this project is **18.69** percent. Compared with the firm's cost of capital, this project is acceptable.

The BA-55 calculator will handle up to 10 periods of unequal net cash flows in addition to the net investment when computing net present values and internal rates of return. The tenth payment is entered by pressing $\boxed{\text{STO}}$ $\boxed{\;\cdot\;}$ after the payment amount has been keyed in. Also note that the calculator does internal rate of return calculations the same way you do—with an iterative trial-and-error process. Hence, it normally takes some time—up to a minute or so—for the internal rate of return to be computed and displayed.

ADDITIONAL READINGS AND REFERENCES

Bailey, A. D., and Jensen, D. L. "General Price Level Adjustments in the Capital Budgeting Decision." *Financial Management* 6 (Spring 1977): 26–32.

Baumol, William J., and Quandt, Richard E. "Investment and Discount Rates under Capital Rationing—A Programming Approach." *The Economic Journal* 75 (June 1965): 317–329.

Ben-Shahar, Haim, and Sarnat, Marshall. "Reinvestment and the Rate of Return on Common Stocks." *Journal of Finance* 21 (Dec. 1966): 737–742.

Bower, Richard S., and Jenks, Jeffrey M. "Divisional Screening Rates." *Financial Management* 4 (Autumn 1975): 42–49.

Brigham, Eugene F. "Hurdle Rates for Screening Capital Expenditure Proposals." *Financial Management* 4 (Autumn 1975): 17–26.

Cooley, Philip L., Roenfeldt, Rodney L., and Chew, It-Keong. "Capital Budgeting Procedures under Inflation." *Financial Management* 4 (Winter 1975): 18–27.

Fogler, H. Russell. "Ranking Techniques and Capital Rationing." *Accounting Review* 47 (Jan. 1972): 134–143.

Hawkins, Clark A., and Adams, Richard A. "A Goal Programming Model for Capital Budgeting." *Financial Management* 3 (Spring 1974): 52–57.

Joy, O. Maurice. "Abandonment Values and Abandonment Decisions: A Clarification." *Journal of Finance* 31 (Sept. 1976): 1225–1228.

Lewellen, Wilbur G., Lanser, Howard P., and McConnell, John J. "Payback Substitutes for Discounted Cash Flow." *Financial Management* 2 (Summer 1973): 17–23.

Litzenberger, Robert H., and Joy, O. M. "Decentralized Capital Budgeting Decisions and Shareholder Wealth Maximization." *Journal of Finance* 30 (June 1975): 993–1002.

Lorie, James H., and Savage, Leonard J. "Three Problems in Rationing Capital." *Journal of Business* (Oct. 1955).

Mao, James C. T. "Survey of Capital Budgeting: Theory and Practice." *Journal of Finance* 25 (May 1970): 349–360.

Nelson, Charles R. "Inflation and Capital Budgeting." *Journal of Finance* 31 (June 1976): 923–931.

Robichek, A., and Van Horne, James C. "Abandonment Value and Capital Budgeting." *Journal of Finance* 22 (Dec. 1967): 577–589.

Van Horne, James C. "A Note on Biases in Capital Budgeting Introduced by Inflation." *Journal of Financial and Quantitative Analysis* 6 (Jan. 1971): 653–658.

Williams, John Daniel, and Rakich, Jonathan S. "Investment Evaluation in Hospitals." *Financial Management* 2 (Summer 1973): 30–35.

Mutually Exclusive Investments Having Unequal Lives

REPLACEMENT CHAINS

Chapter 10 discussed a number of capital budgeting decision models. When mutually exclusive investments were considered, it was implicitly assumed that the alternative projects had *equal* lives. In actual practice, however, this may not be the case. When two or more mutually exclusive alternatives have *unequal* lives, neither the net present value nor the internal rate of return method yields reliable accept-reject information unless the projects are being evaluated for an equal period of time. If, for example, a firm adopts the longer lived of two projects simply on the basis of net present value or internal rate of return data, it essentially ignores any alternative investment opportunities that might have been available at the end of the shorter-lived project.

Suppose a firm is considering two mutually exclusive investments, I and II. Project I requires an initial outlay of $2,000 and is expected to generate a 5-year stream of net cash flows of $600 per year. Project II also requires an initial outlay of $2,000 but is expected to generate a 10-year stream of net cash flows of $375 per year. The firm has a 10 percent cost of capital.

Table 10A-1 shows that the net present value of Project I is $274.60 and the net present value of Project II is $304.37. Thus, the net present value criterion suggests that Project II should be chosen over Project I.

The expected life of Project II is twice as long as that of Project I. Therefore, the two net present values calculated in Table 10A–1 are not really comparable. At this point the firm must also consider what might happen if Project I were replaced with a similar 5-year life project at the end of 5 years. In other words, it would create a *replacement chain* for the shorter-lived project. Suppose, for example, the firm estimates that replacing Project I with a similar project at the end of 5 years would cost $2,100 and, like Project I, would generate annual net cash flows of $600. This results in a new stream of cash flows for Project I, as shown in Table 10A–2. The new net present value for

TABLE 10A-1   Cash Flows for Projects I and II

	PROJECT I		PROJECT II	
Year	Net Investment	Net Cash Flow	Net Investment	Net Cash Flow
0	$2,000	—	$2,000	—
1		$600		$375
2		600		375
3		600		375
4		600		375
5		600		375
6		—		375
7		—		375
8		—		375
9		—		375
10		—		375

$$NPV_I = -\$2,000 + \$600(3.791)$$
$$= \$274.60 .$$

$$NPV_{II} = -\$2,000 + \$375(6.145)$$
$$= \$304.37 .$$

Project I is higher than that for Project II, thus indicating—correctly—that Project I should be chosen over Project II.

Many times it is not possible to get a series of projects (such as Project I with its replacement at the end of 5 years) that will have an identical time duration to that of the longer-lived project (II). For example, one project might have a life of 15 years, whereas an alternative requires replacement every 8 years. Hence, the shorter-lived project together with its replacement have a 16-year duration, whereas the longer-lived project has a 15-year life. Such a comparison will normally be acceptable, since the discrepancy occurs for only 1 year that is 15 years in the future. In present value terms, this will not have much impact.

TABLE 10A-2   Replacement Chain Cash Flows for Project I Compared with Project II

	PROJECT I WITH REPLACEMENT		PROJECT II	
Year	Net investment	Net cash flow	Net investment	Net cash flow
0	$2,000	—	$2,000	—
1		$600		$375
2		600		375
3		600		375
4		600		375
5	2,100	600		375
6		600		375
7		600		375
8		600		375
9		600		375
10		600		375

$$NPV_I = -\$2,000 + \$600(6.145) - \$2,100(0.621)$$
$$= \$382.80 .$$

$$NPV_{II} = -\$2,000 + \$375(6.145)$$
$$= \$304.37 .$$

The importance of time discrepancies such as these depends on the following:

- The number of years of the discrepancy. The fewer the years of the discrepancy, the less important it is.
- The number of years into the future the discrepancy occurs. The further into the future, the less important the discrepancy is.
- The relationship between the rate of return on future investments and the cost of capital. When the rate of return on future investments is equal to the cost of capital, these investments have an NPV = 0. Under these circumstances, the discrepancy can be ignored.

EQUIVALENT ANNUAL ANNUITIES

An alternative approach for dealing with the problem of mutually exclusive investments having unequal lives is to use the equivalent annual annuity approach. This technique can solve the problem of time discrepancies often encountered when using the replacement chain approach.

For example, consider the case of a firm that needs to replace an aging piece of machinery. One alternative would be to buy new Machine A having a 9-year life. Another alternative would be to buy new Machine B with a 5-year life. In this case, the time discrepancy between A and B is significant—4 years. Commonly, this problem is dealt with by developing a string of replacement chains out to a year when both machines would need replacement. The common denominator year in this case is 45 years—indicating nine investments in B and five investments in A.

In cases like this, the equivalent annual annuity approach is often easier to use. In our example, assume the new Machine A will require a net investment of $34,500 and generate net cash flows of $7,000 per year for 9 years. Machine B will require a net investment of $25,000 and generate net cash flows of $8,000 per year for 5 years. The firm's cost of capital is 10 percent. In order to make our decision on the basis of the equivalent annual annuity criterion, we use the following three steps:

1. First, compute the net present value of each machine over its original expected economic life:

$$
\begin{aligned}
\text{NPV}_A &= -\$34,500 + \$7,000(\text{PVIFA}_{0.10,9}) \\
&= -\$34,500 + \$7,000(5.759) \\
&= \$5,813 \ . \\
\text{NPV}_B &= -\$25,000 + \$8,000(\text{PVIFA}_{0.10,5}) \\
&= -\$25,000 + \$8,000(3.791) \\
&= \$5,328 \ .
\end{aligned}
$$

As these calculations indicate, if the possibility of the replacement of Machine B at the end of 5 years is not considered, Machine A would appear to be the best alternative because of its greater net present value.

2. Next, divide the net present value for each machine computed in Step 1 by the PVIFA factor for the project's original life. This gives the *equivalent annual annuity:*

$$\text{Equivalent annual annuity (A)} = \frac{\$5,813}{\text{PVIFA}_{0.10,9}}$$

$$= \frac{\$5,813}{5.759}$$

$$= \$1,009.38 .$$

$$\text{Equivalent annual annuity (B)} = \frac{\$5,328}{\text{PVIFA}_{0.10,5}}$$

$$= \frac{\$5,328}{3.791}$$

$$= \$1,405.43 .$$

3. The equivalent annual annuity method assumes that each machine will be replaced an infinite number of times into the future and will therefore provide these annual annuities in perpetuity. As perpetuities, these equivalent annual annuities can be valued (at present) by dividing the annuity amount by the cost of capital:

$$\text{NPV}_A(\text{assuming infinite replacement}) = \frac{\$1,009.38}{0.10}$$

$$= \$10,093.80 .$$

$$\text{NPV}_B(\text{assuming infinite replacement}) = \frac{\$1,405.43}{0.10}$$

$$= \$14,054.30 .$$

Machine B should be acquired, since it has the highest net present value when evaluated over an infinite replacement horizon.

In general, the equivalent annual annuity method will give the same decision as the replacement chain technique. Its advantage is that it is often computationally simpler, and it simplifies the handling of the time discrepancies that frequently arise in the replacement chain method.

PROBLEMS*

1. The Smith Pie Company is considering two mutually exclusive investments that would increase its capacity to make strawberry tarts. The firm uses a 12 percent cost of capital to evaluate potential investments. The two projects have the following costs and cash flow streams:

---

*Problems in color have check answers provided at the end of the book.

Year	Alternative A	Alternative B
0	– $30,000	– $30,000
1	10,500	6,500
2	10,500	6,500
3	10,500	6,500
4	10,500	6,500
5	—	6,500
6	—	6,500
7	—	6,500
8	—	6,500

a. Using this data, calculate the net present value for Projects A and B.
b. Create a replacement chain for Alternative A. Assume that the cost of replacing A will be $30,000 and that the replacement project will generate cash flows of $10,500 for years 5 through 8. Using these figures, recompute the net present value for Alternative A.
c. Which of the two alternatives should be chosen, A or B? Why?

2. Use the equivalent annual annuity method to solve Problem 1. How does your answer compare with the one obtained in Problem 1?

CHAPTER 11

Capital Budgeting and Risk

A FINANCIAL DILEMMA

Washington Public Power Supply System (Whoops)

The capital budgeting process discussed in the previous two chapters is, in reality, quite simple. If the present value of a project's net cash flows exceeds the outlays required (the net investment), a project is acceptable and should be undertaken. The real difficulty is developing realistic estimates of the costs and benefits from a project. The problems a firm may encounter can stem from an incomplete analysis of a project (the Lockheed case) or from a lack of sufficient concern for the profitability of the firm (Braniff's apparent preoccupation with growth and market share).

In addition to these problems, it must be recognized that nearly all projects have some element of risk—the chance that the actual cash flows will differ from the forecasted ones. This is the case for the Washington Public Power Supply System—now referred to as "Whoops" in the financial community.

In the 1970s a consortium of eighty-eight utilities in the Pacific Northwest agreed to build five nuclear power plants to meet the rapidly growing need for energy in the region. The projected cost of the five plants was $5 billion. Unfortunately, the sharp increases in energy costs in the late 1970s and early 1980s caused the growth in demand for electricity to drop rapidly. The consortium finally canceled two of the five units in the face of declining demand and postponed completion of a third unit for up to 5 years. The cost of these two canceled units will be over $7 billion to customers of the eighty-eight utilities over the next 30 years. In addition to their declining demand, the cost of the units rose from the initial $5 billion to over $24 billion.

This example illustrates one of the painful realities of making capital budgeting decisions—cash flows and costs from a project will rarely meet projections exactly. This is to be expected, since nearly all capital investments contain an element of risk. Although risk cannot be eliminated, a capable financial manager should try to determine at the outset what risks are being assumed when a project is undertaken. What is the worst case outcome? How likely is this outcome? What actions can be taken to reduce this risk? How will investors react to this risk? Given the answers to these questions, risky projects can be properly evaluated. This chapter examines these important questions.

GLOSSARY OF NEW TERMS

Certainty equivalent the amount of cash someone would require with certainty at a point in time in order to make him or her indifferent between that certain amount and an amount expected to be received with risk at the same point in time.

Hurdle rate the minimum acceptable rate of return from an investment project. For projects of average risk, it is usually equal to the firm's cost of capital.

Risk-adjusted discount rate a discount rate that reflects the risk associated with a particular project. In capital budgeting, a higher risk-adjusted rate is used to discount cash flows for riskier projects, while a lower risk-adjusted rate is used to discount cash flows for less risky projects.

Simulation a financial planning tool that models some event, such as the cash flows from an investment project. A computerized simulation is one technique used to assess the risk associated with a particular project.

INTRODUCTION

In Chapter 5 we discussed the nature of risk and its influence on financial decision making. The greater the risk associated with an investment, the greater the return required. This basic principle applies in the capital budgeting area.

In the previous two chapters, investment projects were evaluated using the firm's weighted cost of capital (required rate of return). This approach implicitly assumes that all projects being considered are of equal risk and that this risk is the same as that for the firm as a whole. When a project has more or less than an average risk level, it is necessary to adjust the analysis to account for this risk level.

TOTAL PROJECT RISK VERSUS PORTFOLIO RISK

When analyzing the risk associated with a capital expenditure, it is important to distinguish between the *total project risk* and the *portfolio*, or *beta, risk* of that investment. By total project risk we mean the chance that a project will perform below expectations—possibly resulting in losses from the project and for the firm. In the worst case, these losses could be so severe as to cause the firm to fail.

In contrast, a project that has a high level of total project risk may not affect the portfolio risk of the firm at all. Consider the case of oil and gas exploration companies. The firms know that any wildcat well they drill will cost about $2 million and have only a 10 percent chance of success. Successful wells produce profits of $24 million. Unsuccessful wells produce no profits at all, and the entire investment will be a loss. If each firm only drilled one well, there would be a 90 percent chance the firm would fail (the total project risk would be very high). In contrast, if one firm drilled one hundred wildcat wells, the risk of failure from all wells would be very low because of the portfolio risk reduction that results from drilling many wells. In this case the expected return of the firm would be as follows:

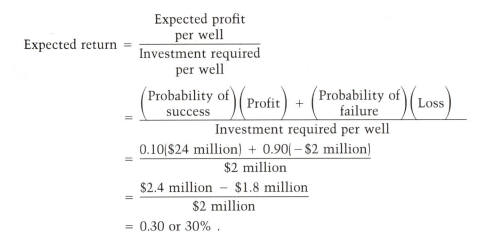

$$\text{Expected return} = \frac{\text{Expected profit per well}}{\text{Investment required per well}}$$

$$= \frac{\left(\begin{array}{c}\text{Probability of}\\\text{success}\end{array}\right)\left(\text{Profit}\right) + \left(\begin{array}{c}\text{Probability of}\\\text{failure}\end{array}\right)\left(\text{Loss}\right)}{\text{Investment required per well}}$$

$$= \frac{0.10(\$24 \text{ million}) + 0.90(-\$2 \text{ million})}{\$2 \text{ million}}$$

$$= \frac{\$2.4 \text{ million} - \$1.8 \text{ million}}{\$2 \text{ million}}$$

$$= 0.30 \text{ or } 30\% .$$

This return is achieved with very little risk relative to that facing a firm drilling a single well. As this example illustrates, the risk of drilling any individual well can be diversified away very effectively. Consequently, these risks are not market related, and they should have little, if any, impact on the beta risk of the firm. That risk remains unchanged and approximately equal to the market risk facing other oil and gas exploration companies.

This example has shown that an investment with high total project risk does not necessarily have to possess high beta risk. Of course, it is possible for a project to have both high total project risk and high beta risk. For example, a grocery store chain (which typically has low beta risk) might decide to develop and market a new line of small business computers. Because of the large number of competitors in this business and because of the grocery chain's lack of expertise, this investment can be expected to have a high level of total project risk. At the same time, the beta risk of this investment is likely to be high relative to that of the grocery chain, because business computer sales expand rapidly during boom periods and slow down dramatically during recessions.

From a capital budgeting perspective, the portfolio (beta) risk of a project is certainly important, because the beta of a firm influences the returns required by investors in that firm and hence the value of the firm's shares.

Total project risk is also important to consider in most cases for several reasons. There are a number of relatively undiversified investors, including the owners of small firms, for whom total project and total firm risk is important. Also, it is the total risk of the firm—not just the beta risk—that determines the risk of firm failure and potential bankruptcy. Stockholders, creditors, managers, and other employees are all interested in preventing the tragedy of total firm failure.

Consequently, in the evaluation of an investment, it is important to consider both the total project risk and the impact of the project on the beta risk of the firm. In the next section we examine a number of techniques that can be used to account for total project risk in the capital budgeting process. We conclude the chapter with a discussion of techniques to use when evaluating the beta risk of a project.

ADJUSTING FOR TOTAL PROJECT RISK

Several different techniques are used to analyze total project risk. These include the *subjective* or *informal approach*, the *net present value/payback approach*, the *risk-adjusted discount rate approach (RADR)*, the *hurdle rate approach*, the *certainty equivalent approach*, the *simulation approach*, and *sensitivity analysis*.

SUBJECTIVE OR INFORMAL APPROACH

Frequently, investment decisions are made based upon the decision maker's subjective feelings about a project's risk in relation to expected return. If a firm is evaluating two mutually exclusive investments having approximately equal net present values, the decision maker will probably choose the less risky one. This informal approach to decision making is commonly used because it is both simple and inexpensive.

If two projects under consideration have significantly different net present values as well as different levels of perceived risk, the decision becomes more complicated. In these cases the decision maker must determine—again subjectively—whether the additional risk of a project will be offset by sufficiently higher returns.

Even though subjective decision making is often useful, more precise methods yield more valuable information in many cases.

NET PRESENT VALUE/PAYBACK APPROACH

Many firms combine net present value (NPV) with payback (PB) when analyzing project risk. As noted in Chapter 10, the project payback period is the length of time required to recover the net investment. Since cash flow estimates tend to become more uncertain farther into the future, applying a payback cutoff point can help reduce this degree of uncertainty. For example, a firm may decide not to accept projects unless they have positive net present values *and* have paybacks of less than some stated number of years.

Like the subjective or informal approach, the net present value/payback method is both simple and inexpensive. It does suffer from some notable weaknesses, however. First, the choice of which payback criterion should be applied is purely subjective and is not directly related to the variability of returns from a project. Some investments may have relatively certain cash flows far into the future, whereas others may not. The use of a single payback cutoff point fails to allow for this. Second, some projects are more risky than others during their start-up periods; the payback criterion also fails to recognize this. Finally, this approach may cause a firm to reject some actually acceptable projects. In spite of these weaknesses, however, some firms have found this approach helpful when screening investment alternatives.

RISK-ADJUSTED DISCOUNT RATE APPROACH

The risk-adjusted discount rate approach (RADR) adjusts for risk by varying the rate at which expected net cash flows are discounted when determining a project's net present value. In the net present value approach, net cash flows of all projects are discounted at the firm's cost of capital. If some projects are riskier than others, however, most investors will require a higher rate of return on these projects to compensate for the increased risk.

In the risk-adjusted discount rate approach, net cash flows for each project are discounted at a risk-adjusted rate, k^*. The magnitude of k^* depends on the relationship between the risk of the individual project and the overall risk of the firm. To compute k^*, the *risk-free rate*, r_f—that is, a required rate of return associated with investment projects characterized by certain cash flow streams—is used. United States Treasury securities are good examples of risk-free investments, because there is no chance that investors will not get the dollar amount of interest and the principal repayment on schedule. Thus, the yield on U.S. Government securities, such as 90-day Treasury Bills, is used as the risk-free rate.

Most companies are not in business to invest in risk-free securities; individual investors can do that just as well. Instead, companies assume some amount of risk, expecting to earn higher returns than those available on risk-free securities. The difference between the risk-free rate and the firm's required rate of return (cost of capital) is an *average risk premium* to compensate investors for the fact that the company's assets are risky. This relationship is expressed algebraically as follows:

$$\Theta = k - r_f, \tag{11.1}$$

where Θ is the average risk premium for the firm; r_f, the risk-free rate; and k, the required rate of return for projects of average risk, that is, the firm's cost of capital.

The cash flows from a project having greater than average risk are discounted at a higher rate, k^*—that is, a risk-adjusted discount rate—to reflect the increased riskiness. Risk premiums applied to individual projects are commonly established *subjectively*. For example, some firms establish a small number of *risk classes* and then apply a different *risk premium* to each class. Average-risk projects, such as equipment replacement decisions, might be evaluated at the firm's cost of capital; medium-risk projects, such as facility expansions, might be assigned a risk premium of 3 percent *above* the firm's cost of capital; and high-risk projects, such as investments in totally new lines of business or the introduction of new products, might be assigned a risk premium of 8 percent *above* the firm's cost of capital.

Although the risk-class approach saves time in the analysis stage, it can lead to suboptimal decisions, since the risk premiums themselves are usually subjectively determined, and no explicit consideration is given to the variation in returns of the projects assigned to individual classes. In short, the risk-class approach is most useful when evaluating relatively small projects that are frequently repeated. In these cases, much is known about the projects' potential returns, and it is probably not worth the effort to try to compute more "precise" risk premiums.

Advantages of the risk-adjusted discount rate approach   The risk adjusted discount rate approach has several advantages, including the following:

- It allows the decision maker to evaluate projects more efficiently by assigning each one a definite level of risk. Projects that initially may seem undesirable because they have lower expected returns might become more attractive if they are shown to have lower risk levels that could help to offset some other high-risk investments.

- The technique provides the decision maker with a single number on which to base accept-reject decisions, thereby eliminating the problem of having to make a risk-return tradeoff at decision time.

HURDLE RATE APPROACH

The hurdle rate approach is similar to the risk-adjusted discount rate method except that the hurdle rate method is used with the internal rate of return decision criterion instead of the net present value. If k_A^* is defined as the risk-adjusted required return for Project A instead of the risk-adjusted discount rate, the hurdle rate for Project A is k_A^*. If a project's internal rate of return is greater than the hurdle rate, the project is acceptable; if the internal rate of return is less than the hurdle rate, the project is unacceptable.

This approach has the same strengths and weaknesses as the risk-adjusted discount rate approach. However, decision makers often prefer the hurdle rate method because the accept-reject criterion is in the form of rates of return rather than net present values. As mentioned in Chapter 10, many business decision makers are more comfortable with criteria stated in the form of rates of return.

CERTAINTY EQUIVALENT APPROACH

Another approach that can be used to deal with project risk uses certainty equivalents. A certainty equivalent factor is the ratio of the amount of cash someone would require with certainty at a point in time in order to make him or her indifferent between that certain amount and an amount expected to be received with risk at the same point in time. The project is adjusted for risk by converting the expected risky cash flows to their certainty equivalents and then computing the net present value of the project. The risk-free rate, r_f—not the firm's cost of capital, k—is used as the discount rate for computing the net present value. This is done because the cost of capital is a *risky* rate, reflecting the firm's average risk, and using it would result in a double counting of risk.

Certainty equivalent factors range from 0 to 1.0. The higher the factor, the more certain the expected cash flow. For example, one project might offer expected cash flows over its 5-year life as follows:

Year	Expected NCF	Certainty Equivalent Factor(α)	Certainty Equivalent Cash Flow
0	– $10,000	1.0	– $10,000
1	+ 5,000	0.9	+ 4,500
2	+ 6,000	0.8	+ 4,800
3	+ 7,000	0.7	+ 4,900
4	+ 4,000	0.6	+ 2,400
5	+ 3,000	0.4	+ 1,200

The initial outlay of $10,000 is known with certainty. It might be for the purchase price of a piece of equipment. Hence, the certainty equivalent factor for year 0 is 1.0, and the certainty equivalent cash flow is – $10,000 (– $10,000 × 1.0). The $5,000 cash inflow in year 1 is viewed as being somewhat risky. Consequently, the decision maker has assigned a certainty equivalent factor of 0.9 to the net cash flow in year 1. Multiplying $5,000 times the 0.9 certainty equivalent factor yields a certainty equivalent cash flow of $4,500. This means that the decision maker would be indifferent between receiving the promised, risky $5,000 a year from now or receiving $4,500 with certainty at the same time. A similar interpretation is given to the certainty equivalent factors and certainty equivalent cash flows for years 2 through 5.

Algebraically, the certainty equivalent factors, α, for the cash flows expected to be received during each time period, t, are expressed as follows:

$$\alpha_t = \frac{\text{Certain return}}{\text{Risky return}} . \tag{11.2}$$

For example, in period 1 the certainty equivalent factor is calculated as follows:

$$\alpha_1 = \frac{\$4,500}{\$5,000}$$
$$= 0.9 .$$

The certainty equivalent factors are used to compute a certainty equivalent net present value as follows:

$$\text{NPV} = -\text{NINV}(\alpha_0) + \sum_{t=1}^{n} \frac{\text{NCF}_t \alpha_t}{(1 + r_f)^t} , \tag{11.3}$$

330

where α_0 = Certainty equivalent factor associated with the net investment (NINV) at time 0.

n = Expected economic life of the project.

α_t = Certainty equivalent factor associated with the net cash flows (NCF) in each period, t.

r_f = Risk-free rate.

Notice in this example that the certainty equivalent factors decline into the future. This reflects the fact that *most* cash flows are viewed as being more risky the farther into the future they are projected to occur.[1] This point is discussed in more detail in Chapter 5. In Table 11–1 we have computed the certainty equivalent net present value for this project assuming an 8 percent risk-free rate. It equals $4,753, and the project is therefore acceptable.

The certainty equivalent approach of considering risk is viewed as being conceptually sound for the following reasons:

- The decision maker can adjust separately each period's cash flows to account for the specific risk of those cash flows. This is normally not done when the risk-adjusted discount rate approach is applied.[2]

- Decision makers must introduce their own risk preferences directly into the analysis. Consequently, the certainty equivalent net present value provides an unambiguous basis for making a decision. A positive net present value means the project is acceptable to that decision maker, and a negative net present value indicates it should be rejected.

SIMULATION APPROACH

Computers have made it both feasible and relatively inexpensive to apply simulation techniques to capital budgeting decisions. A simulation is a finan-

TABLE 11–1 Calculation of Certainty Equivalent Net Present Value

Year	Expected NCF	Certainty Equivalent Factor(α)	Certainty Equivalent Cash Flow	$PVIF_{0.08,t}$	Present Value of Cash Flows
0	– $10,000	1.0	– $10,000	1.000	– $10,000
1	+ 5,000	0.9	+ 4,500	0.926	+ 4,167
2	+ 6,000	0.8	+ 4,800	0.857	+ 4,114
3	+ 7,000	0.7	+ 4,900	0.794	+ 3,891
4	+ 4,000	0.6	+ 2,400	0.735	+ 1,764
5	+ 3,000	0.4	+ 1,200	0.681	+ 817
				Certainty Equivalent NPV =	+ $ 4,753

[1] Different individuals may have different certainty equivalent factors, depending on each individual's relative risk aversion. Risk aversion is a function of many factors, including wealth, age, and the nature of a firm's reward structure.

[2] It is possible, however, to find a risk-adjusted discount rate that will provide results identical (that is, with the same risk-adjusted net present value) to those obtained from the certainty equivalent approach.

cial planning tool that models some event. When simulation is used in capital budgeting, it requires that estimates be made of the probability distribution of each cash flow element (revenues, expenses, and so on). If, for example, a firm is considering introducing a new product, the elements of a simulation might include the number of units sold, market price, unit production costs, unit selling costs, the purchase price of the machinery needed to produce the new product, and the cost of capital. These probability distributions are then entered into the simulation model to compute the project's net present value probability distribution.

Recall that net present value is defined as follows:

$$NPV = \sum_{t=1}^{n} \frac{NCF_t}{(1 + k)^t} - NINV \, ,$$

where NCF_t is the net cash flow in period t and NINV, the net investment. In any period, NCF_t may be computed as follows:

$$NCF_t = [n(p) - n(c + s) - D](1 - t) + D \, , \tag{11.4}$$

where n is the number of units sold; p, the price per unit; c, the unit production cost (excluding depreciation); s, the unit selling cost; D, the annual depreciation; and t, the firm's marginal tax rate. Using Equation 11.4, it is possible to simulate the net present value of the project. Based on the probability distribution of each of the elements that influence the net present value, one value for each element is selected at random.

Assume, for example, that the following values for the input variables are randomly chosen: $n = 2,000$; $p = \$10$; $c = \$2$; $s = \$1$; $D = \$2,000$ and $t = 50\%$, or 0.50. Inserting these values into Equation 11.4 gives the following calculations:

$$NCF_t = [2,000(\$10) - 2,000(\$2 + \$1) - \$2,000](1 - 0.50) + \$2,000$$
$$= (\$20,000 - \$6,000 - \$2,000) \times 0.50 + \$2,000$$
$$= \$8,000 \, .$$

Assuming that the net investment is equal to the purchase price of the machinery ($10,000, in this example), that the net cash flows in each year of the project's life are identical, that $k = 10\%$, and that the project has a 5-year life, the net present value of this particular iteration of the simulation can be computed as follows:

$$NPV = \frac{\$8,000}{(1 + 0.10)^1} + \frac{\$8,000}{(1 + 0.10)^2} + \frac{\$8,000}{(1 + 0.10)^3}$$
$$+ \frac{\$8,000}{(1 + 0.10)^4} + \frac{\$8,000}{(1 + 0.10)^5} - \$10,000$$
$$= \$8,000 \times 3.791 - \$10,000$$
$$= \$20,328 \, .$$

FIGURE 11–1   An Illustration of the Simulation Approach

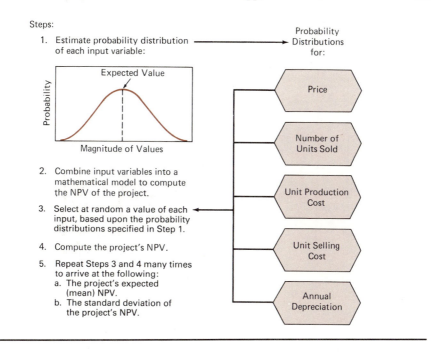

In an actual simulation, the computer program is run a number of different times, using different randomly selected input variables in each instance. Thus, the program can be said to be repeated, or *iterated*, and each run is termed an *iteration*.[3] In each iteration, the net present value for the project would be computed accordingly. Figure 11–1 illustrates a typical simulation approach.

The results of these iterations are then used to plot a probability distribution of the project's net present values and to compute a mean and a standard deviation of returns.[4] This information provides the decision maker with an estimate of a project's expected returns, as well as its risk. Given this information, it is possible to compute the probability of achieving a net present value that is greater or less than any particular value.

For example, assume that the simulation for the project previously illustrated results in an expected net present value of $12,000, with a standard deviation of $6,000. The probability of the project's having a net present value of $0 or less can now be found. The value of $0 is -2.0 standard deviations below the mean:

$$z = \frac{\$0 - \$12,000}{\$6,000}$$

$$= -2.0 .$$

[3]Often one hundred or more iterations of a simulation model are performed.

[4]Regardless of the shape of the probability distribution for the individual variables used in the simulation, the net present value probability distribution will often be normally, or near normally, distributed.

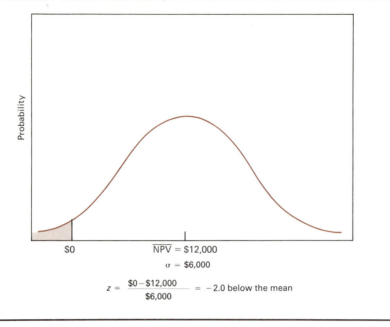

Probability

$0 $\overline{\text{NPV}}$ = $12,000

σ = $6,000

$$z = \frac{\$0 - \$12,000}{\$6,000} = -2.0 \text{ below the mean}$$

where z = the number of standard deviations.

It can be seen from Table V at the back of the book that the probability of a value less than -2.0 standard deviations from the mean is 2.28 percent. Thus, there is a 2.28 percent chance that the actual net present value for this project will be negative. Figure 11–2 shows the probability distribution of this project's net present value. The shaded area under the curve represents the probability that the project will have a net present value of $0 or less.

The simulation approach is a powerful one because it explicitly recognizes all of the interactions among the variables that influence a project's net present value. It provides both a mean net present value and a standard deviation that can help the decision maker analyze tradeoffs between risk and expected return.[5] Unfortunately, it can take considerable time and effort to gather the information necessary for each of the input variables and to correctly formulate the model. This limits the feasibility of simulation to very large projects. In addition, the simulation examples illustrated assumed that the values of the input variables were independent of one another. If this is not true—if, for example, the price of a product has a large influence on the number sold—then this interaction must be incorporated into the model, introducing even more complexity.

_____

[5]Simulation may also be applied to other decision models, such as the internal rate of return or payback approaches. In these cases the mathematical relationships involved in the simulation have to be respecified.

SENSITIVITY ANALYSIS

Sensitivity analysis is a procedure by means of which the change in net present value is calculated for a given change in one of the cash flow elements, such as product price. In other words, a decision maker can determine *how sensitive* a project's return is to changes in a particular variable.

Because sensitivity analysis is derived from the simulation approach, it also requires the definition of all relevant variables that influence the net present value of a project. The appropriate mathematical relationships between these variables must also be defined in order that the cash flow from the project may be estimated and the net present value computed. Rather than dealing with the entire probability distribution for each of the input variables, however, sensitivity analysis allows the decision maker to use only the "best estimate" of each variable to compute the net present value.

The decision maker can then ask various "what if" questions in which the project's net present value is recomputed under various conditions. For example, the best estimate of a product's price might be $10. The net present value of the project could be computed using this input together with best estimates of all the other variables. The next step would involve asking a question like, What if we cannot charge more than $8 per unit? The net present value could then be recomputed using the $8 price and the best estimates for each of the other input variables to determine the effect of the $8 price on the NPV.

Sensitivity analysis can be applied to any variable to determine the effect of changes in one or more of the inputs on a project's net present value. This process provides the decision maker with a formal mechanism for assessing the possible consequences of various scenarios.

It is often useful to construct sensitivity curves to summarize the impact of changes in different variables on the net present value of a project. A sensitivity curve has the project's net present value on the vertical axis and the variable of interest on the horizontal axis. For example, Figure 11–3 shows

FIGURE 11–3 Illustrative Sensitivity Curves

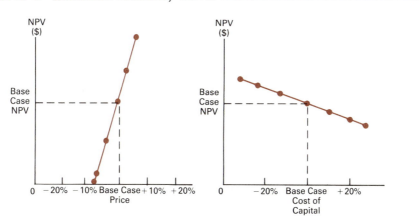

335

the sensitivity curves for two variables, sales price and cost of capital for a project.

The steep slope of the price-NPV curve indicates that the net present value is very sensitive to changes in the price for which the product can be sold. If the product price is approximately 8 percent below the base case, or initial analysis, estimate, the net present value of the project drops to $0, and the project becomes unacceptable for further price declines. In contrast, the relatively flat cost of capital-NPV curve indicates that the net present value is not very sensitive to changes in the firm's cost of capital. Similar curves could be constructed for project life, salvage value, units sold, operating costs, and other important variables.

Using electronic worksheets for sensitivity analysis   The development of low-cost business and personal microcomputers has revolutionized the application of a number of financial management tools. Sensitivity analysis had been a tool used only by large firms with extensive computer capabilities. Now the availability of computer software that can be used on small business and personal computers has extended the access to these techniques to nearly everyone.

Electronic worksheets, such as the popular VISICALC®, have made the application of sensitivity analysis techniques very simple and inexpensive.[6] Once the base case has been defined and entered in the worksheet, it is very easy to ask hundreds of "what if" type of questions. For example, assume that revenues from a project were expected to be $20,000 in year 1 and to grow by 10 percent annually over the 5-year life of the project. This relationship would be entered into the electronic worksheet along with similar relationships for all other factors that go into the determination of the annual net cash flows from the project. The net present value of the base case is computed by the worksheet. Now, what if the revenues will grow only by 5 percent annually, instead of 10 percent? Only one change must be made on the worksheet (redefine the growth rate to 5 percent), and the worksheet will automatically recompute each period's net cash flows and the net present value of the project. This process can be repeated very rapidly, literally hundreds of times, to develop a profile of how sensitive the project is to changes in the individual components of the project's cash flows.

The analyst may discover that the project's net present value is not very sensitive to different levels of operating cost but is very sensitive to different assumptions about price or quantity sold. Using this information, the analyst can decide whether the risk of the project is within acceptable limits.

ADJUSTING FOR BETA RISK IN CAPITAL BUDGETING

The risk adjustment procedures previously discussed are appropriate when the firm believes that a project's total risk is the relevant risk to consider in evaluating the project, and when it is assumed that the returns from the proj-

---

[6]VISICALC®, Personal Software, Inc., 1330 Bordeaux Drive, Sunnyvale, CA (1981).

ect being considered are highly positively correlated with the returns from the firm as a whole. Therefore, these methods are appropriate only when internal firm diversification benefits, which might change the firm's total risk (or the systematic portion of total risk), are not present.

The *beta* concept can also be used to determine risk-adjusted discount rates for individual projects. This approach is most appropriate for a firm whose stock is widely traded and for whom there is very little chance that bankruptcy will occur. (The probability of bankruptcy is a function of total risk, not just systematic risk.)

Just as the systematic risk (beta) of a portfolio of securities can be computed as the weighted average of the individual security betas, a firm may be considered as a portfolio of assets, each having its own measure of systematic risk (beta). From this perspective the systematic risk of the firm is simply the weighted average of the systematic risk of the individual assets.

For example, consider the security market line shown in Figure 11–4. The firm has a beta of 1.2 and uses only internally generated equity capital.[7] The

FIGURE 11–4 Risk-adjusted Discount Rates and the SML

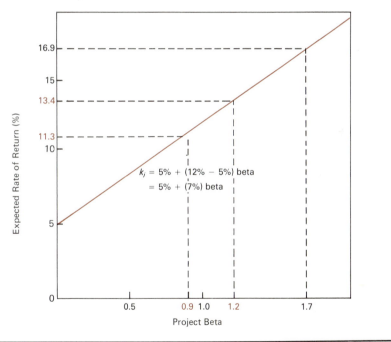

The equation shown on the figure:

$$k_j = 5\% + (12\% - 5\%) \text{ beta}$$
$$= 5\% + (7\%) \text{ beta}$$

Y-axis: Expected Rate of Return (%)
X-axis: Project Beta

---

[7]If the firm also uses debt capital, the following procedure is used to estimate the required return on the equity-financed portion of a project. This cost of equity would have to be adjusted to account for the additional risk arising from the use of debt and would be averaged with the cost of debt, using weights for debt and equity consistent with the optimal capital structure for the firm (or a division of the firm) to arrive at an estimate of the project's systematic risk-adjusted cost of capital. For a further discussion of this point, see Thomas E. Copeland and J. Fred Weston. *Financial Theory and Corporate Practice*, 2nd ed. Reading, Mass.: Addison-Wesley, 1983, chap. 12.

market risk premium is 7 percent. When considering projects of average risk—that is, projects that are highly correlated with the firm's returns on its existing assets and that have a beta similar to the firm's beta (1.2)—the firm should use the computed 13.4 percent cost of equity from Figure 11–4. When considering projects having estimated betas greater than 1.2, it should use a higher cost of equity. For example, if a project's subjectively estimated beta is 1.7, its required return would be 16.9 percent, or 5% + (1.7 × 7%), and this would be used as the risk-adjusted discount rate for that project.

Figure 11–5 illustrates the difference between the use of a single weighted cost of capital and risk-adjusted discount rates for project evaluation. In this case, Projects 1, 2, 3, and 4 are being evaluated by the firm. Using the weighted cost of capital approach, the firm would adopt Projects 3 and 4. However, if the firm considered the differential levels of systematic risk for the four alternatives, it would accept Projects 1 and 3 and reject Projects 2 and 4. In general, *the risk-adjusted discount rate approach is considered preferable to the weighted cost of capital approach when the projects under consideration differ significantly in their risk characteristics.*

The one problem remaining with this suggested procedure involves the determination of beta values for individual projects. Thus far, the most workable approach available is the use of *surrogate market information.* For example, if an aluminum firm is considering investing in the leisure-time product industry, the beta for this new project could be computed using the average beta for a sample of firms engaged principally in the leisure product

FIGURE 11–5   Risk-adjusted Discount Rate versus Weighted Cost of Capital _____

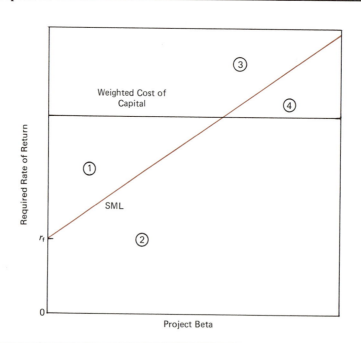

industry. Although the beta for the aluminum firm might be 1.3, resulting in a required equity return on projects of average risk of 14.1 percent, or 5% + (1.3 × 7%), according to Figure 11–4, this would not be the appropriate rate for leisure product projects. Assuming a beta of 0.9 for leisure product firms, the leisure product projects would be required to earn an equity return of only 11.3 percent or 5% + (0.9 × 7%), because of the lower average level of systematic risk associated with leisure product projects. This assumes that the leisure product projects are financed in the same manner as are the firms used to generate the surrogate betas. (See Footnote 7 for a further discussion of this point.)

DIVISIONAL COSTS OF CAPITAL

The approach just outlined can also be used to compute the required rate of return (cost of capital) for investments being evaluated by a firm's various divisions. For divisions that have lower (higher) systematic risk than others, the required returns for projects adopted by these divisions should be lower (higher) than the required returns for the firm as a whole.

For example, West Coast Power is an electric utility that has a calculated beta of 0.91. The firm has three divisions: the electric power generating and distribution division, which has 70 percent of the firm's assets; an oil and gas exploration division, which has 20 percent of the assets; and a transportation and barge division, which has 10 percent of the assets. Using surrogate market information, the beta for each division is estimated as shown here:

	Estimated Divisional Beta	Proportion of Firm's Assets	Weighted Average Beta
Electric power	0.75	0.70	0.53
Exploration	1.30	0.20	0.26
Transportation	1.20	0.10	0.12
		Weight average firm beta =	0.91

Note that the weighted average of the divisional betas is equal to the firm's overall beta—in this case, 0.91.

Conglomerate firms that compete in many different product and geographical markets, such as Ling Temco Vought or Gulf and Western Industries, often estimate separate divisional costs of capital. These divisional costs of capital reflect both the differential required returns of equity investors, estimated from the security market line, and the differential debt-carrying capacity of each division. For example, the parent company may have a debt-to-total-assets ratio of 60 percent. Individual divisions within the firm may compete against other firms that typically have higher or lower debt-to-total-assets ratios. In computing each divisional cost of capital, many firms try to reflect both the differential divisional risks and the differential normal debt ratios for each division.

SUMMARY

- The *risk* of an investment project is defined in terms of the potential *variability* of its returns. When only one return is possible—for example, as with U.S. Government securities held to maturity—there is no risk. When more than one return is possible for a particular project, it is risky.

- Risk is also influenced by the possibility of investment *diversification.* If a proposed project's returns are not *perfectly correlated* with the returns from the firm's other investments, the total risk of the firm may be reduced by accepting the proposed project. This is known as the *portfolio effect.*

- There are several ways in which a decision maker can adjust for differential project risk in capital budgeting, including the *subjective* or *informal approach,* the *net present value/payback approach,* the *risk-adjusted discount rate approach,* the *hurdle rate approach,* the *certainty equivalent approach,* the *simulation approach,* and *sensitivity analysis.* The risk-adjusted discount rate approach is widely used by firms that attempt to consider differential project risk in their capital budgeting procedures. It requires that a *risk premium* be computed for each project or group of projects so that an appropriate risk-adjusted discount rate can be applied when evaluating a project's cash flows. The widely used hurdle rate approach is similar to the risk-adjusted discount rate approach. The simulation approach is the most expensive of the techniques discussed in this chapter; it is normally applied only when large projects are being analyzed. The widespread availability of inexpensive and powerful computer software such as electronic worksheets has made the use of sensitivity analysis far more accessible to small- and medium-sized firms than was previously possible.

- When a project differs significantly in its *systematic risk* profile (as measured by *beta*) from the systematic risk of the total firm, a risk-adjusted discount rate appropriate for that project can be computed using the security market line relationship between risk and required return from the capital asset pricing model.

- The decision to employ some risk analysis technique to evaluate an investment project depends on the project's size and the additional cost of applying such a technique as compared with the perceived benefits. For small projects, only the simpler risk adjustment techniques should be used; for major projects that have above- or below-normal risk it is worthwhile to analyze the project's risk as precisely as possible. Failure to fully analyze the risk of a large project could result in bad investment decisions and even substantial losses.

Developing and Applying Risk-Adjusted Discount Rates in a Diversified Company

William J. Regan
Vice-President and Treasurer
Norman Dmuchowski
Manager of Financial Planning
American Natural Resources Co.

American Natural Resources is an integrated natural gas operation that transports gas from major producing areas, sells gas (wholesale) to several nonaffiliated distributing companies in nine states, stores gas underground in fields in Michigan, and sells gas (retail) to over 1 million customers. In addition, some of the firm's subsidiaries are engaged in gas exploration and production activities. American Natural also has a coal production and marketing subsidiary and a coal gasification subsidiary, and in 1977 it acquired Associated Truck Lines, a regional trucking firm. At the end of 1982 the firm's total assets exceeded $1.1 billion, and it had revenues of over $3.1 billion.

With its diversity of investments, American Natural is faced with the problem of evaluating investment alternatives that may differ significantly with respect to their relative risk. Should all projects be evaluated using the same discount rate, that is, the firm's cost of capital? We believe the answer to this question is no, if the projects differ in terms of their risk characteristics.

In practice, it is often difficult to estimate specific risk-adjusted discount rates to apply to each project. One way to resolve this problem is to estimate separate discount rates for each subsidiary of a diversified firm such as ours.

The approach used at American Natural Resources is based on the capital asset pricing model (CAPM). The risk-adjusted discount rate, k_j, applied in each division, is based on the security market line (SML):

$$k_j = r_f + \text{beta}_j \, (k_m - r_f) \, .$$

The expected risk-free rate, r_f, and the expected market rate of return, k_m, are forecasted using a simulation model that considers historical returns on various asset classes and the market consensus for economic prospects that are implied by the current inflation rate and yields on U.S. Government securities of various maturities.

Next it is necessary to estimate the beta that best reflects the systematic risk of each of American Natural's subsidiaries. Since the common stock of American Natural's subsidiaries is not traded, it is not possible to estimate beta in the traditional way.

One approach we use is to identify companies with publicly traded stock that are engaged entirely (or almost entirely) in the type of operation undertaken by a subsidiary. An average of the betas for these comparative companies can be used as a surrogate measure of the beta for each subsidiary. We use sources such as *Value Line*, Merrill Lynch, and Barr Rosenberg when selecting betas of companies most similar to each of our subsidiaries to be used as surrogates.

Next, these betas are adjusted to remove the impact of the particular financial structure used in each firm. The average of these "unlevered" betas is then determined for each industry group for which American Natural Resources has a subsidiary. This surrogate unlevered beta is used to compute a risk-adjusted discount rate for each subsidiary using the security market line. These divisional risk-adjusted rates are then used to discount the tax-adjusted operating cash flows from investment proposals in each subsidiary.

We see several advantages in this approach, including the following:

- The discount rates for all the subsidiaries are comparable, since they are all based on the same assumptions and market expectations.

- The discount rates are developed for different investment life periods and reflect investor expectations of inflation and the real interest rate over the specific periods.

- The discount rates can be updated periodically to reflect changing investor expectations and industry risk.

- The procedure can also be used to estimate discount rates for potential acquisitions or atypical projects that American Natural Resources might consider.

QUESTIONS AND TOPICS FOR DISCUSSION

1. How does the basic net present value model of capital budgeting deal with the problem of project risk? What are the shortcomings of this approach?

2. How would you define *risk* as it is used in a capital budgeting analysis context?

3. Recalling the discussion in Chapter 5, when is the standard deviation of a project's cash flows an appropriate measure of project risk? When is the coefficient of variation an appropriate measure?

4. How does the basic net present value capital budgeting model deal with the phenomenon of increasing risk of project cash flows over time?

5. Describe how certainty equivalent cash flow estimates can be derived for individual project cash flows.

6. Will all individuals apply the same certainty equivalent estimates to the cash flows from a project? Why or why not?

7. When should a firm consider the portfolio effects of a new project?

8. What are the primary advantages and disadvantages of applying *simulation* to capital budgeting risk analysis?

9. On average, the expected value of returns from each $1 of premiums paid on an insurance policy is less than $1; this is due to the insurance company's administrative costs and profits. In spite of this fact, why do so many individuals and organizations purchase insurance policies?

10. Computer simulation is used to generate a large number of possible outcomes for an investment project. Most firms invest in a particular project only once, however. How can a computer simulation model be helpful to the typical decision maker who is making a one-time-only investment decision?

11. Under what circumstances do you think the use of divisional required rates of return (costs of capital) is likely to improve the capital budgeting decision process?

PROBLEMS*

1. Aunt Bessie has discovered an old lithograph of Andrew Johnson at a local flea market. The dealer is asking a price of $20. Recognizing the potential value of this item, Aunt Bessie buys the lithograph. Given the condition of the lithograph, Aunt Bessie has assigned the following probability distribution to the lithograph's ultimate selling price when she offers it to a local dealer:

Probability	Selling Price
0.05	$ 50
0.25	75
0.35	125
0.20	150
0.15	200

a. Draw a bar graph indicating the lithograph's prospective selling price.
b. What is the expected selling price?
c. What is the standard deviation of the selling price?

2. The Topless Auto Company, a maker of convertible cars, has estimated the probability distribution of its annual net cash flows as follows:

Probability	Cash Flows (In Thousands of Dollars)
0.10	$100
0.20	175
0.40	250
0.20	325
0.10	400

a. Compute the expected annual cash flow.
b. Compute the standard deviation of annual cash flows.
c. Compute the coefficient of variation of annual cash flows.

(NOTE: The calculation of the standard deviation and the coefficient of variation is covered in Chapter 5.)

*Problems in color have check answers provided at the end of the book.

343

3. A new project has expected annual net cash flows of $200,000 with a standard deviation of $125,000. The distribution of annual net cash flows is approximately normal.
   a. What is the probability of the project's having negative annual net cash flows?
   b. What is the probability that annual net cash flows will be greater than $350,000?

4. Two projects have the following expected net present values and standard deviations of net present values:

Project	Expected Net Present Value	Standard Deviation
A	$50,000	$25,000
B	10,000	8,000

   a. Using the standard deviation criterion, which project is riskier?
   b. Using the coefficient of variation criterion, which project is riskier?
   c. Which criterion do you think is appropriate to use in this case? Why?

5. American Steel Corporation is considering two investments. One is the purchase of a new smelter costing $100 million. The expected net present value of this project is $20 million. The other alternative is the purchase of a supermarket chain, also costing $100 million. It too has an expected net present value of $20 million. The firm's management is interested in reducing the variability of its earnings.
   a. Which project should the company invest in?
   b. What assumptions did you make to arrive at this decision?

6. Western Kodiak is a producer of home movie equipment. The firm is considering two investments having the following cash flow streams:

Year	Project A	Project B
0	– $50,000	– $30,000
1	+ 20,000	+ 15,000
2	+ 20,000	+ 5,000
3	+ 10,000	+ 5,000
4	+ 5,000	+ 5,000
5	+ 5,000	+ 40,000

Western Kodiak uses a combination of the net present value approach and the payback approach to evaluate investment alternatives. It requires that all projects have a positive net present value when cash flows are discounted at 10 percent and that all projects have a payback no longer than 3 years. Which project or projects should the firm accept? Why?

7. Tiny Tin Enterprises is the maker of small metal lighting fixtures. It is considering expanding into the growing laser copier business. Tiny Tin estimates that this expansion will cost $2.5 million and will generate a 20-year stream of expected net cash flows amounting to $500,000 per year. The weighted cost of capital for Tiny Tin is 15 percent.
   a. Compute the net present value of the laser copier project using Tiny Tin's weighted cost of capital and the expected cash flows from the project.
   b. Using the risk-adjusted discount rate approach, Tiny Tin's management has

344

decided that this project has substantially more risk than average and has decided that it requires a 24 percent expected rate of return on projects like this.
Recompute the risk-adjusted net present value of this project.

8. Apple Jacks, Inc., produces a cheap wine. The firm is considering expanding into
the snack food business. This expansion will require an initial investment in new
equipment of $100,000. The equipment will be depreciated on a straight line basis
over a 10-year period to an estimated salvage value of $20,000. The expansion
will require an increase in working capital for the firm of $20,000. The equipment
is eligible for the 10 percent investment tax credit.

Revenues from the new venture are forecasted at $100,000 per year for the first
5 years and $110,000 per year for years 6 through 10. Cash operating costs from
the new venture are estimated at $60,000 for the first 5 years and $65,000 for
years 6 through 10. It is assumed that at the end of year 10 the snack food equipment will be sold for its book value.

The firm's marginal tax rate is 40 percent. The required return for projects of
average risk has been estimated as 13 percent.

a. Compute the project's net present value, assuming that it is an average risk
investment.

b. If management decides that all product line expansions have above average
risk and should therefore be evaluated at a 24 percent required rate of return,
what will be the risk-adjusted net present value of the project?

9. The Seminole Production Company is analyzing the investment in a new line of
business machines. The initial outlay required is $35 million. The net cash flows
expected from the investment are as follows:

Year	Net Cash Flow
1	$ 5 million
2	8 million
3	15 million
4	20 million
5	15 million
6	10 million
7	4 million

The firm's cost of capital (used for projects of average risk) is 15 percent.

a. Compute the net present value of this project assuming it possesses average
risk.

b. Because of the risk inherent in this type of investment, Seminole has decided
to employ the certainty equivalent approach. After considerable discussion,
management has agreed to apply the following certainty equivalents to the
project's cash flows:

Year	α_t
0	1.00
1	0.95
2	0.90
3	0.80
4	0.60
5	0.40
6	0.35
7	0.30

345

If the risk-free rate is 9 percent, compute the project's certainty equivalent net present value.

c. On the basis of this analysis, should the project be accepted?

10. A simulation model similar to the one described in this chapter has been constructed by the ZEP Corporation to evaluate the largest of its new investment proposals. After many iterations of the model, ZEP's management has arrived at an expected net present value for Project A of $1.4 million. The standard deviation of the net present value has been estimated from the simulation model results to be $0.8 million.

   a. What is the probability that the project will have a negative net present value?
   b. What is the probability that the project will have a net present value greater than $3.0 million?

11. The Buffalo Snow Shoe Company is considering manufacturing radial snow shoes, which are more durable and offer better traction. Buffalo estimates that the investment in manufacturing equipment will cost $250,000 and will have a 10-year economic life. The equipment is eligible for a 10 percent investment tax credit. Buffalo will depreciate the equipment on a straight line basis to a $0 estimated salvage value over a 10-year period. The estimated selling price of each pair of shoes will be $50. Buffalo anticipates that it can sell 5,000 pairs a year at this price. Unit production and selling costs (exclusive of depreciation) will be about $25. The firm's marginal tax rate is 40 percent. A cost of capital of 12 percent is thought to be appropriate to analyze a project of this type.

   Buffalo has decided to perform a sensitivity analysis of the project before making a decision.

   a. Compute the expected net present value of this project.
   b. Buffalo's president does not believe that 5,000 pairs of the new snow shoes can be sold at a $50 price. He estimates that a maximum of 3,000 pairs will be sold at this price. How does the change in the estimated sales volume influence the net present value of the project?

12. The Jacobs Company is financed entirely with equity. The beta for Jacobs has been estimated to be 1.0. The current risk-free rate is 10 percent, and the expected market return is 15 percent.

   a. What rate of return should Jacobs require on a project of average risk?
   b. If a new venture is expected to have a beta of 1.6, what rate of return should Jacobs demand on this project?
   c. The project in question requires an initial outlay of $10 million and is expected to generate a 10-year stream of annual net cash flows of $2.3 million. Evaluate the project using Jacob's required return for projects of average risk.
   d. Evaluate the project using the risk-adjusted rate computed in Part b.

Capital Budgeting

Four years ago the First National Bank of Macungie installed an automated teller machine (ATM) at one of its branches. The machine had the capacity to accept deposits, make withdrawals, and handle inquiries regarding account balances. Not long afterward, one of its competitors, the Second State Bank, installed its own ATM and called it "Bon Ami" (good friend). It can do everything the First National's ATM can do, and more—including transferring customers' funds between checking and savings, handling address changes and other customer service requests, and accepting utility bill payments.

Since the Second State Bank installed its Bon Ami machine, First National has lost a number of customers. As a result, First National is considering purchasing a new, more efficient, and more productive ATM and naming it "Amigo Plus" because it will handle even more transactions than its competitor's Bon Ami.

When First National purchased its first ATM, it cost $50,000 and was estimated to have a useful economic life of 10 years. The bank took full advantage of the 10 percent investment tax credit at that time* and has been depreciating its ATM on a straight line basis (over 10 years) to an estimated book salvage of $0. The current actual salvage value of the old ATM is $10,000.

Amigo Plus will cost $70,000 and have an expected economic life of 6 years. The bank plans to claim the investment tax credit to which it is entitled and to depreciate the new ATM on a 5-year ACRS basis. The bank believes that its Amigo Plus will attract new customers, which are expected to generate $19,000 in new revenues during the first year. Revenues from these new customers are expected to grow at 5 percent per year over the 6-year life of the new ATM. Cash operating costs to service these customers (exclusive of any costs to maintain the ATM) are expected to be $5,000 during the first year and to increase at a rate of 6 percent per year over the new machine's 6-year life. As an additional benefit, annual maintenance costs on the new ATM will be $2,000 per year *less* than the annual maintenance costs on the old ATM.

First National has a 40 percent marginal tax rate, and its weighted cost of capital is 12 percent.

1. Compute the net investment required to purchase the new ATM. (Consider the cost of the new ATM, the salvage value of the old ATM, and the tax consequences associated with buying the new ATM and disposing of the old one.)

2. Compute the annual incremental net cash flows for each year of the project's expected 6-year-life.

---

*Prior to the ACRS, assets held for 3 to 4 years were eligible for one third of the ITC; assets held for 5 to 6 years were eligible for two thirds of the ITC. Thus, if an asset were sold before 7 years, there was a *recapture* of a portion of the ITC. In this case, two thirds of the original ITC will be recaptured, or $3,333.

3. Compute the net present value of this project, assuming the ATM to be of average risk.

4. Based on the calculations performed in Questions 1 through 3, should First National purchase the new ATM?

5. Assume that First National requires projects to have paybacks of less than 4 years. Under these conditions, should it purchase the new ATM?

6. The bank's board of directors requires that a risk-adjusted discount rate be used to evaluate any investments that are seen as expanding the bank's services. Assume that the board considers the new ATM as falling into this category, since it will handle an increased number of transactions, and that the board requires an additional risk premium of 3 percent to be used when evaluating the project. Under these conditions, should the bank purchase the new ATM?

7. Finally, assume that the bank develops a simulation model to analyze this project. The model produces an expected net present value of $4,800 with a standard deviation of $2,800. The board is willing to tolerate a 5 percent chance that the project will have a net present value less than $0. Under these conditions (and assuming the net present value probability distribution is approximately normal), should First National purchase the new ATM?

ADDITIONAL READINGS AND REFERENCES

Adler, Michael. "On Risk-Adjusted Capitalization Rates and Valuation by Individuals." *Journal of Finance* 25 (Sept. 1970): 819–836.

Bierman, Harold, Jr., and Hass, Jerome E. "Capital Budgeting under Uncertainty: A Reformation." *Journal of Finance* 28 (March 1973): 119–130.

Bonini, Charles P. "Capital Investment under Uncertainty with Abandonment Options." *Journal of Financial and Quantitative Analysis* 12 (March 1977): 39–54.

Hertz, David B. "Risk Analysis in Capital Investment." *Harvard Business Review* 42 (Jan.–Feb. 1964): 95–106.

Lessard, Donald R., and Bower, Richard S. "An Operational Approach to Risk Screening." *Journal of Finance* 28 (May 1973): 321–338.

Lewellen, Wilbur G., and Long, Michael S. "Simulation versus Single-Value Estimates in Capital Expenditure Analysis." *Decision Sciences* 3 (1973): 19–33.

Myers, S. C. "Procedures for Capital Budgeting under Uncertainty." *Industrial Management Review* (Spring 1968).

Paine, Neil R. "Uncertainty and Capital Budgeting." *Accounting Review* 39 (April 1964): 330–332.

Robichek, A. A., and Myers, S. C. "Conceptual Problems in the Use of Risk-Adjusted Discount Rates." *Journal of Finance* 21 (Dec. 1966): 727–730.

Robichek, Alexander A. "Interpreting the Results of Risk Analysis." *Journal of Finance* 30 (Dec. 1975): 1384–1386.

Tuttle, D. L., and Litzenberger, R. H. "Leverage, Diversification, and Capital Market Effects on a Risk-Adjusted Capital Budgeting Framework." *Journal of Finance* 23 (June 1968): 427–443.

Weston, J. Fred. "Investment Decisions Using the Capital Asset Pricing Model." *Financial Management* 2 (Spring 1973): 25–33.

PART FIVE

The Cost of Capital, Capital Structure, and Dividend Policy

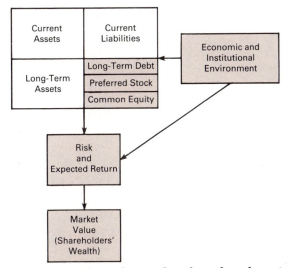

This section considers three closely related topics—the cost of capital (Chapter 12), capital structure (Chapter 13), and dividend policy (Chapter 14). The cost of capital is an important input in the capital budgeting decision process. This market-determined cost of funds also directly influences the value of a firm's securities. The cost of capital cannot be considered in isolation. The capital structure of a firm directly affects its cost of capital. A more debt-laden capital structure will at some point increase the risk of the firm's securities and increase the overall cost of capital to the firm. This results in a reduction in the value of the firm. Chapter 13 looks at the determinants of an "optimal" capital structure—one that is consistent with the objective of shareholder wealth maximization. Finally, the dividend policy of a firm can provide important information to investors that ultimately may affect the firm's risk and cost of capital as perceived by investors.

CHAPTER 12

The Cost of Capital

A FINANCIAL DILEMMA

Cost of Equity Capital for the
Public Service Company of New Mexico

The Public Service Company of New Mexico (PNM) is the largest investor-owned electric utility in the state of New Mexico. As a public utility, PNM is closely regulated by the New Mexico Public Service Commission and the Federal Energy Regulatory Commission (FERC). As a part of any major rate case filing, PNM must establish its cost of capital.

In a typical rate case, there is very little controversy about the cost of preferred stock and debt. As we shall see in this chapter, the calculation of these costs is straightforward. In contrast, there is normally extensive controversy regarding the cost of equity.

In PNM's 1981 filing before the FERC, seven witnesses submitted cost of equity capital testimony. A listing of their recommendations follows:

Witness	Representing	Recommendation
Basil Copeland	City of Gallup, New Mexico	13.75%
Matityahu Marcus	Plains Electric Cooperative	14.80%
Philip Winter	General Services Administration	Range of 15.30–16.40%
Kirk Randall	FERC staff	15.81%
Cornelius Prior	Kidder Peabody for PNM	17.50%
R. Charles Moyer	PNM	17.81%
Mack Wathen	PNM	17.80%

The cost of equity was estimated from a low of 13.75 percent to a high of 17.81 percent. Having heard volumes of conflicting testimony on the issue, the FERC was faced with the dilemma of making a final recommendation.

This chapter develops the principles and models that can be used to compute a firm's cost of debt, preferred stock, and common stock. All these models require the use of some judgment by the analyst. This is particularly true in the case of the cost of common equity. The cost of common equity cannot be estimated with the precision possible in the case of debt and preferred stock. However, the analyst aware of the basic principles contained in this chapter can estimate it more accurately than is implied in the testimony presented in PNM's rate case.

GLOSSARY OF NEW TERMS

Beta   a measure of a stock's price and total return volatility relative to the volatility of prices and returns in the securities markets as a whole.

Capital Asset Pricing Model (CAPM)   a theory that formally describes the nature of the risk–required return tradeoff in finance. It provides one method of computing a firm's cost of equity capital.

Investment opportunity curve   a graph or listing showing a firm's investment opportunities (projects) ranked from highest to lowest expected rate of return.

Marginal cost of capital   the weighted after-tax cost of the next dollars of capital the firm expects to raise to finance new investment projects.

Optimal capital budget   the level of capital spending at which a firm's investment opportunity curve just intersects its marginal cost of capital curve.

INTRODUCTION

Chapters 9 through 11 considered the capital budgeting decisions of a firm. One of the key variables in capital expenditure analysis is the cost of capital. This chapter discusses the concept of the cost of capital and develops approaches that can be used to measure this important variable.

The *cost of capital* is concerned with what a firm has to pay for the capital—that is, the debt, preferred stock, retained earnings, and common stock—it uses to finance new investments. It also can be thought of as the rate of return required by investors in the firm's securities. As such, the firm's cost of capital is determined in the capital markets and is closely related to the degree of risk associated with new investments, existing assets, and capital structure. In general, the greater the risk of a firm as perceived by investors, the greater the return investors will require and the greater the cost of capital will be.

The cost of capital can also be thought of as the minimum rate of return required on new investments undertaken by the firm.[1] If a new investment earns an internal rate of return that is greater than the cost of capital, the value of the firm increases. Correspondingly, if a new investment earns a

---

[1]Technically, this statement assumes that the risk of the new investments is equal to the risk of the firm's existing assets. Also, when used in this context, the cost of capital refers to a weighted cost of the various sources of capital used by the firm. The computation of the weighted cost of capital is considered later in this chapter.

return less than the firm's cost of capital, the firm's value decreases.

This chapter discusses the nature of the tradeoff between risk and required return made by investors in a firm's securities, the measurement of the cost of individual capital components, and the weighted cost of capital and its use in the capital budgeting process. Chapter 13 continues by considering the relationship between capital structure and the cost of capital.

NATURE OF RISK PREMIUMS

Throughout finance, numerous tradeoffs must be made between risk and required return. In capital budgeting, for example, companies require higher returns on projects perceived as "high risk" than on projects considered to be "low risk." This discussion focuses on the relationship between the risk and required return on a firm's securities.

The required return on any security may be thought of as consisting of a riskless, or risk-free, rate of return, r_f, plus a premium for the risk inherent in that security:

$$\text{Required return} = r_f + \text{Risk premium} . \tag{12.1}$$

The riskless rate of return is normally measured by the rate of return on risk-free securities, such as short-term U.S. Treasury securities. This rate varies over time and is influenced by two key factors:

- The expected inflation rate.
- The supply and demand for funds in the overall economy.

When investors expect a high inflation rate and the implied loss in the purchasing power of their money, they will demand a higher rate of return on their investments—not only in risk-free securities, but in risky securities as well. Similarly, if the anticipated demand for investment funds exceeds the anticipated supply at current interest rates, the rate of return required by investors will increase to create a new, higher equilibrium rate of return. These two factors are the primary determinants of returns on risk-free securities. The returns required on all other securities also are influenced by the risk of those securities.

There are four major risk components that determine the risk premium on a specific security at any point in time:

- The business risk of the firm.
- The financial risk of the firm.
- The marketability risk of the security.
- The length of maturity of the security (interest rate risk).

The *business risk* of a firm refers to the variability in the firm's operating earnings (EBIT). It is determined by the variability in the firm's sales revenues and operating costs and by the amount of operating leverage the firm uses in producing sales.

Financial risk refers to the additional variability in a company's earnings

352

per share that results from the use of fixed-cost sources of funds, such as debt and preferred stock. In addition, the financial risk premium includes a premium to compensate for the increased potential risk of bankruptcy that arises from the use of debt financing.

Marketability risk refers to the ability of an investor to buy and sell a company's securities quickly and easily without a significant loss of value. For example, AT&T's shares are readily marketable any time at, or very near to, the current market price. Other, less widely owned securities that are not traded on an organized exchange or traded actively in the over-the-counter market usually do not have such a ready market. This may cause time delays in the sale of the securities and necessitate price concessions. Generally the less marketable a security, the higher its required rate of return.

Interest rate risk refers to the variability in the rate of return or yield on securities (such as bonds or preferred stocks) that arises from changes in interest rates. As interest rates rise, the prices of fixed income securities fall, causing current holders of these securities to realize a lower rate of return, or yield, (than was expected at the time the security was purchased) when they sell the securities.

Finally, a firm's cost of funds may increase at any point in time with increases in the amount of needed financing. For example, a company might be able to sell 1 million new shares of common stock at $25 per share. If the firm sought to sell an additional 1 million shares, however, it would probably have to offer them at a lower price in order to attract enough buyers. This would, of course, increase the cost of the funds raised by the firm. In addition, as a firm seeks increasing amounts of capital from investors, there is a point at which the investors begin to question the firm's ability to effectively manage the large number of investment projects to be financed with these funds.

Although the foregoing concepts provide a useful background for analyzing the cost of a firm's capital, they are not directly applicable to measuring the cost of capital for specific sources of funds. Before considering how the cost of capital may be estimated, it is necessary to examine the relationship between the costs of various capital sources.

RELATIVE COSTS OF CAPITAL

Figure 12–1 illustrates the general risk-return tradeoff between investors' required rates of return and various sources of funds. As was noted, the risk-free rate, r_f, is usually measured as the rate of return on short-term U.S. Treasury securities. Longer-term U.S. Government bonds normally command a higher rate than shorter-term debt, because bond prices vary more than prices of shorter-term debt securities over time, depending on changes in interest rates. Thus, if interest rates rise, the price of long-term bonds falls, resulting in losses for any investor who must sell the security. Investors normally require a premium to compensate for this *interest rate risk*.

Long-term debt securities of the U.S. government are always less risky than corporate long-term debt securities of the same maturity. The reason, of course, is that there is a finite probability, however small, that the firm will default on its obligation to pay interest and principal. Since the government

FIGURE 12–1   **General Risk–Required Return Tradeoff**

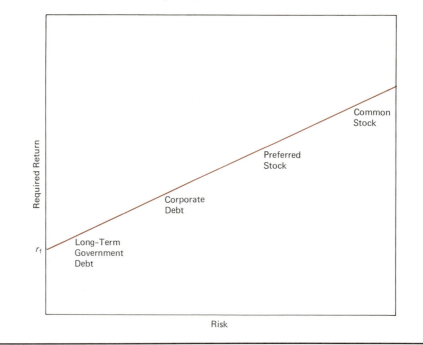

controls the money supply, it can always meet its financial obligations by printing more money. The actual difference in returns, or yields, between government debt and good-quality corporate debt (AAA rated) is usually less than 1 percent and sometimes less than 0.5 percent. For example, in early 1983 the average yield on AAA corporate bonds was 11.39 percent, and the average yield on long-term U.S. Treasury bonds was 10.87 percent. Companies with high default risk must offer high coupon interest rates to investors in order to sell their debt issues. This is because the market recognizes that these high default risk companies are more likely to have difficulty meeting their obligations than low default risk companies.

Preferred stock is normally riskier than debt. The claims of preferred stock-holders on the firm's assets and earnings are junior to those of debtholders. Also, dividends on preferred stock are more likely to be cut or omitted than interest on debt. Consequently, investors in the market usually demand a higher return on preferred stock than on debt.

Finally, common stock is the most risky of the types of securities considered here, because dividends paid to common stockholders are made from cash remaining after interest and preferred dividends have been paid. Thus, the common stock dividends are the first to be cut when the firm encounters difficulties. Therefore, because there is a greater degree of uncertainty associated with common stock dividends than with the interest on debt or preferred stock dividends, common stock dividends are judged more risky. In addition, the market price fluctuations of common stocks tend to be wider than those of preferred stocks or long-term debt. As a result of this higher risk, investors' required return on common stock is higher relative to preferred stock and debt. Over the years the differences between returns realized from long-term debt and common stock investments have averaged roughly 5 to 6 percent.[2]

So far this section has shown that a particular security's risk affects the return required by investors. The analysis must be taken one important step farther, however. If capital markets are to clear (that is, supply equals demand), the firm must offer returns consistent with investor expectations. Suppose, for example, that a firm offers a security for sale in the capital markets at a return that is less than investors in general expect. Obviously, not enough buyers will come forth. Unless the firm increases the return (by dropping the price, raising the interest or dividend rate, and so on), the securities will remain unsold, and the firm will not be able to raise its capital. Thus, *the cost of capital to the firm is equal to the equilibrium rate of return demanded by investors in the capital markets for securities with that degree of risk.*

COMPUTING THE COMPONENT COSTS OF CAPITAL

Firms usually raise funds in "lumpy" amounts; for example, a firm may sell $50 million in bonds to finance capital expenditures at one point in time, and it may use retained earnings or proceeds from the sale of stock to finance capital expenditures later on. In spite of this tendency to raise funds in lumpy amounts from various sources at different points in time, the weighted (or composite) cost of funds, not the cost of any particular component of funds, is the cost we are interested in for capital budgeting purposes. Another way of saying this is that *it is generally incorrect to associate any particular source of financing with a particular project;* that is, the investment and the financing decisions should be separate.

Consider, for example, the case of a firm that is financed 50 percent with debt and 50 percent with equity. The after-tax cost of equity is 16 percent, and the after-tax cost of debt is 10 percent. The firm has two plants, A and B, which are identical in every respect. The manager of Plant A proposes to acquire a new automated packaging machine costing $10 million. A bank has offered to loan the firm the needed $10 million at a rate that will give the firm a 10 percent after-tax cost. The internal rate of return for this project has been estimated to be 12 percent. Since the rate of return exceeds the cost of funds (debt) used to finance the machine, the manager of Plant A argues that the investment should be made.

The manager of Plant B now argues that she too should be allowed to make

[2]See Roger C. Ibbotson and Rex A. Sinquefield. *Stocks, Bonds, Bills, and Inflation: The Past and the Future.* Charlottesville, Va.: Financial Analysts Research Foundation, 1982.

a similar investment. Unfortunately, she is reminded that the firm has a target capital structure of 50 percent debt and 50 percent equity and that her investment will have to be financed with equity in order for the firm to maintain its target capital structure. Since the cost of equity is 16 percent and the project only offers a 12 percent return, the investment is denied for Plant B.

The point of this illustration is that two projects that are economically identical were treated very differently, simply because the method of financing the project was tied to the accept-reject decision. To avoid problems of this type, the capital expenditure decision is usually based on a composite capital cost—that is, each project is assumed to be financed with debt and equity in the proportion in which it appears in the target capital structure. In this case, the composite cost of capital is 13 percent, computed as follows:

Source of Capital	After-tax Cost	Proportion	Composite Cost
Debt	10%	0.5	5%
Equity	16	0.5	8
		Weighted cost of capital =	13%

In this example neither project should be accepted, since the cost of capital exceeds the projects' expected rates of return.

This section develops and applies methods a firm can use to compute the cost of its major component sources of capital—debt, preferred stock, retained earnings, and new common equity. These component costs are then combined into a weighted cost of capital that can be used in making capital budgeting and capital structure decisions.

COST OF DEBT

The cost of debt capital to the firm is the rate of return required by investors. For a debt issue, this rate of return, k_d, equates the present value of all expected future receipts—interest, I, and principal repayment, M— with the offering price, P_0, of the debt security:

$$P_0 = \sum_{t=1}^{n} \frac{I}{(1 + k_d)^t} + \frac{M}{(1 + k_d)^n} .$$ (12.2)

Most *new* long-term debt issued by companies is sold at or close to par value (normally $1,000 per bond), and the coupon interest rate is set at the rate required by investors.[3] When debt is issued at par value, the pretax cost of debt, k_d, is equal to the coupon interest rate:

$$k_d = \text{Coupon interest rate} .$$ (12.3)

[3]When debt is issued at par value, the coupon interest rate is equal to the yield to maturity.

356

Interest payments made to investors, however, are deductible from the firm's taxable income. Therefore, the *after-tax* cost of debt, k_i, issued at par is computed by multiplying the coupon interest rate by 1 minus the firm's marginal tax rate, t:

$$k_i = k_d(1 - t) . \tag{12.4}$$

To illustrate the cost of debt computation, suppose that National Telephone and Telegraph sells $100 million of 8.5 percent first mortgage bonds at par. Assuming a corporate marginal tax rate of 40 percent, the after-tax cost of debt is computed as follows:

$$k_i = k_d(1 - t) = 8.5 (1 - 0.4)$$
$$= 5.1\% .$$

Equation 12.4 assumes that a firm sells the debt to yield *net proceeds*, after the cost of issuance, of $1,000 per bond. However, because of these issue costs, many bonds provide the firm with net proceeds that are less than the $1,000 par value of the bond. In addition, there have been an increasing number of bonds sold at prices considerably below par (called *deep discount bonds*). These bonds have coupon rates substantially less than prevailing market rates. They are discussed in Chapter 16.

In these cases, the computation of the pretax cost of debt is quite similar to the calculation of the yield to maturity on a bond as presented in Chapter 4. (The "Calculator Applications" section in Chapter 4 illustrates how to solve for the yield to maturity on a bond using a financial calculator.) For example, suppose a firm sells a series of 20-year, $1,000 par value bonds. The price to the public is $755, and the bonds provide a coupon rate of interest of 7 percent ($70 interest per year). (These bonds would be called *deep discount bonds*.) The issue costs per bond are $10 each. Hence, the net proceeds to the firm are as follows:

Net proceeds = $1,000 par value − $245 discount − $10 issue costs
= $745 .

The pretax cost of debt to this firm is equal to the discount rate, which equates the present value of all future interest payments ($70 per year for 20 years) plus the repayment of principal ($1,000) at the end of 20 years with the net proceeds to the firm, or

$$\$745 = \$70(\text{PVIFA}_{k_d,20}) + \$1,000(\text{PVIF}_{k_d,20}) .$$

By trial and error, try 10 percent:

$$\$745 = \$70(8.514) + \$1,000(0.149)$$
$$= \$745 .$$

Therefore, the pretax cost of debt is 10 percent. Assuming a 40 percent tax rate, the after-tax cost is as follows:[4]

$$k_i = 10\%(1 - 0.4)$$
$$= 6\% .$$

COST OF PREFERRED STOCK

The cost of preferred stock to the firm is the rate of return required by investors on preferred stock issued by the company. Because many preferred stocks are perpetuities,[5] it is possible to use the simplified preferred stock valuation model developed in Chapter 4:

$$P_0 = \frac{D_p}{k_p} , \qquad (12.5)$$

where P_0 is the preferred stock price; D_p, the annual preferred dividend; and k_p, the investors' required rate of return. The cost of preferred stock, k_p, is given by the following equation:

$$k_p = \frac{D_p}{P_{net}} . \qquad (12.6)$$

In calculating preferred stock cost, the price that should be used, P_{net}, is the net proceeds to the firm, that is, the proceeds from the sale of the stock after subtracting *flotation costs.*

To illustrate, suppose Midwestern Airlines just issued 30 million shares of $2.75 cumulative preferred stock at a price to the public of $25 a share. Assuming flotation costs of $1 a share, the cost of preferred stock is calculated as follows:

$$k_p = \frac{\$2.75}{\$25 - \$1}$$
$$= 0.115, \text{ or } 11.5\% .$$

Since payments by the firm to preferred stockholders are in the form of dividends, they are not tax deductible so the after-tax cost of preferred stock is equal to the pretax rate.

Preferred stock is similar to long-term debt in that both types of securities

---

[4]The tax benefits of interest deductibility are only available for firms that are making profits. For a firm losing money, the tax rate in Equation 12.4 is *zero,* and the pretax cost, k_d, is the same as the after-tax cost, k_i.

[5]An increasing number of preferred stock offerings are callable, or have a fixed maturity. In these cases, the computation of the cost of the preferred is identical to that for bonds; that is, it is necessary to solve for the discount rate, k_p, which equates the present value of future promised dividends plus the present value of the retirement value (usually the par or stated value) of the preferred stock with the net proceeds to the firm.

normally involve fixed, uniform payments per period to the holders. In general, investors are required to pay income taxes on both interest and dividends. However, the issuing company can only deduct interest from its taxable income. As a result, in most situations in which a profitable company (with a 46 percent marginal tax rate) is choosing to leverage with either debt or preferred stock, it will prefer to issue debt, because its after-tax cost is roughly one half that of preferred stock.

COST OF INTERNAL EQUITY CAPITAL

Like the cost of debt and preferred stock, the cost of equity capital to the firm is the equilibrium rate of return required by the firm's common stock investors.

Firms raise equity capital in two ways:

- *Internally*, through retained earnings.
- *Externally*, through the sale of new common stock.

The cost of internal equity to the firm is less than the cost of new common stock, because the sale of new stock requires the payment of flotation costs.

The concept of the cost of internal equity (or simply *equity*, as it is commonly called) can be developed using several different approaches. The first considered here is based on the dividend valuation model.

DIVIDEND VALUATION MODEL APPROACH

Briefly reviewing from Chapter 4, the dividend valuation model (or the dividend capitalization model, as it is often referred to) for common stock valuation (Equation 4.18) is as follows:

$$P_0 = \sum_{t=1}^{\infty} \frac{D_t}{(1 + k_e)^t},$$ (12.7)

where P_0 is the stock's present value or current market price; D_t, the dividend received in period t; and k_e, the return required by investors. This equation shows that k_e, the required return and thus the cost of equity capital, equates the present value of all expected future dividends with the current market price of the stock. In principle, the cost of equity capital can be calculated by solving Equation 12.7 for k_e. In practice, however, the expected future dividends are not known and cannot be estimated with the same degree of confidence as preferred stock dividends and debt interest. As a result, the theoretically correct general form of the dividend valuation model is generally not very useful in calculating the cost of equity capital.

If the firm's future per-share dividends are expected to grow each period perpetually at a constant rate, g, the dividend valuation model can be written as follows:

$$P_0 = \sum_{t=1}^{\infty} \frac{D_0(1 + g)^t}{(1 + k_e)^t},$$ (12.8)

359

where D_0 is the dividend in the current period $(t = 0)$. Assuming that the cost of equity, k_e, is greater than the expected dividend growth rate, g, Equation 12.8 can be transformed algebraically to the following equation:

$$P_0 = \frac{D_1}{k_e - g},$$ (12.9)

where $D_1 = D_0(1 + g)$.

Equation 12.9 can be rearranged to obtain an expression for calculating the cost of equity, assuming that dividends are expected to grow perpetually at a rate g per year:[6]

$$k_e = \frac{D_1}{P_0} + g.$$ (12.10)

To illustrate the use of Equation 12.10, suppose the Fresno Company's common stock is currently selling at $25 a share. Its present dividend, D_0, is $2 a share, and the expected dividend growth rate is 7 percent. The investors' required return (that is, the firm's cost of equity) is calculated as follows:

$$k_e = \frac{\$2(1.07)}{\$25} + 0.07$$

$$= 0.156, \text{ or } 15.6\% .$$

In addition to being used for the constant growth case, the dividend valuation model also can be used to estimate the cost of equity capital for the no-growth case. If a stock pays a current dividend that is expected to remain constant perpetually, the appropriate valuation model follows:

$$P_0 = \frac{D}{k_e},$$ (12.11)

and the cost of equity capital is calculated as follows:

$$k_e = \frac{D}{P_0}.$$ (12.12)

To illustrate, suppose the Mountaineer Railroad pays a dividend of $1.50, which is expected to remain constant forever. The firm's common stock is presently selling at $10 a share. Using these figures, the cost of equity capital is calculated as follows:

---

[6]The growth rate that is relevant is the rate expected by investors. This normally is estimated by examining historical growth rates, as well as projected future growth rates provided by security analysts such as *Value Line* and Merrill Lynch.

$$k_e = \frac{D}{P_0}$$

$$= \frac{\$1.50}{\$10}$$

$$= 0.15, \text{ or } 15\% .$$

The dividend valuation model also can be used to value common stocks that are expected to pay dividends that grow at variable rates in the future. For example, a young high technology company could be expected to show a period of relatively rapid growth followed by a continuing period of more normal growth. Using the dividend valuation model and defining g_1 as an above-normal growth rate expected by investors and security analysts over the first m years and g_2 as a normal, perpetual, expected growth rate beginning in year $m + 1$, the current stock price is determined as follows:

$$P_0 = \sum_{t=1}^{m} \frac{D_0(1 + g_1)^t}{(1 + k_e)^t} + \frac{P_m}{(1 + k_e)^m} \tag{12.13}$$

$$= \sum_{t=1}^{m} \frac{D_0(1 + g_1)^t}{(1 + k_e)^t} + \frac{1}{(1 + k_e)^m} \times \frac{D_{m+1}}{k_e - g_2} . \tag{12.14}$$

The cost of equity capital can be estimated by solving Equation 12.14 by trial and error.

For example, Avtec Corporation is a rapidly growing producer of microcircuit boards used in the aerospace industry. Its stock is currently selling for $10.95 per share. Current dividends, D_0, are $1.00 per share and are expected to grow at a rate of 10 percent per year over the next 4 years and 6 percent annually thereafter. Avtec's cost of internal equity, k_e, can be found by solving Equation 12.14 as follows:

$$\$10.95 = \sum_{t=1}^{4} \frac{\$1.00(1 + 0.10)^t}{(1 + k_e)^t} + \frac{1}{(1 + k_e)^4} \times \frac{D_5}{k_e - 0.06}$$

$$= \frac{\$1.10}{(1 + k_e)^1} + \frac{\$1.21}{(1 + k_e)^2} + \frac{\$1.33}{(1 + k_e)^3}$$

$$+ \frac{\$1.46}{(1 + k_e)^4} + \frac{1}{(1 + k_e)^4} \times \frac{\$1.55}{k_e - 0.06}$$

$$= \$1.10(\text{PVIF}_{k_e,1}) + \$1.21(\text{PVIF}_{k_e,2}) + \$1.33(\text{PVIF}_{k_e,3})$$

$$+ \$1.46(\text{PVIF}_{k_e,4}) + (\text{PVIF}_{k_e,4}) \frac{\$1.55}{k_e - 0.06} .$$

A trial value of 17 percent for k_e yields the following:

$$\$10.95 = \$1.10(0.855) + \$1.21(0.731) + \$1.33(0.624) + \$1.46(0.534)$$

$$+ 0.534 \left(\frac{\$1.55}{0.17 - 0.06} \right)$$

$$= \$10.95 .$$

Thus, Avtec's cost of equity is 17 percent.

In principle, the general dividend valuation model approach can be used to estimate the cost of equity capital for any expected dividend pattern. In practice, there are many stocks that have not only exhibited rather constant growth rates in the past, but look as though they will continue to do so in the future. For these stocks the constant growth form of the dividend capitalization model is appropriate, and the expected growth rate often can be estimated from historical data.

CAPITAL ASSET PRICING MODEL (CAPM) APPROACH

Another technique that can be used to estimate the cost of equity capital is the *Capital Asset Pricing Model* (CAPM), as discussed in Chapter 5. The CAPM formally describes the risk–required return tradeoff for securities. Equation 12.1 illustrates that the rate of return required by investors consists of a risk-free return, r_f, plus a premium compensating the investor for bearing the risk. This risk premium varies from stock to stock.

Obviously, there is less risk associated with an investment in a stable stock, such as AT&T, than in the stock of a small wildcat oil drilling firm, W. As a result, an investor in the drilling stock requires a higher return than the AT&T investor. Figure 12–2 illustrates the difference in required rates of return (or the cost of internal equity) for the two securities. The relationship illustrated in this figure is the *security market line* (SML). The SML depicts the risk–required return relationship in the market for all securities.

Recall from Chapter 5 that the security market line is defined in Equation 5.14 as follows:[7]

$$k_j = r_f + b_j(k_m - r_f) , \tag{12.15}$$

where k_j = the required rate of return on any Security j, r_f = the expected risk-free rate; b_j = the beta (systematic risk) measure for Security j; and k_m = the expected return on the market portfolio. Hence, the value $k_m - r_f$ equals the market risk premium, or the risk premium applicable to a stock of average (beta = 1.0) risk.

The SML concept is based upon investors' expectations regarding a security's risk and return characteristics. Required returns for any individual security are also dependent upon expected future levels of interest rates and the expected return on the market as a whole. These expected values are determined as follows:

▪ *The risk-free rate (r_f).* The rate for r_f that is most frequently used in computing the required return for a security is the 3- or 6-month U.S. Treasury Bill rate. (Some practitioners prefer to use a long-term government bond rate instead.)

---

[7] In Equation 5.14 we used a hat (∧) over the r_f and k_m variables to indicate these are *expected* values. For simplicity, the hats are dropped here, but it should be kept in mind that we are still dealing with expected values for these variables.

362

FIGURE 12–2 Security Market Line (SML)

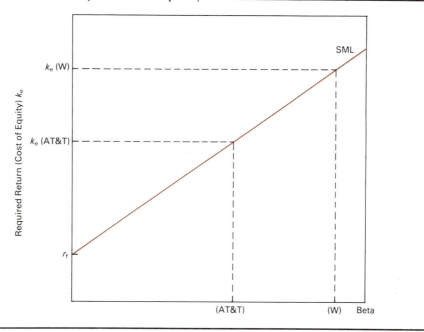

- *The expected market return (k$_m$).* The expected market return is the return investors expect to earn in the future on an average stock—namely, one whose beta is 1.0. The average market return for stocks during the time period from 1926 to 1981 was about 11.4 percent per year.[8] These actual returns have varied substantially, depending on the holding periods assumed. Recent research indicates that future expected market returns should be in the 20 percent range, and the average market risk premium should be in the 5 to 7 percent range.[9]

The firm's beta, b$_j$ Beta is normally estimated by using historical values of the relationship between a security's returns and the market returns. The *Value Line Investment Survey* and brokerage firms such as Merrill Lynch regularly compute and provide betas.[10]

Consider the following example. General Motors' beta has been estimated in Chapter 5 as 0.97. If 6-month U.S. Treasury Bill rates are 9.5 percent and the market return is estimated as 16 percent, the firm's cost of equity may be computed as follows:

$$k_e = r_f + b_j(k_m - r_f)$$
$$= 9.5 + 0.97(16.0 - 9.5)$$
$$= 15.8\% \; .$$

[8]Ibbotson and Sinquefield, p. 71.
[9]Ibid., p. 68.
[10]Because of statistical biases inherent in the historical computation of betas, these reported betas are often adjusted to provide a better estimate of future betas.

When it seems likely that the basic risk characteristics of a firm will change significantly—perhaps because of a merger or product line expansion or contraction—the historical beta may be of little use as a forecast of the firm's future systematic risk characteristics. Under these circumstances, different methods have to be used to estimate the required future returns for the security.

The SML concept is one more tool that may be used in computing the firm's cost of equity capital, k_e. If all of the parameters required of the model are correctly estimated $(r_f, k_m, and\ b_j)$, the model should give a reasonably accurate estimate of k_e. Many analysts find it useful to compute k_e in more than one way to arrive at some consensus about the rate of return investors require on a security.

It should be recalled from Chapter 5 that the beta measure of risk considers only the systematic risk or market risk of a stock. Poorly diversified investors may be more interested in total risk than in systematic risk. When this is true, the CAPM may understate required returns of those investors.

In addition, even when the beta concept can be expected to measure investment risk correctly, it is often difficult to obtain correct measures of the inputs needed to apply the model. The CAPM is an expectational model. Hence, the correct inputs must be based on market expectations about the future risk-free rate, as well as the future market risk premium. The increase in interest rate volatility has caused an increase in the volatility of bonds relative to stocks during the late 1970s and the 1980s. This has resulted in a market risk premium that tends to vary substantially and has made it more difficult to estimate. Finally, investors are faced with a whole range of risk-free rates—from 30-day Treasury Bills to 20-year Treasury Bonds. There is disagreement over which measure of the risk-free rate should be used.

OTHER APPROACHES FOR ESTIMATING THE COST OF EQUITY CAPITAL

This subsection begins by considering a shortcut method of estimating the cost of equity capital based on actual historical returns and ends by discussing nondividend-paying stocks.

Studies analyzing the historical returns earned by common stock investors have found that the returns from average risk common stock investments over the years have averaged 5 to 7 percentage points higher than returns on corporate debt issues. Thus, the cost of equity capital for an average risk company (a firm with a beta of about 1.0) can be approximated by adding 5 to 7 percentage points to the company's current cost of debt. Many analysts use this shortcut method as a reference. Whenever possible, however, the other more precise methods should be used.

For stocks that do not pay dividends, the dividend capitalization model is obviously an inappropriate valuation model and therefore cannot be used directly to determine the cost of equity capital. Investors in nondividend-paying stocks expect to sell the stock in the future at a higher price than the present price, realizing a capital gain. Investors' expectations about the future price are incorporated into the following valuation model:[11]

$$P_0 = \frac{P_t}{(1 + k_e)^t} ,$$

(12.16)

where P_t is the expected stock price at time t. In principle, a firm could use this valuation model to determine its cost of equity capital. In practice, however, this would be difficult to do, since the company would probably have no way of determining the P_t expectations of investors. Instead, the cost of equity capital for nondividend-paying stocks should be determined either by using the Capital Asset Pricing Model or by estimating k_e for comparable dividend-paying stocks in their industry.

For many stocks the cost of equity capital obtained from the dividend capitalization model, the risk premium on debt approach, and the CAPM will generally be in approximate agreement with each other. If substantial differences do exist, further analysis is required. It should be emphasized that the calculation of the cost of equity capital requires the exercise of good judgment by the financial manager.

COST OF EXTERNAL EQUITY CAPITAL

The cost of external equity is greater than the cost of internal equity for the following reasons:

- Flotation costs associated with new shares are usually high enough that they cannot realistically be ignored.

- The selling price of the new shares to the public must be less than the market price of the stock before the announcement of the new issue, or the shares cannot be expected to sell. Before any announcement, the current market price of a stock usually represents an equilibrium between supply and demand. If supply is increased (all other things being equal), the new equilibrium price will be lower.

When a firm's future dividend payments are expected to grow at a constant rate of g per period forever, the cost of external equity, k_e', is defined as follows:

$$k_e' = \frac{D_1}{P_{net}} + g ,$$

(12.17)

where P_{net} is the net proceeds to the firm on a per-share basis. To illustrate, consider the Fresno Company example used in the "Cost of Internal Equity Capital" section, where $P_0 = \$25$, $D_0 = \$2$, $g = 0.07$, and $k_e = 15.6$ percent.

Assuming that new common stock can be sold at \$24 to net the company

---

[11]If investors in a nondividend-paying stock expected the company to begin paying dividends at some future date, a form of the dividend capitalization model could be constructed to reflect these expectations.

TABLE 12–1   Formulas for Computing Component Costs

Cost of debt

$k_i = k_d(1 - t) = $ Coupon interest rate $\times (1 - $ Tax rate).

Cost of preferred
stock

$$k_p = \frac{\text{Preferred dividend}}{\text{Net proceeds to the company}}$$

$$= \frac{D_p}{P_{net}}.$$

Cost of internal
common equity

1. Dividend capitalization model approach—the case of perpetual dividends growing at a constant rate:

$$k_e = \frac{\text{Next year's expected dividend}}{\text{Common stock price}} + \text{Expected dividend growth rate}$$

$$= \frac{D_1}{P_0} + g.$$

2. Capital Asset Pricing Model Approach:

$k_e = $ Risk-free return + Risk premium

$\quad = r_f + \text{beta } (k_m - r_f).$

Cost of external
common equity

$$k'_e = \frac{\text{Next year's expected dividend}}{\text{Net proceeds to company, per share}} + \frac{\text{Expected dividend}}{\text{growth rate}}$$

$$= \frac{D_1}{P_{net}} + g.$$

$23 a share after flotation costs, k'_e is calculated as follows:

$$k'_e = \frac{D_1}{P_{net}} + g$$

$$= \frac{\$2.14}{\$23} + 0.07$$

$$= 0.163, \text{ or } 16.3\% .$$

Because of the relatively high cost of newly issued equity, many companies try to avoid this means of raising capital. The question of whether or not a firm should raise capital with newly issued common stock depends on its investment opportunities.[12]

Table 12–1 summarizes the cost of capital formulas developed in the preceding sections.

WEIGHTED COST OF CAPITAL

Firms calculate their cost of capital in order to determine a discount rate that may be used for evaluating proposed capital expenditure projects. Recall that

---

[12]This discussion is continued in the section on determining the optimal capital budget.

the purpose of capital expenditure analysis is basically to determine which *proposed* projects the firm should *actually* undertake. Therefore, it is logical that *the capital whose cost is measured and compared with the expected benefits from these proposed projects should be the next or marginal capital the firm raises.* Typically, companies estimate the cost of each capital component as the cost they expect to have to pay on these funds during the coming year.[13]

In addition, as a firm evaluates proposed capital expenditure projects, it normally does not specify the proportions of debt and equity financing for each individual project. Instead, each project is presumed to be financed with the same proportion of debt and equity contained in the company's target capital structure.

Thus, the appropriate after-tax cost of capital figure to be used in capital budgeting is not only based on the next capital to be raised but is also weighted by the proportions of the capital components in the firm's long-range target capital structure. Thus, this figure is called the *weighted, or overall, cost of capital.*

The general expression for calculating the weighted cost of capital, k_a, follows:

$$k_a = \begin{pmatrix} \text{Equity} \\ \text{fraction} \\ \text{of} \\ \text{capital} \\ \text{structure} \end{pmatrix} \begin{pmatrix} \text{Cost} \\ \text{of} \\ \text{equity} \end{pmatrix} + \begin{pmatrix} \text{Debt} \\ \text{fraction} \\ \text{of} \\ \text{capital} \\ \text{structure} \end{pmatrix} \begin{pmatrix} \text{Cost} \\ \text{of} \\ \text{debt} \end{pmatrix} \quad \textbf{(12.18)}$$

$$= \left(\frac{E}{D + E}\right)(k_e) + \left(\frac{D}{D + E}\right)(k_i),$$

where D is debt and E is equity in the target capital structure.[14]

To illustrate, suppose a company has a current (and target) capital structure of 75 percent equity and 25 percent debt. (The proportions of debt and equity should be the proportions in which the firm intends to raise funds in the future.) For a firm that is not planning a change in its target capital structure, these proportions should be based on the current *market value weights* of the individual components (debt, preferred stock, and common equity). The company plans to finance next year's capital budget with $75 million of retained earnings ($k_e = 15\%$) and $25 million of long-term debt ($k_d = 10\%$). Assume a 40 percent marginal tax rate. Using these figures, the weighted cost of cap-

---

[13]Stated another way, the cost of the capital acquired by the firm in earlier periods—that is, the *historical* cost of capital—is *not* used as the discount rate in determining next year's capital expenditures.

[14]If the target capital structure contains preferred stock, a preferred stock term is added to Equation 12.18. In this case Equation 12.18 becomes the following:

$$k_a = \left(\frac{E}{E + D + P}\right)(k_e) + \left(\frac{D}{E + D + P}\right)(k_i) + \left(\frac{P}{E + D + P}\right)(k_p).$$

ital being raised to finance next year's capital budget is calculated as follows:

$$k_a = 0.75 \times 15.0\% + 0.25 \times 10.0\% \times (1 - 0.40)$$
$$= 12.75\% \ .$$

DETERMINING THE WEIGHTED (MARGINAL) COST OF CAPITAL SCHEDULE

In the previous section the computation of the weighted (marginal) cost of capital was based on the assumption that the firm would only get equity funds from internal sources and that all debt could be acquired at a 10 percent pretax cost. This procedure for computing the weighted (marginal) cost of capital must be modified if the firm anticipates selling new common stock (having a higher component cost) or issuing additional increments of debt securities at successively higher costs in order to finance its capital budget.

To illustrate, suppose the Major Foods Corporation is developing its capital expenditure plans for the coming year. The company's schedule of potentially acceptable capital expenditure projects (defined by management as projects having an internal rate of return greater than or equal to 10 percent) for next year is as follows:

Project	Amount (In Millions of Dollars)	Internal Rate of Return
A	$4.0	13.8%
B	8.0	13.5
C	6.0	12.5
D	5.0	12.0
E	8.0	11.0
F	4.0	10.0

These projects are all closely related to the company's present business and have the same degree of risk as its existing assets.

The firm's current capital structure (as well as its targeted future capital structure) consists of 40 percent debt, 10 percent preferred stock, and 50 percent common equity measured on the basis of the current market value of debt and equity in the capital structure. The company can raise up to $5 million in debt funds at a pretax cost of 9 percent; debt amounts exceeding $5 million will cost 10 percent. Preferred stock can be raised at an after-tax cost of 10 percent. Major Foods' marginal tax rate is 40 percent.

Major Foods expects to generate $10 million of retained earnings over the coming year. Its present dividend rate, D_0, is $2 per share. The firm's common stock now is selling at $25 per share, and new common stock can be sold to net the firm $24 per share.[15]

---

[15]The net proceeds per share depend on the number of shares sold. As a very general rule, underwriters are reluctant to sell new shares in an amount that exceeds 10 to 15 percent of a company's existing shares.

Over the past several years Major Foods' earnings and dividends have grown at an average of 7 percent per year, and this growth rate is expected to continue for the foreseeable future. The company's dividend payout ratio has been, and is expected to remain, more or less constant.

Given this information, Major Foods' weighted (marginal) cost of capital can be calculated for the coming year:

Step 1 **Calculate the cost of capital for each individual component—the cost of debt, the cost of preferred stock, and the cost of equity.**

Cost of debt:

$k_i = k_d(1 - t) = 9.0 \times 0.6 = 5.4\%$ for the first \$5 million of debt .

$k_i = k_d(1 - t) = 10.0 \times 0.6 = 6.0\%$ for debt exceeding \$5 million .

Cost of preferred stock:

$k_p = 10\%$ (given) .

Cost of equity:

Internal (retained earnings—\$10 million):

$$k_e = \frac{D_0(1 + g)}{P_0} + g$$

$$= \frac{\$2(1.07)}{\$25} + 0.07 = 0.156, \text{ or } 15.6\% .$$

External (new common stock—amounts above \$10 million):

$$k'_e = \frac{\$2(1.07)}{\$24} + 0.07 = 0.159, \text{ or } 15.9\% .$$

Step 2 **Compute the weighted (marginal) cost of capital for each increment of capital raised.**

Major Foods should raise funds in proportion to its target capital structure from its lowest cost sources first. In this case, these sources are retained earnings (15.6 percent after-tax cost), preferred stock (10 percent after-tax cost), and the first \$5 million in debt (5.4 percent after-tax cost). When these sources are exhausted, the company should consider using the higher cost sources—external equity (15.9 percent after-tax cost) and additional debt (6.0 percent after-tax cost) together with preferred stock.

How much total financing—retained earnings, preferred stock, and debt—can be done before the \$5 million in low cost debt is exhausted and Major must acquire additional debt funds at the higher cost? Since we know that the target capital structure consists of 40 percent debt, the total financing, X, that this will support is equal to the amount of low cost debt available divided by the debt fraction in the capital structure:

$$X = \frac{\text{Amount of low cost debt available}}{\text{Debt fraction of capital structure}}$$

$$= \frac{\$5 \text{ million}}{0.40}$$

$$= \$12.5 \text{ million} .$$

This $12.5 million level represents a *break point* in the marginal cost of capital schedule. Beyond $12.5 million in total financing, the weighted (marginal) cost of capital will rise, because higher cost debt must now be used. Of this $12.5 million in total financing, $5 million will be debt, $1.25 million (10 percent of the total) will be preferred stock, and $6.25 million will be retained earnings.[16] The cost of this first block of funds is as follows:

$$k_a = 0.40 \times 5.4\% + 0.10 \times 10\% + 0.50 \times 15.6\%$$

$$= 10.96\% .$$

Beyond the first $12.5 million in funds, Major can use higher cost debt (6 percent after-tax cost), preferred stock (10 percent after-tax cost), and retained earnings (15.6 percent after-tax cost) until all retained earnings are exhausted. Of the total amount of retained earnings available ($10 million), $6.25 million has been used, leaving $3.75 million. The total financing that can be supported with the retained earnings is as follows:

$$X = \frac{\text{Amount of retained earnings available}}{\text{Equity fraction of capital structure}}$$

$$= \frac{\$3.75 \text{ million}}{0.5}$$

$$= \$7.5 \text{ million} .$$

This $7.5 million level represents the next break point in the weighted (marginal) cost of capital schedule. Of this $7.5 million in total financing, $3.75 million will be retained earnings, $0.75 million will be preferred stock, and $3 million will be debt. The cost of this second block of funds will be as follows:

---

[16]In this case the first break point was defined by the amount of low cost debt available. It is possible that retained earnings could be exhausted before all low cost debt is used. For example, if only $5 million in retained earnings were available, the first break point would occur at $10 million, or $5 million equity/0.5. Only $4 million of low cost debt would be used in this increment, leaving $1 million for the next increment. This next increment would be $2.5 million, or $1 million debt/0.4.

FIGURE 12–3   Weighted (Marginal) Cost of Capital Schedule for Major Foods

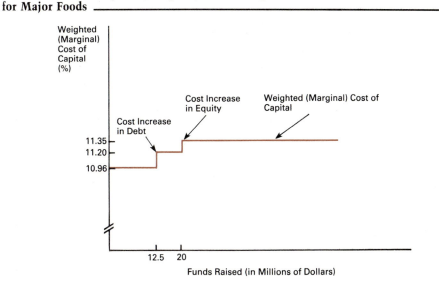

$$k_a = 0.40 \times 6.0 + 0.10 \times 10\% + 0.50 \times 15.6\%$$
$$= 11.20\% \ .$$

Beyond the second block, all additional funds raised will be with high cost debt, new common stock, and preferred stock. The weighted cost of these funds is as follows:

$$k_a = 0.40 \times 6.0 + 0.10 \times 10\% + 0.50 \times 15.9\%$$
$$= 11.35\% .$$

Figure 12–3 provides a graph of the weighted (marginal) cost of capital schedule for Major Foods.

The weighted (marginal) cost of capital schedule can now be used to determine the optimal capital budget for Major Foods. This is illustrated in the next section.

DETERMINING THE OPTIMAL CAPITAL BUDGET

The *optimal capital budget* can be determined by comparing the expected project returns to the company's marginal cost of capital schedule. This is accomplished by first plotting the returns expected from the proposed capital expenditure projects against the cumulative funds required. The resulting graph is called an *investment opportunity curve*. Next, the previously calculated k_a for the three capital "packages" are combined to determine the company's *marginal cost of capital curve*. The optimal capital budget is indicated

FIGURE 12–4   Determining the Optimal Capital Budget

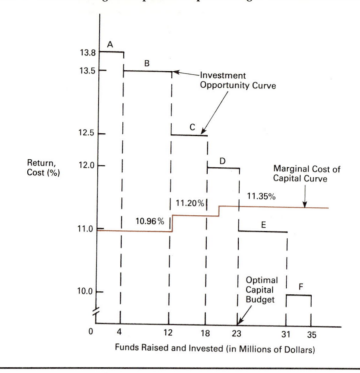

Funds Raised and Invested (in Millions of Dollars)

by the point at which the investment opportunity curve and the marginal cost of capital curve intersect, as shown in Figure 12–4.

Specifically, the Major Foods Corporation's optimal capital budget totals $23 million and includes Projects A, B, C, and D. Projects E and F are excluded, because their returns are expected to be below the 11.35 percent cost of funds. Acceptance of Projects E and F would result in a decrease in the firm's value. In principle, the optimal capital budget maximizes the value of the firm.

It should be noted that this procedure assumes that all projects being considered are of equal (average) risk. If this is not the case, one of the capital budgeting under risk techniques discussed in Chapter 11 must be incorporated into the procedure described.

THE COST OF DEPRECIATION-GENERATED FUNDS

One very large source of funds for many firms is funds generated from depreciation. Also, some firms may generate funds from the sale of assets from time to time. What is the cost of these funds? Since the firm always has the option to either reinvest these funds in the firm or to return them to the stockholders as dividends and to retire outstanding debt, the appropriate opportunity cost of these funds is the firm's weighted (marginal) cost of capital.

With respect to the marginal cost of capital schedule in Figure 12–3, it is generally agreed that these funds have an opportunity cost equal to the first "block" of funds, that is, 10.96 percent. If $10 million in depreciation-generated funds were available, the first block of funds would increase from $12.5 million to $22.5 million, and all other blocks would also be shifted to the right by $10 million.

SUMMARY

- A firm's *cost of capital* is defined as the rate the firm has to pay for the debt, preferred stock, common stock, and/or retained earnings it uses to finance its new investments in assets. The cost of capital is the rate of return required by investors in the firm's securities. Cost of capital can also be thought of as the minimum rate of return required on new investments undertaken by the firm.

- The higher the risk of a security, the higher the return required by investors. In general, common stock is more risky than preferred stock; preferred stock is more risky than corporate debt securities, and corporate debt securities are more risky than government debt securities. Investors' required returns generally decrease in the same order.

- A firm's *cost of debt capital*, k_d, is the rate of return required by investors. The after-tax cost of debt, k_i, issued at par is calculated as follows:

$$k_i = k_d(1 - t) = \text{Coupon interest rate}(1 - t),$$

where t is the firm's marginal tax rate.

- A firm's *cost of preferred stock*, k_p, is the rate of return required by the preferred stock investors. It is calculated as follows:

$$k_p = \frac{D_p}{P_{net}},$$

where D_p is the preferred dividend and P_{net}, the preferred stock price net of flotation costs on new issues. Preferred stock is used relatively infrequently as a source of capital, because its cost is normally about twice that of debt. This is due to the fact that interest on debt is a tax-deductible expense for the firm, whereas dividends on stock are not.

- A firm's *cost of equity capital* is defined as the rate of return required by its common stock investors. Equity capital can be raised *internally* through retained earnings and *externally* through the sale of new common stock.

- A firm's *cost of internal equity* can be determined by either the dividend valuation model or the Capital Asset Pricing Model (CAPM). Using the dividend valuation model and assuming that dividends perpetually grow at a rate of g per year, the following equation for calculating the cost of equity capital, k_e, is obtained:

$$k_e = \frac{D_1}{P_0} + g \,.$$

Using the CAPM, the cost of equity capital can be calculated as follows:

$$k_e = r_f + b(k_m - r_f) \,,$$

where r_f is the risk-free rate; b (beta), the relative measure of the stock's return volatility; and k_m, the expected return on the market.

- A firm's *cost of external equity*, k'_e, when dividends are expected to grow perpetually at a constant rate, is as follows:

$$k'_e = \frac{D_1}{P_{net}} + g \,,$$

where P_{net} is the net proceeds to the firm on a per-share basis.

- Firms normally use an after-tax *weighted cost of capital* to evaluate proposed capital expenditure projects. Each project is presumed to be financed with the same proportion of debt and equity contained in the company's target capital structure. The general formula for calculating the weighted cost of capital, k_a, is as follows:

$$k_a = \begin{pmatrix} \text{Equity} \\ \text{fraction} \\ \text{of} \\ \text{capital} \\ \text{structure} \end{pmatrix} \begin{pmatrix} \text{Cost} \\ \text{of} \\ \text{equity} \end{pmatrix} + \begin{pmatrix} \text{Debt} \\ \text{fraction} \\ \text{of} \\ \text{capital} \\ \text{structure} \end{pmatrix} \begin{pmatrix} \text{Cost} \\ \text{of} \\ \text{debt} \end{pmatrix} \,.$$

- The *optimal capital budget* maximizes the value of the firm and occurs at the point where the firm's *investment opportunity curve* and *weighted marginal cost of capital curve* intersect. The investment opportunity curve is obtained by plotting the returns expected from proposed capital expenditure projects against the cumulative funds required.

- The cost of depreciation generated funds is equal to the weighted cost of the firm's first "block" of funds.

The Cost of Equity Capital to El Paso Electric Company

Samuel C. Hadaway
Director of Economic Research Division
Public Utility Commission of Texas

This Focus on Corporate Practice example provides excerpts from testimony presented in September 1982 regarding the cost of equity capital for the El Paso Electric Company (EPEC). The testimony is presented in the typical question-and-answer format of a utility rate case.

Q. **Would you please explain the purpose of this portion of your testimony?**

A. This section is intended to identify the general principles involved in determining the rate of return on equity, or the minimum return required by marginal investors to induce them to purchase shares of a company's common stock.

Specifically, the cost of equity is the minimum price that must be paid to investors for the use of their money. Equity capital is a resource—just like debt funds, labor, fuel, and so on—that has a cost, or rent, attendant with its usage. By identifying the cost of this resource and allowing a utility the opportunity to earn at approximately this rate, consumers are required to pay only for the actual cost of the money invested in plant and facilities. At the same time, however, because the cost of equity capital is determined by assessing the risk to which the capital is exposed, the required return to the utility shareholder is the same as might be expected on other investments of similar risk. If equity capital is authorized to earn this opportunity cost, a company should experience little difficulty raising additional funds. In short, by allowing a utility company to earn its cost of equity, consumers pay only for the actual cost of money, stockholders receive neither windfall gains nor is their investment confiscated, and the return is sufficient to attract new capital so that service can be maintained and expanded as needed.

Q. **How is the cost of equity capital determined?**

A. The cost of capital is a function of two things: the time value of money and the risk to which the capital will be exposed. In other words, the cost of all capital can be generally described as follows:

$$\text{Cost of capital} = \text{Risk-free rate} + \text{Risk premium}.$$

It is obvious that in this model, the more risky the use to which capital is put, the greater the required return; and alternatively, a less risky use of capital will command a lower return.

Q. **How do investors view El Paso Electric Company as compared with other electrics?**

A. The two predominant features of EPEC as compared with other electrics are the nature (nuclear) and massive size of its construction program (Palo Verde) relative to total capitalization, and the extremely heavy external financing requirements caused by the program's size and the company's poor internal cash generation. With the Palo Verde investment's representing about 75 percent of the company's total capital, investors view the company's planning process with skepticism and note that Palo Verde "will remain burdensome in the absence of successful efforts to sell down its participation to a more manageable level."[17] Beyond the sheer size of Palo Verde relative to all the other assets of the company, the annual growth in asset size itself is a further concern. The company has added new plant equal to over 25 percent of capitalization in each of the last several years, even though a clear danger signal goes out to the investment community when annual construction expenditures exceed 10 to 15 percent of capital in any one year. These kinds of management decisions during a period of historically all time high capital costs have raised serious investor doubts. . . .

Q. **How have you gone about estimating the cost of equity to El Paso Electric Company?**

A. In conjunction with the previous section's general background materials on capital market conditions, the electric utility industry, and EPEC as a part of that industry, I have considered explicitly three independent approaches to the issue of estimating the company's cost of equity. In the first approach, the comparable earnings method, I have examined the returns of firms judged to be similar in risk to EPEC in an attempt to determine what investors expect from these alternate investments. Next, I have performed a conventional discounted cash flow (DCF) analysis. This analysis attempts to replicate market expectations and impute investors' required returns from EPEC. A final test is to determine whether a risk premium, or additional return, is required by investors for holding common stock instead of long-term bonds. . . .

[NOTE: At this point the testimony discusses the three approaches just identified, and a cost of equity capital recommendation is derived from each. The DCF analysis is based on Equation 12.10, the constant growth model.]

Q. **In your DCF analysis, what is the appropriate dividend yield for El Paso Electric?**

A. When an investor purchases a share of stock, he is buying expected future dividends and price appreciation. Therefore, the dividend yield component of the DCF model should be computed by dividing the dividends expected to be received in the coming year, D_1, by the current market price, P_0. EPEC's present quarterly dividend is $0.335. Consistent with the past year and as estimated by the company in its response to the staff's request for information, EPEC is expected to increase its quarterly dividend to $0.35 in September 1983. Therefore, I have used $1.335 per share in my calculation as representative of the dividend ex-

---

[17]Standard and Poor's *Creditweek*. July 26, 1982.

pected to be received in the coming 2 months (three quarters at $0.335 and one quarter at $0.35). The market price of the company's stock has ranged from $10.00 to $12.50 during 1982, and between $11.50 and $12.25 since mid-August. Given these data, a midpoint price of $11.875 since mid-August seems appropriate to use for P_0 in the DCF model.

Q. **Why have you used a recent price rather than a long-term average price?**

A. A recent market price has been selected because the cost of equity is a current and forward-looking concept, and a recent market price is a better indication of investors' present requirements than would be a historical point estimate (such as end of test year) or a long-run average. Based on these values, the market presently expects a dividend yield of approximately 11.4 percent ($1.355/$11.875) from EPEC's common stock. . . .

[NOTE: This dividend yield is later adjusted to 12.0 percent to account for issue costs on new equity.]

Q. **Please describe the growth, g, component of the DCF model.**

A. In using the DCF model to estimate a company's cost of equity, we are not concerned with the rate at which the firm will actually grow (that is primarily a function of regulatory actions, management ability, weather, economic conditions, and chance); rather, at issue in the DCF model is the growth expectations that investors have embodied in the current price of the stock. Furthermore, the DCF model technically maintains that investors are concerned with the expected increase in dividends into infinity; in other words, their emphasis is on average long-term growth rather than short-run growth. Consequently, in estimating the growth component of the DCF model, the analyst is attempting to determine what investors think long-term growth will be.

Q. **What factors influence investors' expectations of a company's growth?**

A. In addition to the fundamental operating characteristics of the specific company, investors typically analyze the company as an integral part of its particular industry. The overall characteristics and growth expectations for the industry are considered, as well as the company's relative position in that industry. Thus, when analyzing an electric utility, one would expect investors to consider growth prospects for the specific company in question, as well as for the electric industry as a whole.

Q. **How have you analyzed the growth expectations of El Paso Electric's investors?**

A. I have approached estimating EPEC's expected growth rate in two specific ways and have also made a general review of other information upon which investors might rely in forming their expectations for EPEC's future. First, the internal growth expected from earnings retention and long-term earned rates of return (the *br method*) is evaluated. Then historical growth rates in dividends, and the earnings and book values that support dividend growth, are examined. In addition to these two specific methods of evaluating growth expectations, I will also discuss additional industry and economic factors that may affect investors' perceptions of EPEC's long-term future prospects. . . .

[NOTE: After an extensive analysis of these growth factors, the final recommendation is made.]

Q. **From this analysis, what growth rate in EPEC's dividends do you believe is appropriate in the DCF model, and what is the resulting DCF estimate of the fair rate of return on EPEC's equity capital?**

A. My long-run DCF growth estimate is presented as a range of values in the upper end of the br result and is similar to historic values for dividends and book value growth. The specific range is 4.5 to 5.0 percent. In combination with the 12.0 adjusted yield developed in the previous section, this range of possible expected growth rates produces the following cost of equity estimates for El Paso Electric:

$$k_e = \frac{D_1}{P_0} + g \, .$$

$$k_1 = 12.0\% + 4.5\% \qquad k_2 = 12.0\% + 4.75\% \qquad k_3 = 12.0\% + 5.0\%$$
$$\quad = 16.5\% \, . \qquad\qquad\quad = 16.75\% \, . \qquad\qquad\quad = 17.0\% \, .$$

My specific recommendation is the midpoint of the range, with my best DCF point estimate for the cost of EPEC equity at 16.75 percent.

QUESTIONS AND TOPICS FOR DISCUSSION

1. How do retained earnings differ from other sources of financing?

2. Does the retained earnings figure shown on a firm's balance sheet necessarily have any relationship to the amount of retained earnings the firm can generate in the coming year? Explain.

3. Why is corporate long-term debt more risky than government long-term debt?

4. Why do investors generally consider common stock to be more risky than preferred stock?

5. Should a firm pay cash dividends in a year in which it raises external common equity?

6. Discuss the meaning of an *optimal* capital budget.

7. Evaluate the statement, Depreciation-generated funds have no explicit cost and therefore should be assigned a zero cost in computing a firm's cost of capital.

8. Describe how to derive the "break points" in the marginal cost of capital schedule.

PROBLEMS*

1. Calculate the after-tax cost of a $25 million debt issue that Pullman Manufacturing Corporation (40 percent marginal tax rate) is planning to place privately with a large insurance company. This long-term issue will yield 9⅜ percent to the insurance company.

*Problems in color have check answers provided at the end of the book.

2. Husky Enterprises recently sold an issue of 10-year maturity bonds. The bonds were sold at a deep discount price of $655 each. After flotation costs, Husky received $646.45 each. The bonds have a $1,000 maturity value and pay $50 interest at the end of each year. Compute the after-tax cost of debt for these bonds if Husky's marginal tax rate is 40 percent.

3. Calculate the after-tax cost of preferred stock for Bozeman-Western Airlines, Inc., which is planning to sell $10 million of $5.75 cumulative preferred stock to the public at a price of $50 a share. Flotation costs are estimated to be $2 a share. The company has a marginal tax rate of 40 percent.

4. St. Joe Trucking has sold an issue of $6 cumulative preferred stock to the public at a price of $60 per share. After flotation costs, St. Joe netted $57 per share. The company has a marginal tax rate of 40 percent.
   a. Calculate the after-tax cost of this preferred stock offering assuming this stock is a perpetuity.
   b. If the stock is callable in 5 years at $66 per share, and investors expect it to be called at that time, what is the after-tax cost of this preferred stock offering? (Compute to the nearest whole percent.)

5. The following financial information is available on Fargo Fabrics, Inc.:

Current per-share market price	$20.25
Current per-share dividend	$ 1.12
Current per-share earnings	$ 2.48
Beta	0.90
Expected return on the market	14.0%
Risk-free rate	7.0%

Past 10 years earnings per share:

19X1	$1.39	19X6	$1.95
19X2	1.48	19X7	2.12
19X3	1.60	19X8	2.26
19X4	1.68	19X9	2.40
19X5	1.79	19Y0	2.48

This past earnings growth trend is expected to continue for the foreseeable future. The dividend payout ratio has remained approximately constant over the past 9 years and is expected to remain at current levels for the foreseeable future.
   Calculate the cost of equity capital using the following methods:
   a. The dividend capitalization model approach.
   b. The Capital Asset Pricing Model approach.
   HINT: To estimate g, calculate the average of the first 3 years of earnings and the average of the last 3 years of earnings; then use these averages to estimate the growth rate for the 7-year period of 19X2 to 19X9. This "smooths out" random fluctuations in earnings growth from year to year.

6. The stock of Alpha Tool sells for $10.25 per share. Its current dividend rate, D_0, is $1 per share. Analysts and investors expect Alpha to increase its dividends at a 10 percent rate for each of the next 2 years. This annual dividend growth rate is expected to decline to 8 percent for years 3 and 4, and then to settle down to 4 percent per year forever. Calculate the cost of internal equity for Alpha Tool.

7. The Hartley Hotel Corporation is planning a major expansion. Hartley is financed 100 percent with equity and intends to maintain this capital structure after the expansion. Hartley's beta is 0.9. The expected market return is 16 percent and the risk-free rate is 10 percent. If the expansion is expected to produce an internal rate of return of 17 percent, should Hartley make the investment?

8. Wentworth Industries is 100 percent equity financed. Its current beta is 0.9. The expected market rate of return is 15 percent, and the risk-free rate is 10 percent.
   a. Calculate Wentworth's cost of equity.
   b. If Wentworth changes its capital structure to 30 percent debt, it estimates that its beta will increase to 1.1. The after-tax cost of debt will be 7 percent. Should Wentworth make the capital structure change?

9. The Ewing Distribution Company is planning a $100 million expansion of its chain of discount service stations to several neighboring states. This expansion will be financed, in part, with debt issued with a coupon interest rate of 15 percent. The bonds have a 10-year maturity and a $1,000 face value, and they will be sold to net Ewing $990 after issue costs. Ewing's marginal tax rate is 40 percent.

   Preferred stock will cost Ewing 14 percent after taxes. Ewing's common stock pays a dividend of $2 per share. The current market price per share is $15, and new shares can be sold to net $14 per share. Ewing's dividends are expected to increase at an annual rate of 5 percent for the foreseeable future. Ewing expects to have $20 million of retained earnings available to finance the expansion.

   Ewing's target capital structure is as follows:

Debt	20%
Preferred stock	5
Common equity	75

   Calculate the weighted cost of capital that is appropriate to use in evaluating this expansion program.

10. Pacific Intermountain Utilities Company has a present capital structure (that the company feels is optimal) of 50 percent long-term debt, 10 percent preferred stock, and 40 percent common equity. For the coming year the company has determined that its optimal capital budget can be externally financed with $70 million of 10 percent first-mortgage bonds sold at par and $14 million of preferred stock costing the company 11 percent. The remainder of the capital budget will be financed with retained earnings. The company's common stock is presently selling at $25 a share, and next year's common dividend, D_1, is expected to be $2 a share. The company has 25 million common shares outstanding. Next year's net income available to common stock (including net income from next year's capital budget) is expected to be $106 million. The company's past annual growth rate in dividends and earnings has been 6 percent. However, a 5 percent annual growth in earnings and dividends is expected for the foreseeable future. The company's marginal tax rate is 40 percent.

    Calculate the company's weighted cost of capital for the coming year.

11. Panhandle Industries, Inc., currently pays an annual common stock dividend of $2.20 per share. The company's dividend has grown steadily over the past 9 years from $1.10 to its present level; this growth trend is expected to continue. The company's present dividend payout ratio, also expected to continue, is 40 percent. In addition, the stock presently sells at 8 times current earnings (that is, its "P/E multiple" is 8).

    Panhandle Industries' stock has a beta of 1.15, as computed by a leading investment service. The present risk-free rate is 7.0 percent, and the expected return on the stock market is 13.0 percent.
    a. Suppose an individual investor feels that 12 percent is an appropriate required rate of return for the level of risk this investor perceived for Panhandle Industries. Using the dividend capitalization model and the Capital Asset Pricing

Model approaches, determine whether this investor should purchase Panhandle Industries' stock.

b. Calculate the company's cost of equity capital using both the dividend capitalization model approach and the Capital Asset Pricing Model approach.

12. Colbyco Industries has a target capital structure of 60 percent common equity, 30 percent debt, and 10 percent preferred stock. The cost of retained earnings is 15 percent, and the cost of new equity (external) is 16 percent. Colbyco anticipates having $20 million of new retained earnings available over the coming year. Colbyco can sell $15 million of first-mortgage bonds with an after-tax cost of 9 percent. Its investment bankers feel the company could sell $10 million of debentures with a 9.5 percent after-tax cost. Additional debt would cost 10 percent after tax and be in the form of subordinated debentures. The after-tax cost of preferred stock financing is estimated to be 14 percent.

Compute the marginal cost of capital schedule for Colbyco, and determine the break points in the schedule.

AN INTEGRATIVE CASE PROBLEM

Cost of Capital

The Marietta Corporation, a large manufacturer of mufflers, tail pipes, and shock absorbers, is presently carrying out its financial planning for next year. In about 2 weeks, at the next meeting of the firm's board of directors, Frank Bosworth, vice-president of finance, is scheduled to present his recommendations for next year's overall financial plan. He has asked Donna Botello, manager of financial planning, to gather the necessary information and perform the calculations for the financial plan.

The company's divisional staffs, together with corporate finance department personnel, have analyzed several proposed capital expenditure projects. The following is a summary schedule of acceptable projects (defined by the company as projects having internal rates of return greater than 8 percent):

Project	Investment Amount (In Millions of Dollars)	Internal Rate of Return
A	$10.0	25%
B	20.0	21
C	30.0	18
D	35.0	15
E	40.0	14
F	40.0	12
G	40.0	10
H	20.0	9

All projects are expected to have 1 year of negative cash flow followed by positive cash flows over their remaining years. In addition, next year's projects involve modifications and expansion of the company's existing facilities and products. As a result, these projects are considered to have approximately the same degree of risk as the company's existing assets.

Botello feels that this summary schedule and detailed supporting documents provide her with the necessary information concerning the possible capital expenditure projects for next year. She now can direct her attention to obtaining the data necessary to determine the cost of the capital required to finance next year's proposed projects.

The company's investment bankers indicated to Bosworth in a recent meeting that they feel the company could issue up to $50 million of 9 percent first-morgage bonds at par next year. The investment bankers also feel that any additional debt would have to be subordinated debentures with a coupon of 10 percent, also to be sold at par. The investment bankers rendered their opinion after Bosworth gave an approximate estimate of the size of next year's capital budget, and after he estimated that approximately $100 million of retained earnings would be available next year.

Both the company's financial management and the investment bankers consider the present capital structure of the company, shown in the following table, to be optimal (assume that book value and market value are equal):

Debt	$ 400,000,000
Shareholders' equity:	
Common stock	150,000,000
Retained earnings	450,000,000
	$1,000,000,000

Botello has assembled additional information, as follows:

- Marietta common stock is presently selling at $21.00 a share.

- The investment bankers also have indicated that an additional $75 million in new common stock could be issued to net the company $19 a share.

- The company's present annual dividend is $1.32 a share. However, Bosworth feels fairly certain that the board will increase it to $1.41 a share next year.

- The company's earnings and dividends have doubled over the past 10 years. Growth has been fairly steady, and this rate is expected to continue for the foreseeable future. The company's marginal tax rate is 40 percent.

Using the information provided, answer the following questions. (NOTE: Disregard depreciation in this case.)

1. Calculate the cost of each component source of capital.

2. Calculate the marginal cost of capital for the various intervals, or "packages," of capital the company can raise next year. Plot the marginal cost of capital curve.

3. Using the marginal cost of capital curve from Question 2, and plotting the investment opportunity curve, determine the company's optimal capital budget for next year.

4. Should Project G be accepted or rejected? Why?

5. What factors do you feel might cause Bosworth to recommend a different capital budget than the one obtained in Question 3?

ADDITIONAL READINGS AND REFERENCES

Alberts, W. W., and Archer, S. H. "Some Evidence on the Effect of Company Size on the Cost of Equity Capital." *Journal of Financial and Quantitative Analysis* 8 (March 1973): 229–245.

Ang, James S. "Weighted Average versus True Cost of Capital." *Financial Management* 2 (Autumn 1973): 56–60.

Archer, Stephen H., and Faerber, LeRoy G. "Firm Size and the Cost of Equity Capital." *Journal of Finance* 21 (March 1966): 69–84.

Arditti, Fred D., and Tysseland, Milford S. "Three Ways to Present the Marginal Cost of Capital." *Financial Management* 2 (Summer 1973): 63–67.

Boudreaux, Kenneth J., Long, Hugh W., Ezzell, John R., Porter, R. Burr, BenHorim, Moshe, and Shapiro, Alan C. "The Weighted Average Cost of Capital: A Discussion." *Financial Management* (Summer 1979): 7–23.

Brigham, E. F., and Pappas, J. "Rates of Return on Common Stock." *Journal of Business* 42 (July 1969).

Brigham, Eugene F., and Smith, Keith V. "The Cost of Capital to the Small Firm." *The Engineering Economist* 13 (Fall 1967): 1–26.

Ezzell, John R., and Porter, R. Burr. "Flotation Costs and the Weighted Average Cost of Capital." *Journal of Financial and Quantitative Analysis* 11 (Sept. 1976): 403–414.

Fama, Eugene F., and Miller, Merton H. *The Theory of Finance.* New York: Holt, Rinehart and Winston, 1972.

Gordon, Myron. *The Investment, Financing, and Valuation of the Corporation.* Homewood, Ill.: Irwin, 1962.

Gordon, Myron J., and Halpern, Paul J. "Cost of Capital for a Division of a Firm." *Journal of Finance* 29 (Sept. 1974): 1153–1163.

Haley, C. W., and Schall, L. D. *The Theory of Financial Decisions,* 2nd ed. New York: McGraw-Hill, 1979.

Lawrence, David W. "The Effects of Corporate Taxation on the Cost of Equity Capital." *Financial Management* (Spring 1976): 52–57.

Lewellen, W. G. *The Cost of Capital.* Dubuque, Iowa: Kendall-Hunt, 1976.

Lewellen, Wilbur G. "A Conceptual Reappraisal of Cost of Capital." *Financial Management* 3 (Winter 1974): 63–70.

Lintner, John. "The Cost of Capital and Optimal Financing of Corporate Growth." *Journal of Finance* 18 (May 1963): 292–310.

Loosigian, Allan M. *Interest Rate Futures.* Princeton, N.J.: Dow Jones Books, 1980.

McDonald, John G. "Market Measures of Capital Cost." *Journal of Business Finance* 2 (Autumn 1970): 27–36.

Nantell, Timothy J., and Carlson, C. Robert. "The Cost of Capital as a Weighted Average." *Journal of Finance* 30 (Dec. 1975): 1343–1355.

Powers, Mark J., and Vogel, David J. *Inside the Financial Futures Markets.* New York: Wiley, 1981.

Solomon, Ezra. *The Theory of Financial Management.* New York: Columbia University Press, 1963.

APPENDIX 12A

Introduction to Financial Futures

GLOSSARY OF NEW TERMS

Financial futures contract a commitment to receive or deliver a specified dollar amount of a financial instrument at a definite time in the future at a current agreed-upon price.

Hedging a transaction that limits the risk associated with market price fluctuations for a particular investment position.

Long hedge the process of buying a futures contract to protect a current position from a loss due to a decrease in interest rates or an increase in prices.

Margin a required deposit of money to insure that a future commitment will be fulfilled. The deposit amount is usually expressed as a percentage of the future contract's worth.

Margin call the process of requesting additional funds in order to meet the required minimum margin level. These funds may be needed because of an adverse change in market prices or a change in margin requirements.

Short hedge the process of selling a futures contract to protect a current position from a loss due to an increase in interest rates or a decrease in prices.

Speculators individuals or institutions who assume the risk that hedgers are attempting to avoid.

INTRODUCTION

Chapter 12 discusses the relationship between cost of capital and risk, namely, the cost of capital to a firm increases as risk increases. During the 1970s and early 1980s, financial markets in the United States have been characterized by relatively large and rapid interest rate fluctuations. This volatility has increased the level of risk financial market participants must bear.

The financial futures markets offer financial managers a method of lowering risk.

The area of financial futures has grown rapidly in recent years. The financial futures contracts actively traded include U.S. Treasury security futures (bills, notes, and bonds), Government National Mortgage Association (GNMA) bond futures, bank certificate of deposit futures, Eurodollar futures, futures based on various stock market indexes, and foreign currency futures.

FUTURES MARKET TERMINOLOGY

Most transactions that individuals enter into take place in the *cash*, or *spot*, market. For example, farmers who sell melons at roadside stands near their farms are dealing in the spot market. Suppose these farmers also grow wheat, and in December they become concerned that the price of wheat may decline from its present level by the time they harvest and sell their wheat next summer. To protect against this possible price decline, they could sell wheat futures contracts. By *selling futures contracts*, the farmers agree to deliver a certain quantity and quality of wheat at a specified time in the future (sometime during July, for example). The prices the farmers will receive for their wheat in July are agreed upon at the time they sell the contracts in December. Therefore, they have "locked in" the future prices they will receive for their wheat; in other words, the farmers have *hedged* their wheat position.

The buyer of a wheat futures contract might be a cereal company that will have to purchase wheat next summer and is concerned about the possibility of a rise in the price of wheat. Alternatively, the buyer of a July wheat futures contract in December might be an individual who simply feels that the price of wheat will increase by July and that he or she can make a profit by trading wheat futures. This individual is referred to as a *speculator* in the parlance of the futures market. Speculators assume the risk that hedgers are attempting to avoid, in return for possible profits.

BASICS OF FINANCIAL FUTURES

A *financial futures contract* is a legally binding agreement to receive or deliver a specified dollar amount of a particular financial instrument at a definite future time at a current agreed-upon price. For example, the seller of a 10-year U.S. Treasury Notes futures contract agrees to deliver $100,000 worth of U.S. Treasury Notes on the last business day of a predetermined future month. The price the seller will receive for the U.S. Treasury Notes in the future is agreed upon at the time the contract is executed. (Actually, less than 1 percent of the sellers of futures contracts make delivery of the commodity or security; usually the sellers buy back the futures contract prior to the delivery date.) Table 12A-1 shows the contract highlights for the 10-year U.S. Treasury futures.

Participants in the financial futures market can either *buy* or *sell* futures contracts. Buyers of futures contracts are said to be *long* the futures, and sellers are said to be *short* the futures.

TABLE 12A–1 Contract Highlights: 10-Year U.S. Treasury Futures

Trading unit	U.S. Treasury Notes with $100,000 face value.
Deliverable grade	U.S. Treasury Notes that have an actual maturity of not less than 6½ years and not greater than 10 years.
Delivery method	By Federal Reserve book entry transfer system. Invoice is adjusted for coupon rates and maturity dates. Accrued interest is prorated.
Settlement	Equal to the futures price times a conversion factor, where the conversion factor is based on the price at which a deliverable note would yield 8 percent.
Price basis	$1/32$ of a point ($31.25) per contract. Contract will be quoted as percentage of par.
Trading limits	$64/32$ of a point ($2,000) per day.
Last day of trading	The last trading day shall be the business day prior to the last 7 business days of the delivery month.
Last delivery day	The last business day of the delivery month.
Delivery months	March, June, September, and December.
Ticker symbol	TY

SOURCE: Reproduced with permission from *Ten Year Treasury Futures*, Chicago Board of Trade (1982).

Suppose an individual expects interest rates to decrease within the next year. The decrease in interest rates will generally cause bond prices to increase. By *buying* a bond futures contract, the individual can make a profit if interest rates do in fact decrease between the time the contract is bought and the delivery month (or when the contract is sold). Table 12A–2 shows the prices of several U.S. Treasury Bond futures contracts, as of July 9, 1982, and March 31, 1983. Between July 1982 and March 1983, interest rates on U.S. Treasury Bonds dropped from about 14 percent to about 10.5 percent. To illustrate the profit that could have been made, consider a person who bought a June 1983 U.S. Treasury Bond futures contract in July 1982 for $62^{28/32}$ percent of par. The price of the $100,000 par value contract was $62,875. By March 1983 this contract was selling for $75^{31/32}$ percent of par, or $75,968.75, and the buyer would have had a profit of approximately 21 percent on the purchase ($13,093.75 divided by $62,875). Buyers and sellers of futures con-

TABLE 12A–2 Prices of U.S. Treasury Bond Futures Contracts*

	PRICE†	
MATURITY DATE	July 9, 1982	March 31, 1983
June 1983	62–28	75–31
September 1983	63–02	75–14
December 1983	63–08	75–01
March 1984	63–14	74–22

*The approximate current yield on U.S. Treasury Bonds was 14 percent as of July 1982 and 10.5 percent as of March 1983.
†Prices are quoted in thirty seconds of 100 percent of par value. A quote of 62–28 equals $62,875.
SOURCE: *Wall Street Journal*, July 12, 1982, and April 1, 1983.

tracts are not required to pay the entire contract price when the contract is initially executed. Instead, they are only required to make a partial deposit, or *margin*. Margins are typically less than 10 percent of the contract's price. As a result, the 21 percent profit figure in this example easily could have been considerably higher because of margin leverage.

The seller of the June 1983 U.S. Treasury Bond futures contract in July 1982 would have lost approximately 21 percent on the sale by March 1983. The seller was expecting interest rates to increase.

Participants in the financial futures markets either *hedge* or *speculate*. In *hedging*, market participants take a futures position approximately equal but opposite to their current commitment in the market. Hedgers protect themselves from market changes by the fact that losses on one side of the position are covered by the gains on the opposite side. Although no hedged position is perfect insurance against risk, hedging does allow investors more protection than does their simply trusting the market to move in their favor.

The following is an example of hedging in the financial futures market. Suppose the manager of a pension fund expects interest rates to increase, causing the pension fund's bond portfolio to decrease in value. To hedge, or protect the value of the fund's assets against this possible interest rate rise, the manager could sell bond futures. Then, if interest rates do in fact rise, the decrease in the value of the fund's bond portfolio will be offset by the profit made on the bond futures. The bond futures that were sold when interest rates were relatively low will decrease in value as interest rates increase. The futures then could be bought back at the lower price, enabling a profit to be made. This example is called a *short hedge*, because the pension fund manager owned the bonds and sold, or *shorted*, the futures contract.

A *long hedge* can be illustrated as follows. Suppose a financial manager anticipates receiving 1 year from now some funds that are to be invested in long-term bonds. If the financial manager expects interest rates to decline over the next year, causing long-term bond prices to rise, he or she could *buy*, or go long in, U.S. Treasury Bond futures. Then, if interest rates do in fact decline, the profit from the bond futures purchase would offset the increased price of the bonds that have to be purchased. This example is called a *long hedge*, because the financial manager bought, or was *long* in, the futures contract and did not own the bonds.

In both of these hedging examples, financial managers used the futures market to lower their level of risk exposure. In effect, they were able to transfer a portion of their risk to another market participant. If this other party involved in the transaction does not have a position to hedge, he or she is termed a *speculator*.

FIXED-INCOME FUTURES AND HEDGING

The fixed-income futures that are available include U.S. Treasury Bills, U.S. Treasury Notes, U.S. Treasury Bonds, certificates of deposit, and GNMAs. Fixed-income futures are widely used by market participants desiring to hedge against the risk of volatile interest rates.

An actual example of fixed-income futures hedging involves the underwriting of a $1.0 billion note and debenture issue for IBM by an underwriting team lead by Salomon Brothers and Merrill Lynch in October 1979.[1] Apparently, the underwriters were concerned about the possibility of an interest rate rise that would cause the IBM securities to decline in value before being sold by the underwriters.

In this situation, the underwriters would want to sell bond futures contracts. Then, if interest rates did rise, the yield on the bonds for issue would become unattractive, causing their price to fall, and the underwriters would have to absorb this loss. However, the price of the bond futures would also have dropped. Thus, the underwriters' commitment to deliver bonds at a fixed price in the future would earn them a gain, since they would be able to buy back the bonds at a reduced price in the market and then sell them at the higher, fixed price. Alternatively, the underwriters could buy back the bond futures at the lower price.

Although the IBM underwriters did not reveal their hedging technique, it has been suggested that they sold short either U.S. Treasury Bond futures or GNMA futures. Therefore, when interest rates did rise (due to the Federal government's move to tighten credit), these underwriters realized a gain from their short position. This gain helped to almost completely offset the loss they faced as a result of the decreased issuing price of the IBM bonds.

In the IBM example, the underwriters were successful in transferring their capital loss to the futures buyers. However, if interest rates had not changed, the price of the bond futures contract would have remained stable. As a result, neither the futures buyer nor seller would have made a gain or loss. If interest rates had declined, however, the underwriters would have transferred their capital gain to the futures buyers. Therefore, for every hedged transaction in which there is a "winner," there also exists a "loser."

STOCK-INDEX FUTURES

Futures contracts based on different stock market indexes have been traded since 1982. By the spring of 1983, futures contracts based on the *Standard and Poor's 500 Market Index*, the *New York Stock Exchange Index*, and the *Value Line Stock Index* were available.

Stock-index futures can be used to protect equity investments. Like other financial futures, stock-index futures are financial instruments contracted for future delivery. However, instead of actually delivering stock shares, stock-index contracts held to maturity simply expire. At the expiration date, the buyers' and sellers' accounts are settled, based on the present level of the particular stock index.

Hedgers can buy stock-index futures contracts based on their expectations of future market movements. For example, portfolio managers who expect a temporary downturn in the stock market could sell stock-index futures instead of liquidating large blocks of stock in their portfolios. In this instance, if the stock market index does drop, the gain made from buying back the futures contract at a lower price will help offset the decline in the market value of the stock being held.

Futures transactions also allow financial managers to operate quickly in

[1]*Business Week* (Oct. 29, 1979): 50.

rapidly changing stock market environments, because a single futures trans-action is easier to accomplish than deciding which individual stocks to trade. In addition, futures transactions costs are generally lower than those for com-parable security transactions.

Speculators can also participate in the stock-index futures market. For ex-ample, if speculators expect the stock market to increase, they can buy a futures contract. If the index does rise, the value of the contract increases, resulting in a profit.

QUESTIONS AND TOPICS FOR DISCUSSION

1. What is a financial futures contract?
2. What is the difference between a hedger and a speculator?
3. What is the difference between a short hedge and a long hedge?
4. If speculators expect interest rates to decline, would they want to buy or sell bond futures? Explain.

CHAPTER 13

The Capital Structure Decision

Coors Versus Anheuser-Busch

When a firm has a high level of business risk, it usually seeks to balance this risk with a lower level of financial risk by employing lower levels of debt in its capital structure. The question of determining an optimal capital structure—one that will maximize the value of the firm—is an important one in financial management. Although it is usually not possible to derive a precise answer to this question, it is possible to identify a range of the capital structure over which a firm's cost of capital is likely to be near its minimum, resulting in a value for the firm that is likely to be near its maximum.

Nevertheless, some firms either choose to or are forced to operate outside this range. For example, the brewing industry is characterized by relatively high levels of operating leverage and subsequently high levels of business risk. The industry as a whole has a debt-to-total-assets ratio that averages a modest 40 percent. Coors has the reputation of being very conservative; it seeks to avoid debt financing whenever possible and has a debt-to-total-assets ratio of only 20 percent (with practically no long-term debt). In contrast, Anheuser-Busch (whose stock symbol is BUD) has a debt-to-total-assets ratio of about 45 percent.

On one hand, most analysts would probably conclude that Coors does not use financial leverage as effectively as it could and that this results in lower earnings and stock prices than might otherwise be possible. On the other hand, they would probably compliment BUD for using an appropriate amount of debt, resulting in a reasonable amount of risk and a stock price that is more nearly optimal from a capital structure standpoint. (In early 1983 the price-earnings ratio for Coors was 10 times, whereas it was 12 times for BUD.)

This chapter analyzes the capital structure decision and attempts to identify a firm's optimal capital structure—one consistent with the maximization of shareholder wealth.

GLOSSARY OF NEW TERMS

Capital structure   the amount of permanent short-term debt, long-term debt, preferred stock, and common equity used to finance a firm.

Financial structure   the amount of current liabilities, long-term debt, preferred stock, and common equity used to finance a firm.

Indifference point   that level of EBIT where the earnings per share of a firm are the same, regardless of which of two alternative capital structures is employed.

Optimal capital structure   the capital structure that minimizes a firm's weighted cost of capital and, therefore, maximizes the value of the firm.

Target capital structure   the proportions of permanent short-term debt, long-term debt, preferred stock, and common equity that a firm *desires* to have in its capital structure.

INTRODUCTION

Kaiser Aluminum reported the following in a recent annual report:[1]

> An improved capital structure is critical to improving overall financial flexibility, and management's target in this area had been to lower the debt portion of Kaiser Aluminum's capital structure from the 1973 level of approximately 50 percent to below 40 percent, a goal that was achieved at the end of 1978 . . . Having achieved its initial goal, management has reevaluated the corporation's position in the light of current conditions and has set a new debt-to-capital ratio goal of about 35 percent, recognizing that the ratio will shift above or below this figure in any given year, depending largely upon earnings and capital spending levels.

This chapter considers how a firm like Kaiser Aluminum analyzes its capital structure decision. *Capital structure* is defined as the amount of permanent short-term debt,[2] long-term debt, preferred stock, and common stock used to finance a firm. In contrast, *financial structure* refers to the amount of total current liabilities, long-term debt, preferred stock, and common stock used to finance a firm. Thus, capital structure is part of the financial struc-

---

[1]*Annual Report.* Kaiser Aluminum and Chemical Corporation, 1978, p. 15.
[2]*Permanent* short-term debt is contrasted with *seasonal* short-term debt.

ture, representing the permanent sources of the firm's financing. This chapter deals only with the total permanent sources of a firm's financing; the decision about what proportions of debt should be long-term and short-term is considered in Chapter 18.

To illustrate the capital structure concept, suppose that a company currently has $10 million in permanent short-term debt, $40 million in long-term debt outstanding, $10 million in preferred stock, and $40 million in common stock. In this case the company's current capital structure is said to be "50 percent debt, 10 percent preferred stock, and 40 percent common stock."[3] Thus, capital structure pertains to the permanent debt, preferred stock, and equity portion of the balance sheet.

This chapter emphasizes the firm's long-range *target capital structure*, that is, the capital structure at which the firm ultimately plans to operate. For most companies the current and target capital structures are virtually identical, and calculating the target structure is a straightforward process. Occasionally, however, companies find it necessary to change from their current capital structure to a different target. (This was the case in the Kaiser Aluminum example cited.) The reasons for such a change may involve a change in the company's asset mix (and a resulting change in its risk), an increase in competition that may imply more risk, or simply a desire to move closer to an optimal capital structure that will maximize the firm's value.

For example, Tenneco, Inc., the Houston-based conglomerate, was primarily engaged in the natural gas transmission business in the early 1960s. Natural gas transmission is a regulated business with a relatively low level of business risk, so firms like Tenneco can normally incur relatively large amounts of debt to make their capital structures relatively leveraged.

During the mid- and late 1960s Tenneco increased its business risk level by acquiring a number of firms in nonregulated industries. At this time Tenneco management consulted with the company's investment bankers and adopted a target capital structure of approximately 50 percent permanent debt—down considerably from the 70 percent debt levels of the early 1960s. It took several years for the firm to reach this target, because it continued paying dividends and did not issue large amounts of new common stock. By year-end 1982, the company had decreased its debt percentage to about 50 percent of its total capitalization. Thus, the company lowered its level of financial risk because of an increase in business risk.

One reason why firms are concerned about their capital structure is that there appears to exist in practice (given the laws on the tax deductibility of interest) a capital structure at which the *cost* to the firm *of* its employed *capital* is minimized. At this minimum-cost capital structure, the net present value of new investment projects is maximized, and, as a result, the incremental increase in the firm's value also is maximized. This minimum-cost capital structure is therefore called the *optimal* capital structure.

This chapter considers the factors that influence the determination of an

---

[3]Companies normally do not distinguish in their capital structure between whether common equity is obtained by retained earnings or new common stock. In other words, only the *total* common shareholders' equity is considered, not the *relative* amounts in the common stock, contributed capital in excess of par, and retained earnings accounts.

optimal capital structure and examines the relationship between capital structure, a firm's cost of capital, and the value of the firm.

FINANCIAL LEVERAGE, CAPITAL STRUCTURE, AND EARNINGS PER SHARE

One basic issue regarding capital structure involves the question of whether a firm should use debt or equity financing. This question logically should be viewed from the standpoint of the firm's stockholders, and the answer depends essentially on the firm's level of operating income.

Consider the Yuma Corporation with a present capital structure consisting only of common stock (35 million shares). Assume that Yuma is considering an expansion and is evaluating two alternative financing plans.[4] Plan 1, equity financing, would involve the sale of an additional 15 million shares of common stock at $20 each. Plan 2, debt financing, would involve the sale of $300 million of 10 percent long-term debt.

If the firm adopts Plan 1, it remains totally equity financed. If, however,

TABLE 13-1   EBIT-EPS Analysis—Yuma Corporation (All Figures Except Per-Share Amounts Are in Millions of Dollars)*

	EBIT = $75	EBIT = $125
Equity Financing (Plan 1)		
EBIT	$ 75	$ 125
Interest	—	—
EBT	$ 75	$ 125
Taxes @ 40%	30	50
EAT	$ 45	$ 75
Shares outstanding	50	50
EPS	$0.90	$1.50
% change in EBIT		+66.67%
% change in EPS		+66.67%
Debt Financing (Plan 2)		
EBIT	$ 75	$ 125
Interest	30	30
EBT	$ 45	$ 95
Taxes @ 40%	18	38
EAT	$ 27	$ 57
Shares outstanding	35	35
EPS	$0.77	$1.63
% change in EBIT		+66.67%
% change in EPS		+112%

*EBIT = earnings before interest and taxes; EBT = earning before taxes; EAT = earnings after taxes; EPS = earnings per share.

[4]Preferred stock is not included in this example, because it merely complicates the matter. Because preferred stock is a fixed income security, it would be treated much like debt in this example.

FIGURE 13–1   EBIT-EPS Analysis

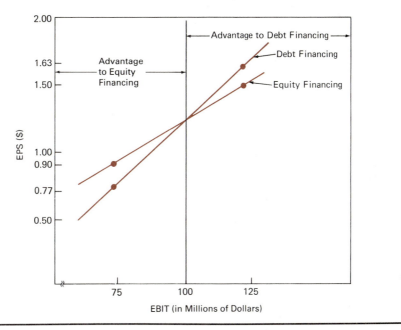

the firm adopts Plan 2, it becomes partially debt financed (leveraged). Because Plan 2 involves the use of financial leverage, this financing issue is basically one of whether it is in the best interests of the firm's existing stockholders to employ financial leverage.

An analytical technique called *EBIT-EPS analysis*[5] can be used to help determine when debt financing is advantageous and when equity financing is advantageous. Table 13–1 illustrates the calculation of EPS at two different assumed levels of EBIT for both financing plans. Since the relationship between EBIT and EPS is linear, the two points calculated in Table 13–1 can be used to graph the relationship for each financing plan; this is shown in Figure 13–1.

In this example, earnings per share at EBIT levels less than $100 million are higher using the equity financing alternative. Correspondingly, at EBIT levels greater than $100 million, earnings per share are higher with debt financing. The $100 million figure is called the *EBIT-EPS indifference point*. By definition, the earnings per share for the debt and equity financing alternatives are equal at the EBIT-EPS indifference point:

$$\text{EPS (debt financing)} = \text{EPS (equity financing)} . \qquad \textbf{(13.1)}$$

This equation may be rewritten as follows:

[5]To review briefly, EBIT is earnings before interest and taxes, or operating income; EPS is earnings per share.

$$\frac{(EBIT - \text{Interest for debt alternative})(1 - \text{Tax rate}) - \text{Preferred dividends}}{\text{Number of common shares for debt alternative}}$$

$$= \frac{\begin{array}{c}(EBIT - \text{Interest for equity alternative}) \times \\ (1 - \text{Tax rate}) - \text{Preferred dividends}\end{array}}{\text{Number of common shares for equity alternative}} .$$

$$\frac{(EBIT - I_d)(1 - t) - P}{N_d} = \frac{(EBIT - I_e)(1 - t) - P}{N_e} , \qquad \textbf{(13.2)}$$

where EBIT is earnings before interest and taxes, I_d is the firm's total interest payments if the debt alternative is chosen, I_e is the firm's total interest payments if the equity alternative is chosen, and N_d and N_e represent the number of common shares outstanding for the debt and equity alternatives, respectively. The firm's effective tax rate is indicated as t, and P is the amount of preferred dividends for the firm. This equation may be used to calculate directly the EBIT level at which earnings per share for the two alternatives are equal. The data from the example shown in Table 13–1 yield the EBIT level of $100 million at the indifference point:

$$\frac{(EBIT - \$30)(1 - 0.4) - 0}{35} = \frac{(EBIT - \$0)(1 - 0.4) - 0}{50} .$$

$$50(0.6 \; EBIT - \$18) = 35 \times 0.6 \; EBIT .$$

$$30 \; EBIT - \$900 = 21 \; EBIT .$$

$$9 \; EBIT = \$900 .$$

$$EBIT = \$100 .$$

Note that in the equity alternative, a 67 percent increase in EBIT (from $75 million to $125 million) results in a 67 percent increase in earnings per share (from $0.90 to $1.50) or a degree of financial leverage of 1.0. In the debt alternative, a 67 percent increase in EBIT results in a 112 percent increase in earnings per share or a degree of financial leverage of 1.67. A similar magnification of earnings per share will occur if EBIT declines. This wider variation in earnings per share, which occurs with the debt financing alternative, is an illustration of *financial risk*, since financial risk is defined as the increased variability in earnings per share due to the firm's use of debt. All other things being equal, an increase in the proportion of debt financing is said to increase the financial risk of the firm.

FINANCIAL LEVERAGE AND STOCK PRICES

A more important question involves the impact of financial leverage on the firm's common stock price. Specifically, which financing alternative results in the higher stock price? Suppose the Yuma Corporation is able to operate at the $125 million EBIT level. Then, if the company chooses the debt financing alternative, its EPS will equal $1.63, and if it chooses the equity alternative, its EPS will be $1.50. But the stock price depends on the price-earnings (P/E) ratio that the stock market assigns to each alternative. Suppose the stock market assigns a P/E ratio of 10.0 to the company's common stock if the equity alternative is chosen, and a P/E ratio of 9.8 if the debt alternative is chosen. The common stock price, P_0, can be calculated for both alternatives as follows:

$$P_0 = \text{(P/E ratio)(EPS)} .$$

Equity alternative:

$$P_0 = (10.0)(\$1.50) = \$15 .$$

Debt alternative:

$$P_0 = (9.8)(\$1.63) = \$15.97, \text{ or approximately } \$16 .$$

These calculations show that in this case the stock market places a higher value on the company's stock if the debt alternative is chosen rather than the equity alternative. Notice that the stock market assigned a slightly lower PE ratio to the debt alternative. The stock market recognized the increased financial risk associated with the debt alternative, but this increased risk was more than offset by the increased EPS possible with the use of debt.

To carry the Yuma Corporation example one important step farther, suppose the company, while operating at the $125 million EBIT level, chooses an even higher debt capital structure, which causes its EPS to increase to $2.25. Suppose further that the stock market feels that this high debt capital structure significantly increases the company's financial risk—to the point where bankruptcy could occur if EBIT levels turned downward in a recession. If the stock market assigns a P/E of 6.0, for example, the stock price would be $13.50, or $2.25 × 6.0, and it would be clear that this change in capital structure is not desirable.

In summary, the firm can potentially show increased earnings to its stockholders by increasing its level of financial risk. However, since increases in risk tend to increase the cost of capital (which is analogous to a decrease in the P/E ratio), the firm's management has to assess the tradeoff between the higher earnings per share for its stockholders and the higher costs of capital. This important point is discussed further in this chapter.

COST OF CAPITAL AND ITS RELATIONSHIP TO CAPITAL STRUCTURE

The preceding chapter developed the concept of a weighted cost of capital. This section continues to explore that topic by examining the functional relationship between the cost of capital and the firm's capital structure.

Assuming that the right-hand side of the balance sheet contains only permanent debt and common equity, leverage may be defined as the relative amount of debt in the firm's capital structure and measured by the debt ratio $D/(D + E)$, where D is debt and E is equity.

The first step in this analysis considers the relationship between the cost of debt and capital structure. All other things being equal, investors in debt consider the debt less risky if the firm has a low, rather than high, proportion of debt in its capital structure. As the proportion of debt in the capital structure increases, investors require a higher return on the more risky debt. And since the firm's cost of capital is the investor's required return, the cost of debt increases as the proportion of debt increases.

The precise relationship between the cost of debt and the debt ratio is difficult to determine. This is due to the fact that it is impossible to observe the cost of debt at two different capital structures (at the same time) for a single firm. Nevertheless, there is good evidence that the cost of debt increases rather slowly for moderate amounts of debt. There is some point at which the capital markets consider any new debt "excessive" and therefore much more risky. The cost of debt curve in Figure 13–2 illustrates such a relationship. The actual region where the cost of debt begins to increase more rapidly varies by firm and industry, depending on the firm's level of business risk.

The next step in this analysis focuses on the relationship between the cost of equity capital and capital structure. When a firm has a low debt ratio, any equity employed is less risky than equity used when the firm is financed with a relatively high proportion of debt. Earlier in this chapter it was shown that the greater the fraction of debt used, the greater the variability in earnings per common share. In addition, the greater the fraction of debt used, the greater the risk of bankruptcy. Because the returns expected by stockholders in the form of present and future dividends depend partly on current earnings, it can be concluded that variability in earnings per common share can result in variability of the returns to investors, that is, greater risk. Thus, it can be

FIGURE 13–2   Cost of Debt Capital as a Function of Capital Structure

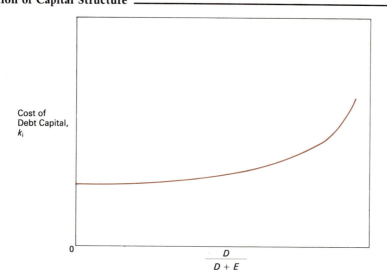

FIGURE 13–3   Cost of Equity Capital as a Function of Capital Structure

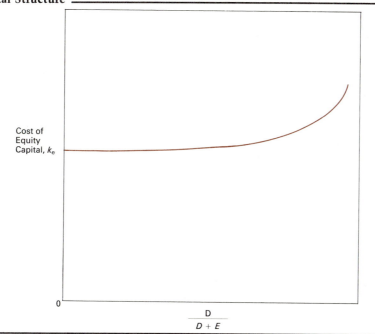

stated that investors' required returns and the cost of equity capital increase as the relative amount of debt used to finance the firm increases.

Once again, the exact nature of the relationship between the cost of equity and the debt ratio is difficult to determine in practice. However, there is agreement that the cost of equity capital increases at a relatively slow rate as the debt proportion increases up to moderate amounts. Then, in the range where additional debt is viewed as "excessive" and much more risky, the cost of equity increases more rapidly. This is shown in Figure 13–3. As was true in the debt illustration, the region where the cost of equity capital begins to increase more rapidly varies by firm and industry.

The relationship between the weighted cost of capital, k_a, and the debt proportion can now be considered. The following equation (Equation 12.18),

$$k_a = \left(\frac{E}{D + E}\right)(k_e) + \left(\frac{D}{D + E}\right)k_i \,,$$

can be used to calculate k_a for any debt ratio, provided that the values of k_e and k_i at that debt ratio are known. Since the relationships between the debt ratio and k_i and k_e have been developed, the relationship between k_a and the debt ratio follows accordingly. The k_a curve, shown in Figure 13–4, begins at $k_a = k_e$, since by definition the weighted cost of capital for an all-equity firm equals the cost of equity. As even small increments of debt are used, k_a becomes lower; as the debt proportion continues to increase from moderate to excessive, k_a "bottoms out" and then begins to increase. The resulting saucer-shaped curve contains a point at which the firm's overall cost of capital is minimized and its value maximized. This point is the firm's *optimal capital*

FIGURE 13–4   **Overall Cost of Capital as a Function of**
Capital Structure

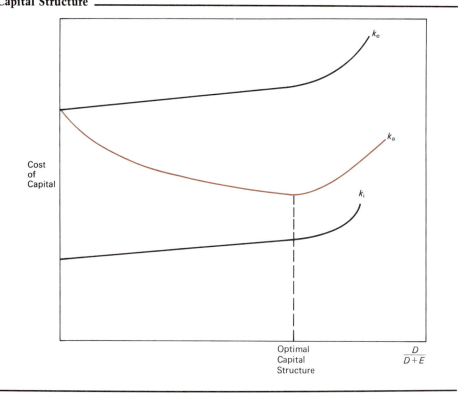

FIGURE 13–5   **Value of the Firm as a Function of**
Capital Structure

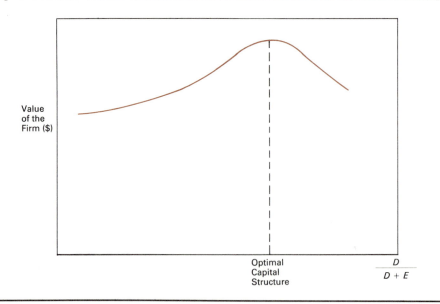

structure. If the firm is thought of as a cash flow generator, it can be seen that the lower the discount rate (the weighted cost of capital), the higher the firm's value; this is shown in Figure 13–5.

Given the importance of an optimal capital structure, it is logical to ask how a firm knows when it is operating at its optimal capital structure. Unfortunately, the answer is that the firm cannot determine this exactly. This is not a great problem, however, since the optimal capital structure, in practice, is best depicted as a range of values. Many companies are able to conclude that they are operating near their optimal range by examining how their interest costs behave as their debt proportion is increased. Comparison with other companies in the industry should also help a firm determine whether it can safely increase its proportion of "moderate" debt and reduce its weighted cost of capital.

DETERMINING AN OPTIMAL CAPITAL STRUCTURE: AN INTEGRATIVE APPROACH

The tools of EBIT-EPS analysis and the theory of an optimal capital structure can help a firm decide on an appropriate capital structure. This section utilizes an example to develop a 5-step procedure designed to assist financial managers in making capital structure decisions.

Balboa Department Stores has been 100 percent financed with equity funds since the firm was founded. While analyzing a major expansion program, the firm has decided to consider alternative capital structures. In particular, it has been suggested that the firm should use this expansion program as an opportunity to increase the long-term debt-ratio from the current level of 0 percent to a new level of 30 percent. Interest on the proposed new debt will amount to $100,000 per year.

Step 1 Compute the expected level of EBIT after the expansion. Based on Balboa's past operating experience and a projection of the impact of the expansion, it estimates its expected EBIT to be $500,000 per year under normal operating circumstances.

Step 2 Estimate the variability of this level of operating income. Based on the past performance of the company over several business cycles, the standard deviation of operating income is estimated to be $200,000 per year. (Operating income is assumed to be normally distributed, or at least approximately so.)

Step 3 Compute the indifference point between the two financing alternatives—add new debt or maintain the all-equity capital structure. Using the techniques of EBIT-EPS analysis previously discussed, the indifference point is computed to be $300,000.

Step 4 Analyze these estimates in the context of the risk the firm is willing to assume.

After considerable discussion, it has been decided that the firm is willing to accept a 25 percent chance that operating earnings in any year will be below the indifference point, and a 5 percent chance that

401

the firm will have to report a loss in any year. To complete this analysis, it is necessary to compute the probability that operating earnings will be below the indifference point, that is, the probability that EBIT will be less than $300,000. This is equivalent on the standard normal curve to the following:

$$z = \frac{\$300,000 - \$500,000}{\$200,000}$$
$$= -1.0 ,$$

or 1.0 standard deviation below the mean. The probability that EBIT will be less than 1.0 standard deviation below the mean is 15.87 percent; this is determined from Table V at the end of the book. Thus, on the basis of the indifference point criterion, the proposed new capital structure appears acceptable. The probability of incurring losses must now be analyzed. This is the probability that EBIT will be less than the required interest payments of $100,000. On the standard normal curve, this corresponds to the following:

$$z = \frac{\$100,000 - \$500,000}{\$200,000}$$
$$= -2.0 ,$$

or 2.0 standard deviations below the mean. The probability that EBIT will be less than 2.0 standard deviations below the mean is 2.28 percent, as shown in Table V. According to this criterion, the proposed capital structure also seems acceptable.

If either or both of these tests had shown the proposed capital structure to have an unacceptable level of risk, the analysis would have been repeated for lower levels of debt than the proposed 30 percent rate. Similarly, since the proposed capital structure has exceeded the standards set by the firm, management might want to consider even higher levels of debt than the proposed 30 percent.

Step 5   Examine the market evidence to determine whether the proposed capital structure is too risky in relation to the following: the firm's level of business risk, industry norms for leverage ratios and coverage ratios, and the recommendations of the firm's investment bankers.

This step is undertaken only after a proposed capital structure has met the "internal" tests for acceptability. As was observed earlier, financial leverage is a two-edged sword: it enhances expected returns, but it also increases risk. If the increase in perceived risk is greater than the increase in expected returns, the firm's weighted cost of capital may rise instead of fall, and the firm's value will decline.

It is important to note that there is no need for a firm to feel constrained by industry standards in setting its own capital structure. If, for example, a firm has traditionally been more profitable than the average firm in the industry, or if a firm's operating income is more stable than the operating income of the average firm, a higher level of financial leverage probably can be tolerated. The final choice of a capital structure involves a careful analysis of expected future returns and risks relative to other firms in the industry.

SUMMARY

- *Capital structure* is defined as the relative amount of permanent short-term debt, long-term debt, preferred stock, and common stock used to finance a firm. The capital structure decision is important to the firm, because there exists in practice a capital structure at which the *cost of capital* is minimized. This minimum-cost capital structure is the *optimal* capital structure, because the value of the firm is maximized at this point.

- *EBIT-EPS analysis* is an analytical technique that can be used to help determine the circumstances under which a firm should employ financial leverage. Basically, it involves calculating earnings per share at different levels of EBIT for debt and equity financing plans. This information may then be used to graph earnings per share versus EBIT to determine the EBIT levels at which financial leverage is advantageous to the firm.

- The *indifference point* in EBIT-EPS analysis is that level of EBIT where earnings per share are the same, regardless of which of two alternative capital structures is used. At EBIT levels greater than the indifference level, more financially levered capital structures will produce higher levels of earnings per share; at EBIT levels less than the indifference point, less financially levered capital structures will produce higher levels of earnings per share.

- A firm can analyze its capital structure decision by performing an EBIT-EPS analysis, computing the risk of unfavorable financial leverage at its expected level of operating income, and analyzing financial leverage ratios and coverage ratios for other firms in the industry. A careful evaluation of these facts, together with an analysis of the firm's business risk, can assist in making the final determination regarding the desirability of a proposed capital structure.

QUESTIONS AND TOPICS FOR DISCUSSION

1. Discuss the meaning of an *optimal* capital structure.
2. What is the relationship between the value of a firm and the cost of capital?
3. In practice, how can a firm determine whether or not it is operating at (or near) its optimal capital structure?
4. Why does the marginal cost of capital increase as the amount of financing increases?
5. What are the major limitations of EBIT-EPS analysis as a technique to determine the optimal capital structure?
6. Under what circumstances should a firm use *more* debt in its capital structure than is used by the "average" firm in the industry? When should it use *less* debt than the "average" firm?

7. Why do public utilities typically have capital structures with about 50 percent debt, whereas major oil companies average about 25 percent debt in their capital structures?

PROBLEMS*

1. Taco Castle is a regional fast-food chain with a present capital structure consisting only of common stock (10.0 million shares). The company is planning a major expansion into several neighboring states. At this time the company is undecided between the following two financing plans (assume a 40 percent marginal tax rate):

- Equity financing. Under this plan, an additional 5.0 million shares of common stock will be sold at $10 each.

- Debt financing. Under this plan, $50 million of 10 percent long-term debt will be sold.

One piece of information the company desires for its decision analysis is an EBIT-EPS analysis.
a. Calculate the EBIT-EPS indifference point.
b. Graphically determine the EBIT-EPS indifference point.
HINT: Use EBIT = $10 million and $25 million.
c. What happens to the indifference point if the interest rate on debt increases and the common stock sales price remains constant?
d. What happens to the indifference point if the interest rate on debt remains constant and the common stock sales price increases?

2. Two capital goods manufacturing companies, Rock Island and Davenport, are virtually identical in all aspects of their operations—product lines, amount of sales, total size, and so on. The two companies differ only in their capital structures, as shown here:

	Rock Island	Davenport
Debt (8%)	$400 million	$100 million
Common equity	$600 million	$900 million
Number of common shares outstanding	30 million	45 million

Each company has $1,000 million ($1 billion) in total assets.
Capital goods manufacturers are typically subject to cyclical trends in the economy. Suppose that the EBIT level for both companies is $100 million during an expansion and $60 million during a recession. (Assume a 40 percent tax rate for both companies.)
a. Calculate the earnings per share for both companies during expansion and recession.
b. Which stock is riskier? Why?
c. At what EBIT level are the earnings per share of the two companies identical?
d. Calculate the common stock price for both companies during an expansion if the stock market assigns a price-earnings ratio of 10 to Davenport and 9 to Rock Island.

3. The Wellington Steel Company is considering opening a new subsidiary in Denver, to be operated as a separate company. The company's financial analysts expect the new facility's average EBIT level to be $6 million per year. At this time the com-

*Problems in color have check answers provided at the end of the book.

pany is considering the following two financing plans (use a 40 percent marginal tax rate in your analysis):

Plan 1. Equity financing. Under this plan, 2 million common shares will be sold at $10 each.

Plan 2. Debt-equity financing. Under this plan, $10 million of 12 percent long-term debt and 1 million common shares at $10 each will be sold.

  a. Calculate the EBIT-EPS indifference point.
  b. Calculate the expected EPS for both financing plans.
  c. What factors should the company consider in deciding which financing plan to adopt?
  d. Which plan do you recommend the company adopt?

4. This problem is an extension of Problem 3. Suppose Wellington Steel adopts Plan 2, and the Denver facility does initially operate at an annual EBIT level of $6 million.

  a. What is the times interest earned ratio?
  b. If the lenders require that the new company maintain a times interest earned ratio equal to 3.5 or greater, by how much could the EBIT level drop and the company still be in compliance with the loan agreement?

5. This problem is an extension of Problem 3. Suppose the expected annual EBIT level of $6 million is normally distributed with a standard deviation of $2 million. What is the probability that the EPS will be negative in any given year, if Plan 2 is selected?

6. Canyon Instruments Corporation has determined the following costs of debt and equity capital for various fractions of debt in its capital structure:

Debt Fraction	k_e	k_i
0.00	12.00	—
0.10	12.05	4.8
0.30	12.10	4.9
0.40	12.20	5.0
0.45	12.40	5.2
0.50	12.80	5.7
0.60	15.00	7.0

  a. Based on these data, determine the company's optimal capital structure.
  b. Suppose the company's actual capital structure is 50 percent debt and 50 percent equity. How much higher is k_a at this capital structure than at the optimal value of k_a?
  c. Is it necessary in practice for the company to know precisely its optimal capital structure? Why?

7. High Sky, Inc., a hot air balloon manufacturing firm, currently has the following simplified balance sheet:

Assets		Liabilities and Capital	
Total assets	$1,100,000	Bonds (10% interest)	$ 600,000
		Common stock at par ($3), 100,000 shares outstanding	300,000
		Contributed capital in excess of par	100,000
		Retained earnings	100,000
		Total liabilities and capital	$1,100,000

The company is planning an expansion that is expected to cost $600,000. It can be financed with new equity (sold to net the company $4 per share) or with the sale of new bonds at an interest rate of 11 percent. (The firm's marginal tax rate is 40 percent.)

a. Compute the indifference point between the two financing alternatives.

b. If the expected level of EBIT for the firm is $240,000 with a standard deviation of $50,000, what is the probability that the debt financing alternative will produce higher earnings than the equity alternative? (EBIT is normally distributed.)

c. If the debt alternative is chosen, what is the probability that the company will have negative earnings per share in any period?

ADDITIONAL READINGS AND REFERENCES

Alberts, W. W., and Archer, S. H. "Some Evidence on the Effect of Company Size on the Cost of Equity Capital." *Journal of Financial and Quantitative Analysis* 8 (March 1973): 229–245.

Archer, Stephen H., and Faerber, LeRoy G. "Firm Size and the Cost of Equity Capital." *Journal of Finance* 21 (March 1966): 69–84.

Barges, Alexander. *The Effect of Capital Structure on the Cost of Capital.* Englewood Cliffs, N.J.: Prentice-Hall, 1963.

Brigham, E.F., and Pappas, J. "Rates of Return on Common Stock." *Journal of Business* 42 (July 1969).

Fama, Eugene F., and Miller, Merton H. *The Theory of Finance.* New York: Holt, Rinehart and Winston, 1972.

Gordon, Myron. *The Investment, Financing, and Valuation of the Corporation.* Homewood, Ill.: Irwin, 1962.

Haley, C. W., and Schall, L. D. *The Theory of Financial Decisions*, 2nd ed. New York: McGraw-Hill, 1979.

Krouse, Clement G. "Optimal Financing and Capital Structure Programs for the Firm." *Journal of Finance* 27 (Dec. 1972): 1057–1072.

Lee, Wayne Y., and Barker, Henry H. "Bankruptcy Costs and the Firm's Optimal Debt Capacity: A Positive Theory of Capital Structure." *Southern Economic Journal* 43 (April 1977): 1453–1465.

Lewellen, W. G. *The Cost of Capital.* Dubuque, Iowa: Kendall-Hunt, 1976.

Lintner, John. "The Cost of Capital and Optimal Financing of Corporate Growth." *Journal of Finance* 18 (May 1963): 292–310.

Marsh, P. "Choice between Equity and Debt: An Empirical Study." *Journal of Finance* 37 (March 1982): 121–144.

Masulis, Ronald W. "The Impact of Capital Structure Change on Firm Value: Some Estimates." *Journal of Finance* 38 (March 1983): 107–126.

Miller, M. H. and Modigliani, Franco. "Some Estimates of the Cost of Capital to the Electric Utility Industry." *American Economic Review* (June 1966): 333–391.

Modigliani, F., and Miller, M. "The Cost of Capital, Corporation Finance, and the Theory of Investment." *American Economic Review* (June 1958): 261–297.

Schwartz, Eli, and Aronson, J. Richard. "Some Surrogate Evidence in Support of the Concept of Optimal Capital Structure." *Journal of Finance* 22 (March 1967): 10–18.

Scott, David F., and Martin, John D. "Industry Influence on Financial Structure." *Financial Management* 4 (Spring 1975): 67–73.

Solomon, Ezra. "Leverage and the Cost of Capital." *Journal of Finance* 18 (May 1963): 273–279.

Solomon, Ezra. *The Theory of Financial Management.* New York: Columbia University Press, 1963.

Theoretical Perspectives on Capital Structure and Valuation

INTRODUCTION

Chapter 13 shows that a firm's overall cost of capital is a function of the debt fraction in its capital structure. This is illustrated in Figure 13–4; the debt fraction at which the overall cost of capital is minimized is the *optimal* capital structure, because at this fraction, the firm's value is maximized.

This appendix considers some additional theoretical perspectives on capital structure and valuation. Two different theories, the *net income theory* and the *net operating income theory*, of capital structure and firm valuation are considered. Then the classical work of Merton Miller and Franco Modigliani is discussed.

Two prominent finance researchers, Franco Modigliani and Merton Miller (MM), showed in 1958 that under certain assumptions, a firm's overall cost of capital, and therefore its value, is *independent* of capital structure.[1] On the surface, the Chapter 13 results and the MM results would seem to contradict each other. As it turns out, however, the two viewpoints are not really contrary. The key to the analysis is in the assumptions made by MM.

NET INCOME THEORY OF CAPITAL STRUCTURE AND VALUATION

The *net income theory* of capital structure and valuation assumes that the cost of debt and the cost of equity remain constant as the firm's capital structure changes. In addition, the pretax cost of debt, k_d, is lower than the cost

---

[1]Franco, Modigliani, and Merton Miller. "The Cost of Capital, Corporation Finance, and the Theory of Investment." *American Economic Review* 48 (June 1958): 261–296.

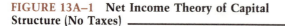

FIGURE 13A–1   Net Income Theory of Capital Structure (No Taxes)

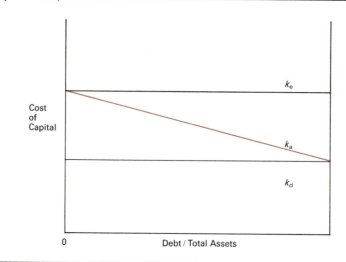

of equity, k_e, because debt is less risky than equity. Therefore, as a firm increases its leverage by increasing its level of debt relative to equity, the overall cost of capital, k_a, declines. This is shown in Figure 13A–1. The importance of this lowered overall cost of capital is that the value of the firm is calculated by discounting the present value of its expected future cash flows by its overall cost of capital. Therefore, the more debt a firm has in its capital structure, the lower its overall cost of capital and therefore the higher its value.

NET OPERATING INCOME THEORY OF CAPITAL STRUCTURE AND VALUATION

The *net operating income theory* of capital structure and valuation assumes that the cost of debt and the overall cost of capital are constant regardless of a firm's leverage position. However, as a firm increases its relative debt level, the cost of equity capital increases. The reason the cost of equity capital increases is that stockholders require a higher return due to the increased risk imposed by the additional debt. The net operating income theory further assumes that the increased cost of equity capital exactly offsets the benefit of the lower cost of debt so that the overall cost of capital does not change with changes in capital structure. This is illustrated in Figure 13A–2.

The net operating income theory assumes that a firm's value is calculated by discounting its expected future operating income by its overall cost of capital. Since this theory assumes that the overall cost of capital is independent of capital structure, it follows that the firm's value is independent of capital structure.

408

FIGURE 13A–2   Net Operating Income Theory of Capital Structure (No Taxes)

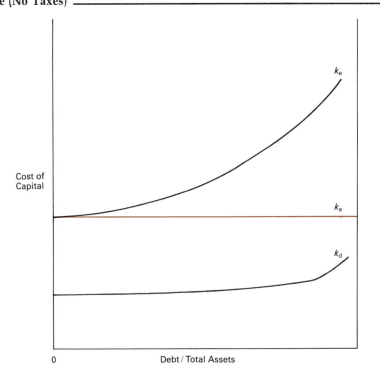

MM ANALYSIS

The preceeding sections describe two different theories of valuation and capital structure. One, the net income theory, states that the value of the firm increases as the level of debt in its capital structure increases. The other, the net operating income theory, says that the value of the firm is independent of capital structure. Obviously, the two theories contradict each other, and both cannot be correct.

In their analysis, MM argued that the net income theory of capital structure and valuation is not possible in perfect capital markets in which their assumptions hold. MM use the notion of *arbitrage* to support their claims. *Arbitrage* is the process of simultaneously buying and selling the same or equivalent securities in different markets. For example, suppose that at a given moment, gold is selling at $400 an ounce in New York and $405 an ounce in London. Arbitragers would quickly and simultaneously buy gold in New York and sell it in London, thereby making a profit. In the process, however, they would bid up the New York price and bid down the London price, eliminating the price differential. Interestingly, the existence of arbitragers keeps the prices of the same or equivalent securities approximately equal in different markets.

409

In their analysis, MM assumed that *perfect* capital markets exist. This implies the following:

- There are no transactions costs for buying and selling securities.
- A sufficient number of buyers and sellers exists in the market, so no single person can have a significant influence on security prices.
- Relevant information is readily available for individuals and is costless to obtain.
- All investors can borrow or lend at the same rate.

MM made several other assumptions. They assumed all investors are rational and have homogeneous expectations of a firm's earnings. Firms operating under similar conditions will face the same degree of business risk. This assumption is called the *homogenous risk class assumption*. The final assumption made by MM is that there are no income taxes. In some of their work, MM relax this assumption and consider their analysis in a world in which income taxes exist.

MM argue that the net income theory is not possible. Suppose two firms in the same industry differed only in that one was *levered* (that is, it had some debt in its capital structure) and the other was *unlevered* (that is, it had no debt in its capital structure). By simply changing its capital structure, the unlevered firm would require a reward (in the form of an increase in the firm's value) from stockholders for doing so. However, in the perfect capital market without transactions costs, MM argue that stockholders would not reward the firm for increasing its debt. Stockholders could change *their own* financial debt-equity structure without cost to receive an equal return. Therefore, stockholders would not increase their opinion of the value of an unlevered firm just because it took on some debt.

The MM major argument against the net income approach is the arbitrage process. If one of two unlevered firms with identical business risk took on some debt, then according to the net income theory, its value should increase and therefore so would the value of its stock. MM suggest that under these circumstances, investors will sell the overpriced stock of the levered firm. They can then use an arbitrage process of borrowing, buying the unlevered firm's stock and investing the excess funds elsewhere. Through these costless transactions, investors can increase their return without increasing their risk. Hence, they have substituted their own personal financial leverage for corporate leverage. MM argue that this arbitrage process will continue until the selling of the levered firm's stock drives down its price to the point where it is equal to the unlevered firm's stock price, which has been driven up due to increased buying.

The arbitrage process occurs so rapidly that the market values of the levered and unlevered firms are equal. Thus, MM conclude that the value of a firm is independent of its capital structure in perfect capital markets with no income taxes.

The major criticisms of the MM analysis are based on the assumptions made. First, MM assume costless transactions, which do not exist. Investors pay a cost for their transactions in the market and therefore would want to limit them. Also, MM assume that personal and corporate leverage are equally risky. However, an individual with an investment in a levered company stands to lose only the stock investment. In contrast, if the investor borrows and invests funds, he or she can lose both the stock investment and the borrowed funds, as well as still be held responsible for paying off the debt.

The assumption that individuals and corporations can borrow and lend at the same rate is also not necessarily true. And if the borrowing costs are not similar, the arbitrage process may not be possible.

Later in their analysis, MM allow income taxes to exist. When income taxes and the costs associated with bankruptcy (legal and accounting costs, costs from the loss of customer confidence, and so on) are assumed to exist, the MM results are essentially the same as the capital structure results shown in Figure 13–4.

QUESTIONS AND TOPICS FOR DISCUSSION

1. What are the differences between the net income theory and the net operating income theory of capital structure and firm valuation?
2. What is arbitrage?
3. Do the research results of Modigliani and Miller differ from the capital structure material discussed in Chapter 13? Explain.

CHAPTER 14

Dividend Policy

A FINANCIAL DILEMMA

Penn Central: Part I

As a matter of policy, many firms pay out a relatively stable amount of their earnings to shareholders in the form of dividends. In general, a firm will increase dividend payments only when it is confident that it can sustain the improved earnings prospects and, by extension, continue to pay dividends at the higher rate. By the same token, firms are usually reluctant to reduce dividend payments during short-term earnings declines. This policy, however, can add to a firm's problems when it is faced with a serious long-term decline in profitability.

In 1968 Penn Central's restated earnings showed losses of $20 million. Even though the firm had only $100 million in internally generated funds, which were needed for a $300 million capital improvement program, it continued to pay $55 million in dividends during that year. The company's president, Stuart Saunders, maintained that good stockholder relations were extremely important and used this as a rationale for continuing a dividend policy that was beginning to look questionable. At that time he was also trying to build Penn Central into a diversified corporation and felt that a high dividend payout would keep the firm's price-earnings ratio high, making it both easier and cheaper to accomplish new mergers.

In 1969, faced with losses of nearly $120 million, Penn Central paid out another $43 million in dividends. Meanwhile, the firm's sources of internal funds fell $635 million short of meeting its total cash needs. In essence, Penn Central borrowed money in 1968 and 1969 to meet dividend payments. On June 21, 1969, the firm was forced to declare bankruptcy. Although Penn Central's dividend policy was certainly not the only factor responsible for this outcome, it did contribute to the firm's cash crisis, which ultimately led to the bankruptcy decision.

This chapter discusses the elements of a sound dividend policy and how this policy can contribute to the overall firm objective of maximizing shareholder wealth.

GLOSSARY OF NEW TERMS

Declaration date   the day on which the directors of a company declare a dividend.

Ex-dividend date   the date on which the right to the most recently declared dividend no longer goes along with the sale of the stock. The ex-dividend date is four business days prior to the *record date.*

Insolvency   a situation in which either a firm's liabilities exceed its assets or it is unable to pay its creditors as required.

Passive residual theory   a theory of dividend policy that suggests that a firm should retain its earnings as long as there are investment opportunities available that promise a rate of return higher than the required rate of return.

Record date   the date on which a firm makes a list from its stock transfer books of those shareholders who are eligible to receive the declared dividend.

Stock dividend   a payment of additional shares of common stock to stockholders.

Treasury stock   common stock that has been reacquired by the issuing company.

INTRODUCTION

The value of a firm is influenced by three types of financial decisions:

- Investment decisions.
- Financing decisions.
- Dividend decisions.

While each is presented as a separate topic in this and most financial management textbooks,[1] it is important to realize that the three are interdependent in a number of ways. For example, the investments made by a firm determine the level of future earnings and future potential dividends; capital structure influences the cost of capital, which in turn determines in part the number of acceptable investment opportunities; and dividend policy influences the amount of equity capital in a firm's capital structure (via the retained earnings account) and, by extension, influences the cost of capital.

There are a number of factors that influence a firm's choice of a dividend policy. Ideally a firm should choose a dividend policy that is most likely to *maximize shareholder wealth.* Thus, dividend policy affects how investors perceive—and value—a firm. However, this is not the only consideration—legal and internal decision-making constraints also play important roles.

This chapter begins by examining the factors that influence a firm's choice of dividend policy. Next, it considers the pros and cons of a number of differ-

---

[1] In this text investment decisions are dealt with in Chapters 9 through 11 and 19 through 21, and financing decisions are discussed in Chapters 13, 15 through 18, and 22.

ent dividend policies. And, finally, it discusses the mechanics of dividend payments, along with stock dividends and share repurchase plans.

DETERMINANTS OF DIVIDEND POLICY

Dividend policy determines how the earnings of a firm are distributed. Earnings are either retained and reinvested in the firm, or they are paid out to shareholders. In recent years the retention of earnings has been a major source of equity financing for private industry. In 1981 corporations retained over $44 billion in earnings, while issuing only $23.5 billion in new common stock.

As Table 14–1 shows, this division between new stock issues and retained earnings has tended to vary over time. However, retained earnings (in the aggregate) are more important than new stock issues as a source of equity.

On the one hand, retained earnings can be used to stimulate growth in future earnings and as a result can influence future share values. On the other hand, dividends provide stockholders with tangible current returns. Many factors combine to determine the dividend policy of a firm; these are examined in the following sections.

LEGAL CONSTRAINTS

Most states have laws that regulate the dividend payments a firm chartered in that state can make. These laws basically state the following:

- A firm's capital cannot be used to make dividend payments.

TABLE 14–1 **Earnings Retention and New Common Stock Issues**

Year	Earnings Retained (in Billions of Dollars)	New Common Stock Issues (in Billions of Dollars)
1981	$44.4	$23.5
1980	38.9	16.8
1979	54.5	7.7
1978	62.2	7.5
1977	53.7	7.9
1976	36.9	8.3
1975	29.1	7.4
1974	13.4	4.0
1973	32.3	7.6
1972	30.5	10.7
1971	22.8	9.5
1970	14.8	7.0
1965	30.0	1.5
1960	12.1	1.7
1955	13.1	2.2
1950	7.2	0.8

SOURCE: *Federal Reserve Bulletin*, various issues, and *Economic Report of the President*, 1983.

- Dividends must be paid out of a firm's present and past *net* earnings.
- Dividends cannot be paid when the firm is insolvent.

The first restriction is termed the *capital impairment restriction.* In some states *capital* is defined as including only the par value of common stock; in others, *capital* is more broadly defined to also include the contributed capital in excess of par account (sometimes called *capital surplus*).

For example, the Johnson Tool and Die Company has the following capital accounts on its balance sheet:

Common stock ($5 par; 100,000 shares)	$ 500,000
Contributed capital in excess of par	400,000
Retained earnings	200,000
Total common stockholders' equity	$1,100,000

If the company is chartered in a state that defines capital as the par value of common stock, then it can pay out a total of $600,000 ($1,100,000 − $500,000 par value) in dividends. If, however, the company's home state restricts dividend payments to retained earnings alone, then Johnson Tool and Die could only pay dividends up to $200,000. Regardless of the dividend laws, however, it should be realized that dividends are paid from a firm's *cash* account with an offsetting entry to the *retained earnings* account.

The second restriction, called the *net earnings restriction*, requires that a firm have generated earnings *before* it is permitted to pay any cash dividends. This prevents the equity owners from withdrawing their initial investment in the firm and impairing the security position of any of the firm's creditors.

The third restriction, termed the *insolvency restriction*, states that an insolvent company may not pay cash dividends. When a company is insolvent, its liabilities exceed its assets. Payment of dividends would interfere with the creditors' prior claims on the firm's assets and thus is prohibited.

These three restrictions affect different types of companies in different ways. New firms, or small firms with a minimum of accumulated retained earnings, are most likely to feel the weight of these legal constraints when determining their dividend policies, whereas well-established companies with histories of profitable performances and large retained earnings accounts are less likely to be influenced by them.

TAX CONSTRAINTS

Whereas the legal restrictions explained above tend to encourage corporations to retain their earnings, the IRS Code—specifically Sections 531 through 537—has an opposite effect. In essence, the code prohibits corporations from retaining an excessive amount of profits for the purpose of protecting stockholders from paying taxes on dividends received. Dividend payments are considered taxable income. If a corporation decides to retain its earnings in anticipation of providing growth and future capital appreciation for its investors, the investors are not taxed until their shares are sold. In addition, taxes levied on long-term capital gains are generally lower than the taxes on an equivalent amount of dividend income.

If the IRS rules that a corporation has accumulated excess profits to protect its stockholders from having to pay personal income taxes on dividends, the firm has to pay a heavy penalty tax on those earnings. It is the responsibility of the IRS to prove this allegation, however. Some companies are more likely to raise the suspicions of the IRS than others. For example, small closely held corporations whose shareholders are in high marginal tax brackets, firms that pay consistently low dividends, and those that have large amounts of cash and marketable securities are good candidates for IRS review.

RESTRICTIVE COVENANTS

Restrictive covenants generally have more impact on dividend policy than do the legal constraints just discussed. These covenants are contained in bond indentures, term loans, short-term borrowing agreements, lease contracts, and preferred stock agreements.

These restrictions basically limit the total amount of dividends a firm can pay. Sometimes they may state that dividends cannot be paid at all until a firm's earnings have reached a specified level. For example, the term loan agreement that Atlas Corporation has with the Manufacturers Hanover Trust prohibits the payment of dividends without the prior approval of the bank.

In addition, *sinking fund requirements*, which state that a certain portion of a firm's cash flow must be set aside for the retirement of debt, sometimes limit dividend payments. Also, dividends may be prohibited if a firm's net working capital (current assets − current liabilities) or its current ratio does not exceed a certain predetermined level.

LIQUIDITY CONSIDERATIONS

Dividend payments are cash outflows. Thus, the more liquid a firm is, the more able it is to pay dividends. Even if a firm has a past record of high earnings that have been reinvested, resulting in a large retained earnings balance, it may not be able to pay dividends unless it has sufficient liquid assets, primarily cash.[2] Liquidity is likely to be a problem during a business downturn, when both profits and cash flows often decline. Rapidly growing firms with many profitable investment opportunities often find it difficult to maintain adequate liquidity and pay dividends at the same time.

BORROWING CAPACITY AND ACCESS TO THE CAPITAL MARKETS

Liquidity is desirable for a number of reasons. Specifically, it provides protection in the event of a financial crisis. It also provides the flexibility needed to take advantage of unusual financial and investment opportunities. There are other ways of achieving this flexibility and security, however. For example, companies frequently establish lines of credit and revolving credit agree-

---

[2]For example, John A. Brittain found that corporate dividend payments are positively related to a firm's liquidity. See John A. Brittain. *Corporate Dividend Policy*. Washington, D. C.: Brookings, 1966, pp. 184–187.

ments with banks, allowing them to borrow on short notice.[3] Large well-established firms are usually able to go directly to credit markets with either a bond issue or a sale of commercial paper. The more access a firm has to these external sources of funds, the better able it will be to make dividend payments.

A small firm whose stock is closely held and infrequently traded often finds it difficult (or undesirable) to sell new equity shares in the markets. As a result, retained earnings are the only source of new equity. When a firm of this type is faced with desirable investment opportunities, the payment of dividends is often inconsistent with the objective of maximizing the value of the firm.

EARNINGS STABILITY

Most large widely held firms are reluctant to lower their dividend payments, even in times of financial stress. Thus, a firm with a history of stable earnings is usually more willing to pay a higher dividend than a firm with erratic earnings.

A firm whose cash flows have been more or less constant over the years can be fairly confident about its future and frequently reflects this confidence in higher dividend payments.

GROWTH PROSPECTS

A rapidly growing firm usually has a substantial need for funds to finance the abundance of attractive investment opportunities. Instead of paying large dividends and then attempting to sell new shares to raise the equity investment capital it needs, this type of firm usually retains larger portions of its earnings and avoids the expense and inconvenience of public stock offerings.

INFLATION

In an inflationary environment, funds generated by depreciation are often not sufficient to replace a firm's assets as they become obsolete. Under these circumstances a firm may be forced to retain a higher percentage of earnings to maintain the earning power of its asset base.

Inflation also has an impact on a firm's working capital needs. In an atmosphere of rising prices, *actual* dollars invested in inventories and accounts receivable tend to increase in order to support the same *physical* volume of business.[4] And, because the dollar amounts of accounts payable and other payables requiring cash outlays are higher with rising prices, transaction cash balances normally have to be increased. Thus, inflation can force a firm to retain more earnings as it attempts to maintain its same relative preinflation working capital position.

---

[3]See Chapter 22 for a more detailed discussion of this topic.

[4]The ultimate impact of inflation on a firm's liquidity depends on whether or not the firm is able to pass these higher costs on to its customers in the form of higher prices.

SHAREHOLDER PREFERENCES

In a closely held corporation with relatively few stockholders, management may be able to set dividends according to the preferences of its stockholders. For example, assume that the majority of a firm's stockholders are in high marginal tax brackets. They probably favor a policy of high earnings retention, resulting in eventual capital gains (which are taxed at substantially lower rates than cash dividends), over a high payout dividend policy. However, high earnings retention implies that the firm has enough acceptable capital investment opportunities to justify the low payout dividend policy. In addition, recall that the IRS does not permit corporations to retain excessive earnings if they have no legitimate investment opportunities. Also, a policy of high retention when investment opportunities are not available is inconsistent with the objective of maximizing shareholder wealth.

In a large corporation whose shares are widely held, it is nearly impossible for a financial manager to take individual shareholders' preferences into account when setting dividend policy. Some wealthy stockholders prefer retention and capital gains, while other stockholders who are in lower marginal tax brackets, or who depend upon dividends as a source of current income, prefer a higher dividend rate. Therefore, when a firm's ownership is diverse, management should consider investment opportunities, cash flow needs, access to the financial markets, and other related factors when setting dividend policy. Those stockholders who do not find this policy acceptable can sell their shares and buy stock in other firms that are more attractive to them.

It has been argued that firms tend to develop their own "clientele" of investors (this is known in finance as the "clientele effect"). Some companies, such as public utilities, which typically pay out 70 percent or more of earnings as dividends, have traditionally attracted investors who desire a high dividend yield, while growth firms, like Diebold (which recently has had a dividend payout ratio of 17 percent), have tended to attract investors who prefer retention and possible capital gains.

PROTECTION AGAINST DILUTION

If a firm adopts a policy of paying out a large percentage of its annual earnings as dividends, it may need to sell new shares of stock from time to time to raise the equity capital needed to invest in potentially profitable projects. If existing investors do not or cannot acquire a proportionate share of the new issue, controlling interest in the firm is *diluted*. Some firms choose to retain more of their earnings and pay out lower dividends rather than risk dilution.

There are alternatives to high earnings retention, however; one of these involves raising external capital in the form of debt. This increases the financial risk of the firm, however, ultimately raising the cost of equity capital and lowering share prices.[5] If the firm feels that it already has an optimal capital structure, a policy of obtaining all external capital in the form of debt is likely to be counterproductive, unless sufficient new equity capital is retained or acquired in the capital markets to offset the increased debt.

---

[5]See Chapters 4, 12, and 13.

DIVIDEND POLICY AND FIRM VALUE

There are two major schools of thought among finance scholars regarding the effect dividend policy has on a firm's value. While Merton Miller and Franco Modigliani argue that dividend policy does not have a significant effect on a firm's value,[6] Myron Gordon, David Durand, and John Lintner argue that it does.[7] Each of these viewpoints is discussed in the following sections.

ARGUMENTS FOR THE IRRELEVANCE OF DIVIDENDS

The group led by Miller and Modigliani (MM) contends that a firm's value is determined solely by its investment decisions, and that the dividend payout ratio is a mere detail. They maintain that the effect of any particular dividend policy can be exactly offset by other forms of financing, such as the sale of new common equity shares. This argument depends on a number of key assumptions, however, including the following:

- *No taxes.* Under this assumption, investors are indifferent about whether they receive either dividend income or capital gains income.

- *No transaction costs.* This assumption implies that investors in the securities of firms paying small or no dividends can sell (at no cost) any number of shares they wish in order to convert capital gains into current income.

- *No flotation costs.* If firms did not have to pay flotation costs on the issue of new securities, they could acquire needed equity capital at the same cost, regardless of whether they retained their past earnings or paid them out as dividends. The payment of dividends sometimes results in the need for periodic sales of new stock.

- *Existence of a fixed investment policy.* According to MM, the firm's investment policy is not affected by its dividend policy. Furthermore, MM claim that it is investment policy, *not* dividend policy, that really determines a firm's value.

MM realize that there is considerable empirical evidence that changes in dividend policy do influence stock prices. As discussed in this chapter, many firms favor a policy of reasonably stable dividends. An increase in dividends conveys a certain type of *information* to the shareholders—namely, that management expects future earnings to be higher. Similarly, a cut in dividends is viewed as conveying unfavorable information about the firm's earnings prospects. MM argue that this *informational content* of dividend policy influences share prices, and *not* the pattern of dividend payments *per se.*

[6]Merton Miller and Franco Modigliani. "Dividend Policy, Growth and the Valuation of Shares." *Journal of Business* 34 (Oct. 1961): 411–433.

[7]Myron Gordon. "The Savings, Investment and Valuation of a Corporation." *Review of Economics and Statistics* (Feb. 1962): 37–51; Myron Gordon. *The Investment, Financing and Valuation of the Corporation.* Homewood, Ill.: Irwin, 1962; David Durand. "Bank Stocks and the Analysis of Covariance." *Econometrica* (Jan. 1955): 30–45; John Lintner. "Dividends, Earnings, Leverage, Stock Prices and the Supply of Capital to Corporations." *Review of Economics and Statistics* (Aug. 1962): 243–269.

Furthermore, MM argue that each firm tends to develop its own clientele of investors. For example, investors who seek capital gains income will be attracted to low dividend payout securities, whereas investors who favor large current income—in other words, high dividends—will be attracted to high dividend payout securities. Thus, a firm that changes its dividend policy could lose some stockholders to other firms with a more appealing dividend policy. This, in turn, may cause a temporary reduction in the price of the firm's stock. Other investors, however, who prefer the newly adopted dividend policy will view the firm as being undervalued and will purchase more shares. In the MM world, these transactions occur instantaneously and at no cost to the investor, the net result being that a stock's value remains unchanged.

ARGUMENTS FOR THE
RELEVANCE OF DIVIDENDS

Scholars belonging to the second school of thought argue that share values are indeed influenced by the division of earnings between dividends and retention. Basically, they contend that the MM propositions are reasonable—given MM's restrictive assumptions—but that dividend policy becomes important once these assumptions are removed.

Specifically, Gordon asserts that shareholders who are risk averse may prefer some dividends over the promise of future capital gains, because dividends are regular, certain returns, while future capital gains are less certain. According to Gordon, dividends reduce investors' uncertainty, causing them to discount a firm's future earnings at a lower rate, thereby increasing the firm's value. In contrast, failure to pay dividends increases investors' uncertainty, which raises the discount rate and lowers share prices. Although there is some empirical evidence in support of this argument, it is difficult to decide which is more valid—the MM informational content of dividends approach or the Gordon uncertainty resolution approach.

Of course, if the assumption of no transaction costs for investors is removed, then investors care whether they are paid cash dividends or receive capital gains. In the MM world, investors who own stocks paying low or no dividends could periodically sell a portion of their holdings to satisfy current income requirements. In actuality, however, brokerage charges and odd-lot differentials make such liquidations expensive and imperfect substitutes for regular dividend payments.

Removal of the no-tax assumption also makes a difference to shareholders, since capital gains are taxed at a lower rate than dividends, and capital gains taxes may be deferred until the stock is sold. In his study of dividend policy from 1920 to 1960, John A. Brittain found evidence in support of this proposition.[8] In general, he found that rising tax rates tend to reduce dividend payout rates.

The existence of flotation costs on new equity sales also tends to make earnings retention more desirable. Given a firm's investment policy, the payout of earnings the firm needs for investments requires it to raise external

[8]John A. Brittain. *op. cit.*, especially chap. 4.

420

equity. External equity is more expensive, however, because of flotation costs. Thus, the use of external equity will raise the firm's cost of capital and reduce the value of the firm. In addition, the cost of selling small issues of equity to meet investment needs is likely to be prohibitively high for most firms. Thus, firms that have sufficient investment opportunities to profitably utilize their retained funds tend to favor retention.[9]

Many practitioners believe that dividends are important, both for their informational content and because external equity capital is more expensive than retained equity. Thus, when establishing an optimal dividend policy, a firm should consider shareholder preferences along with investment opportunities and the relative cost of retained equity versus externally raised equity.

DIVIDEND POLICIES

It has been shown that there are a number of practical considerations that influence a firm's board of directors in determining an "optimal" dividend policy. Next, several alternative dividend strategies are discussed.

PASSIVE RESIDUAL POLICY

The passive residual policy suggests that a firm should retain its earnings as long as it has investment opportunities that promise higher rates of return than the required rate. For example, assume a firm's shareholders could invest their dividends in stocks of similar risk with an expected rate of return (dividends plus capital gains) of 18 percent. This 18 percent figure, then, would constitute the required rate of return on the firm's retained earnings.[10] As long as the firm can invest these earnings to earn more than this required rate, it should not pay dividends (according to the passive residual policy), since such payments would require either that the firm forgo some acceptable investment opportunities or raise necessary equity capital in the more expensive external capital markets.

Interpreted literally, the residual theory implies that dividend payments will vary from year to year, depending on available investment opportunities. There is, however, strong evidence that most firms try to maintain a rather stable dividend payment record over time. However, this does not mean that firms ignore the principles of the residual theory in making their dividend decisions, because dividends can be smoothed out from year to year in two ways.[11] First, a firm can choose to retain a larger percentage of earnings dur-

---

[9]This argument provides the basis for the passive residual or marginal theory of dividends discussed later in this chapter.

[10]This is the rate of return that must be earned on the equity-financed portion of new investments. To earn this return on equity, new investments must earn an overall rate of return equal to the weighted cost of capital—reflecting the fact that all investments are made with a mix of debt and equity funds in the proportions of the target capital structure.

[11]Robert C. Higgins. "The Corporate Dividend-Saving Decision." *Journal of Financial and Quantitative Analysis* (March 1972): 1531–1538, provides empirical support for the view that each period's dividends are a function of longer-term trends.

ing years when funding needs are large. If the firm continues to grow, it can manage to do this without reducing the dollar amount of the dividend. Second, a firm can borrow the funds it needs, temporarily raise its debt-to-equity ratio, and avoid a dividend cut in this way. Because issue costs are lower for large offerings of long-term debt, long-term debt capital tends to be raised in large, lumpy sums. If a firm has many good investment opportunities available to it during a particular year, this type of borrowing is preferable to cutting back on dividends. The firm will need to retain earnings in future years to bring its debt-to-equity ratio back in line. A firm that has many good investment opportunities for a number of years may eventually be forced to cut its dividend and/or sell new equity shares to meet financing requirements and maintain an optimal capital structure.

The residual theory also suggests that "growth" firms will normally have lower dividend payout ratios than firms in mature nongrowth industries. For example, many public utilities, such as American Electric Power, Potomac Electric Power, and Public Service Company of New Mexico, tend to have rather high payout ratios. In contrast, growth firms like Digital Equipment and Litton Industries tend to have rather low payout ratios. Table 14–2 summarizes the recent dividend payout ratios for these firms.

STABLE DOLLAR DIVIDEND POLICY

There is much evidence to indicate that most firms—and stockholders—prefer reasonably stable dividend policies. This stability is characterized by a rather strong reluctance to reduce the dollar amount of dividends from one period to the next. Similarly, increases in the dollar dividend rate are normally not made until the firm's management is satisfied that future earnings will be high enough to justify the larger dividend. Thus, while dividend rates tend to follow increases in earnings, they also tend to lag behind them to a certain degree.

Figure 14–1 illustrates the relationship between corporate dividends and profits since 1929. It is apparent from this chart that aggregate dividend payments fluctuate much less widely than corporate earnings do. There has been a strong upward trend in the amount of dividends paid, with very few years showing significant reductions. This is in sharp contrast to the more erratic record of corporate earnings. Note, for example, that during the Great Depression (for example, 1933), reluctance to reduce dividend payments resulted in

TABLE 14–2   Recent Dividend Payout Ratios for Six Firms

Firm	Dividend Payout Ratio (%)
American Electric Power	95
Potomac Electric Power	74
Public Service Company of New Mexico	80
K-Mart	54
Litton Industries	17
Digital Equipment	0

SOURCE: Annual reports of individual companies.

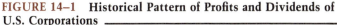

FIGURE 14–1 **Historical Pattern of Profits and Dividends of U.S. Corporations**

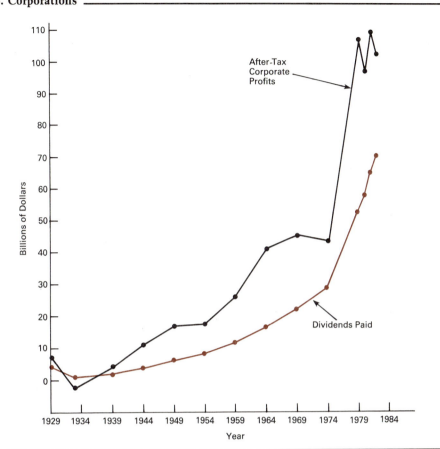

SOURCE: Economic Report of the President, 1983.

total corporate dividends *exceeding* total corporate earnings. Between 1931 and 1933, in fact, many firms continued to pay dividends in spite of overall negative earnings.

More specifically, Figure 14–2 shows the dividend and earnings history of the Owens-Corning Company. Once again, it can be seen that there has been an upward trend in dividends over time. It is clear, however, that dividend increases tend to lag earnings increases. Annual dividend payments are also more stable than earnings figures. Note, for instance, the dramatic growth in earnings in 1976, 1977, and 1978, which resulted from the increased demand for fiberglass insulating products, and compare this with the very modest increase in dividends during these years. When earnings declined in 1980, 1981, and 1982, the $1.20 dividend rate was maintained.

There are many reasons why investors prefer stable dividends. For instance, many investors feel that dividend changes possess *informational content*— they equate changes in a firm's dividend levels with profitability. A cut in dividends may be interpreted to indicate that the firm's long-run profit poten-

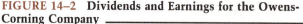

FIGURE 14–2   Dividends and Earnings for the Owens-Corning Company

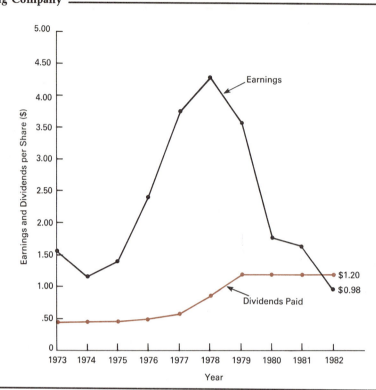

SOURCE: Annual Reports for Owens-Corning Company.

tial has declined. Similarly, a dividend increase is seen as a verification of the expectation that future profits will increase.[12]

In addition, many shareholders need and depend on a constant stream of dividends for their cash income requirements. While they can sell off some of their shares as an alternative source of current income, associated transaction costs and odd-lot charges make this an imperfect substitute for steady dividend income.

Some managers feel that a stable and growing dividend policy tends to reduce investor uncertainty concerning future dividend streams. They believe investors will pay a higher price for the stock of a firm that pays stable dividends, thereby reducing the firm's cost of equity.

And, finally, stable dividends are legally desirable. Many regulated financial institutions—such as bank trust departments, pension funds, and insurance companies—are limited as to the types of common stock they are allowed to own. To qualify for inclusion in these "legal lists," a firm must have a record of continuous and stable dividends. The failure to pay a dividend or the reduction of a dividend amount can result in removal from these lists. This, in

[12]Sometimes, however, an increase in a firm's dividend payout ratio may be interpreted to mean the firm no longer has a large number of high-return investment opportunities available to it.

turn, reduces the potential market for the firm's shares and may lead to price declines. For example, in 1982 (a very bad year for farm equipment producers), John Deere experienced a dramatic decline in earnings (97 percent in the second quarter alone). In spite of projected earnings of only $1.00 per share for the year, the company was expected to continue paying at the $2.00 per share yearly rate to preserve its 26-year record of no dividend cuts.

OTHER DIVIDEND PAYMENT POLICIES

Some firms have adopted a *constant payout ratio* dividend policy. A firm that uses this approach pays out a certain percentage of each year's earnings—for example, 40 percent—as dividends. If the firm's earnings vary substantially from year to year, dividends also will fluctuate. (The late Penn Central Company had adopted this type of dividend payout policy at one time.)

As shown in Table 14-3, aggregate dividend payout ratios for U. S. corporations generally have averaged in the 40 to 50 percent range, although recent (1980 to 1982) figures have been in excess of 60 percent.

This finding supports the notion that firms try to maintain fairly constant payout ratios over time. On a year-to-year basis, however, these payout ratios have varied substantially. For example, the aggregate payout ratio was about 63 percent during 1970, a recession year, and only 31 percent during 1948, a year of relative prosperity. Because of the reluctance to reduce dividends, payout ratios tend to increase when profits are depressed and decrease as profits increase.

Other firms choose to pay a *small regular quarterly dividend plus year-end extras.* This policy is especially well suited for a firm with a volatile earnings record, volatile year-to-year cash needs, or both. Even when earnings are low, the firm's investors can count on their regular dividend payments. When earnings are high and there is no immediate need for these excess funds, the firm declares a year-end extra dividend. This policy gives management the flexibility to retain funds as needed and still satisfy investors who desire to receive some "guaranteed" level of dividend payments. U.S. Steel, Du Pont, and General Motors have all followed this policy from time to time. Figure

TABLE 14–3   Aggregate Dividend Payout Ratios for U.S. Corporations

Years	Percentage of After-Tax Earnings Paid Out as Dividends
1940–1944	44.1
1945–1949	35.7
1950–1954	41.3
1955–1959	44.0
1960–1964	48.9
1965–1969	46.6
1970–1974	52.6
1975–1979	46.9
1980–1982	62.7

SOURCE: Economic Report of the President, 1983.

FIGURE 14–3   **Dividends and Earnings for General Motors** ————————————

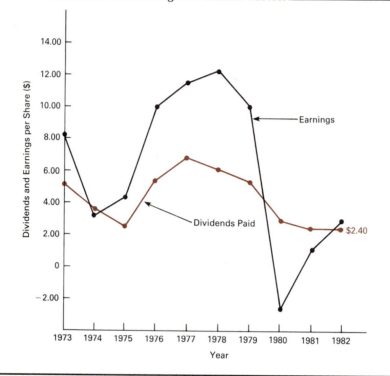

SOURCE: Annual Reports of General Motors.

14–3 shows how this policy has affected General Motors. While actual dividend payments have varied dramatically from year to year (compare this figure, for example, with Figure 14–2, which shows Owens-Corning's dividends), they have not fallen below $2.40, the "regular" rate in effect in 1975. (This regular rate was temporarily increased in 1979 but subsequently reduced back to $2.40.)

HOW DIVIDENDS ARE PAID

In most firms, the board of directors holds quarterly or semiannual meetings to evaluate the firm's past performance and decide the level of dividends to be paid during the next period. Changes in the amount of dividends paid have tended to be made rather infrequently—especially in firms that follow a stable dividend policy—and only after there is clear evidence that the firm's future earnings are likely to be either permanently higher or permanently lower than previously reported levels.

Most firms follow a dividend declaration and payment procedure similar to that outlined in the following paragraphs. This procedure usually revolves around a *declaration date*, an *ex-dividend date*, a *record date*, and a *payment date*.

Figure 14–4 is a time line that illustrates the Dickinson Company's dividend payment procedure. The firm's board of directors meets on the *decla-*

FIGURE 14–4   Key Dates in the Dickinson Company's Dividend Payment Procedure

April 15		May 11	May 15		May 29
Declaration Date		Ex–Dividend Date	Record Date		Payment Date

ration date—April 15—to consider future dividends. They *declare* a dividend on that date, which will be payable to *shareholders of record* on the *record date* May 15. On that date, the firm makes a list from its stock transfer books of those shareholders who are eligible to receive the declared dividend.

The major stock exchanges require four *business days* prior to the record date for recording ownership changes. The day that begins this 4-day period is called the *ex-dividend date*—in this case, May 11, as long as May 15 occurs on a Friday. Investors who purchase stock prior to May 11 are eligible for the May 15 dividend; investors who purchase stock on or after May 11 are not entitled to the dividend. On May 11, the ex-dividend date, the stock price can be expected to decline by the amount of the dividend, since this much value has been removed from the firm.

The *payment date* is normally 2 to 4 weeks after the record date; in this case, May 29. On this date, Dickinson mails dividend payments to the holders of record.

Figure 14–5 is a typical dividend announcement. It contains information

FIGURE 14–5   Sample Public Dividend Announcement

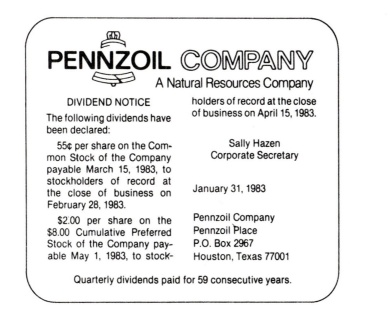

PENNZOIL COMPANY
A Natural Resources Company

DIVIDEND NOTICE

The following dividends have been declared:

55¢ per share on the Common Stock of the Company payable March 15, 1983, to stockholders of record at the close of business on February 28, 1983.

$2.00 per share on the $8.00 Cumulative Preferred Stock of the Company payable May 1, 1983, to stockholders of record at the close of business on April 15, 1983.

Sally Hazen
Corporate Secretary

January 31, 1983

Pennzoil Company
Pennzoil Place
P.O. Box 2967
Houston, Texas 77001

Quarterly dividends paid for 59 consecutive years.

on the company making the dividend, the payment date, the record date, and the declaration date. It also specifies the amount of the quarterly dividend payment per common share. And, because regular, stable dividend payments are important to many investors, it notes that the firm has made consecutive quarterly dividend payments for 59 years.

STOCK DIVIDENDS

A stock dividend is the payment of additional shares of stock to common stockholders. It involves making a transfer from the retained earnings account to the other stockholders' equity accounts.

For example, the Colonial Copies Company has the following common stockholders' equity:

Pre–Stock Dividend Common Stockholders' Equity	
Common stock ($5 par, 100,000 shares)	$ 500,000
Contributed capital in excess of par	1,000,000
Retained earnings	5,000,000
Total common stockholders' equity	$6,500,000

Suppose the firm declares a 10 percent stock dividend and existing shareholders receive 10,000 (10% × 100,000) new shares. Since stock dividend accounting is usually based on the predividend market price, a total of $200,000 (10,000 shares × an assumed market price of $20 per share) is transferred from the firm's retained earnings account to the other stockholders' equity accounts. Of this $200,000, $50,000 ($5 par × 10,000 shares) is added to the common stock account, while the remaining $150,000 is added to the contributed capital in excess of par account. Following the stock dividend, Colonial has the following common stockholders' equity:

Post–Stock Dividend Common Stockholders' Equity	
Common stock ($5 par, 110,000 shares)	$ 550,000
Contributed capital in excess of par	1,150,000
Retained earnings	4,800,000
Total common stockholders' equity	$6,500,000

The net effect of this transaction is to increase the number of outstanding shares and to redistribute funds among the firm's capital accounts. The firm's total stockholders' equity remains unchanged, and each shareholder's proportionate claim to the firm's earnings remains constant. For example, if Colonial Copies Company has 100,000 shares outstanding prior to a 10 percent stock dividend, and its total earnings are $200,000 ($2 per share), a stockholder who owns 100 shares has a claim on $200 of the firm's earnings. Following the 10 percent stock dividend, earnings per share decline to $1.82 ($200,000/110,000 shares). The stockholder who originally owned 100 shares now has 110 shares but continues to have a claim on only $200 (110 shares × $1.82 per share) of the firm's earnings.

Because each shareholder's proportionate claim on a firm's net worth and earnings remains unchanged in a stock dividend, the market price of each share of stock should decline in proportion to the number of new shares issued. In the Colonial Copies example, a $20 pre–stock dividend price should result in a post–stock dividend price decline to $18.18:

$$\text{Post–stock dividend price} = \frac{\text{Original price}}{1 + \dfrac{\text{Percent stock}}{\text{dividend rate}}} = \frac{\$20}{1 + 0.10}$$

$$= \$18.18 \, .$$

If a stockholder's wealth prior to the dividend is $2,000 (100 shares × $20 per share), postdividend wealth also should remain at $2,000 (110 shares × $18.18 per share).

In essence, all a stock dividend does is increase the number of pieces of paper in the stockholders' hands. Nevertheless, there are a number of reasons why firms declare stock dividends. First, a stock dividend may have the effect of broadening the ownership of a firm's shares, since existing shareholders often sell their stock dividends.[13] Second, in the case of a firm that already pays a cash dividend, a stock dividend results in an effective increase in cash dividends, providing that the per-share dividend rate is not reduced. (It is rare for a firm to declare a stock dividend and reduce its cash dividend rate at the same time.) And, finally, the declaration of stock dividends effectively lowers the per-share price of a stock, thereby possibly broadening its investment appeal. Investors seem to prefer stocks selling in approximately the $15 to $70 price range, since more investors will be financially capable of purchasing 100-share round lots.[14] Round lots of 100 shares are more desirable for investors to own because there are lower transactions costs associated with their purchase and sale.

STOCK SPLITS

Stock splits are similar to stock dividends in that they have the effect of increasing the number of shares of stock outstanding and reducing the price

---

[13]See C. Austin Barker, "Evaluation of Stock Dividends." *Harvard Business Review* (July–Aug. 1958): 99–114, for an empirical confirmation of this point.

[14]For an empirical view of the effects of stock dividends and splits on share values, see C. Austin Barker. *op. cit.;* also Keith B. Johnson. "Stock Splits and Price Change." *Journal of Finance* (Dec. 1966): 675–686; W. H. Hausman, R. R. West, and J. A. Langay. "Stock Splits, Price Changes and Trading Profits: A Synthesis." *Journal of Business* (Jan. 1971): 69–77; E. Fama, R. Fisher, M. Jensen, and R. Roll. "The Adjustment of Stock Prices to New Information." *International Economic Review* (Feb. 1969): 1–21.

of each outstanding share. From an accounting standpoint, stock splits are accomplished by reducing the par value of existing shares of stock and increasing the number of shares outstanding. For example, in a 2-for-1 stock split, the number of shares would be doubled. Although stock splits have an impact similar to stock dividends, they are normally not considered an element of a firm's dividend policy. Therefore, they are discussed in more detail in Chapter 16.

SHARE REPURCHASES AS DIVIDEND DECISIONS

According to the residual theory of dividend policy, a firm that has more funds than it needs for investments should pay a cash dividend to shareholders. Some firms, however, prefer to repurchase outstanding shares rather than pay cash dividends.

Firms carry out share repurchase programs in a number of ways. For example, a company may buy directly from its stockholders in what is termed a *tender offer*, or it may purchase the stock in the open market, or it may privately negotiate purchases from large holders, such as institutions.

Repurchased shares become known as *treasury stock*. Treasury stock is often used to facilitate mergers and acquisitions; to satisfy the conversion provisions of some preferred stock and debentures, as well as the exercise of warrants; and to meet the need for new shares in executive stock options and employee stock purchase plans. From the stockholders' perspective, share repurchases increase earnings per share for the remaining outstanding shares and also increase stock prices, assuming that investors continue to apply the same *price to earnings (P/E) multiple* to the earnings per share before and after repurchase.[15] The P/E multiple is equal to the price per share divided by the earnings per share. For example, if a stock sells for $40 per share and earns $8 per share, its P/E multiple is 5 times (40/8). The P/E multiple indicates the value placed by investors on a dollar of a firm's earnings. It is influenced by a number of factors, including earnings prospects and investors' perceptions regarding a firm's risk.

For example, the Jetzon Corporation has earnings of $5 million and 1 million shares currently outstanding. The company plans to distribute $2 million—in either the form of cash dividends or share repurchases. The market price of the stock is $30 (after accounting for the impact of the expected $2 dividend distribution.)

Assume that the firm decides to repurchase some of its shares by making a tender offer to acquire 62,500 shares at $32 per share ($32 × 62,500 = $2 million). How will this affect the remaining stockholders? If the P/E multiple remains the same before and after the repurchase (P/E = $30/$5, or 6 times), the value of the shares before and after repurchase will be as follows:

---

[15]If a stock repurchase results in a substantial increase in the debt-to-equity ratio, the new P/E multiple may be lower because of increased financial risk.

	Before Repurchase	After Repurchase
Net earnings	$5,000,000	$5,000,000
Shares outstanding	1,000,000	937,500
Earnings per share	$5.00	$5.33
Price-earnings ratio	6×	6×
Market price (ex-dividend)	$30	$32
Expected dividend	$2	$0

If the firm had chosen to declare a cash dividend instead, shareholder wealth would have been $32 per share ($30 ex-dividend price + $2 dividend). The repurchase of $2 million worth of shares still results in shareholder wealth of $32, but $2 of this total represents capital gains, which are taxed at a lower rate. Thus, stockholders who prefer current income will favor cash dividends, whereas those who prefer capital gains will favor share repurchases.[16]

Normally a firm will announce its intent to buy back some of its own shares so that investors will know why there is sudden additional trading in the stock. An announcement of repurchase is also useful to current shareholders, who may not want to sell their shares before they have had an opportunity to receive any capital gains expected to result from the repurchase

FIGURE 14–6 Sample Share Repurchase Announcement

---

[16]In addition to the lower tax rate on capital gains, capital gains have the benefit of permitting the investor to decide *when* these gains are taken. This permits the investor to postpone any tax from the repurchase transaction until sometime in the future.

program. Figure 14–6 is an example of a repurchase announcement for an employee stock purchase plan.

Although a stock repurchase seems like a desirable way of distributing a firm's earnings, repurchases are deterred to a large degree by the IRS. Specifically, the IRS will not permit a firm to follow a policy of regular stock repurchases as an alternative to cash dividends, because repurchase plans convert cash dividends (which are taxed at an ordinary rate) to capital gains (which are taxed at a lower rate). The IRS looks upon regular repurchases as essentially equivalent to cash dividends and requires that they be taxed accordingly.

SUMMARY

- *Dividend policy* determines the ultimate distribution of a firm's earnings between retention (reinvestment) and cash dividend payments to stockholders. Retained earnings provide investors with a source of potential future earnings growth, whereas dividends provide them with a current distribution.

- A number of factors influence a firm's choice of dividend policy. These include the following:

1. Legal constraints prohibiting dividends that impair capital.
2. Tax constraints prohibiting the excess accumulation of profits.
3. Restrictive covenants, bond indentures, and other financing agreements.
4. The need for liquidity.
5. Borrowing capacity and access to the capital markets.
6. Earnings stability.
7. Capital expansion opportunities.
8. Inflation.

Shareholders' preferences also may influence a firm's choice of dividend policy. These are determined by stockholders' tax positions and their desire to maintain control of the firm.

Some of these factors favor high dividends, while others imply a lower payout policy. The board of directors should weigh these factors in each instance and arrive at the best possible dividend policy.
- Under a restrictive set of assumptions articulated by Miller and Modigliani (MM), the value of a firm is solely dependent on its investment decisions. Under these conditions, dividend policy does not affect the value of the firm. Once the MM assumptions are removed, dividend policy may affect firm value because of the informational content of dividends and because external equity capital is more expensive to acquire than retained earnings.

- There are a number of alternative dividend policies, including the following:

1. The passive residual approach.
2. The stable dollar dividend approach.

3. The constant payout ratio approach.

4. The policy of paying a small, regular dividend plus year-end extras.

There is ample evidence to indicate that many firms favor a stable dividend policy.

- *Stock dividends* are sometimes used in lieu of (and in conjunction with) cash dividends. The net effect of stock dividends is to leave the total value of the firm unchanged while increasing the number of shares outstanding and broadening the ownership base.

- Some firms employ *share repurchase plans* instead of paying cash dividends. Although the purchase of *treasury stock* should not affect before-tax shareholder wealth, repurchases do convert shareholder benefits from ordinary income (dividends) to capital gains. Thus, the IRS imposes certain limitations on share repurchases.

Stock Splits and Stock Dividends·

Lawrence Ingrassia
Staff Reporter of The Wall Street Journal

Which is the better value—50 shares of BBDO International Inc. stock at $68 a share, or 100 shares at $34 a share?

There is no difference, you say? Try telling that to BBDO. On the advice of its investment bankers and of brokers who follow the company closely, BBDO recently declared a 2-for-1 stock split.

The reason is investor psychology. Individuals who play the market prefer stocks that aren't too expensive; and at more than $60 a share, BBDO's stock was getting a bit costly. "We wanted to do what we could to make our stock attractive to investors, and the 'right' trading range is $20 to $40 a share," explains Steve Kahler, executive vice president of BBDO, an advertising holding company.

A flurry of stock splits and stock dividends is expected this year because the bull market has pushed many stock prices out of the trading range preferred by individual investors. Procter & Gamble Co., Dun & Bradstreet Corp., Dow Jones & Co., Network Systems Corp., Wallace Computer Service Inc. and Intergraph Corp. are just a few of the companies that have declared or proposed stock splits in the past couple of months.

"By the second half of this year, I expect to see splitting activity start picking up, and it probably will be quite heavy in 1984," predicts Stan West, vice president of the New York Stock Exchange's business-research division. Historically, he notes, stock splits and stock dividends increase six months to a year after a bull market.

SIGN OF BULLISHNESS

Stock splits can accomplish a variety of corporate purposes. They generally increase the number of shareholders and the trading volume, as well as signal that management is bullish about a company's prospects.

But mostly, a split caters to the psychology of shareholders. For one thing, it makes them feel as if they're getting something—more shares—for nothing.

And, by lowering the per-share price, splits make it easier for individuals to buy round lots of 100 shares. "Small investors don't like to buy 35 shares or 72 shares—they like to buy 100 shares so they feel they're big shots," says Robert Stovall, a senior vice president at Dean Witter Reynolds Inc.

Individual investors also firmly believe that stocks that split are good buys, although it is a matter of debate whether a stock split or stock dividend actually improves a stock's price.

In themselves, stock splits or stock dividends don't change the value of the investor's holdings. The owner gets additional shares, but the market price of the shares is reduced so that the total value of the holdings is the same when the split is effected. (The basic difference between a split and dividend is that in a split the par, or stated, value of the stock changes and in a dividend it doesn't.)

Studies of stocks that split disagree on whether splits lead to faster price gains. "The logic of a split is that it should have no effect. All you're doing is taking a piece of paper and tearing it up," says Eugene Fama, a professor of finance at the University of Chicago's Graduate School of Business. A 1970 study by Prof. Fama of New York Stock Exchange stocks that split from 1926 to 1960 showed that "a split per se had no effect on the price of a stock," although the simultaneous announcement of other good news—such as a dividend increase—can help a stock's price.

But in contrast to Prof. Fama's conclusions, a Big Board study found that stocks that split 3 for 2 or more from 1963 to 1980 "increased 2½ times faster (in price) than nonsplitting stocks in the seven years surrounding the split," the exchange's Mr. West says.

THE MARKET REACTS

The price of BBDO International's stock has increased to $68 a share from $61 a share bid in over-the-counter trading on Nov. 30, the day the company's board proposed the 2-for-1 split. "The market seemed to like it . . . but who knows whether (the increase) has to do with the split or not?" says Mr. Kahler, adding that BBDO also announced that it intended to raise its quarterly dividend and that last fall it got Chrysler Corp. as a new advertising account.

Walgreen Co. shareholders also fared well after a 2-for-1 split last February reduced the stock's price to $23 a share; it steadily rose to more than $50 a share. Happy with that performance, Walgreen declared a 100% stock dividend, payable Feb. 11.

But the split may be coincidental to the price increase, says Daniel

Stock Splits
And Dividends

Splits of 3-for-2 or More,
Dividends of 50% or More
By NYSE Companies

Source: New York Stock Exchange

435

Jorndt, vice president and treasurer of Walgreen. "There's a significant point that has to be made," Mr. Jorndt says. "Stocks that split are generally of companies that are doing well. So a company's earnings and prospects of future earnings tend to drive a stock toward a split. It's sort of the chicken or the egg deal. . . . A split in itself doesn't do anything."

Indeed, a split doesn't help a stock price if the company's economic fortunes take a turn for the worse. Weatherford International Inc., an oil-field-services concern, had a 3-for-2 split in April 1981, when the oil-drilling business still was booming. Weatherford's stock price has since slumped to $13 a share from the post-split price of nearly $25, and the main reason is the industrywide recession.

When considering their own portfolios, some corporate executives don't place much importance on stock splits. "As an individual investor, (a split) doesn't mean anything to me. If I want to buy a stock and it's at $50 a share, I will," says Richard Fisher, vice president for finance and treasurer at Network Systems. Nonetheless, the maker of high-speed computer communications equipment declared a 2-for-1 split, payable April 27, to reduce its stock price from around $40 a share to $20 a share. "Brokers have told us that the best place for stock to sell is the $15 to $25 range," he adds.

Stock splits, perhaps not coincidentally, are good for brokers. Not only do they generate interest and increase trading in a stock, but they also increase commissions in another way. Because of the way most commission schedules are set up in the brokerage business, there is a higher commission on a trade, of, say, 75 shares at $10 a share than on a trade of 10 shares at $75 a share, even though the dollar value of the trades is the same.

Splits also can serve a purpose for companies that have little stock outstanding or whose management owns a large amount of stock in the company. By splitting its stock, a company can increase the float, or amount of stock in the public's hands. Care Corp., a nursing-home operator, had a 4-for-1 split last week, partly because about 60% of the company's 500,000 shares outstanding were controlled by insiders and relatives, leaving only 200,000 shares for trading by others. In addition to lowering the stock price to around $20 a share, the split increased the float to 800,000 shares, notes Charles Bloom, vice president and treasurer. As a result, he adds, "there has been an increase in trading."

*Reprinted by permission of *The Wall Street Journal* © Dow Jones and Company, Inc. (1983). All Rights Reserved. (January 27, 1983), p. 56.

QUESTIONS AND TOPICS FOR DISCUSSION

1. What legal and tax restrictions limit the amount of cash dividends that may be paid by a firm?

2. What other "external" factors limit a firm's ability to pay cash dividends?

3. What is the likely impact of a highly inflationary economy on a firm's ability to

pay dividends? Would you expect this impact to be greater or smaller for a rapidly expanding firm? Why?

4. How can the "passive residual" view of dividend policy be reconciled with the tendency of most firms to maintain a constant or steadily growing dividend payment record?

5. Why do many managers prefer a stable dollar dividend policy to a policy of paying out a constant percentage of each year's earnings as dividends?

6. Under what circumstances would it make sense for a firm to borrow money in order to make its dividend payments?

7. Some people have suggested that it is irrational for a firm to pay dividends and sell new stock in the same year, since the cost of newly issued equity is greater than the cost of retained earnings. Do you agree? Why or why not?

8. Why do many firms choose to issue stock dividends? What is the value of a stock dividend to a shareholder?

9. What are the tax limitations on the practice of share repurchases as a regular dividend policy?

10. In the theoretical world of Miller and Modigliani, what role does dividend policy play in the determination of share values?

11. What role do most practitioners think dividend policy plays in determining share values?

PROBLEMS *

1. Jacobs Corporation earned $2 million after tax. The firm has 1.6 million shares of common stock outstanding.
   a. Compute the earnings per share of Jacobs.
   b. If Jacobs's dividend policy calls for a 40 percent payout ratio, what are the dividends per share?

2. Drew Financial Associates currently pays a quarterly dividend of 50 cents per share. This quarter's dividend will be paid to stockholders of record on Friday, February 22, 19X1. Drew has 200,000 common shares outstanding. The retained earnings account has a balance of $15 million before the dividend, and Drew holds $2.5 million in cash.
   a. What is the ex-dividend date for this quarter?
   b. Drew's stock traded for $22 per share the day prior to the ex-dividend date. What would you expect the stock price to open at on the ex-dividend date? Give some reasons why this might not occur.
   c. What is the effect of the dividend payment on Drew's cash, retained earnings, and total assets?

3. Winkie Baking has just announced a 100 percent stock dividend. The annual cash dividend per share was $2.40 before the stock dividend. Winkie intends to pay $1.40 per share on each of the new shares. Compute the percentage increase in the cash dividend rate that will accompany the stock dividend.

4. Wolverine Corporation plans to pay a $3 dividend per share on each of its 300,000 shares next year. Wolverine anticipates earnings of $6.25 per share over the year. If the company has a capital budget requiring an investment of $4 million over

*Problems in color have check answers provided at the end of the book.

the year and it desires to maintain its present debt to total assets (debt ratio) of 0.40, how much external equity must it raise? Assume Wolverine's capital structure includes only common equity and debt and that debt and equity will be the only sources of funds to finance capital projects over the year.

5. Tulia Dairy pays a $2.50 cash dividend and earns $5 per share. The cash dividend has recently been increased to $2.65 per share, *and* a 3 percent stock dividend has been declared. What is the effective rate of increase in the dividends for Tulia as a result of this action?

6. The Mori Egg Noodle Company has the following equity accounts on its balance sheet:

Common stock ($10 par, 200,000 shares)	$2,000,000
Contributed capital in excess of par	1,000,000
Retained earnings	4,000,000
Total common stockholders' equity	$7,000,000

   a. What is the maximum amount of dividends that may be paid by the Mori Company if the capital impairment provisions of state law are limited to the following?
      i. The par value of common stock.
      ii. The par value and the capital in excess of par accounts.
   b. What other factors may limit Mori's ability to pay dividends?

7. Champoux Hair Factory, Inc., has earnings before interest and taxes of $100,000. Annual interest amounts to $40,000, and annual depreciation is $40,000. Taxes are computed at a 40 percent rate. Existing bond obligations require the payment of $20,000 per year into a sinking fund.
   Champoux wishes to pay a $1 per-share dividend on the existing 20,000 shares. The firm's bond indenture prohibits the payment of dividends unless the cash flow (before dividends and sinking fund payments) is greater than the total of dividends, interest, and sinking fund obligations.
   a. Can Champoux pay the proposed dividend?
   b. What is the maximum dividend per share that may be paid?

8. Lenberg Lens Company believes in the "dividends as a residual" philosophy of dividend policy. This year's earnings are expected to total $5 million. Being a very conservative company, Lenberg is financed solely with common stock. The required rate of return on retained earnings is 12 percent, whereas the cost of newly raised capital is 14 percent because of flotation costs.
   a. If Lenberg has $3 million of investment projects having expected returns greater than 12 percent, what total amount of dividends should Lenberg pay?
   b. If Lenberg has $6 million of investment projects having expected returns greater than 14 percent, what total amount of dividends should Lenberg pay?
   c. What factors, other than its belief in the residual theory of dividends, should Lenberg consider in setting its dividend policy in Part b?

9. Phoenix Tool Company and Denver Tool Company have had a very similar record of earnings performance over the past 8 years. Both firms are in the same industry and, in fact, they compete directly with each other. The two firms have nearly identical capital structures. Phoenix has a policy of paying a constant 50 percent of each year's earnings as dividends, whereas Denver has sought to maintain a constant dollar dividend policy, with changes in the dollar dividend payment occurring infrequently. The record of the two companies follows:

	PHOENIX			DENVER		
Year	EPS	Dividend	Average Market Price	EPS	Dividend	Average Market Price
19X1	$2.00	$1.00	$20	$2.10	$0.75	$18
19X2	2.50	1.25	24	2.40	0.75	22
19X3	1.50	1.25	15	1.60	0.75	17
19X4	1.00	0.50	10	0.90	0.75	14
19X5	0.50	0.25	8	0.50	0.50	10
19X6	−1.25	nil	8	−1.10	0.50	10
19X7	1.00	0.50	10	1.10	0.75	14
19X8	1.50	0.75	14	1.45	0.75	17

The president of Phoenix wonders what accounts for Denver's current (19X8) higher stock price, in spite of the fact that Phoenix currently earns more per share than Denver and frequently has paid a higher dividend.

a. What factors can you cite that might account for this phenomenon?

b. What do you suggest as an optimal dividend policy for both Phoenix and Denver that might lead to increases in both of their share prices? What are the limitations of your suggestions?

10. The Emco Steel Company has experienced a slow (3 percent per year) but steady increase in earnings per share. The firm has consistently paid out an average of 75 percent of each year's earnings as dividends. The stock market evaluates Emco primarily on the basis of its dividend payout, since growth prospects are modest.

Emco's management presents a proposal to the board of directors that would require the outlay of $50 million to build a new plant in the rapidly expanding Florida market. The expected annual return on the investment in this plant is estimated to be in excess of 30 percent, more than twice the current company average. To finance this investment, a number of alternatives are being considered. They include the following:

a. Finance the expansion with externally raised equity.

b. Finance the expansion with 50 percent externally generated equity and 50 percent internally generated equity. This alternative would necessitate a dividend cut for this year only.

c. Finance the expansion with a mix of debt and equity similar to their current relative proportions in the capital structure. Under this alternative, dividends would not be cut. Rather, any equity needs in excess of that which could be provided internally would be raised through a sale of new common stock.

Evaluate these various financing alternatives with reference to their effects on the dividend policy and common stock values of the company.

11. The Sweet Times Candy Company has the following equity accounts on its balance sheet:

Common stock ($1 par, 500,000 shares)	$ 500,000
Contributed capital in excess of par	2,000,000
Retained earnings	13,000,000
Total common stockholders' equity	$15,500,000

The current market price of the firm's shares is $50.

439

a. If the firm declares a 10 percent stock dividend, what will be the impact on the firm's equity accounts?

b. If the firm currently pays no cash dividend, what is the impact of a 10 percent stock dividend on the wealth position of the firm's existing stockholders?

c. If the firm currently pays a cash dividend of $1 per share, and this per-share dividend rate does not change after the 10 percent stock dividend, what impact would you expect the stock dividend to have on the wealth position of existing shareholders?

12. Striker's Match Company reported the following financial data:

Net earnings	$3,000,000
Shares outstanding	1,000,000
Earnings per share	$3
Market price per share (ex-dividend)	$40
Expected dividend per share	$2

Striker is considering distributing $2 million to existing stockholders, either as cash dividends or through the repurchase of outstanding shares. The repurchase plan is favored by some of the company's wealthiest and most influential stockholders.

If the shares are repurchased, the company would make a tender offer for 47,619 shares at a price of $42. Alternatively, the firm could pay a $2 dividend, after the payment of which each share would sell for $40.

a. Ignoring taxes, what impact does the choice of a dividend payment or share repurchase plan have on the wealth position of the firm's shareholders?

b. If most shareholders are in a very high marginal tax bracket, which alternative is favored?

c. What are the limitations on the repurchase alternative as an element of the firm's dividend policy?

ADDITIONAL READINGS AND REFERENCES

Ben-Zion, Uri, and Shalit, Sol S. "Size, Leverage, and Dividend Record as Determinants of Equity Risk," *Journal of Finance* 30 (June 1975): 1015–1026.

Black, F., and Scholes, M. "The Effects of Dividend Yield and Dividend Policy on Common Stock Prices and Returns." *Journal of Financial Economics* 1 (May 1974): 1–22.

Elton, Edwin J., and Gruber, Martin J. "Marginal Stockholder Tax Rates and the Clientele Effect." *Review of Economics and Statistics* 52 (Feb. 1970): 68–74.

Fama, E., and Miller, M. *The Theory of Finance.* New York: Holt, Rinehart and Winston, 1972.

Friend, Irwin, and Puckett, Marshall. "Dividends and Stock Prices." *American Economic Review* 54 (Sept. 1964): 656–682.

Gordon, Myron J. "Dividends, Earnings and Stock Prices." *Review of Economics and Statistics* 41 (May 1959): 99–105.

Higgins, Robert C. "The Corporate Dividend-Savings Decision." *Journal of Financial and Quantitative Analysis* 7 (March 1972): 1527–1541.

Johnson, Keith B. "Stock Splits and Price Changes." *Journal of Finance* 21 (Dec. 1966): 675–686.

Lintner, J. "Distribution of Income of Corporations among Dividends, Retained Earnings and Taxes." *American Economic Review* (May 1956): 97–113.

Litzenberger, R. H., and Ramaswamy, K. "The Effect of Personal Taxes and Dividends on Capital Asset Prices: Theory and Empirical Evidence." *Journal of Financial Economics* (June 1979): 163–195.

Loomis, C. J. "A Case for Dropping Dividends." *Fortune Magazine* (June 1968).

Millar, James A., and Fielitz, Bruce D. "Stock-Split and Stock-Dividend Decisions." *Financial Management* 2 (Winter 1973): 35–45.

Miller, M. H., and Modigliani, F. "Dividend Policy, Growth and the Valuation of Shares." *Journal of Business* (Oct. 1961): 411–433.

___. "Some Estimates of the Cost of Capital to the Electric Utility Industry." *American Economic Review* 56 (June 1966): 333–391.

Norgaard, R., and Norgaard, C. "A Critical Examination of Share Repurchase." *Financial Management* (Spring 1974): 44–51.

Pettway, Richard H., and Malone, R. Phil. "Automatic Dividend Reinvestment Plans of Nonfinancial Corporations." *Financial Management* 2 (Winter 1973): 11–18.

Steward, Samuel S., Jr. "Should a Corporation Repurchase Its Own Stock?" *Journal of Finance* (June 1976): 911–921.

Walter, James E. "Dividend Policies and Common Stock Prices." *Journal of Finance* 11 (March 1956): 29–41.

___. *Dividend Policy and Enterprise Valuation.* Belmont, Calif.: Wadsworth Publishing Co., 1967.

Watts, Ross. "The Information Content of Dividends." *Journal of Business* 46 (April 1973): 191–211.

West, Richard R., and Brouilette, Alan B. "Reverse Stock Splits." *Financial Executive* 38 (Jan. 1970): 12–17.

PART SIX

Sources of Intermediate- and Long-Term Funds

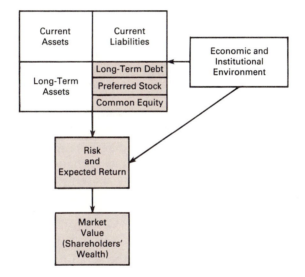

The decision to acquire long-term assets requires that sources of financing be arranged to fund these asset acquisitions. In this part of the book, the major sources of intermediate- and long-term financing are discussed. Chapter 15 deals with term loans and leasing. Chapter 16 looks at long-term debt, preferred stock, and common stock; Chapter 17 considers convertible securities and warrants. Choosing the right mix of financing alternatives can help a firm balance risk, increase returns, and thereby maximize shareholder wealth.

CHAPTER 15

Term Loans and Leases

A FINANCIAL DILEMMA

Billie Sol Estes: A Case of Insecure "Secured" Loans

In the late 1950s Billie Sol Estes, a West Texas fertilizer dealer and grain storage elevator operator, found that he was faced with growing liabilities to his major supplier, Commercial Solvents. To raise additional funds to continue his operation, he convinced a number of wealthy local farmers to buy ammonia storage tanks on credit from a firm that was secretly controlled by Estes.

Estes leased the tanks, and the lease payments were set equal to the loan payments he needed in order to pay for the tanks. The farmers borrowed about 80 percent of the cost of the tanks, and Estes reimbursed them for their 20 percent equity contribution in the purchase. Although some storage tanks were actually delivered, most of them were merely "phantom" tanks that Estes used to secure a number of loans. He then resold these loans to several financial institutions.

When the institutions came to check on the security of their loans, Estes merely showed them some of the few tanks he actually held. He accommodated those institutions who wanted to see the serial numbers on their tanks by simply screwing or welding correct serial numbers onto the existing tanks as they were needed.

When Estes's financial empire finally crumbled, the lending institutions with whom he was involved ended up losing in excess of $25 million on their so-called secured loans.

A truly secured loan depends on the character of the borrower and a program to carefully monitor the quality of the security. This chapter considers a number of intermediate-term sources of financing for a firm.

GLOSSARY OF NEW TERMS

Affirmative loan covenant a portion of a loan agreement that outlines actions a firm's management *agrees to take* as conditions for receiving the loan.

Amortization schedule   a schedule of periodic payments of interest and principal owed on a debt obligation.

Balloon loan   a loan that requires a large final payment greater than each of the periodic (principal and interest) payments.

Bullet loan   a loan that requires only the periodic payment of interest during the term of the loan, and a final single repayment of principal at maturity.

Chattel mortgage   a lien on personal property, such as machinery, as security for the repayment of a loan.

Compensating balance   a certain percentage of a loan balance that the borrower keeps on deposit with a bank as a requirement of a loan provided by the bank.

Conditional sales contract   a financing agreement in which the seller of a piece of equipment retains title until all payments have been made.

Direct lease   a lease that is initiated when a firm acquires the use of an asset that it did not previously own.

Financial lease   a *noncancelable* agreement that obligates the lessee to make payments to the lessor for a predetermined period of time. These payments are usually sufficient to amortize the full cost of the asset plus provide the lessor with a reasonable rate of return on the investment in the asset.

Lease   a contract that allows an individual or a firm to make economic use of an asset for a stated period of time without obtaining an ownership interest in it.

Lessee   the user and renter of the property in a lease transaction.

Lessor   the property owner who collects rental payments from the lessee in a lease transaction.

Leveraged lease   a type of financial lease in which the lessor borrows up to 80 percent of the cost of the leased asset on a nonrecourse basis from a group of lenders. The lessor receives the full tax benefits of ownership. This is also sometimes called a *third-party equity lease* or a *tax lease.*

Negative loan covenant   a portion of a loan agreement that outlines actions a firm's management *agrees not to take* during the term of the loan.

Operating lease   a *cancelable* lease agreement that provides the lessee with the use of an asset on a period-by-period basis. This is sometimes called a *service* or *maintenance lease,* especially if the lessor provides maintenance services as part of the lease contract.

Restrictive loan covenant   a portion of a loan agreement that limits the scope of certain actions a firm may take during the term of the loan.

Safe harbor lease   a special category of tax transfer leases created by the ERTA of 1981. These were phased out beginning in 1982 to be replaced by *finance leases.*

Sale and leaseback   a lease that is initiated when a firm sells an asset it owns to another firm and simultaneously leases the asset back for its own use.

Term loan   any debt obligation having an initial maturity between 1 and 10 years. This is often referred to as *intermediate-term credit.*

INTRODUCTION TO TERM LOANS

A *term loan,* or *intermediate-term credit,* is defined as any debt obligation having an initial maturity between 1 and 10 years. It lacks the permanency characteristic of long-term debt.

Term loans constitute the major source of intermediate-term financing. They are made available by a wide variety of financial intermediaries, including commercial banks, insurance companies, pension funds, small business investment companies, government agencies, and equipment suppliers. Since term loans are privately negotiated between the borrowing firm and the lending institution, they are less expensive than public offerings of common stock or bonds. The issuing firm in a public offering pays the registration and issue expenses necessary to sell the securities. For small- to moderate-sized offerings these expenses can be large in relation to the funds raised. For example, one study indicated that the total flotation cost as a percentage of the gross proceeds for a $500,000 debt issue was 8 percent; for a $500,000 common stock issue, it was about 16 percent. These costs dropped to 1.4 percent for a $10 million debt issue and 6.9 percent for a $10 million common stock issue.[1] Because of this potential cost advantage, term loans are well suited for financing small additions to plant facilities and equipment, such as a new piece of machinery, or moderate increases in working capital needs.

Term loans are also preferable to short-term loans, because they provide the borrower with a certain degree of security. Rather than having to be concerned about whether a short-term loan will be renewed, the borrower can have a term loan structured in such a way that the maturity coincides with the economic life of the asset being financed. Thus, the cash flows generated by the asset can service the loan without putting any additional financial strain on the borrower.

Terms loans can be used to finance a moderate increase in working capital under these circumstances:

- The cost of a public offering is too high.
- The firm intends to use the term debt only until its earnings are sufficient to amortize the loan.
- The desired increase is relatively long term but not permanent.

REPAYMENT PROVISIONS

A term loan agreement usually requires that the principal be *amortized* over the life of the loan. This means that the firm is required to pay off the loan in installments rather than in one lump sum. This has the effect of reducing the risk to the lender that the borrower will be unable to retire the loan in one lump sum when it comes due. Amortization of principal is also consis-

---

[1] For further information on issue costs, see Securities and Exchange Commission. *Cost of Flotation of Registered Equity Issues, 1963–1965.* Washington, D.C.: USGPO, 1979); Irwin Friend. *Investment Banking and the New Issues Market.* Cleveland: World Publishing, 1967. See also Chapter 16 of this text.

tent with the idea that term loans are not a permanent part of a firm's capital structure.

The amortization schedule of a term loan might require the firm to make equal quarterly, semiannual, or annual payments of principal and interest. For example, assume a firm borrows $100,000 payable over 8 years, with an interest rate of 9 percent per annum on the unpaid balance. The repayment schedule calls for eight equal annual payments, the first occurring at the end of year 1.

Equation 3.15 from Chapter 3 can be rewritten as follows:

$$PVAN = R(PVIFA_{i,n})$$

$$R = \frac{PVAN}{PVIFA_{i,n}}.$$

Given the present value of the annuity (PVAN) = $100,000, the interest rate (i) = 9 percent, the number of time periods (n) = 8, and the $PVIFA_{0.09,8}$ from Table IV, the annual payment, R, is computed as follows:

$$R = \frac{\$100,000}{5.535}$$

$$= \$18,067.$$

By making eight annual payments of $18,067 to the lender, the borrower will just pay off the loan and provide the lender with a 9 percent return. Table 15–1 shows the principal and interest for each year's annuity payment. (The "Calculator Applications" section in Chapter 3 illustrates the use of a financial calculator to compute a loan amortization schedule similar to the one in Table 15–1.)

TABLE 15–1   Sample Loan Amortization Schedule*

End of Year (1)	Annual Annuity Amount (2)	Interest† (3)	Principal Repayment‡ (4)	Remaining Balance (5)
0	$ 0	$ 0	$ 0	$100,000
1	18,067	9,000	9,067	90,933
2	18,067	8,183	9,884	81,049
3	18,067	7,294	10,773	70,276
4	18,067	6,324	11,743	58,533
5	18,067	5,267	12,800	45,733
6	18,067	4,116	13,951	31,782
7	18,067	2,860	15,207	16,575
8	18,067	1,492	16,575	0
	$144,536	$44,536	100,000	

*Figures in the table have been rounded. Rounding is done to yield a zero ending loan balance. If the table reported payments in terms of both dollars *and* cents, and if fractional cents were permitted, no rounding would be necessary.
†Interest each period is equal to 0.09 times the remaining balance from the previous period; for example, interest in year 1 equals 0.09 × $100,000 = $9,000, and interest in year 2 equals 0.09 × $90,933 = $8,183.
‡The principal repayment each period equals the annual annuity amount ($18,067) minus the per-period interest from Column 3.

Over the life of this loan the firm will make total payments of $144,536. Of this, $100,000 is the repayment of the principal, and the other $44,536 is interest. It is important to know what proportions of a loan payment are principal and interest, since interest payments are tax deductible.

In this example the repayment schedule calls for equal periodic payments to the lender consisting of both principal and interest. Other types of repayment schedules are also possible, including the following:

- The borrower might be required to make equal reductions in the principal outstanding each period, with the interest being computed on the remaining balance for each period.

- The borrower might be required to make equal periodic payments over the life of the loan that only partially amortize the loan, leaving a lump payment that falls due at the termination of the loan period (this is called a *balloon loan*).

- The borrower might be required to make a single principal payment at maturity while making periodic (usually quarterly) interest payments only over the life of the loan (this is called a *bullet loan*).[2]

INTEREST COSTS

The interest rate charged on a term loan depends on a number of factors, including the general level of interest rates in the economy, the size of the loan, the maturity of the loan, and the borrower's credit standing. Generally, interest rates on intermediate-term loans tend to be slightly higher than interest rates on short-term loans because of the higher risk assumed by the lender. Also, large term loans tend to have lower rates than small term loans, because the fixed costs associated with granting and administering a loan do not vary proportionately with the size of the loan. In addition, large borrowers often have better credit standings than small borrowers. An interest rate between 0.25 and 2.5 percent above the prime rate is common for term loans obtained from banks.

The interest rate on a small term loan is usually the same throughout the loan's lifetime. In contrast, many larger term loans specify a *variable* interest rate, which depends on the bank's prime lending rate. For example, if a loan is initially made at 0.5 percent above the prime rate, the loan agreement might specify that the interest charged on the remaining balance will continue to be 0.5 percent above the prevailing rate. Thus, whenever the prime rate is increased, the loan rate also increases; if the prime rate declines, so does the interest rate on the loan.

COMPENSATING BALANCES

It is not uncommon for a bank to require a borrowing firm to keep a percentage of its loan balance—for example, 20 percent—on deposit as a compensat-

---

[2]These three repayment patterns are illustrated in the "Problems" section at the end of this chapter.

ing balance. If this balance is greater than the amount the firm would normally keep on deposit with the bank, this requirement effectively increases the firm's cost of the loan.[3]

EQUITY PARTICIPATIONS

The interest rate charged on a term loan also may be influenced by a desire on the part of the lending institution to take an equity position (often called a "kicker") in the company as an additional form of compensation. This is usually accomplished through the issue of a *warrant* by the borrower to the lender. A warrant is an option to purchase a stated number of shares of a company's common stock at a specified price sometime in the future.[4] If the company prospers, the lending institution shares in this prosperity on an equity basis. The issuance of warrants in conjunction with a term loan is common when the loan has an above-normal level of risk but the lending institution feels the borrower has promising growth potential. Alternatively, the borrower may issue warrants to secure a more favorable lending rate.

SECURITY PROVISIONS AND PROTECTIVE COVENANTS

The security provisions and protective covenants specified by a term loan agreement are often determined by the borrower's credit standing: the weaker the credit standing, the more restrictive the protective covenants.

SECURITY PROVISIONS

In general, security requirements apply more often to intermediate-term loans than to short-term loans. This is due to the fact that longer-term loan contracts tend to have more default risk. Security provisions are also dependent on the size of the borrowing firm. For example, term loans to small firms tend to be secured more often than term loans to large firms.

The sources of security for a term loan include the following:

- An assignment of payments due under a specific contract.
- An assignment of a portion of the receivables or inventories.
- The use of a floating lien on inventories and receivables.
- A pledge of marketable securities held by the borrower.
- A mortgage on property, plant, or equipment held by the borrower.
- An assignment of the cash surrender value of a life insurance policy held by the borrower for its key executives.

---

[3]Compensating balances are discussed in more detail in Chapter 22.
[4]Chapter 17 contains a more complete discussion of warrants.

AFFIRMATIVE COVENANTS

An affirmative covenant is a portion of a loan agreement that outlines actions the borrowing firm *agrees to take* during the term of the loan. Typical affirmative covenants include the following:

- The borrower agrees to furnish periodic financial statements to the lender, including a balance sheet, income statement, and a sources and uses of funds statement. These may be furnished monthly, quarterly, or annually and are frequently required to be audited. Pro forma cash budgets and projections of the costs needed to complete contracts on hand also may be required.

- The borrower agrees to carry sufficient insurance to cover insurable business risk.

- The borrower agrees to maintain a minimum amount of net working capital (current assets − current liabilities).

- The borrower agrees to maintain management personnel who are acceptable to the financing institution.

NEGATIVE COVENANTS

A negative covenant outlines actions that the borrowing firm's management *agrees not to take* without prior written consent of the lender. Typical negative covenants include the following:

- The borrowing firm agrees not to pledge any of its assets as security to other lenders, as well as not to factor (sell) its receivables. This type of agreement is called a *negative pledge clause* and is found in nearly all unsecured loans. It is designed to keep other lenders from interfering with the immediate lender's claims on the assets of the firm.

- The borrower is prohibited from making mergers or consolidations. In addition, it may not sell or lease a major portion of its assets without written approval of the lender.

- The borrower is prohibited from making or guaranteeing loans to others that would impair the lender's security.

RESTRICTIVE COVENANTS

Rather than requiring or prohibiting certain actions on the part of the borrower, *restrictive covenants* merely *limit their scope*. These are typical restrictive covenants:

- Limitations on the amount of dividends a firm may pay.
- Limitations on the level of salaries, bonuses, and advances a firm may give to employees.

These restrictions, in essence, force the firm to increase its equity capital base, thereby increasing the security for the loan.

Other restrictive covenants might include the following:

- Limitations on the total amount of short- and long-term borrowing the firm may engage in during the period of the term loan.

- Limitations on the amount of funds the firm may invest in new property, plant, and equipment. (This restriction usually applies only to those investments that cannot be financed from internally generated funds.)

And, finally, a firm that has outstanding long-term debt may be restricted as to the amount of debt it can retire without also retiring a portion of the term loan.

These restrictions are quite common, but the list is not all-inclusive. For example, a standard loan agreement checklist published by a large New York city bank lists thirty-four commonly used covenants. In general, covenants included in a loan agreement are determined by the particular conditions surrounding the granting of the term loan, including the credit record of the borrower and the maturity and security provisions of the loan.

For example, Atlas Corporation has a $22 million term loan with Manufacturers Hanover Trust, payable in eight equal quarterly installments which began in 1982. The loan was arranged on June 30, 1978. The agreement required Atlas to maintain consolidated tangible net worth (book value minus intangible assets) of not less than $30 million, consolidated working capital of not less than $10 million, and a current ratio of 1.5:1 after excluding amounts owed under the loan agreement that mature within 1 year. The company was also required to maintain a ratio of consolidated long-term debt to consolidated tangible net worth of not more than 1.25:1 through June 29, 1980, and a ratio of not more than 1:1 thereafter. In addition, Atlas could not make any cash dividend payments without the bank's consent. The loan was secured by virtually all the assets of the firm's Minerals Division.

DEFAULT PROVISIONS

All term loans have *default provisions* that permit the lender to insist that the borrower repay the entire loan immediately under certain conditions. The following are examples:

- The borrower fails to pay interest, principal, or both as specified by the terms of the loan.

- The borrower materially misrepresents any information on the financial statements required under the loan's affirmative covenants.

- The borrower fails to observe any of the affirmative, negative, or restrictive covenants specified within the loan.

A borrower who commits any of these common acts of default will not necessarily be called on to repay a loan immediately, however. Basically, a lender will only use a default provision as a last resort, seeking in the meantime to make some agreement with the borrower, such as working out an acceptable modified lending plan with which the borrower is more able to comply. Normally, a lender will call a loan due only if no reasonable alternative is available or if the borrower is facing near-certain failure.

SUPPLIERS OF TERMS LOANS

There are numerous sources of term loans, including commercial banks, insurance companies, pension funds, commercial finance companies, government agencies, and equipmment suppliers. Many of these sources are discussed in the following sections.

COMMERCIAL BANKS AND SAVINGS AND LOAN ASSOCIATIONS

Many commerical banks and some savings and loan associations are actively involved in term lending. For example, about one-third of all commercial and industrial loans made by commercial banks are term loans.

In spite of this level of activity, banks generally tend to favor loans having relatively short maturities—that is, less than 5 years—although some banks will make loans having lifetimes as long as 10 years or more. In addition, some banks limit their term lending to existing customers. Often banks will form *syndicates* to share large term loans. This not only limits the risk exposure for any one bank, but also complies with laws that limit the size of *unsecured* loans made to single customers.

LIFE INSURANCE COMPANIES AND PENSION FUNDS

Whereas commercial banks tend to prefer shorter-term loans, insurance companies and pension funds are most interested in longer-term commitments, for example, 10 to 20 years. As a result, it is common for a bank and an insurance company to share a term loan commitment. Under this type of arrangement, the bank might agree to finance the first 5 years of a loan, with the insurance company's financing the loan for the remaining years. This can also be advantageous to the borrower, since banks can generallly charge a lower rate of interest for loans having shorter maturities.

From the borrowing firm's perspective, term loan agreements with pension funds and insurance companies have one significant limitation. If a firm decides to retire a term loan with a bank, it may usually do so without penalty. Because insurance companies are interested in having their funds invested for longer periods of time, however, prepayment of an insurance company term loan may involve some penalties.

Term loans from insurance companies and pension funds are usually secured, often with a mortgage on an asset such as a building. These mortgage-secured loans are rarely made for amounts greater than 65 to 75 percent of the value of the collateral, however.

And, finally, term loans from life insurance companies and pension funds tend to have slightly higher stated rates of interest than bank term loans. This is because (1) they are generally made for longer maturities and (2) there are no compensating balance requirements.

Small business adminstration (SBA)

The Small Business Administration (SBA), an agency of the Federal government, was established in 1953 to make credit available to small businesses that cannot reasonably obtain financing from private sources.

Normally an SBA loan is secured by a mortage on the firm's plant and equipment, third-party guarantees, or an assignment of accounts receivable and/or inventories.

The SBA makes three major types of loans:

- Direct loans.
- Participation loans.
- Economic opportunity loans.

Direct loans are financed by the SBA, and, since funds are quite limited, these loans are usually made only when the applicant firm cannot borrow from private sources at reasonable rates.

A *participation loan* is obtained from a local bank, with the SBA guaranteeing up to 90 percent of it. The SBA prefers participation loans over direct loans. Typical SBA loans range between $20,000 and $40,000 and have a maximum 10-year maturity. In addition, they usually carry an interest rate that is considerably below the rate that would be charged for a similar non-SBA loan. A rate about 1 percent higher than the U.S. Treasury Bond rate is quite common. Like other term loans, SBA loans must normally be amortized, that is, paid off in periodic (usually monthly) installments.

Economic opportunity loans have been made available since 1970 to assist economically and socially disadvantaged individuals who own their own firms.

Small business investment companies (SBICs)

Small business investment companies (SBICs) are licensed by the government to make both equity and debt investments in small firms. They raise their capital by borrowing from the SBA and other sources.

The SBICs take an equity interest in the small firms they loan funds to, hoping to profit from their growth and prosperity. Unlike SBA loans, which are made to any eligible credit-worthy small business, SBICs specialize in providing funds to firms that have above-average growth potential. Naturally, these firms often have above-average risk as well. Thus, the interest charge on an SBIC loan is generally somewhat higher than that on a normal bank term loan. SBIC loans have maturities as long as 10 to 20 years.

Industrial development authorities (IDA's)

Many states and municipalities have organized IDAs to encourage new firms to locate in their area or to assist existing firms with expansion plans. In a typical financing plan, a local IDA sells tax-exempt municipal revenue bonds and uses the proceeds to build a firm's new facility. It then leases the plant to the firm, collecting lease payments from the firm that are large enough to pay the principal and interest on the municipal revenue bonds. Because bonds of this nature are tax exempt, the interest on them is generally lower than the interest on bonds issued directly by a private corporation. As a result, an IDA can charge a firm an attractively low lease rate. In 1981 nearly $7.6 billion in loans were issued by state and local government IDAs.[5]

Corporate outlays for pollution control investments amounted to nearly 2.5 percent of all capital outlays in 1982 and totaled nearly $8 billion. The growing need to finance pollution control expenditures has led to the development of *pollution control revenue bonds,* which are issued by municipalities. Proceeds from these bonds are used to acquire pollution control equipment,

FIGURE 15–1   Announcement of a Pollution Control Revenue Bond

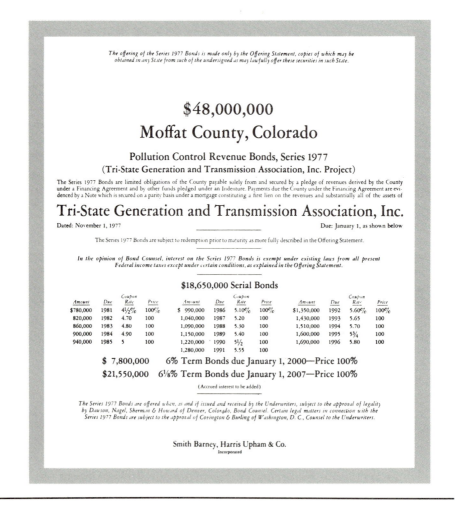

The offering of the Series 1977 Bonds is made only by the Offering Statement, copies of which may be obtained in any State from such of the undersigned as may lawfully offer these securities in such State.

$48,000,000
Moffat County, Colorado

Pollution Control Revenue Bonds, Series 1977
(Tri-State Generation and Transmission Association, Inc. Project)

The Series 1977 Bonds are limited obligations of the County payable solely from and secured by a pledge of revenues derived by the County under a Financing Agreement and by other funds pledged under an Indenture. Payments due the County under the Financing Agreement are evidenced by a Note which is secured on a parity basis under a mortgage constituting a first lien on the revenues and substantially all of the assets of

Tri-State Generation and Transmission Association, Inc.

Dated: November 1, 1977   Due: January 1, as shown below

The Series 1977 Bonds are subject to redemption prior to maturity as more fully described in the Offering Statement.

In the opinion of Bond Counsel, interest on the Series 1977 Bonds is exempt under existing laws from all present Federal income taxes except under certain conditions, as explained in the Offering Statement.

$18,650,000 Serial Bonds

Amount	Due	Coupon Rate	Price	Amount	Due	Coupon Rate	Price	Amount	Due	Coupon Rate	Price
$780,000	1981	4½%	100%	$ 990,000	1986	5.10%	100%	$1,350,000	1992	5.60%	100%
820,000	1982	4.70	100	1,040,000	1987	5.20	100	1,430,000	1993	5.65	100
860,000	1983	4.80	100	1,090,000	1988	5.30	100	1,510,000	1994	5.70	100
900,000	1984	4.90	100	1,150,000	1989	5.40	100	1,600,000	1995	5¾	100
940,000	1985	5	100	1,220,000	1990	5½	100	1,690,000	1996	5.80	100
				1,280,000	1991	5.55	100				

$ 7,800,000   6% Term Bonds due January 1, 2000—Price 100%

$21,550,000   6⅛% Term Bonds due January 1, 2007—Price 100%

(Accrued interest to be added)

The Series 1977 Bonds are offered when, as and if issued and received by the Underwriters, subject to the approval of legality by Dawson, Nagel, Sherman & Howard of Denver, Colorado, Bond Counsel. Certain legal matters in connection with the Series 1977 Bonds are subject to the approval of Covington & Burling of Washington, D. C., Counsel to the Underwriters.

Smith Barney, Harris Upham & Co.
Incorporated

---

[5]In 1968 Congress limited the use of IDA bonds to small issues ($1 million, generally) and certain exempt facilities, including pollution control facilities.

which is then sold or leased to local industries. Because interest payments on pollution control revenue bonds are tax-free to investors, a firm's cost is much lower than it would be if these investments had to be financed with conventional debt or equity.

Figure 15–1 is an announcement of a pollution control revenue bond for Moffat County, Colorado. These bonds were used to finance pollution control construction expenditures incurred by the Tri-State Generation and Transmission Association. The average coupon rate of interest for this issue is about 5.3 percent. By comparison, the interest rate for taxable AA-rated bonds during this same period was about 8½ percent.

The Moffat County bonds are *serial* bonds; that is, some matured as early as 1981, while others remain outstanding until 2007. Thus, this issue constitutes a mixture of intermediate- and long-term financing.

EQUIPMENT LOANS

When a firm procures a loan to finance new equipment, it may use the equipment itself as collateral for an intermediate-term loan. These loans are called *equipment financing loans.*

Equipment financing loans are commonly made for readily marketable equipment. These loans are normally made for somewhat less than the market value of the equipment, and the difference provides a margin of safety for the lender. This difference may range between 20 and 30 percent for readily marketable and mobile equipment, such as trucks or cars. The amortization schedule for an equipment financing loan is usually tied closely to the asset's economic life.

There are several potential sources of equipment financing, including commercial banks, sales finance companies, equipment sellers, and insurance companies and pension funds. Commercial banks are often the least expensive source of such financing—especially when compared with sales finance companies. The equipment seller may provide financing either directly or through a captive finance subsidiary (that is, the seller's own financing subsidiary). Although at first glance, an equipment seller may appear to charge a very modest interest rate, it is often difficult to make a meaningful comparison between the rates charged by a supplier and other financing sources such as commercial banks. This is because the selling firm might price the equipment in such a way as to conceal part of the cost of carrying its credit customers; that is, noncash customers may pay relatively higher prices than cash customers.

There are two primary security instruments used in connection with equipment financing loans: the *conditional sales contract* and the *chattel mortgage.* Each of these is discussed in the following sections.

CONDITIONAL SALES CONTRACT

When a conditional sales contract (sometimes called a *purchase money mortgage*) is used in an equipment financing transaction, the seller retains title until the buyer has made all payments required by the financing contract.

Conditional sales contracts are used almost exclusively by equipment sellers. At the time of purchase, the buyer normally makes a down payment to the seller and issues a promissory note for the balance of the purchase price. The buyer then agrees to make a series of periodic payments (usually monthly or quarterly) of principal and interest to the seller until the note has been paid off. When the last payment has been made, the title to the equipment passes to the buyer. In the case of default, the seller may repossess the asset.

CHATTEL MORTGAGE

A chattel mortgage is a lien on property other than real estate. Chattel mortgages are most common when a commercial bank or sales finance company makes a direct equipment financing loan. It involves the placement of a lien against the property by the lender. Notification of the lien is filed with a public office in the state where the equipment is located. Given a valid lien, the lender may repossess the equipment and resell it if the borrower defaults on the loan payment.

INTRODUCTION TO LEASING

A promotional brochure from the Warner and Swasey Financial Corporation states, "The value of a machine is in the use, not its ownership." This is true in the sense that whereas a firm may wish to acquire the *use* of an asset needed in the production of goods and the providing of services, it is not absolutely necessary to acquire legal title to the asset. Leasing is a means of obtaining economic use of an asset for a specific period of time without obtaining an ownership interest in the asset. In the lease contract, the property owner *(lessor)* agrees to permit the property user *(lessee)* to make use of the property for a stated time. In return, the lessee agrees to make a series of periodic payments to the lessor.

Leasing as a source of intermediate- and long-term financing has become increasingly popular since World War II. Prior to that time most lease contracts were written for real estate and farm property. Today there are few major firms that are not involved in leasing. Leased assets range from transportation equipment (such as railroad rolling stock, trucks, automobiles, airplanes, and ships) to computers, medical equipment, specialized industrial equipment, energy transmission equipment, and mining equipment. Some firms lease entire power-generating plants and aluminum reduction mills. In the hotel and motel industry, leases may even include bathroom fixtures, paintings, furniture, and bedding.

The volume of leasing activity has been expanding at about twice the rate of the country's GNP growth since 1970. By the early 1980s, about 20 percent of all capital outlays were financed through leases. In 1983 an estimated $200 billion of equipment had been leased.

Many types of firms originate leases. These include commercial banks, savings and loan institutions, investment banks, industrial companies, finance companies, and automotive firms.

Because of the growing importance and widespread acceptance of lease financing, the contemporary financial manager should have a good understanding of this financing method. The following sections discuss the characteristics of various types of leases and develop a lease analysis model from the perspective of the lessor. Later sections consider the tax and accounting treatment of leases and the advantages and disadvantages of leases. Finally, a lease analysis model is developed from the perspective of the lessee.

TYPES OF LEASES

Leases are classified in a number of ways. "True leases," which are the primary focus of this chapter, are traditional leases in which the lessor is considered to hold the legal title to the leased asset. The asset user, the lessee, has no ownership interest in the asset. *Operating leases* and various types of *financial*, or *capital*, *leases* are subcategories of true leases. In addition, the Economic Recovery Tax Act (1981) and the Tax Equity and Fiscal Responsibility Act (1982) created additional unique leasing arrangements, called *safe harbor leases*, *tax benefit transfer leases*, and *"finance" leases*. These special lease arrangements are discussed at the end of the chapter.

OPERATING LEASES

An *operating lease*, sometimes called a *service* or *maintenance lease*, is an agreement that provides the lessee with use of an asset on a period-by-period basis. Normally the payments under an operating lease contract are insufficient to recover the full cost of the asset for the lessor. As a result, the contract period in an operating lease tends to be somewhat less than the usable economic life of the asset, and the lessor expects to recover the costs (plus a return) from renewal rental payments, the sale of the asset at the end of the lease period, or both.

The most important characteristic of an operating lease is that it may be canceled at the option of the lessee as long as the lessor is given sufficient notice. Even though the lessee may be required to pay a penalty to the lessor upon cancelation, this is preferable to being compelled to keep an asset that is expected to become obsolete in the near future. For example, many firms lease their computers under an operating lease arrangement. (Of course, the lessor charges a rental that is consistent with expectations of the asset's economic life.)

Most operating leases require the lessor to maintain the leased asset. In addition, the lessor is normally responsible for any property taxes owed on the asset and for providing appropriate insurance coverage. The costs of these services are built into the lease rate.

FINANCIAL, OR CAPITAL, LEASES

A *financial lease*, also termed a *capital lease*, is a noncancelable agreement.[6] The lessee is required to make payments throughout the lease period,

---

[6]This chapter focuses primarily on financial leases rather than operating leases, because financial leases represent more permanent obligations. The analysis techniques discussed at the end of this chapter, however, are equally applicable to both operating and financial leases.

whether or not the asset continues to generate economic benefits. Failure to make payments could eventually force the lessee into bankruptcy.

With financial leases, the lessee is generally responsible for maintenance of the asset. The lessee may also have to pay insurance and property taxes. The total payments over the lease period are sufficient to amortize the original cost of the asset and provide a return to the lessor. Some financial leases provide for a renewal or repurchase option at the end of the lease; these are limited by the IRS.

A financial lease may originate either as a *sale and leaseback* or as a *direct lease.*

Sale and leaseback   A sale and leaseback occurs when a company sells an asset to another firm and immediately leases it back for its own use. In this transaction the lessor normally pays a price close to the asset's fair market value. The lease payments are set at a level that will return the full purchase price of the asset to the lessor, plus provide a reasonable rate of return. The sale and leaseback is advantageous to the lessee for the following reasons:

- The lessee receives cash from the sale of the asset, which may be reinvested elsewhere in the firm or used to increase the firm's liquidity.

- The lessee can continue using the asset, even though it is owned by someone else.

A good illustration of a sale and leaseback transaction was Pan American World Airways' decision in 1980 to sell and lease back its 59-story headquarters building to Metropolitan Life Insurance Company for $400 million. The sale was prompted by a continuing stream of losses from its airline operations. In the first half of 1980, Pan Am had losses of over $141 million. The sale was expected to give Pan Am a $340 million cash infusion after deducting selling costs of $10 million and the $50 million outstanding mortgage balance.

Direct lease   A direct lease is initiated when a firm acquires the use of an asset that it did not previously own. The lease may be with the manufacturer of the asset or a financial institution. In the latter instance, the user-lessee first determines the following:

- What equipment will be leased.
- Which manufacturer will supply the equipment.
- What options, warranties, terms of delivery, installation agreements, and service agreements will have to be made.
- What price will be paid for the asset.

The lessee then contacts a financial institution and works out the terms of the lease, after which the institution (which then becomes the lessor) acquires the asset for the lessee and the lessee starts making the lease payments. Under this arrangement the lessee is usually responsible for taxes, insurance, and maintenance.

Leveraged leases

Approximately 85 percent of all financial leases currently written in the United States are leveraged leases.[7] Also known as *third-party equity leases* and *tax leases*, leveraged leases are designed to provide financing for assets that require large capital outlays (greater than $300,000) and have economic lives of 5 years or more.

A leveraged lease is a three-sided agreement among the lessee, the lessor, and the lenders. The *lessee* selects the leased asset, receives all the income generated from its use, and makes the periodic lease payments. The *lessor* (normally a financial institution, such as a leasing company or a commercial bank) acts either for itself or as a trustee for an individual or a group of individuals to provide the equity funds needed to purchase the asset. The *lenders* (usually banks, insurance companies, trusts, pension funds, or foundations) lend the funds needed to make up the asset's full purchase price. Specifically, the lessor normally supplies 20 to 40 percent of the purchase price, and the lenders provide the remaining 60 to 80 percent.

Figure 15–2 is an announcement of a leveraged lease that was arranged by Salomon Brothers for Kansas City Southern Lines. In this case, the Ford Motor Credit Company acted as the lessor and provided equity funds of $4,728,974 to acquire 450 boxcars, which were leased to Kansas City Southern Lines. Debt funds of $10,072,198 were provided by a number of institutional lenders.

In a leveraged lease the long-term money is supplied to the lessor by the lenders on a nonrecourse basis; that is, the lenders cannot turn to the lessor for repayment of the debt in the event of default. Normally the lender receives mortgage bonds secured by the following:

- A first lien on the asset.
- An assignment of the lease.
- An assignment of the lease rental payments.
- Occasionally, a direct guarantee from the lessee or a third party (such as the government, in the case of merchant vessel financing).

Because the lenders do not have recourse to the lessor in the event of default, the lessor's risk exposure is limited to the 20 to 40 percent equity contribution.

As the owner of the asset, the lessor reports the lease payments as gross income. For tax purposes the lessor is entitled to the full value of the 10 percent investment tax credit. The lessor receives additional benefits from the tax-deductible interest and accelerated depreciation. As a result, the lessor incurs very large tax losses and receives large cash inflows during the early years of the lease.

Because the lessor receives the entire investment tax credit in addition to having the accelerated depreciation tax shield while making a relatively small equity investment, the lessor can provide a very attractive lease rate to

---

[7]Edward W. Reed et al. *Commercial Banking.* Englewood Cliffs, N.J.: Prentice-Hall, 1976, p. 244.

FIGURE 15–2   Announcement of a Leveraged Lease Financing Arrangement

This announcement appears as a matter of record only.

$14,801,172

Kansas City Southern Lines

15 Year Leveraged Lease of 450 Boxcars
Equity Funds of $4,728,974 were provided by

Ford Motor Credit Company

Debt Funds of $10,072,198 were provided by
various institutional lenders.

The undersigned arranged the financing for
this leveraged lease transaction.

Salomon Brothers   ITEL CORPORATION

the lessee. Lease rates of 4 to 6 percent are not uncommon when AAA borrowing rates are 9 to 10 percent. Figure 15–3 is a diagram of a typical leveraged lease arrangement.

Lessees who do not anticipate that their taxable income will be sufficient to allow them to take advantage of the tax benefits of ownership are most likely to use leveraged leases for large transactions. These include firms with low profit levels, large tax loss carryforwards, or large amounts of tax-exempt income. The lessee effectively gives up the tax benefits of ownership in exchange for more favorable lease rates.[8]

DETERMINING THE LEASE PAYMENTS: THE LESSOR'S PERSPECTIVE

The Wallace Company (lessee) desires to lease a piece of equipment valued at $100,000 from the Gray Company (lessor) for a period of 5 years. Under

---

[8]The first "Focus on Corporate Practice" example at the end of this chapter illustrates a leveraged lease transaction.

FIGURE 15–3   **Diagram of a Typical Leveraged Lease**

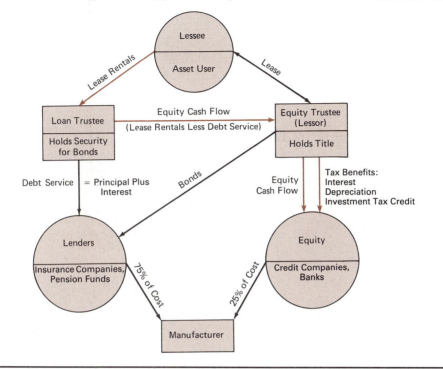

the terms of the lease, payments are to be made at the beginning of each of the 5 years. The Gray Company expects to sell the asset for an estimated salvage value of $20,000 at the end of the 5-year period. If Gray requires an 11 percent before-tax return on the lease[9] (exclusive of any benefits that may accrue from claiming the investment tax credit or using the depreciation tax shield), what will be the annual lease payments?[10]

These payments are computed as follows:

Step 1   Compute the lessor's net investment; in this case, the $100,000 initial outlay minus the present value of the salvage at the end of year 5:

Initial outlay	$100,000
Less: Present value of $20,000 salvage	
at 11% ($20,000 × 0.593)	11,860
Net investment	$ 88,140

---

[9]If the required return were stated in terms of an after-tax return, considering depreciation, the investment tax credit, and any ownership costs for which the lessor is responsible (such as maintenance, insurance, or property taxes), this analysis would have to be modified to reflect these additional costs and benefits of ownership.

[10]The procedure discussed in this section illustrates a *general* approach that can be applied to all financial leases. In the case of leveraged leases, however, the existence of nonrecourse debt complicates matters. For an example of leveraged lease analysis, see Reed et al. *op. cit.*, pp. 246–247.

(If the lessor were eligible to take an investment tax credit on the asset, the net investment would be reduced accordingly.)

Step 2 Compute the annual lease payments using the appropriate interest factor for the present value of an annuity (PVIFA from Table IV). Since lease payments are normally made at the beginning of each year, they constitute an *annuity due*. Thus, the last four payments, which occur at the ends of years 1 through 4, are discounted, whereas the present value of the first payment, made at the *beginning* of year 1, is not discounted. Taking the PVIFA for 11 percent and 5 years and multiplying by (1 + 0.11) gives the required PVIFA for an annuity due. If R is the annual lease payment, the present value of the lease payments may be set equal to the net investment to determine the required R, as follows:

$$\text{Net investment} = R(\text{PVIFA}_{0.11,5})(1 + 0.11)$$
$$\$88,140 = R(3.696)(1.11)$$
$$\$88,140 = R(4.103)$$
$$R = \$21,482 \ .$$

Thus, the Wallace Company will have to make an annual lease payment of $21,482 to the Gray Company at the beginning of each year.

TAX STATUS OF TRUE LEASES

Annual lease payments are tax deductible for the lessee if one crucial criterion is met; namely, the IRS must agree that a contract is truly a lease and not just an installment loan being called a lease. Before embarking on a lease transaction, all involved parties should obtain an opinion from the IRS regarding the tax status of the proposed lease. The opinion of the IRS normally revolves primarily around the following general rules:

- The remaining useful life of the equipment at the end of the lease term must be the greater of 1 year or 20 percent of its originally estimated useful life.

- Leases in excess of 30 years are *not* considered to be leases for tax purposes.

- The lease payments must provide the lessor with a reasonable return on the investment. At this point in time, a range of 8 to 16 percent would probably be viewed as reasonable. This profit potential must exist apart from the transaction's tax benefits.

- Renewal options must be reasonable; that is, the renewal rate must be closely related to the economic value of the asset for the renewal period.

- If the lease agreement specifies a purchase option at the end of the lease period, the purchase price must be based on the asset's fair market value at that time.

- In the case of a leveraged lease, the lessor must provide a minimum of 20 percent equity.

- Limited use property (valuable only to the lessee) may not be leased.

If the IRS does not agree that a contract is truly a lease, taxes are applied as if the property had been sold to the lessee and pledged to the lessor as security for a loan. The reason for the IRS retrictions previously cited is that the IRS wants to prohibit lease transactions that are set up purely to speed up tax deductions. For example, a building would normally be depreciated over 15 years under ACRS depreciation rules. It would be possible to set up a lease over a 3-year period that allowed the lessee to effectively write off the cost of the building for tax purposes over 3 years. This would increase tax deductions for the lessee at the expense of tax receipts to the U.S. Treasury. These IRS guidelines are designed to prevent this type of abuse.

Finally, it should be noted that under Section 48(d) of the IRS Code, the investment tax credit may be taken by either the lessor or the lessee, or shared between the two. In leveraged leases the investment tax credit is normally taken by the lessor, but this is not required per se by the IRS. In general, the two parties to a lease have considerable latitude in working out a mutually acceptable agreement concerning the investment tax credit.

LEASES AND ACCOUNTING PRACTICES

In recent years firms have tended to disclose more information regarding lease obligations.

In November 1976 the Financial Accounting Standards Board (FASB) issued *Standard No. 13*, which *requires* lessees to capitalize certain types of leases, primarily financial or capital leases. The capitalized value of a lease is determined by computing the present value of all required lease payments, discounted at a rate equal to the lessee's incremental borrowing rate for a secured loan over a term similar to the lease.[11] Table 15–2 illustrates this procedure.

TABLE 15–2 Accounting Treatment of Leases

Assets		Liabilities	
Lease property under capital leases less accumulated amortization	$1,500	Current: Obligations under capital leases*	$ 150
		Long term: Obligations under capital leases*	1,350
	$1,500		$1,500

*The $150 represents lease payments due during the next year. The $1,350 represents the present value of lease payments due beyond 1 year in the future.

[11]In certain circumstances it is possible for a firm to use a lower rate. See FASB *Standard No. 13* for a more detailed discussion.

In addition to making these balance sheet adjustments, a firm must show the following in the footnotes to the financial statements:[12]

- *For financial leases:*

1. The gross amount of assets reported under financial leases as of the date of the balance sheet by major classes according to nature or use.

2. The amount of accumulated lease amortization.

3. Future minimum lease payments as of the date of the latest balance sheet presented, in total and for each of the next 5 fiscal years.

- *For operating leases:*

1. Future minimum rental payments required as of the date of the latest balance sheet presented, in total and for each of the following 5 fiscal years.

2. The rental expense for each period for which an income statement is presented.

The lessee also must indicate in the notes to the financial statements the existence and terms of renewal or repurchase options and escalation clauses, any restrictions imposed by leases (such as restrictions on dividends, additional debt, or further leasing), and any contingent rental obligations.

The effect of these new disclosure requirements is to lower a firm's reported return on investment and to increase the reported debt-to-equity ratios of those firms that have acquired portions of their assets through leasing. In the past some analysts argued that one of the advantages of leasing was that it provided "off–balance sheet" financing and tended to increase a firm's capacity to borrow. Whether or not this was true, the new lease-reporting requirements should eliminate this distortion, facilitate clearer analysis of a firm's financial condition, and make it easier to make comparisons among firms.

ADVANTAGES AND DISADVANTAGES OF LEASING

There are a number of potential advantages to leasing. However, the prudent financial manager also should be aware of the disadvantages.

ADVANTAGES

Perhaps the major advantage of leasing is that it provides *flexible financing.* Most lease arrangements tend to have fewer restrictive covenants than loan agreements. In addition, leasing is well suited to piecemeal financing. A firm that is acquiring assets over time may find it more convenient to lease them than to negotiate term loans or sell securities each time it makes a new capital outlay.

---

[12]The requirements presented here are not inclusive; they merely summarize the most significant disclosures.

In the case of real estate leasing, the lessee may *effectively be able to depreciate land.* Since the lease payments will reflect both the lessor's investment in any buildings *and* the cost of the land, the lessee is able to effectively depreciate the land by deducting the full amount of the lease payment for tax purposes. To keep this benefit in perspective, however, it should be noted that the lessee also loses any salvage value associated with the property at the end of the lease.

The lessee also may be able to make *lower payments* because of the tax benefits enjoyed by the lessor. This is especially important in the case of a leveraged lease, when the lessee is a firm with insufficient taxable income to take advantage of the tax benefits of ownership.

In addition, it *may* be possible for the lessee to *avoid some of the risks of obsolescence* associated with ownership. The lessor will charge a lease rate intended to provide a specified return on the required net investment. The net investment is equal to the cost of the asset minus the present value of the expected salvage value at the end of the lease. If the actual salvage is less than originally expected, the lessor bears the loss.

For the small or marginally profitable firm, *leasing is often the only available source of financing,* since the title to leased property remains with the lessor and reduces the lessor's risk in the event of failure. If the lessee does fail, the lessor can quickly recover the leased property.

Leasing tends to *smooth out expenses* for the lessee. Since lease payments are a constant annual outlay, whereas ACRS depreciation expenses are large in the early years of ownership and less in later years, earnings tend to appear more stable when assets are leased rather than owned. In addition, reported earnings per share are normally higher in the early years of a lease as compared with ownership because of the use of ACRS depreciation when the asset is owned.

Leasing is said to provide *100 percent financing,* whereas most borrowing requires a down payment. Because lease payments are normally made in advance of each period, this 100 percent financing benefit is diminished by the amount of the first required lease payment.

From the lessee's perspective, leases can *increase a firm's liquidity.* For example, a sale and leaseback transforms some of a firm's fixed assets into cash in exchange for an obligation to make a series of fixed future payments.

And, finally, leasing gives some plant or divisional managers additional *flexibility in acquiring assets* if lease agreements are not subject to internal capital expenditure constraints. In recent years local school districts, municipalities, and the Department of the Navy, among other organizations, have used leasing to circumvent capital outlay restrictions.

DISADVANTAGES

The primary disadvantage of leasing is *cost.* For a firm with a strong earnings record, good access to the credit markets, and the ability to take advantage of the tax benefits of ownership, leasing is often a more expensive alternative. Of course, the actual cost difference between ownership and leasing depends on a number of factors and varies from case to case.

Another disadvantage of leasing is the *loss of the asset's salvage value.* In real estate this loss can be substantial. A lessee may also have *difficulty getting approval to make property improvements* on leased real estate. If the improvements substantially alter the property or reduce its potential range of uses, the lessor may be reluctant to permit them.

In addition, if a leased asset (with a financial lease) becomes obsolete or if the capital project financed by the lease becomes uneconomical, *the lessee may not cancel the lease without paying a substantial penalty.*

LEASE-BUY ANALYSIS: THE LESSEE'S PERSPECTIVE

Financial theorists and model builders have devoted a substantial amount of time and effort to developing an analytical framework within which the differential costs associated with leasing versus buying can be compared. At least fifteen different approaches to the problem have been suggested, and there is considerable disagreement as to which one is the best.[13] In spite of this abundance of models, the perplexed financial manager can take some comfort in the fact that the practical effects resulting from the differences in the models tend to be small, since few real-world decisions are changed as a result of which lease-buy model is chosen.[14]

One of the most commonly used approaches to the analysis of a lease versus purchase decision assumes that the appropriate comparison should be between *leasing* and *borrowing to buy.* Advocates of this approach argue that a financial lease is much like a loan in that it requires a series of fixed payments. Failure to make lease payments, like failure to make loan payments, may result in bankruptcy.

The basic approach of this lease-buy analysis model involves the computation of the present value cost associated with leasing and the present value cost associated with borrowing to buy. *The objective is to choose the alternative having the lowest present value cost.*

For example, the First National Bank has decided that it needs to acquire a new data processing system to handle the paperwork associated with the provision of many new services. To date, the bank has done an economic analysis of the acquisition and found that the new system has a positive net present value.

The bank wishes to determine whether the new data processing system should be purchased or leased. The complete system will cost $1,000,000 if it is purchased. The bank plans to keep the system for 7 years. It will be depreciated over 5 years using ACRS depreciation rates. The system is eligible for the 10 percent investment tax credit (ITC). At the end of 7 years the actual salvage is expected to be $100,000.

If purchased, the system can be financed with a 7-year, 20 percent interest

---

[13]Basically, the various models differ as to which discount rate should be used to evaluate various components of the cash flows and as to which cash flows should be considered.

[14]Evidence of this is presented in a paper by Arthur Gudikunst and Gordon Roberts. "Empirical Analysis of Lease-Buy Decisions," presented at the 1975 Meeting of the Eastern Finance Association.

loan of $900,000 ($1,000,000 cost less the ITC). The loan requires 7 *equal annual* end-of-year payments consisting of principal and interest. If the system is leased, the lessor will receive the benefit of the ITC. This financial lease will require 7 beginning-of-year lease payments of $210,000 each.

The bank's marginal tax rate is 40 percent for ordinary income and 25 percent for capital gains. Under both financing alternatives, the bank will be responsible for all operating, maintenance, insurance, and property tax payments associated with the system.

Tables 15–3 and 15–4 present an analysis of the leasing versus borrowing and buying decision. Table 15–3 provides the data necessary to compute the present value cost of borrowing and buying. The first step in this analysis requires the calculation of the annual loan payments. The asset costs $1,000,000, but First National is eligible to receive the 10 percent ($100,000) ITC. Because of this, First National would need to borrow $900,000 at an interest rate of 20 percent. The annual end-of-year payment on this loan is computed as follows:

$$\text{Payment} = \frac{\$900,000}{\text{PVIFA}_{0.20,7}}$$
$$= \frac{\$900,000}{3.605}$$
$$= \$249,653 \ .$$

Columns 2 through 5 in Table 15–3 show the loan amortization schedule, while Column 6 shows the annual depreciation expense. Tax-deductible expenses, consisting of interest and depreciation, are shown in Column 7. The tax shield benefits from Column 7 are computed in Column 8. Column 9 shows the after-tax value of the estimated salvage—in this case, it is equal to the salvage value ($100,000) times (1 − the marginal tax rate of 40 percent). Column 10 summarizes the cash outflows associated with ownership, which equal the total loan payments (Column 2) minus tax shield benefits (Column 8) minus the after-tax salvage value (Column 9). The present value cost of borrowing and buying is computed in Column 12 by multiplying the cash outflows (Column 10) by the present value interest factors (Column 11). In this case, the after-tax cost of borrowing, 12 percent, is used, since the cash flows that are being evaluated are known with relative certainty. Specifically, the payments of principal and interest are fixed by the terms of the loan agreement, and the depreciation schedule is also predetermined. This justifies using a discount rate below the firm's weighted cost of capital. The salvage value is also thought to be relatively certain, so the same after-tax cost of borrowing is used to compute the present value of the expected salvage value.[15] The after-tax cost of borrowing is also used to evaluate the cost of leasing, since lease payments are known in advance and thus are not subject to much uncertainty.

---

[15]In cases where the salvage value is less certain, many analysts feel that a higher discount rate—such as the firm's weighted cost of capital—should be used to adjust for the uncertainty associated with the estimate of the salvage value.

TABLE 15–3 Present Value Analysis of the Borrowing and Buying Decision for the First National Bank

End of Year (1)	Total Payment (2)	Interest @ 20% (3)	Principal Reduction (4)	Remaining Balance (5)	ACRS Depreciation* (6)
0	—	—	—	$900,000	—
1	$249,653	$180,000	$ 69,653	830,347	$142,500
2	249,653	166,069	83,584	746,763	209,000
3	249,653	149,353	100,300	646,463	199,500
4	249,653	129,293	120,360	526,103	199,500
5	249,653	105,221	144,432	381,671	199,500
6	249,653	76,334	173,319	208,352	—
7	249,653	41,670	207,983	0†	
					$950,000

*The ACRS depreciation rates are applied to the installed cost of an asset less one-half of the ITC, or $1,000,000 less $50,000. The ACRS rates are 15, 22, 21, 21, and 21 percent, respectively, over the 5-year depreciation life of the system.

†The actual balance in this example works out to $369. This is due to (1) rounding of the present value interest factor for an annuity in Table IV when computing the annual payment and (2) rounding of the interest and principal payments to the nearest dollar. In the absence of rounding, the remaining balance would compute to $0 at the end of year 7. The exact payment using a calculator is $249,681.53.

Table 15–4 provides the data necessary to compute the present value cost of leasing. Column 2 shows the beginning-of-year lease payments. The tax shield resulting from the deductibility of each year's lease payments is received 1 year after a payment is made (that is, when the taxes are paid) and is shown in Column 3.[16] The after-tax cash flow of leasing, computed as the difference between the lease payment (Column 2) and the tax shield from the lease payment (Column 3), is shown in Column 4. Finally, the present value cost of leasing is computed in Column 6 by using the 12 percent present value interest factors in Column 5.

With the information computed in these two tables, First National can make a *reasoned* decision between leasing and buying the new data processing system. Since the present value *cost* of leasing is $690,144 and the present value *cost* of ownership is only $602,403, ownership is preferred to leasing.

This general procedure can be used to evaluate any lease versus buy decision once it has been determined by standard capital budgeting techniques that an asset should be acquired.[17]

[16]This treatment assumes that taxes are paid once a year at the end of the year and that lease payments are made at the beginning of the tax year. In reality, with quarterly tax payments, the delay in receiving the benefits of lease payment tax deductibility is much less than 1 year.

[17]Some finance professionals argue that the type of lease-buy analysis presented here is inherently biased against the leasing alternative. Because a financial lease is a fixed financial obligation much like debt, the debt alternative compared should be a loan with the same present value of payments as those in the lease case. If this is done, it is argued, there will be a more accurate reflection of the impact of leasing on the debt capacity and capital structure of the firm. However, this modified approach to lease-buy analysis is not likely to alter the decision reached in the example.

TABLE 15–3   (cont.)

Tax-Deductible Expenses (3) + (6) (7)	Tax Saving 0.40 × (7) (8)	After-Tax Salvage Value, S(1 − 0.4) (9)	Cash Outflow if Owned (2) − (8) − (9) (10)	$PVIF_{0.12,t}$ (11)	Present Value Cost of Borrowing and Buying (10) × (11) (12)
—	—	—	—	1.000	—
$322,500	$129,000	—	$120,653	0.893	$107,743
375,069	150,028	—	99,625	0.797	79,401
348,853	139,541	—	110,112	0.712	78,400
328,793	131,517	—	118,136	0.636	75,134
304,721	121,888	—	127,765	0.567	72,443
76,334	30,534	—	219,119	0.507	111,093
41,670	16,668	$60,000	172,985	0.452	78,189
					$602,403

SAFE HARBOR LEASING

The Economic Recovery Tax Act (1981) established a separate category of leases called *safe harbor leases*. Safe harbor leases meet the criteria of Section 168(f)(8) of the IRS Code. If both the lessor and the lessee agree to apply safe harbor provisions to a lease, the tax guidelines for true leases do not apply. Safe harbor leasing can be applied to any property that qualifies for the ITC.

TABLE 15–4   Present Value Analysis of the Leasing Decision for First National Bank

End of Year (1)	Lease Payment (2)	Tax Shield 0.4(2)* (3)	After-Tax Cash Flow If Leased (2) − (3) (4)	$PVIF_{0.12,t}$ (5)	Present Value Cost of Leasing (5) × (4) (6)
0	$210,000	—	$210,000	1.000	$210,000
1	210,000	$84,000	126,000	0.893	112,518
2	210,000	84,000	126,000	0.797	100,422
3	210,000	84,000	126,000	0.712	89,712
4	210,000	84,000	126,000	0.636	80,136
5	210,000	84,000	126,000	0.567	71,442
6	210,000	84,000	126,000	0.507	63,882
7	—	84,000	(84,000)	0.452	(37,968)
					$690,144

Advantage of owning over leasing = Present value cost of leasing − Present value cost of owning
= $690,144 − $602,403
= $87,741

Indicated decision: Select the alternative with the lowest present value cost. Hence, the asset should be owned (Advantage = $87,741).

*The lease payment in Column 2 is multiplied by 0.4, the firm's tax rate.

The asset must be leased within 3 months of acquisition. In the case of safe harbor leases, it is permissible for the lessee to be the legal owner of the leased property. The lessee can acquire title for a nominal sum, such as $1, at the end of the lease.

In practice, safe harbor leases and the closely related *tax benefit transfer leases* were nothing more than vehicles to transfer tax benefits from the lessee (who presumably cannot use them) to the lessor (who has considerable tax liabilities). Indeed, the intent of Congress when the safe harbor provisions were included in the ERTA was to provide a vehicle for firms with poor performance to realize the benefits of the ITC and ACRS depreciation, and therefore to encourage new investment by these firms.

For example, Ford Motor Company generated between $100 million and $200 million in tax benefits (depreciation deductions and ITCs) as a result of investing approximately $1 billion in new equipment and tooling in 1981. Since Ford was losing money, however, it could not use these benefits to reduce taxes. Fortunately, the new tax law permitted Ford to sell its benefits and receive needed cash immediately. IBM, a profitable company, bought the Ford benefits in November 1981.

The transaction by which tax benefits are sold is a safe harbor lease. In the example, Ford sold the equipment and tooling it acquired in 1981 to IBM. IBM then leased the equipment and tooling back to Ford. As a result, IBM can take the ITCs and ACRS depreciation deductions on the equipment. These credits and deductions will reduce IBM's Federal income taxes, and, as a result, IBM was willing to pay Ford for the benefits. Since Ford could not use the benefits because of its losses, the benefits were essentially worthless unless Ford sold them. The sale and leaseback arrangement, which is part of most safe harbor leases, actually involves no exchange of cash except the initial payment by IBM to Ford for the value of the transferred tax benefits. Instead, IBM agrees to make annual payments on a loan from Ford (to finance IBM's initial purchase of the assets) that *exactly* equal Ford's annual lease payments to IBM; that is, the payments are a *wash*. The net effect is that Ford receives cash for tax benefits it cannot use, and IBM receives needed tax benefits to reduce its Federal income tax liability.

The safe harbor provisions were intended primarily to assist distressed firms. However, the sale of tax credits became widespread by even financially sound firms. By the end of 1981, leases for more than $20 billion in property had been arranged under safe harbor. Indeed, the use of safe harbor leases to transfer tax benefits between firms became so widespread that there was a fear this could effectively mean the end of significant corporate taxation. Firms with tax liabilities would simply buy tax credits from other firms that were unable to use them fully. For example, in 1981 General Electric (GE), through its credit subsidiary, leased enough property (much of it under safe harbor leasing provisions) to generate $340 million in ITCs. Together with other tax credits GE had earned, the firm was able to reduce its tax bill to $50 million on net income before taxes of over $2.6 billion.

Because of the potential revenue losses to the Federal Government, the Tax Equity and Fiscal Responsibility Act (TEFRA) of 1982 modified the original safe harbor leasing rules and created a new tax-oriented lease called the *finance lease.*

FINANCE LEASE

To avoid the full impact of safe harbor leasing on the tax revenues of the U.S. Treasury, the TEFRA provided for a phasing out of safe harbor leasing for most equipment by January 1, 1984. Between July 2, 1982, and January 1, 1984, a set of modified safe harbor leasing rules applied. Beginning on January 1, 1984, and continuing through January 1, 1986, a class of *limited finance leases* was established.[18] After January 1, 1986, *unlimited finance leases* will be permitted. Some major provisions of these finance leases follow:

- Finance leases generally are available for new ACRS recovery property (excluding public utility property) that is eligible for the ITC.

- Tax benefits will be passed from the lessor to the lessee in the form of reduced rents. (During the transitional period the vehicle for a transfer of tax benefits is either a reduction of rents or a lump-sum payment, as in the Ford-IBM case).

- The lessor may only reduce 50 percent of its tax liability in 1984 and 1985 as a result of safe harbor leases and finance leases. This limitation expires for property leased after September 30, 1985, for taxable years beginning after that date.

- A lessee may lease only 40 percent of otherwise eligible property until December 31, 1985, when this limitation expires.

- Effective January 1, 1984, a fixed-price purchase option of at least 10 percent of the original asset cost is permitted.

- Finance leases *may* cover limited-use property.

- The asset must be leased within 90 days of acquisition.

- The lessor may use regular ACRS depreciation rates.

- The lessor may only claim 20 percent of the ITC in the year the property is placed in service and 20 percent in each of the next 4 years. This provision expires for assets placed in service after September 30, 1985.

- Tax benefits may not be carried back by the lessor.

Under the new *finance lease* provisions of the TEFRA, it appears that most firms will have considerable latitude to "sell" unusable tax benefits to firms that can make use of them.

SUMMARY

- *Term loans*, or *intermediate-term credit*, include any debt obligation having an initial maturity between 1 and 10 years.

- Term loans, being privately negotiated between the borrower and the lender, tend to be cheaper than public security offerings, since flotation costs

---

[18]*Finance leases* as described here are not to be confused with the true *financial*, or *capital*, leases discussed earlier in the chapter.

on small to medium-sized public offerings are high. Thus, term loans are a good source of funds for financing small and medium-sized increases in working capital or for financing the acquisition of a piece of equipment.

- Term loans are normally amortized by a series of installments. The interest rate ranges between 0.25 to 2.5 percent above the prime rate. Many term loan agreements require that some specific asset be pledged as *security*. In addition, the borrowing firm may have to agree to certain *affirmative*, *negative*, and *restrictive covenants* governing its actions during the loan period.

- Term loans are supplied by several institutions, including commercial banks (frequently the cheapest supplier of term funds), life insurance companies and pension funds (who prefer making loans having longer maturities), the Small Business Administration, small business investment companies, municipal or state industrial development authorities, and sales finance companies.

- Term loans that are secured by a lien on a piece of equipment are called *equipment financing loans*. They are made by the lending institutions previously named, as well as by equipment sellers or *captive finance subsidiaries*. The two primary security instruments used in equipment financing are the *conditional sales contract* and the *chattel mortgage*.

- A *lease* is a written agreement that permits the *lessee* to use a piece of property owned by the *lessor* in exchange for a series of periodic lease or rental payments.

- An *operating lease* provides the lessee with the use of an asset on a period-by-period basis. An operating lease *may be canceled* at the lessee's option. Most operating leases are written for a relatively short period of time, normally less than 5 years.

- A *financial lease* is a *noncancelable* agreement that obligates the lessee to make payments to the lessor for a predetermined period of time. There are two major types of financial leases: *sale and leaseback* agreements and *direct leases*. *Leveraged leases*, also called *tax leases*, have become increasingly common due to the effects of the investment tax credit. Approximately 85 percent of the financial leases written today are leveraged leases.

- Subject to a series of IRS guidelines, firms that lease a portion of their assets may deduct the full amount of the lease payment for tax purposes.

- Recent decisions by the Financial Accounting Standards Board (FASB) require that financial leases be capitalized and shown on the lessee's balance sheet.

- Leasing offers a number of potential advantages, including flexibility, the effective depreciation of land, and tax benefits (in some cases). It also may be the only source of financing available to many marginally profitable firms. It has a number of potential disadvantages, too, however. For example, leasing tends to be more costly than ownership for a firm with a good earnings record and good access to the capital markets.

- A number of analytical models are available to assist the lessor in determining what lease payments to charge. Other models are available to assist

472

the lessee in determining which is the less expensive source of financing—leasing or borrowing to buy.

- *Safe harbor leasing* provisions and *finance leases* are not true leases, but simply a means for firms to transfer tax benefits (ACRS depreciation and ITC) from firms that cannot use them to firms that can.

Leveraged Lease Financing and the San Diego Gas and Electric Company

R. Lee Haney
Financial Analysis Supervisor
San Diego Gas and Electric Company

San Diego Gas and Electric (SDGE) is a large utility operating in southern California. It is engaged in the generation and distribution of electricity for residential, commercial, municipal, and industrial users in the city and nearly all of the county of San Diego, plus some surrounding areas. It also distributes natural gas in San Diego County. In 1977 the firm had total assets of over $1.4 billion and revenues of over $388 million. Because of its location in rapidly growing southern California, SDGE has experienced more demand for its services than most other utilities, and this in turn has created huge capital investment requirements. This example illustrates one of the more innovative approaches used to handle the financing of these capital needs.

In June 1973, SDGE began engineering and design work for a 292-megawatt oil-fired steam electric generating unit at its Encina Power Plant. Construction began in July 1976, and the unit was put into commercial operation in October 1978.

Rather than being owned by SDGE, this unit was financed with a leveraged lease. Traditionally, leasing has been used to finance general-purpose, movable assets, such as airplanes, computers, ships, and railroad rolling stock. As this example illustrates, leasing is increasingly being used to finance fixed special-purpose assets.

In August 1978 SDGE (lessee) and Bank AmeriLease, Inc. (lessor), a subsidiary of Bank of America, concluded a $133.3 million leveraged lease for the Encina generating unit. Under the agreement, SDGE sold the power plant to Bank AmeriLease and leased it back for an initial 25-year period—with options for three 5-year renewals. The figure below is an announcement of this agreement.

Why did SDGE choose to lease this power plant rather than own it? First, the effective cost of the lease was under 6 percent, which is substantially less than the cost of conventional financing. The firm's weighted cost of debt and equity capital was 10.93 percent. In addition, the entire lease payment is an operating expense for tax purposes, resulting in an even lower after-tax cost.

How can a leveraged lease provide financing at such a low cost? First, the equity participant in the transaction contributed only 31.6 percent of the cost, with the balance of 68.4 percent's being financed through borrowings from loan participants. Hence, the lease transaction provides greater leverage than would be possible if SDGE owned the asset, since SDGE uses 50 percent debt in its capital structure. Second, leveraged leasing may provide lower costs when the lessee (SDGE) cannot fully utilize the investment tax credit and other tax benefits of ownership. In

August 29, 1978   **$133,269,956**

THE ENCINA–5 PROJECT

LEVERAGED LEASE FINANCING

SAN DIEGO GAS & ELECTRIC COMPANY

*As Lessee of a 292 (net) megawatt oil–fired steam
electric generating plant at Carlsbad, California.*

*The undersigned acted as sole agents for the placement of
$91,080,000 of Loan Certificates, Series A, and advised the
Lessee in the placement of $42,189,956 of Owner Certificates
issued in connection with the financing of the Encina–5 Project.*

BLYTH EASTMAN DILLON & CO.
        INCORPORATED

              MERRILL LYNCH WHITE WELD CAPITAL MARKETS GROUP
                    MERRILL LYNCH, PIERCE, FENNER & SMITH INCORPORATED

contrast, the equity investors can take advantage of 100 percent of the ownership tax benefits, even though they have contributed only 31.6 percent of the cost. The benefits of increased leverage and the utilization of tax deductions and credits results in a lower, blended cost of funds to the lessor. This lower cost of funds is passed through to the lessee in the form of lower lease rentals.

Another advantage of the leveraged lease was the fact that SDGE was able to avoid going to the capital market for conventional financing. The firm was able to forgo a $50 million bond issue previously planned for late 1978 and to reduce other debt and preferred financing in 1979. This resulted in an improvement in interest and fixed-charge coverages. On the negative side, however, it should be noted that bond rating agencies view a lease of this type as an obligation comparable to debt. In their coverage calculations, a leveraged lease is treated simply as a lower cost debt obligation. Thus, the benefit of improved coverage ratios is only achieved to the extent that the lease cost is less than the equivalent borrowing cost, as was true in this case.

Leveraged lease financing is a growing, viable alternative source of financing for a wide range of investment projects, especially when the investing firm is unable to take full advantage of the tax benefits of ownership.

Equipment Leasing

Terry J. Winders
President
FIRST LEASE and Equipment Consulting Corporation

As economic cycles have become shorter and less predictable, increased emphasis is being placed on controlling costs and effecting good cash management. Modern methods of financing capital equipment are evaluated more by the return on investment and the useful life of the equipment than by only the cost of borrowing. Leasing of capital equipment (personal property) has become an alternative that can provide a form of financing that reduces cash flow and improves short-term profits.

When the short-term cost of money exceeds long-term costs, cash is at a premium, and thoughts turn to 100 percent financing and a reduction of payment size to avoid negative cash flows. Equipment leasing serves a variety of needs for businesses, but none so great as the need to preserve cash and reduce the drain on reserves with adjustable rental payments.

Equipment leasing is generally categorized by two major headings: *a tax-motivated lease* and a *non–tax-motivated lease.* That is to say, the rentals (payments) on the equipment leased will or will not be reduced by the value of certain tax incentives such as accelerated depreciation, ITC, and energy tax credits. A nontax lease generally has only the value of the equipment at lease termination to reduce the size of rentals or payments.

A *nontax lease* generally is considered to take on the appearance of a contract of sale, because the ownership remains with the seller until all payments have been received, and then title is transferred for a stated amount. This stated amount is called a *purchase option.* The existence of a purchase option prohibits the lease from being a tax lease, because the IRS, through its Revenue Ruling 55–540 (as amended by 75–21 April 11, 1975), has stated that a purchase option that can be determined to be a bargain (less than the market value at the time of title transfer) proves that the true benefits of ownership rest with the purchaser. Therefore, the seller or financial institution holding title during the lease is prevented from taking the advantages of tax incentives. A nontax lease generally is used when it is important for the ownership of the equipment to remain with the lessor (seller/financial institution) until the lessee (customer) has completed the lease term. If the lessor has elected to take the value of the equipment at lease termination into account when determining the rental stream for the period of time the lessee has requested, it is ordinarily true that the lease payments will be lower than in the case of a conditional sale or a loan that would require the customer to completely pay for the equipment over the term of use. For example, nontax leases are used when "cost plus" contracts are negotiated during the construction of real property. Contracts usually do not allow a contractor to call "interest" on equipment loans a

476

cost, but they do allow rentals as a cost. Therefore, a contractor reduces expenses and increases profits by leasing equipment instead of borrowing to purchase.

True tax leases only offer fair market options at termination of the rental period to protect the lessor's right to depreciation and to bargain for ITC rights. Also, inflation and market conditions may make the actual value of the equipment much greater at lease termination than was predicted, thereby giving additional profits to the lessor. Occasionally technology and market conditions reduce equipment values; although a lessee may make all rental payments on time, the lessor will lose, because the equipment is worth less at termination than was expected. An example of a true lease would be a lease on a commercial aircraft where the carrier, having an extremely large capital budget, would find that the amount of ITCs and accelerated depreciation from purchasing many aircraft greatly exceeded the carrier's ability to absorb these benefits. A lease arranged for 80 percent of the useful life of the equipment would allow the carrier to have reduced rental payments and, at the same time, have use of the equipment for revenue generation over the greater part of the asset's useful life. The value of this reduced cash flow over the term of the lease might more than make up for the additional cost to purchase the aircraft at lease termination if inflation increased its value beyond original assumptions.

Equipment leasing began in earnest in the 1960s with the establishment of the ITC and the ability of lessors to leverage their position. They leveraged their position by borrowing a large portion of the cost of the equipment, leaving them with a minor equity position and still having the ability to take full advantage of tax credits. This is accomplished by using the strength of the credit of the lessee, pledging the payment stream from the lease to the lender, allowing a lien on the equipment (collateral), and thereby remaining not liable for the loan (a nonrecourse loan). The debt for the lease remains off the balance sheet for the lessor because of the nonrecourse nature of the loan.

The sophisticated software necessary to juggle all the variables on an equipment lease—such as delivery date, state tax bracket, Federal tax bracket, county tax bracket, residual assumptions, ITC, and equipment life—came into being in the 1960s. The software was refined during the 1970s to allow its use on transactions as low as $10,000. The sophistication of the software packages available today and the broad understanding of pricing techniques have expanded the use of equipment leasing from the industrial marketplace to the agricultural marketplace and also to foreign markets.

In 1981 the Economic Recovery Tax Act attempted to support ailing companies by allowing a *safe harbor lease.* This was a lease that would allow tax benefits to pass to a lessor while the lessee retained most of the benefits of ownership. In 1982 fear for the loss of tax revenues caused Congress to pass the Tax Equity and Fiscal Responsibility Act, thereby restricting the safe harbor election to extreme cases (such as a $150,000 exclusion for farmers) and also restricting the amount of safe harbor leasing any customer or lessor could engage in. Major leasing companies thereby returned to "guideline leasing" (rules established by IRS Revenue Ruling 55–540) in late 1982 except for extreme cases or leases to farmers.

The 1982 act also created a new format of leasing called a *finance lease* to take effect in varying stages with many restrictions. The finance leases combine some of the advantages of both guideline and non-tax leases. However, tremendous pressure is being placed on Congress to repeal or seriously modify this type of lease before it becomes the only method of tax-oriented leasing in January 1986.

QUESTIONS AND TOPICS FOR DISCUSSION

1. Under what circumstances might a firm prefer intermediate-term borrowing to either long- or short-term borrowing?

2. Discuss the advantages and disadvantages of the following types of term loans:
   a. Those that require equal periodic payments.
   b. Those that require equal periodic reductions in outstanding principal.
   c. Balloon loans.
   d. Bullet loans.

3. What are the major factors that influence the effective cost of a term loan?

4. Define the following and give an example of each:
   a. Affirmative covenants.
   b. Negative covenants.
   c. Restrictive covenants.

5. What institutions are the primary suppliers of business term loans?

6. Define the following:
   a. A conditional sales contract.
   b. A chattel mortgage.

7. Under what conditions would a firm prefer the following?
   a. A "fixed-rate" term loan from a bank.
   b. A "floating-rate" term loan, with the rate tied to the bank's prime rate?

8. What are the primary differences between operating leases and financial leases?

9. How does a leveraged lease differ from a nonleveraged financial lease? What type of firm or organization is most likely to take advantage of the leveraged lease financing option? What type of individual or financial institution is most likely to act as the lessor in a leveraged lease?

10. From a tax perspective, what are the primary requirements in a lease transaction that must be met in order for the IRS to consider the transaction a genuine lease? Why is a favorable IRS ruling regarding the tax status of a lease important to both the lessor and the lessee?

11. One advantage that has often been claimed of lease financing is that it creates "off–balance sheet" financing. Evaluate this benefit in light of FASB *Opinion No. 13.*

12. How can leasing allow a firm to effectively "depreciate" land?

13. What effect does leasing have on the stability of a firm's reported earnings?

14. It has been argued that leasing is almost always more expensive than borrowing and owning. Do you think this is true? Why or why not? Under what circum-

stances is leasing likely to be more desirable than direct ownership?

15. What was the major objective of safe harbor leasing?

16. Distinguish between *financial,* or *capital, leases* and the *finance leases* established under the TEFRA of 1982.

PROBLEMS *

1. Lobo Banks normally provides term loans that require repayment in a series of equal annual installments. If a $10 million loan is made, what would be the annual end-of-year payments, assuming the following?
   a. A 9 percent loan for 10 years.
   b. A 9 percent loan for 8 years.
   c. A 6 percent loan for 8 years.

2. Set up the amortization schedule for a 5-year, $1 million, 8 percent term loan that requires equal annual end-of-year payments. Be sure to distinguish between the *interest* and the *principal* portion of each payment.

3. Set up the amortization schedule for a 5-year, $1 million, 8 percent bullet loan. How is the principal repaid in this type of loan?

4. A firm receives a $2 million, 5-year loan at a 10 percent interest rate. The loan requires annual payments of $250,000 per year (at the end of each year) for years 1 to 4.
   a. What payment is required at the end of year 5?
   b. What would you call this type of loan?
   c. How does it differ from the loan in Problem 2?

5. A $5 million, 5-year loan bears an interest rate of 7 percent. The loan repayment plan calls for five annual end-of-year payments. Each payment is to include an equal amount of principal repayment ($1 million per year) plus accrued interest. Set up the amortization schedule for this loan. Be sure to distinguish between the *interest* and the *principal* portions of each annual payment.

6. Huskie Bank has provided the Mucklup Manufacturing Company with a 2-year term loan for $100,000 at a stated annual rate of interest of 8 percent. Interest for the entire 2-year period must be prepaid; that is, the loan's total interest payments must be made at the same time the loan is granted. Mucklup is required to repay the entire $100,000 principal balance at the end of the 2-year period.
   Compute the effective annual percentage cost of the loan.

7. The James Company has been offered a 4-year loan from its bank in the amount of $100,000 at a stated interest rate of 10 percent per year. The loan will require four equal end-of-year payments of principal and interest plus a $30,000 balloon payment at the end of the fourth year.
   a. Compute the amount of each of the end-of-year payments.
   b. Prepare a loan amortization schedule detailing the amount of principal and interest in each year's payment.
   c. What is the effective interest rate on this loan? Prove your answer.
   HINT: Each year's payment may be computed by solving for the annuity payment of a 4-year, 10 percent annuity that has a present value of $70,000—the amount of the loan that is amortized by the four yearly payments—and adding to that amount the interest on the unpaid balloon portion of the loan.

* Problems in color have check answers provided at the end of the book.

8. Ajax Leasing Services has been approached by Gamma Tools to provide lease financing for a new automated screw machine. The machine will cost $220,000 and have an economic life of 5 years. The estimated salvage value of the machine will be $20,000. If Ajax requires an 8 percent before-tax rate of return on this investment, what annual (beginning-of-year) lease payment should be required?

9. The First National Bank of Springer has established a leasing subsidiary. A local firm, Allied Business Machines, has approached the bank to arrange lease financing for $10 million in new machinery. The economic life of the machinery is estimated to be 20 years. The estimated salvage value at the end of the 20-year period is $0. The machinery is eligible for the 10 percent investment tax credit. The tax credit is assumed to be immediately available at the time the asset is acquired. Allied Business Machines has indicated a willingness to pay the bank $1 million per year at the *end* of each year for 20 years under the terms of a financial lease.

   a. If the bank retains the benefit of the investment tax credit, depreciates the machinery on a straight line basis over 20 years to a $0 estimated salvage value, and has a 40 percent marginal tax rate, what *after-tax* rate of return will the bank earn on the lease?

   b. In general, what effect would the use of ACRS depreciation by the bank have on the rate of return it earns from the lease?

10. Jessup Corporation wants to acquire a $200,000 computer. Jessup has a 40 percent marginal tax rate. The computer has an estimated life of 10 years and would be depreciated on a straight line basis to a *book* salvage value of $0 if Jessup owned the computer. Actual *cash* salvage value is estimated to be $20,000. A 10 percent investment tax credit is available to Jessup at the time it acquires the computer. If the computer is leased, it is assumed that the lessor would claim the 10 percent investment tax credit.

   Jessup could borrow the needed funds ($200,000 less $20,000 investment tax credit) at a 10 percent rate. The loan would require annual end-of-year principal plus interest payments of $29,294. Alternatively, the asset could be leased at an annual rate of $28,000, payable at the beginning of each of the 10 years.

   a. Using Jessup's after-tax cost of borrowing as the discount rate, compute the present value cost of leasing.

   b. Compute the present value cost of borrowing and buying the computer.

   c. Which alternative is more attractive? Why?

11. a. What effect would the use of ACRS depreciation have on your answers to Problem 10?

    b. Assume Jessup does not have enough taxable income to take advantage of the 10 percent investment tax credit. What effect would that have on the firm's decision? How would the present value cost of borrowing and buying change?

12. The following stream of after-tax cash flows are available to you as a potential equity investor in a leveraged lease:

End of Year	Cash Flow (After Tax)	End of Year	Cash Flow (After Tax)
0	−50	6	0
1	+30	7	−5
2	+20	8	−10
3	+15	9	−15
4	+10	10	+10
5	+5		

The cash flow in year 0 represents the initial equity investment. The high positive cash flows in years 1 to 5 result from the tax shield benefits from the investment tax credit, accelerated depreciation, and interest deductibility on the nonrecourse debt. The negative cash flows in years 6 to 9 are indicative of the cash flows generated in a leveraged lease after the earlier-period tax shields have been utilized. The positive cash flow occurring in year 10 is the result of the asset's salvage value.

    a. What problems would you encounter in computing the equity investor's rate of return on this investment?

    b. If, as a potential equity investor, you require an 8 percent after tax rate of return on investments of this type, should you make this investment?

13. The Jacobs Company desires to lease a numerically controlled milling machine costing $200,000. Jacobs has asked both First Manufacturers Bank Leasing Corp. and Commercial Associates, Inc. (a commercial finance company), to quote an annual lease rate. Both leasing companies now require a 20 percent pretax rate of return on this type of lease. Suppose First Manufacturers estimates the machine's salvage value at the end of the lease to be $30,000, and Commercial Associates estimates salvage to be $80,000. Based on this information and disregarding the investment tax credit, what annual (beginning-of-year) lease payments will each leasing company require, if the lease term is 5 years?

14. Atlas Leasing Services has been approached by Boulder Fabricating Co., a small metal fabricator, to provide lease financing for a new press. The machine will cost $150,000 and is expected to have a $50,000 salvage value at the end of a 5-year lease. Atlas Leasing considers salvage value in determining lease payments, because the company feels it cannot be competitive without doing so. If Atlas Leasing desires a 20 percent before-tax rate of return on this lease, what annual (end-of-year) lease payment should be required? The machine is eligible for a 10 percent investment tax credit, and Atlas plans to take it. Atlas considers investment tax credits in determining lease payments.

15. The First National Bank of Great Falls is considering a leveraged lease agreement involving some mining equipment with the Big Sky Mining Corporation. The bank (40 percent tax bracket) will be the lessor; the mining company, the lessee (0 percent tax bracket); and a large California pension fund, the lender. Big Sky is seeking $50 million, and the pension fund has agreed to lend the bank $40 million at 10 percent. The bank has agreed to repay the pension fund $4 million of principal each year plus interest. (The remaining balance will be repaid in a balloon payment at the end of the fifth year.) Several tax matters are pertinent to the analysis: (1) the equipment is eligible for a 10 percent investment tax credit, and the bank plans to take it; and (2) the equipment will be depreciated on a straight line basis over a five-year estimated useful life with no expected salvage value. Assuming Big Sky has agreed to annual lease payments of $10 million, calculate the bank's initial cash outflow and its first 2 years of cash inflows.

Lease and Term Loan Analysis

Bay Products Corporation of North America (BPCNA) currently has no computer facilities. Recent growth in the firm's operations has led management to consider the possibility of adding an in-house mid-size computer to its accounting and financial departments. BPCNA management has called in consultants from a number of computer firms to assist it in designing a useful and cost-effective system. After considering a number of alternatives, BPCNA decided that the DATAMAX 1000 computer, offered by Data Equipment, Inc., best meets its current and projected future needs.

BPCNA evaluated the desirability of the acquisition of the DATA-MAX 1000 computer using its normal capital budgeting procedures. It found that the computer has a large positive expected net present value.

Jim Horn, a new management trainee in the financial planning office, has recently been reading about the boom in the leasing industry. He feels that if leasing is growing as rapidly as it seems, there must be some significant advantages to the leasing alternative to ownership.

If purchased, the new computer will cost $100,000. The computer has an estimated economic life of 6 years and is therefore eligible for the 10 percent investment tax credit. BPCNA would depreciate the computer on a 5-year ACRS basis to a $0 estimated salvage value. If purchased, the computer could be financed with a 6-year loan of $90,000 (the $100,000 asset cost minus the investment tax credit equals the net outlay required) at a 10 percent annual percentage rate of interest. The loan calls for six equal annual end-of-year payments of principal and interest.

If BPCNA decides to lease the computer, it will not receive the investment tax credit. Under the terms of the financial lease, BPCNA would be required to make six beginning-of-year lease payments of $22,000 each. BPCNA believes that its after-tax cost of borrowing, estimated to be 6 percent, is the appropriate rate to use to evaluate the cash flows from borrowing and buying and from leasing. BPCNA's marginal tax rate is 40 percent.

Under both the lease alternative and the borrow and buy alternative, BPCNA will contract with a computer service company to handle the estimated annual service and maintenance.

1. Compute the present value cost of borrowing and buying the computer.
2. Compute the present value cost of leasing the computer.
3. Which alternative should BPCNA accept? What other factors might be considered?
4. If BPCNA can borrow the needed funds from a bank in the form of a bullet loan carrying a 10 percent interest rate, what effect would this have on the decision to lease or buy?
5. What effect would the use of straight line depreciation have on the lease-buy decision? (Answer verbally; no calculations are needed. Ignore the bullet loan assumption in Question 4.)

6. If, at the end of 6 years, the computer is expected to have an actual salvage value of $10,000, what would be the impact on the present value cost of borrowing and buying?

ADDITIONAL READINGS AND REFERENCES

Anderson, Paul F., and Martin, John D. "Lease vs Purchase Decisions: A Survey of Current Practice." *Financial Management* (Spring 1977): 41–47.

Athanasopoulas, Peter J., and Bacon, Peter W. "The Evaluation of Leveraged Leases." *Financial Management* 9 (Spring 1980): 76–80.

Bower, Richard S. "Issues in Lease Financing." *Financial Management* 2 (Winter 1973): 25–34.

Gordon, Myron J. "A General Solution to the Buy or Lease Decision: A Pedagogical Note." *Journal of Finance* 29 (March 1974): 245–250.

Gritta, R. D. "The Impact of the Capitalization of Leases on Financial Analysis." *Financial Analysts Journal* (March–April 1974): 47–52.

Johnson, Robert W., and Lewellen, Wilbur G. "Analysis of the Lease-or-Buy Decision." *Journal of Finance* 27 (Sept. 1972): 815–823.

Keller, Thomas F., and Peterson, Russell J. "Optimal Financial Structure, Cost of Capital and the Lease-or-Buy Decision." *Journal of Business Finance and Accounting* 1 (Autumn 1974): 405–414.

Moyer, R. Charles. "Lease Evaluation and the Investment Tax Credit: A Framework for Analysis." *Financial Mangement* 4 (Summer 1975): 39–44.

Nantell, Timothy J. "Equivalence of Lease versus Buy Analyses." *Financial Management* 2 (Autumn 1973): 61–65.

Nelson, A. Thomas. "Capitalized Leases—The Effect on Financial Ratios." *Journal of Accountancy* 116 (July 1963): 49–58.

Ofer, Aharon R. "The Evaluation of the Lease vs Purchase Alternatives." *Financial Management* (Summer 1976): 67–74.

Roberts, Gordon S., and Gudikunst, Arthur C. "Equipment Financial Leasing Practices and Costs: Comment." *Financial Management* 7 (Summer 1978): 79–81.

Roenfeldt, Rodney L., and Osteryoung, Jerome S. "Analysis of Financial Leases." *Financial Management* 2 (Spring 1973): 74–87.

Smith, Pierce R. "A Straightforward Approach to Leveraged Leasing." *Journal of Commercial Bank Lending* (July 1973): 19–39.

Sorensen, Ivar, and Johnson, Ramon. "Equipment Financial Leasing Practices and Costs: An Empirical Study." *Financial Management* (Spring 1977): 33–40.

Vanderwicker, P. "The Powerful Logic of the Leasing Boom." *Fortune* (Nov. 1973): 132–136.

Zinbarg, Edward D. "The Private Placement Loan Agreement." *Financial Analysts Journal* 31 (July–Aug. 1975): 33–35.

CHAPTER 16

Long-Term Debt, Preferred Stock, and Common Stock

A FINANCIAL DILEMMA

Hershey Foods: A Semisweet Offering

On February 26, 1979, Hershey Foods announced that it planned to sell $75 million of new 30-year debenture bonds. The firm planned to use the proceeds from these bonds to repay bank borrowings incurred when it purchased the Friendly Ice Cream Corporation.

On the same day, Moody's Investors Services, a major bond-rating agency, announced that it was downgrading Hershey's senior debt obligations from an AA to an A rating. Apparently, Moody's felt that Hershey's additional planned "permanent" debt increased the firm's risk.

Because its bonds have been downgraded, Hershey Foods will now have to pay more for any additional funds it borrows. This may not necessarily be undesirable, however, since the firm's new, more leveraged capital structure might result in a lower weighted cost of capital.

For a firm to make the appropriate capital structure decisions, its management must be familiar with the characteristics, advantages, and disadvantages of various forms of long-term financing. This chapter examines the alternatives of common stock, preferred stock, and long-term debt in this light.

GLOSSARY OF NEW TERMS

Bond rating   an evaluation of a bond's probability of default. This is performed by an outside rating agency, such as Standard and Poor's or Moody's.

Bond refunding   a situation that occurs when a firm redeems a callable bond issue and sells a generally lower interest cost issue to take its place.

Call feature   a provision that permits an issuer of bonds (and sometimes preferred stock) to retire the obligation prior to its maturity.

Call premium   the difference between a bond's call price and its par value.

Call price   the price at which a bond may be retired, or called, prior to its maturity.

Competitive bidding   the process of selling a new security offering to the highest bidding underwriting syndicate.

Convertible bond   a bond that may be converted into common stock at the holder's option.

Cumulative dividends   a typical feature of preferred stock that requires any past-due preferred stock dividends to be paid before any common stock dividends can be paid.

Direct placement   the sale of an entire security offering to one or more institutional investors rather than the general public. This is also termed a *private placement.*

Flotation cost   the cost of issuing new securities. This includes both underwriting expenses and other issue expenses, such as printing and legal fees.

Income bond   a bond that pays interest only if the firm earns sufficient income.

Indenture   the contract between the issuing firm and the lenders in a debt obligation.

Investment banker   a financial institution that underwrites and sells new securities. In general, investment bankers assist firms in obtaining new financing.

Listed security exchanges   organized secondary security markets that operate at designated places of business. The New York Stock Exchange (NYSE) is an example of a listed security exchange.

Negotiated underwriting   a process whereby a firm wishing to sell new securities to the public negotiates the terms of the underwriting with the investment banker or bankers.

Over-the-counter (OTC) securities markets   a network of security dealers connected by a communications system of telephones and computer terminals that provides price quotations on individual securities.

Par value   an arbitrary value assigned to common stock or preferred stock by the issuing firm. In the case of a bond, the par value is usually $1,000 and represents the amount of principal borrowed and due at maturity.

Preemptive right   a provision contained in some corporate charters that gives common stockholders the right to buy on a pro rata basis any new common shares sold by the firm.

Prospectus   a document that contains a vast amount of information about a company's legal, operational, and financial position. It is prepared for the benefit of prospective investors in a new security issued by the firm.

Purchasing syndicate   a *group* of investment bankers who agree to underwrite a new security issue in order to spread the risk of underwriting.

Right a short-term option issued by a firm that permits an existing stock-holder to buy a specified number of shares of common stock at a specified price (the subscription price), usually below the current market price.

Rights offering the sale of new shares of common stock by distributing stock purchase *rights* to a firm's existing shareholders. This is also termed a *privileged subscription.*

Securities and Exchange Commission (SEC) the government regulatory agency responsible for administering Federal securities legislation.

Senior debt debt that has a higher claim to a firm's earnings and/or assets than junior debt.

Stock split the issuance of a number of new shares in exchange for each old share held by a stockholder.

Subordinated debenture a bond that has a claim on the issuing firm's assets that is junior to other forms of debt in the event of a liquidation. The claims of subordinated debenture holders can be met only *after* all the claims of senior creditors have been met.

Trustee the bondholders' representative in a public debt offering. The trustee is responsible for monitoring the borrower's compliance with the terms of the indenture.

Underwriting a process whereby a group of investment bankers agrees to purchase a new security issue at a set price and then offer it for sale to the general public.

Underwriting spread the difference between the selling price to the public of a new security offering and the proceeds received by the offering firm. This is also termed an *underwriting discount.*

INTRODUCTION

Long-term debt, preferred stock, and common stock are the major sources of capital for a firm. Long-term debt and preferred stock are classified as *fixed income securities*, because they involve relatively constant distributions of interest or dividend payments to their holders. For example, Houston Lighting and Power Company sold $50 million of long-term debt in 1971, at which time it agreed to pay its lenders an interest rate of 7.5 percent or $75 a year for each $1,000 of debt outstanding. Since then the company has continued to pay this interest rate, even though market interest rates have fluctuated. Similarly, AT&T issued $1.37 billion of preferred stock in 1971. Its investors paid $50 per share, and the company agreed to pay an annual dividend of $4 per share. Since that time, AT&T has continued to pay this amount, even though common stock dividends have been increased several times.

Common stock, on the other hand, is a *variable income security*, because the dividends paid on common stock tend to fluctuate. For example, in 1975 Tucson Electric Power Company sold new common shares when annual dividends were $0.84 per share. By mid-1983 the annual rate was $2.20 per share, having been raised several times during the intervening years.

Common stock also differs from long-term debt and preferred stock in that its market price tends to fluctuate considerably, thus causing returns on common stock investments to vary more widely over time than returns on preferred stock or long-term debt.

The fixed-income securities—long-term debt and preferred stock—also differ from each other in several ways. For example, the interest paid to long-term lenders is a tax-deductible expense for the borrowing company, whereas dividends paid to preferred stockholders are not. Legally, long-term debtholders are considered creditors, whereas preferred stockholders are considered owners. Thus, a firm is not legally required to pay dividends to its preferred stockholders, and the failure to do so has less serious consequences than does the failure to meet interest obligations on long-term debt. In addition, long-term debt has a specific *maturity*, whereas preferred stock is often *perpetual*.

The next three major sections of this chater are devoted to detailed discussions of each of these three sources of capital. The remaining two major sections deal with capital markets and the role of investment bankers.

LONG-TERM DEBT

Although a company incurs a certain amount of financial risk when it engages in long-term borrowing, it can gain the advantages of positive financial leverage by earning a higher rate of return on its assets than the rate of interest it has to pay for its borrowed funds.[1] Many large U.S. companies operating near their optimal capital structures have up to 40 percent or more long-term debt in their capital structures. As long as a firm does not use an excessive amount of long-term debt, the benefits of favorable financial leverage are likely to outweigh the disadvantages of increased financial risk.

When a company borrows money in the capital markets, it issues long-term debt securities to investors. These are usually sold in denominations of $1,000 and constitute a promise by the issuing company to repay a certain amount of money (the $1,000 principal) on a particular date (the maturity date) and to pay a specified amount of interest at fixed intervals (usually twice a year). Most debt has a *par value* of $1,000, and debt prices are often expressed as a percentage of that value. For example, a market price listing of "87" indicates that a $1,000 par value bond may be purchased for $870.

There are many different types of long-term debt. The type or types a company chooses to use will depend on its own particular financial situation and the characteristics of the industry as a whole.

TYPES OF LONG-TERM DEBT

Long-term debt is generally classified according to whether or not it is secured by specific physical assets of the issuing company. Secured debt issues are usually called *mortgage bonds*, and issues that are not secured by specific

---

[1]Financial leverage is discussed in Chapter 7.

assets are called *debentures* or, occasionally, *debenture bonds.* The term *bond* is often used to denote any type of long-term debt security.

At the present time, utility companies are the largest users of mortgage bonds. In recent years the use of mortgage bonds relative to other forms of long-term debt has declined, while the use of debentures has increased. Since debentures are unsecured, their quality depends on the general credit-worthiness of the issuing company. As a result, they are usually issued by large, financially strong firms.

The yield differential between the mortgage bond and debenture alternatives is another example of the risk-return tradeoff that occurs throughout finance. For example, suppose Midstates Oil Company could issue either mortgage bonds or debentures. If the mortgage bonds could be sold with a 10 percent interest rate, the debentures would have to be sold at a higher rate—for example, 10.3 percent—to attract investors. This is due to the fact that investors require a higher return on debentures, which are backed only by the unmortgaged assets of the company and the company's earning power, than they do on mortgage bonds, which are secured by specific physical assets as well as the company's earning power.

Debt issues are also classified according to whether they are *senior* or *junior.*[2] Senior debt has a higher priority claim to a firm's earnings and/or assets than junior debt. Occasionally the actual name of the debt issue will contain a "junior" or "senior" qualifier. In most instances, however, identification of how a particular company's debt issues are ranked requires an analysis of the restrictions placed on the company by the purchasers of the issue.

Unsecured debt also may be classified according to whether it is *subordinated* to other types of debt. In the event of a liquidation or reorganization, the claims of *subordinated debenture holders* are considered only *after* the claims of *unsubordinated debenture holders.* In general, subordinated debentures are junior to other types of debt, including bank loans, and may even be junior to *all* of a firm's other debt.

Equipment trust certificates are used largely by railroad and trucking companies. The proceeds from these certificates are used to purchase specific assets, such as railroad rolling stock. The certificate holders own the equipment and lease it to the company. Technically, equipment trust certificates are not true bonds, even though they are guaranteed by the issuing company, because the interest and principal are paid by the *trustee* (the financial institution responsible for looking after the investors' interests). Even so, they are classified as debt because they have all of the characteristics of debt.

Collateral trust bonds are backed by stocks or bonds of other corporations. This type of financing is principally of historical interest; it is used today primarily by holding companies. A holding company may, for example, raise needed funds by pledging the stocks and/or bonds of its subsidiaries as collateral. In this arrangement the holding company serves as the *parent* company. The subsidiary borrows from the parent, and the parent borrows from the capital markets. This makes good sense, because the parent company can

---

[2]The senior-junior classification scheme is also used in connection with preferred and common stock. Preferred stock is junior to long-term debt and senior to common stock.

generally get more favorable terms for its debt in the capital markets than the subsidiary.

Income bonds are also largely of historical interest, although they are still occasionally used today. Income bonds promise to pay interest only if the issuing firm earns sufficient income; if it does not, no interest obligation exists. These securities are rarely issued directly. Instead, they often are created in reorganizations following bankruptcy and are normally issued in exchange for junior or subordinated issues. Thus, unsecured income bonds are generally considered to be "weak" securities.

Pollution control bonds and *industrial revenue bonds* are issued by local governments rather than corporations. The interest paid to purchasers of municipal bonds is tax exempt, and the interest rate is typically less than what a corporation would have to pay. The interest payments are guaranteed by the corporation for whose benefit the bonds are issued.

Original issue deep discount bonds are newly issued bonds that have coupon interest rates lower than the current market rate and therefore sell at discounts from par value. These bonds are discussed in the first "Focus on Corporate Practice" later in this chapter.

FEATURES OF LONG-TERM DEBT

Long-term debt has a number of unique features. Several of these are discussed in the following paragraphs.

Indenture   An indenture is a contract between a firm that issues long-term debt securities and the lenders. In general, an indenture does the following:

- It thoroughly details the nature of the debt issue.
- It carefully specifies the manner in which the principal must be repaid.
- It lists any restrictions that are placed on the firm by the lenders. These restrictions are called *covenants,* and the firm must satisfy them to keep from defaulting on its obligation.[3] Typical restrictive covenants include the following:

1. A minimum coverage, or times interest earned ratio, the firm must maintain.

2. A minimum level of working capital the firm must maintain.

3. A maximum amount of dividends the firm can pay on its preferred and common stock.

4. Other restrictions that effectively limit how much leasing and issuing of additional debt the firm may do.

Trustee   Since the holders of a large firm's long-term debt issue are likely to be widely scattered geographically, the Trust Indenture Act of 1939 requires that

---

[3]A company defaults on its debt when it does not pay interest or required principal on time. When default occurs, the debt is often said to be "triggered," meaning that the entire principal amount comes due immediately. This could result in bankruptcy.

a trustee represent the debtholders in dealings with the issuing company. A trustee is usually a commercial bank or trust company that is responsible for insuring that all the terms and convenants set forth in the indenture agreement are adhered to by the issuing company. The issuing company must pay the trustee's expenses.

Call feature   A call feature is an optional retirement provision that permits the issuing company to redeem, or *call*, a debt issue prior to its maturity date at a specified price termed the *redemption*, or *call*, *price*. Many firms use the call feature because it provides them with the potential flexiblity to retire debt prior to maturity if, for example, interest rates decline.

The call price is greater than the par value of the debt, and the difference between the two is the *call premium*. During the early years of an issue the call premium is usually equal to about 1 year's interest. Some debt issues specify *fixed* call premiums, whereas others specify *declining* call premiums. For example, in 1982 the El Paso Natural Gas Company issued 16.7 percent, 20-year debentures. During 1982 the company could have retired all or part of this issue at 116.7 percent of par value, and during 1983 the redemption price dropped to 115.77 percent of par. Similar reductions in the redemption price are scheduled for each year up to the year 2000.

Many bonds are not callable at all for several years after the initial issue date. This situation is referred to as a *deferred call*.

Details of the call feature are worked out before the debt is sold in the negotiations between the underwriters and the issuing company. Since a call feature gives the company significant flexibility in its financing plans, while at the same time potentially depriving the lenders of the advantages they would gain from holding the debt until maturity, the issuing company has to offer the investors compensation in the form of the call premium in exchange for the call privilege. In addition, the interest rate on a callable debt issue is usually slightly higher than the interest rate on a similar noncallable issue.

Because of the interest savings that can be achieved, a firm is most likely to call a debt issue when prevailing interest rates are appreciably lower than those that existed at the time of the original issue. When a company calls a relatively high interest issue and replaces it with a lower interest issue, the procedure is called *bond refunding*. This topic is discussed in the appendix to this chapter.

Sinking fund   Usually lenders will require that a borrowing company gradually reduce the outstanding balance of a debt issue over its life instead of having the entire principal amount come due on a particular date 20 or 30 years into the future. The usual method of providing for a gradual retirement is a sinking fund, so called because a certain amount of money—for example, 3 percent of the total issue—is put aside annually, or "sunk," into a *sinking fund account*. In practice, however, a company can also satisfy its sinking fund requirements either by purchasing a portion of the debt each year in the open market or, if the debt is callable, by using a lottery technique to determine which actual numbered certificates will be called and retired within a given year. The alternative chosen depends on the current market price of the debt issue. In general, if current interest rates are above the issue's coupon rate, the current market price of the debt will be less than $1,000, and the company should meet its sinking fund obligation by purchasing the debt in the open market. If, on the other hand, market interest rates are lower than the issue's coupon rate, and if the market price of the debt is above the call price, the company should use the call procedure.

Conversion feature Some debt issues (and some preferred stock issues) have a conversion feature that allows the holder to exchange the security for the company's common stock at the option of the holder. The features of convertible securities are discussed in Chapter 17.

Typical sizes of debt issues Debt issues sold to the public through underwriters are usually in the $25 to $200 million range, although very large firms occasionally borrow up to $500 million or more at one time. Since the use of an underwriting group in a public offering involves considerable expense, it is usually uneconomical for a company to make a public offering of this nature for debt issues less than about $25 million. *Private placements*, however, frequently involve lesser amounts of money—for example, $5 to $10 million—since the entire debt issue is purchased by a single investor, such as an insurance company.

Maturity The typical maturity on long-term debt is about 20 to 30 years. Occasionally companies borrow money for as long as 40 years. On the other end of the scale, companies in need of financing often are willing to borrow for only about 10 years, especially if they feel that interest rates are temporarily high, as was true in the environment of the late 1970s and until mid-1982—an environment characterized by high rates of inflation and historically high interest rates. By the spring of 1983, many large companies were again issuing fixed-rate debt securities with 25- and 30-year maturities.

From an accounting standpoint, debt obligations maturing in more than 1 year are usually classified as long-term debt on the balance sheet.

BOND RATINGS

Debt issues are rated according to their relative degree of risk by various financial companies, including Moody's Investors Services and Standard and Poor's Corporation (S&P). These agencies consider a variety of factors when rating a firm's securities, including earnings stability, coverage ratios, the relative amount of debt in the firm's capital structure, and the degree of subordination, as well as past experience. According to Moody's rating scale, the highest-quality–lowest-risk issues are rated Aaa, and the scale continues down through Aa, A, Baa, Ba, B, Caa, Ca, and C. On the Standard and Poor's ratings scale, AAA denotes the highest-quality issues, and this rating is followed by AA, A, BBB, BB, B, and so on. S&P also has various C and D classifications for high-risk issues; the vast majority of debt issues, however, fall into one of the A or B categories. Figure 16–1 shows Moody's and S&P's bond-rating definitions.

Table 16–1 gives some examples of capital structure and coverage ratios for various debt ratings. In general, as the debt rating decreases from AAA to

FIGURE 16–1 Moody's and Standard and Poor's Bond-Rating Definitions

KEY TO MOODY'S CORPORATE RATINGS*

Aaa

Bonds which are rated Aaa are judged to be of the best quality. They carry the smallest degree of investment risk and are generally referred to as "gilt edge." Interest payments are protected by a large or by an exceptionally stable margin and principal is secure. While the various protective elements are likely to change, such changes as can be visualized are most unlikely to impair the fundamentally strong position of such issues.

Aa

Bonds which are rated Aa are judged to be of high quality by all standards. Together with the Aaa group they comprise what are generally known as high grade bonds. They are rated lower than the best bonds because margins of protection may not be as large as in Aaa securities or fluctuation of protective elements may be of greater amplitude or there may be other elements present which make the long term risks appear somewhat larger than in Aaa securities.

A

Bonds which are rated A possess many favorable investment attributes and are to be considered as upper medium grade obligations. Factors giving security to principal and interest are considered adequate but elements may be present which suggest a suscepti- bility to impairment sometime in the future.

Baa

Bonds which are rated Baa are considered as medium grade obligations, i.e., they are neither highly protected nor poorly secured. Interest payments and principal security ap- pear adequate for the present but certain protective elements may be lacking or may be characteristically unreliable over any great length of time. Such bonds lack outstanding investment characteristics and in fact have speculative characteristics as well.

Ba

Bonds which are rated Ba are judged to have speculative elements; their future cannot be considered as well assured. Often the protection of interest and principal payments may be very moderate and thereby not well safeguarded during both good and bad times over the future. Uncertainty of position characterizes bonds in this class.

B

Bonds which are rated B generally lack characteristics of the desirable investment. As- surance of interest and principal payments or of maintenance of other terms of the con- tract over any long period of time may be small.

Caa

Bonds which are rated Caa are of poor standing. Such issues may be in default or there may be present elements of danger with respect to principal or interest.

Ca

Bonds which are rated Ca represent obligations which are speculative in a high degree. Such issues are often in default or have other marked shortcomings.

Continued

C

Bonds which are rated C are the lowest rated class of bonds and issues so rated can be regarded as having extremely poor prospects of ever attaining any real investment standing.

---

*Moody's applies numerical modifers, 1, 2 and 3 in each generic rating classification from Aa through B in its corporate bond rating system. The modifier 1 indicates that the security ranks in the higher end of its generic rating category; the modifier 2 indicates a mid-range ranking; and the modifier 3 indicates that the issue ranks in the lower end of its generic rating category. SOURCE: *Moody's Bond Record*, March 1983. Reprinted by permission of Moody's Investors Service, Inc.

STANDARD & POOR'S CORPORATE AND MUNICIPAL DEBT-RATING DEFINITIONS

AAA

Debt rated AAA has the highest rating assigned by Standard & Poor's. Capacity to pay interest and repay principal is extremely strong.

AA

Debt rated AA has a very strong capacity to pay interest and repay principal and differs from the higher rated issues only in small degree.

A

Debt rated A has a strong capacity to pay interest and repay principal although it is somewhat more susceptible to the adverse effects of changes in circumstances and economic conditions than debt in higher rated categories.

BBB

Debt rated BBB is regarded as having an adequate capacity to pay interest and repay principal. Whereas it normally exhibits adequate protection parameters, adverse economic conditions or changing circumstances are more likely to lead to a weakened capacity to pay interest and repay principal for debt in this category than in higher rated categories.

BB, B, CCC, CC

Debt rated BB, B, CCC and CC is regarded, on balance, as predominently speculative with respect to capacity to pay interest and repay principal in accordance with the terms of the obligation. BB indicates the lowest degree of speculation and CC the highest degree of speculation. While such debt will likely have some quality and protective characteristics, these are outweighed by large uncertainities or major risk exposures to adverse conditions.

C

The rating C is reserved for income bonds on which no interest is being paid.

D

Debt rated D is in default, and payment of interest and or repayment of principal is in arrears.

Continued

FIGURE 16–1 continued

Plus (+) or Minus (−)

The ratings from "AA" to "B" may be modified by the addition of a plus or minus sign to show relative standing within the major rating categories.

SOURCE: *Standard & Poor's Bond Guide*, March 1983. Reprinted by permission of Standard and Poor's.

lower ratings, the percentage of long-term debt in the capital structure increases and the coverage ratio decreases.

As a general rule, "triple A" issues yield the lowest interest rates at any given time. This is another example of the risk–return tradeoff in finance. Since the perceived default risk difference between companies rated A and B is usually less during periods of economic prosperity than during recessionary periods, the interest rate spread between A- and B-rated issues also tends to be smaller during periods of economic prosperity.

INFORMATION ON DEBT FINANCING ACTIVITIES

Every business day financial newspapers contain information on debt financing activities. For example, The *Wall Street Journal* devotes at least one page to financing activities in the bond market. This page contains announcements by underwriters concerning the characteristics of the new issues presently being offered.

TABLE 16–1 Selected Examples of Capital Structure and Coverage Ratios for Various Debt Ratings

Company	Standard and Poor's Debt Rating*	Long-Term Debt to Total Capitalization†	Operating Income Divided by Interest Expense†
IBM Corp.	AAA	12.7%	18.6 times
General Electric	AAA	10.2	7.9
Mobil Corp.	AA	17.3	10.9
Dayton Hudson	AA	26.4	7.7
Textron	AA −	18.7	7.9
Deere & Co.	A +	21.0	2.5
Monsanto	A	22.3	6.5
RCA Corp.	BBB +	45.3	2.5
Ford Motor	BBB +	24.1	1.4
Goodyear Tire & Rubber	BBB	30.4	3.8
International Harvester	CCC	57.2	0.03

*As of March 1983.
†As of December 31, 1981.
SOURCES: *Standard & Poor's Bond Guide*, March 1983; *Standard & Poor's 500 Stock Market Encyclopedia*, Spring 1983.

The *Wall Streeet Journal* also contains information on the secondary debt markets, including price quotations for the widely traded corporate debt issues listed on the New York Stock Exchange. The next section is devoted to understanding these price quotations.

UNDERSTANDING BOND QUOTATIONS[4]

The majority of existing debt issues of U.S. corporations are traded over the counter. However, many widely traded issues are listed on the major exchanges. Price quotations for debt issues traded on the New York Stock Exchange are published daily in the *Wall Street Journal*. Table 16–2 shows a selected list from that source on two different dates in 1982 and 1983.

Bond prices are quoted as a percentage of their par value (usually $1,000). For example, the closing price of the Toledo Edison issue on April 14, 1983, was $782.50 per $1,000 bond. The *8.80s05* after the AT&T (American Telephone & Telegraph) means that the debt issue has a contract, or coupon, interest rate of 8.80 percent. Thus, a holder of the issue receives $44 in interest per bond every 6 months for a total of $88 (8.8% × $1,000) each year. This debt issue, or series (the *s* stands for "series"), matures in the year 2005, hence, the *05* listing. The current yield is calculated by dividing the annual

TABLE 16–2 Selected Listing of Bond Quotations
New York Exchange

Bonds	Cur Yld	Vol	High	Low	Close	Net Chg
SELECTED BOND QUOTATIONS—JULY 9, 1982						
Alld C zr98s	—	18	13⅞	13¼	13½	+¼
ATT 8.80s05	14	203	63¾	63	63⅝	+⅜
duPnt 8.45s04	14	16	60½	60½	60½	+¾
Exxon 6s97	12	71	53	52⅛	52⅛	−⅛
IntHrv 9s04	29	52	30¾	30	30¾	+1⅜
TolEd 9.65s06	16	40	59⅛	59⅛	59⅛	+1⅛
UCarb 14½s91	15	9	98⅞	97	98⅞	+1⅞

SOURCE: *Wall Street Journal*, July 12, 1982.

Bonds	Cur Yld	Vol	High	Low	Close	Net Chg
SELECTED BOND QUOTATIONS—APRIL 14, 1983						
AlldC zr98s	—	32	21⅝	21½	21⅝	+⅛
ATT 8.80s05	11	584	83	81⅝	83	+1
duPnt 8.45s04	11	85	79	78	78	+½
Exxon 6s97	8.9	254	67⅜	66¼	67⅜	+1⅛
IntHrv 9s04	16	252	57⅞	56¾	57⅞	+1⅝
TolEd 9.65s06	12	10	78¼	78¼	78¼	+1¼
UCarb 14½s91	13	60	113	113	113	+1

SOURCE: *Wall Street Journal*, April 15, 1983.

[4]In this discussion the term *bond* includes mortgage bonds, debentures, and notes.

interest by the day's closing price; for example, $88/$830 = 11%. However, current yield is only an approximation of the true yield, given by the yield to maturity.[5]

USERS OF LONG-TERM DEBT

Most large and medium-sized companies finance some portion of their fixed assets with long-term debt. This debt may be in the form of either secured bonds or unsecured debentures. Utilities rely on debt capital to a large degree and, as a group, are the largest users of secured bonds; the *first mortgage bonds* of a utility are typically a safe, low-risk investment. Manufacturing companies, in contrast, rely on debt capital to varying degrees and generally use unsecured debt more often than secured debt.

Many large companies have virtually continuous capital expenditure programs. Usually a company will plan to finance at least partially any new assets with long-term debt. Since it is generally uneconomical to borrow small amounts of long-term capital, however, companies that have ongoing construction programs often gradually "draw down" on their short-term revolving credit agreements. Then, once every couple of years or so, a firm of this type will enter the capital markets and sell long-term debt. At that time a portion of the proceeds is used to repay the short-term borrowings, and the cycle begins again. This procedure is called *funding* short-term debt; as a result, long-term debt is sometimes referred to as *funded debt.*

Most established companies attempt to maintain reasonably constant proportions of long-term debt and common equity in their capital structures. During the course of a company's normal profitable operations, though, long-term debt is gradually retired as it matures, and the retained earnings portion of common equity is increased. This in turn decreases the debt-to-equity ratio. Thus, to maintain their desired capital structures, companies have to raise long-term debt capital periodically. This gradual refunding of debt, along with the tax deductibility of interest, accounts for the fact that about 85 to 90 percent of the external long-term capital raised in the United States is in the form of debt.

ADVANTAGES AND DISADVANTAGES OF LONG-TERM DEBT FINANCING

From the issuing firm's perspective, the major advantages of long-term debt include the following:

- Its relatively low after-tax cost due to the tax deductibility of interest.
- The increased earnings per share possible through financial leverage.
- The ability of the firm's owners to maintain greater control over the firm.

The following are the major disadvantages of long-term debt financing, from the firm's perspective:

- The increased financial risk of the firm resulting from the use of debt.

[5]Chapter 4 contains a discussion of yield to maturity calculations.

496

- The restrictions placed on the firm by the lenders.

From the investors' viewpoint, debt securities in general offer stable returns and thus are considered to be relatively low-risk investments compared with common stock investments. Since debtholders are creditors, however, they do not participate in any increased earnings the firm may experience. In fact, during periods of relatively high inflation, holders of existing debt find that their *real* interest payments decrease, because the nominal interest payments remain constant.

PREFERRED STOCK

As a source of capital for a firm, preferred stock occupies an intermediate position between long-term debt and common stock. Like common stock, preferred stock is part of the stockholders' equity. Like long-term debt, it is considered a fixed-income security, although preferred stockholders receive dividends instead of interest payments. Since the issuing firm usually does not promise repayment at a specific date, preferred stock tends to be a more permanent form of financing than long-term debt. Dividends on preferred stock, like interest payments on long-term debt, normally remain constant over time.

Due to increases in corporate tax rates, the popularity of preferred stock financing has declined in recent decades. Dividends cannot be deducted from income for corporate income tax purposes, whereas interest payments are tax deductible. This means that for a company paying almost half of its income in taxes, the after-tax cost of preferred stock is approximately twice as great as that of long-term debt, assuming that the pretax preferred stock and long-term debt rates are about the same and that the company makes no change in its capital structure.[6]

Preferred stock bears its name because it usually has preference, or priority, over common stock with regard to the company's dividends and assets. For example, if a company's earnings in a given year are insufficient to pay dividends on preferred stock, the company is not permitted to pay dividends on its common stock. In the event of a liquidation following bankruptcy, the claims on the firm's assets by preferred stockholders are subordinate to those of creditors but have priority over those of common stockholders.

FEATURES OF PREFERRED STOCK

Like long-term debt, preferred stock has its own unique distinguishing characteristics. A number of these are discussed here.

---

[6]For a given company at a particular time, preferred stock will often cost slightly more than long-term debt, even on a pretax basis, because investors require a higher return to compensate them for the greater risk involved with preferred stock. (See Chapter 12 for a further discussion of this topic.) In contrast, preferred dividends received by corporate investors qualify for the 85 percent intercompany dividend exclusion, whereas interest income does not. Thus, a preferred stock offering that is largely purchased by other corporations may have a lower yield than similar debt offerings.

Selling price and par value   The selling price, or issue price, is the per-share price at which preferred stock shares are sold to the public. At the present time, the most common selling price is $25 per share. In the past, $100 per share was a more common issue price.

The par value is the value assigned to the stock by the issuing company, and it is frequently the same as the initial selling price. No relationship necessarily exists between the two, however. A preferred stock sold at $25 per share may have a $25 par value, $1 par value, or no par value at all. Regardless of what a preferred stock's actual par value is, however, the preferred stockholders are entitled to their issue price plus dividends in the event of liquidation after the claims of creditors have been paid in full.

Preferred stock usually is designated by its dividend amount rather than its dividend percentage. For example, suppose Intermountain Power Company has a series of preferred stock that pays an annual dividend of $2.20, has a $1 par value, and was initially sold to the public at $25 per share. An investor would most likely refer to the stock as "Intermountain Power's $2.20 preferred."

Cumulative feature   Most preferred stock is cumulative. This means that if, for some reason, a firm fails to pay its preferred dividend, it cannot pay dividends on its common stock until it has satisfied all preferred dividends in arrears. The principal reason for this feature is that investors are generally unwilling to purchase preferred stock that is not cumulative.

Participation   Stock is said to be *participating* if the holders share in any increased earnings the company might experience. Virtually all preferred stock, however, is *nonparticipating;* that is, the preferred dividend remains constant, even if the company's earnings increase. Any dividend increases resulting from higher earnings accrue directly to the common stockholders.

Maturity   Preferred stock is technically part of a firm's equity capital. As such, some firms issue preferred stock that is intended to be *perpetual,* that is, a permanent portion of the stockholders' equity having no specific maturity date. Many preferred stock investors, however, desire sinking fund provisions, which guarantee that the issue will be retired over a specified time period. For example, AMAX Incorporated issued preferred stock in 1977, intending to retire it by 1985. Because of the stock's relatively short maturity, AMAX was able to sell portions of the issue to insurance and finance companies that probably would not have purchased the issue otherwise.[7]

Call feature   Like long-term debt, preferred stock can sometimes be redeemed, or *called,* at the issuing firm's option at some specified price. Suppose, for example, that Atlantic Public Service Company issues a $2.10 series of preferred stock that is sold at $25 per share. A typical call provision might allow the company to retire all or part of the issue at $27.10 during the third year, at $26.80 during the fourth year, at $26.50 during the fifth year, and so

[7]*Business Week* (June 27, 1977):97.

on until the price reaches $25 during the tenth year. (In this example the stock is not callable during the first 2 years after issue.)

Whereas the call feature allows the issuing company a measure of flexibility in its financing plans, the call feature is generally not attractive to investors. Thus, a firm usually must also provide investors with a *call premium*, or the difference between the call price and the original selling price, should it decide to attach a call feature to its preferred stock.

The probability that a firm will exercise the call privilege is likely to increase during times when market interest rates have decreased below those that existed at the time of issue. After calling the original issue, the firm can replace it with a lower cost issue.

Voting rights   As a general rule, preferred stockholders are not entitled to vote for the company's board of directors. However, special voting procedures frequently take effect if the company omits its preferred dividends or incurs losses for a period of time. In such a case, the preferred stockholders often vote as a separate group to elect one or more members of the company's board of directors. This insures that the preferred holders will have direct representation on the board.

Preference stock   Occasionally, companies that issue preferred stock also issue *preference stock*, which is junior to preferred stock. For example, Tenneco Inc. has both cumulative preference and cumulative preferred stock in its capital structure. The preference stock is defined by the company as a third class, or order, of preferred stock. Therefore, the preference stock is entitled to dividends after the first preferred and second preferred holders receive their dividends.

TRADING OF PREFERRED SHARES

Following the initial sale of preferred stock by a firm, investors who purchase the shares may decide to sell them in the secondary markets. Large issues of actively traded preferred stock are listed on the major stock exchanges, such as the New York and the American stock exchanges. However, a majority of preferred stock issues are rather thinly traded, and these are traded over the counter.

USERS OF PREFERRED STOCK

Utility companies are the most frequent users of preferred stock financing, largely because of the financing constraints placed on them by regulatory agencies. For example, a regulatory agency might require that the utilities under its control limit their use of mortgage bond financing to 60 percent of the amount of new assets. The regulatory agency might also require that these assets be financed with at least 30 percent common equity. Thus, many utilities use preferred stock for about 10 percent of their capitalization. This permits them to satisfy the regulatory agency requirements and to maximize their use of financial leverage by employing a fixed-income security. In addition, utilities are permitted by their regulatory agencies to consider preferred dividends as an expense for rate making purposes.

Within the last 25 years or so, preferred stock (usually convertible) has been rather widely used in mergers and acquisitions. Frequently, acquiring companies issue preferred stock in exchange for the common stock of acquired companies. This is, in effect, another example of financial leverage, and it can cause an increase in the earnings per common share of the acquiring company.[8]

Other occasional users of preferred stock financing are capital-intensive companies undertaking expansion programs. These companies may choose preferred stock as a means of securing long-term financing for the following reasons:

- Their capital structures and various other restrictions prevent the judicious use of additional long-term debt.

- Depressed common stock prices and the potential dilution of per-share earnings may cause them to decide against external common equity financing.

Often these same companies have relatively low marginal tax rates (because of losses, accelerated depreciation, and investment tax credits) that make the after-tax cost of preferred stock not appreciably different from that of long-term debt. For example, Chrysler, International Harvester, and U.S. Steel, as well as a number of airlines, are recent issuers of preferred stock.

In 1982 large commercial banks were another group of preferred stock users. These banks, including BankAmerica, Chase Manhattan, and Manufacturers Hanover, issued variable-rate preferred stock, partly to get additional equity into their capital structures.

ADVANTAGES AND DISADVANTAGES OF PREFERRED STOCK FINANCING

From the issuing company's perspective, the principal advantage of preferred stock is that preferred dividend payments are potentially flexible. Omitting a preferred dividend in difficult times usually results in less severe consequences than omitting an interest payment on long-term debt.

In addition, preferred stock financing can increase a firm's degree of financial leverage. However, financial analysts may regard the issuance of preferred stock as equivalent to debt. In this case, the company is viewed as having used up a portion of its "debt capacity." Or, in effect, the company has leveraged with preferred stock rather than long-term debt—at approximately twice the after-tax cost.

From the investors' perspective, companies who purchase the preferred stock of other companies accrue certain tax advantages resulting from the 85 percent exclusion of intercompany dividends from Federal income taxes. For example, an insurance company in the 46 percent tax bracket can invest in the preferred stock of another company and pay taxes equal to only about 6.9

---

[8]Chapter 23 contains a more detailed discussion of the use of preferred stock in mergers.

percent of the preferred dividend income.[9] In contrast, the same insurance company would be required to include all the interest received in its taxable income.

The principal disadvantage of preferred stock financing is its high after-tax cost as compared with long-term debt, since dividends cannot be deducted for income tax purposes. This means that the after-tax cost to the firm for preferred stock is usually about twice as high as the after-tax cost of long-term debt, assuming that the firm's capital structure remains constant. As a result, most companies considering long-term financing with fixed-income securities choose long-term debt over preferred stock.

COMMON STOCK

A firm's common stockholders are its true owners. Common stock is a *residual form of ownership* in that the claims of common stockholders on the firm's earnings and assets are considered only *after* the claims of governments, debtholders, and preferred stockholders have been met. Common stock is considered a *permanent* form of long-term financing, since, unlike debt and some preferred stock, common stock has no maturity date.

Unlike long-term debt and preferred stock, which are fixed income securities, common stock is a *variable income security.* Common stockholders are said to participate in a firm's earnings, because they may receive a larger dividend if earnings increase in the future, or their dividend may be cut if earnings drop.

COMMON STOCK AND ACCOUNTING

Common stock appears on the right-hand side of a firm's balance sheet as part of the stockholders' equity. This is shown in Table 16–3.

Stockholders' equity includes both preferred stock (if any exists) and common stock. The total equity attributable to the common stock of the Law-

TABLE 16–3   Lawrence Company Stockholders' Equity, December 31, 19X5 (in Thousands of Dollars)

STOCKHOLDERS' EQUITY

Preferred stock; $25 par value; authorized, 2,000,000 shares; issued and outstanding, 1,500,000 shares	$ 3,750
Common stock; $2 par value; authorized, 10,000,000 shares; issued and outstanding, 6,675,000 shares	13,350
Contributed capital in excess of par value*	28,713
Retained earnings	38,257
Total stockholders' equity	$84,070

*The *contributed capital in excess of par* account has several other frequently used names, including *capital surplus* and *additional paid-in capital.* Many accountants feel that the expression *capital surplus* is misleading, because it implies that the firm has excess capital.

[9]This 6.9 percent figure is calculated by multiplying the portion of dividends that is subject to taxes, namely, 15 percent, by 46 percent.

rence Company is equal to the total stockholders' equity less the preferred stock:

$$\$84,070,000 - \$3,750,000 = \$80,320,000 \; .$$

In other words, the sum of the common stock account, contributed capital in excess of par value account, and retained earnings account equals the total common stockholders' equity.

The *book value* per share of common stock is calculated as follows:

$$\text{Book value per share} = \frac{\text{Total common stockholders' equity}}{\text{Number of shares outstanding}} \; .$$

In the case of the Lawrence Company,

$$\text{Book value per share} = \frac{\$80,320,000}{6,675,000}$$
$$= \$12.03$$

A common stock's book value is calculated on the basis of balance sheet figures and does not necessarily have any relationship to the common stock's *market value*, which is based primarily on expectations concerning general economic conditions and the firm's future earnings.

The balance in the common stock account is calculated by multiplying the number of shares actually outstanding by the *par value*, an arbitrary value assigned to shares of common stock.[10] To continue with this example, the Lawrence Company has 6,675,000 shares outstanding and a $2 par value, resulting in a balance of $13,350,000.

To illustrate the nature of the contributed capital in excess of par value account, suppose Lawrence decides to raise an additional $12 million in external equity capital by selling 600,000 common shares at $20 each.[11] The amount credited to the common stock account is $1,200,000 (600,000 shares times the $2 par value). The remainder of the $12 million is added to the contributed capital in excess of par value account. In other words, this account contains capital that is paid into the firm in excess of the par value when common stock is issued.

Additions to the retained earnings account occur as a result of earnings that are retained in the business, as opposed to earnings that are paid out to the stockholders as dividends. Retained earnings, which are internally generated funds, are an important source of capital for business. They account for roughly 60 percent of all capital sources to U.S. business, and externally

---

[10]At one time par value was considered important for any possible liquidation proceedings, but today it has little, if any, real significance. Par value is normally a low figure and tends to be less than $5 per share. Occasionally companies issue stock with no par value. In these instances the balance in the common stock account is a "stated value."

[11]Before sales of the new shares, a reasonable price level might be about $21 or $22 per share. (This example ignores flotation costs.)

raised capital constitutes the other 40 percent. Of these externally raised funds, only about 10 percent (or 4 percent of the total funding) comes from new common stock financing, and even less comes from the sale of new preferred stock.

STOCKHOLDER RIGHTS

Common stockholders have a number of general rights, including the following:

- The right to share equally on a per-share basis in any dividends paid.
- The right to share equally on a per-share basis in any assets remaining after senior claims are satisfied in a liquidation.
- The right to vote on stockholder matters.
- The right to share proportionately in any new stock sold. (This is called the *preemptive right*.)

Whereas all stockholders have dividend and liquidation rights, in addition to voting rights (unless the stock is specifically nonvoting), preemptive rights exist in a relatively small minority of firms at the present time. (Voting rights and preemptive rights are discussed in detail in the appendix to this chapter.)

UNDERSTANDING STOCK QUOTATIONS

Table 16–4 shows a partial listing of NYSE stocks from the *Wall Street Journal*. Beginning at the left-hand side, the first two columns show the stock's price range during the previous 52 weeks. For example, the per-share stock price of Bristol-Myers ranged between $52.125 and $74.375. The column immediately to the right of the stock name shows the current annual dividend rate; for example, the Bristol-Myers annual rate is $2.40 per share. The next column shows the dividend percentage yield; for Bristol-Myers, the figure is 3.3 (calculated as the annual dividend divided by the closing price, or $2.40/ $72.00 = 3.3%). Then the price-earnings (P/E) ratio (the current price divided by the last 12 months' earnings) is shown. The P/E ratio indicates how much investors are willing to pay for $1 of earnings from the firm. The P/E multiple is influenced by a number of factors, including the risk of the firm and projections of future earnings. The next figure is the sales volume in hundreds of shares; in this case, 97,800 shares of Bristol-Myers common stock were traded on Monday, March 28, 1983. The next three columns list the high, low, and closing prices for the day; the final column shows the net change for the day, or the difference between this day's closing price and the closing price on the previous business day (or the last day on which a trade took place). For the day, Bristol-Myers traded between $72.00 and $73.25; closing at $72.00 per share, down $0.75 per share for the day.

Quotations on most over-the-counter (OTC) stocks are given in terms of their "bid" and "asked" prices. The "bid" price is the price dealers are willing to pay for a security, and the "asked" price is the price at which dealers are willing to sell. The difference between the two prices is the dealer's "spread," or gross profit margin. For example, on Thursday, April 14, 1983, the stock

TABLE 16–4 **Partial Listing of Stock Market Quotations**

52 WEEKS High	Low	Stock	Div.	Yld %	P-E Ratio	Sales 100s	High	Low	Close	Net chg.
37¼	23¼	BrigSt	1.36a	4.2	14	89	32¾	32½	32¾	+ ½
74⅜	52⅛	BristM	2.40	3.3	14	978	73¼	72	72	− ¾
77¼	56	BrstM	pf 2	2.6	..	6	77	76½	77	− ¼
23⅜	17½	BritPt	1.50e	7.6	4	32	19¾	19⅝	19¾..	...
17½	7½	Brock	.10	1.1	16	176	9⅛	8⅞	9	+ ⅛
19½	12⅝	Brckwy	1.32	6.9	9	57	19¼	19¼	19¼..	...
31½	23⅜	BkyUG	2.90	10.	6	285	28½	28⅛	28⅜..	...
22½	16⅞	BkUG	pf2.47	12.	..	2	21⅜	21⅜	21⅜	− ⅛
33¼	26	BkUG	pf3.95	12.	..	2	32¼	32¼	32¼	− ¼
17⅜	9¾	BwnSh	.20	1.2	..	33	16½	15⅞	16½	+ ⅞
70½	27	BwnGp	1.96	2.8	12	201	70	68	70	+ 1¾
43⅜	16¼	BrwnF	s .80	2.1	18	723	38⅞	38	38	− ½
28½	16⅛	Brnswk	1	3.7	..	156	27½	27	27¼..	...
44⅜	23¼	BrshW	s .80	1.8	35	59	u45	44¾	44¾	+ ⅜
17	10¼	BucyEr	.88	6.3	11	309	14	13½	14	+ ⅜
17¼	7¼	Bundy	.60	3.9	18	18	15½	15½	15½	− ⅛
18⅝	14¼	BunkrH	2.16	12.	..	8	18⅜	18¼	18⅜..	...
34¾	17	BurlInd	1.52	4.4	24	275	34¾	34⅜	34⅜	− ⅜
75⅜	34¼	BrlNth	1.52	2.1	10	526	73¾	72¾	73	− ⅝
6¾	4⅞	BrlNo	pf .55	8.8	..	4	6⅜	6¼	6¼	− ¼
21	16¾	BrlN	pf 2.13	10.	..	8	20⅝	20⅝	20⅝..	...
26½	15⅝	Burndy	.76	3.2	19	453	24⅛	23⅛	24⅛	+ ¾
49⅞	29⅝	Burrgh	2.60	5.6	17	1257	47⅛	46½	46⅝	− ⅜
19¼	8⅛	ButlrIn	.52	2.8	17	13	18⅞	18⅝	18¾	+ ⅛
12	7½	Buttes		..	..	37	8¼	8¼	8¼..	...

SOURCE: *Wall Street Journal*, March 29, 1983.

of Air Wisconsin closed on the OTC market at "14 bid, 14½ asked." The dealer's "spread," or gross profit margin, was $0.50.

OTHER FEATURES OF COMMON STOCK

This section covers other topics related to the ownership of common stock, including *common stock classes, stock splits, stock dividends,* and *stock repurchases.*

Common stock classes Occasionally a firm may decide to create more than one class of common stock. The reason for this may be that the firm wishes to raise additional equity capital by selling a portion of the existing owners' stock while at the same time maintaining control of the firm. This can be accomplished by creating a separate class of *nonvoting stock.* Typically so-called Class A common stock is nonvoting, whereas Class B has voting rights; the classes are normally otherwise equal. The Ford Motor Company is an example of a large, widely held company that has more than one class of common stock. Ford's 12.7 million shares of "Class B stock" are entirely held by Ford family interests. This class has 40 percent of the total voting power. Ford's 107.8 million shares of "common stock" are held by the public and have 60 percent of the total voting power. The two classes are otherwise equal.

504

Stock splits   If management feels that the firm's common stock should sell at a lower price to attract more purchasers, it can effect a *stock split*. There seems to be a general feeling in the finance community that the optimum price range for a share of common stock should be very roughly $15 to $70. Consequently, if a stock rises above this range, management may decide on a stock split to get the price back to a more desirable trading level.

For example, the per-share price of Proctor & Gamble common stock rose from the $60s to the $110s between 1980 and 1982. Then in January 1983, with the stock trading at about $120, the stock split 2 for 1. Following the split, the stock traded in the $60 range.

A stock split does not necessarily have to be 2 for 1. Splits of 3 for 1, 3 for 2, and so on are not uncommon. Frequently companies choose to raise their dividend levels at the time of a split. Prior to the split, Proctor & Gamble's annual dividend was $4.20 per share; after the split, the dividend was raised to $2.40 per share, which amounted to $4.80 per share on the presplit shares.

Many investors believe stock splits are an indication of good financial health. The mere splitting of a stock, however, should not be taken in and of itself as evidence that the stock will necessarily perform well in the future.

During 1965 to 1982, an average of about 100 stock splits per year occurred on organized exchanges in the United States, with a higher than average number occurring during years when stock prices were relatively high.

From an accounting standpoint, when a stock is split, its par value is changed accordingly. For example, when the split is 2 for 1, the par value is reduced by one-half, and the number of shares is doubled. No changes occur in the firm's account balances or capital structure.

Reverse stock splits   Reverse stock splits are stock splits in which the number of shares is decreased. They are used to bring low-priced shares up to more desirable trading levels. For example, assume the management of Ajax Steel, whose stock has dropped to about $4 per share, is concerned that potential investors might be unwilling to buy the stock because of the relatively large percentage commission on low-priced stocks, as well as the stigma that is attached to them. One alternative it might choose is a 1-for-5 reverse stock split, which could bring the stock price back up to about $20 per share. It should be obvious, however, that the reverse stock split itself will not cure any ills Ajax might be experiencing.

Many investors feel reverse stock splits indicate poor corporate health. For this reason they are relatively uncommon.

Stock dividends   A stock dividend is a dividend to stockholders that consists of additional shares of stock instead of cash. Normally stock dividends are in the 2 to 10 percent range—that is, the number of shares outstanding is increased by 2 to 10 percent. From an accounting standpoint, stock dividends involve a transfer from the retained earnings account to the common stock and additional paid-in capital accounts.[12]

Stock repurchases   From time to time companies repurchase some of their

---

[12]Chapter 14 contains a more detailed discussion of stock dividends.

own shares. One reason for this is to make stock available for use in mergers or the exercise of executive stock options. Repurchased stock is called *treasury stock.*

Occasionally, a firm may repurchase stock because management feels the current market price is low enough to make the stock a good investment. This practice became popular during the late 1970s, when the markets were depressed. For example, IBM purchased some 4 million of its shares in March 1977.

In isolated cases a company may sell off a portion of its assets and use the proceeds to repurchase stock. Gulf Oil did this in late 1972 by selling a number of marginal assets for $331 million and then, in March 1973, repurchasing 13 million common shares for $341 million.

ADVANTAGES AND DISADVANTAGES OF COMMON STOCK FINANCING

One of the major advantages of common stock financing is that no fixed dividend obligation exists, at least in principle. In practice, however, dividend cuts are relatively uncommon for companies paying a "regular" dividend, a fact that implies that corporate management generally views a firm's current level of dividends as a minimum for the future. Nevertheless, common stock financing does allow firms a greater degree of flexibility in their financing plans than fixed-income securities do. Thus, common stock is less risky to the firm than fixed income securities. Limits on additional debt and the maintenance of working capital levels are only two of the constraints imposed on a firm when fixed-income security financing is employed.

In addition, common stock financing can be advantageous for a firm whose capital structure contains more than an optimal amount of debt. Under these circumstances, common stock financing can lower the firm's weighted cost of capital.

From the investors' perspective, however, common stock is a riskier investment than debt securities or preferred stock. Because of this, investors in common stock require relatively high rates of return, and this means that the firm's cost for common stock financing is high compared with fixed-income securities.

From another perspective, external common stock financing frequently results in an initial dilution of per-share earnings, particularly if the assets acquired with the proceeds of the financing do not produce earnings immediately. Table 16–5, which contains figures for Tucson Electric Power Company for 1976 and 1975, illustrates this point.

TABLE 16–5   Example of Diluted Per-Share Earnings as a Result of Common Stock Financing

	YEAR ENDED SEPTEMBER 30	
	1976	1975
Net income available for common stock	$25,821,000	$20,673,000
Average number of common shares outstanding	15,600,000	12,122,007
Earnings per average share of common stock	$1.66	$1.71

Notice that whereas the firm's net income increased in 1976 over 1975, its earnings per share declined because of the new shares issued. Thus, the additional issue of common shares can dilute the original owners' claims on the firm's earnings. If, on the other hand, the new assets earn a higher rate of return than the existing assets, the original owners will benefit from the increased earnings. Also, the problem of diluted earnings should only be temporary if the firm is investing wisely and should have no adverse consequences in a well-informed market.

A final disadvantage of external equity financing involves the relatively high flotation costs associated with common stock sold to the public.[13]

SELECTED CAPITAL MARKET TOPICS

This section presents several capital market topics. Capital markets are usually classified as either *primary* or *secondary* markets. New securities are issued in the primary markets, and the firms issuing these securities receive the proceeds from their sale, thus raising new capital. Outstanding securities are traded in the secondary markets, where owners of these securities may sell them to other investors. The corporations whose securities are traded in the secondary markets do not share in the proceeds from these sales.

Although primary and secondary markets are separate, they are closely related. Smoothly functioning secondary markets aid the primary markets, because investors tend to be more willing to purchase new securities when they know they can sell them in the secondary market. In fact, the potential liquidity available in the secondary markets may make investors more willing to accept slightly lower returns on their investments, thereby lowering the cost companies have to pay for their funds.

LISTED SECURITY EXCHANGES AND OVER-THE-COUNTER MARKETS

Secondary markets can be further classified as either listed security exchanges or over-the-counter (OTC) markets. Listed security exchanges operate at designated places of business and have requirements governing the types of securities they can list and trade. The OTC security markets do not have centralized places of business, but rather exist as networks of security dealers connected by a communications system of telephones and terminals with price quotations.

Listed security exchanges   The New York Stock Exchange (NYSE), sometimes called the *Big Board*, is the oldest and largest stock exchange in the United States. Over 1,900 common and preferred stocks and over 800 bonds are listed on the NYSE. For a company's stock to be listed and traded on the NYSE, the company must meet certain minimum requirements with regard to the number of shares of stock outstanding, the number of shareholders, the geo-

---

[13]Flotation costs are discussed in detail later in this chapter.

graphical distribution of shareholders, the value of assets, the market value of shares, and the net income level. As a result, only the largest U.S. companies tend to be listed on the NYSE.

The NYSE is composed largely of security firms that purchase memberships, or *seats*. The cost of these seats varies, depending on the securities industry outlook.

The other organized national exchange is the American Stock Exchange (ASE or AMEX), which, like the NYSE, is located in New York City. The companies listed on the AMEX are smaller on average than those listed on the NYSE.

In addition to the national exchanges, there are a number of *regional* exchanges located around the country. The two largest are the Midwest Stock Exchange in Chicago and the Pacific Stock Exchange in San Francisco and Los Angeles. In general, regional exchanges list stocks of companies located in their geographical areas. Many large companies are listed on both the NYSE and one or more regional exchanges.

Trading activities on the NYSE and several of the regional exchanges—including the Midwest, Pacific, Philadelphia, Boston, and Cincinnati exchanges—are listed together and reported in the financial press as the *NYSE Composite Transactions*. Eventually an electronic communications network called the *Intermarket Trading System* will connect all the major U.S. stock exchanges.

Over-the-counter markets   Securities that are not listed on exchanges are said to be traded "over the counter" (OTC). In general, these include stocks of small and relatively unknown companies, although many bank and insurance company stocks, a majority of corporate bonds and preferred stocks, and most U.S. Treasury and municipal bonds are traded in OTC markets. Security firms that deal in OTC stocks and actually carry inventories in certain stocks play an important role in the smooth functioning of OTC markets, and they are said to "make a market" in the securities they inventory.

On each business day the *Wall Street Journal* contains a full page of price quotations on OTC stocks having some national interest. Much of this page is devoted to quotations from the NASDAQ tape, the automated quotation system of the National Association of Security Dealers. This system has helped to more fully integrate the OTC market at the national level.

In addition to the listings contained in the *Wall Street Journal*, the financial pages of newspapers around the country contain price quotations on OTC stocks of companies located in their areas.

UNDERSTANDING THE FINANCIAL PAGES

The *Wall Street Journal* and the business sections of daily newspapers in larger cities contain economic and security market news. This subsection discusses *stock market indexes, margin trading*, and *short selling*.

Stock market indexes   Stock market indexes give a broad indication of how the stock market, or a segment of the stock market, performed during a particular day. The most frequently quoted stock market index is the Dow Jones

Industrial Average (DJIA), which is based on the stock prices of thirty large, well-established industrial corporations.[14] The DJIA is calculated by adding the prices of the thirty stocks and dividing by some number that reflects stock dividends and splits. When a radio announcer says, "The market was up 5 points today," the announcer means the DJIA was up 5 points. A 1-point movement in the DJIA is equal to about a 7 cent per share movement in the price of an average stock.

The Dow Jones Transportation Average is based on twenty major railroad, airline, and trucking stocks, and the Dow Jones Utility Average is derived from fifteen major utility stocks. The DJIA is combined with the transportation and the utility averages to form the Dow Jones Composite Average.

The *Standard and Poor's 500* Stock Price Index (S&P 500) is another frequently quoted stock market index that is significantly broader than the DJIA. It is compiled from the stock prices of 400 leading industrial firms, twenty transportation firms, forty utilities, and forty financial institutions. The S&P 500 is a *market value–weighted index.* This means, for example, that a stock whose total market value is $20 million influences the index twice as much as a stock whose total market value is $10 million.

Margin trading   Securities purchased with funds borrowed from brokers are said to be *bought on margin.* Investors may have *cash accounts* and *margin accounts* with their brokers. In the case of a cash account, the investor pays the full purchase price of any securities bought; in the case of a margin account, the investor puts up only a portion of the total price (that is, the margin), and the broker lends the investor the remaining portion. Margin trading is designed to increase returns available to investors, but it also increases risk, similar to the impact financial leverage has on corporations. The margin percentage is regulated by the Federal Reserve System.

Short selling   Most investors purchase a security (that is, take a *long* position), hope the price will increase during the holding period, and sell it at some future date. However, it is also possible for investors to sell securities they do not own and buy them back later. This is termed *short selling* or taking a *short* position. When making a short sale, the investor borrows the securities to be sold from another investor. When the securities are bought back later by the short seller, they are delivered to the investor that initially loaned them. If the short seller is able to sell a security first at a relatively high price and buy it back later at a lower price, a profit is realized.

REGULATION OF THE SECURITY MARKETS

Both the individual states and the Federal government regulate the securities business. Beginning with Kansas in 1911, each of the fifty states (with the exception of Delaware) has passed so-called blue sky laws. The term *blue sky*

---

[14]Dow Jones and Company is a financial company that publishes the *Wall Street Journal.* Every Monday the *Wall Street Journal* lists the companies that make up the Dow Jones averages on the second-to-last page. Every day the values of all the major stock market indexes are listed in the *Wall Street Journal* and in the financial section of most major newspapers.

came about when some risky securities were called nothing more than "pieces of blue sky." In spite of these state laws, many investors received incomplete and even fraudulent security information during the 1920s. This fact, combined with the 1929 stock market crash and the general reform spirit of the 1930s, led to the enactment of two principal pieces of security legislation—the Securities Act of 1933 and the Securities Exchange Act of 1934. This Federal legislation has been aimed primarily at insuring full disclosure of security information.

The Securities Act of 1933 requires any firm offering *new* securities to the public to make a complete disclosure of all pertinent facts regarding these securities; the Securities Exchange Act of 1934 expanded the coverage to include trading in *existing* securities. The 1934 act also created the Securities and Exchange Commission (SEC), which is responsible for administering the Federal securities legislation. These Federal laws make no judgments regarding the quality of securities issues; they simply require full disclosure of the facts.[15]

Any company that plans to sell an interstate security issue totaling over $500,000 and having a maturity greater than 270 days is required to register the issue with the SEC.[16] The procedure involves the preparation of a *registration statement* and a *prospectus*. The registration statement contains a vast amount of information about the company's legal, operational, and financial position; the prospectus summarizes the information contained in the registration statement and is intended for the use by potential investors.

After a company has filed a registration statement and prospectus, there is normally a waiting period of 20 days before the SEC approves the issue and the company can begin selling the securities. During the waiting period the company may use a preliminary prospectus in connection with the anticipated sale of securities. This preliminary prospectus is often called a "red herring" because it contains a statement, usually marked in red, saying that the prospectus is "not an offer to sell."

Many capital market participants have complained over the years about the large amount of paperwork and the resulting delays that the SEC rules apparently caused. In 1982 the SEC began allowing companies to file one initial registration statement, called a "shelf registration," for a variety of future securities the company plans to sell at any time within 2 years. After the initial shelf registration, no additional SEC paperwork is necessary when the company chooses to sell its securities. Shelf registrations are designed to decrease the amount of SEC paperwork and thereby increase the efficiency of the capital-raising process. By late 1982 it was estimated that 20 percent of the funds raised in the United States since March 1982 involved shelf registrations.[17]

The Securities Exchange Act of 1934 also made it possible for the govern-

---

[15]In recent years some states have prohibited the sale of certain securities on the grounds of poor quality rather than any problems associated with the disclosure of information.

[16]Security issues of the Federal government and nonprofit organizations do not have to be registered with the SEC. Bank and railroad issues are also exempt, since these industries are regulated by other government agencies.

[17]*Wall Street Journal* (November 2, 1982): 42.

ment to regulate "insider" trading. Any time a director, officer, or major stockholder—that is, an "insider"—of a large corporation trades in that corporation's securities, this fact must be reported to the SEC. This information is available to the public and is used by some investors in deciding which stocks to buy or sell. This aspect of the 1934 act attempts to prevent insiders from secretly trading securities on the basis of private information.

ROLE OF THE INVESTMENT BANKER

Investment bankers are financial intermediaries who bring together suppliers and users of long-term funds in the capital markets. Whenever a large corporation is considering raising funds in the capital markets, it will almost always enlist the services of an investment banker. In fact, most large industrial corporations have ongoing relationships with their investment bankers.

The investment banker is well qualified to advise the corporation on a variety of matters, including the following:

- Long-range financial planning.
- The timing of security issues.
- The purchase of securities.
- The marketing of securities.
- The arrangement of private loans and leases.
- The negotiation of mergers.

In summary, the investment banker is an important source of financial market expertise.

HOW SECURITIES ARE SOLD

Firms can sell securities in the primary capital markets in one of three ways:

- By selling securities through investment bankers to the public in a *public cash offering.*
- By placing a debt or stock issue with one or more large investors in a *private*, or *direct*, *placement.*
- By selling common stock to existing stockholders through a *rights offering.*

Investment bankers usually assist firms in all three methods of sale. Figure 16–2 is a flowchart that outlines the various methods and steps for the sale of corporate securities.

Public cash offerings Normally, when a corporation wishes to issue new securities and sell them to the public, it makes an arrangement with an investment banker whereby the investment banker agrees to purchase the entire issue at a set price. This is called *underwriting.* The investment banker then resells the issue to the public at a higher price.

Underwriting can be accomplished either through *negotiations* between the underwriter and the issuing company or by *competitive bidding.* A *ne-*

FIGURE 16–2   How Securities Are Sold: A Flowchart

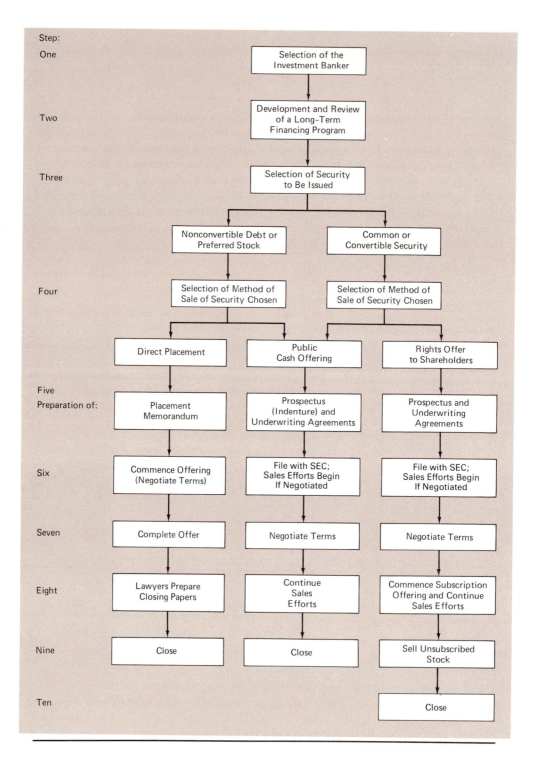

gotiated underwriting is simply an arrangement between the issuing firm and its investment bankers. Most large industrial corporations turn to investment bankers with whom they have had ongoing relationships. In competitive bidding the firm sells the securities to the underwriter (usually a group) that bids the highest price. Many regulated companies, such as utilities and railroads, are required by their regulatory commissions (for example, the Federal Energy Regulatory Commission, the Interstate Commerce Commission, and state regulatory bodies) to sell new security issues in this way.

An investment banker who agrees to underwrite a security issue assumes a certain amount of risk and, in turn, requires compensation in the form of an *underwriting discount* or *underwriting spread*, computed as follows:

Underwriting spread = Selling price to public − Proceeds to company .

Examples of underwriting spread amounts are shown in Table 16–6.

It is difficult to compare underwriting spreads for negotiated and competitive offerings, since it rarely happens that two offerings are brought to market at the same time that differ only in the ways in which they are underwritten. Generally underwriters receive lower spreads for competitive bidding utility issues than for negotiated industrial offers. This is primarily due to the fact that utilities have tended to have a lower level of risk than industrial companies.

Security issues sold to the public through underwriters normally exceed $25 million in size; amounts totaling $250 million are not uncommon.

TABLE 16–6 Sample Underwriting Spreads for Selected Issues, 1982 to 1983

Company	Issue Size (In Millions of Dollars)	Underwriting Spread (%)	S&P Rating*
Debt Issues			
First Interstate Bancorp.	$100	0.63	AA
CIGNA Corporation†	100	1.00	AA
Corning Glass Works†	100	1.00	A
U.S. Leasing International†	30	2.00	BBB
Jerrico, Inc.	40	1.88	BB
Petro-Lewis	85	3.35	B
Sunshine Mining Company	30	3.68	B
Common Stock Issues			
El Paso Electric Company	$57.5	3.26	
Ryder System, Inc.	83.4	3.88	
Southwest Airlines	34.7	3.89	
Service Corporation International	48.26	4.48	
Adage, Inc.	10.0	6.26	
Atlantic Southeast Airlines	5.2	8.00	

*Standard and Poor's (S&P) bond-rating scale is AAA (for the highest quality issues), AA, A, BBB, BB, B, CCC, CC, C.
†Convertible issues.

Due to the size of these issues, individual investment bankers usually are not able to underwrite an entire issue by themselves. Normally a group of underwriters, called a *purchasing syndicate,* agrees to underwrite the issue in order to spread the risk.[18] Sometimes the purchasing syndicate can sell an entire issue to large institutional investors;[19] this is often true with high-quality debt issues. On other occasions—particularly with large debt issues or equity issues—the underwriters organize a *selling group* of security firms to market the issue to the public. It is not uncommon for a selling group responsible for marketing a large issue to number over 100 security firms.

An important part of the negotiations between the issuing firm and the investment banker is the determination of the security's selling price. It is in the best interests of both the issuing firm and the underwriter to have the security "fairly priced." If the security is underpriced, the issuing firm will not raise the amount of capital it could have, and the underwriter may lose a customer. If the security is overpriced, the underwriter may have difficulty selling the issue, and investors who discover that they paid too much may choose not to purchase the next issue offered by either the corporation or the underwriter.

Occasionally, with smaller company issues, the investment banker agrees to help market the issue on a "best efforts" basis rather than underwriting it. Under this type of arrangement the investment banker is under no further obligation to the issuing company if some of the securities cannot be sold. The investment banker functions as a *dealer* in an underwriting situation and as a *broker* in a best efforts situation. In a best efforts offering the investment banker does not assume the risk that the securities will not be sold at a favorable price.

Private placements Many industrial companies choose to *directly,* or *privately, place* debt or preferred stock issues with one or more institutional investors instead of having them underwritten and sold to the public. In these cases, investment bankers who act on behalf of the issuing company receive a "finder's fee" for finding a buyer and negotiating the terms of the agreement.

The private market is an important source of long-term debt capital, especially for smaller corporations. Between 1953 and 1970, the 500 largest U.S. industrial corporations raised 37 percent of their debt in the private market; during the same period the smaller industrial corporations raised roughly 75 percent of their financing needs in this way.[20]

Private security placements have a number of advantages:

- They can save on flotation costs by eliminating underwriting costs.

- They can avoid the time delays associated with the preparation of registration statements and with the waiting period.

---

[18]In most cases one to three underwriters agree to manage an issue, handling all legal matters, advertising, and so on. These firms are the *managing underwriters.*

[19]Institutional investors include life insurance companies, pension funds, mutual funds, and commercial banks.

[20]See Eli Shapiro and Charles R. Wolf. *The Role of Private Placements in Corporate Finance.* Boston: Harvard University, Graduate School of Business Administration, 1972.

- They can offer greater flexibility in the writing of the terms of the contract (called the *indenture*) between the borrower and the lender.

An offsetting disadvantage is that, as a very general rule, interest rates for private placements are about one-eighth of a percentage point *higher* than they are for debt and preferred issues sold through underwriters. For small-sized debt and preferred stock issues—that is, those that are less than about $20 million—the percentage cost of underwriting becomes fairly large. Because of this, these smaller-sized issues are frequently placed privately with institutional investors.

Rights offerings and standby underwritings   Firms may sell their common stock directly to their existing stockholders through the issuance of *rights*, which entitle the stockholders to purchase new shares of the firm's stock at a *subscription price* below the market price. (Rights offerings are also called *privileged subscriptions*.) Each stockholder receives one right for each share owned; in other words, if a firm has 100 million shares outstanding and wishes to sell an additional 10 million shares through a rights offering, each right entitles the holder to purchase 0.1 shares, and it takes 10 rights to purchase one share.[21]

When selling stock through a rights offering, firms usually enlist the services of investment bankers, who urge rights holders to purchase the stock. In an arrangement called a *standby underwriting*, the investment banker agrees to purchase—at the subscription price—any shares that are not sold to rights holders. The investment banker then resells the shares. In a standby underwriting the investment banker bears risk and is compensated by an underwriting fee.

Flotation costs   Flotation costs are the costs involved in issuing new securities. The total flotation cost of a security issue sold through underwriters is calculated as follows:

$$\text{Total flotation cost} = \text{Underwriting spread} + \text{Company's issue expenses}.$$

The company's issue expenses are usually considerably less than the underwriting spread. For example, when Service Corporation International sold 1.35 million shares of common stock in 1983, the underwriting spread was $2,160,000, and the issue expenses were $280,564.

Flotation costs can vary widely, depending on the type of the security being offered, the quality of the security, and the size of the issue. Common stock flotation costs range from about 2 percent to as high as 20 percent or more, whereas flotation costs on good quality debt issues fall into roughly the 0.5 to 3 percent range. Table 16–6 shows the underwriting spreads for several 1982–1983 issues.

Generally, flotation costs are higher for common stock than for preferred stock issues, and flotation costs of preferred stock are higher than those of debt issues. One reason for this is the amount of risk each type of issue in-

---

[21]Rights and rights offerings are discussed in greater detail in the appendix to this chapter.

volves. Common stocks usually involve more risk for underwriters than preferred stock, and preferrred stock involves more risk than debt. Stock prices are subject to wider price movements than debt prices. Another reason for these differences in flotation costs is that investment bankers usually incur greater marketing expenses for common stock than for preferred stock or debt issues. Common stock is customarily sold to a large number of individual investors, whereas debt securities are frequently purchased by a much smaller number of institutional investors.

Flotation costs also depend on the quality of the issue. Low quality debt issues, for example, tend to have higher percentage flotation costs than high quality issues, since underwriters bear more risk with the former and therefore require greater compensation. And, finally, flotation costs are dependent on the size of the issue—they tend to be higher for small-sized issues, all other things being equal, since underwriters have various fixed expenses (such as advertising expenses, legal fees, registration statement costs, and so on) that are incurred regardless of the issue's size.

SUMMARY

GENERAL

- *Long-term debt, preferred stock,* and *common stock* are major sources of capital for a firm.

- Long-term debt and preferred stock are classified as *fixed-income securities,* because interest (on long-term debt) and dividends (on preferred stock) tend to remain constant over time.

- *Capital markets*—the markets for long-term financial assets—can be classified as either *primary* or *secondary.* New securities are issued in the primary markets, whereas existing securities are traded in the secondary markets.

LONG-TERM DEBT

- Long-term debt is generally classified according to whether or not it is *secured* by specific physical assets of the issuing company. Secured debt issues are *mortgage bonds,* whereas debt issues backed only by unmortgaged assets and the company's earning power are *debentures.*

- Long-term debt usually has the following features:

1. The *indenture,* or the contract between the issuing company and the debtholders.

2. The *trustee,* who represents the debtholders in dealings with the company.

3. The *call feature,* which gives the issuing company the option to retire the debt prior to maturity.

4. The *sinking fund requirement,* which, in practice, means the company must gradually reduce the outstanding balance of the debt issue over its life.

- Bond *refunding* occurs when a company redeems a callable issue and sells a lower cost issue to take its place.

- The major advantages of long-term debt financing include the following:

1. Its low after-tax cost to the company due to the tax deductibility of the interest paid out.

2. The increased earnings per share possible through financial leverage.

- The major disadvantage of long-term debt financing is the increased financial risk of the firm.

Preferred stock

- Preferred stock occupies an intermediate position between long-term debt and common stock as a source of capital. Like common stock, preferred stock is part of the stockholders' equity, and preferred stockholders receive returns in the form of dividends. Preferred stock is also similar to long-term debt in that preferred dividends, like the interest on long-term debt, usually remain constant over time.

- Preferred stock usually has the following features:

1. The *selling price,* or *issue price,* is the per-share price at which the shares are sold to the public.

2. The *par value* is an arbitrary value assigned to the stock by the issuing company.

3. Most preferred stock is *cumulative*—that is, dividends on common stock cannot be paid as long as any past or present preferred dividends remain unpaid.

4. Virtually all preferred stock is *nonparticipating*—that is, preferred stock does not share in any increased earnings of the firm.

5. Some preferred stock is *perpetual*, whereas other preferred stock is gradually retired by the firm.

6. Preferred stock is often *callable.*

- From the issuing company's perspective, preferred stock financing is advantageous due to the potential flexibility of preferred dividend payments.

- The principal disadvantage of preferred stock financing is that dividends are not tax deductible, which causes the after-tax cost of preferred stock to the firm to be higher than the cost of long-term debt, all other things being equal.

Common stock

- The common stockholders are the true owners of the firm, and, as such, common stock is a permanent form of financing. Common stockholders participate in the firm's earnings, potentially receiving larger dividends if earnings rise or smaller dividends if earnings drop.

- Stockholder rights include the following:

1. The right to dividends.

2. The right to any assets remaining after senior claims are satisfied in a liquidation.

3. Voting rights.

4. The *preemptive right,* or the right to share proportionately in any new stock sold. This right is available in some firms but not in others.

- If a company's common stock price rises above the price range considered optimal, the company's management can effect a *stock split* to get the price back to a more desirable trading level.

- *Treasury stock* is stock that has been repurchased by the issuing company.

- Common stock permits a firm more flexibility in its financing plans than fixed-income securities do, because, in principle, no fixed-dividend obligation exists.

Capital markets and
investment banking

- Listed exchanges, such as the New York and American stock exchanges, have designated places of business, as well as various trading regulations and listing requirements. The over-the-counter markets do not have designated places of business, but instead exist through a telephone and computer communications network.

- The Securities Act of 1933 and the Securities Exchange Act of 1934 are the principal pieces of securities legislation in the United States. The 1933 act require. .omplete disclosure of information on *new* securities, and the 1934 act expands this coverage to include *existing* securities. The Securities Exchange Act of 1934 also created the Securities and Exchange Commission (SEC), which is responsible for administering Federal securities legislation.

- *Investment bankers* are financial intermediaries that bring together suppliers and users of long-term funds in the capital markets. The principal service provided by investment bankers is the *underwriting* of securities. Underwriting is an insurance function whereby an investment banker agrees to purchase an entire issue at a specific price. The underwriters, usually a group called a *purchasing syndicate,* then resell the issue to the public at a slightly higher price. Since they assume a certain amount of risk when they agree to underwrite a security issue, underwriters earn the difference between the proceeds to the company and the selling price; this is called the *underwriting spread,* or the *underwriting discount.*

- Industrial corporations usually sell their securities through *negotiated underwritings,* whereas utilities and railroads frequently are required by law to sell their new security issues to the highest bidder in *competitive bidding.*

- Some security issues are *privately,* or *directly, placed* with institutional investors instead of being sold to the public through underwriters. The private market is an important source of debt financing for smaller firms.

- Firms may also choose to sell their common stock to their existing stockholders through a *rights offering,* or *privileged subscription.* Rights entitle stockholders to purchase new shares at a *subscription price* that is below the market price. Underwriters usually assist in rights offerings by agreeing to purchase any unsold shares; this is called a *standby underwriting*.

■ *Flotation costs* are the costs of issuing new securities. They are generally higher for common stock issues than for preferred stock issues, which, in turn, are higher than those for debt issues. Flotation costs tend to be inversely proportional to the issue's quality, since underwriters bear more risk with lower quality issues and therefore require greater compensation.

Original Issue Deep Discount Bonds

Thomas R. Mongan
Senior Vice-President
First City National Bank of Houston

Original issue deep discount (OID) bonds are newly issued bonds that have coupon interest rates that are lower than the current market rates and therefore sell at discounts from par value.

The first publicly traded OID bond of a major, highly rated U.S. company was issued in early March 1981 by Martin Marietta Corporation. This issue was followed by a large number of additional OID bonds from such companies as Northwest Industries, Inc., J. C. Penney Company, Allied Corporation, General Electric Credit Corp., and BankAmerica, to name a few.

The Northwest Industries issue is a 7 percent coupon, 30-year bond that was sold at a 47 percent discount from par value, or $527.50 per bond, in late March 1981. These bonds had an initial yield to maturity of 13.5 percent, and at the time, if Northwest Industries had issued regular coupon bonds sold at par, it would have had to pay about 14.5 percent. Thus, the company saved approximately 1 percent on its borrowing costs by issuing the OID bonds.

Some of the OID bonds pay no interest and are therefore called *zero coupon bonds.* For example, in April 1982 Allied Corporation issued several zero coupon bonds with different maturities, including one issue maturing in August 1998 that was originally sold at 12.5 percent of par, or $125 each. (This bond is listed in Table 16–2.)

From the viewpoint of the corporate issuer, there are several advantages to issuing OID bonds:

- The cost of capital for OID bonds is less than that for regular coupon bonds. (The Northwest Industries example illustrates this.) The issuing company has low or zero interest cash outflows. In addition, OID bonds typically do not have sinking fund obligations; therefore, no principal repayments have to be made prior to maturity.

- Each year the issuing company is allowed to amortize a portion of the total discount amount for tax purposes.[22] This results in a positive cash flow for the issuing company. To illustrate, suppose a company sells $100 million par value of OID bonds for $50 million. If the company is allowed to amortize (that is, expense) $2 million in a given year, and it is in the 46 percent tax bracket, it saves $920,000 in Federal income taxes and thus receives a positive cash inflow as a result of the amorti-

---

[22]The OID bond purchaser must report a portion of the discount as taxable income each year. This causes a negative cash flow as taxes are paid. As a result, the purchasers of OID bonds have primarily been tax-exempt investors such as pension funds and individual retirement accounts.

zation. (If the amortization cash inflow exceeds the interest cash outflow, the issuing company actually has a net cash *inflow* as a result of issuing debt!)

There are also at least two disadvantages of issuing OID bonds:

- The OID bonds are effectively noncallable by the issuing company, because call prices are above 100 percent of par value, and OID bonds sell at less than 100 percent of par value.

- At maturity, the issuing company is required to make a large lump-sum cash outlay, which is not tax deductible.

In some months during 1981 and 1982, OID bonds accounted for about 25 percent of the new funds raised in the U.S. domestic bond market. However, by 1983 OID bonds had declined in importance, partly because of the decline in long-term interest rates.

Standard and Poor's Bond-rating Process

(When the rating agencies, such as Moody's or Standard and Poor's, rate the quality of the securities of a firm, they perform an in-depth analysis of the financial and operating condition of the firm. This "Focus on Corporate Practice" example outlines the key factors considered by Standard and Poor's when rating the securities of industrial companies.)

INDUSTRIAL COMPANY RATING METHODOLOGY PROFILE

I. **Industry risk:** Defined as the strength of the industry within the economy and relative to economic trends. This also includes the ease or difficulty of entering this industry, the importance of any diversity of the earnings base and the role of regulation and legislation.
   A. Importance in the economic cycle.
   B. Business cyclicality; earnings volatility, lead-lag and duration, diversity of earnings base, predictability and stability of revenues and earnings.
   C. Economic forces impacts; high inflation, energy costs and availability, international competitive position, social-political forces.
   D. Demand factors; real growth projections relative to GNP and basis for projections, maturity of markets.
   E. Basic financial characteristics of the business: fixed or working capital intensive; importance of credit as a sales tool.
   F. Supply factors: raw materials, labor, over/under utilized plant capacity.
   G. Federal, state, foreign regulation.
   H. Potential legislation.

    I. Fragmented or concentrated business.

    J. Barriers to entry/ease of entry.

II. **Issuer's industry position—market position:** The company's sales position in its major fields and its historical protection of its position and projected ability for the future.

    A. Ability to generate sales.

    B. Dominant and stable market shares.

    C. Marketing/distributing requirements of business—strengths, weaknesses, national, international, regional.

    D. R&D—degree of importance—degree of obsolescence—short or long product life.

    E. Support/service organization.

    F. Dependence on major customers/diversity of major customers.

    G. Long-term sales contracts/visibility of revenues/backlogs/prepayments (*e.g.*, subscriptions).

    H. Product diversity.

III. **Issuer's industry position—operating efficiency:** This covers the issuer's historical operating margins and assesses its ability to maintain or improve them based upon pricing or cost advantages.

    A. Ability to maintain or improve margins.

    B. Pricing leadership.

    C. Integration of manufacturing operations.

    D. Plant and equipment: modern and efficient or old and obsolete. Low or high cost producer.

    E. Supply of raw material.

    F. Level of capital and employee productivity.

    G. Labor; availability, cost, union relations.

    H. Pollution control requirements and impact on operating costs.

    I. Energy costs.

IV. **Management evaluation:**

    A. The record of achievement in operations and financial results.

    B. Planning—extent, integration and relationship to accomplishments. Both strategic and financial. Plan for growth—both internal and external.

    C. Controls—management, financial and internal auditing.

    D. Financing policies and practices.

    E. Commitment, consistency and credibility.

    F. Overall quality of management; line of succession—strength of middle management.

    G. Merger and acquisition considerations.

    H. Performance vs. peers.

V. **Accounting quality:** Overall accounting evaluation of the methods employed and the extent to which they overstate or understate financial performance and position.

    A. Auditor's qualifications.

    B. LIFO vs. FIFO inventory method.

    C. Goodwill and intangible assets.

    D. Recording of revenues.

    E. Depreciation policies.

    F. Nonconsolidated subsidiaries.

    G. Method of accounting and funding for pension liabilities. Basic posture of the pension plan assumptions.

    H. Undervalued assets such as LIFO reserve.

VI. **Earnings protection:** Key measurements indicating the basic long-term earnings power of the company including:

    A. Returns on capital.

    B. Pretax coverage ratios.

    C. Profit margins.

    D. Earnings on asset/business segments.

    E. Sources of future earnings growth.

    F. Pension service coverage.

    G. Ability to finance growth internally.

    H. Inflation-adjusted earning capacity.

VII. **Financial leverage and asset protection:** Relative usage of debt, with due allowance for differences in debt usage appropriate to different types of businesses.

    A. Long-term debt and total debt to capital.

    B. Total liabilities to net tangible stockholders' equity.

    C. Preferred stock/capitalization.

    D. Leverage implicit in off-balance sheet financing arrangments, production payments, operating rentals of property, plant and equipment, nonconsolidated subsidiaries, unfunded pension liabilities, etc.

    E. Nature of assets.

    F. Working capital management—accounts receivable, inventory, and accounts payable turnover.

    G. Level, nature and value of intangible assets.

    H. Off-balance sheet assets such as undervalued natural resources or LIFO reserve.

VIII. **Cash flow adequacy:** Relationship of cash flow to leverage and ability to internally meet all business cash needs.

    A. Evaluation of size and scope of total capital requirements and capital spending flexibility.

    B. Evaluation of variability of future cash flow.

    C. Cash flow to fixed and working capital requirements.

    D. Cash flow to debt.

    E. Free cash flow to short-term debt and total debt.

IX. **Financial flexibility:** Evaluation of the company's financing needs, plans, and alternatives and its flexibility to accomplish its financing program under stress without damaging creditworthiness.

A. Relative financing needs.

B. Projected financing plan.

C. Financing alternatives under stress—ability to attract capital.

D. Capital spending flexibility.

E. Asset redeployment potentials—nature of assets and undervalued liabilities.

F. Nature and level of off-balance sheet assets or liabilities. This would include unfunded vested pension benefits and LIFO reserves.

G. High level of short-term debt/high level of floating rate debt.

H. Heavy or unwieldy debt service schedule (bullet maturities in future)—either of debt or sinking fund preferred stock.

I. Heavy percentage of preferred stock as a percentage of total capital.

J. Overall assessment of near-term sources of funds as compared to requirements for funds/internal financial self-sufficiency/need for external financing.

K. Ownership/affiliation.

SOURCE: *Standard and Poor's Credit Overview: Corporate and International Ratings.* New York: Standard and Poor's, 1982, pp. 90–91. Reprinted by permission of Standard and Poor's Corporation.

QUESTIONS AND TOPICS FOR DISCUSSION

1. Define the following terms:
   a. Bond.
   b. Mortgage bond.
   c. Debenture.
   d. Indenture.
   e. Trustee.
   f. Income bond.

2. Explain the call feature of long-term debt and preferred stock.

3. Suppose a company simultaneously sold two long-term debt issues at par: $9\frac{1}{8}$ percent senior debentures and $9\frac{3}{8}$ percent senior subordinated debentures. What risk-return tradeoff would an investor face who was considering one of these issues?

4. What is the relationship between par value, market value, and book value for the following?
   a. For long-term debt.
   b. For preferred stock.
   c. For common stock.

5. In what ways is preferred stock similar to long-term debt? In what ways is it similar to common stock?

6. Does the retained earnings figure on a company's balance sheet indicate the amounts of funds the company has available for current dividends or capital expenditures? Explain fully.

7. What is treasury stock, and what is it used for?

524

8. Suppose an associate of yours (who has just lost money in the stock market) comments that the stock exchanges should be shut down because "all people do is lose money in the stock market." What would your response be?

9. What is the general purpose of Federal and state regulation of security markets?

10. What are the basic provisions of the Securities Act of 1933 and the Securities Exchange Act of 1934?

11. What are the ways in which firms can sell their securities in the primary capital markets?

12. What factors influence the flotation cost percentage on security issues?

PROBLEMS*

1. Consider the Burlington Northern common stock listed in Table 16–4 (symbolized as BrlNth). Determine the following in regard to Burlington Northern:
   a. Current (1983) dividend per share.
   b. Dividend yield.
   c. Price-earnings ratio.
   d. Closing price on March 28, 1983.
   e. Closing price on the previous business day.
   f. Volume of shares traded on March 28, 1983.

2. Consider the Exxon bond listed in Table 16–2. Determine the following in regard to this bond:
   a. Coupon interest rate.
   b. Maturity date (year).
   c. Closing price (dollar amount) on April 14, 1983.

3. What was the approximate initial yield to maturity on Allied Corporation's zero coupon bonds (listed in Table 16–2) issued in April 1982 for $125 and maturing in August 1998 for $1,000?

4. This problem refers to the bonds listed in Table 16–2.
   a. Suppose an investor had purchased International Harvester's 9s04 on July 9, 1982 and sold them on April 14, 1983. What percentage rate of return would she have earned on her investment? (Disregard interest received during the holding period.)
   b. Suppose an investor had purchased Union Carbide's 14½s91 on July 9, 1982, and sold them on April 14, 1983. What percentage rate of return would he have earned on his investment? (Disregard interest received during the holding period.)
   c. Why are the returns calculated in Parts a and b different?

5. Baylor Minerals, Inc., is considering issuing additional long-term debt to finance an expansion. At the present time the company has $50 million in 10 percent debentures outstanding. Its after-tax net income is $10 million, and the company is in the 50 percent tax bracket. The company is required by the debenture holders to maintain its overall coverage ratio at 3.5 or greater.
   a. What is the present coverage (times interest earned) ratio?
   b. How much additional 10 percent debt can the company issue now and remain "covered"? (Assume for this calculation that earnings before interest and taxes remains at its present level.)

*Problems in color have check answers provided at the end of the book.

c. If the interest rate on additional debt is 12 percent, how much unused "debt capacity" does the company have?

6. In 1983 Andrews Oil Corporation sold units at $1,000 each consisting of a 20-year, 10¾ percent, $1,000 principal amount debenture plus 7 shares of the company's stock. At the time of issue the company's stock was selling at $15 a share.

    a. Set up the equation for calculating an investor's yield to maturity on the debentures.

    b. Calculate an investor's expected current interest yield on the debentures.

7. An insurance company in a 40 percent tax bracket is considering an investment in either the bonds or preferred stock of National Telephone and Telegraph. The bonds currently yield 9.0 percent, and the preferred stock yields 9.3 percent.

    a. What after-tax yield can the insurance company expect on the two types of securities?

    b. Should the investment decision be based only on expected return? Discuss.

8. The per-share price range for the common stock of General Motors (GM) for 1982 was 34 to 64½, whereas the price for GM's $3.75 preferred stock fluctuated between 27⅛ and 37½. The common stock paid $2.40 in dividends during the year. Assume that you held both the common and the preferred stock for 1 year.

    a. Calculate your percentage returns, assuming that you were lucky enough to have bought both stocks at their lows and sold them at their highs.

    b. Calculate your percentage returns, assuming that you were unlucky enough to have bought both stocks at their highs and sold them at their lows.

    c. What general conclusions can you draw about the relative variability of returns, or *risk*, of the two stocks?

9. The balance sheet and income statement of Eastland Products, Inc., are as follows:

BALANCE SHEET, DECEMBER 31, 19X1 (IN MILLIONS OF DOLLARS)

Current assets	$ 40	Current liabilities	$ 20
Fixed assets, net	110	Long-term debt	40
		Preferred stock	10
		Common stock ($1 par)	5
		Contributed capital in excess	
		of par value	20
		Retained earnings	55
Total assets	$150	Total liabilities and equity	$150

INCOME STATEMENT FOR YEAR ENDED DECEMBER 31, 19X1 (IN MILLIONS OF DOLLARS)

Sales	$120
Cost of goods sold	80
EBIT	$ 40
Interest	5
EBT	$ 35
Taxes (40%)	14
Net income	$ 21

ADDITIONAL INFORMATION:

Total preferred dividends	$1 million
Total common dividends	$10 million
Market price of common stock	$32 a share
Number of common shares authorized	10 million

Using these data, calculate the following:

a. Earnings per common share.

b. The common stock price-earnings ratio.

c. The common stock book value (per share).

d. The coverage (times interest earned) ratio.

e. The firm's capital structure.

f. The firm's current dividend yield (common stock).

g. The current dividend payout ratio (common stock).

h. How much of the retained earnings total was added during 19X1?

10. Show the new balance sheet of Eastland Products (Problem 9) after the company sells 1 million new common shares in early 19X2 to net $28 a share. Part of the proceeds, $10 million, is used to reduce current liabilities, and the remainder is temporarily deposited in the company's bank account. Later this remainder (along with additional long-term debt financing) will be invested in new manufacturing facilities.

ADDITIONAL READINGS AND REFERENCES

Ang, J. S. "The Two Faces of Bond Refunding." *Journal of Finance* 30 (June 1975): 869–874.

Bear, Robert M., and Curley, Anthony J. "Unseasoned Equity Financing." *Journal of Financial and Quantitative Analysis* 10 (June 1975): 311–325.

Bierman, Harold. "The Bond Refunding Decision." *Financial Management* 1 (Summer 1972): 22–29.

Bowlin, O. D. "The Refunding Decision: Another Special Case in Capital Budgeting." *Journal of Finance* 21 (March 1966): 55–68.

Brown, Bowman. "Why Corporations Should Consider Income Bonds." *Financial Executive* 35 (Oct. 1967): 74–78.

Caks, John. "The Coupon Effect on Yield to Maturity." *Journal of Finance* 32 (March 1977): 103–115.

Dyl, E. A., and Joehnk, M.D. "Competitive versus Negotiated Underwriting of Public Utility Debt." *Bell Journal of Economics* 7 (Autumn 1976): 680–689.

Ederington, Louis. "Negotiated versus Competitive Underwritings of Corporate Bonds." *Journal of Finance* 31 (March 1976): 17–26.

Elsaid, H. H. "The Function of Preferred Stock in the Corporate Financial Plan." *Financial Analysts Journal* (July–Aug. 1969): 112–117.

Fisher, Lawrence. "Determinants of Risk Premiums on Corporate Bonds." *Journal of Political Economy* 67 (June 1959): 217–237.

Furst, Richard W. "Does Listing Increase the Market Price of Common Stocks?" *Journal of Business* 43 (April 1970): 174–180.

Gray, W. S. "Future Structure of the Market System." *Financial Analysts Journal* 36 (March 1980): 14–18.

Hickman, W. B. *Corporate Bonds: Quality and Investment Performance.* Occasional Paper 59, New York: National Bureau of Economic Research, 1957.

Ibbotson, R. R. "Price Performance of Common Stock New Issues." *Journal of Financial Economics* 2 (Sept. 1975): 235–272.

Johnson, Rodney, and Klein, Richard. "Corporate Motives in Repurchases of Discounted Bonds." *Financial Management* 3 (Autumn 1974): 44–49.

Karna, Adi S. "The Cost of Private versus Public Debt Issues." *Financial Management* 1 (Summer 1972): 65–67.

Pinches, George E., and Mingo, Kent A. "A Multivariate Analysis of Industrial Bond Ratings." *Journal of Finance* 28 (March 1973): 1–18.

Reilly, Frank K., and Joehnk, Michael D. "The Association between Market-Determined Risk Measures for Bonds and Bond Ratings." *Journal of Finance* 31 (Dec. 1976): 1387–1403.

Silver, Andrew. "Original Issue Deep Discount Bonds." *Federal Reserve Bank of New York Quarterly Review* (Winter 1981–1982): 18–28.

Bond Refunding, Stockholder Voting Rights, and Rights Offerings

GLOSSARY OF NEW TERMS

Cumulative voting   a voting procedure by which stockholders may cast multiple votes for a single board of directors candidate. Cumulative voting makes it easier for stockholders with minority views to elect sympathetic board members.

Ex-rights   a stock sells ex-rights when stock purchasers no longer receive the *rights* along with the shares purchased.

Rights-on   a stock sells rights-on when purchasers receive the *rights* along with the shares purchased.

INTRODUCTION

This appendix considers three additional topics related to bonds and stocks:

- Bond refunding analysis.
- Stockholder voting rights.
- Analysis of rights offerings.

BOND REFUNDING ANALYSIS

Bond refunding occurs when a company redeems a callable issue and sells a lower cost issue to take its place.[1] The decision of whether or not to refund

---

[1]Callable preferred stock also can be refunded. The same considerations and analysis apply to both debt and preferred stock.

a particular debt issue is usually based on a capital budgeting (present value) analysis. The principal benefit, or cash inflow, is the present value of the after-tax interest savings over the life of the issue. The principal investment, or cash outflow at the time of refunding, consists primarily of the call premium and the flotation cost of the new debt.

Bond refunding differs from other capital expenditure projects in one very important way: the cash inflows are known with considerably more certainty than the cash flows from a typical capital expenditure project and thus are less risky. As a result, the weighted cost of capital is not used. Instead, the *after-tax cost of the new debt* is believed to be a more appropriate discount rate for bond refunding analysis.

As an illustration of bond refunding, consider the following example. The APCO Company issued $100 million of 30-year, 10 percent debt 5 years ago. In the meantime, interest rates have declined, and the firm's management feels the decline has bottomed out. The debt issue is now callable at 107 percent of par. The company could refund the old issue with a new 25-year, 8 percent, $100 million issue. Flotation costs on the new issue would be 0.5 percent, or $500,000, whereas the unamortized flotation costs on the old issue are $450,000. If APCO decided to call the old issue and refund it, both issues would be outstanding for a 3-week period, resulting in overlapping interest payments. The company's marginal tax rate is 50 percent. For purposes of discounting, the after-tax cost of new debt is $0.08 \times (1 - 0.5) = 0.04$.

To determine whether APCO should refund the old issue, a bond refunding analysis is carried out.

Step 1   The interest savings (cash inflows) are calculated:[2]

Annual interest, after tax = Issue size × Interest rate × (1 − Tax rate)
Annual interest, old issue = $100 million × 10% × 0.5 = $5 million
Annual interest, new issue = $100 million × 8% × 0.5 = $4 million
    Annual after-tax interest savings $1 million

$$\text{Present value of interest savings} = \text{Annual after-tax interest} \times \text{PVIFA}_{0.04,25}$$
$$= \$1 \text{ million} \times 15.622$$
$$= \$15.622 \text{ million} .$$

Step 2   The net investment (*net cash* outflow at time 0) is calculated. This involves computing the after-tax call premium, the flotation cost of the new issue, the flotation cost of the old issue, and the overlapping interest.

The after-tax call premium is calculated as follows:

$$\text{Call premium, after-tax} = \$7 \text{ million} \times (1 - 0.5)$$
$$= \$3.5 \text{ million} .$$

The call premium is a cash outflow.

---

[2]This calculation assumes that interest is received once a year at year-end. Actually, interest is paid every 6 months. However, the two results are not materially different.

The flotation cost of the new issue is 0.5 percent, or $500,000. This amount cannot be deducted from APCO's current period income for tax purposes. Instead, it must be capitalized and amortized over the life of the debt issue, because the benefits that accrue to a firm as a result of a flotation cost expenditure occur over the life of the issue. Thus,

$$\begin{array}{l}\text{Present value of}\\\text{flotation cost}\\\text{of new issue}\end{array} = \text{Flotation cost} - \text{Present value tax effect}$$

$$= \text{Flotation cost} - \left(\begin{array}{c}\text{Annual after-tax}\\\text{savings from}\\\text{amortization}\end{array} \times \text{PVIFA}_{0.04,25}\right)$$

$$= \text{Flotation cost} - \left(\frac{\text{Flotation cost}}{\text{Number of years}} \times \text{Tax rate}\right.$$

$$\left. \times \ \text{PVIFA}_{0.04,25}\right)$$

$$= \$500,000 - \left(\frac{\$500,000}{25} \times 0.5 \times 15.622\right)$$

$$= \$500,000 - \$156,220$$

$$= \$343,780 \ .$$

The present value of the flotation cost of the *new* issue is a net cash outflow.

APCO has been amortizing the flotation cost of the old issue over its life. If it refunded the issue, the company would no longer receive the benefits from the old issue's flotation cost and could therefore write off the remaining unamortized flotation cost at the time of refunding. Because of the write-off, however, APCO would lose the benefits of the old flotation cost over the remaining life of the issue. Thus,

$$\begin{array}{l}\text{Present value of}\\\text{flotation cost of old}\\\text{issue}\end{array} = \begin{array}{c}\text{Present value,}\\\text{lost benefits,}\\\text{old flotation cost,}\\\text{after tax}\end{array} - \begin{array}{c}\text{Present value,}\\\text{write-off of old}\\\text{flotation cost,}\\\text{after tax}\end{array}$$

$$= \left(\frac{\text{Old flotation cost}}{\text{Number of years}} \times \text{Tax rate} \times \text{PVIFA}_{0.04,25}\right)$$

$$- \ (\text{Old flotation cost} \times \text{Tax rate})$$

$$= \left(\frac{\$450,000}{25} \times 0.5 \times 15.622\right) - (\$450,000 \times 0.5)$$

$$= \$140,598 - \$225,000$$

$$= - \ \$84,402 \ .$$

The flotation cost effect of the old issue is a net cash inflow at the time of refunding.

In most bond refundings it is necessary for a firm to sell the new issue and receive the proceeds before paying off the old lenders. Both issues are usually outstanding for less than a month. Thus, the interest expense on the new issue during the overlapping period is considered a cost, or part of the refunding investment. In APCO's case, this expense is calculated as follows:

$$\begin{array}{c}\text{Overlapping} \\ \text{interest}\end{array} = \begin{array}{c}\text{Size of} \\ \text{issue}\end{array} \times \begin{array}{c}\text{Annual interest rate} \\ \text{of new issue,} \\ \text{after tax}\end{array} \times \begin{array}{c}\text{Fraction of year} \\ \text{both issues} \\ \text{outstanding}\end{array}$$

$$= \$100 \text{ million} \times 0.04 \times \frac{3}{52}$$

$$= \$230{,}769 \ .$$

The overlapping interest is a cash outflow.

In summary, the net investment is calculated as follows:

Call premium	$3,500,000
Present value of flotation cost, new issue	343,780
Present value of flotation cost, old issue	(84,402)
Overlapping interest	230,769
Net investment (cash outflow)	$3,990,147

Step 3   Finally, the net present value of refunding is calculated as follows:

$$\text{Net present value of refunding} = \begin{array}{c}\text{Present value,} \\ \text{interest savings}\end{array} - \begin{array}{c}\text{Present value,} \\ \text{net investment}\end{array}$$

$$= \$15.622 \text{ million} - \$3.990 \text{ million}$$

$$= \$11.632 \text{ million} \ .$$

Because the net present value is positive, APCO should call its old issue and refund it with the new one.[3]

STOCKHOLDER VOTING RIGHTS

A firm's stockholders elect its board of directors by means of either a *majority* or a *cumulative* voting procedure. Majority voting is similar to the voting that takes place in political elections; namely, if two slates of people are running for the board, the one that receives more than 50 percent of the votes wins. With majority voting it is possible that a group of stockholders with a minority viewpoint will have no representation on the board.

---

[3]Financial analysts can normally determine the *approximate* net present value of refunding by comparing the present value of the interest savings with the after-tax cost of the call premium. However, as is true with any shortcut method, caution should be exercised.

Cumulative voting, in contrast, makes it easier for stockholders with minority views to elect sympathetic board members. (Because of the potential inequities of majority voting, cumulative voting is required in some states and permitted in all fifty states.) In cumulative voting, each share of stock represents as many votes as there are directors to be elected. For example, if a firm is electing seven directors, a particular holder of 100 shares would have 700 votes and could cast all of them for *one* candidate, thereby increasing that candidate's chances of being elected to the board. The following formula can be used to determine the minimum number of shares or votes necessary to elect a certain number of directors:

$$\text{Number of shares} = \frac{\begin{array}{c}\text{Number of} \\ \text{directors} \\ \text{desired}\end{array} \times \begin{array}{c}\text{Number of} \\ \text{shares} \\ \text{outstanding}\end{array}}{\begin{array}{c}\text{Number of directors} \\ \text{being elected}\end{array} + 1} + 1 .$$

Of course, it is possible that not all the shareholders will vote their shares. In this case, the calculation is based on the number of shares actually voting rather than the number of shares outstanding.

Consider the following example. The Markham Company has eleven members on its board and 1 million shares of common stock outstanding. If seven members were up for reelection in a given year and all the shares were voted, the number of shares necessary to elect one director would be as follows:

$$\frac{1 \times 1,000,000}{7 + 1} + 1 = 125,001 .$$

In addition to electing the board of directors, a firm's stockholders may vote from time to time on various other matters, such as whether to retain a particular auditing firm or increase the number of shares authorized.

The election of directors and other voting normally occurs at the annual stockholders' meeting. Since it is usually not possible for all stockholders to attend, management—or anyone else—can solicit votes by *proxy*. Normally, a stockholder can expect to receive a single proxy statement from the firm's management requesting that stockholders follow management's recommendations. In the rather unlikely event that another group of stockholders sends out its own proxy statement, a *proxy fight* is said to occur. Proxy fights are most common when a company is performing poorly.

ANALYSIS OF RIGHTS OFFERINGS

In addition to the sale of new common stock through underwriters, new equity capital can be raised through a *rights offering*. In a rights offering the firm's existing stockholders are given an opportunity to purchase a fraction of the new shares equal to the fraction they currently own. For example, if a company has 10 million shares outstanding and decides to sell 1 million additional shares through a rights offering, each shareholder is entitled to purchase 0.1 new share for each share presently owned. (The *rights* themselves are really the documents describing the offer. Each stockholder receives one right for each share currently held.)

In a rights offering, shareholders have the opportunity to maintain their original ownership percentage. Hence, rights offerings are used in equity financing by companies whose charters contain the *preemptive right*. In addition, rights offerings *may* be used as a means of selling common stock in companies in which preemptive rights do not exist. The number of rights offerings has gradually declined over the years because of the large amount of paperwork associated with them.[4]

The following example illustrates what a rights offering involves. The Miller Company has 10 million common shares outstanding and plans to sell an additional 1 million shares via a rights offering. In this case, each right entitles the holder to purchase 0.1 share, and it takes 10 rights to purchase 1 share. The company has to decide on a *subscription price*—that is, the price the rightholder will have to pay per new share. The subscription price has to be less than the market price, or rightholders will have no incentive to subscribe to the new issue. As a general rule, subscription prices are 5 to 20 percent below market prices. If the Miller Company's stock is selling at $40 per share, a reasonable subscription price might be $35 per share.

VALUATION OF RIGHTS

Because a right represents an opportunity to purchase stock below its market value, the right itself has a certain value, which is calculated under two sets of circumstances:

- The *rights-on* case.
- The *ex-rights* case.

A stock is said to "trade with rights-on" when the purchasers receive the rights along with the shares they purchase. In contrast, a stock is said to "trade ex-rights" when the stock purchasers no longer receive the rights.

For example, suppose the Miller Company announced on May 15 that shareholders of record as of Friday, June 20, will receive the rights. This means that anyone who purchased stock on or before Monday, June 16, will receive the rights, and anyone who purchased stock on or later than June 17 will not.[5] The stock trades with rights up to and including June 16 and goes ex-rights on June 17, the *ex-rights date*. On that date the stock's market value falls by the value of the right, all other things being equal.

The theoretical, or formula, value of a right for the rights-on case can be calculated using the following equation:

$$R = \frac{M_o - S}{N + 1},$$

where R is the theoretical value of the right; M_o, the rights-on market price

---

[4] *Barron's* (May 2, 1977):11.
[5] A stock purchaser becomes a "shareholder of record" 4 *trading* days after purchase.

of the stock; S, the subscription price of the right; and N, the number of rights necessary to purchase 1 new share. In the Miller Company example, the right's theoretical value is $0.45:

$$R = \frac{\$40 - \$35}{10 + 1}$$
$$= \$0.45 \ .$$

The theoretical value of a right when the stock is trading ex-rights can be calculated by using the following equation:

$$R = \frac{M_e - S}{N} \ ,$$

Where M_e is the ex-rights market price of the stock; S, the subscription price of the right; and N, the number of rights necessary to purchase 1 new share. If the Miller stock were trading ex-rights, the theoretical value of a right would be as follows:

$$R = \frac{\$39.55 - \$35}{10}$$
$$= \$0.45 \ .$$

(Notice that M_e is lower than M_o by the amount of the right.)

Some shareholders may decide not to use their rights because of lack of funds or for some other reason. These stockholders can sell their rights to other investors who wish to purchase them. Thus, a market exists for the rights, and a market price is established for them. Generally, the market price is higher than the theoretical value, since investors who are optimistic about the stock's short-run performance often "bid up" the price of the right because they can earn a higher return by purchasing the rights than by purchasing the stock because of the leverage rights provide. In general, the premium of market value over theoretical value decreases as the rights expiration date approaches. A right is worthless after its expiration date.

QUESTIONS AND TOPICS FOR DISCUSSION

1. What is *bond refunding?* At what relative level of interest rates is bond refunding most likely to occur? Explain.
2. What is the difference between majority voting and cumulative voting?
3. What is the *preemptive right* of common stockholders? In what type of company is the preemptive right important? Unimportant?

PROBLEMS*

1. The Springfield Gas and Electric Company is considering refunding $50 million of 11 percent debt with an 8 percent, 20-year debt issue. The existing, or old, issue

*Problems in color have check answers provided at the end of the book.

also matures in 20 years and is now callable at 108 percent of par. The unamortized flotation cost on the old issue is $400,000 and the flotation cost of the new issue is 0.875 percent. The company estimates that both issues will be outstanding for 4 weeks, resulting in overlapping interest. The company has a weighted cost of capital of 10.0 percent and a 50 percent marginal tax rate. In addition, the company's financial management feels as though the present interest rate decline has nearly bottomed out. Calculate the net present value of the refunding, and make a recommendation to management on whether or not to refund.

2. Suppose you have accumulated a sizable investment (100,000 common shares) in Alpine Land and Development Company. You are dissatisfied with the performance of the present management and are considering running for the board of directors. The company has a nine-member board and a total of 1,500,000 common shares outstanding. Assume that all shares will be voted in the upcoming election and that four of the nine board members are up for reelection.
   a. If the voting procedure is cumulative, what is the minimum number of shares necessary to insure your election to the board? Is it possible for you to be elected with fewer votes? Explain.
   b. Suppose a close friend of yours also owns a good deal of Alpine and shares your feelings about the present management. If the voting procedure is cumulative, how many shares are necessary to elect both you and your friend to the board?
   c. If the voting procedure is majority, how many votes are necessary for election in Parts a and b of this problem? Explain your answer.

3. Oswego Manufacturing Company has decided to sell additional common stock through a rights offering. The company has 50 million shares outstanding and plans to sell an additional 5.0 million shares through the rights offering. Each shareholder will receive 1 right for each share currently held, and thus each right will entitle shareholders to purchase 0.1 share. Oswego's common stock is currently selling at $50 a share, and the subscription price of the rights will be $45 a share.
   a. Calculate the theoretical value of the right for both the *rights-on* and the *ex-rights* cases.
   b. How much is the market price of the company's stock expected to drop on the *ex-rights* date, all other things being equal? Why?
   c. If the market price of Oswego's common stock increases to $52 a share, what will the theoretical value of the right be (rights-on)?
   d. Discuss the trend of the right's market price over its life, assuming the company's common stock continues to trade in the $50 range. (No numerical calculations are necessary for this part of the problem.)

CHAPTER 17

Convertible Securities and Warrants

A FINANCIAL DILEMMA

Expanded Uses of Warrants in the 1980s

The early 1980s have been characterized as a period of "creative financings" because of the unusual financing methods employed by some companies. Warrants were used as part of some of these creative financings.

In January 1983 International Harvester used a bond swap in an attempt to strengthen its balance sheet. The holders of various Harvester bonds swapped their old bonds for new bonds with warrants. For example, a holder of $2,000 (principal value) in old bonds paying 9 percent coupon interest was offered $1,000 in new bonds paying 18 percent. Even though the holders would lose no interest income, they had to decide if the receipt of warrants was sufficient to compensate them for the loss of principal at maturity. Harvester's financial managers and investment bankers also had to decide whether the swap was in the best interests of the company's stockholders.

In another unusual warrant transaction, Trans World Corporation (June 1982) issued warrants in connection with a common stock offering. The company sold 1.8 million units, which consisted of 1 common share and 1 warrant. The company referred to the warrants as "dual-option warrants," because the holders could either exercise the warrants for common stock *or* preferred stock.

As a result of the recession in 1982, many companies became unable to service their debt. Some of these companies were able to obtain additional working capital loans as well as restructure their existing debt, that is, extend the repayment period. However, the banks, after assessing the high level of risk associated with making the additional loans to troubled companies, wanted higher returns than interest income alone could provide. Accordingly, some banks demanded and received warrants in return for the restructuring and additional loans. Then, if the company did return to profitability, the

537

banks had an opportunity to earn a high return on the warrants by selling them.

This chapter considers the features and characteristics of both warrants and convertible securities. An understanding of these features and characteristics is necessary to evaluate the impact on shareholder wealth of issuing these types of securities.

GLOSSARY OF NEW TERMS

Conversion premium   the amount by which the market value of a convertible security exceeds the higher of its conversion value or straight-bond (preferred) value.

Conversion price   the effective price an investor pays for common stock when the stock is obtained by converting a convertible security.

Conversion ratio   the number of common shares an investor obtains by converting a convertible security.

Conversion (stock) value   the value of a convertible security, based on the value of the underlying shares of common stock.

Convertible security   a fixed-income security that may be exchanged for a firm's common stock at the holder's option. The two most common types of convertible securities are *convertible preferred stock* and *convertible debentures*.

Exercise price   the price at which the holder of a warrant can purchase the issuing company's common stock.

Straight-bond, or investment, value   the value a convertible debt security would have if it did not possess the conversion feature.

Warrant   a company-issued long-term option to purchase a specified number of shares of the firm's stock at a particular price during a specified time period.

INTRODUCTION

In addition to long-term debt, preferred stock, and common stock, a firm has two other primary forms of financing available to it: *convertible securities* and *warrants*. A convertible security is a fixed-income security, such as a debenture or a share of preferred stock, that may be exchanged for the firm's common stock at the holder's option.[1] A warrant is an option to purchase

---

[1]Convertible bonds are usually unsecured debentures. However, in February 1983 Pan American World Airways issued $135 million of convertible secured trust notes maturing in 1998. Pan Am used some of its planes as collateral for the notes. Apparently, Pan Am and its investment bankers felt that securing this convertible issue was necessary in order to sell it to investors. Pan Am lost $485 million in 1982.

shares of the company's common stock for a particular price during a specified period of time. Warrants are usually sold to investors as part of a *unit* that consists of a fixed-income security with a warrant attached. The issuance of convertible securities, warrants, or both often makes it easier for a firm to sell its fixed-income securities, especially during tight money periods. This chapter describes the features of convertible securities and warrants and considers the circumstances in which they are used. It also develops and illustrates valuation models for both convertibles and warrants.

CONVERTIBLE SECURITIES

Both debentures and preferred stock can have convertibility or conversion features. When a company issues convertible securities, its usual intention is the future issuance of common stock. To illustrate, suppose the Beloit Corporation issues 2 million shares of $2.75 convertible preferred stock at a price of $50 a share. After the sale, the company receives gross proceeds of $100 million. Because of the convertibility feature, the company can expect to issue shares of common stock in exchange for the redemption of the convertible preferred stock over some future time period. In the case of Beloit's convertible preferred, each share can be exchanged for 2 shares of common stock; that is, it is convertible into 2 shares of common stock. Thus, if all the preferred shares are converted, the company in effect will have issued 4 million new common shares, and the preferred shares no longer will appear on Beloit's balance sheet. No additional funds are raised by the company at the time of conversion.

FEATURES OF CONVERTIBLE SECURITIES

As an introduction to the terminology and features of convertible securities, consider a $200 million, 25-year issue of 9 percent convertible subordinated debentures sold by Deere and Company in 1983. Convertible securities are exchangeable for common stock at a stated *conversion price*. In the case of the Deere issue, the conversion price is $40. This means that each $1,000 debenture is convertible into common stock at $40 a share.

The number of common shares that can be obtained when a convertible security is exchanged is determined by the conversion ratio, which is calculated as follows:

$$\text{Conversion ratio} = \frac{\text{Par value of security}}{\text{Conversion price}}. \qquad \textbf{(17.1)}$$

In the case of Deere and Company's convertible subordinated debentures, the conversion ratio is the following:

$$\text{Conversion ratio} = \frac{\$1,000}{\$40}$$
$$= 25.$$

Thus, each $1,000 Deere debenture can be exchanged for 25 shares of common stock. Although the conversion ratio may change one or more times during the life of the conversion option, it is more common for it to remain constant.

Normally, the conversion price is set about 20 percent above the common stock's market price prevailing at the time of issue. For example, at the time Deere issued its convertible debentures, the market price of its common stock was about $33 a share. The $7 difference between the conversion price and the market price represents a 21 percent premium.

Holders of convertible securities are protected against dilution by the company. For example, suppose Deere and Company were to split its common stock 2 for 1. The conversion price (and therefore the conversion ratio) would be adjusted so that the holders would not be disadvantaged by the split. Specifically, in the Deere case the new conversion price would be $20, and the new conversion ratio would be 50.

REASONS FOR ISSUING
CONVERTIBLE SECURITIES

Three principal and interrelated reasons exist for issuing convertibles:

- To "sweeten" the sale of fixed-income securities, permitting a firm to raise funds with a lower interest rate or preferred dividend rate.

- To sell common stock in the future at a higher price than the price prevailing at the time of original issue.

- To acquire and use low cost capital for a period of time until the full benefits of the financing can be reflected in the company's earnings.

Each of these three reasons will be discussed.

Frequently investors prefer fixed-income convertible securities over similar issues that are not convertible. This is because investors are able to combine the relatively secure and stable interest payments or preferred dividends with the appreciation potential of common stock ownership. Hence, the convertibility feature "sweetens" the deal.

Benefits also accrue to the issuing company in the form of lower interest payments or dividends. This occurs because investors are willing to accept the conversion privilege as part of their overall return. As an example, consider again the Deere and Company 9 percent convertible subordinated debentures. At the time Deere sold these convertibles, the company would have had to pay about 12 percent interest on any nonconvertible debt it issued. Thus, the convertibility feature is saving Deere about $6 million a year [(0.12 − 0.09) × $200 million] in interest expense. Typically, firms can issue convertible securities with interest rates or dividend yields about 3 percent below straight issues, that is, issues without convertibility features.

Another reason firms issue convertible securities is effectively to sell common stock at a higher price than the market price prevailing at the time of issue. Suppose a company needs additional equity financing because of a relatively high proportion of fixed-income securities in its capital structure. If the company's management feels the price of its common stock is temporarily depressed, one alternative is to consider issuing a convertible security. With the conversion price typically set about 20 percent above the market price at the time of issue, the use of a convertible security effectively gives the issuing company the potential for selling common stock above the existing market price. However, for the sale to be successful, conditions in the future must be such that investors will want to exercise their conversion option. Also, if the market price rises considerably above the conversion price, it may turn out that the company would have been better off to wait and sell common stock directly rather than sell the convertible issue at all.

The third reason for issuing convertible securities centers around the fact that the earnings resulting from a particular external financing issue may not begin for some time after financing occurs. For example, the construction and start-up period for a major expansion may be several years. During this period the company may desire debt or preferred stock financing. Eventually, once the expansion is fully operational and producing income, the company may want to achieve its original goal of additional common stock financing. The delayed issue of common stock minimizes the dilution in earnings per share that results from the immediate issuance of common stock.

VALUATION OF CONVERTIBLE SECURITIES

Because convertible securities possess certain characteristics of both common stock and fixed-income securities, their valuation is more complex than that of ordinary nonconvertible securities. The actual market value of a convertible security is a function of both the *common stock value*, or *conversion value*, and the value as a fixed-income security, or *straight-bond* or *investment value*. Each of these is discussed here.[2]

Conversion value   The conversion value, or stock value, of a convertible bond is defined as the conversion ratio times the common stock's market price:

$$\text{Conversion value} = \text{Conversion ratio} \times \text{Stock price} . \qquad (17.2)$$

To illustrate, assume a firm offers a convertible bond that can be exchanged for 40 shares of common stock. If the market price of the firm's common stock is $20 per share, the conversion value is $800. If the market price of the common stock rises to $25 per share, the conversion value becomes $1,000. And if the stock price rises to $30 per share, the conversion value becomes $1,200. In the case of Deere and Company's convertible bonds, the conversion value was 25 × $33, or $825, at the time of issue.

Straight-bond value   The straight-bond value, or investment value, of a convertible debt issue is the value it would have if it did not possess the conversion feature. Thus, it is equal to the sum of the present value of the interest

---

[2]For simplicity, only convertible debt is considered in this discussion, although the principles apply to convertible preferred stock as well.

annuity plus the present value of the expected principal repayment:

$$\text{Straight-bond value} = \sum_{t=1}^{m} \frac{\text{Interest}}{(1 + k_d)^t} + \frac{\text{Principal}}{(1 + k_d)^m}, \qquad (17.3)$$

where k_d is the current yield to maturity for *nonconvertible* debt issues of similar quality and maturity; t, the number of years; and m, the time to maturity.

Considering again Deere and Company's 9 percent, 25-year convertible debentures, the bond value at the time of issue is calculated as follows, assuming that 12 percent is the appropriate discount rate (and that interest is paid annually):

$$
\begin{aligned}
\text{Straight-bond value} &= \sum_{t=1}^{25} \frac{\$90}{(1.12)^t} + \frac{\$1,000}{(1.12)^{25}} \\
&= \$90(\text{PVIFA}_{0.12,25}) + \$1,000(\text{PVIF}_{0.12,25}) \\
&= \$90(7.843) + \$1,000(0.059) \\
&= \$705.87 + \$59 \\
&= \$764.87 .
\end{aligned}
$$

Market value   The market value of a convertible debt issue is usually somewhat above the higher of the conversion or the straight-bond value. This is illustrated in Figure 17–1.

The difference between the market value and the higher of the conversion or the straight-bond value is the *conversion premium* for which the issue sells. This premium tends to be largest when the conversion value and the straight-bond value are nearly identical. This set of circumstances allows investors to participate in any common stock appreciation while at the same time having some degree of downside protection, because the straight-bond value can represent a "floor" below which the market value will not fall.[3] The Deere and Company convertible debentures described in this section were offered to the public at $1,000 per bond and were quickly bought up by investors. In this case, investors were willing to pay $1,000 for an issue having a conversion value of approximately $825 and a bond value of about $765. The $1,000 market value contained a premium of $175 over the conversion value (which was higher than the bond value).

CONVERTING CONVERTIBLE SECURITIES

Conversion can occur in one of two ways:

- It may be *voluntary* on the part of the investor.
- It can be effectively *forced* by the issuing company.

Whereas voluntary conversions can occur at any time prior to the expiration of a conversion feature, forced conversions occur at specific points in time.

---

[3]The straight-bond value may fall if long-term interest rates rise, however.

FIGURE 17–1   Convertible Debenture Valuation at Different Stock Prices*

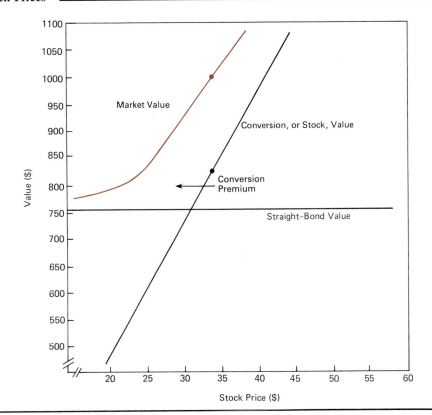

*Conversion ratio = 25; straight-bond value = $765.

The method most commonly used by companies to force conversion is the exercise of the *call* privilege on the convertible security. For example, consider the Trans World Corp. 12 percent convertible bonds maturing in 2005, which the company decided to call for redemption in 1983. The bonds had a conversion ratio of 41.66, and the market price of Trans World common stock at the time of the call was $34 per share. Thus, the conversion value was approximately $1,416 per bond. The call price—which was set and agreed upon by both the borrower and the lender at the time of the original issue—was $1,102 per bond.

Holders of the Trans World convertibles had two alternatives under these circumstances:

▪ Conversion, in which case the holder would receive common stock having a market value of $1,416 per bond.

▪ Redemption, in which case the holder would receive $1,102 in cash for each bond.

The conversion alternative was the obvious choice, since even those investors who did not wish to hold the common stock could sell it upon conversion for more money than they would receive from redemption. Trans World Corp. viewed the call as an opportunity to remove $57.6 million in long-term debt from its balance sheet without having to redeem the bonds for cash and to save $6.9 million a year in interest expense.[4]

Another way in which a company can effectively force conversion is by raising its dividend on common stock to a high enough level that holders of convertible securities are better off converting them and receiving the higher dividend.

Conversion of a significant proportion of a convertible security issue may take place immediately prior to the time the conversion ratio is scheduled to drop. For example, suppose the conversion ratio on a particular convertible debenture is scheduled to drop from 50 to 45 as of December 1 of this year. This means that the convertible debenture may be exchanged for 50 common shares before December 1 and 45 shares after that date (ignoring trading date considerations). To receive the greater number of shares, some investors may choose to convert before December 1. If a conversion ratio is scheduled to decline, the date and the amount of the change in the ratio is specified at the time the original security is issued.

WARRANTS

As mentioned earlier in this chapter, a warrant is an option to purchase a specific number of shares of the issuing company's common stock at a particular price during a specified time period. Warrants are frequently issued in conjunction with an offering of debentures or preferred stock. In these instances, like convertibles, warrants serve to "sweeten," or function as an "equity kicker," for fixed-income security offerings.

However, during the early 1980s, the various ways in which warrants were used as a financing device seemed to expand. For example, warrants were used in connection with bond swaps, equity offerings, and debt restructurings.[5]

FEATURES OF WARRANTS

To illustrate some of the features of financing with warrants, consider American Express, which sold 900,000 warrants in 1982 to raise approximately $11.4 million (less flotation costs). Each warrant allowed the purchase of 1 common share at $55. The warrants sold for $12.625 each.

The *exercise price* of a warrant is the price at which the holder can purchase common stock of the issuing company. The exercise price—which normally remains constant over the life of the warrant—is usually between 10 and 30 percent above the market price of the common stock prevailing at the time of issue. The exercise price of the American Express warrants is $55, approximately 21 percent above the $45.50 per-share market price of the common stock at the time of issue.

---

[4]*Wall Street Journal* (March 24, 1983):42.
[5]The Financial Dilemma at the beginning of this chapter gives examples of these financings.

The *expiration date* of the American Express warrants is February 28, 1987, meaning that the life of these warrants is 5 years. Typically, the life of a warrant is between 5 and 10 years, although on occasion the life can be longer or even perpetual.

The management of American Express hopes that the common share price will rise above the $55 level and remain there, expecially until after the warrants expire, since this would mean that the firm could reasonably expect holders to exercise their warrants. If this happened, American Express would receive funds totaling $49.5 million (900,000 warrants times $55 per warrant) at expiration. Thus, the company would realize its goal of raising additional capital at the time of exercise. This is in contrast to a convertible bond or preferred stock, because with convertible securities the company does not receive additional funds at the time of conversion.

If a warrant is issued as part of a unit with a fixed-income security, the warrant is usually *detachable* from the debenture or preferred stock. This means that purchasers of the units have the option of selling the warrants separately and continuing to hold the debenture or preferred stock.[6] As a result, other investors can purchase and trade warrants.

Prior to 1970, warrants were usually not used as a financing vehicle by large, established firms. In April of that year, however, AT&T sold $1.6 billion of 30-year debentures with warrants to buy 31.4 million common shares at $52 each through May 15, 1975. The use of warrant financing by AT&T undoubtedly caused other large, established firms to consider warrants. Also before 1970, warrants normally were listed either on the American Stock Exchange or traded over the counter, since the New York Stock Exchange would not list them. However, with the AT&T warrants the NYSE changed its policy and began to list warrants of NYSE companies if the warrants met certain requirements, including a life greater than 5 years. For example, Chrysler, Eastern Air Lines, and Mattel, among others, have warrants that are traded on the NYSE. The American Express warrants are traded on the American Stock Exchange.

Holders of warrants do not have the rights of common stockholders, such as the right to vote for directors or receive dividends, until they exercise their warrants.

REASONS FOR ISSUING WARRANTS

The primary reason for issuing warrants is to sell common stock in the future. Warrants also are used to "sweeten" fixed-income security offerings by giving investors an opportunity to participate in any common stock price appreciation. Just as with convertible securities, warrants also can permit a company to sell common stock at a price above the price prevailing at the time of original issue. In addition, warrants allow a company to sell common stock in the future without incurring underwriting costs at the time of sale.

---

[6] It is normally illogical to consider selling the fixed-income security immediately after purchase unless economic conditions change. An investor who desires only the warrant could purchase it separately.

VALUATION OF WARRANTS

In general, a warrant's value is a function of the outlook for the issuing company and the economy as a whole. The warrant's value is also dependent upon the difference betweeen the exercise price and the common stock's market price. In this connection, the formula value of a warrant is defined by the following equation:

$$\begin{matrix}\text{Formula value} \\ \text{or a warrant}\end{matrix} = \text{Max}\left\{0; \left(\begin{matrix}\text{Common stock} \\ \text{market price} \\ \text{per share}\end{matrix} - \begin{matrix}\text{Exercise} \\ \text{price} \\ \text{per share}\end{matrix}\right) \times \begin{matrix}\text{Number of shares} \\ \text{obtainable with} \\ \text{each warrant}\end{matrix}\right\}. \quad (17.4)$$

At the time of issue, a warrant's exercise price is greater than the common stock price. Even though the calculated formula value may be negative, it is considered to be zero, since securities cannot sell for negative amounts. For example, the American Express warrants had an exercise price of \$55 when the firm's common stock price was \$45.50 per share. Each warrant entitled the holder to 1 share, and the formula value was zero:

$$\begin{aligned}\text{Formula value} &= \text{Max}\ \{0;\ (\$45.50 - \$55)(1)\} \\ &= 0\ .\end{aligned}$$

During the winter of 1983, however, the price of American Express common stock reached a high of \$70.75 per share, and, at the same time, the warrants traded at \$27.25 each. The formula value at this time was calculated as follows:

$$\begin{aligned}\text{Formula value} &= \text{Max}\ \{0;(\$70.75 - \$55)(1)\} \\ &= \$15.75\ .\end{aligned}$$

Thus, the warrant market price of \$27.25 represented a *premium* of \$11.50 over the formula value.

In general, investors consider warrants to be worth more than their formula

TABLE 17–1 Market Price Data for American Express Common Stock and Warrants, 1982–1983*

Common Stock Market Price Per Share	Warrant Market Price	Warrant Formula Value	Premium Over Formula Value
46	12¾	0	12¾
48⅜	13	0	13
58½	17⅝	3½	14⅛
64⅛	21¾	9⅛	12⅝
70¾	27¼	15¾	11½

*The two market prices occurred simultaneously; for example, when the common stock price was 58½, the warrant price was 17⅝.

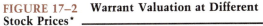

FIGURE 17–2   Warrant Valuation at Different Stock Prices*

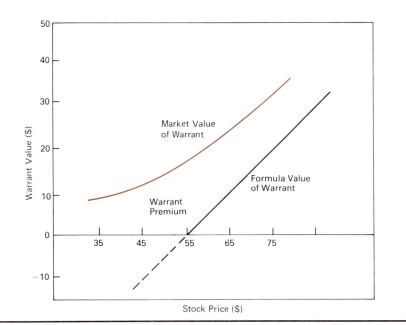

*Warrant exercise price = $55.

value. This is due to leverage. The leverage effect of warrants is shown in Table 17–1, which lists actual 1982–1983 stock market data for American Express common stock and warrants, as well as Figure 17–2, which graphically plots these values.

As Table 17–1 and Figure 17–2 show, the premium over the formula value reaches a maximum when the warrant exercise price is equal to the common stock price, because, at this point, the opportunities for high percentage returns on investment are greatest. This is not only true for the American Express warrants; it is also true in general. The reason for this is that when the exercise price is equal to the common stock price, warrant investors have the potential for large absolute (and percentage) gains if the stock price increases. At the same time, their potential losses are limited to the price paid for the warrant.

To illustrate the leverage opportunities warrants provide, suppose an investor purchased American Express common stock at $46 per share and sold it at $70.75 per share. The investor's return would be calculated as follows:[7]

$$\text{Rate of return} = \frac{\text{Ending price} - \text{Beginning price}}{\text{Beginning price}} \times 100$$

$$= \frac{\$70.75 - \$46}{\$46} \times 100$$

$$= 54\% \ .$$

[7]These two returns are not annualized, and the return on the common stock investment does not consider any dividends the investor might have received during the holding period.

At the same time, the investor could have purchased the warrants instead, buying them at $12.75 each and selling them at $27.25; the return would have been as follows:

$$\text{Rate of return} = \frac{\$27.25 - \$12.75}{\$12.75} \times 100$$
$$= 114\% .$$

As can be seen, an investment in the warrants would have yielded greater returns. This *potential* for high returns encourages investors to pay prices exceeding formula values for warrants. This premium over formula value decreases as the stock price moves beyond the warrant exercise price, because the opportunity for greater returns decreases.

Another important factor in warrant valuation is the length of time remaining before the warrants expire. To illustrate, consider the market price of the AT&T warrants just after their issue and just prior to expiration, holding the AT&T stock price constant. The warrants were issued in May 1970 and expired in May 1975. In May 1970 and in February 1975, AT&T common stock traded in the $48 per share range. The warrants traded in the $9.50 range in May 1970 and in the $1 range in February 1975. The difference can be attributed to the time remaining before expiration.

ACCOUNTING FOR CONVERTIBLE SECURITIES AND WARRANTS

Companies that have convertible securities and warrants outstanding are required by *Accounting Principles Board Opinion 15* to calculate and report to stockholders two earnings-per-share figures—*primary* and *fully diluted.* Primary earnings per share are basically calculated by dividing net income available to common stock by the number of common shares outstanding. The fully diluted figure is a calculation of what earnings per share would have been if convertibles had been converted and warrants had been exercised during the accounting period.[8]

When a company has significant amounts of convertibles and warrants outstanding, the fully diluted figure is usually less than the primary figure and, as such, serves as a better indicator of the company's future earnings per share.

SUMMARY

Table 17–2 summarizes the similarities among and differences between convertibles and warrants.

---

[8]These calculations can be relatively complex. For example, warrants are assumed to be exercised only if the market price of the common stock is above the warrant's exercise price.

TABLE 17–2   Summary Comparison of Convertibles and Warrants (When Warrants Are Issued as Part of a Fixed-Income Security Offering) _____

Similarities

1. The intention is the future issuance of common stock at a price higher than that prevailing at the time of the convertible or warrant issue.
2. Both convertibles and warrants can serve to "sweeten" fixed-income security offerings, thereby making the securities easier to sell.
3. Both the convertibility option and the attachment of warrants result in interest expense or preferred dividend savings for the issuing company.

Differences

1. The company receives additional funds at the time warrants are exercised, whereas no additional funds are received at the time convertibles are converted.
2. The fixed-income security remains on the company's books after the exercise of warrants; in the case of convertibles, the fixed-income security is exchanged for common stock and taken off the company's books.
3. Because of the call feature, convertible securities potentially give the company more control over when the common stock is issued.

CONVERTIBLE SECURITIES

- *Convertible* debt or preferred stock securities are exchangeable for a company's common stock at the option of the holder.

- The price at which a convertible security is exchangeable for common stock is the *conversion price.*

- The number of common shares that can be obtained when a convertible security is exchanged is the *conversion ratio,* which is calculated by dividing the par value of the security by the conversion price.

- At the time of issue, the conversion price normally exceeds the market price of the common stock by about 20 percent.

- Convertible securities possess characteristics of both common stock and fixed-income securities. Their market value is a function of both their stock, or conversion, value and their value as a fixed-income security. The *conversion value* is calculated by multiplying the conversion ratio by the current stock price.

WARRANTS

- A *warrant* is an option to purchase shares of a company's common stock at a particular price during a specific time period. Warrants frequently are issued as part of a fixed-income security offering. Warrants also are issued as part of more "creative" financing packages.

- The *exercise price* of a warrant is the price at which the holder can purchase common stock of the issuing company.

- Warrants are issued for the following reasons:

1. To sell common stock in the future at a higher price than the price at the time of original issue.

2. To "sweeten" fixed-income security offerings.

3. To sell common stock in the future without incurring underwriting costs at the time of sale.

▪ The *formula value* of a warrant depends on the number of common shares each warrant is entitled to and the difference between the common stock market price and the warrant exercise price. Warrants normally sell at a premium over their formula value.

QUESTIONS AND TOPICS FOR DISCUSSION

1. In what ways are convertible securities and warrants similar? Dissimilar?

2. What is the relationship between the conversion price and the conversion ratio for convertible securities?

3. Why do companies issue convertible securities?

4. Why do investors purchase convertible securities?

5. What is the relationship between conversion value, bond value, and market value for a convertible security?

6. How can a company effectively force conversion of a convertible security?

7. What is the relationship between a warrant's formula value and its market value? When is the premium over the formula value usually the greatest?

PROBLEMS·

1. The Vermillion Corporation has debentures outstanding (par value = $1,000) that are convertible into the company's common stock at a price of $25 per share. The convertibles have a coupon interest rate of 6 percent and mature 20 years from now. In addition, the convertible debenture is callable at 107 percent of par value. The company has a marginal tax rate of 40 percent.

   a. Calculate the conversion value if Vermillion's common stock is selling at $20 a share.

   b. Calculate the bond value, assuming that straight debt of equivalent risk and maturity is yielding 9 percent.

   c. Using the answers from Parts a and b, what is a realistic estimate of the market value of the convertible debentures? (No calculation is necessary for this part of the problem.)

   d. What is the conversion value if the company's common stock price increases to $35 a share?

   e. Given the situation presented in Part d, what is a realistic estimate of the market value of the convertible debenture? (No calculation is necessary for this part of the problem.)

   f. What is the minimum common stock price that will allow the Vermillion management to use the call feature of the debentures to effectively force conversion?

   g. Suppose that increased expectations concerning inflation cause the yield on straight debt of equivalent risk and maturity to reach 10 percent. How will this affect the bond value of the convertible?

·Problems in color have check answers provided at the end of the book.

2. In December 1982 Eastman Kodak issued $275 million of 8¼ percent convertible debentures due in 2007. The debentures are convertible into common stock at $102.25 a share. The company's common stock was trading at about $83 a share at the time the convertibles were issued.

   a. How many shares of common stock can be obtained by converting one $1,000 par value debenture; that is, what is the conversion ratio?

   b. What was the conversion value of this issue at the time these debentures were originally issued?

   c. By what percentage was the conversion price above the stock price at the time these debentures were originally issued?

3. The Portsmouth Corporation has warrants presently outstanding, and each warrant entitles the holder to purchase 1 share of the company's common stock at an exercise price of $20 a share. If the market price of the warrants is $7 and the common stock price is $24 a share, what is the premium over the formula value for the warrants?

4. Charter Corporation, a petroleum and insurance company, has warrants to purchase common stock outstanding. Each warrant entitles the holder to purchase 1 share of the company's common stock at an exercise price of $10 a share. Both the common stock and the warrants are traded on the New York Stock Exchange. The warrants expire on September 1, 1988. In 1983, when the company's common stock was trading at about $11.50 a share, the warrants were trading at $6 each.

   a. What was the formula value of the warrants at that time?

   b. What was the premium over the formula value at that time?

   c. What are the reasons investors were willing to pay more than formula value for these warrants at that time?

   d. Suppose that in August 1988, the Charter common stock is still trading at $11.50 a share. What do you think the warrant price would be then? Why?

   e. The Charter Corporation paid an annual dividend of $1 a share, as of 1983, to its common shareholders. Do warrant holders receive dividends?

5. The Wickersham Manufacturing Company, whose present balance sheet is summarized here, is considering issuing $100 million of 6 percent subordinated debentures (par value = $1,000), which are convertible into common stock at a price of $40.

Balance Sheet
(In Millions of Dollars)

Current assests	$200	Current liabilities	$100
Fixed assets, net	300	Long-term debt	150
Total assets	$500	Common equity	250
		Total liabilities and equity	$500

   a. Show the pro forma balance sheet for the issuance of the convertibles prior to conversion. Assume the proceeds are invested in new plant and equipment, and disregard flotation costs.

   b. Show the pro forma balance sheet, assuming conversion of the entire issue.

   c. How much additional money will the company raise at the time of conversion?

6. The capital structure of Whitefield Mills, Inc., is as follows:

Long-term debt	$250 million
Common stock, $1 par	25 million
Contributed capital in excess of par value	150 million
Retained earnings	350 million
	$775 million

The company has decided to raise additional capital by selling $75 million of 8 percent debentures with warrants attached. Each $1,000 debenture will have 25 warrants attached, and each warrant will entitle the holder to purchase 1 share of common stock at $30.

a. Show the company's new capital structure after the sale of debentures and the exercise of all the warrants. Assume that no other changes in capital structure occur between now and the time the warrants are exercised.

b. What condition is necessary in order for the warrants to be exercised?

c. How much total money will the company raise as a result of this security issue, if all warrants are exercised?

7. You own 10 Bitterroot Industries, Inc., 5 percent convertible debentures due in 2005. The conversion ratio of the debentures is 30, and the debentures are callable at $1,070 each. You bought the debentures when they originally were issued in 1975 for $1,000 each. At that time, Bitterroot common stock was selling at $28.50 a share, and now it is up to $44 a share. The convertible debentures are now selling at $1,320 each.

Last week you received a notice from Bitterroot Industries stating that the company is calling the debentures.

a. What are your alternatives?

b. Which alternative should you choose?

8. One of Merrill Lynch's convertible issues is its 9¼ percent debentures due in 2005. These debentures are convertible into common stock at $40 a share.

a. In March 1983 Merrill Lynch common stock was trading at $78 a share. At approximately what price do you think the convertible debentures were trading? Why?

b. At the time you work this problem, there is a good chance that these Merrill Lynch convertibles will have been called for redemption. What are the reasons why this issue might be called?

9. Calculate the percentage return that could have been earned by an investor who purchased American Express common stock at $58½ and sold it at $70¾. Compare this return with the return that could have been earned by investing in American Express warrants over the same time period. When the common was at $58½, the warrant was at $17⅝, and when the common was at $70¾, the warrant was at $27¼.

10. Calculate the after-tax component cost of capital, k_c, for a 7.5 percent convertible debenture sold at par and due to mature in 25 years. The conversion ratio is 25, and conversion is expected to occur at the end of 10 years, when the common stock price is expected to be $54 a share. The company has a 40 percent marginal tax rate.

HINT: Try $k_c = 7.0\%$.

ADDITIONAL READINGS AND REFERENCES

Alexander, G. J., and Stover, R. D. "Effect of Forced Conversions on Common Stock Prices." *Financial Management* 9 (Spring 1980): 39–45.

Baumol, William J., Malkiel, Burton G., and Quandt, Richard E. "The Valuation of Convertible Securities." *Quarterly Journal of Economics* 80 (Feb. 1966): 48–59.

Black, Fischer. "Fact and Fantasy in the Use of Options." *Financial Analysts Journal* 31 (July–Aug. 1975): 36–41.

Black, Fischer, and Scholes, Myron. "The Pricing of Options and Corporate Liabilities." *Journal of Political Economy* 81 (May–June 1973): 637–654.

Black, Fischer, and Scholes, Myron. "The Valuation of Option Contracts and a Test of Market Efficiency." *Journal of Finance* 27 (May 1972): 399–417.

Brigham, Eugene F. "Analysis of Convertible Debentures: Theory and Some Empirical Evidence." *Journal of Finance* 21 (March 1966): 35–54.

Chen, Andrew H. J. "A Model of Warrant Pricing in a Dynamic Market." *Journal of Finance* 25 (Dec. 1970): 1041–1059.

Frank, Werner G., and Weygandt, Jerry J. "Convertible Debt and Earnings per Share: Pragmatism vs. Good Theory." *Accounting Review* 45 (April 1970): 280–289.

Pinches, George E. "Financing with Convertible Preferred Stocks, 1960–1967." *Journal of Finance* 25 (March 1970): 53–64.

Rush, David F., and Melicher, Ronald W. "An Empirical Examination of Factors Which Influence Warrant Prices." *Journal of Finance* 29 (Dec. 1974): 1449–1466.

Schwartz, Eduardo S. "The Valuation of Warrants: Implementing a New Approach." *Journal of Financial Economics* 4 (Jan. 1977): 79–94.

Shelton, J. P., "The Relation of the Price of a Warrant to the Price of Its Associated Stock." *Financial Analysts Journal* (May–June 1967): 143–151; (July–Aug. 1967): 88–99.

Smith, C. W. "Option Pricing: A Review." *Journal of Financial Economics* 3 (Jan.–March 1967): 3–52.

Soldofsky, Robert M. "Yield-Rate Performance of Convertible Securities." *Financial Analysts Journal* 27 (March–April 1971): 61–65.

Stanton, T. C., and Maxwell, P. H. "Warrants: A Cost of Capital Perspective." *Financial Executive* 48 (1980): 27–31.

Walter, James E., and Que, Agustin V. "The Valuation of Convertible Bonds." *Journal of Finance* 28 (June 1973): 713–732.

Options

GLOSSARY OF NEW TERMS

Call   an option to *buy* shares of a particular stock at a set price.

Covered option   an option written by an investor who owns the underlying stock. This is in contrast to an *uncovered*, or *naked*, option.

Exercise price   the price at which an option holder can purchase or sell a company's stock. This also is termed the *striking price*.

Option   a contract that gives its holder the right to buy or sell a stated number of shares of stock at a set price during a specified time period.

Option premium   the market price of an option contract.

Put   an option to *sell* shares of a particular stock at a set price.

INTRODUCTION

An *option* is a contract that gives its holder the right to buy or sell shares (usually 100) of a particular stock at a set price during a specified time period. Options have existed for many years, but their popularity has greatly increased since formal listing and trading of options began on the Chicago Board Options Exchange (CBOE) in April 1973. Several exchanges now list options, the two most important ones being the CBOE and the American Stock Exchange.

TERMINOLOGY OF OPTIONS

Options are classified as either *call* or *put* options. A call is an option to *buy* a particular stock, whereas a put is an option to *sell* it. The set price at which the stock can be purchased or sold is the *exercise* or *striking price*, and the specified time period during which the option may be exercised ends on the *expiration date*. In the United States, trading in a particular option begins 9 months prior to the expiration date. Thus, the maximum possible option life is 9 months. The market price of an option contract is called the *option premium*.

HOW OPTIONS ARE USED

Investors who feel that a particular stock's price is likely to increase in the near future might *buy* a call option on that stock (assuming that options on the stock are traded). In contrast, investors who feel that a particular stock's price is likely to decrease might *buy* a put option on that stock.

Instead of buying a put, investors who feel that a particular stock's price is likely to decrease might *sell*, or *write*, a call option on that stock. If the call writer *owns* the underlying stock, the option is said to be *covered*; otherwise it is *uncovered*, or *naked*.[1]

Investors who buy calls have the potential of making high percentage returns on their investments. In contrast, the maximum possible amount they can lose is the price they paid for the options. To illustrate, suppose an investor pays $250 for an option to purchase 100 shares of RCX Corporation at $30 per share when the stock is selling at that price. If the stock price goes up to $40 per share, for example, the call with an exercise price of $30 will sell at $10 or more per share (for a total of at least $1,000), with the amount over $10 depending partially on how much time remains before the option expires. Thus, the investor in the call will roughly quadruple the investment (that is, $1,000/$250), whereas the stock investor will realize a return of 33 percent [that is, ($4,000 − $3,000)/$3,000]. In contrast, if the stock drops from $30 to $20, the call purchaser will lose virtually all of the $250 (that is, a loss of approximately 100 percent) invested, whereas the investor who has purchased 100 shares of the stock will lose $1,000 (that is, a loss of approximately 33 percent).

There are a number of circumstances in which an investor might choose to buy a put. For example, assume Henry Cassel owns a stock that he feels is temporarily overpriced, but he does not want to sell the stock because of its long-term prospects. One alternative (besides selling and buying back later) is to buy a put. At the time Mr. Cassel buys the put, he pays the put price (that is, the premium). If Mr. Cassel is correct and the stock does drop in price, the option premium will increase, and he will make a profit by either selling the put or exercising it. The purchase of a put option provides the investor with perfect protection against a price decline. The cost of this protection is the put premium.

Instead of buying a put, Mr. Cassel could have chosen to *write* (or *sell*) a call. In this instance, at the time Mr. Cassel writes the call, he receives the proceeds (that is, the premium). If Mr. Cassel is correct and the stock does drop in price, the option premium also will decrease, and he will make a profit by either buying the call back at a lower price or letting it expire.

Another situation in which an investor might choose to buy a put is to

---

[1] If a put writer is *short* the underlying stock, the option is said to be *covered*.

protect an unrealized gain. Suppose, for example, Betty Owens has a gain on a stock she owns and would like to sell now at the present price. There are two possible reasons why she would not simply sell the stock now: (1) to defer her capital gains taxes until the next year or (2) to defer selling until her holding period exceeds 1 year and she is eligible for capital gains treatment on her stock sale. By buying a put, Ms. Owens can eliminate the risk of a price decline. If the stock goes down between now and when it is sold, the lost revenues from the sale of the stock can be made up from the increase in the put premium. The put is sold at the higher price when the stock is sold.

The writing of *naked options* (that is, when the call option writer does not own the underlying stock) generally is considered quite risky. As a result, investors who desire to write naked options have to meet certain requirements of their brokerage firm with respect to their total portfolio value.

Table 17A–1 lists a number of options quotations that can be used to illustrate the mechanics of options trading. For example, the buyer or holder of an Alcoa 35 call option had the right to purchase 100 shares of Alcoa common stock at $35 per share prior to the expiration date, which is the Saturday following the third Friday of the month listed (in this case, either April, July, or October 1983). Expiration dates are 3 months apart, and options are normally not written for time periods longer than 9 months. Specifically, the closing price on February 17, 1983, of an Alcoa October 35 call is listed as 3¼. This means that a buyer at that price would have had to pay $325 plus commission for the right to buy 100 shares of Alcoa common stock at $35 per share prior to the third Saturday in October 1983. In actuality the buyer probably would not have exercised the option, since most options are not exercised. Instead, buyers usually sell their options prior to the expiration date rather than buy the stock at the exercise price.

Looking further at the data in Table 17A–1, it can be seen that the Alcoa closing price was $32.50 per share. The Alcoa 30 call was said to be "in the money," because the striking price was less than the stock's market price. The Alcoa 35 call was an "out-of-the-money" option, because the striking price was greater than the stock's market price. When the striking price and market price are equal, the option is "at the money."

An option's premium, or price, depends on a number of factors, the two most important of which are the exercise price and the length of time before the option's expiration date. The options listed in Table 17A–1 that have higher exercise prices sell at lower prices. This is due to the fact that buyers have to pay more money to exercise options with higher exercise prices, and thus these options have less value to potential buyers. Also, the longer the time remaining until the option expires, the higher the option price.

Trading on new options with different striking prices commences as stock prices move up or down. For example, if Alcoa's stock price were to drop to the $25 per share range, trading would begin in Alcoa 25 options. The striking price varies by multiples of $5 for stocks selling below $100 per share and by multiples of $10 for stocks trading above $100 per share.

The companies on whose stocks the options are written do not receive any of the funds exchanged. Instead, these funds are transferred between buyers and sellers of options, with brokers receiving the commissions.

556

TABLE 17A–1 Selected Options Quotations, Thursday, February 17, 1983*

OPTION & NY CLOSE	STRIKE PRICE	CALLS—LAST			PUTS—LAST		
		Apr.	Jul.	Oct.	Apr.	Jul.	Oct.
Alcoa	 25	r	r	r	r	r	¼
32½	 30	3½	4¾	5⅝	¾	1½	r
32½	 35	1	2 11-16	3¼	r	r	r
Am Tel	 50	16¾	s	s	r	s	s
67⅜	 55	12¼	12⅛	s	1-16	5-16	s
67⅜	 60	7¼	8	s	⅜	1	s
67⅜	 65	2¾	4⅛	5	1½	2½	3¼
67⅜	 70	1 1-16	2	3	4⅜	5¼	6
67⅜	 75	5-16	⅞	1⅞	r	r	r

r—Not traded. s—No option offered.
Last is premium (purchase price).

*Closing prices of all options. Sales unit usually is 100 shares. Security description includes exercise price. Stock close is New York or American exchange final price.
SOURCE: *Wall Street Journal* (February 18, 1983).

The number of stocks on which options are listed has increased since 1973. Options serve an important function in the securities markets in that they provide certain investors and speculators with securities having the risk, return, and maturity characteristics they desire.

QUESTIONS AND TOPICS FOR DISCUSSION

1. Define the following terms:
   a. Option.
   b. Call.
   c. Put.
   d. Exercise (striking) price.
   e. Option premium.
   f. Covered option.
   g. Uncovered (naked) option.
2. What are the similarities and differences between options and warrants?
3. What factors are important in determining option prices?
4. What are the factors investors should consider in deciding whether to buy a put or sell a call on stocks they own?
5. Will option premiums in general be higher at a time when interest rates are relatively high, compared with a time when interest rates are relatively low, all other things being equal?

PART SEVEN

The Management of Working Capital

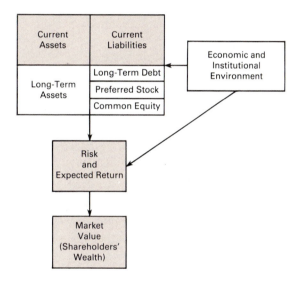

This part of the book considers the financial management of a firm's current assets and current liabilities. This is called *working capital management.* Chapter 18 provides an overview of working capital management, with emphasis on the risk-return tradeoffs that are implied. Chapter 19 deals with the management of cash and marketable securities; Chapter 20, with accounts receivable; and Chapter 21, with inventories. Chapter 22 looks at current liabilities and the sources of short-term credit. Working capital management influences both the risk of a firm and its expected returns. As such, it is an important determinant of firm value.

CHAPTER 18

Working Capital Management: An Overview

A FINANCIAL DILEMMA

Going Broke While Making a Profit[*]

At the beginning of the year, John Stickler was in good spirits. He was president of Cactus Creations, a firm that manufactured decorative planters for $6 each and sold them for $8 each, and demand was strong in the growing Sunbelt region. Stickler kept a 30-day inventory, paid his bills promptly, and billed his customers on terms of net 30 days (that is, payments were due in 30 days). Sales forecasts had been accurate, and a steady increase was anticipated over the next year.

On January 1, the firm's books read as follows:

Cash = $8,000.
Inventory = $6,000.
Receivables = $8,000.

In January Stickler sold 1,000 planters, produced at a cost of $6,000, and collected receivables of $8,000. Janurary's profits totaled $2,000.

On February 1 the firm's books read as follows:

Cash = $10,000.
Inventory = $6,000.
Receivables = $8,000.

February sales increased to an expected 1,500 units. To maintain a 30-day inventory, production was increased to 2,000 units at a cost of $12,000. All January receivables were collected, and profits through February totaled $5,000.

---

[*]Adapted from "How to Go Broke. . . . While Making a Profit." *Business Week* (April 28, 1956): 46–54.

On March 1 the account balances were as follows:
   Cash = $6,000.
   Inventory = $9,000.
   Receivables = $12,000.
March sales increased to 2,000 units. Collections from February were made on time. Production was increased to 2,500 to maintain a 2,000-unit inventory. Profits for the month totaled $4,000 ($9,000 year to date).
   On April 1 the books read as follows:
   Cash = $3,000.
   Inventory = $12,000.
   Receivables = $16,000.
Sales increased to 2,500 units in April; Stickler was overjoyed. Customers continued to pay on time. Production was increased to 3,000 units to maintain a 2,500-unit inventory. Profits for the month totaled $5,000 ($14,000 year to date). Stickler headed for a long-deserved vacation in the islands.
   On May 1 the books read as follows:
   Cash = $1,000.
   Inventory = $15,000.
   Receivables = $20,000.
In May sales exploded to new records—3,000 units—and production was increased to 3,500. Profits for the first 5 months of the year were $20,000. Then Stickler got an unexpected call from his accountant, telling him to come home as quickly as possible. The firm was out of cash.
   On June 1 Cactus Creations' accounts had the following balances:
   Cash = $0.
   Inventory = $18,000.
   Receivables = $24,000.
Stickler came home, confused and perplexed, and immediately arranged a meeting with his banker.
   This example illustrates the importance of proper planning and management of a firm's working capital. This chapter is the first of five chapters dealing with this important area.

GLOSSARY OF NEW TERMS

Net working capital   the difference between a firm's current assets and current liabilities.

Working capital   a firm's total investment in current assets.

INTRODUCTION

The management of working capital concerns decisions involving a firm's current assets and current liabilities—what they consist of, how they are used, and how their mix affects the risk versus return characteristics of the firm. The term *working capital* normally denotes the firm's *total* investment in current assets, whereas *net working capital* denotes the *difference* between the firm's current assets and current liabilities. From a conceptual standpoint it is useful to view *working capital* as the firm's *gross* investment in current assets and *net working capital* as the amount of current assets that is supported, or financed, by noncurrent sources of funds.

Effective working capital management is crucial to a firm's long-run growth and survival. If, for example, a firm lacks the working capital needed to expand production and sales, it may lose revenues and profits. A firm that does not have enough working capital may be unable to pay bills on time and will incur the costs associated with a deteriorating credit rating, a potential forced liquidation of assets, and possible bankruptcy.

Working capital management is a continuing process that involves a number of day-to-day operations and decisions that determine the following:

- The firm's level of current asset investment.
- The proportions of short-term and long-term debt the firm will use to finance its assets.
- The level of investment in each type of current asset.
- The specific sources and mix of short-term credit (current liabilities) the firm should employ.

This chapter, which is the first of five dealing with this important area of finance, considers the *aggregate* level of current assets and current liabilities a firm may employ. The following three chapters detail the optimal level of investment in each of the major current asset accounts—specifically, Chapter 19 deals with cash and marketable securities; Chapter 20, with accounts receivable; and Chapter 21, with inventories. Finally, Chapter 22 covers the specific sources and appropriate mixes of short-term credit.

IMPORTANCE OF WORKING CAPITAL

Working capital differs from *fixed* capital in terms of the time required to recover the investment in a given asset. In the case of fixed capital, or long-term assets (such as land, buildings, and equipment), a firm usually needs several years or more to recover the initial investment. In contrast, working capital is turned over, or circulated, at a relatively rapid rate. Investments in inventories and accounts receivable usually are recovered during a firm's normal operating cycle, when inventories are sold and receivables are collected.

A manufacturing firm's operating cycle consists of three primary activities—purchasing resources, manufacturing the product, and distributing (selling) the product. These activities create funds flows that are both unsynchronized and uncertain. They are unsynchronized because cash disbursements (for example, payments for resource purchases) usually take place before cash receipts (for example, collection of receivables). They are uncertain because future sales and costs, which generate the respective receipts and disbursements, cannot be forecasted with complete accuracy. If the firm is to function properly, it has to invest funds in various short-term assets

FIGURE 18–1   Operating Cycle of a Typical Manufacturing Firm _____

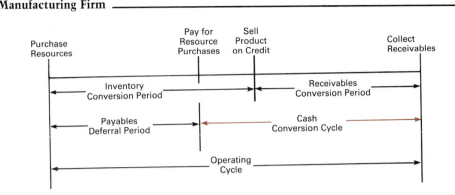

(working capital) during this cycle. It has to maintain a *cash balance* to pay the bills as they come due. In addition, the firm must invest in *inventories* to fill customer orders promptly and to permit efficient operation of the manufacturing process. And, finally, the firm invests in *accounts receivable* to extend credit to its customers.

Figure 18–1 illustrates the operating cycle of a typical manufacturing firm.[1] The length of the operating cycle is equal to the length of the inventory and receivables conversion periods. The inventory conversion period is the length of time required to produce and sell the product. The receivables conversion period represents the length of time required to collect the sales receipts (receivables). The payables deferral period is the length of time the firm is able to defer payment on its various resource purchases (for example, materials, wages, and taxes). Finally, the cash conversion cycle represents the *net time interval* between the collection of cash receipts from product sales and the cash payments for the firm's various resource purchases.

The cash conversion cycle shows the time interval over which additional nonspontaneous sources of working capital financing must be obtained in order to carry out the firm's activities.[2] An increase in the length of the operating cycle, without a corresponding increase in the payables deferral period, lengthens the cash conversion cycle and creates further working capital financing needs for the firm.

A firm's net working capital position is not only important from an internal standpoint; it is also widely used as one measure of the firm's *risk. Risk*, as used in this context, deals with the probability that a firm will encounter financial difficulties, such as the inability to pay bills on time. All other

_____

[1]The following discussion is based on Verlyn D. Richards and Eugene J. Laughlin. "A Cash Conversion Cycle Approach to Liquidity Analysis." *Financial Management* 9 (Spring 1980): 32–38.

[2]Spontaneous sources of financing (such as trade credit offered by suppliers) automatically expand (contract) as the firm's volume of purchases increases (decreases). Nonspontaneous sources of financing (such as bank loans), in contrast, do not automatically expand or contract with the volume of purchases. This concept is discussed further in Chapter 22, which deals with sources of short-term funds.

TABLE 18–1   Aggregate Assets of U.S. Manufacturing, Wholesaling, and Retailing Corporations

Assets	Manufacturing, 3rd Quarter 1982* (in millions of dollars)	(%)	Wholesale Trade, 4th Quarter 1981* (in millions of dollars)	(%)	Retail Trade, 4th Quarter 1981* (in millions of dollars)	(%)
Cash	$ 39,172	2.4%	$ 18,106	5.7%	$ 14,877	5.1%
U.S. government and other securities	35,586	2.2	6,575	2.1	3,425	1.2
Receivables	245,803	15.3	94,581	29.6	40,013	13.7
Inventories	295,960	18.4	106,748	33.4	112,602	38.6
Other current asets	46,762	2.9	11,466	3.6	10,588	3.6
Total current assets†	$ 663,284	41.3%	$237,475	74.3%	$181,505	62.3%
Net property, plant, and equipment	$ 631,131	39.3%	$ 56,592	17.7%	$ 86,590	29.7%
Other assets	312,992	19.5	25,360	7.9	23,473	8.1
Total assets†	$1,607,407	100.0%	$319,426	100.0%	$291,568	100.0%

*Latest period for which data is available.
†In some cases, totals may differ slightly from the sums of individual entries because of rounding.
SOURCE: *Quarterly Financial Report for Manufacturing, Mining, and Trade Corporations.* Federal Trade Commission (3rd Quarter 1982).

things being equal, the more net working capital a firm has, the more likely that it will be able to meet current financial obligations. Since net working capital is one measure of risk, a firm's net working capital position affects its ability to obtain debt financing. Many loan agreements with commercial banks and other lending institutions contain a provision requiring the firm to maintain a minimum net working capital position. Likewise, bond indentures also often contain such provisions.

The magnitude and relative importance of working capital investment is shown in Table 18–1, which lists aggregate asset data for various sectors of the economy. In the manufacturing sector, for example, current assets constituted 41.3 percent of the total assets of all U.S. manufacturing corporations. Among the wholesaling and retailing sectors, the percentages were even higher—74.3 and 62.3 percent respectively.

Table 18–2 shows that considerable variation also exists among different industries within the manufacturing sector. For the six industries shown, current assets as a percentage of total assets range from 20.6 to 60.2 percent.

LEVELS OF
WORKING CAPITAL INVESTMENT

The size and nature of a firm's investment in current assets is a function of a number of different factors, including the following:

564

TABLE 18–2   Distribution of Aggregate Assets in Various Manufacturing Industries

	Petroleum and Coal Products	Motor Vehicles and Equipment	Food and Kindred Products	Printing and Publishing	Electrical and Electronic Equipment	Textile Mill Products
Cash	0.9%	2.2%	2.6%	4.8%	3.1%	4.0%
Marketable securities	1.7	3.4	2.2	3.2	2.9	2.4
Receivables—net	9.0	11.4	14.4	20.6	19.9	25.3
Inventories—net	7.1	15.1	18.9	10.4	25.3	26.1
All other current assets	1.8	4.4	3.0	4.8	4.2	2.4
Total current assets*	20.6%	36.6%	41.2%	43.8%	55.4%	60.2%
Fixed assets—net	55.8%	35.1%	35.1%	33.7%	26.3%	34.6%
All other noncurrent assets	23.6	28.3	23.7	22.5	18.3	5.2
Total assets*	100.0%	100.0%	100.0%	100.0%	100.0%	100.0%

*In some cases, totals may differ slightly from the sums of individual entries because of rounding.
SOURCE: *Quarterly Financial Report for Manufacturing, Mining, and Trade Corporations.* Federal Trade Commission (3rd Quarter 1982).

- The type of products manufactured.

- The length of the operating cycle.

- The sales level (since higher sales require more investment in inventories and receivables).

- Inventory policies (for example, the amount of safety stocks maintained, that is, inventories needed to meet higher than expected demand or unanticipated delays in obtaining new inventories).

- Credit policies.

- How efficiently the firm manages current assets. (Obviously, the more effectively management economizes on the amount of cash, marketable securities, inventories, and receivables employed, the smaller the working capital requirements.)

For the purposes of discussion and analysis, these factors are held constant for the remainder of this chapter. Instead of focusing on these factors, this section examines the risk-return tradeoffs associated with alternative levels of working capital investments.

PROFITABILITY VERSUS RISK TRADEOFF FOR ALTERNATIVE LEVELS OF WORKING CAPITAL INVESTMENT

Before deciding on an appropriate level of working capital investment, a firm's management has to evaluate the tradeoff between expected profitability and the risk that it may be unable to meet its financial obligations. Profitability is measured by the rate of return on total assets, that is, EBIT/total assets. As mentioned earlier in this chapter, the risk that the firm will en-

FIGURE 18–2   Three Alternative Working Capital Investment Policies

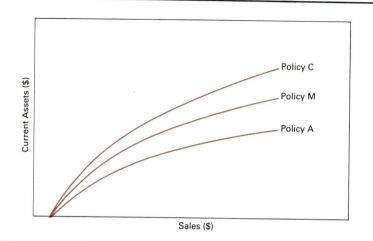

counter financial difficulties is related to the firm's net working capital position.

Figure 18–2 illustrates three alternative working capital policies.[3] Each curve in the figure demonstrates the relationship between the firm's investment in current assets and sales for that particular policy.

Policy C represents a *conservative* approach to working capital management. Under this policy the firm holds a relatively large proportion of its total assets in the form of current assets. Since the rate of return on current assets normally is assumed to be less than the rate of return on fixed assets,[4] this policy results in a *lower expected profitability* as measured by the rate of return on the firm's total assets. Assuming that current liabilities remain constant, this type of policy also increases the firm's net working capital position, resulting in a *lower risk* that the firm will encounter financial difficulties.

In contrast to Policy C, Policy A represents an *aggressive* approach. Under this policy the firm holds a relatively small proportion of its total assets in the form of lower yielding current assets and thus has relatively less net working capital. As a result, this policy yields a *higher expected profitability* and a *higher risk* that the firm will encounter financial difficulties.

Finally, Policy M represents a *moderate* approach, since expected profitability and risk levels fall between those of Policy C and Policy A.

---

[3]The relationship between current assets and sales is drawn as a concave, *curvilinear* function, since it is assumed that economies of scale exist in the holding of current assets. In other words, increases in sales normally should require less than proportionate increases in current assets, particularly for cash and inventories. The amount of the firm's *fixed* assets is held constant in the following discussion.

[4]This assumption is based on the principle that the lower an asset's risk, the lower its expected return. Current assets are normally less risky than fixed assets, since they can be converted into cash more easily and with less potential loss in value. Therefore, current assets should have lower expected returns.

TABLE 18–3   Profitability and Risk of Alternative Working Capital Investment Policies for the Ohio Engineering Company (in Millions of Dollars)

	AGGRESSIVE	MODERATE	CONSERVATIVE
	Relatively Small Investment in Current Assets	Moderate Investment in Current Assets	Relatively Large Investment in Current Assets
Current assets (C/A)	$35	$40	$45
Fixed assets (F/A)	30	30	30
Total assets (T/A)	$65	$70	$75
Current liabilities (C/L)	$20	$20	$20
Forecasted sales	$100	$100	$100
Expected EBIT	$10	$10	$10
Expected rate of return on total assets (EBIT ÷ T/A)	15.38%	14.29%	13.33%
Net working capital position (C/A − C/L)	$15	$20	$25
Current ratio (C/A ÷ C/L)	1.75	2.0	2.25

These three approaches may be illustrated with the following example. The Ohio Engineering Company, a manufacturer of steel-making equipment, has forecasted sales next year to be $100 million and EBIT to be $10 million. The firm has fixed assets of $30 million and current liabilities totaling $20 million.

Ohio Engineering is considering three alternative working capital investment policies:

- An *aggressive* policy consisting of $35 million in current assets.

- A *moderate* policy consisting of $40 million in current assets.

- A *conservative* policy consisting of $45 million in current assets.

Assume that sales and EBIT remain constant under each policy.[5] Table 18–3 contains the results of the three proposed policies.

The aggressive policy would yield the highest expected rate of return on total assets, 15.38 percent, whereas the conservative policy would yield the lowest rate of return, 13.33 percent. The aggressive policy also would result in a lower net working capital position ($15 million) than would the conservative policy ($25 million).

Using net working capital as a measure of risk, the aggressive policy is most risky, and the conservative policy is the least risky. The current ratio is another measure of a firm's ability to meet financial obligations as they come due. The aggressive policy would yield the lowest current ratio, and the conservative policy would yield the highest current ratio.

---

[5] In practice, however, this assumption may not be completely realistic, since a firm's sales are usually a function of its inventory and credit policies. Higher levels of finished goods inventories and a more liberal credit extension policy—both of which increase a firm's investment in current assets—may also lead to higher sales. This effect can be incorporated into the analysis by modifying the sales and EBIT projections under the various alternative working capital policies. Although changing these projections would affect the numerical values contained in Table 18–3, it should not affect the general conclusions concerning the profitability versus risk tradeoffs.

OPTIMAL LEVEL OF WORKING CAPITAL INVESTMENT

The optimal level of working capital investment is the level that is expected to maximize shareholder wealth. It is a function of several factors, including the variability of sales and cash flows and the degree of operating and financial leverage employed by the firm. Thus, no single working capital investment policy is necessarily optimal for all firms.

PROPORTIONS OF SHORT-TERM AND LONG-TERM FINANCING

Not only does a firm have to be concerned about the *level* of current assets; it also has to determine the *proportions* of short- and long-term debt to use in financing these assets. This decision also involves tradeoffs between profitability and risk.

Sources of debt financing are classified according to their *maturities*. Specifically, they can be categorized as being either *short term* or *long term*, with short-term sources having maturities of 1 year or less and long-term sources having maturities of greater than 1 year.[6]

COST OF SHORT-TERM VERSUS LONG-TERM DEBT

Recall from Chapter 2 that the *term structure of interest rates* was defined as the relationship among interest rates of debt securities that differ in their length of time to maturity. This relationship (the *yield curve*) is examined in Appendix 18A. Historically, as illustrated in Appendix 18A, long-term interest rates generally have exceeded short-term rates (see Figure 18A–2).

Also, because of the reduced flexibility of long-term borrowing relative to short-term borrowing, the *effective* cost of long-term debt may be higher than the cost of short-term debt, even when short-term interest rates are equal to or greater than long-term rates. With long-term debt, a firm incurs the interest expense even during times when it has no immediate need for the funds, such as during seasonal or cyclical downturns. With short-term debt, in contrast, the firm can avoid the interest costs on unneeded funds by paying off (or not renewing) the debt. In summary, the cost of long-term debt is generally higher than the cost of short-term debt.

RISK OF LONG-TERM VERSUS SHORT-TERM DEBT

Borrowers (firms) have different attitudes toward the relative risk of long-term versus short-term debt than do lenders. Whereas lenders normally feel that risk increases with maturity, firms feel that there is more risk associated with short-term debt. The reasons for this are twofold.

First, there is always the chance that a firm will not be able to refund its short-term debt. When a firm's debt matures, the company either pays off the debt as part of a debt reduction program or arranges new financing. At the

---

[6]In this discussion the term *long-term financing* includes any *intermediate-term financing*.

time of maturity, however, the firm could be faced with financial problems resulting from such events as strikes, natural disasters, or recessions that cause sales and cash inflows to decline. Under these circumstances the firm may find it very difficult or even impossible to obtain the needed funds. This could lead to operating and financial difficulties. The more frequently a firm must refinance debt, the greater the risk of its not being able to obtain the necessary financing.

Second, short-term interest rates tend to fluctuate more over time than do long-term interest rates (see Figure 18A–2). As a result, a firm's interest expenses and expected earnings after interest and taxes are subject to more variation (risk) over time with short-term debt than with long-term debt.

PROFITABILITY VERSUS RISK TRADEOFF FOR ALTERNATIVE FINANCING PLANS

A company's need for financing is equal to the sum of its fixed and current assets.[7] Current assets can be divided into the following two categories:

- *Permanent* current assets.
- *Fluctuating* current assets.

Fluctuating current assets are those that are affected by the seasonal or cyclical nature of demand. For example, a firm must make larger investments in inventories and receivables during peak selling periods than during other periods of the year. Permanent current assets are those that are held to meet the firm's minimum long-term needs. Figure 18–3 illustrates a typical firm's financing needs over time. The fixed assets and permanent current assets lines are upward sloping, indicating that the investment in these assets and, by extension, financing needs tend to increase over time for firms whose sales are increasing.

One way in which firms can meet their financing needs is by using a *matching approach* in which the maturity structure of the firm's liabilities is made to correspond exactly to the life of its assets. This is illustrated in Figure 18–4. As can be seen, fixed and permanent current assets are financed with long-term debt and equity funds, whereas fluctuating current assets are financed with short-term debt.[8] Application of this approach is not as simple as it appears, however. In practice the uncertainty associated with the lives of individual assets makes the matching approach a difficult one to implement.

Figures 18–5 and 18–6 illustrate two other financing plans. Figure 18–5 shows a *conservative* approach, which uses a relatively high proportion of long-term debt. The relatively low proportion of short-term debt in this ap-

---

[7]The following discussion assumes a constant amount of equity financing.

[8]This analysis does not consider "spontaneous" sources of short-term credit, such as accounts payable. Since spontaneous short-term credit is virtually cost-free when used within reasonable limits, a firm normally will employ this type of credit to the fullest extent possible before using "negotiated" sources of short-term credit, such as bank loans. Since none of the conclusions concerning the tradeoff between profitability and risk are affected by ignoring spontaneous sources of short-term credit, it need not be considered here.

FIGURE 18–3   **Financing Needs over Time**

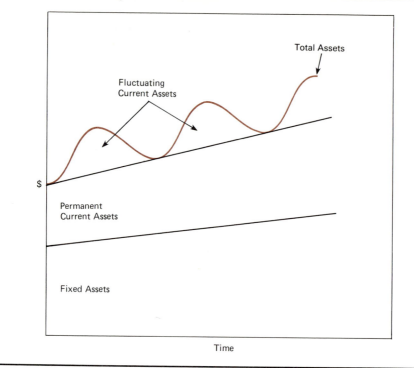

FIGURE 18–4   **Matching Approach to Asset Financing**

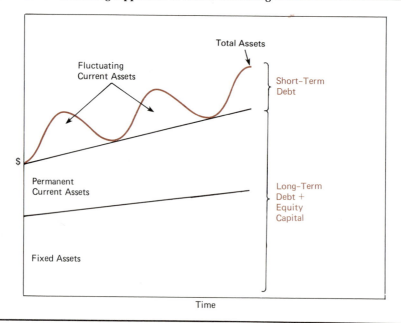

FIGURE 18–5   Conservative Approach to Asset Financing

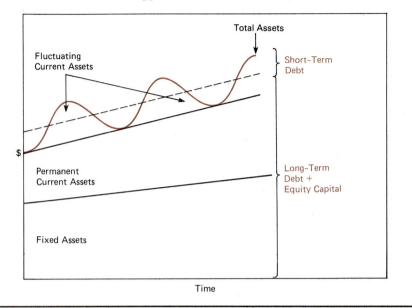

proach reduces the risk that the firm will be unable to refund its debt, and it also reduces the risk associated with interest rate fluctuations. At the same time, however, this approach cuts down on the expected returns available to stockholders, since the cost of long-term debt is generally greater than the cost of short-term debt.

Figure 18–6 illustrates an *aggressive* approach, which uses a relatively high proportion of short-term debt. A firm that uses this particular approach must refund debt more frequently, and this increases the risk that it will be unable to obtain new financing as needed. In addition, the greater possible fluctuations in interest expenses associated with this financing plan also add to the firm's risk (variability in earnings). These higher risks are offset by the higher expected after-tax earnings that result from the lower costs of short-term debt.

Consider again the Ohio Engineering Company, which has total assets of $70 million and common shareholders' equity of $28 million on its books. Forecasted sales for next year are $100 million, and expected earnings before interest and taxes (EBIT) are $10 million. Interest rates on the company's short-term and long-term debt are 8 and 10 percent respectively.

Ohio Engineering is considering three different combinations of short-term and long-term debt financing:

- An *aggressive* plan consisting of $30 million in short-term debt (STD) and $12 million in long-term debt (LTD).

- A *moderate* plan consisting of $20 million in short-term debt and $22 million in long-term debt.

- A *conservative* plan consisting of $10 million in short-term debt and $32 million in long-term debt.

571

FIGURE 18–6   **Aggressive Approach to Asset Financing**

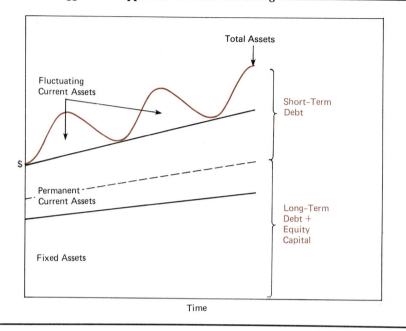

Table 18–4 shows the data for each of these alternative proposed financing plans. From the standpoint of profitability, the aggressive financing plan would yield the highest expected rate of return to the stockholders—11.43 percent—whereas the conservative plan would yield the lowest rate of return—10.71 percent. In contrast, the aggressive plan would involve a greater degree of risk that the firm will be unable to refund its debt, since it assumes $30 million in short-term debt and the conservative plan assumes only $10 million in short-term debt. This is further substantiated by the fact that the firm's net working capital position and current ratio would be lowest under the aggressive plan and highest under the conservative plan—indicating that the degree of risk that the firm will be unable to meet financial obligations would be greater with the aggressive plan. The moderate financing plan represents a middle-of-the-road approach, and the expected rate of return and risk level are between the aggressive and the conservative approaches. In summary, both expected profitability and risk increase as the proportion of short-term debt increases.[9]

[9]This example assumes that the costs of short-term and long-term debt would be the same for each of the three financing policies. In practice, however, this would probably not be the case, since lenders generally require higher interest rates before making loans involving higher risks. Thus, a firm following an aggressive financing policy probably will have to pay slightly higher interest rates on debt than will a firm following a conservative policy. This effect can be incorporated into the analysis by modifying the interest rates on short-term and long-term debt under the various financing policies. This would affect the numerical values in the example, but it should not affect the general conclusions concerning the profitability versus risk tradeoffs.

TABLE 18–4 Profitability and Risk of Alternative Financing Policies for the Ohio Engineering Company (in Millions of Dollars)

	AGGRESSIVE	MODERATE	CONSERVATIVE
	Relatively Large Amount of Short-Term Debt	Moderate Amount of Short-Term Debt	Relatively Small Amount of Short-Term Debt
Current assets (C/A)	$40	$40	$40
Fixed assets (F/A)	30	30	30
Total assets (T/A)	$70	$70	$70
Current liabilities (STD)(C/L) (interest rate, 8%)	$30	$20	$10
Long-term liabilities (LTD)(interest rate, 10%)	12	22	32
Total liabilities (60% of T/A)	$42	$42	$42
Common stock	28	28	28
Total liabilities and common stock	$70	$70	$70
Forecasted sales	$100	$100	$100
Expected EBIT	10	10	10
Less: Interest:			
STD, 8%	2.4⎫	1.6⎫	0.8⎫
LTD, 10%	1.2⎭ 3.6	2.2⎭ 3.8	3.2⎭ 4.0
Taxable income	$6.4	$6.2	$6.0
Less: Taxes (50%)	3.2	3.1	3.0
Net income after taxes	$3.2	$3.1	$3.0
Expected rate of return on common stock	11.43%	11.07%	10.71%
Net working capital position (C/A − C/L)	$10	$20	$30
Current ratio (C/A ÷ C/L)	1.33	2.0	4.0

OPTIMAL PROPORTIONS OF SHORT-TERM AND LONG-TERM DEBT

As it is the case with working capital investment policy, no one combination of short- and long-term debt is necessarily optimal for all firms. In choosing a financing policy that maximizes shareholder wealth, a firm's financial manager also must take into account various other factors, such as the variability of sales and cash flows, which affect the valuation of the firm.

OVERALL WORKING CAPITAL MANAGEMENT

Until now this chapter has analyzed the working capital investment and financing decisions independently of one another in order to examine the profitability-risk tradeoffs associated with each, assuming that all other factors are held constant. Effective working capital management, however, also re-

TABLE 18–5   Alternate Working Capital Investment and Financing Policies for the Ohio Engineering Company (in Millions of Dollars)

	AGGRESSIVE	MODERATE	CONSERVATIVE
	Relatively *Small* Investment in Current Assets; Relatively *Large* Amount of Short-Term Debt	Moderate Investment in Current Assets; Moderate Amount of Short-Term Debt	Relatively *Large* Investment in Current Assets; Relatively *Small* Amount of Short-Term Debt
Current assets (C/A)	$35	$40	$45
Fixed assets (F/A)	30	30	30
Total assets (T/A)	$65	$70	$75
Current liabilities (STD) (C/L) (interest rate, 8%)	$30	$20	$10
Long-term liabilities (LTD) (interest rate, 10%)	9	22	35
Total liabilities (60% of T/A)	$39	$42	$45
Common stock	26	28	30
Total liabilities and common stock	$65	$70	$75
Forecasted sales	$100	$100	$100
Expected EBIT	10	10	10
Less: Interest:			
STD, 8%	2.4 ⎫ 3.3	1.6 ⎫ 3.8	0.8 ⎫ 4.3
LTD, 10%	0.9 ⎭	2.2 ⎭	3.5 ⎭
Taxable income	$6.7	$6.2	$5.7
Less: Taxes (50%)	3.35	3.1	2.85
Net income after taxes	$3.35	$3.1	$2.85
Expected rate of return on common stock	12.88%	11.07%	9.50%
Net working capital position (C/A − C/L)	$ 5	$20	$35
Current ratio (C/A ÷ C/L)	1.17	2.0	4.5

quires the consideration of the *joint* impact of these decisions on the firm's profitability and risk.

Referring to the Ohio Engineering Company again, assume that the firm is 60 percent debt financed (both short term and long term) and 40 percent financed with common stock. Ohio Engineering is evaluating three alternative working capital investment and financing policies. The *aggressive* policy would require a relatively *small* investment in current assets, $35 million, and a relatively *large* amount of short-term debt, $30 million. The *conservative* policy would require a relatively *large* investment in current assets, $45 million, and a relatively *small* amount of short-term debt, $10 million. The firm also is considering a middle-of-the-road approach, which would involve a *moderate* investment in current assets, $40 million, and a *moderate* amount of short-term debt, $20 million.

Table 18–5 shows the data for each approach. The aggressive working capital policy is expected to yield the highest return on shareholders' equity, 12.88 percent, whereas the conservative policy is expected to yield the lowest return, 9.50 percent. The net working capital and current ratio are lowest under the aggressive policy and highest under the conservative policy, indicating that the aggressive policy is the most risky. The moderate policy yields an expected return and risk level that is somewhere between the aggressive and the conservative policies.

Whereas this type of analysis will not directly yield the optimal working capital investment and financing policies a firm should choose, it can give the financial manager some insight into the profitability-risk tradeoffs of alternative policies. With an understanding of these tradeoffs, the financial manager should be able to make better decisions concerning the working capital policy that will lead to a maximization of shareholder wealth.

SUMMARY

- *Working capital* represents a firm's investment in current assets.

- *Net working capital* is the difference between current assets and current liabilities.

- *Working capital management* is concerned with determining the *aggregate amount* and *composition* of a firm's current assets and current liabilities.

- Working capital decisions affect both the *expected profitability* and the *risk* of a firm. In this context, *risk* refers to the probability that the firm will encounter financial difficulties, such as the inability to meet current financial obligations.

- When the level of working capital is increased, both the expected profitability and the risk are lowered. Similarly, when the level of working capital is decreased, both the expected profitability and the risk are increased.

- When the proportion of short-term debt used is increased, both the expected profitability and the risk are increased. Similarly, when the proportion of short-term debt used is decreased, both the expected profitability and the risk are lowered.

- Effective working capital management requires that the working capital investment and financing decisions be analyzed simultaneously so that their *joint* impact on the firm's expected profitability and risk can be evaluated.

- No one working capital investment and financing policy is necessarily *optimal* for all firms. To select the working capital policy that maximizes shareholder wealth, a financial manager should consider additional factors, including the inherent variability in sales and cash flows and the degree of operating and financial leverage employed.

QUESTIONS AND TOPICS FOR DISCUSSION

1. Describe the difference between working capital and net working capital.

2. Why does the typical firm need to make investments in working capital?

3. Discuss the profitability versus risk tradeoffs associated with alternative levels of working capital investment.

4. Why is it possible for the cost of long-term debt to exceed the cost of short-term debt, even when short-term interest rates are higher than long-term rates?

5. Describe the matching approach for meeting the financing needs of a firm. What is the primary difficulty in implementing this approach?

6. Discuss the profitability versus risk tradeoffs associated with alternative combinations of short-term and long-term debt used in financing a firm's assets.

7. Why is no one working capital investment and financing policy necessarily optimal for all firms? What additional factors need to be considered in establishing a working capital policy?

8. **a.** Which of the following working capital financing policies subjects the firm to greater risk?
   i. Financing permanent current assets with short-term debt.
   ii. Financing fluctuating current assets with long-term debt.
   b. Which policy will produce the higher expected profitability?

PROBLEMS*

1. Consider again the comprehensive example involving the Ohio Engineering Company (Table 18–5). In this example it was assumed that forecasted sales and expected EBIT, as well as the interest rates on short-term and long-term debt, were independent of the firm's working capital investment and financing policies. However, these assumptions are not always completely realistic in practice. Sales and EBIT are generally a function of the firm's inventory and receivables policies. Both of these policies, in turn, affect the firm's level of investment in working capital. Likewise, the interest rates on short-term and long-term debt are normally a function of the riskiness of the firm's debt as perceived by lenders and, hence, are affected by the firm's working capital investment and financing decisions. Recompute Ohio Engineering's rate of return on common stock under the following set of assumptions concerning sales, EBIT, and interest rates for each of the three different working capital investment and financing policies.

Policy	Forecasted Sales (In Millions of Dollars)	Expected EBIT (In Millions of Dollars)	Interest Rate STD (%)	LTD (%)
Aggressive	$ 98	$ 9.8	8.5	10.5
Moderate	100	10.0	8.0	10.0
Conservative	102	10.2	7.5	9.5

2. The Welsh Manufacturing Company balance sheet for the year ended 19X3 follows:

*Problems in color have check answers provided at the end of the book.

	December 31, 19X3 (In Thousands of Dollars)	
Assets		
Cash		$ 3,810
Marketable securities		2,700
Accounts receivable		27,480
Inventories		41,295
Plant and equipment	$64,650	
Less: Accumulated depreciation	17,100	
Net plant and equipment		47,550
Total assets		$122,835
Liabilities and Owners' Equity		
Accounts payable		$ 14,582
Current portion of long-term debt		3,000
Accrued wages		1,200
Accrued taxes		3,600
Other current liabilities		2,200
Long-term debt		33,000
Common stock ($10 par)		19,500
Capital contributed in excess of par		15,000
Retained earnings		30,753
Total liabilities and owners' equity		$122,835

a. Determine Welsh's working capital investment.

b. Determine Welsh's *net* working capital investment.

3. National Electric Company, a manufacturer of various types of electrical equipment, is examining its working capital investment policy for next year. Projected fixed assets and current liabilities for next year are $20 million and $18 million, respectively. Sales and EBIT are a function of the firm's investment in working capital—particularly its investment in inventories and receivables. The firm is considering the following three different working capital investment policies:

Working Capital Investment Policy	Investment in Current Assets (In Millions of Dollars)	Projected Sales (In Millions of Dollars)	EBIT (In Millions of Dollars)
Aggressive (small investment in current assets)	$28	$59	$5.9
Moderate (moderate investment in current assets)	30	60	6.0
Conservative (large investment in current assets)	32	61	6.1

a. Determine the following for each of the working capital investment policies:
   i. Rate of return on total assets (that is, EBIT/total assets).
   ii. *Net* working capital position.
   iii. Current ratio.

b. Describe the profitability versus risk tradeoffs of these three policies.

4. National Electric Company also is investigating the use of various combinations of short-term and long-term debt in financing its assets. Assume that the firm has decided to employ $30 million in current assets, along with $20 million in fixed assets, in its operations next year. Given this level of current assets, anticipated sales and EBIT for next year are $60 million and $6 million, respectively. The firm's income tax rate is 50 percent. Equity funds (common stock and retained earnings) will be used to finance $25 million of its assets, with the remainder being financed by short-term and long-term debt. National is considering implementing one of the following financing policies:

Financing Policy	Amount of Short-Term Debt (In Millions of Dollars)	Interst Rate LTD (%)	STD (%)
Aggressive (large amount of short-term debt)	$24	8.5	5.5
Moderate (moderate amount of short-term debt)	18	8.0	5.0
Conservative (small amount of short-term debt)	12	7.5	4.5

  a. Determine the following for each of the financing policies:
    i. Rate of return on shareholders' equity.
    ii. *Net* working capital position.
    iii. Current ratio.
  b. Evaluate the profitability versus risk tradeoffs of these three policies.
5. National Electric Company also wishes to analyze the *joint impact* of its working capital investment and financing policies on shareholder return and risk. Again, assume that the firm has $20 million in fixed assets. Also, the firm's financial structure consists of short-term and long-term debt and common equity. National wishes to maintain a debt to total assets ratio of 50 percent, where debt consists of both short-term and long-term sources. The following information was developed for the three policies under consideration:

Working Capital Investment and Financing Policy	Investment in Current Assets (in Millions of Dollars)	Amount of STD (in Millions of Dollars)	Projected Sales (in Millions of Dollars)	EBIT (in Millions of Dollars)	Interest Rate LTD (%)	STD (%)
Aggressive	$28	$24	$59	$5.9	8.5	5.5
Moderate	30	18	60	6.0	8.0	5.0
Conservative	32	12	61	6.1	7.5	4.5

  a. Determine the following for each of the three working capital investment and financing policies:
    i. Rate of return on shareholders' equity.
    ii. *Net* working capital position.
    iii. Current ratio.
  b. Evaluate the profitability versus risk tradeoffs associated with these three policies.

6. Educational Toys, Inc. (ETI), has highly seasonal sales and financing requirements. The firm's balance sheet on December 31, 19X0, (*now*) is as follows:

Assets (In Millions of Dollars)		Liabilities (In Millions of Dollars)	
		Short-term debt	$ x
Current assets	$20	Long-term debt	y
Fixed assets	34	Net worth (equity)	30
Total assets	$54	Total liabilities and equity	$54

ETI has made the following projections of its asset needs and net additions to
retained earnings (that is, equity) for the next 3 years:

Year	Quarter	Fixed Assets (in Millions of Dollars)	Current Assets (In Millions of Dollars)	Net Additions To Retained Earnings (in Millions of Dollars)
19X1	1 (March 31)	$36	$20	$0
	2 (June 30)	36	24	0
	3 (Sept. 30)	36	30	1
	4 (Dec. 31)	36	24	1
19X2	1 (March 31)	38	24	0
	2 (June 30)	38	28	0
	3 (Sept. 30)	38	36	1
	4 (Dec. 31)	38	28	2
19X3	1 (March 31)	40	28	0
	2 (June 30)	40	32	0
	3 (Sept. 30)	40	38	1
	4 (Dec. 31)	40	30	2

Assuming that ETI does not plan to sell any preferred or new common stock over
the next 3 years,
   a. Determine ETI's quarterly total assets and *total* (short-term and long-term)
      debt requirements for the next 3 years.
   b. Plot the firm's *fixed, current,* and *total* assets over time on a graph.
7. Assume that ETI (see Problem 6) follows a *matching* approach in financing its
   assets. In other words, long-term debt will be used to finance its fixed and permanent current assets, and short-term debt will be used to finance its fluctuating
   current assets. The costs of short-term and long-term debt to ETI under this plan
   are 6 and 8 percent per annum (that is, 1.5 and 2 percent per quarter), respectively.
   Using this information, determine the following:
   a. The amount of short-term and long-term debt outstanding each quarter.
   b. ETI's total interest costs over the 3-year period under this approach.
8. ETI (see Problem 6) also is considering other financing plans. One plan under
   consideration is a *conservative* policy. Under this policy the firm would determine its *maximum* debt requirements for the coming year and finance this entire

amount with long-term debt at an interest rate of 8 percent per annum on December 31 of each year. Any funds in excess of its seasonal (quarterly) needs would be invested in short-term interest-bearing securities to yield a 4 percent per annum rate of return. Using this information, determine the following:

a. The amount of long-term debt ETI would have to borrow each year.

b. ETI's *net* interest costs over the 3-year period under this conservative policy.

9. Finally, ETI (see Problem 6) also is considering an *aggressive* policy. Under this policy the firm would determine its *minimum* debt requirements for the coming year on December 31 of each year and finance one-half of this amount with long-term debt, with the remainder being financed by short-term debt. The costs of short-term and long-term debt under this policy are 6 and 8 percent per annum, respectively. Using this information, determine the following:

a. The amount of short-term and long-term debt outstanding each quarter.

b. ETI's total interest costs over the 3-year period under this aggressive policy.

10. Greenwich Industries has forecasted its monthly needs for working capital (net of spontaneous sources such as accounts payable) for 19X3 as follows:

Month	Amount	Month	Amount
January	$7,500,000	July	$6,000,000
February	6,000,000	August	7,500,000
March	3,000,000	September	8,500,000
April	2,500,000	October	9,000,000
May	3,500,000	November	9,500,000
June	4,500,000	December	9,000,000

Short-term borrowing (that is, a bank line of credit) costs the firm 10 percent, and long-term borrowing (that is, term loans) costs the firm 12 percent. Any funds in excess of its monthly needs can be invested in interest-bearing marketable securities to yield 8 percent per annum.

a. Suppose the firm follows a *conservative* policy by financing the *maximum* amount of its working capital requirements for the coming year with long-term borrowing and investing any excess funds in short-term marketable securities. Determine Greenwich's *net* interest costs during 19X3 under this policy.

b. Suppose the firm follows an *aggressive* policy by financing *all* its working capital requirements for the coming year with short-term borrowing. Determine Greenwich's interest costs during 19X3 under this policy.

c. Discuss the profitability versus risk tradeoffs associated with these conservative and aggressive working capital financing policies.

ADDITIONAL READINGS AND REFERENCES

Beranek, William. *Working Capital Management.* Belmont, Calif.: Wadsworth, 1968.

Bierman, H., Chopra, K., and Thomas, J. "Ruin Considerations: Optimal Working Capital and Capital Structure." *Journal of Financial and Quantitative Analysis* 10 (March 1975): 119–128.

Cargill, Thomas F. "The Term Structure of Interest Rates: A Test of the Expectations Hypothesis." *Journal of Finance* 30 (June 1975): 761–771.

Carleton, Willard T., and Cooper, Ian A. "Estimation and Uses of the Term Structure of Interest Rates." *Journal of Finance* 31 (September 1976): 1067–1083.

Cossaboom, R. A. "Let's Reassess the Profitability-Liquidity Tradeoff." *Financial Executive* (May 1971): 46–51.

Knight, W. D. "Working Capital Management—Satisficing versus Optimization." *Financial Management* (Spring 1972): 33–40.

Malkiel, B. G. *The Term Structure of Interest Rates: Expectations and Behavior Patterns.* Princeton, N.J.: Princeton University Press, 1966.

Mehta, Dileep. *Working Capital Mangement.* Englewood Cliffs, N.J.: Prentice-Hall, 1974.

Modigliani, Franco, and Sutch, Richard. "Debt Management and the Term Structure of Interest Rates: An Empirical Analysis." *Journal of Political Economy* 75 (August 1967): 569–589.

Richards, Verlyn, and Laughlin, Eugene J. "A Cash Conversion Cycle Approach to Liquidity Analysis." *Financial Management* 9 (Spring 1980): 32–38.

Smith, Keith V. *Readings on the Management of Working Capital.* St. Paul, Minn.: West Publishing, 1980.

Smith, Keith V. "State of the Art of Working Capital Management." *Financial Management* (Autumn 1973): 50–55.

Stancill, James. *The Management of Working Capital.* Scranton. Pa.: Intext Educational Publishers, 1971.

Van Horne, James C. "A Risk-Return Analysis of a Firm's Working-Capital Position." *Engineering Economist* 14 (Winter 1969): 71–89.

Welter, Paul. How to Calculate Savings Possible through Reduction of Working Capital." *Financial Executive* (Oct. 1970): 50–58.

The Term Structure of Interest Rates

INTRODUCTION

In the financial markets there is a wide range of interest rates associated with the many different types of credit transactions. Securities[1] are available that offer investors considerably different rates of return[2] depending on such factors as default risk, maturity, marketability, and tax status. The focus of this appendix is on the differential yields of securities with different maturities. The *term structure of interest rates* is defined as the relationship at a given point in time among interest rates of debt securities that differ only in the length of time to maturity.

Plotting interest rates (percent) on the vertical axis and length of time to maturity (years) on the horizontal axis results in a *yield curve.* Two yield curves for U.S. Government securities are shown in Figure 18A–1.[3] Note the different shapes of the two yield curves. The yield curve for August 1982 is *downward sloping,* indicating that the longer the time to maturity, the lower the yield on the security. The yield curve for January 1983, in contrast, is *upward sloping,* meaning that the longer the time to maturity, the higher the yield on the security.[4]

---

[1] The terms *security, debt security, debt, debt instrument, bond, loan, funds, financing,* and so on will be used interchangeably throughout the appendix to refer to a credit obligation between a borrower and lender. A borrower or lender can be an individual, business firm, or financial institution.

[2] The terms *rate of return, interest rate, rate, yield,* and so on will be used interchangeably throughout the appendix to refer to the percentage yield to maturity that is earned on a security when it is held to maturity.

[3] The primary reason for examining U.S. Government securities is that we are able to hold many of the factors affecting yields, such as default risk, constant. Corporate debt security issues, even for the same company, often differ significantly with respect to sinking fund provisions, call features, conversion features, degree of subordination, and whether or not they are secured by specific physical assets. Hence, these bond issues differ with respect to risk. Thus, it is difficult to use them in making yield versus time to maturity comparisons. However, the same general conclusions concerning the term structure of interest rates still apply to these securities.

[4] Upward and downward sloping yield curves are not the only possible shapes. At various times in the past, the yield curve has been relatively flat and also has been "hump" shaped, that is, high intermediate-term yields and low short-term and long-term yields.

FIGURE 18A–1 Yield Curves Showing the Term Structure of Interest Rates for U.S. Treasury Securities (August 1982 and January 1983) _____

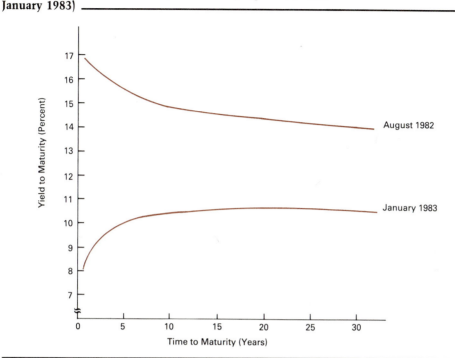

SOURCE: *Federal Reserve Bulletin* (October 1982 and March 1983)

In general, from a historical perspective, the yield curve has been upward sloping much more often than downward sloping. As can be seen in Figure 18A–2, long-term interest rates (as measured by the yields on AAA corporate bonds) have exceeded short-term interest rates (as measured by the yields on prime commercial paper) over much of the last 50 years.

THEORIES OF THE
TERM STRUCTURE OF INTEREST RATES

Three main theories have been proposed to explain the shape of the yield curve:[5]

- Liquidity premium theory.
- Expectations theory.
- Market segmentation theory.

[5]This section draws heavily on Jack Clark Francis. *Investment: Analysis and Management*, 3rd ed. New York: McGraw-Hill, 1980, chap. 10. See also Sergei Dobrovolsky. *The Economics of Corporate Finance*. New York: McGraw-Hill, 1971, chap. 15.

583

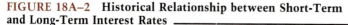

FIGURE 18A–2   Historical Relationship between Short-Term and Long-Term Interest Rates

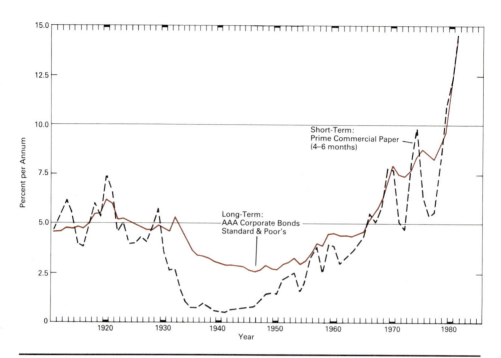

SOURCE: *Historical Chart Book.* Board of Governors of the Federal Reserve System (1982).

LIQUIDITY PREMIUM THEORY

The liquidity premium theory holds that the yields on long-term securities should average higher than the yields on short-term securities. In other words, in the absence of other factors, the yield curve should be upward sloping.

This theory is based on the risk preferences of both lenders and borrowers. Lenders, it is argued, prefer short-term over long-term debt because of the higher interest rate risk and default risk associated with long-term debt. This preference is reflected in a willingness by lenders to accept lower yields on short-term debt as compared with long-term debt. Borrowers (primarily business firms), in contrast, prefer to finance their fixed-asset acquisitions (for example, plants and equipment) with long-term funds. Compared with short-term debt, long-term financing reduces the risk that the borrower will be unable to refund the short-term debt when it comes due for renewal periodically and the risk of having to pay uncertain (for example, possibly higher) interest rates at renewal time. Consequently, borrowers are willing to pay higher interest rates for long-term funds as compared with short-term funds.

EXPECTATIONS THEORY

Long-term interest rates, according to the expectations theory, are a function of the expected future short-term interest rates. Specifically, when interest rates are in equilibrium, the n-period long-term rate is postulated to be equal to the geometric mean[6] of the expected 1-period rates for periods 1, 2, 3, . . ., n. Only the current period (that is, period 1) short-term rate is known. The other expected short-term rates for periods 2, 3, . . ., n are for securities that will exist in the future and hence are not observable at the present time (that is, at time 0).

If future short-term interest rates are expected to rise, long-term interest rates must be above the current short-term rate for the geometric mean relationship among interest rates to hold. This would produce an upward sloping yield curve. Conversely, if future short-term interest rates were expected to fall, long-term rates would have to be below the current short-term rate, thus producing a downward sloping yield curve.

Many economic and political conditions can cause expected future short- and long-term interest rates to rise or fall, thus affecting the shape of the yield curve. Examples include expected future government deficits or surpluses, changes in the rate of inflation, changes in Federal Reserve monetary policy (that is, the rate of growth of the money supply), and cyclical business conditions.

MARKET SEGMENTATION THEORY

Another theory used to explain the shape of the yield curve is based on market segmentation. According to this theory, the securities markets are segmented by maturity. Furthermore, interest rates within each maturity segment are determined more or less independently by the supply and demand interactions of the segment's borrowers and lenders. If strong borrower demand exists for long-term funds and these funds are in short supply, the yield curve will be upward sloping. Conversely, if strong borrower demand exists for short-term funds and these funds are in short supply, the yield curve will be downward sloping.

Several factors limit the choice of maturities by lenders and borrowers. One such restriction is the legal regulations that limit the types of investments commercial banks, savings and loan associations, insurance companies, and other financial institutions are permitted to make. Another limitation faced by lenders is the desire (or need) to match the maturity structure of their liabilities with assets of equivalent maturity. For example, insurance companies and pension funds, because of the long-term nature of their contractual obligations to clients, primarily are interested in making long-term investments. Commercial banks and money market funds, in contrast, are primarily short-term lenders, because a large proportion of their liabilities are in the form of deposits that can be withdrawn on demand. Similarly, borrow-

---

[6] A geometric mean of n rates of return $(X_1, X_2, . . . , X_n)$ is equal to $\overline{X} = [(1 + X_1)(1 + X_2) . . . (1 + X_n)]^{1/n} - 1$. Geometric means are commonly used when dealing with multiperiod compound interest and growth rates.

ers, such as business firms, limit their choice of debt maturities when they attempt to match the maturity composition of their debt capital with their asset structure. (Recall the matching approach discussed in Chapter 18.)

SUMMARY

At any point in time, the term structure of interest rates is the result of the interaction of the factors previously described. Each of the three theories is descriptive of reality, and each can be supported by empirical data. All three theories are useful in explaining the shape of the yield curve.

QUESTIONS AND TOPICS FOR DISCUSSION

1. Define *yield curve.*
2. What financial variables are held constant when a yield curve is constructed? Why are these variables held constant?
3. What are two reasons why the yield curve might be upward sloping? Downward sloping?
4. Explain how a downward sloping yield curve might affect the financing plans of a firm. Assume the downward sloping curve can be best explained in the context of the expectations theory of interest rates.

CHAPTER 19

The Management of Cash and Marketable Securities

A FINANCIAL DILEMMA

Managing Uncle Sam's Money*

When Wayne Granquist, former associate director of the Office of Management and Budget, was trying to convince Dick Cavanagh to leave private industry for a government career, Cavanagh wanted to know exactly what his new job would involve. In reply, Granquist asked Cavanagh to check his personal records to see how long it took the IRS to cash his quarterly income tax check. Cavanagh found that it took an unusually long 22 days. He accepted the job, knowing that he would be working on improving the government's cash management procedures.

In doing some research, Cavanagh found that the government pays its bills earlier than necessary and ends up paying $118 million in interest on the money it *borrows* to make the quick payments. He also found that the government is slow in collecting money owed to it, taking 23 days to bill buyers of goods from the nation's strategic stockpiles and 9 more days to cash the payment checks once they are received. In addition, Cavanagh found that the government has an average of $1.5 billion on deposit in banks around the country earning *no interest*.

Since then, Cavanagh and Granquist have worked hard to develop plans to improve the government's cash management procedures. This chapter considers some of these techniques.

*Adapted from "Putting Uncle's Cash to Work." *Time* (June 5, 1978).

GLOSSARY OF NEW TERMS

Bank draft an order to pay that is similar to a check, except that it is not payable on demand. Instead, a bank draft is payable when the issuing firm accepts it.

Banker's acceptance a short-term debt instrument issued by a firm as part of a commercial transaction. Payment is guaranteed by a commercial bank.

Commercial paper short-term, unsecured promissory notes. Commercial paper is generally issued by large, well-known corporations and finance companies.

Concentration banking the use of decentralized collection centers and local banks to collect accounts receivable. This speeds up a firm's collections.

Default risk the risk that a borrower will fail to make interest payments, principal payments, or both on a loan.

Float the difference between an account balance as shown on the bank's books and as shown on the firm's books. Float represents the net effect of the delays in the payment of checks the firm writes and the collection of checks the firm receives.

Lockbox a post office box maintained by a bank to speed up the collection of receivables.

Repurchase agreement an arrangement with a bank or securities dealer in which an investor acquires certain short-term securities subject to a commitment that the securities will be repurchased by the bank or securities dealer on a specified date.

Wire transfer the process of electronically sending funds from one bank to another through the Federal Reserve System.

Zero-balance system a payment system that uses a master disbursing account that services all other disbursing accounts. A zero balance is maintained in all but the master account until payments must be made.

INTRODUCTION

Cash and marketable securities are the most liquid of a company's assets. *Cash* is the sum of the currency a company has on hand and the funds on deposit in a bank checking account or accounts. Cash is the medium of exchange that permits management to carry on the various functions of the business organization. In fact, the survival of a company can depend on the availability of cash to meet financial obligations on time.

Marketable securities consist of short-term investments a firm makes with its temporarily idle cash that can be readily sold and converted into cash when needed. Unlike cash, however, marketable securities provide the firm with interest income.

Referring to Table 18–1 in Chapter 18, it can be seen that cash and marketable securities accounted for only about 2.4 and 2.2 percent, respectively, of the total assets of all U.S. manufacturing corporations, ranking well behind inventories and receivables. Even though liquid asset balances tend to be small compared with other categories of current assets, they nevertheless must be managed efficiently if the firm is to operate profitably and minimize the risk of insolvency.

Cash management involves much more than simply paying bills and receiving payments for goods and services. It is a much broader function that is concerned with determining the following:

- The optimal size of the firm's liquid asset balance.

- The most efficient methods of controlling the collection and disbursement of cash.

- The appropriate types and amounts of short-term investments the firm should make.

This chapter examines these decisions in detail.

LIQUID ASSET BALANCE

There are three primary reasons why firms hold liquid asset balances.[1]

- First, since cash inflows and outflows are not perfectly synchronized, liquid asset balances are necessary to serve as a buffer between these flows. This reason is the *transactions motive*.[2]

- Second, since future cash flows and the ability to borrow additional funds on short notice are often uncertain, liquid asset balances are necessary to meet unexpected requirements for cash. This is the *precautionary motive*.

- Finally, a firm generally has to hold cash balances in order to compensate the bank (or banks)[3] for the services provided. These are called *compensating balances*.

The following sections consider the importance of cash from a number of perspectives.

CASH FLOWS AND THE CASH BUDGET

Virtually every activity within a firm generates cash flows. As shown in Figure 19–1, the firm's cash balance is affected by every transaction that involves either a cash inflow or a cash outflow. Cash inflows, or *receipts*, occur when customers pay for their purchases, when the firm obtains bank loans, when it sells new issues of debt and equity securities, and when it sells (or

---

[1] G. A. Pogue, R. B. Faucett, and R. N. Bussard. "Cash Management: A Systems Approach." *Industrial Management Review* 11 (Feb. 1970): 55–74.

[2] In *The General Theory of Employment, Interest and Money* (New York: Harcourt, Brace, 1935), economist John Maynard Keynes identified three primary reasons why people hold cash—the transactions motive, the precautionary motive, and the speculative motive. Within the *business firm*, the first two motives for holding cash are much more important than the latter one.

[3] Many medium and large firms use the services of more than one bank.

FIGURE 19–1   **Cash Flows within a Typical Firm***

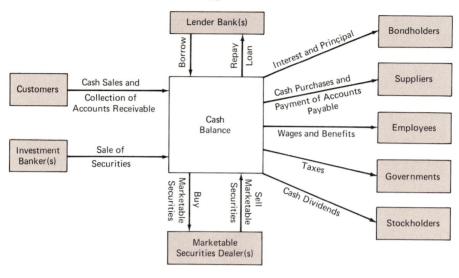

*Arrows indicate the *direction* of cash flows.

collects interest on) marketable securities. Cash outflows, or disbursements, occur when the firm makes payments to suppliers, when the firm pays wages to employees, taxes to governments, interest and principal to bondholders, and cash dividends to shareholders, and when the firm repays bank loans and purchases marketable securities. Thus, the cash balance at the end of any given period is the result of many interrelated activities.

Cash flows differ with respect to their degree of *certainty*. In general, future outflows are more certain than future inflows. Most expenditures (outflows) are directly controllable by the firm and, as a result, can be more easily fore-casted. For example, outflows for such items as raw materials, labor, dividends, debt repayments, and capital equipment are determined primarily by management decisions and usually are known in advance of their occurrence. Inflows, in contrast, occur partly as a result of decisions made outside the firm and thus are usually more difficult to control and forecast. For example, cash inflows from sales depend primarily on the buying decisions of custom-ers, as well as on when they make their payments.

The first step in efficient cash management is the development of a *cash budget* showing the forecasted cash receipts and disbursements over the plan-ning horizon of the firm. Many larger firms prepare a series of cash budgets, each one covering a different time period. For example, a firm may prepare daily cash budgets for the next 5 working days, weekly cash budgets for the next 10 weeks, and monthly cash budgets for the next 12 months. The daily and weekly forecasts are used in making short-term decisions, such as deter-mining the amount of marketable securities the firm should purchase or sell. The monthly projections are used in longer range planning, such as determin-ing the amount of bank loans the firm will need.[4]

[4]Chapter 8 contains a discussion of how cash budgets are developed.

A complete cash budget also contains a forecast of any cumulative cash shortages or surpluses expected during each of the budgeting subperiods—which is the kind of information needed in making cash management decisions. Knowledge of a potential cash shortage ahead of time gives the financial manager ample opportunity to investigate alternative sources of financing and to choose the least costly one. All other things being equal, lending institutions prefer to make loans to firms that have demonstrated an ability to anticipate their future cash needs. Firms that seem to be faced with frequent cash "emergencies" generally have more difficulty getting loans. Similarly, advance knowledge of a cash surplus allows the financial manager to invest in appropriate marketable securities.

CORPORATE-BANK RELATIONS

A firm's bank provides it with a variety of both tangible and intangible services. The most significant tangible services include the following:

- Disbursement and payroll checking accounts.
- Collection of deposits.
- Cash management.
- Lines of credit, term loans, or both.
- Handling of dividend payments.
- Registration and transfer of the firm's stock.[5]

The most important intangible banking service is the availability of future credit if and when the need arises. Other intangible services include the following:

- Supplying credit information.
- Providing consulting advice on such matters as economic conditions, mergers, and international business.

A bank is compensated for the services it provides by charging the firm explicit fees and/or requiring the maintenance of a minimum cash balance, or *compensating balance,* in its checking account. The bank can use this compensating balance to make other loans or investments, and the interest income realized is *compensation* for the various services rendered to the firm. Although some banks require firms to maintain *absolute* minimum compensating balances, most stipulate minimum *average* balances.

In determining the profitability and appropriate level of a corporate client's compensating balance, the bank compares the estimated income from and the costs of the firm's account. To determine the estimated income, the average account balance (less required reserves) over a period of time is multiplied by the return the bank can earn on the deposits. Any fees collected for services rendered are added to this income. The estimated costs of the account are obtained by multiplying the number of each type of transaction the

---

[5]An interesting sample survey of corporate-bank relationships, including the types of services provided by banks to their corporate customers, is discussed in W. L. Reed. "Profits from Better Cash Management." *Financial Executive* 40 (May 1972): 40–56.

firm makes per period (such as payroll checks, vendor checks, customer payments, and other deposits) by the bank's cost per item of each type of transaction; the costs of any intangible services provided to the firm are then added to this figure. Due to competition among banks and differences in the methods used to compute account income and costs, compensating balance requirements for a given level of account activity vary from bank to bank. As a result, a firm should occasionally do some "comparison shopping" to determine whether its present bank is offering the best fee schedule and compensating balance requirement currently available.

OPTIMAL LIQUID ASSET BALANCE

When a firm holds liquid asset balances, whether in the form of currency, bank demand deposits, or marketable securities, it is in effect investing these funds. To determine the optimal investment in liquid assets, the firm must weigh the benefits and costs of holding these various balances.

A minimum compensating balance requirement on the part of the bank essentially imposes a *lower limit* on the firm's optimal level of liquid asset balances. When the firm holds liquid assets in excess of this lower limit, it incurs an *opportunity cost.* The opportunity cost of excess liquid assets, held in the form of bank deposits, is the return the firm could earn on these funds in their next best use, such as in the expansion of other current or fixed assets. The opportunity cost of liquid asset balances, held in the form of marketable securities, is the income that could be earned on these funds in their next best alternative use in the firm *less* the interest income received on the marketable securities.

Given the opportunity cost of holding liquid asset balances, why would a firm ever maintain a bank balance exceeding the compensating balance requirements? The answer is that these balances help the firm avoid the "shortage" costs associated with inadequate liquid asset balances.[6]

Shortage costs can take many different forms, including the following:

- Forgone cash discounts.
- Deterioration of the firm's credit rating.
- Higher interest expenses.
- Possible financial insolvency.

Many suppliers offer customers a cash discount for prompt payment. Having to forgo this cash discount can be quite costly to the firm. In addition, the credit-worthiness of a firm is at least partially determined by the current and quick ratios—both of which can be affected by an inadequate liquid asset balance. This, in turn, can cause the firm's credit rating to deteriorate and make loans on favorable terms more difficult for the firm to secure in the future. The credit rating also can fall if the firm fails to pay bills on time because of inadequate cash. This can make future credit difficult to obtain from suppliers. If the firm has inadequate liquid asset reserves, it may have to meet unforeseen needs for cash by short-term borrowing, and it may be

---

[6]See William Beranek. *Analysis for Financial Decisions.* Homewood, Ill.: Irwin, 1963, chap. 11.

FIGURE 19–2   Optimal Liquid Asset Balance _____

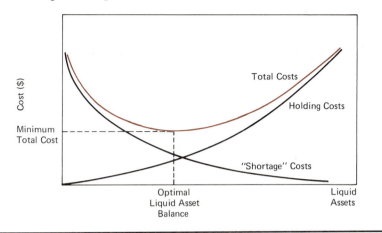

unable to negotiate for the best terms—including the lowest possible interest rate—if its credit rating is questionable. Finally, an inadequate liquid asset balance increases the firm's risk of insolvency, since a serious recession or natural disaster would be more likely to reduce the firm's cash inflows to the point where it could not meet contractual financial obligations.

An inverse relationship exists between a firm's liquid asset balance and these shortage costs: the larger a firm's liquid asset balance, the smaller its associated shortage costs. The opportunity holding costs, in contrast, increase as a firm's liquid asset balance is increased. As shown in Figure 19–2, the optimal liquid asset balance occurs at the point where the sum of the opportunity holding costs and the shortage costs is minimized. Admittedly, many of these shortage costs are difficult to measure. Nevertheless, a firm should at least attempt to evaluate the tradeoffs among these costs in order to economize on cash holdings.

CONTROLLING THE COLLECTION AND DISBURSEMENT OF CASH

The cash collection and disbursement processes provide a firm with two areas to attempt to economize on cash holdings. For example, if sales average $5 million per day and the company can speed up collections by only *1 day*, the cash balance will increase by $5 million, and these released funds can be invested in other current assets or in fixed assets. If this additional cash can be invested in projects yielding a 10 percent return, it will generate added income of $500,000 per year (10% × $5 million).

A firm's cash balance as shown on the bank's books generally differs from that shown on the firm's own books. This difference is known as *float* and represents the net effect of the delays in the payment of checks the firm writes and the collection of checks the firm receives. Checks written by the firm result in *disbursement*, or *positive*, float; that is, an excess of bank net collected balances over the balances shown on the firm's books. In contrast, checks received by the firm and deposited in its account result in *deposit*, or *negative*, float; that is, an excess of book balances over bank net collected balances. Often a firm cannot withdraw the deposited funds until the bank *clears* the checks. In other words, the firm's bank must first collect the funds from the other banks upon which the checks are drawn. The amount of time in which a check clears depends on the geographical proximity of the bank that receives the check and the bank on which it is drawn. In general, checks take a maximum of 2 days to clear through the Federal Reserve System. Checks processed through bank clearinghouses may take longer.[7]

The primary objective of cash collection involves expediting collections and reducing the lag between the time customers pay their bills and the time the checks are collected. In contrast, the primary objective of cash disbursement is to slow payments so that the firm can keep the funds in the bank as long as possible. Expediting collections and slowing disbursements helps increase the firm's cash balance and provide it with funds to use for other profitable investments.

EXPEDITING COLLECTIONS

Figure 19–3 illustrates the main steps in the cash collection process. The total time involved in this process is a combination of mailing time, company processing time, and check-clearing time, each of which may vary depending on where the firm's customers and their respective banks are located.[8] Some methods available for reducing the collection time are discussed in the following paragraphs.

Decentralized collection centers and concentration banks Figures 19–4 and 19–5 illustrate two alternative cash collection systems. In the centralized system (Figure 19–4), customers are instructed to send their payments to the

FIGURE 19–3   **Cash Collection Process**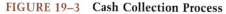

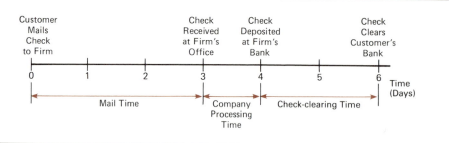

---

[7]Although most banks do not put holds on checks of large corporate clients, they often do on checks of individuals and small business customers. A *Wall Street Journal* article (January 12, 1983, p. 29) cited Citibank's (First National City Bank of New York's) policy as typical; "Its holds range from 3 business days for a local check to as long as 15 days for a check drawn on a small-town bank in a distant state."

[8]The particular times shown in Figure 19–3 are merely illustrative. Actual times will vary. (This is also true for Figures 19–7 and 19–8.)

FIGURE 19–4   Centralized Collection System

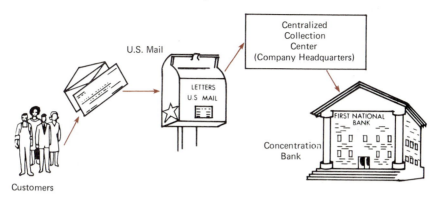

firm's headquarters. In the *decentralized* system (Figure 19–5), customers mail their payments to a nearby collection center, which is strategically located to minimize mail delay. The collection center then deposits the checks in a local bank and reports this information to the firm's headquarters. Since most of the checks are drawn on banks that are located in the same geographical area as the collection center, check-clearing time and deposit float are reduced. Each business day, funds in excess of the amount necessary to compensate the local bank for its services are transferred to an account in a *concentration bank*, where the firm maintains a disbursement account upon which checks are written.

A tradeoff exists between the number of collection centers and the potential savings realized. The more collection centers used, the less time required to convert customers' checks into collected balances. However, these savings from faster collections are offset by the direct fees involved, the opportunity costs of the compensating balances the firm must maintain at each local bank, or both. The financial manager must weigh the tradeoffs involved in

FIGURE 19–5   Decentralized Collection System

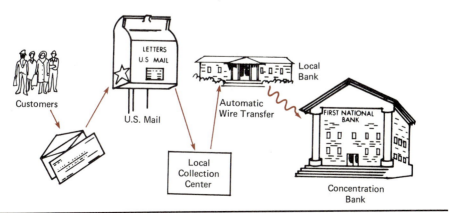

both savings and costs in deciding on the appropriate number and location of collection centers.

Lockboxes Figure 19–6 illustrates the lockbox collection system. A lockbox is a post office box maintained by a local bank for the purpose of receiving a firm's remittances. Customers mail payments to this post office box, which is usually no more than a few hundred miles away.[9] For example, Monsanto, a large chemical firm, maintains 22 lockboxes around the country. The bank empties the box several times each working day, deposits the payments in the firm's account, puts the checks into the clearing system, and sends the firm a list of the payments received each day. Not only does the lockbox reduce mailing time, it also eliminates company processing time, since the checks are deposited and begin the clearing process *before* the company's accounting department processes the payments received rather than after processing them. The bank normally charges a fee for this service, requires a compensating balance, or both. Funds in excess of the bank's compensating balance requirement are transferred each day to a disbursement account in a concentration bank.

The decision to establish a lockbox collection system requires a comparison of the associated benefits and costs. If the earnings on the funds released by the acceleration of collections exceed the forgone returns on the required compensating balances, the service fees charged by the lockbox bank, or both, the establishment of a lockbox collection system is profitable.

If the number of checks being handled is small and the dollar amount of each check is large, a lockbox arrangement is very beneficial to the firm.

FIGURE 19–6 Lockbox Collection System _____

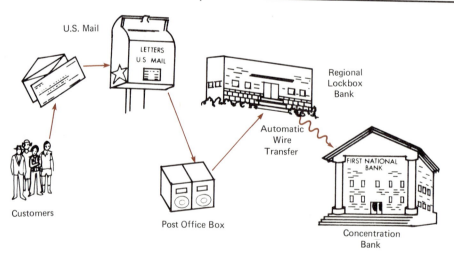

U.S. Mail

Regional Lockbox Bank

Automatic Wire Transfer

Customers

Post Office Box

Concentration Bank

---

[9]Determining the optimal location of lockboxes is a complex problem. For some solutions, see Ferdinand K. Levy. "An Application of Heuristic Problem Solving to Accounts Receivable Management." *Management Science* 12 (Feb. 1966): B-236–B-244; Alan Kraus et al. "The Lock-Box Location Problem." *Journal of Bank Research* 1 (Autumn 1970): 51–58.

Under these conditions the bank's work load is light, and the associated service fees, compensating balances, or both, are small. However, when large numbers of checks with small dollar amounts are involved—for example, in the case of oil company credit cards—a lockbox system may not be profitable. Under these conditions the service fees, opportunity costs, or both, on the required compensating balances may exceed the earnings the firm realizes from having the funds available a few days earlier.

The lockbox decision can be illustrated with the following example. The Pacific Company, located in Los Angeles, currently receives and processes all customer payments at its corporate headquarters (that is, a *centralized* system). The firm is considering establishing a bank lockbox collection system for seven southeastern states—Florida, North Carolina, South Carolina, Tennessee, Alabama, Georgia, and Mississippi—which would be located in Atlanta. The lockbox would reduce average mailing time for customer payments from 3 days to 1½ days, and it would reduce check processing and clearing time from 5 days to 2½ days.

The average daily collections from the southeastern region total $250,000 per working day, and the average number of payments received total 800 per working day (assume 250 working days per year). A bank in Atlanta has agreed to process the payments for an annual fee of $15,000 plus $0.10 per payment received. This bank would not require a compensating balance. Assuming an 8 percent opportunity cost for released funds, should Pacific use the lockbox collection system?

Under the present collection system, an average of 8 days elapses between the time a customer mails a payment to Pacific and the time the check is collected (3 days' mailing time + 5 days' processing and clearing time). In the lockbox collection system this time would be reduced to 4 days (1½ days' mailing time + 2½ days' processing and clearing time). The difference between the two systems is 4 days, thereby releasing $1 million in cash (4 × $250,000). The firm would realize expected annual earnings on the released funds of $80,000 ($1 million × 8%) under the lockbox system. The annual cost of the lockbox system would be $15,000 (the fixed cost charged by the bank) plus $20,000 (the variable cost of 800 checks per day × 250 working days per year × $0.10 per check), or $35,000. Since the earnings on the released funds would exceed the service fees charged by the bank, Pacific should employ the lockbox collection system.

Wire transfers and depository transfer checks Once deposits enter the firm's banking network, the objective is to transfer surplus funds (that is, funds in excess of any required compensating balances) from its local (collection) bank accounts to its concentration (disbursement) bank account or accounts. Two methods used to perform this task are *wire transfers* and *depository transfer checks*.

With a *wire transfer*, funds are sent from a local bank to a concentration bank electronically through the Federal Reserve System or a private bank wire system. Wire transfers are the fastest way of moving funds between banks, since the transfer takes only a few minutes and the funds become immediately available (that is, they can be withdrawn) by the firm upon receipt of the wire notice at the concentration bank. Wire transfers eliminate the mailing and check-clearing times associated with other funds transfer methods. Some firms leave standing instructions with their local (collection) banks to automatically wire surplus funds on a periodic basis (for example, daily, twice a week, and so on) to their concentration bank. Also, some firms specify in their sales contracts that customers must wire their payments on the due dates.

Wire transfer of funds is available to member banks of the Federal Reserve System and to nonmember banks through their correspondent banks. The cost to corporate customers of a wire transfer at most banks is $2 to $4. For a firm with multiple collection centers that use wire transfers on a daily basis, the annual costs can be substantial. Consequently, this method of transferring funds should be used only when the incremental value of having the funds immediately available exceeds the additional cost.

A *depository transfer check* is an unsigned, nonnegotiable check drawn on the local collection bank and payable to the concentration bank. As it deposits customer checks in the local bank each day, the collection center mails a depository transfer check to the concentration bank authorizing it to withdraw the deposited funds from the local bank. Upon receipt of the depository transfer check, the firm's account at the concentration bank is credited for the designated amount. Depository transfer checks are processed through the usual check-clearing process. While the use of depository transfer checks does not eliminate mailing and check-clearing time, it does insure the movement of funds from the local collection center banks to the concentration bank in a timely manner. Also, the cost of this method of transferring funds is low; often the only cost involved is postage.

Recently, an *automated depository transfer check system* has been established. This system eliminates the mail float involved in moving the funds from the local bank to a concentration bank. Funds transferred by use of this automated system can become available for use by the firm in as little as 1 day.

Special handling of large remittances   Firms that receive individual remittances in the multimillion-dollar range may find it more profitable to use special courier services to pick up these checks from customers (rather than having their customers mail the checks) and present them for collection to the banks upon which they are drawn.

Use of preauthorized checks   A preauthorized check resembles an ordinary check except that it does not require the signature of the person (or firm) on whose account it is being drawn. This system is especially useful for firms that receive a large volume of payments of a fixed amount each period. Insurance companies, savings and loans, charitable institutions, and leasing firms make extensive use of this collection procedure. When preauthorized checks are used, the payer agrees to allow the payee (the firm that is owed the money) to write a check on the payer's account and deposit that check immediately for collection at an agreed-upon time. Preauthorized checks have the advantages of completely eliminating the mail float, reducing billing and collecting expenses, and making the cash flows for both parties highly predictable. Many payers like preauthorized check systems because they do not have to bother to write a check each month.

SLOWING DISBURSEMENTS

Figure 19–7 illustrates the principle steps involved in the cash disbursement process. Several ways in which a firm can slow disbursements and keep funds in the bank for longer periods of time are discussed in the following paragraphs.

Scheduling and centralizing payments   A firm should pay bills *on time*—not before or after they are due. Payments made ahead of time lower the firm's average cash balance, whereas late payments can impair the firm's credit rating or fail to qualify for a cash discount.

Centralizing payments from disbursement accounts maintained at a concentration bank helps minimize the amount of idle funds a firm must keep in local field offices and divisional bank accounts. A number of firms have set up *zero-balance* systems to use disbursement float more effectively. In a zero-balance system a *master*, or *concentration*, *account* is set up to receive all deposits coming into the zero-balance system. As checks clear through the zero-balance accounts on which they are issued, funds are transferred to these accounts from the master account. These disbursement accounts are called zero-balance accounts because exactly enough funds are transferred into them daily to cover the checks that have cleared, leaving a zero balance at the end of the day. In general, all disbursements for accounts payable, payroll, and whatever other purposes the firm desires are issued from these zero-balance accounts. For a zero-balance system to operate effectively, the firm must have a well-developed network for reporting deposits and disbursements, as well as a close working relationship with its bank.

Drafts   A draft is similar to a check, except it is not payable on demand. Instead, when a draft is transmitted to a firm's bank for collection, the bank must present the draft to the firm for acceptance before making payment. Once the draft has been accepted, the firm can deposit the necessary funds to cover the payment.

The use of drafts rather than checks permits a firm to keep smaller balances in its disbursement accounts, since funds do not have to be deposited in them until the drafts are presented for payment. Normally, drafts are more expensive to use than checks. However, the lower account balances and higher processing costs cause banks to impose service charges on firms using

FIGURE 19–7   Cash Disbursement Process —————————————

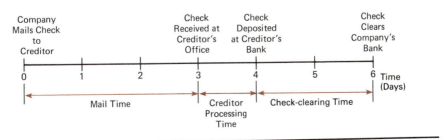

599

FIGURE 19–8   Amount of Dividend Checks Clearing a Sample Account Each Day

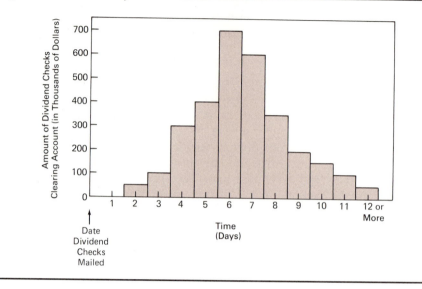

drafts; this cost must be included in the analysis of the benefits and costs of using drafts to pay bills.

Synchronizing transfers with check clearings   The balance in a disbursement account shown on the bank's books normally will be greater than the balance shown on the firm's books. This disbursement float is due to the various delays between the time when checks are written and when they are cleared (see Figure 19–7). Given accurate estimates of the size of a float and the number of days before a typical check is deposited and cleared, as shown in Figure 19–8, a firm can maintain a negative book balance and invest the float in interest-bearing securities. Sufficient funds then can be transferred into the disbursement account each day to cover the checks that are expected to clear. This approach obviously requires complete, timely record keeping and accurate forecasting.

Maximizing check-clearing float   Some firms make payments to suppliers from checking accounts located a long distance from the supplier. For example, an East Coast supplier might be paid with checks drawn on a West Coast bank. This increases the time required for the check to clear through the banking system.

INVESTING IN MARKETABLE SECURITIES

Rather than let their cash reserves build up in excess of daily cash requirements, many firms invest in interest-bearing short-term marketable securities. Given the higher interest rates (and yields) of recent years, firms have become much more conscious of the sizable opportunity costs (that is, lost income) of idle cash balances. Determining the level of liquid assets that should be invested in marketable securities depends on several factors, including these:[10]

- The interest to be earned over the expected holding period.
- The transaction costs involved in buying and selling the securities.
- The variability of the firm's cash flows.

In addition to the desire to earn interest income on their liquid asset balances, there are two primary reasons why firms hold marketable securities:

- As a *precautionary* measure.
- As a way of temporarily investing cash that is being *accumulated* for a variety of purposes.

Marketable securities serve as added protection against unforeseen cash needs that could exceed the firm's cash balance. They also provide the firm with a means of accumulating funds needed for fixed outlays that are required on specific dates, such as quarterly dividend and income tax payments, capital expenditures, and repayments of loans or bond issues. These accumulated funds also may help the firm handle seasonal fluctuations in cash flows. For example, a firm may wish to hold a large amount of marketable securities during surplus months and "draw down" on them during deficit months. A firm may also need to hold temporarily in marketable securities the proceeds from a new debt or equity securities offering prior to using these funds for expansion.

CHOOSING MARKETABLE SECURITIES

A firm may choose among many different types of securities when deciding where to invest excess cash reserves. In determining which securities to include in its portfolio, the firm should consider a number of criteria, including the following:

- Default risk.
- Marketability.
- Maturity date.
- Rate of return.

Each of these is discussed in this section.

Default risk   A firm usually will invest in marketable securities that have little or no default risk. U.S. Treasury securities have the lowest default risk, followed by securities of other U.S. government agencies and, finally, by corporate and municipal securities. Various financial reporting agencies, including Moody's Investors Service and Standard and Poor's, compile and publish

---

[10]Appendix 19A discusses two quantitative models that may be used to determine the optimal division of liquid asset balances between cash and marketable securities.

information concerning the safety ratings of the various corporate and municipal securities. There is a positive relationship between a security's expected return and risk. Since a firm must be concerned with selecting marketable securities having minimal default risk, it has to be willing to accept relatively low expected yields on marketable securities.

Marketability   A firm usually buys marketable securities that can be sold on short notice for a price that is fairly close to the amount paid for them. Thus, there are two dimensions to a security's marketability, or *liquidity*–namely, the time required to sell the security and the price realized from the sale. If a long period of time, a high transaction cost, or a significant price concession is required to dispose of a security, the security has poor marketability and is generally not considered suitable for inclusion in a marketable securities portfolio. Naturally, there is a tradeoff involved here between risk and return. Generally, a highly marketable security has a smaller degree of risk that the investor will incur a loss, and consequently it usually has a lower expected yield than one with limited marketability.

Maturity date   Firms usually limit their marketable securities purchases to issues that have relatively short maturities. Recall that prices of debt securities decrease when interest rates rise and increase when interest rates fall. For a given change in interest rates, prices of long-term securities fluctuate more widely than short-term securities with equal default risk. Thus, an investor who holds long-term securities is exposed to a greater risk of loss if the securities have to be sold prior to maturity. This is known as *interest rate risk*. For this reason, most firms generally do not buy marketable securities that have more than 180 to 270 days remaining until maturity, and many firms restrict most of their temporary investments to those maturing in less than 90 days. Since the yields on securities with short maturities often are lower than the yields on securities with longer maturities, a firm has to be willing to sacrifice yield to avoid interest rate risk.

Rate of return   Although the rate of return, or yield, also is given consideration in selecting securities for inclusion in the firm's portfolio, it is less important than the other three criteria just described. The desire to invest in securities that have minimal default and interest rate risk and that are readily marketable usually limits the selection to those having relatively low yields.

TYPES OF MARKETABLE SECURITIES

Firms normally confine their marketable securities investments to "money market" instruments, that is, those high-grade (low default risk) short-term debt instruments having original maturities of 1 year or less. Money market instruments that are suitable for inclusion in a firm's marketable securities portfolio include U.S. Treasury issues, other Federal agency issues, negotiable certificates of deposit, commercial paper, repurchase agreements, bankers' acceptances, money market mutual funds, and bank money market accounts. Each of these will be discussed. (In some cases, firms also will use long-term bonds having 1 year or less remaining to maturity as "marketable" securities and treat them as money market instruments.)

Table 19–1 lists the characteristics and yields of these various money market instruments. As can be seen in the last three columns of the table, yields on these securities vary considerably over time. Yields are a function of a number of factors, including the state of the economy, the rate of inflation, and government monetary and fiscal policies.

United States Treasury issues   United States Treasury Bills are the most popular marketable securities. They are sold at weekly auctions through Federal Reserve Banks and their branches and have standard maturities of 91 days, 182 days, and 1 year. Once they are issued, Treasury Bills can be bought and sold in the secondary markets through government securities dealers. There is a large and active market for Treasury Bills, which means that a firm can easily dispose of them when it needs cash.

The advantages of Treasury issues include short maturities, a virtually default-free status, and ready marketability. Their primary disadvantage lies in the fact that their yields are normally the lowest of any marketable security.

The Treasury also issues notes that have original maturities of from 1 to 7 years and bonds that have maturities over 7 years. As these securities approach their maturity dates, they become, in effect, short-term instruments that are then suitable for inclusion in a firm's marketable securities portfolio.

Other Federal agency issues   A number of Federal government–sponsored agencies issue their own securities, including the "big five"—the Federal Home Loan Bank, the Federal Land Banks, the Federal Intermediate Credit Bank, the Bank for Cooperatives, and the Federal National Mortgage Association. Although each of these agencies guarantees its own securities, they do not constitute a legal obligation on the part of the U.S. government. Nevertheless, most investors consider them to be very low risk securities, and they sell at yields slightly above U.S. Treasury securities but below other money market instruments. Since these securities are traded in the secondary markets through the same dealers who handle U.S. Treasury securities, they are readily marketable should a firm need to dispose of them before maturity.

Negotiable certificates of deposit   Commercial banks are permitted to issue certificates of deposit (CDs), which entitle the holder to receive the amount deposited plus accrued interest on a specified date. At the time of issue, maturities on these instruments range from 30 days to 18 months. Once issued, CDs become *negotiable*, meaning they can be bought and sold in the secondary markets. Since CDs of the largest banks are handled by government securities dealers, they are readily marketable and thus are suitable for inclusion in a firm's marketable securities portfolio. Yields on CDs are generally above the rates on Federal agency issues having similar maturities.

Commercial paper   Commercial paper consists of short-term unsecured promissory notes that are issued by large, well-known corporations and finance companies. Some finance companies, such as General Motors Accep-

TABLE 19–1 Characteristics and Yields of Money Market Instruments

INSTRUMENT	DENOMINATIONS	MATURITIES	MARKETABILITY		YIELDS* (%) December 1980	YIELDS* (%) November 1982
U.S. Treasury Bills	Various denominations from $10,000 to $1,000,000	91 days, 182 days, 52 weeks	Highly organized secondary market	(3 months) (6 months)	15.49 14.64	8.07 8.34
Federal agency issues	Numerous denominations from $1,000 to $1,000,000	Wide variation in maturities from several days to more than 10 years	Well-established secondary market for short-term securities of "big five" agencies		—	—
Negotiable certificates of deposit	$25,000 to $1,000,000	1 to 18 months	Fairly good secondary market	(1 month) (3 months) (6 months)	19.24 18.65 17.10	8.82 8.95 9.13
Commercial paper	$5,000 to $5,000,000 or more in multiples of $1,000	2 or 3 days to 270 days	Weak secondary market	(1 month) (3 months) (6 months)	18.95 18.07 16.49	8.66 8.69 8.72
Repurchase agreements	Varying amounts; no standard denominations	1 day to several months	Good, since borrower agrees to repurchase securities at a fixed price		—	—
Bankers' acceptances	Varying amounts, depending on the size of the commercial transaction	30 to 180 days	Good, although less extensive than for most other instruments	(3 months)	17.96	8.76
Money market mutual funds	Minimum of $1,000 is usually required; no standard denominations	Redeemable at any time	Good, since the fund agrees to redeem shares at any time	Yields vary from fund to fund, but they usually exceed the yield available on Treasury Bills.		
Bank money market accounts	Minimum of $2,500 required	Normally redeemable at any time (by law, banks reserve the right to require 7 days' written notice for withdrawals)	Good, except in rare instances when a bank might impose a 7-day written notice requirement	—		

SOURCE: *Federal Reserve Bulletin*, Table 1:35, various issues.

604

tance Corporation (GMAC) and C.I.T. Financial Corporation, which issue large amounts of commercial paper regularly, sell it directly to investors. Industrial, utility, and transportation firms and smaller finance companies, which issue commercial paper less frequently and in smaller amounts, sell their commercial paper through commercial paper dealers. Maturities on commercial paper at the time of issue range from 2 or 3 days to 270 days.

The secondary market for commercial paper is weak, although it is sometimes possible to make arrangements with the issuer or commercial paper dealer to repurchase the security prior to maturity. This weak secondary market, combined with a somewhat higher default risk, results in higher yields on commercial paper than on most other money market instruments.

Repurchase agreements   A repurchase agreement, or "repo," is an arrangement with a bank or securities dealer in which the investor acquires certain short-term securities subject to a commitment from the bank or dealer to repurchase the securities on a specified date. Securities used in this agreement can be government securities, CDs, or commercial paper. Their maturities tend to be relatively short, ranging from 1 day to several months, and are designed to meet the needs of the investor.

The yield on a repo is slightly less than the rate that can be obtained from outright purchase of the underlying security. The repo rate approximates the rate on Federal funds, which is the rate used when banks borrow from other banks. Repurchase agreements are very safe investments, since the bank or securities dealer with whom the agreement is arranged *and* the issuer of the security both would have to default before the investor would incur a loss.

Bankers' acceptances   A bankers' acceptance is a short-term debt instrument issued by a firm as part of a commercial transaction. Payment is guaranteed by a commercial bank. Bankers' acceptances are commonly used financing instruments in international trade, as well as in certain lines of domestic trade.

These instruments vary in amount, depending on the size of the commercial transaction. A secondary market exists in which these acceptances can be traded should a bank or investor choose not to hold them until maturity, which usually ranges between 30 and 100 days at the time of issue. Bankers' acceptances are relatively safe investments, since both the bank and the borrower are liable for the amount due at maturity. Their yields are comparable to the rate available on CDs.

Money market mutual funds   Many of the higher yielding marketable securities described are only available in relatively large denominations. For example, negotiable CDs usually come in amounts of $100,000 or more. As a result, a smaller firm that has only limited funds to invest at any given time is often unable to obtain the higher yields offered on these securities. An alternative is a *money market mutual fund* that pools the investments of many other small investors and invests in large-denomination money market instruments. By purchasing shares in a money market fund, such as Dreyfus Liquid Assets or Merrill Lynch Ready Assets, a smaller firm can approach the higher yields offered on large-denomination securities. In addition, most of these funds offer limited check-writing privileges, which enables firms to earn interest on invested funds until their checks clear and provides liquidity.

Bank money market accounts   Early in 1983 banks were permitted to offer checking accounts with yields comparable to those on money market mutual funds.

SUMMARY

- A firm holds liquid asset balances for the following primary reasons:

1. To conduct transactions.

2. For precautionary purposes.

3. To compensate its bank or banks for various services rendered.

- To manage cash effectively, a firm must first develop a *cash budget* showing all of the forecasted cash inflows and outflows over the planning horizon.

- A firm's optimal liquid asset balance depends on both the opportunity cost of holding excess balances and the "shortage" costs associated with not having enough needed cash available.

- The primary objective in controlling cash collections is to reduce the delay between the time when the customer mails the payment and when it becomes a collected balance. Methods for reducing collection time include decentralized collection centers and concentration banks, lockboxes, wire transfers, depository transfer checks, preauthorized checks, and special handling of large remittances.

- The primary objective in controlling cash disbursements is to slow payments and keep the firm's funds in the bank as long as possible. Techniques for slowing disbursements include scheduling and centralizing payments, using drafts rather than checks, and synchronizing transfers of cash to disbursement accounts with check clearings.

- The primary criteria a firm should use in selecting *marketable securities* include *default risk, marketability* (or *liquidity), maturity date,* and *rate of return.* The most commonly used marketable securities include U.S. Treasury issues, other Federal agency issues, negotiable certificates of deposit, commercial paper, repurchase agreements, bankers' acceptances, money market funds, and bank money market accounts.

Zero-Balance Banking

Carl J. Lange
Vice-President and Controller
Sysco Corporation

Sysco Corporation, a food distributor with 1982 revenues of $1.7 billion, has developed a banking system network for its 65 self-supporting distribution centers, which are geographically located in 44 of the 48 contiguous United States.

The corporate headquarters office in Houston acts as a central bank to each of the distribution centers, which purchase, resell, and deliver items to the purchaser. The distribution centers pay for the items with a check drawn on an out-of-state bank, which maximizes the float on the check before its clearing in the banking system. Each day the bank notifies the headquarters treasurer of the total amount of the checks that have been processed. Then each day the treasurer reimburses the bank for the exact amount. Each week the treasurer informs the distribution center accounting department of the total amount of checks cleared each day during the week.

The distribution centers deposit all monies collected each day with a local bank and notify the headquarters treasurer of the amount available. The treasurer then wire transfers the money from the local bank to the headquarters bank.

The headquarters accounting department sends the distribution center a monthly report showing the daily deposits and withdrawals and calculates the balance either owed or loaned to the headquarters. Interest, based on the current prime rate, is computed on a daily basis and charged or credited to each distribution center on the last day of each month.

The bank balance is always zero in the distribution accounts, but the outstanding checks at the end of each month will equal a negative amount in the cash account in the distribution center's general ledger.

QUESTIONS AND TOPICS FOR DISCUSSION

1. Define the following terms:
   a. Demand deposits.
   b. Compensating balance.
   c. Disbursement float.
   d. Deposit float.
   e. Lockbox.
   f. Wire transfer.
   g. Depository transfer check.
   h. Zero-balance system.
   i. Draft.

2. What are the primary reasons why a firm holds a liquid asset balance?

3. Describe the methods available to a firm for expediting the collection of cash.

4. Describe the techniques available to a firm for slowing disbursements.

5. What are the primary criteria in selecting marketable securities for inclusion in a firm's portfolio?

6. What types of marketable securities are most suitable for inclusion in a firm's portfolio? What characteristics of these securities make them desirable investments for temporarily idle cash balances?

7. Describe the cost tradeoffs associated with maintaining the following:
   a. Excessive liquid asset balances.
   b. Inadequate liquid asset balances.

8. Describe the primary services a bank provides to a firm. How is the bank compensated for these services?

PROBLEMS*

NOTE: When converting annual data to daily data or vice versa in these exercises, assume there are 360 days per year.

1. Dexter Instrument Company's sales average $3.0 million per day.
   a. If Dexter could reduce the time between customers' mailing their payments and the funds' becoming collected balances by 2.5 days, determine the increase in the firm's average cash balance.
   b. Assuming that these additional funds can be invested in marketable securities to yield 8.5 percent per annum, determine the annual increase in Dexter's (pretax) earnings.

2. Exman Company performed a study of its billing and collection procedures and found that an average of 8 days elapses between the time when a customer's payment is received and when the funds become usable by the firm. The firm's *annual* sales are $450 million.
   a. Assuming that Exman could reduce the time required to process customer payments by 1.5 days, determine the increase in the firm's average cash balance.
   b. Assuming that these additional funds could be used to reduce the firm's outstanding bank loans (current interest rate is 8 percent) by an equivalent amount, determine the annual pretax savings in interest expenses.

3. The High-Rise Construction Company, located in Houston, receives large remittances (that is, progress payments) from customers with whom it has contracts. These checks are frequently drawn on New York City banks. If the checks are deposited in High-Rise's Houston bank, the funds will not become collected balances and usable by the firm until 2 *business* days later. In other words, deposits made on Monday become available for use on Wednesday, and deposits made on Friday become available to the firm on the following Tuesday. However, if High-Rise sends an employee to New York with the check and she presents it for payment at the bank upon which it is drawn, the funds will be available immediately (that is, the same day) to the firm. Assuming that High-Rise can earn 6 percent on short-term investments and that the cost of sending an employee to New York to present the check for payment is $350, determine the following:
   a. The net (pretax) benefit to the firm of using this special handling procedure for a $1 million check received on the following days:

*Problems in color have check answers provided at the end of the book.

    i. Monday.

    ii. Friday.

    Why do the answers to Parts i and ii differ?

b. The amount of a check on which the firm just "breaks even" (that is, the net pretax benefit equals zero) using this special handling procedure, assuming that the check is received on the following days:

    i. Monday.

    ii. Friday.

4. International Oil Company currently processes all its credit card payments at its domestic headquarters in Chicago. The firm is considering establishing a lockbox arrangement with a Los Angeles bank to process its payments from ten western states (California, Nevada, Arizona, Utah, Oregon, Washington, Montana, Wyoming, Colorado, and Idaho). Under the arrangement, the average mailing time for customer payments from the western region would be reduced from 3.0 days to 1.5 days, whereas check-processing and clearing time would be reduced from 6.0 days to 2.5 days. Annual collections from the western region are $172.8 million. The total number of payments received annually is 4.8 million (an average of 400,000 credit card customers × 12 payments per year). The Los Angeles bank will process the payments for an annual fee of $75,000 plus $0.05 per payment. No compensating balance will be required. Assume that the funds released by the lockbox arrangement can be invested elsewhere in the firm to yield 10 percent before taxes. The establishment of a lockbox system for the western region will reduce payment-processing costs at the Chicago office by $50,000 per year. Using this information, determine the following:

    a. The amount of funds released by the lockbox arrangement.

    b. The annual (pretax) earnings on the released funds.

    c. The annual fee International must pay to the Los Angeles bank for processing the payments.

    d. The annual *net* (pretax) benefits International Oil will receive by establishing this lockbox arrangement with the Los Angeles bank.

5. International Oil (see Problem 4) also has received a proposal from a Salt Lake City bank to set up a lockbox system for the firm. Average mailing time for checks in the western region would be reduced to 2 days under the proposal from the Salt Lake City bank, and check-processing and clearing time would also average 2.5 days. The Salt Lake City bank would not charge any fees for processng the payments, but it would require International Oil to maintain a $1,500,000 average compensating balance with the bank—funds that normally would be invested elsewhere in the firm (yielding 10 percent) and not kept in a noninterest-bearing checking account.

    a. Determine the annual *net* (pretax) benefits to International Oil of establishing a lockbox system with the Salt Lake City bank.

    b. Which of the two lockbox systems (if any) should the firm select?

6. Japanese Motors, a major importer of foreign automobiles, has a subsidiary (Japanese Motor Credit Company, or JMCC) that finances dealer inventories, as well as retail installment purchases of the company's cars. With respect to the financing of retail purchases, JMCC currently employs a centralized billing and collection system. Once a customer's credit has been approved at one of the subsidiary's 50 local branch offices, the information is forwarded to JMCC headquarters (located in Los Angeles), and the customer is issued a book of payment coupons. Each month during the life of the installment contract, the customer mails a coupon stub along with the payment to the Los Angeles office. The average mailing, processing, and check-clearing time with the present collection system is 8 days.

In an effort to reduce this collection time, JMCC is considering establishing a decentralized collection system. Under this system customers would be instructed to mail their payments to the nearest local branch office, which would then deposit the checks in a local bank and report this information to JMCC headquarters in Los Angeles. As the checks cleared in the local banks, funds would be sent each day to JMCC's central bank in Los Angeles. This decentralized collection system would reduce both mailing time and check-clearing time and reduce the average collection time to 5 days.

JMCC's annual installment collections are $792 million. Implementation of the decentralized collection system is expected to reduce collection costs at the Los Angeles headquarters by $100,000 a year compared with the currently employed centralized collection system. However, branch office collection costs are expected to *rise* by $225,000 if the decentralized system is implemented. JMCC's Los Angeles bank currently requires the firm to maintain a $250,000 balance as compensation for depositing customer payments. Compensating balances at the 50 local banks that JMCC would employ with the decentralized collection system are expected to total $500,000. Any funds released under the decentralized collections system would be used to reduce the firm's debt, which currently carries an interest rate of 7.5 percent.

Using this information, determine the annual *net* pretax benefits JMCC would realize by implementing a decentralized collection system.

7. J-Mart, a nationwide department store chain, processes all its credit sales payments at its suburban Detroit headquarters. The firm is considering the implementation of the lockbox collection system with an Atlanta bank to process monthly payments from its southeastern region. Annual credit sales collections from the region are $60 million. The establishment of the lockbox system would reduce mailing, processing, and check-clearing time from 8 days currently to 3.5 days, reduce company processing costs by $25,000 per year, and reduce the compensating balance of its Detroit bank by $200,000. The Atlanta bank would not charge any fee for the lockbox service but would require J-Mart to maintain a $500,000 compensating balance. Funds released by the lockbox arrangement could be invested elsewhere in the firm to earn 15 percent before taxes. Determine the following:
   a. The amounts of funds released by the lockbox arrangement.
   b. The annual (pretax) earnings on the released funds.
   c. The annual *net* (pretax) benefits to J-Mart of establishing the lockbox system with the Atlanta bank.

8. Peterson Electronics uses a decentralized collection system whereby customers mail their payments to one of six regional collection centers. The checks are deposited each working day in the collection center's local bank, and a depository transfer check for the amount of the deposit is mailed to the firm's concentration bank in New York. An average of 5 days elapse between the time the checks are deposited in the local bank and the time the funds become collected funds (and available for disbursements) at the concentration bank. Peterson is considering using wire transfers instead of depository transfer checks in moving funds from the six collection centers to its concentration bank. Wire transfers would reduce the elapsed time *by* 3 days. Depository transfer checks cost $0.25 (including postage), and wire transfers cost $4.00. Assume there are 250 working days per year. Peterson can earn 9 percent before taxes on any funds that are released through more efficient collection techniques. Determine the net (pretax) benefit to Peterson of using wire transfers if annual sales are as follows:
   a. $24 million.
   b. $240 million.

9. Wisconsin Paper Company is considering etablishing a zero-balance system for its payroll account. The firm pays its employees every 2 weeks on Friday (that is, 26 pay periods per year). Currently the firm deposits the necessary funds in the payroll account on Friday to cover the total amount of the checks written each pay period, which averages $1 million. However, the firm has found that the majority of the checks did not clear the payroll account until the following week. A typical distribution of when the checks clear the payroll account is as follows:

Day	Amount of Funds Clearing Payroll Account
Friday	$ 300,000
Monday	450,000
Tuesday	150,000
Wednesday	100,000
Total	$1,000,000

Assume that the firm can earn 6 percent on any funds released from its payroll account using a zero-balance system.

a. Determine the annual pretax returns the firm would realize from the use of a zero-balance system for its payroll account.

b. What additional information is necessary to make a decision concerning the desirability of establishing such a system?

ADDITIONAL READINGS AND REFERENCES

Archer, Stephen H. "A Model for the Determination of Firm Cash Balances." *Journal of Financial and Quantitative Analysis* 1 (March 1966): 1–11.

Batlin, C. A., and Hinko, Susan. "Lockbox Management and Value Maximization." *Financial Management* 10 (Winter 1981): 39–44.

Baumol, William J. "The Transactions Demand for Cash: An Inventory Theoretic Approach." *Quarterly Journal of Economics* 65 (Nov. 1952): 545–556.

Daellenbach, Hans G. "Are Cash Management Optimization Models Worthwhile?" *Journal of Financial and Quantitative Analysis* (Sept. 1974): 607–626.

Donaldson, Gordon. "Strategy for Financial Emergencies." *Harvard Business Review* (Nov.–Dec. 1969): 67–79.

Jones, R. "Face to Face with Cash Management: How One Company Does It." *Financial Executive* (Sept. 1969): 37–39.

Miller, Merton H., and Orr, Daniel. "A Model of the Demand for Money by Firms." *Quarterly Journal of Economics* 80 (Aug. 1966): 413–435.

Nauss, Robert M., and Markland, Robert E. "Solving Lockbox Location Problems." *Financial Management* 8 (Spring 1979): 21–31.

Orgler, Yair. *Cash Management: Models and Methods.* Belmont, Calif.: Wadsworth Publishing, 1970.

Searby, Frederick W. "Use Your Hidden Cash Resources." *Harvard Business Review* 46 (March–April 1968): 71–80.

Sethi, Suresh P., and Thompson, Gerald L. "Application of Mathematical Control Theory to Finance: Modeling Simple Dynamic Cash Balance Problems." *Journal of Financial and Quantitative Analysis* 5 (Dec. 1970): 381–394.

APPENDIX 19A

Cash Management Models

INTRODUCTION

Various quantitative models have been developed for determining the optimal division of a firm's liquid asset balance between cash and marketable securities. These models vary in complexity, depending partly on the assumptions made about the firm's cash flows. The simpler *deterministic* models assume that cash payments occur at a *uniform certain rate* over time. The more complex *probabilistic* or *stochastic* models assume that cash balances fluctuate from day to day in a *random* or unpredictable manner. Two of these cash management models are examined in more detail below.

DETERMINISTIC CASH MANAGEMENT MODEL

The simplest models for determining a firm's optimal cash balance are based on the deterministic economic order quantity (EOQ) model of inventory theory.[1] This basic model makes the following assumptions:

- Cash payments (outflows) occur over time at a known uniform rate of T dollars per period.

- Periodically, whenever a firm's cash balance falls to zero, C dollars of marketable securities are sold, and the funds are deposited in the firm's checking account.

- Replenishment transactions take place instantaneously.

These assumptions yield the sawtoothed pattern shown in Figure 19A–1. In

---

[1] The inventory model was first applied to cash management by William J. Baumol in "The Transactions Demand for Cash: An Inventory Theoretic Approach." *Quarterly Journal of Economics* 66 (Nov. 1952): 545–556. See Dileep R. Mehta. *Working Capital Management.* Englewood Cliffs, N.J.:Prentice-Hall, 1974, chap. 6, for a further discussion of cash management models.

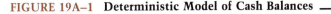

FIGURE 19A–1 Deterministic Model of Cash Balances

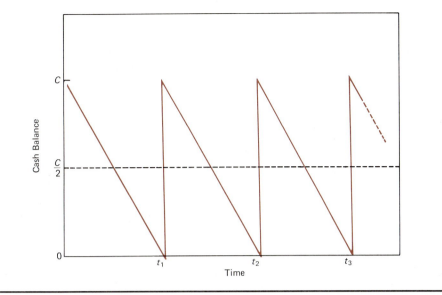

this diagram, replenishment of the firm's cash balance occurs at points t_1, t_2, t_3, and so on. Note that the firm's average cash balance under these assumptions is $C/2$ dollars.

Every time a firm sells marketable securities, it incurs a *transaction cost*. This cost includes the time the financial officer needs to make the trade and process the necessary paperwork, as well as any brokerage fees involved. The basic deterministic model assumes that the transaction cost is a *fixed* cost equal to b dollars per transaction, and that it is independent of the amount of marketable securities sold. A total of T/C transactions are needed to meet the firm's cash needs over the period. Transaction costs over the period are equal to the number of transactions, T/C, multiplied by the cost per transaction, b.

The firm incurs a *holding cost* on funds held as cash balances, which is equal to the interest forgone on marketable securities investments. The basic deterministic model assumes that funds invested in marketable securities can earn an interest rate of i percent per period. The holding cost to the firm of selling C dollars of marketable securities periodically and maintaining an average cash balance of $C/2$ dollars is equal to the average cash balance, $C/2$, multiplied by the opportunity interest rate, i.

Total costs involved in periodically selling C dollars of marketable securities and depositing these funds in the firm's checking account are equal to the sum of the transaction and holding costs:

$$\text{Total Cost} = \left(\frac{T}{C} \times b\right) + \left(\frac{C}{2} \times i\right). \qquad \textbf{(19A.1)}$$

613

The value of C that minimizes the total cost function given in Equation 19A.1 is as follows:[2]

$$C^* = \sqrt{\frac{2bT}{i}}.$$

(19A.2)

Equation 19A.2 contains a number of implications for cash management. First, the inverse relationship between C^* and i indicates that a firm should hold less liquid asset balances in cash (and correspondingly more in marketable securities) at higher interest rates on marketable securities. As i increases, so do the opportunity costs of holding a large average cash balance, $C/2$. Second, the fact that C^* increases with the *square root* of T indicates that the firm's optimal average cash balance, $C^*/2$, increases less than proportionately as cash payments (outflows) rise. This means that economies of scale are present. Thus, for example, when the firm's cash payments, T, over a given time period increase by 100 percent, the optimal average cash balance increases by only about 41 percent.

PROBABILISTIC CASH MANAGEMENT MODEL

When a firm's cash balance is assumed to fluctuate randomly from day to day, more complex models from control theory are useful in determining the optimal cash balance.[3] In the probabilistic model, transactions take place that either increase (cash receipt) or decrease (cash payment) the firm's cash balance. Transactions are assumed to be 1 unit in size.[4] The probabilities that a transaction will either increase or decrease the firm's cash balance by 1 unit are each assumed to be 0.50. Under these assumptions, the firm's cash balance moves upward or downward over time in a random manner, as shown in Figure 19A–2.

Instead of continually buying and selling marketable securities to maintain cash balances at some desired level, such as z in Figure 19A–2, the firm allows its cash balance to randomly fluctuate between *lower* (zero) and *upper* (h) limits. As long as the cash balance stays within this range, no marketable securities transactions take place. When the cash balance falls to zero (the lower limit),[5] the firm should *sell z* units of marketable securities. This ac-

---

[2]The optimal value of C is found by differentiating Equation 19A.1 with respect to C, setting the derivative equal to zero, and solving the resulting expression for C.

[3]Control theory was first applied to cash management by Merton H. Miller and Daniel Orr. "A Theory of the Demand for Money by Firms." *Quarterly Journal of Economics* 80 (Aug. 1966): 413–435. See Mehta, *op. cit.*, chap. 6 and Bibliography, for references to additional work in this area.

[4]"One unit" can be used to represent 1 dollar, 1 (hundred) dollars, 1 (thousand) dollars, and so on.

[5]The lower limit does not necessarily have to be set at zero. Any positive cash balance could be used as a lower bound on the firm's cash balance. A nonzero lower limit is necessary when the sale of securities is not instantaneous, as is assumed in the model.

FIGURE 19A–2 **Probabilistic Model of Cash Balances**

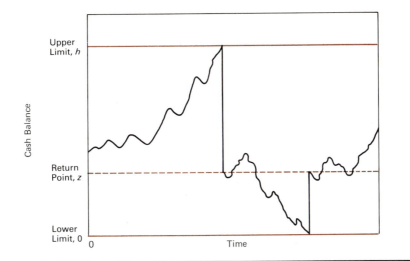

tion will *increase* the cash balance to z units. Similarly, when the cash balance rises to h (the upper limit), the firm should *purchase* $h - z$ units of marketable securities. This action will *decrease* the cash balance to z units. In both cases, z is referred to as the *return point*.

As is the case with the deterministic cash management model previously described, the cost per transaction, b, of selling (or purchasing) marketable securities is assumed to be fixed and independent of the amount of securities sold (or bought). Unlike the deterministic model, however, the number of transactions per period in the probabilistic model is a *random variable* that varies from period to period, depending on the pattern of cash balance changes. Thus, transaction costs per period are a function of the *expected* number of security transactions that take place during the period.

The percentage holding cost, i, per period, of liquid assets held in the form of cash (or checking account deposits) is the *daily* interest rate that can be earned on marketable securities investments. Unlike in the deterministic model, however, the average cash balance in the probabilistic model is a *random variable* that varies from period to period, depending on the cash flow pattern. As a result, holding costs per period are a function of the *expected* average cash balance.

Expected total costs of the cash balance return point policy previously described are equal to the sum of *expected* transaction costs and *expected* holding costs. The values of z (return point) and h (upper limit) that minimize the expected total cost function are calculated as follows:

$$z^* = \sqrt[3]{\frac{3b\sigma^2}{4i}} \, , \tag{19A.3}$$

$$h^* = 3z^* \, , \tag{19A.4}$$

615

where σ^2 is the variance of the changes in the firm's cash balance for the given period.[6] It can be shown that the *expected* average cash balance under this return point policy is equal to $\frac{4}{3} z^*$.

This model has some interesting implications for cash management. First, the optimal return point, z^*, is directly related to b and inversely related to i, which is consistent with what might be expected and analogous to the relationship between C^* and these variables in the deterministic model. Second, the return point and the expected average cash balance are directly related to the variability of the cash flows. All other things being equal, firms whose cash flows are subject to greater variation from period to period should maintain larger average cash balances.

Miller and Orr tested their model using 9 months of data for the cash balances, purchases, and sales of securities for a large industrial firm. When the decisions of the model were compared with those actually made by the firm's treasurer, it was found that the model produced average daily cash balances of only $160,000—a greater than 40 percent reduction from the $275,000 average carried by the treasurer.

USING CASH MANAGEMENT MODELS

As is apparent from this discussion, these cash management models are based on a number of simplifying assumptions. They also require the estimation of several parameters in actual applications by a particular firm. In some circumstances the assumptions in the models, difficulties in obtaining accurate estimates of the parameters, or both, may make it impractical to actually implement these specific models. Nevertheless, they are still valuable tools, since they provide the financial manager with insights into the cost tradeoffs that are involved in effective cash management.

PROBLEMS*

1. Schultz Brewing Company's forecasted cash transactions for the next year are $8 million. The cost of selling marketable securities each time the firm needs to replenish its cash balance (that is, its bank checking account) is $200. Marketable securities investments yield the firm 8 percent. Assuming that the deterministic EOQ model applies to this situation, determine the following:
   a. The optimal amount of marketable securities that the firm should periodically sell.
   b. The average cash balance for the firm.
   c. The frequency with which the firm will need to sell marketable securities (assume 360 days per year).
   d. The total cost per year of this policy.

2. The Bongo Board Company believes that the probability of its cash balances' increasing on any day is equal to the probability of their decreasing. The standard deviation of daily net cash balances is estimated to be $800. The current interest

---

[6]The "variance" is a measure of the *variability* or *dispersion* in the distribution of changes in the firm's cash balance. Variance is equal to the square of the standard deviation.
*Problems in color have check answers provided at the end of the book.

rate on marketable securities is 9 percent, and the company incurs a fixed cost of $75 each time transfers are made from the cash account to the marketable securities account and vice versa.

If the company wants to use a control limit model to direct transfers between cash and marketable securities, compute the following (assuming a 360-day year):

a. The return point.
b. The optimal upper control limit.
c. The firm's expected average cash balance.

CHAPTER 20

The Management of Accounts Receivable

A FINANCIAL DILEMMA

W. T. Grant

W. T. Grant, formerly one of the largest retailers in the United States, began to experience financial problems as early as 1973. The firm had opened a number of new discount department stores, but sales volumes and profit levels were not adequate to support this rapid expansion. In mid-1975 Grant reported losses of $177.3 million for the year ending January 1975. Rumors quickly spread regarding Grant's long-term viability, and suppliers became reluctant to provide any additional trade credit to the firm.

In September 1975 W. T. Grant called a meeting of its major suppliers for the purpose of encouraging them to ship needed Christmas merchandise. At this meeting many suppliers reported that their "factors" would no longer buy Grant's receivables.* As a result, Grant entered the critical Christmas selling season with a shortage of merchandise. On October 3, 1975, the firm declared bankruptcy, and it was liquidated in early 1976.

The decision of the factors, not the suppliers, to refrain from extending additional credit was the final straw that led to W. T. Grant's collapse. This chapter discusses the credit-granting decision of firms. It details the principles of a sound credit policy and provides the analytical tools necessary to evaluate proposed changes in this policy.

GLOSSARY OF NEW TERMS

Bad-debt loss ratio the proportion of the total receivables volume that is never collected by the firm.

Factors are financial institutions that buy the accounts receivable of suppliers on a nonrecourse basis. They charge a fee of 1.0 to 3.0 percent on the receivables purchased, and in exchange they assume the risk of nonpayment and handle the bookkeeping and collections activities. The specific nature of the services factors provide is discussed in Chapter 22.

Credit period   the length of time a credit customer has to pay the account in full.

Discount period   the length of time a credit customer has to pay the account and still be eligible to take the cash discount.

Seasonal datings   credit terms under which the buyer of seasonal merchandise is encouraged to take delivery well before the peak sales period. Payment on the purchases is deferred until after the peak sales period.

INTRODUCTION

Accounts receivable consist of the credit a firm grants its customers when selling goods or services. They take the form of either *trade credit*, which the firm extends to other firms, or *consumer credit*, which the firm extends to its ultimate consumers.

Although somewhat less liquid than either cash or marketable securities, accounts receivable constitute a major current asset for most firms.[1] Table 18–1 in Chapter 18 shows that accounts receivable make up 15 percent of the total assets of manufacturing firms and nearly 30 percent of the total assets of firms engaged in wholesale trade.

For a firm to grant credit to its customers, it has to do the following:

- Establish credit and collection policies.
- Evaluate individual credit applicants.

As we will see in this chapter, the success of a firm's credit policies can have a very significant impact on the total performance of the firm. For example, Monsanto's credit manager has estimated that a 1-day reduction in the average collection period for the firm's receivables increases its cash flow by $10 million and improves profits by $1 million.

ESTABLISHING CREDIT AND COLLECTION POLICIES

When a firm decides to extend credit to customers, it essentially is making an investment decision, namely, an investment in accounts receivable.[2] Like the decision to invest in any other type of asset, the establishment of an *optimal credit extension policy* requires the firm to examine and attempt to measure the *marginal costs* and *marginal returns* associated with a number of alternative policies. Also, as in any other investment decision, the primary

---

[1] *Liquidity* refers to the ease and speed with which an asset can be converted into cash—the most liquid of all assets—without a significant price concession.

[2] From the *customer's* perspective, credit represents a form of short-term financing known as *accounts payable.* This is discussed in more detail in Chapter 22. Considering it in yet another way—specifically, in the context of the *sources and uses of funds* statement—credit represents a *use* of funds by the selling firm and a *source* of funds to its customers. (See Chapter 8 for a review of this topic.)

goal of accounts receivable management should be to maximize shareholder wealth. Therefore, a firm should be willing to increase its investment in accounts receivable as long as the marginal returns obtained from each additional dollar of receivables investment exceed the associated marginal costs of the investment.

What are the marginal returns and costs associated with a more liberal extension of credit to the firm's customers? With respect to returns, a more liberal extension of credit presumably stimulates sales and leads to increased gross profits, assuming that all other factors (such as economic conditions, prices, production costs, and advertising expenses) remain constant. Offsetting these increased returns are several types of credit-related marginal costs, including the opportunity costs of the additional capital funds that are employed to support the higher level of receivables. Checking new credit accounts and collecting the higher level of receivables also results in additional costs for the firm. And finally, a more liberal credit policy frequently results in increased bad-debt expenses, since a certain number of new accounts are likely to fail to repay the credit that is extended to them.

In determining an optimal credit extension policy, the firm's financial manager must consider a number of major controllable variables that can be used to alter the level of receivables, including the following:

- Credit standards.
- Credit terms.
- Collection effort.

Each of these is discusssed in the sections that follow.

CREDIT STANDARDS

Credit standards are the criteria the firm uses to screen credit applicants in order to determine which of its customers should be offered credit, and how much. The process of setting credit standards allows the firm to exercise a degree of control over the "quality" of accounts accepted.[3] The quality of credit extended to customers is a multidimensional concept involving the following:

- The time a customer takes to repay the credit obligation, *given that it is repaid.*
- The probability that a customer will fail to repay the credit extended to it.

The *average collection period* serves as one measure of the promptness with which customers repay their credit obligations. It indicates the average number of days the firm must wait after making a credit sale before receiving the customer's cash payment. Obviously, the longer the average collection period, the higher the firm's receivables investment and, by extension, its cost of extending credit to customers.

---

[3]*Complete* control over the quality of accounts accepted is generally impossible due to uncertainty about future events (for example, a recession or a strike) that could make it difficult or even impossible for a customer to repay its account with the firm.

TABLE 20–1   Credit Evaluation Data Compiled by the Westchester Furniture Company

Credit Risk Group	Credit Sales ($)	Average Collection Period (Days)	Bad-Debt Loss Ratio (%)
1	900,000	25	—
2	1,100,000	30	0.5
3	400,000	45	3
4	300,000*	60	7
5	100,000*	90	13

*Estimated lost sales due to the fact that no credit is extended to customers in these risk categories.

The likelihood that a customer will fail to repay the credit extended to it is sometimes referred to as *default risk*. The *bad-debt loss ratio*, which is the proportion of the total receivables volume the firm never collects, serves as an overall, or aggregate, measure of this risk. A firm can estimate its loss ratio by examining losses on credit that has been extended to similar types of customers in the past.[4] The higher a firm's loss ratio, the greater the cost of extending credit.

For example, the Westchester Furniture Company is considering making a change in its credit standards. Before reaching any decision, the company must first determine whether such a change would be profitable. The first step in making this decision involves an evaluation of the overall credit-worthiness of the company's existing and potential customers (retailers) using various sources of information.[5] Table 20–1 illustrates the credit sales, average collection period, and loss ratio data for various credit risk groups of the company's customers.

Under its current credit policy, Westchester extends unlimited credit to all customers in Credit Risk Groups 1, 2, and 3 and no credit to customers in Groups 4 and 5, meaning that the customers in these latter two groups must submit payment along with their orders. As a result of this policy, the firm estimates that it "loses" $300,000 per year in sales from Group 4 customers and $100,000 per year in sales from Group 5 customers.

Westchester estimates that its *variable* production, administrative, and marketing costs (including credit department costs) are approximately 75 percent of total sales;[6] that is, the *variable cost ratio* is 0.75. Thus, the profit contribution ratio per dollar of sales is as follows:

$$1.00 - 0.75 = 0.25 .$$

[4]This estimation procedure assumes that the loss ratio does not change significantly over time because of changing economic conditions. Otherwise, the loss ratio should be adjusted to take account of expected future economic changes. This procedure also assumes that credit extension and repayment information is available on a sufficiently large sample of accounts to provide the firm with a reliable estimate of its loss ratio. Without this information, the firm simply has to make an "educated guess" as to the size of the loss ratio.

[5]Some of these sources of information are described later in this chapter.

[6]This analysis assumes that the collection costs for Credit Risk Group 4 customers are the same as for customers in the other groups and are included in credit department costs.

The firm's required pretax rate of return (that is, the opportunity cost) on its receivables investment is 20 percent.

One alternative the firm is considering is to relax credit standards by extending full credit to Group 4 customers. In evaluating this alternative, the firm has to analyze how this policy would affect pretax profits. If the marginal returns of this change in credit standards exceed the marginal costs, pretax profits would increase, and the decision to extend full credit to the Group 4 customers would be a good one.

Table 20–2 contains the results of this analysis. In Step A, the marginal profitability of the additional sales is calculated. Next, the cost of the additional investment in receivables is calculated in Step B.[7] In Step C, the additional bad-debt loss is computed. Finally, in Step D, the net change in pretax profits is determined by deducting the marginal costs computed in Steps B and C from the marginal returns found in Step A. Since this net change is a positive $44,000, the analysis indicates that Westchester should relax its credit standards by extending full credit to the Group 4 customers.

This analysis contains a number of both explicit and implicit assumptions that the firm must be aware of. One assumption is that *the firm has excess capacity* and thus could produce the additional output at a *constant variable cost ratio* of 0.75. If the firm currently is operating at or near full capacity, and additional output could only be obtained by paying more costly overtime rates and/or investing in new facilities, this analysis would have to be modified to take account of these incremental costs. This analysis also assumes that the average collection period of the customers in Groups 1, 2, and 3 would *not increase* once the firm began extending credit to Group 4 custom-

---

[7]Note that we have chosen to use sales value in determining the (opportunity) cost of the additional receivables investment. Disagreement exists in the finance literature concerning the measurement of the incremental investment in accounts receivable (and its associated opportunity cost) arising from a change in the firm's credit standards. Some authors contend that the relevant measure of investment is the dollar *cost* the firm has tied up in the new accounts receivable rather than the total *sales value.* The rationale for this approach is that the "profit" on the sale—that is, the difference betweeen the amount of the accounts receivable and their associated cost—would be nonexistent without the change in credit standards. Hence, no opportunity cost is incurred on this uncollected "profit." Advocates of this approach use variable cost or total cost as a measure of the amount of funds invested in accounts receivable. Other authors claim that the total sales value of the new accounts receivable is indeed the relevant measure of investment in accounts receivable. The rationale for this approach is that the opportunity cost of the increased level of accounts receivable is the return the firm could earn if it reduced accounts receivable back to its original level. In other words, considerations of symmetry require that the opportunity cost of increasing accounts receivable by a given amount should be equal to the returns that could be earned on the funds released from decreasing accounts receivable by the same amount. The interested reader should consult the following references for a more complete discussion of the issues involved: John S. Oh. "Opportunity Cost in the Evaluation of Investment in Accounts Receivable." *Financial Management* 5 (Summer 1976): 32–36; Edward A. Dyl. "Another Look at the Evaluation of Investment in Accounts Receivable." *Financial Management* 6 (Winter 1977): 67–70; Joseph C. Atkins and Yong H. Kim. "Comment and Correction: Opportunity Cost in the Evaluation of Investment in Accounts Receivable." *Financial Management* 6 (Winter 1977): 71–74; Tirlochan S. Walia. "Explicit and Implicit Cost of Changes in the Level of Accounts Receivable and the Credit Policy Decision of the Firm." *Financial Management* 6 (Winter 1977): 75–78; and J. Fred Weston and Pham D. Tuan. "Comment on Analysis of Credit Policy Changes." *Financial Management* 9 (Winter 1980): 59–63.

TABLE 20–2   Westchester Furniture Company's Analysis of the Decision to Relax Credit Standards by Extending Full Credit to Customers in Credit Risk Group 4

Step A. Additional sales	$300,000	
Marginal profitability of additional sales		
= Profit contribution ratio × Additional sales		
= 0.25 × $300,000		$75,000
Step B. Additional investment in receivables		
= Additional average daily sales* × Average collection period		
$= \dfrac{\text{Additional annual sales}}{360} \times 60$		
$= \dfrac{\$300,000}{360} \times 60$	$ 50,000	
Cost of the additional investment in receivables		
= Additional investment in receivables × Required pretax rate of return		
= 50,000 × 0.20		$10,000
Step C. Additional bad-debt loss		
= Bad-debt loss ratio × Additional sales		
= 0.07 × $300,000		$21,000
Step D. Net change in pretax profits		
= Marginal returns − Marginal costs		
= A − (B + C)		
= $75,000 − ($10,000 + $21,000)		+ $44,000

*Standard practice is to assume that there are 360 days per year.

ers. If it became known that the Group 4 customers had 60 days or more to pay their bills with no penalty involved, the Group 1, 2, and 3 customers, who normally pay their bills promptly, might also start delaying their payments. If this occurred, the analysis would have to be modified to account for such shifts. It was also assumed that the required rate of return on the investment in receivables for Group 4 *does not change* as a result of extending credit to these more risky accounts. A case can be made for increasing the required rate of return to compensate for the increased risk of the new accounts. Finally, this example (and subsequent examples in this chapter) assumed that *no change* in inventory investment takes place as a result of changes in the firm's credit policies. We should recognize that this assumption may not always be correct; that is, the management of accounts receivable and inventories cannot always be considered independently of each other. Often a higher level of sales, which results from more liberal credit standards, only can occur if the firm increases its investment in inventories. In summary, for this type of analysis to be valid and to lead to the correct decision, it must include *all* the marginal costs and benefits that result from the decision.

CREDIT TERMS

A firm's *credit terms*, or terms of sale, specify the conditions under which the customer is required to pay the firm for the credit extended to it. These conditions include the *length of the credit period* and the *cash discount* (if any) given for prompt payment, plus any special terms, such as *seasonal datings*.

Credit period   Table 20–3 contains some examples of "typical" credit terms offered by various industries. For example, credit terms of "net 30" mean that the customer has 30 days from the invoice date within which to pay the bill and that no discount is offered for early payment. A firm's credit terms are frequently determined by industry customs, and thus they tend to vary among different industries. The credit period may be as short as 7 days or as long as 6 months. Variation appears to be positively related to the length of time the merchandise is in the purchaser's inventory. For example, manufacturers of goods having relatively low inventory turnover periods, such as jewelry, tend to offer retailers longer credit periods than distributors of goods having higher inventory turnover periods, such as food products.

A firm's credit terms can affect its sales. For example, if the demand for a firm's products depends in part on the firm's credit terms, it should consider lengthening the credit period to stimulate sales. In making this type of decision, however, the firm also must consider its closest competitors. If they lengthen their credit periods, too, every firm may end up having about the same level of sales, a much higher level of receivables investments and costs, and a lower rate of return.

Analyzing the possible effects of an increase in a firm's credit period involves comparing the profitability of the increased sales that are expected to occur with the required rate of return on the additional investment in receivables. Additional bad-debt losses also must be considered. If the firm contin-

TABLE 20–3   Typical Credit Terms in Various Industries

Industry/Product	Credit Terms
Canned goods (general)	1½/10, net 60
Cigars (wholesaler)	Net 7
Decorations (interior)	6/10, net 60
Drugs (manufacturer)	2/10, net 60; 1/10, net 30
Fruits and produce (fresh)	Net 7
Furniture (upholstered)	2/30, net 60; 2/10, net 30
Groceries (wholesaler)	Net 7; C.O.D.; 1/10, net 30
Implements (agricultural)	2/10, net 60 with seasonal dating
Jewelry	5/30, net 4 months
Lumber and building materials (wholesaler)	2/10, net 30
Motors (electric, fractional horsepower)	Net 30
Petroleum (gasoline and lubricating oils)	1/10, net 30
Plumbing and heating (wholesaler)	2/10, net 30
Seeds (vegetable and flower)	1½/10, net 60; 2/10, net 60
Silverware	2/30, net 4 months
Stationery	2/10, net 60
Teas (importer)	3/10, net 4 months
Teas (wholesaler)	2/10, net 120
Textiles (velvet)	6/10, 60 days' dating with dating as of April 15 and October 15

SOURCE: Adapted from Theodore Beckman and Robert Bartels. *Credits and Collections: Management and Theory*, 8th ed. New York:McGraw-Hill, 1969, pp. 697–704. Used with permission of McGraw-Hill Book Company.

ues to accept the same quality of accounts under its lengthened credit terms, no significant change in the bad-debt loss ratio should occur.

For example, Allied Electric Company, a manufacturer of lighting fixtures, is considering changing its credit terms from "net 30" to "net 60." The firm expects sales (all on credit) to increase by about 10 percent from a current level of $2,200,000, and it expects its average collection period to increase from 35 days to 65 days. The bad-debt loss ratio should remain at 3 percent of sales. The firm's variable cost ratio is 0.75, which means that its profit contribution ratio (per dollar of sales) is $1.00 - 0.75 = 0.25$. Allied's required pretax rate of return on investments in receivables is 20 percent.

Table 20-4 contains an analysis of Allied's decision. Many of the calculations in this table are similar to those in Table 20-2, which analyzed the effects of a change in credit standards. As in Table 20-2, no account has been taken of any increase in inventory investment that may be necessary to support this increased level of sales. If inventory investment were increased as a result of this decision, it would be necessary to add an additional cost to the analysis of the effects of a change in credit terms. Specifically, the cost of the additional investment in inventory (computed as the additional inventory investment times the required pretax rate of return) would have to be determined.

The marginal returns ($55,000) computed in Step A represent the marginal profitability of the additional sales generated by the longer credit period. The

TABLE 20-4   Allied Electric Company's Analysis of the Decision to Change Its Credit Terms from "Net 30" to "Net 60"

Step A. Additional sales
$$= \text{Percent increase} \times \text{Present sales}$$
$$= 0.10 \times \$2,200,000 \qquad\qquad\qquad \$220,000$$
Marginal profitability of additional sales
$$= \text{Profit contribution ratio} \times \text{Additional sales}$$
$$= 0.25 \times \$220,000 \qquad\qquad\qquad\qquad\qquad \$55,000$$

Step B. Additional investment in receivables
$$= \text{New average balance} - \text{Present average balance}$$
$$= \frac{\text{New annual sales}}{360} \times \text{New average collection period}$$
$$- \frac{\text{Present annual sales}}{360} \times \text{Present average collection period}$$
$$= \frac{\$2,200,000 + \$220,000}{360} \times 65 - \frac{\$2,200,000}{360} \times 35$$
$$= \$436,944 - \$213,889 \qquad\qquad\qquad \$223,055$$
Cost of the additional investment in receivables
$$= \text{Additional investment in receivables} \times \text{Required pretax rate of return}$$
$$= \$223,055 \times 0.20 \qquad\qquad\qquad\qquad\qquad \$44,611$$

Step C. Additional bad-debt loss
$$= \text{Bad-debt loss ratio} \times \text{Additional sales}$$
$$= \$220,000 \times 0.03 \qquad\qquad\qquad\qquad\qquad \$\ 6,600$$

Step D. Net change in pretax profits
$$= \text{Marginal returns} - \text{Marginal costs}$$
$$= A - (B + C)$$
$$= \$55,000 - (\$44,611 + \$6,600) \qquad\qquad +\$\ 3,789$$

marginal costs (obtained in Steps B and C) consist of the cost of the additional receivables investment ($44,611) and the additional bad-debt losses ($6,600). The net increase in pretax profits (Step D) that would result from the decision to lengthen the credit period would be +$3,789. Thus, the decision would appear to be worthwhile.

Cash discounts   A *cash discount* is a discount offered on the condition that the customer will repay the credit extended within a specified period of time. A cash discount normally is expressed as a percentage discount on the net amount of the cost of goods purchased (usually excluding freight and taxes). The length of the discount period also is specified when discount terms are offered. For example, credit terms of "2/10, net 30" mean that the customer can deduct 2 percent of the invoice amount if payment is made within 10 days from the invoice date. If payment is not made by this time, the full invoice amount is due within 30 days from the invoice date. (In some cases the discount period may begin with the date of shipment or the date of receipt by the customer.) Like the length of the credit period, the cash discount varies among different lines of business.

Cash discounts are offered (or increased) in order to speed up the collection of accounts receivable and, by extension, reduce the firm's level of receivables investment and associated costs.[8] Offsetting these savings or benefits is the cost of the discounts that are taken, which is equal to the lost dollar revenues from the existing unit sales volume.

For example, the Galaxy Record Company is considering instituting a cash discount. The company currently sells to record distributors on credit terms of "net 30" and wants to determine the effect on pretax profits of offering a 1 percent cash discount on terms of "1/10, net 30." The company's average collection period is now 50 days and is estimated to decrease to 28 days with the adoption of the 1 percent cash discount policy. It also is estimated that approximately 40 percent of the firm's customers will take advantage of the new cash discount. Galaxy's annual credit sales are $2,500,000, and the company's required pretax rate of return on receivables investment is 20 percent.

Table 20–5 contains an analysis of Galaxy's proposed cash discount policy. The marginal returns ($30,556) computed in Step A represent the earnings Galaxy expects to realize on the funds released by the decrease in receivables. The marginal costs ($10,000) found in Step B represent the cost of the cash discount. Subtracting the marginal costs from the marginal returns (Step C) yields a net increase in pretax profits of $20,556, indicating that Galaxy should offer the proposed 1 percent cash discount.

Seasonal datings   Seasonal datings are special credit terms that sometimes are offered to retailers when sales are highly concentrated in one or more periods during the year. Under a seasonal dating credit arrangement, the re-

---

[8]The offering of a cash discount also may increase demand and sales, since some potential customers may view it as a form of price cut and be willing to purchase the product at this new, "lower" price. Throughout the ensuing analysis it is assumed that the cash discount is *not* perceived as a price cut and that there is no resulting increase in demand. It is also assumed that offering a cash discount will not reduce the firm's bad-debt loss by any measurable amount.

TABLE 20–5   Galaxy Record Company's Analysis of the Decision to Offer a 1 Percent Cash Discount

Step A. Decrease in average receivables balance

= Present average balance − New average balance

$$= \frac{\text{Annual sales}}{360} \times \text{Present average collection period}$$

$$- \frac{\text{Annual sales}}{360} \times \text{New average collection period}$$

$$= \frac{\$2,500,000}{360} \times 50 - \frac{\$2,500,000}{360} \times 28$$

= \$347,222 − \$194,444   \$152,778

Earnings on the funds released by the decrease in receivables

= Decrease in receivables × Required pretax rate of return

= \$152,778 × 0.20   \$30,556

Step B. Cost of cash discount

= Annual sales × Percentage taking discount × Percentage discount

= \$2,500,000 × 0.40 × 0.01   \$10,000

Step C. Net change in pretax profits

= Marginal returns − Marginal costs

= A − B

= \$30,556 − \$10,000   + \$20,556

---

tailer is encouraged to order and accept delivery of the product well ahead of the peak sales period and then to remit payment shortly after the peak sales period. The primary objective of seasonal dating is to increase sales to retailers who are unable to finance the buildup of inventories in advance of the peak selling period because of a weak working capital position, limited borrowing capacity, or both.

For example, O. M. Scott and Sons, manufacturers of lawn and garden products, has a seasonal dating plan that is tied to the growing season. Payments for winter and early spring shipments are due at the end of April and May, depending on the geographical area, and payments for shipments during the summer months are due in October or November. Payments for purchases made outside the two main selling seasons are due on the 10th of the second month following shipment. A cash discount of 0.6 percent per month is offered to encourage payments in advance of these seasonal dates. The arrangement enables and encourages dealers of lawn and garden products to be fully stocked with Scott products in advance of the peak selling periods.

Seasonal datings also can be used to reduce the manufacturer's inventory storage costs. With a seasonal sales pattern and a uniform production rate throughout the year, large inventory buildups normally occur prior to each selling period. By encouraging retailers to order in advance of these peak periods, a seasonal dating arrangement reduces these inventory buildups and lowers the manufacturer's warehouse storage costs by passing them on to the retailer. A firm considering this type of arrangement, however, should note that seasonal datings will probably not appreciably reduce the required investment. Approximately the same amount of working capital is invested in either case—consisting of receivables investment if seasonal datings are offered and inventory investment if seasonal datings are not offered. Thus, the decision to offer a seasonal dating credit plan involves a comparison of the profitability of the expected increased sales plus any savings in inventory investment and warehouse storage costs versus the required return on the additional investment in receivables.

COLLECTION EFFORT

The collection effort consists of the methods the firm employs in attempting to collect payment on past-due accounts. Some commonly used methods include the following:

- Sending notices or letters informing the customer of the past-due status of the account and requesting payment.
- Telephoning and/or visiting the customer in an effort to obtain payment.
- Employing a collection agency.
- Taking legal action against the customer.

Another approach, which is also effective in some cases, is for the firm to refuse to make new shipments to the customer until the past-due bills are paid. While the objectives of the collection effort are to speed up past-due payments and reduce bad-debt losses, the firm also must avoid antagonizing normally credit-worthy customers who may be past due for some good reason—for example, because of temporary liquidity problems. A collection effort that is too aggressive may reduce future sales and profits if customers begin buying from other firms whose collection policies are more lenient.

When determining which methods to use in its collection effort, a firm has to consider the amount of funds it has available to spend for this purpose. If the firm has a relatively small amount of money available for collecting past-due accounts, it must confine itself to less costly (and less effective) methods, such as sending letters and making telephone calls. If it has a larger budget, the firm can employ more aggressive (and, it is hoped, more effective) procedures, such as sending out representatives to personally contact past-due customers. In general, the larger a firm's collections expenditures, the shorter its average collection period and the lower its level of bad-debt losses. The benefits of additional collection efforts, however, are likely to diminish rapidly at extremely high expenditure levels.

The marginal benefits of the decision to increase collection expenditures consist of the earnings on the funds released from the receivables investment as a result of the shorter average collection period, plus the reduction in bad-debt losses. A firm should increase its collection expenditures only if these marginal benefits are expected to exceed the amount of the additional collection expenditures.

MONITORING ACCOUNTS RECEIVABLE

For a firm to effectively control its receivables investment, the credit manager must monitor the status and composition of these accounts. An *aging of accounts* is a useful monitoring technique.[9] In an aging analysis, the firm's accounts are classified into different categories based on the number of days they are past due. These classifications show both the aggregate amount of receivables and the percentage of the total receivables outstanding in each category. Aging of accounts receivable provides more information than such summary ratios as, for example, the average collection period. Comparing aging schedules at successive points in time (for example, monthly, quarterly, or semiannually) can help the credit manager monitor any changes in the "quality" of the firm's accounts.

EVALUATING INDIVIDUAL CREDIT APPLICANTS

Once a firm has established its credit and collection policies, it can use them as a basis for evaluating individual credit applicants.[10] In general, the credit evaluation process consists of these main steps:

- Gathering relevant information on the credit applicant.
- Analyzing the information obtained to determine the applicant's credit-worthiness.
- Deciding whether to extend credit to the applicant and, if so, determining the amount of the line of credit.

The credit evaluation process is limited by both time and cost. Often a firm may have only a few days—or, in some cases, only a few hours—in which to evaluate a credit request. Delaying this decision too long may result in the loss of a potential customer's order.

The credit evaluation process also is limited by the amount of resources the credit department has. The amount of time and money a firm spends on evaluating a customer's request for credit should depend on the size of the losses the company would experience if it made an incorrect decision. These potential losses stem from either denying credit to a credit-worthy customer or offering credit to a customer who is not credit-worthy. The larger the potential losses, the more time and money the firm should spend on evaluating the credit applicant.

GATHERING INFORMATION ON THE CREDIT APPLICANT

Information for evaluating the credit-worthiness of a customer is available from a variety of sources, including the following:

- Financial statements submitted by the customer.

---

[9]Aging schedules are also discussed in Chapter 6.

[10]Once these policies are established, however, they do not have to remain static over time. The financial manger should review them periodically, making appropriate modifications as dictated by changing economic conditions (for example, rising interest rates), or other circumstances.

- Credit reporting organizations.
- Banks.
- The firm's own prior experience with the customer.

These sources differ with respect to their costs and the reliability of the information they provide.

Financial statements   A firm can ask a credit applicant to supply various kinds of financial information, such as income statements and balance sheets (preferably audited ones), and possibly even a forecasted budget. This information can be used to evaluate the applicant's financial strength—and the applicant's ability to repay credit obligations. Unwillingness on the part of the applicant to supply financial statements may indicate financial weakness and suggest the need for more detailed checking, the outright refusal to extend credit, or both.

Credit reporting organizations   A number of national and local organizations collect information on the financial position and credit standing of business firms. Other companies and lending institutions that are considering extending credit to a firm may obtain information about it from these organizations, usually for a fee. The most widely known organization of this type is Dun and Bradstreet, Inc., which provides its subscribers with a credit reference book and written credit reports on individual business firms. D&B's reference book is published bimonthly and contains the names and ratings of nearly 3 million businesses located in the United States and Canada, including manufacturers, wholesalers, retailers, business services, and other types of businesses that buy regularly on credit.

Table 20–6 is a sample of the type of listing contained in the D&B reference book. The D&B rating, shown in the far right column, consists of two

TABLE 20–6   Sample Listings from the Dun and Bradstreet Reference Book _____

38	Arn... ...tone		
17 61	Asendorf Tin Shop		FF2
76 22	Austen Wes TV Service		EE2
55 41	Backers Service Station		HH2
57 12	Barber Furniture Co Inc		CC1
50 13	Beasleys Automotive	0	FF4
53 11	Beaumont & Hunt, Inc.		BB1
59 41	Bedlans Sporting Goods		DC3
51 91	Bervin Distrg Inc of Beatrice		— —
51 91	Bervin Distributing Inc		CC2
15 21	Blackwell Trenching Service		DD2
15 21	Boeckner Brothers Inc		DC2
54	Boogaarts Fairbury Inc		

SOURCE: Reprinted by permission, Dun and Bradstreet, Inc.

TABLE 20–7 Dun and Bradstreet Rating System

ESTIMATED FINANCIAL STRENGTH			COMPOSITE CREDIT APPRAISAL			
			HIGH	GOOD	FAIR	LIMITED
5A	$50,000,000	and over	1	2	3	4
4A	$10,000,000 to	49,999,999	1	2	3	4
3A	1,000,000 to	9,999,999	1	2	3	4
2A	750,000 to	999,999	1	2	3	4
1A	500,000 to	749,999	1	2	3	4
BA	300,000 to	499,999	1	2	3	4
BB	200,000 to	299,999	1	2	3	4
CB	125,000 to	199,999	1	2	3	4
CC	75,000 to	124,999	1	2	3	4
DC	50,000 to	74,999	1	2	3	4
DD	35,000 to	49,999	1	2	3	4
EE	20,000 to	34,999	1	2	3	4
FF	10,000 to	19,999	1	2	3	4
GG	5,000 to	9,999	1	2	3	4
HH	Up to	4,999	1	2	3	4

GENERAL CLASSIFICATION

ESTIMATED FINANCIAL STRENGTH			COMPOSITE CREDIT APPRAISAL		
			GOOD	FAIR	LIMITED
1R	$125,000	and over	2	3	4
2R	$50,000 to	$124,999	2	3	4

EXPLANATION

When the designation "1R" or "2R" appears, followed by a 2, 3 or 4, it is an indication that the Estimated Financial Strength, while not definitely classified, is presumed to be in the range of the ($) figures in the corresponding bracket, and while the Composite Credit Appraisal cannot be judged precisely, it is believed to fall in the general category indicated

"INV." shown in place of a rating indicates that Dun & Bradstreet is currently conducting an investigation to gather information for a new report. It has no other significance

"FB" (Foreign Branch) Indicates that the headquarters of this company is located in a foreign country (including Canada). The written report contains the location of the headquarters

ABSENCE OF A RATING--THE BLANK SYMBOL

A blank symbol (--) should not be interpreted as indicating that credit should be denied. It simply means that the information available to Dun & Bradstreet does not permit us to classify the company within our rating key and that further inquiry should be made before reaching a credit decision

ABSENCE OF A LISTING

The absence of a listing in the Dun & Bradstreet Business Information File or in the Reference Book is not to be construed as meaning a concern is non-existent, has discontinued business, nor does it have any other meaning. The letters 'NQ' on any written report mean 'not listed in the Reference Book'. The letters 'FBN' on any written report also mean that the business is not listed in the Reference Book and that the headquarters is located in a foreign country

EMPLOYEE RANGE DESIGNATIONS IN REPORTS ON NAMES NOT LISTED IN THE REFERENCE BOOK	KEY TO EMPLOYEE RANGE DESIGNATIONS		
Certain businesses do not lend themselves to a Dun & Bradstreet rating and are not listed in the Reference Book. Information on these names, however, continues to be stored and updated in the D&B Business Information File. Reports are available on these businesses but instead of a rating they carry an Employee Range Designation (ER) which is indicatwe of size in terms of number of employees. No other significance should be attached	ER 1	1000 or more	Employees
	ER 2	500- 999	Employees
	ER 3	100 - 499	Employees
	ER 4	50 - 99	Employees
	ER 5	20 - 49	Employees
	ER 6	10 - 19	Employees
	ER 7	5 - 9	Employees
	ER 8	1 - 4	Employees
	ER N		Not Available

SOURCE: Reprinted by permission, Dun and Bradstreet, Inc.

parts—the firm's estimated financial strength and its composite credit appraisal—and is based on the rating system shown in Table 20–7.

For example, the BB1 rating shown for Beaumont and Hunt, Inc., in Table 20–6 indicates that the firm has an estimated financial strength, or net worth, of $200,000 to $299,999 (Category BB in Table 20–7) and a high composite credit appraisal (Category 1 in Table 20–7).

A D&B credit report provides far more detailed information about a firm's

TABLE 20–8   Dun and Bradstreet Credit Report for Beaumont and Hunt, Inc.

Dun & Bradstreet, Inc.

This report has been prepared for:

BE SURE NAME, BUSINESS AND
ADDRESS MATCH YOUR FILE

ANSWERING
INQUIRY

SUBSCRIBER: 008-001042

THIS REPORT MAY NOT BE REPRODUCED IN WHOLE OR IN PART IN ANY MANNER WHATEVER

CONSOLIDATED REPORT

SUBSCRIBER: 008-001042

```
DUNS:  00-647-3261                DATE PRINTED              SUMMARY
BEAUMONT & HUNT, INC.            OCT 15, 198-          RATING      BB1

120 LEMOINE AVE.                 DEPARTMENT STORE      STARTED     1956
AUGUSTA, GA.  30901                                    PAYMENTS    DISC-PPT
     TEL 404 872-9664            SIC NOS.              SALES       $1,600,000
                                 53 11                 WORTH       $261,791
DANIEL T. BEAUMONT, PRES.                              EMPLOYS     20
                                                       HISTORY     CLEAR
                                                       CONDITION   STRONG
                                                       TREND       UP
```

SPECIAL EVENTS

09/10/8-   Kevin Hunt, Sec/Treas, reported a $3,000 merchandise loss in Sept 8 burglary. Loss is fully insured.

PAYMENTS   {Amounts may be rounded to nearest figure in prescribed ranges}

REPORTED	PAYING RECORD	HIGH CREDIT	NOW OWES	PAST DUE	SELLING TERMS	LAST SALE WITHIN
09/8-	Disc	17000	6000	-0-	2 10 30	1 mo.
08/8-	Ppt	6800	300	-0-	30	2 mos.
	Ppt	5000	2500	-0-	30	1 mo.
07/8-	Disc	12000	2500	-0-	30	2-3 mos.
	Ppt	2500	1000	-0-	30	2-3 mos.
	Ppt	1000	-0-	-0-	EOM	2-3 mos.
02/8-	Disc	10000	500	-0-	2 10 30	1 mo.
	Ppt	3000	500	-0-	2 10 30	1 mo.
	Ppt	1500	-0-	-0-	30	2-3 mos.

CHANGES

05/17/8-   Subject recently expanded its line of merchandise with the addition of sporting goods.

UPDATE

08/10/8-   Aug 10, 198-, Beaumont, Pres. said nine months sales through July 31 were up 10%, profits rising. Concern now employs 20.

FINANCE

02/15/8-   Fiscal statement dated October 31, 198-.

```
Cash            $   75,000       Accts Pay        $  140,510
Accts Rec.         110,746       Accruals             48,636
Inventory          285,465       Fed. & other taxes   26,714
Prepaid              1,240
                ----------                        ----------
   Current         472,451          Current          215,860
Fixt & Equip         5,200       Capital Stock         50,000
                                 Retained Earnings    211,791
                ----------                        ----------
   Total           477,651          Total            477,651
```

Annual sales $1,600,000; net income $48,000; monthly rent $2,500. Lease expires 198-. Fire insurance on mdse & fixt $300,000.
{Above figures from statement provided by Accountant: Fred Mitchell, Augusta, Ga. Prepared from books without audit.}

{CONTINUED}

SOURCE: Reprinted by permission, Dun and Bradstreet, Inc.

financial position than the reference book does. Table 20–8 shows an example of the first page of a credit report for Beaumont and Hunt, Inc. The report contains a summary of trade credit payments to existing suppliers, which can be extremely valuable to firms that are considering extending credit to Beaumont and Hunt. Also included in a typical report are financial data from the firm's balance sheet and income statement, a review of its banking relationships, historical information about the owners, and a description of its operations, including the location of facilities and the kinds of products sold.[11]

The National Association of Credit Management also fills requests for information on the repayment patterns of specific firms. In addition, a number of other organizations collect and disseminate credit information within given industries, such as the toy and furniture industries, as well as within given geographical areas, such as Chicago and New York.

Banks Many banks will assist their business customers in obtaining information on the credit-worthiness of other firms. Through its contacts with other banks, a customer's bank often can obtain detailed information on the payment patterns and financial status of the firm under investigation and pass this information on to a customer.

Prior experience with the customer A firm's prior experience with a credit customer can be extremely useful when deciding whether to continue extending credit, increase the amount of credit it currently grants to the customer, or both. If for example the customer tends to remit payments well beyond the due date and/or if the firm must employ expensive collection methods in obtaining payments, the credit analyst should weigh this unfavorable information in making the credit extension decision.

ANALYZING CREDIT-WORTHINESS AND MAKING THE CREDIT DECISION

Credit analysts ideally should obtain information about an applicant from as many sources as possible, but they also should consider the time and costs involved. Specifically, analysts should weigh the expected returns to be derived from any additional information against the cost involved in obtaining it.

A good way to structure information collection is to proceed *sequentially*, beginning with the least costly and time-consuming sources. If the results of this initial check indicate that more information is needed, the analyst can proceed to additional sources. For example, the analyst may begin by consulting the customer's past credit history with the firm. If further information is needed, the analyst then can check the D&B reference book and/or ask the applicant to supply financial statements and a list of firms that have extended trade credit to it in the past. Finally if still more information is needed, the credit analyst can request a D&B credit report on the applicant

---

[11]The reliability and comprehensiveness of this type of report depend in part on how willing a firm is to supply D&B with pertinent information.

and/or request credit checks through banks and the applicant's trade creditors.

Because a great deal of information usually is available about a credit applicant, the credit manager must be able to sort through this information and extract the key elements that will enable a reliable overall assessment of the applicant's credit-worthiness to be made. There are no magic formulas for making unerring credit decisions, but there are some traditional guidelines available that can serve as a framework for analysis. These guidelines are called the "five Cs of credit":

- Character.
- Capacity.
- Capital.
- Collateral.
- Conditions.

Character refers to the applicant's willingness or desire to meet credit obligations. Past payment patterns are useful in gauging this aspect of credit-worthiness.

Capacity refers to the applicant's ability to meet financial obligations. A reasonable estimate of an applicant's capacity usually can be obtained by examining its liquidity position and projected cash flows.

Capital constitutes the applicant's financial strength, particularly with respect to net worth. Evidence about a firm's capital usually can be obtained by evaluating the balance sheet using financial ratios.

Collateral represents the assets that the applicant may pledge as security for the credit extended to it. However, collateral is seldom a critical consideration, since the primary concern of the firm offering trade credit is the timely repayment of the credit, not foreclosing on the pledged assets.

Conditions refer to the general economic climate and its effect on the applicant's ability to pay. A good credit risk in prosperous times might be unable to make payments during a recession.

Many credit analysts feel that the first two Cs, character and capacity, are the most important only insofar as they help to insure that the firm considering extending credit will not leave anything important out of the analysis.

Numerical credit scoring systems are another technique that has been found useful, particularly in the area of consumer credit.[12] This technique allows the credit granting firm to quantitatively rate various financial and personal characteristics of the applicant, such as the length of time in business, its D&B credit rating, and its current ratio. The total credit score then can be computed based on the characteristics thought to be related to credit-worthiness. The applicant's credit score next is compared with those of other applicants, or with a minimally acceptable cutoff score. Although numerical

---

[12]These credit scoring systems normally are developed using the statistical techniques of either regression or discriminant analysis. A simplified explanation of the use of discriminant analysis in developing credit scoring systems, including a numerical example, can be found in William Beranek, *Analysis for Financial Decisions*, Homewood, Ill.: Irwin, 1963, pp. 327–334.

credit scoring systems can be beneficial in credit screening, they can be difficult and expensive to install.

Guidelines and techniques such as these can aid in the analysis of an applicant's credit-worthiness; the ability to make sound credit decisions, however, ultimately depends on the decision maker's experience and judgment in evaluating the available information.

SUMMARY

- For a firm to extend credit to its customers, it must invest a certain amount of funds in *accounts receivable.*

- A firm should change its credit extension policy only if the *marginal benefits* of the change will exceed the *marginal costs.* A more liberal credit policy normally leads to increased sales and generates marginal benefits in the form of higher gross profits. The marginal costs of this type of policy, however, include the cost of the additional funds invested in accounts receivable, any additional credit checking and collection costs, and increased bad-debt expenses.

- A financial manager can exercise control over the firm's level of receivables investment through three credit policy variables: *credit standards, credit terms,* and the *collection effort.* All three variables can be used to control the average collection period and bad-debt loss ratio.

1. Credit standards are the criteria a firm uses to screen its credit applicants.

2. Credit terms are the conditions under which customers are required to repay the credit extended to them. They specify the length of the credit period and the cash discount (if any) given for early repayment.

3. The collection effort represents the methods used in attempting to collect payment from past-due accounts.

- Evaluating individual credit applicants involves *gathering information* about the applicant, *analyzing this information* to determine the applicant's credit-worthiness, and then *making the credit decision.*

- The amount of information a firm can collect on a credit applicant is limited by both time and cost considerations. In deciding whether to seek more information about an applicant, the credit analyst should weigh the expected returns from more information against the cost of obtaining it.

- Possible sources of relevant information about a credit applicant include financial statements submitted by the applicant, credit reporting organizations (such as Dun and Bradstreet), banks, and the firm's own prior experience with the customer.

- The "five Cs of credit," which include *character, capacity, capital, collateral,* and *conditions,* can be used as credit screening guidelines to help insure that the firm will consider most of the relevant factors in the analysis and decision-making process.

Trade Credit Management at Hiram-Walker

Roy V. Campbell
Corporate Credit Manager
Hiram-Walker

INTRODUCTION

Accounts receivable constitutes one of the largest assets on Hiram-Walker's balance sheet. Our receivables represent 15 percent of our total assets. We sell our various brands of liquor and wine to approximately 8,000 customers (wholesalers and distributors) throughout the world,[13] and the quality of this trade credit is most important to our management. Our credit department, which is located in Windsor, Ontario, has overall responsibility for the granting of trade credit, as well as the collection of receivables.

SOURCES OF CREDIT INFORMATION

Hiram-Walker uses various sources of information in evaluating a credit applicant. For example, each applicant is required to complete a Customer Credit Information Form, which requests information concerning the firm's owners and officers, in addition to banking and trade references. The customer also is required to submit financial statements, preferably audited ones. Since we are not always able to get an audited statement from an applicant, in some cases we will settle for one signed by a company officer. We check credit references supplied by the applicant, particularly those from our competitors in the liquor industry. While we also check bank references, banks usually do not provide us with much usable information.

A Dun and Bradstreet report normally is obtained on each credit applicant. Although the *financial* information in these reports is often out of date and not too helpful, the *historical* information on an applicant and its management can be quite useful. Once a company has established credit with us, our sales representatives in the field are an important source of information about any changes in the structure of the company, such as changes in ownership and/or management, that might affect the decision to continue granting credit.

EVALUATING THE CREDIT APPLICANT

Time is of the essence in reaching a decision on whether or not credit should be granted to a customer. Since Hiram-Walker is in a highly

---

[13]In addition to selling to private companies, Hiram-Walker also distributes its product to various government-controlled and/or government-operated enterprises, such as the Pennsylvania State Liquor Control Board, embassies, and military installations.

competitive industry, lost sales and profits can result if the decision-making process is delayed too long. Much of the checking is done by phone, so we usually can make a decision as soon as we get the customer's financial statements. Typically, the credit granting decision is made within a few days following a request for credit.

One piece of data (from our Customer Credit Information Form) that we consider very important in reaching a decision is the length of time that the customer has been in business. In the past we have found that there is a higher incidence of bankruptcy among more recently established distributors than among older, well-established firms. Standard financial measurements, such as the debt-to-equity ratio and the rate of return on sales, are generally not too useful in evaluating credit applicants. Since many (if not most) liquor distributors are undercapitalized, it is difficult to discriminate among firms with respect to their credit-worthiness on the basis of their debt-to-equity ratios. Also, since more than one-half of liquor distributors' sales represent Federal and state taxes, their rates of return on sales are generally much less than the rates of return earned by firms in other industries. This makes it difficult to determine whether a given credit applicant is earning an "adequate" rate of return on its sales.

In analyzing an applicant's balance sheet, we are primarily concerned with the composition of the firm's debt and the security that has been given for this debt. While banks are the most commonly used source of financing, some distributors obtain financing by factoring their receivables. This indicates to us that the distributor is unable to obtain lower cost bank financing and, by extension, that there may be higher risks involved in extending credit to this customer. Consequently, we are more cautious in extending credit to firms that make extensive use of factoring.

Whenever we find loans payable to the officers of the company on the applicant's balance sheet, it is our policy to require a subordination agreement before extending credit. Such an agreement gives us a priority claim, and hence an added measure of protection, in the event that the distributor is forced into bankruptcy, liquidation, or both. In some instances we may require personal guarantees from the owners and their spouses as a further measure of protection. When a distributor is a subsidiary of a larger company, we often will ask the parent company to guarantee payment of the credit extended to the distributor.

The Uniform Commercial Code limits the extent to which we may use security agreements to protect our receivables. In addition, the Bureau of Alcohol, Tobacco, and Firearms (BATF),[14] whose rules and regulations govern the liquor industry, has ruled informally that security agreements constitute a consignment sale, which is illegal in the industry. Consequently, this credit tool is not available to us in seeking to minimize our risks. In the case of distributors whom we consider high risk, we will give our normal 30-day credit terms provided that they supply us with an irrevocable letter of credit from their bank guarantee-

---

[14]The BATF is part of the Treasury Department of the U.S. government.

ing payment of the account. If they cannot provide such a guarantee, we will only sell to them when their order is accompanied by a certified check.

It is not always possible to judge the credit-worthiness of an applicant based solely on objective factors. Whenever we are planning to grant substantial amounts of credit to a customer, we normally visit their facilities and meet the company's officers, owners, or both. The information obtained from this meeting is used in conjunction with the firm's financial data in making the credit decision.

EVALUATING THE PERFORMANCE OF THE CREDIT DEPARTMENT

When Hiram-Walker extends credit to customers, we incur costs (that is, interest) on funds invested in receivables, as well as any bad-debt costs that may arise if customers fail to pay for the merchandise shipped to them. In evaluating the performance of our credit department, management is particularly interested in the aging summary of our receivables. The aging summary provides information on the amount of receivables that are delinquent, that is, the amount that has not been paid within the normal 30-day credit period. This information aids management in determining how good a job our credit department is doing in selecting credit-worthy accounts and collecting the receivables.

Another measure of our credit department's performance is the amount of credit losses (bad debts) incurred. At Hiram-Walker we have been successful in reducing these losses to the point where they are almost insignificant as a percentage of total sales. In a typical year, for example, we might incur losses of $200,000 on sales of over $1 billion.

QUESTIONS AND TOPICS FOR DISCUSSION

1. What are the marginal returns and costs associated with a more liberal extension of credit to a firm's customers?

2. What are the major credit policy variables a firm can use to control its level of receivables investment?

3. Define the following:
   a. Average collection period.
   b. Bad-debt loss ratio.
   c. Aging of accounts.

4. Discuss at least two reasons why a firm might want to offer seasonal datings to its customers.

5. Describe the marginal costs and benefits associated with each of the following changes in a firm's credit and collection policies:
   a. Increasing the credit period from 7 to 30 days.
   b. Increasing the cash discount from 1 to 2 percent.
   c. Offering a seasonal dating credit plan.
   d. Increasing collection expenditures (and effort).

6. Describe the three steps involved in evaluating individual credit applicants.

7. What are the primary sources of information about the credit-worthiness of credit applicants?

8. Describe the "five Cs of credit" used in evaluating the credit-worthiness of a credit applicant.

9. How does a firm's required rate of return on investment enter into the analysis of changes in its credit and collection policies?

10. A firm is currently selling on credit terms of "net 30," and its accounts receivable average 30 days past due (that is, the firm's average collection period is 60 days). What credit policy variables might the firm consider changing to reduce its average collection period?

11. "The objective of the firm's credit and collection policies should be to minimize its bad-debt losses." Do you agree or disagree with this statement? Explain.

12. Discuss how each of the following factors would tend to affect a firm's credit extension policies:
    a. A shortage of working capital.
    b. An increase in output to the point where the firm is operating at full production capacity.
    c. An increase in the firm's profit margin (that is, its profit contribution ratio).
    d. An increase in interest rates (that is, borrowing costs).

Problems*

(NOTE: Assume 360 days per year when converting from annual to daily amounts or vice versa.)

1. Albert Tool Company sells to retail hardware stores on credit terms of "net 30." Annual credit sales are $15 million and are spread evenly throughout the year. The firm's variable cost ratio is 0.70. Albert's accounts receivable average $1.6 million. Using this information, determine the following for the firm:
    a. Average daily credit sales.
    b. Average collection period.
    c. Average investment in receivables.

2. National Paper Company sells on terms of "net 30." The firm's variable cost ratio is 0.80.
    a. If annual credit sales are $2 million and its accounts average 15 days *overdue*, what is National's investment in receivables?
    b. Suppose that, as the result of a recession, annual credit sales decline by 10 percent to $1.8 million, and customers delay their payments to an average of 30 days *past the due date*. What will be National's new level of receivables investment?

3. Looking back at Tables 20–1 and 20–2, evaluate the impact on the Westchester Furniture Company's pretax profits of extending full credit to the customers in Credit Risk Group 5.

4. Once again, consider the Westchester Furniture Company example. Assume that rising labor and interest costs have increased Westchester's variable cost ratio from 0.75 to 0.80 and its required pretax rate of return on receivables investment from 20 to 25 percent. Reevaluate the effect on Westchester's pretax profits of extending full credit to the customers in Credit Risk Group 4.

*Problems in color have check answers provided at the end of the book.

5. In evaluating the extension of credit to customers in Credit Risk Group 4 in the chapter (Tables 20–1 and 20–2), it was assumed that no increase in inventory investment was required to support the additional $300,000 in annual sales. Suppose instead that an additional inventory investment (that is, raw materials, work-in-process, and finished goods) of $120,000 is required to expand sales by $300,000. Furthermore, assume that Westchester's required (pretax) rate of return on inventory investment is 20 percent. Reevaluate the decision to extend credit to Group 4 customers under these new conditions.

6. Fretter Company, a wholesale distributor of jewelry, sells to retail jewelry stores on terms of "net 120." Its average collection period is 150 days. The firm is considering the introduction of a 5 percent cash discount if customers pay within 30 days. Such a change in credit terms is expected to reduce the average collection period to 108 days. Fretter expects 30 percent of its customers to take the cash discount. Annual credit sales are $6 million. Fretter's variable cost ratio is 0.667, and its required pretax return on receivables investment is 18 percent. Determine the following:
   a. The funds released by the change in credit terms.
   b. The net effect on Fretter's pretax profits.

7. In an effort to speed up the collection of receivables, Baxter Publishing Company is considering increasing the size of its cash discount by changing its credit terms from "1/10, net 30" to "2/10, net 30." Currently, the firm's collection period averages 43 days. Under the new credit terms it is expected to decline to 25 days. Also, the percentage of customers who will take advantage of the cash discount is expected to increase from the current 50 percent to 70 percent with the new credit terms. Bad-debt losses currently average 4 percent of sales and are not expected to change significantly if Baxter changes its credit policy. Annual credit sales are $3.5 million, the variable cost ratio is 60 percent and the required pretax rate of return (that is, the opportunity cost) on receivables investment is 15 percent. Assuming that Baxter does decide to increase the size of its cash discount, determine the following:
   a. The earnings on the funds released by the change in credit terms.
   b. The cost of the additional cash discounts taken.
   c. The net effect on Baxter's pretax profits.

8. The North Carolina Furniture Company (NCFC) manufactures upholstered furniture, which it sells to various small retailers in the Northeast and Midwest on credit terms of "2/10, net 60." The company currently does not grant credit to retailers with a 3 (fair) or 4 (limited) Dun and Bradstreet Composite Credit Appraisal. If NCFC were to extend credit to retailers in the "fair" category, an additional $1.2 million per year in sales could be generated. The estimated average collection period for these customers is 90 days, and the expected bad-debt loss ratio is 6 percent. Approximately 10 percent of these customers are expected to take the cash discount. NCFC's variable cost ratio is 0.70, and its required pretax rate of return on receivables investment is 20 percent. Determine the net change in NCFC's pretax profits from extending credit to retailers in the "fair" category.

9. Michigan Pharmaceuticals, Inc., a wholesale distributor of ethical drugs to local pharmacies, has been experiencing a relatively long average collection period, since many of its customers face liquidity problems and delay their payments well beyond the due date. In addition, its bad-debt loss ratio is high, since a number of pharmacies have closed because of financial difficulties. To avoid these problems in the future, Michigan Pharmaceuticals is considering a plan to *institute more stringent credit standards* to keep the average collection period and bad-debt losses from rising beyond acceptable limits. Specifically, the firm plans

to refuse to grant additional credit to any current customers that are more than 15 days past due on their payments. Such a change in credit policy is expected to reduce current annual sales of $6.5 million by 20 percent, *reduce* the average collection period from 110 days to 75 days, and lower bad-debt losses from 8 to 4 percent. The firm's variable cost ratio is 0.75, and its required pretax return on receivables investment is 15 percent. Determine the net effect of this plan on the pretax profits of Michigan Pharmaceuticals.

10. Madison Electric Company sells on terms of "net 30." Given the following information on its receivables, construct an aging of accounts schedule as of September 1, showing the percentage of accounts that are current, 1 to 30 days past due, 31 to 60 days past due, 61 to 90 days past due, and over 90 days past due. (Assume 30 days in each month.)

Account Number	Invoice Date	Amount Due
1311	August 15	$1,315
1773	July 14	721
1217	July 25	677
1319	August 14	1,711
1814	April 10	325
1713	August 5	917
1443	May 8	493
1144	June 28	211
1972	May 5	755
1011	April 21	377
1619	August 28	1,550
1322	August 13	275
1173	March 5	675
1856	August 12	695
1317	June 10	720

11. Worthington Industries, Inc. estimates that if it spent an additional $15,000 to hire another collection agent in its credit department, it could lower its bad-debt loss ratio to 3.5 perent from a current rate of 4 percent and also reduce its average collection period from 50 to 45 days. (Assume that sales remain unchanged if the agent is hired.) Worthington's annual credit sales are $5 million, and its variable cost ratio is 0.75. The firm's required pretax rate of return on receivables investment (that is, the opportunity cost) is 20 percent. Determine the net effect on Worthington's pretax profits of hiring an additional collection agent.

12. Allied Apparel Company received a large order from Websters Department Stores, which operates a chain of approximately 300 popular-priced department stores located primarily in the New England–Middle Atlantic states area. Allied is considering extending trade credit to Websters. As part of its credit check, Allied obtained Websters's balance sheets and income statements (shown here) for the last 3 years. Webster's Dun and Bradstreet rating is 5A3. A check of several of Websters's trade creditors has revealed that the firm generally takes any cash discounts when they are offered but averages about 30 days overdue on its payments to two suppliers whose credit terms are "net 30."

A Dun and Bradstreet publication entitled *Key Business Ratios* yielded the following information concerning the "average" financial ratios for firms in the same line of business as Websters:

Current assets to current liabilities	2.82
Net income after taxes to sales	1.89%
Net income after taxes to net worth	5.65%
Total liabilities to net worth	1.48

Websters Department Stores, Balance Sheet (in Thousands of Dollars)

	19X1	19X2	19X3
Assets			
Current assets:			
Cash and marketable securities	$ 9,283	$ 13,785	$ 23,893
Accounts receivable (net)	162,825	179,640	140,543
Inventories	119,860	135,191	129,707
Other	1,994	2,190	1,956
Total current assets	$293,962	$330,806	$296,099
Long-term assets:			
Buildings and equipment (net)	$ 27,426	$ 30,295	$ 30,580
Other	11,821	14,794	16,687
Total long-term assets	$ 39,247	$ 45,089	$ 47,267
Total assets	$333,209	$375,895	$343,366
Liabilities and net worth			
Current liabilities:			
Accounts payable	$ 23,637	$ 21,861	$ 15,020
Notes payable	117,010	135,929	165,299
Other	49,273	49,229	29,653
Total current liabilities	$189,920	$207,019	$209,972
Long-term liabilities:			
Debentures	$ 38,001	$ 36,101	$ 35,201
Term loan	—	28,440	29,701
Other	4,986	853	655
Total long-term liabilities	$ 42,987	$ 65,394	$ 65,557
Net worth:			
Common stock	$ 5,576	$ 5,576	$ 5,576
Preferred stock	2,580	2,580	2,580
Retained earnings	92,146	95,326	59,681
Total net worth	100,302	103,482	67,837
Total liabilities and net worth	$333,209	$375,895	$343,366

Websters Department Stores, Income Statement (in Thousands of Dollars)

Sales	$494,550	$556,132	$529,857
Cost of sales	337,580	384,899	390,980
Gross profit	$156,970	$171,233	$138,877
Selling, general, and administrative expenses	133,330	155,494	187,926
Net profit before taxes	$ 23,640	$ 15,739	$ -49,049
Income taxes	7,715	6,222	-14,741
Net income after taxes	$ 15,925	$ 9,517	$ -34,308
Dividends	6,343	6,337	1,337
Additions to retained earnings	$ 9,582	$ 3,180	$ -35,645

In evaluating Websters' application for trade credit, answer the following questions:

a. What positive financial factors would lead Allied to decide to extend credit to Websters?

b. What negative financial factors would lead Allied to decide *not* to extend credit to Webster's?

c. What additional information about Websters would be useful in performing the analysis?

ADDITIONAL READINGS AND REFERENCES

Atkins, Joseph C., and Kim, Yong H. "Comment and Correction: Opportunity Cost in the Evaluation of Investment in Accounts Receivable." *Financial Management* 6 (Winter 1977): 71–74.

Brosky, John J. *The Implicit Cost of Trade Credit and Theory of Optimal Terms of Sale.* New York: Credit Research Foundation, 1969.

Daniels, Frank, et al. "Accounts Receivable and Related Inventory Financing—Worthless Collateral?" *Journal of Commercial Bank Lending* (July 1970): 38–53.

Davis, P. M. "Marginal Analysis of Credit Sales." *Accounting Review* (Jan. 1966): 121–126.

Dyl, Edward A. "Another Look at the Evaluation of Investment in Accounts Receivable." *Financial Management* 6 (Winter 1977): 67–70.

Lewellen, Wilbur G., and Edmister, Robert O. "A General Model for Accounts Receivable Analysis and Control." *Journal of Financial and Quantitative Analysis* (March 1973): 195–206.

Long, Michael S. "Credit Screening System Selection." *Journal of Financial and Quantitative Analysis* 11 (June 1976): 313–328.

Marrah, George L. "Managing Receivables." *Financial Executive* 38 (July 1970): 40–44.

Mehta, Dileep. "The Formulation of Credit Policy Models." *Management Science* (Oct. 1968): B30–B50.

Oh, John S. "Opportunity Cost in the Evaluation of Investment in Accounts Receivable." *Financial Management* 5 (Summer 1976): 32–36.

Schwartz, Robert A. "An Economic Model of Trade Credit." *Journal of Financial and Quantitative Analysis* 9 (Sept. 1974): 643–657.

Soldofsky, R. M. "A Model for Accounts Receivable Management," *Management Accounting* (Jan. 1966): 55–58.

Walia, Tirlochan S. "Explicit and Implicit Cost of Changes in the Level of Accounts Receivable and the Credit Policy Decision of the Firm." *Financial Management* 6 (Winter 1977): 75–78.

Weston, J. Fred, and Tuan, Pham D. "Comment on Analysis of Credit Policy Changes." *Financial Management* 9 (Winter 1980): 59–63.

Wrightsman, Dwayne. "Optimal Credit Terms for Accounts Receivable." *Quarterly Review of Economics and Business* 9 (Summer 1969): 59–66.

CHAPTER 21

Inventory Management

The Bearing Corporation

The Bearing Corporation of America handles a full line of industrial bearings. The firm maintains an inventory of the most frequently used bearings, which constitute about 20 percent of its total product line. It provides other bearings on a special-order basis, because it does not want to use any more funds than necessary in "nonearning" inventory assets.

Currently the firm orders more standard "stock" bearings only when supplies are depleted. This results in an average 1-week period when the firm does not have a particular model available.

As the firm's new financial manager, you have decided to undertake an analysis of Bearing's inventory policies. Specifically, you want to estimate the various inventory-related costs, which include the cost of lost sales from customers who cannot wait for their orders and instead go to other suppliers (that is, stockout costs); the cost of placing and receiving orders; and the cost of carrying inventory. You then will use this information to determine the optimal amount of inventory to keep on hand.

This chapter develops a number of models that can assist you in making this decision.

GLOSSARY OF NEW TERMS

Carrying costs all costs associated with holding items in inventory for a period of time.

Inventory cycle the time between placement of successive orders of an item.

Lead time the time between when an order is placed for an item and when the item actually is received in inventory.

Ordering costs   all costs associated with placing and receiving an order.

Reorder point   the inventory level at which an order should be placed for replenishment of an item.

Stockout costs   the cost of lost sales associated with the inability to fill orders from inventory.

INTRODUCTION

The final category of current assets examined in this text is *inventories*. In a manufacturing firm, inventories serve as a *buffer* between the various phases of the procurement-production-sales cycle. They *uncouple* the various phases by giving the firm flexibility with respect to timing the purchase of raw materials, scheduling production facilities and employees, and meeting fluctuating and uncertain demand for the finished product. Inventories also serve similar purposes in the procurement-sales cycle of a wholesaling or retailing firm.

Table 18–1 in Chapter 18 indicates the size and relative importance of inventories. The total value of inventories represented about 18 and 39 percent of the total assets of firms in the manufacturing and retailing sectors, respectively.

This chapter explores the various types of inventories and their functions, along with the different categories of inventory-related costs. It also develops some models and procedures that can be used in efficiently managing a firm's level of inventory investment. Although financial managers do not have primary responsibility for managing a firm's inventories, they are responsible for seeing that funds are invested wisely within the firm. To perform this function, financial managers must have a good working knowledge of inventory control techniques.

TYPES AND FUNCTIONS OF INVENTORIES

Manufacturing firms generally hold three types of inventories:

- Raw materials inventories.
- Work-in-process inventories.
- Finished goods inventories.

Like any other asset, the holding of inventories constitutes an investment of funds. Determining the optimal level of inventory investment requires that the benefits and costs associated with alternative levels be measured and compared. To do this, it is necessary to determine the specific benefits associated with holding the various types of inventories.

RAW MATERIALS INVENTORIES

Raw materials inventory consists of items a firm purchases for use in its production process. It may consist of basic materials (for example, iron ore for a steel-making operation), manufactured goods (for example, jet engines for an airplane assembly operation), or both. Maintaining adequate raw materials inventories provides a firm with advantages in both purchasing and production. Specifically, the purchasing department benefits by being able to buy needed items in large quantities and take advantage of *quantity discounts* offered by suppliers. In addition, if rising prices, shortages of specific items, or both are forecasted for the future, maintaining a large stock of raw materials insures that the firm will have adequate supplies at reasonable costs.

Knowing that there will be adequate stocks of raw materials available when needed permits the production department to meet production schedules and make the most efficient use of its personnel and facilities. Thus, there are a number of valid reasons why a firm's purchasing and production departments will want to maintain large inventories of raw materials.

WORK-IN-PROCESS INVENTORIES

Work-in-process inventory consists of all items that are presently in the production cycle at some intermediate stage of completion. For example, they may be currently undergoing some type of operation (such as assembly or painting); they may be in transit between operations; or they may be stored somewhere, awaiting the next step in the production cycle.

Work-in-process inventories are a necessary part of modern industrial production systems, since they give each operation in the production cycle a certain degree of independence. This, in turn, aids in the efficient scheduling of the various operations and helps minimize costly delays and idle time. For these reasons a firm's production department will want to maintain reasonable work-in-process inventories. In general, the longer a firm's production cycle, the larger its work-in-process inventory.

FINISHED GOODS INVENTORIES

Finished goods inventory consists of those items that have completed the production cycle and are available for sale. With the exception of large-scale, specialized types of equipment—such as industrial machinery, military armaments, jet airplanes, and nuclear reactors, which are contracted for *before* they are produced—most consumer and industrial products are manufactured and stored in inventory to meet forecasted future sales.

Keeping enough finished goods inventories on hand provides significant benefits for both the marketing and the production departments. From marketing's perspective, large finished goods inventories enable it to fill orders promptly, minimize lost sales, and avoid shipment delays due to stockouts. From production's standpoint, maintaining a large finished goods inventory permits items to be manufactured in large production runs, which helps keep unit production costs low by spreading fixed set-up expenses over large volumes of output.

INVENTORY-RELATED COSTS

At the same time that there are a number of benefits to be realized from holding inventories, there are also a number of costs that must be considered, including the following:

- Ordering costs.
- Carrying costs.
- Stockout costs.

ORDERING COSTS

Ordering costs represent all the costs of placing and receiving an order. They are stated in dollars per order. When a firm is ordering from an external source, these include the costs of preparing the purchase requisition, expediting the order (for example, long distance calls and follow-up letters), receiving and inspecting the shipment, and handling payment. Factors such as an item's price and engineering complexity also affect its ordering costs. When an order is placed for an item that is manufactured *internally* within a firm, ordering costs consist primarily of *production set-up* costs, which are the expenses incurred in getting the plant and equipment ready for a production run.

In practice, the cost per order generally contains both fixed and variable components, since a portion of the cost—such as that of receiving and inspecting the order—normally varies with the quantity ordered. However, many simple inventory control models, such as the EOQ model (which is described later in this chapter), treat cost per order as fixed by assuming that these costs are independent of the number of units ordered.

CARRYING COSTS

Carrying costs constitute all the costs of holding items in inventory for a given period of time. They are expressed either in dollars per unit per period or as a percentage of the inventory value per period. Components of this cost include the following:

- Storage and handling costs.
- Obsolescence and deterioration costs.
- Insurance.
- Taxes.
- The cost of the funds invested in inventories.

Storage and handling costs include the cost of warehouse space. If the firm leases warehouse space, this cost is equal to the rent paid. If the firm owns the warehouse, this cost is equal to the value of the space in its next-best alternative use (that is, the opportunity cost). They also include depreciation on the inventory handling equipment, such as conveyors and forklift trucks, and the wages and salaries paid to warehouse workers and supervisors.

Inventories are valuable only if they can be sold. *Obsolescence costs* represent the decline in inventory value caused by technological or style changes that make the existing product less salable. *Deterioration costs* represent the decline in value caused by changes in the physical quality of the inventory, such as spoilage and breakage.

Another element of carrying cost is the cost of insuring the inventory against losses due to theft, fire, and natural disaster. In addition, the firm must pay any personal property taxes and business taxes required by local and state governments on the value of its inventories.

The *cost of funds invested in inventories* is measured by the *required rate of return* on these funds. Since inventory investments are likely to be of "average risk," the overall weighted cost of capital should be used to measure the cost of these funds. If it is felt that inventories constitute an investment with either above-average or below-average risk, some adjustment in the weighted cost of capital may be necessary to account for this difference in risk. Chapters 5 and 11 discuss the determination of risk-adjusted discount rates. Some firms incorrectly use the rate of interest on borrowed funds as a measure of this cost. This tends to understate the true cost, since a given amount of lower cost debt must be balanced with additional higher cost equity financing. Inventory investment cost constitutes an opportunity cost in that it represents the return a firm forgoes as a result of deciding to invest its limited funds in inventories rather than in some other asset. Thus, for most inventory decisions, the appropriate opportunity cost is the firm's weighted cost of capital.

The cost of carrying inventories can represent a significant cost of doing business. Table 21–1 contains the results of a survey on annual inventory carrying costs, expressed as a percentage of inventory value. This study found that *total* annual carrying costs were in the range of 10 to 24 percent for most of the firms surveyed.

Like ordering costs, inventory carrying costs contain both fixed and variable components. Most carrying costs vary with the inventory level, but a certain portion of them—such as warehouse rent and depreciation on inven-

TABLE 21–1 Inventory Carrying Costs (as a Percentage of Inventory Value)

Cost Category	Low	High
Storage space and equipment	0.5%	10%
Handling costs	1.0	5
Obsolescence and physical loss	0.5	6
Insurance	0.5	2
Taxes	0.25	6
Cost of money	6.0	11

SOURCE: S. Dowst. "You Can't Afford 'Dead Money' Inventories." *Purchasing* (Sept. 17, 1970): 73–76.

tory handling equipment—are relatively fixed over the short run. Most of the simple inventory control models, such as the EOQ model, treat the entire carrying cost as variable.

STOCKOUT COSTS

Stockout costs are incurred whenever a firm is unable to fill orders because the demand for an item is greater than the amount the firm currently has available in inventory. When a stockout in raw materials occurs, for example, stockout costs include the expenses of placing special orders and expediting incoming orders, in addition to the costs of any resulting production delays. A stockout in work-in-process inventory results in additional costs of re-scheduling and speeding production within the plant, and it also may result in lost production costs if work stoppages occur. Finally, a stockout in fin-ished goods inventory may result in the immediate loss of profits if custom-ers decide to purchase the product from another firm, and in potential long-term losses if customers decide to order from other firms in the future.

INVENTORY CONTROL MODELS

Given the significance of the benefits and costs associated with holding in-ventories, it is important that the firm efficiently control the level of inven-tory investment. There are a number of inventory control models available that can help in determining the optimal inventory level of each item. These models range from the relatively simple to the extremely complex. Their de-gree of complexity depends primarily on the assumptions made about the demand or usage for the particular item and the lead time required to secure additional stock.

In the "classical" inventory models, which include both the simpler *deter-ministic* models and the more complex *probabilistic* models, it is assumed that demand is either uniform or dispersed and *independent* over time.[1] In other words, demand is assumed either to be *constant* or to fluctuate over time due to *random* elements. These types of demand situations are common in retailing and some service operations.

The simpler deterministic inventory control models, such as the *economic order quantity* (EOQ) *model*, assume that both demand and lead times are *constant* and known with *certainty*. Thus, deterministic models eliminate the need to consider stockouts. The more complex probabilistic inventory

---

[1]*Dependent* demand models, in contrast, assume that demand tends to be "lumpy," or to occur at specific points in time. Dependent demand tends to occur when products are manufactured in lots, since all the items required to produce the lot are usually withdrawn from inventory at the same time rather than unit by unit. Dependent demand is a direct result of the demand for a "higher level" item. Material requirements planning (MRP) models have been developed to deal with the case of dependent demand. See R. B. Chase and N. J. Aquilano. *Production and Operations Management*, rev. ed. Homewood, Ill.: Irwin, 1977, chap. 9, for a discussion of MRP.

control models assume that demand, lead time, or both are *random variables with known probability distributions.*[2]

BASIC EOQ MODEL

In its simplest form, the EOQ model assumes that annual demand or usage for a particular item is known with certainty. It also assumes that this demand is stationary or uniform throughout the year. In other words, seasonal fluctuations in the rate of demand are ruled out. Finally, the model assumes that orders to replenish the inventory of an item are filled instantaneously. Given a known demand and zero lead time for replenishing inventories, there is no need for a firm to maintain additional inventories, or safety stocks, to protect itself against stockouts.

The assumptions of the EOQ model yield the saw-toothed inventory pattern shown in Figure 21–1. The vertical lines at the 0, T_1, T_2, and T_3 points in time represent the instantaneous replenishment of the item by the amount of the order quantity, Q, and the negatively sloped lines between the replenishment points represent the use of the item. Since the inventory level varies between 0 and the order quantity, average inventory is equal to one-half of the order quantity, or $Q/2$.

This model assumes that the cost of placing and receiving an order is the same for each order and independent of the number of units ordered. It also assumes that the annual cost of carrying 1 unit of the item in inventory is constant regardless of the inventory level. Total annual inventory costs, then, are the sum of ordering costs and carrying costs.[3] The primary objective of

FIGURE 21–1   Certainty Case of the Inventory Cycle

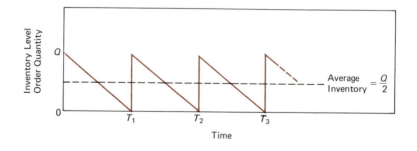

---

[2]Rather than survey all the various inventory control models in depth, this chapter develops the deterministic EOQ model to illustrate the cost tradeoffs involved in determining the optimal inventory level. It then examines the factors that must be considered and the cost tradeoffs involved in developing a probabilistic model, without using mathematical analysis or formal solution techniques.

[3]The *actual* cost of the item (that is, either the price paid for items purchased externally or the production cost for items manufactured internally) is excluded from this analysis, since it is assumed to be constant regardless of the order quantity. This assumptioon is relaxed later when quantity discounts are considered.

the EOQ model is to find the order quantity, Q, that minimizes total annual inventory costs.

Algebraic solution   In developing the algebraic form of the EOQ model, the following variables are defined:

Q = The order *quantity*, in units .
D = The annual *demand* for the item, in units .
S = The cost of placing and receiving an order, or *set-up* cost .
C = The annual cost of *carrying* 1 unit of the item in inventory .

Ordering costs are equal to the number of orders per year multiplied by the cost per order, S. The number of orders per year is equal to annual demand, D, divided by the order quantity, Q. Carrying costs are equal to average inventory, $Q/2$, multiplied by the annual carrying cost per unit, C.
    The total annual cost equation is as follows:

$$\text{Total costs} = \text{Ordering costs} + \text{Carrying costs} . \qquad \textbf{(21.1)}$$

By substituting the variables just defined into Equation 21.1, the following expression is obtained:

Total costs = (Number of orders per year × Cost per order)
              + (Average inventory × Annual carrying cost per unit) ,   **(21.2)**

or, in algebraic terms,

$$\text{Total costs} = \left(\frac{D}{Q} \times S\right) + \left(\frac{Q}{2} \times C\right) . \qquad \textbf{(21.3)}$$

    The EOQ is the value of Q that minimizes the total costs given in Equation 21.3. The standard procedure for finding this value of Q involves calculus.[4] The optimal solution, or EOQ, is equal to the following:

$$Q^* = \sqrt{\frac{2SD}{C}} . \qquad \textbf{(21.4)}$$

    Another item of information that sometimes is useful for planning purposes is the optimal length of one inventory cycle, that is, the time between placements of orders for the item. The optimal length of one inventory cycle, T^*, measured in days, is equal to the economic order quantity, Q^*, divided by the average daily demand, $D/360$ (assuming 360 days per year), as follows:

$$T^* = \frac{Q^*}{D/360} . \qquad \textbf{(21.5)}$$

---

[4]Specifically, the first derivative of Equation 21.3 with respect to Q is set equal to 0, and the equation is solved for Q.

This equation can be rewritten as follows:

$$T^* = \frac{360 \times Q^*}{D} .$$

(21.6)

The following example illustrates the use of the EOQ model. Midwest Department Stores sells Simmons mattresses through its retail outlets located in the Detroit metropolitan area. All inventories are maintained at the firm's centrally located warehouse. Annual demand for the Simmons standard-sized mattress is 3,600 units and is spread evenly throughout the year. The cost of placing and receiving an order is $31.25.

Midwest's annual carrying costs are 20 percent of the inventory value. Based on a wholesale cost of $50 per mattress, the annual carrying cost per mattress is $0.20 \times \$50 = \$10$. Because Simmons maintains a large regional distribution center in Detroit, Midwest can replenish its inventory virtually instantaneously. The firm wishes to determine the number of standard-sized mattresses it should periodically order from Simmons in order to minimize the total annual inventory costs. Substituting $D = 3{,}600$, $S = \$31.25$, and $C = \$10$ into Equation 21.4 yields the following EOQ:

$$Q^* = \sqrt{\frac{2 \times \$31.25 \times 3{,}600}{\$10}}$$

$$= 150 \text{ mattresses} .$$

Using Equation 21.3, we can calculate the total annual inventory costs of this policy:

$$\text{Total costs}^* = \frac{3{,}600}{150} \times \$31.25 + \frac{150}{2} \times \$10$$

$$= \$1{,}500 .$$

Finally, Equation 21.6 can be used to determine Midwest's optimal inventory cycle for these mattresses:

$$T^* = \frac{360 \times 150}{3{,}600}$$

$$= 15 \text{ days} .$$

Thus, the EOQ of 150 mattresses and the optimal inventory cycle of 15 days for this item indicate that Midwest should place an order for 150 mattresses every 15 days.

Graphic solution   The order quantity that minimizes total annual inventory costs can be determined graphically by plotting inventory costs (vertical axis) as a function of the order quantity (horizontal axis). As can be seen in Figure 21–2, annual ordering costs, DS/Q, vary *inversely* with the order quantity, Q, since the number of orders placed per year, D/Q, decreases as

FIGURE 21–2   Graphic Solution of the EOQ Model

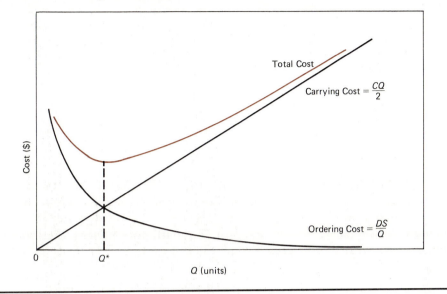

the size of the order quantity increases. Carrying costs, $CQ/2$, vary *directly* with the order quantity, Q, since the average inventory, $Q/2$, increases as the size of the order quantity increases.

The total inventory cost curve is found by vertically summing the heights of the ordering and carrying cost functions. The order quantity corresponding to the lowest point on the total cost curve is the optimal solution—that is, the economic order quantity, Q^*.

EXTENSIONS OF THE BASIC EOQ MODEL

The basic EOQ model just described makes a number of simplifying assumptions, including those pertaining to the demand for the item, replenishment lead time, the behavior of ordering and carrying costs, and quantity discounts. In practical applications of inventory control models, however, some of these assumptions may not be valid. Thus, it is important to understand how different assumptions affect the analysis and the optimal order quantity. The following sections examine what occurs when some of these assumptions are altered.

Nonzero lead time   The basic EOQ model assumes that orders to replenish the inventory of an item are filled instantaneously; that is, the lead time is zero. In practice, however, some time usually elapses between when a purchase order is placed and when the item actually is received in inventory. This lead time consists of the time it takes to manufacture the item, the time it takes to package and ship the item, or both.

If the lead time is *constant* and *known with certainty*, the optimal order quantity, Q^*, is not affected, although the time when an order should be placed is. Specifically, the firm should not wait to reorder until the end of the inventory cycle, when the inventory level reaches zero—such as at points T_1, T_2, and T_3 in Figure 21–3. Instead, the firm should place an order n *days* *prior* to the end of each cycle, n being equal to the replenishment lead time measured in days. The *reorder point* is defined as the inventory level at which an order should be placed for replenishment of an item. Assuming that demand is constant over time, the reorder point, Q_r, is equal to the lead time, n (measured in days), multiplied by daily demand:

$$Q_r = n \times \frac{D}{360},$$

(21.7)

where $D/360$ is daily demand (based on 360 days per year).

For example, if the lead time for standard-sized mattresses ordered by Midwest Department Stores (see the previous section) is 5 days, and annual demand is 3,600 mattresses, an order for 150 mattresses (that is, the economic order quantity) should be placed when the inventory level reaches the following:

$$Q_r = 5 \times \frac{3,600}{360}$$

$$= 50 \text{ mattresses},$$

which occurs on the 10th day of each inventory cycle. Five days later, on the 15th day of the inventory cycle—when the inventory level falls to zero—Midwest will receive the order, and the inventory level will again rise to 150.

Quantity discounts   Large orders often permit a firm to realize substantial per-unit savings (that is, economies of scale) in manufacturing, order processing, and shipping. Many firms encourage their customers to place large orders

FIGURE 21–3   Nonzero Replenishment Lead Time Case of an Inventory Cycle

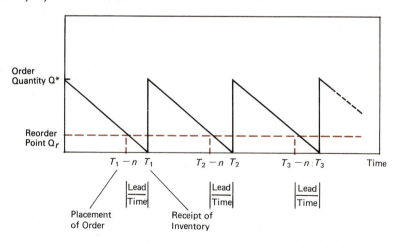

by passing on to them a portion of these savings in the form of *quantity discounts*. With a quantity discount, the cost per unit to the customer is variable and depends on the quantity ordered. The following approach can be used to determine the effect of a quantity discount on the optimal order quantity.

First, the EOQ is determined, using Equation 21.4. Next, the annual *net returns* when the order quantity is increased from the EOQ level up to the order size necessary to receive the discount are calculated.[5] The annual net returns are equal to the discount savings on the annual demand less any increase in annual inventory costs, as defined in Equation 21.3. If the annual net returns are *positive*, the optimal order quantity is the order size necessary to receive the discount; if they are not, the optimal order quantity is the smaller EOQ value.

For example, suppose Simmons offers a 2 percent, or $1, quantity discount per mattress on orders of 600 or more standard-sized mattresses. Midwest wishes to determine the optimal order quantity under these conditions. Midwest's EOQ is 150 mattresses. Thus, the annual net returns of increasing the order quantity from 150 to 600 need to be calculated.

The discount savings on annual demand are defined as follows:

$$\text{Discount savings} = \text{Discount per unit} \times \text{Annual demand} . \quad \textbf{(21.8)}$$

In Midwest's case, this is calculated as follows:

$$\text{Discount savings} = \$1 \times 3{,}600$$
$$= \$3{,}600 .$$

If Midwest were to order the discount order quantity, Q', of 600 mattresses, the carrying cost per unit, C', would be reduced to $9.80 ($49 \times 0.20). Substituting the appropriate quantities into Equation 21.3 yields the following total annual inventory costs:

$$\text{Total costs}' = \frac{3{,}600}{600} \times \$31.25 + \frac{600}{2} \times \$9.80$$
$$= \$187.50 + \$2{,}940$$
$$= \$3{,}127.50 .$$

As calculated earlier, the total annual inventory costs at the EOQ of 150 are $1,500. The *change* in annual inventory costs, Δ Total costs, resulting from the increased order quantity, is calculated as follows:

$$\Delta \text{ Total costs} = \text{Total costs}' - \text{Total costs}^*$$
$$= \$3{,}127.50 - \$1{,}500$$
$$= + \$1{,}627.50 .$$

---

[5]It is assumed that the order quantity necessary to receive a discount is *above* the EOQ level. If this were not the case, the firm would receive the discount automatically when placing an order for the amount of the EOQ.

The annual net returns are equal to the discount savings less the increased inventory costs, or $3,600 − $1,627.50 = $1,972.50. Because the annual net returns in this analysis are positive, Midwest should increase its order quantity from 150 to 600 mattresses and take advantage of the quantity discount.

PROBABILISTIC INVENTORY CONTROL MODELS

Thus far the analysis has assumed that demand or usage is uniform throughout time and known with certainty, as well as that the lead time necessary to procure additional inventory is also a fixed, known value. However, in most practical inventory management problems either (or both) of these assumptions may not be strictly correct. Typically, demand fluctuates over time due to seasonal, cyclical, and "random" influences, and imprecise forecasts of future demands are often all that can be made. Similarly, lead times are subject to uncertainty because of such factors as transportation delays, strikes, and natural disasters. Under these conditions, the possibility of stockouts exists. To minimize the possibility of stockouts and the associated stockout costs, most firms use a standard approach of adding a *safety stock* to their inventory. A safety stock is maintained to meet unexpectedly high demand during the lead time, unanticipated delays in the lead time, or both.

Figure 21–4 shows the inventory pattern characterized by these more realistic assumptions. During the first inventory cycle $(0 - T_2)$, an order to replenish the inventory is placed at T_1, when the inventory level reaches the predetermined order point. The order then is received at T_2. The second cycle $(T_2 - T_4)$ is similar to the first, except for the fact that demand exceeds the normal inventory of the item, and part of the safety stock is consumed during the lead time prior to receipt of the order at T_4. During cycle 3 $(T_4 - T_6)$, demand exceeds the normal inventory plus the safety stock and, as a result, a stockout occurs during the lead time prior to receipt of the order at T_6.

Determining the optimal safety stock and order quantities under these more realistic conditions is a fairly complex process that lies beyond the

FIGURE 21–4   Uncertainty Case of the Inventory Cycle ————————————

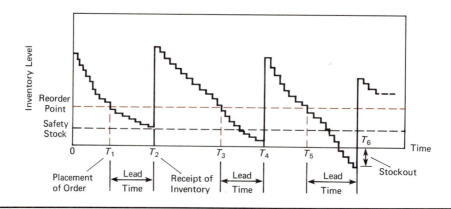

scope of this text.[6] However, the factors that have to be considered in this type of analysis can be briefly identified. All other things being equal, the optimal safety stock increases as the uncertainty associated with the demand forecasts and lead times increases. Likewise, all other things being equal, the optimal safety stock increases as the cost of stockouts increases. Determining the optimal safety stock involves balancing the *expected* costs of stockouts against the cost of carrying the additional inventory.

SUMMARY

- Inventories serve as a *buffer* between the various stages of the manufacturing firm's procurement-production-sales cycle. By uncoupling the various phases of the firm's operations, inventories provide the firm with *flexibility* in timing purchases, scheduling production, and meeting fluctuating, uncertain demand for the finished product.

- Inventory-related costs include *ordering costs, carrying costs,* and *stockout costs.* Ordering costs include all the costs of placing and receiving an order. Carrying costs include the various costs of holding items in inventory, including the cost of funds invested in inventory. Stockout costs are the costs incurred when demand exceeds available inventory, such as lost profits.

- Inventory control models usually are classified into two types: *deterministic,* if demand and lead time are known with *certainty,* and *probabilistic,* if demand and/or lead time are *random variables* with known probability distributions.

- The objective of the deterministic *economic order quantity* (EOQ) *model* is to find the order quantity that minimizes total inventory costs.

- The economic order quantity is equal to $\sqrt{2SD/C}$, where D is the annual demand; S, the fixed cost per order; and C, the annual carrying cost per unit.

- Some of the assumptions made in the basic EOQ model do not necessarily apply in practice. In the event of a nonzero lead time or quantity discounts, for example, the model must be modified.

- Probabilistic inventory control models require consideration of the possibility of *stockouts.* One approach used to handle this problem is to add a *safety stock* to the inventory.

QUESTIONS AND TOPICS FOR DISCUSSION

1. Define the following terms:
   a. Stockout.
   b. Deterministic inventory control models.
   c. Probabilistic inventory control models.

---

[6]See any of the following books for a discussion of these more complex models: H. M. Wagner, *Principles of Operations Research.* Englewood Cliffs, N.J.: Prentice-Hall, 1969; G. Hadley and T. M. Whitin, *Analysis of Inventory Systems.* Englewood Cliffs, N.J.: Prentice-Hall, 1963; and Richard I. Levin and Charles A. Kirkpatrick, *Quantitative Approaches to Management,* 4th ed. New York: McGraw-Hill, 1978.

    d. Safety stock.
    e. Lead time.
    f. Quantity discount.

2. Describe the benefits of holding the following:
    a. Raw materials inventories.
    b. Work-in-process inventories.
    c. Finished goods inventories.

3. Describe the components of carrying costs.

4. How do ordering costs for items purchased externally differ from ordering costs for items manufactured internally within the firm?

5. Describe the nature of stockout costs associated with a stockout in the following:
    a. Raw materials inventories.
    b. Work-in-process inventories.
    c. Finished goods inventories.

6. Describe the assumptions underlying the basic EOQ model.

7. In general terms, describe how to deal with each of the following conditions when determining the optimal inventory level:
    a. Constant (nonzero) replenishment lead time known with certainty.
    b. Quantity discounts.
    c. Demand and replenishment lead time subject to uncertainty.

8. How does the firm's required rate of return on investment enter into inventory decisions?

PROBLEMS*

(NOTE: Assume that there are 360 days per year when converting annual data to daily data or vice versa.)

1. Allstar Shoe Company produces a wide variety of athletic-type shoes for tennis, basketball, and running. Although sales are somewhat seasonal, production is uniform throughout the year. Allstar's production and sales average 1.92 million pairs of shoes per year. The company purchases shoelaces for its entire product line. Shoelaces are bought in lots of 10,000 pairs at a price of $800 per lot. Ordering costs are $20, including the cost of preparing the purchase order and inspecting the shipment when it arrives at the company's warehouse. Annual inventory carrying costs average 15 percent of the inventory value. Assuming that the shoelace manufacturer is located nearby and that orders are filled on the same day they are placed (that is, virtually instantaneously), determine the following:
    a. The EOQ for shoelaces.
    b. The total annual inventory costs of this policy.
    c. The frequency with which Allstar should place its orders for shoelaces.

2. Quick-Copy Duplicating Company uses 110,000 reams of standard-sized paper a year at its various duplicating centers. Its current paper supplier charges $2.00 per ream. Annual inventory carrying costs are 15 percent of inventory value. The costs of placing and receiving an order of paper are $41.25. Assuming that inventory replenishment occurs virtually instantaneously, determine the following:
    a. The firm's EOQ.
    b. The total annual inventory costs of this policy.
    c. The optimal ordering frequency.

*Problems in color have check answers provided at the end of the book.

3. Looking again at the information in Problem 2, compute and plot ordering costs, carrying costs, and total inventory costs for order quantities of 2,000, 4,000, 5,000, 5,500, 6,000, 7,000, and 9,000 reams. Connect the points on each function with a smooth curve, and determine the EOQ from the graph (and the table used in constructing the graph).

4. Suppose Quick-Copy's paper supplier (see Problem 2) offers a 1 percent discount on orders of 10,000 or more reams. Determine the net annual pretax returns to Quick-Copy of taking the discount.

5. Suppose another paper supplier offers Quick-Copy (see Problem 2) the following price discount schedule:

Quantity (Reams)	Price per Ream
0–9,999	$2.000
10,000–19,999	1.985
20,000 and up	1.975

Assuming that Quick-Copy places its order with this other supplier, determine its optimal order quantity.

6. East Publishing Company employs a high-speed printing press in its operations. A typical production run of 5,000 to 50,000 copies of a textbook can be produced in less than 1 day. The manager of the business textbook division is attempting to determine the optimal number of copies of the second editions of its financial management and managerial economics textbooks to produce. Expected annual demand for the two books are 50,000 and 22,500 copies, respectively. Furthermore, the manager does not want to produce more than a 3-year supply of either book, since these textbooks normally are revised after the 3rd year. Setup costs of getting the printing press (and bindery) ready for a production run of a given textbook are $2,500 and $2,000, respectively, for the two books. Annual carrying costs are $0.80 per copy (16 percent annual carrying charge times the $5.00 production cost per copy). For each textbook, determine the following:
   a. The economic order quantity.
   b. The total annual inventory costs.
   c. The optimal ordering frequency.

7. Arizona Instruments uses integrated circuits (ICs) in its business calculators. Its annual demand for ICs is 120,000 units. The ICs cost Arizona Instruments $10 each. The company has determined that the EOQ is 20,000 units. It takes 18 days between when an order is placed and when the delivery is received. Carrying costs are 20 percent of the inventory value. Determine the following:
   a. The optimal ordering frequency .
   b. The average inventory and annual carrying costs.
   c. The reorder point.

8. Suppose Arizona Instruments (see Problem 7) decides to maintain a 3-month safety stock of ICs to meet unexpected demand and possible shipment delays (due to strikes, shortages, and so on) from its supplier. Determine the following:
   a. The amount of safety stock, in units.
   b. The average inventory and annual carrying costs.
   c. The reorder point.

9. *Sensitivity of EOQ Model to Estimation Errors.* The calculation of the EOQ using Equation 21.4 assumes that the values of the parameters of the model (S, C, and

D) are known or can be determined precisely. In actual applications of the model, these parameter values must be estimated and are therefore subject to possible error.

This problem examines the effects of possible estimation errors on the EOQ. Refer again to Problem 2. Determine the *estimated* EOQ and the percentage error between the *estimated* EOQ and the *actual* EOQ, as determined in Problem 2; that is, $[(Q^\cdot_{est} - Q^\cdot_{act}) \div Q^\cdot_{act}] \times 100$ under each of the following conditions:

a. *Estimated* carrying costs are 13.5 percent of inventory value (10 percent less than the *actual* value of 15 percent).

b. *Estimated* ordering costs are $33 per order (20 percent less than the actual value of $41.25).

c. *Estimated* carrying costs and ordering costs are both 20 percent higher than the *actual* costs (18.0 percent and $49.50, respectively).

What conclusions can be drawn from this example concerning the size of the errors in the EOQ value relative to possible errors in estimating the parameters of the model?

10. *Variable Ordering Costs.* The basic EOQ model assumes that ordering costs are fixed and independent of the order quantity. In practice, however, ordering costs can consist of both fixed and variable components. For example, a portion of the costs of receiving and inspecting an order normally will vary with the order quantity.

This problem examines the effects of variable ordering costs on the EOQ. Assume that ordering costs consist of a fixed component, S', and a variable component, $V' \times Q$, where V' is the variable ordering cost per unit. Under this assumption, the total inventory cost equation becomes the following:

Total costs' = Number of orders per year × cost per order + Average inventory × Annual carrying cost per unit

$$= \frac{D}{Q} \times (S' + V'Q) + \frac{Q}{2} \times C$$

$$= \frac{DS'}{Q} + DV' + \frac{QC}{2}.$$

Refer again to Problem 2. Assume that the fixed cost of placing an order, S', is $41.25, and that variable ordering cost per unit, V', is $0.01.

a. Compute and plot ordering costs, carrying costs, and total costs for order quantities of 2,000, 4,000, 5,000, 5,500, 6,000, 7,000, and 9,000 reams. Connect the points on each function with a smooth curve, and determine the EOQ from the graph (and the table used in constructing the graph).

b. How does the answer to Part a compare with the EOQ values determined in Problem 2a? What conclusions can be drawn from this example concerning the effects of variable ordering costs on the EOQ?

ADDITIONAL READINGS AND REFERENCES

Hadley, G., and Whitin, T. M. *Analysis of Inventory Systems.* Englewood Cliffs, N.J.: Prentice-Hall, 1963.

Levin, Richard I., and Kirkpatrick, Charles A. *Quantitative Approaches to Management,* 4th ed. New York: McGraw-Hill, 1978.

Mehta, Dileep R. *Working Capital Management.* Englewood Cliffs, N.J. Prentice-Hall, 1974.

Schiff, Michael. "Credit and Inventory Management: Separate or Together." *Financial Executive* (Nov. 1972): 28–33.

Schiff, Michael, and Leiber, Z. "A Model for the Integration of Credit and Inventory Management." *Journal of Finance* (March 1974): 133–140.

Wagner, H. M. *Principles of Operations Research.* Englewood Cliffs, N.J.: Prentice-Hall, 1969.

CHAPTER 22

Obtaining
Short-Term Funds

A FINANCIAL DILEMMA

Penn Central: Part II

In 1968 Penn Central's restated earnings showed losses of $20 million. In 1969 consolidated losses were nearly $120 million, and sources of internal funds were $635 million short of meeting the firm's total cash needs. In an attempt to handle these cash needs, Penn Central went into the short-term credit market.

During 1968 the firm raised $50 million in short-term money in the Eurodollar market. During 1969 it managed to increase its revolving credit agreement with a group of commercial banks from $100 million to $150 million, and it raised an additional $85 million in long-term debt. During late 1969 the firm raised an additional $59 million in the Eurodollar market at a rate of 10.1 percent—*two times greater* than the firm's return on investment in good times.

In 1970, in order to meet $106 million in sinking fund obligations, the firm mortgaged nearly all remaining unsecured assets, announced plans to sell $100 million in debentures, and sold over $195 million in unsecured commercial paper. When the company announced first-quarter losses in excess of $100 million, it found that it could no longer sell commercial paper, and the $100 million debenture offering was canceled due to lack of investor interest—even though it had a 10.5 percent yield.

Finally, the commercial banks refused to provide Penn Central with the $200 million in short-term credit it had requested in order to continue operations. The banks insisted on a government loan guarantee as a condition for making the loans; when this guarantee was not forthcoming, Penn Central entered bankruptcy proceedings. It had simply run out of cash.

This chapter considers the characteristics, advantages, and disadvantages of various sources of short-term credit. As this example illustrates, short-term borrowing exposes a firm to the constant risk that this credit may not be renewed. As a result, most firms seek a balance between long-term and short-term sources of financing.

GLOSSARY OF NEW TERMS

Discount loan   a loan in which the bank deducts the interest in advance at the time the loan is made.

Factoring   the sale of a firm's accounts receivable to a financial institution known as a *factor*.

Field warehouse financing agreement   a loan agreement in which the inventory that is being pledged as collateral is segregated from the firm's other inventories and stored on the firm's premises under the control of a field warehouse company.

Floating lien   an inventory loan in which the lender receives a security interest or general claim on all of the firm's inventory.

Line of credit   an agreement that permits a firm to borrow funds up to a predetermined limit at any time during the life of the agreement.

Nonrecourse factoring   a factoring arrangement in which the factor assumes the risk of default on the purchased receivables.

Pledging of accounts receivable   a short-term borrowing arrangement with a financial institution in which the loan is secured by the firm's accounts receivable.

Prime rate   the lowest rate normally charged by banks on loans made to their most credit-worthy business customers.

Promissory note   a formal short-term credit obligation that states the amount to be paid and the due date.

Recourse factoring   a factoring arrangement in which the firm remains liable for any receivables not collected by the factor.

Revolving credit agreement   a *binding* agreement that commits a bank to make loans to a firm up to a predetermined credit limit. To obtain this type of commitment from a bank, a firm usually pays a *commitment fee* based on the unused portion of the pledged funds.

Terminal warehouse financing agreement   a loan agreement in which the inventory that is being pledged as collateral is stored in a bonded warehouse operated by a public warehousing company.

Trust receipt   a security agreement under which the borrowing firm holds the inventory and proceeds from the sale of the inventory in trust for the lender. This also is known as *floor planning*.

INTRODUCTION

A firm normally employs a combination of short-term credit and long-term debt and equity in financing its current and fixed assets. The various sources of long-term financing already have been discussed. The focus of this chapter is on the major sources of short-term credit.

Short-term credit includes all of a firm's debt obligations that originally were scheduled for repayment within 1 year.[1] Short-term credit may be either *unsecured* or *secured*.[2] In the case of unsecured short-term debt, a firm obtains credit from the lender without having to pledge any specific assets as collateral, and the lender depends primarily on the cash-generating ability of the firm to repay the debt. If the firm becomes insolvent and declares bankruptcy, the unsecured lender usually stands little chance of recovering all or even a significant portion of the amount owed.

In the case of secured short-term debt, the borrowing firm pledges certain specified assets—such as accounts receivable, inventory, or fixed assets—as collateral.[3] The Uniform Commercial Code, which was adopted by all states during the 1960s, outlines the procedures that must be followed in order for a lender to establish a valid claim on a firm's collateral.

The first step in this process involves the execution of a *security agreement*, which is a contract between the lender and the firm specifying the collateral held against the loan. The security agreement then is filed at the appropriate public office within the state where the collateral is located. Future potential lenders can check with this office to determine which assets the firm has pledged and which are still free to be used as collateral. Filing this security agreement legally establishes the lender's security interest in the collateral. If the borrower defaults on the loan or otherwise fails to honor the terms of the agreement, the lender can seize and sell the collateral to recover the amount owed. Thus, the lender in a secured short-term debt agreement has *two* potential sources of loan repayment: the firm's cash-generating ability and the collateral value of the pledged assets.

In general, firms prefer to borrow funds on an unsecured basis, since the added administrative costs involved in pledging assets as security raise the cost of the loan to the borrower. In addition, secured borrowing agreements can restrict a firm's future borrowing. Many firms are not able to obtain unsecured credit, however, For example, a firm may be financially weak or too new to justify an unsecured loan, or it may want more credit than the lender is willing to give on an unsecured basis. In any of these circumstances, the firm either must provide collateral or it will not receive the loan.

The short-term credit sources available to the firm can be either *spontaneous* or *negotiated*. Spontaneous sources, which include *trade credit, accrued expenses*, and *deferred income*, are discussed in the following sections. Later sections of this chapter consider the various negotiated sources, such as *bank credit, commercial paper, receivables loans*, and *inventory loans*.

---

[1]Short-term credit does *not* always correspond exactly to the current liabilities shown on the firm's balance sheet. Current liabilities also include that portion of long-term debt (such as term loans and mortgages) that is scheduled for repayment during the next year.

[2]Long-term debt also may be either unsecured or secured.

[3]As an alternative to pledging specific assets as collateral for a loan, a firm may get a third party to *cosign*, or *guarantee*, the loan. If the borrower defaults, the third party becomes responsible for repayment. Lenders usually will accept only financially sound third parties, such as a stockholder, supplier, or customer who has a vested interest in the firm's success.

TRADE CREDIT

Whenever a firm receives merchandise ordered from a supplier and then is permitted to wait a specified period of time before having to pay, it is receiving *trade credit*.[4] In the aggregate, trade credit is the most important source of short-term financing for business firms. Smaller firms in particular usually rely heavily on trade credit to finance their operations, because they are often unable to obtain funds from banks or other lenders in the financial markets.

Most trade credit is extended on an *open account* basis. A firm sends a purchase order to a supplier, who then evaluates the firm's credit-worthiness, using various information sources and decision criteria.[5] If the supplier decides to extend the firm credit, it ships the ordered merchandise to the firm, along with an invoice describing the contents of the shipment, the total amount due, and the terms of sale. When the firm accepts the merchandise shipped by the supplier, it in effect agrees to pay the amount due as specified by the terms of sale on the invoice. Once it has been established, trade credit becomes almost automatic and is subject to only periodic reviews by the supplier. Open account trade credit appears on the firm's balance sheet as *accounts payable.*

Promissory notes sometimes are used as an alternative to the open account arrangement. When a firm signs a promissory note, which specifies the amount to be paid and the due date, it is formally recognizing an obligation to repay the credit. A supplier may require a firm to sign a promissory note if it questions the firm's credit-worthiness. Promissory notes usually appear on the firm's balance sheet as *notes payable.*

CREDIT TERMS

Credit terms, or terms of sale, specify the conditions under which a firm is required to repay the credit that a supplier has extended to it. These conditions include the *length* and the *beginning date* of the credit period, the *cash discount* (if any) given for prompt repayment, and any *special terms*, such as *seasonal datings*.[6]

COST OF TRADE CREDIT

Trade credit is considered a *spontaneous* source of financing, since it normally expands as the volume of a firm's purchases increases. For example, suppose a company experiences increased demand for its products. As a result, the company increases purchases from suppliers by 20 percent from an average of $10,000 per day to an average of $12,000 per day. Assuming that these purchases are made on credit terms of "net 30" and that the firm waits

---

[4]If the supplier does not feel the firm is credit-worthy, it can require that payment be made either before the goods are shipped (cash before delivery, or CBD) or upon delivery of the merchandise (cash on delivery, or COD). These are cash sales and do not involve an extension of credit.

[5]These sources and criteria are discussed in Chapter 20.

[6]This topic is discussed in Chapter 20.

until the last day of the credit period to make payment, its average accounts payable outstanding (trade credit) automatically will increase by 20 percent from $300,000 ($10,000 × 30) to $360,000 ($12,000 × 30).

Because the use of trade credit is flexible, informal, and relatively easy to obtain, it is an attractive source of financing for virtually all firms, especially new and smaller firms. To make intelligent use of trade credit, however, a firm should consider the associated costs. Unlike other sources of financing, such as bank loans and bonds, which include explicit interest charges, the cost of trade credit is not always readily apparent. It may appear to be "cost-free" because of the lack of interest charges, but this reasoning can lead to incorrect financing decisions.

Obviously, someone has to bear the cost of trade credit. In extending trade credit, the supplier incurs the cost of the funds invested in accounts receivable, plus the cost of any cash discounts that are taken. Normally, the supplier passes on all or part of these costs to the firm implicitly as part of the purchase price of the merchandise, depending on market supply and demand conditions. If a firm is in a position to pay cash for purchases, it may consider trying to avoid these implicit costs by negotiating lower prices with suppliers.

If the terms of sale include a cash discount, the firm must decide whether or not to take it. If the firm *takes the cash discount*, it forgoes the credit offered by the supplier beyond the end of the discount period. Assuming that the firm takes the cash discount and wants to make maximum use of the credit offered by suppliers, it should pay its bills on the last day of the discount period. Under these conditions trade credit does represent a "cost-free" source of financing to the firm (assuming that no additional discounts are available if the firm pays cash on delivery or cash before delivery).

If the firm *forgoes the cash discount* and pays bills after the end of the discount period, a definite opportunity cost of trade credit is incurred. In calculating the cost of not taking the cash discount, it is assumed that the firm will make maximum use of extended trade credit by paying on the last day of the credit period. Paying after the end of the credit period, or *stretching accounts payable*, subjects the firm to certain other costs; these are considered in the following section.

The effective annual percentage cost of forgoing a cash discount is equal to the discount rate per period times the number of periods per year:

$$\text{Effective annual percentage cost} = \frac{\text{Percentage discount}}{100 - \text{Percentage discount}} \times \frac{360}{\text{Credit period} - \text{Discount period}}. \tag{22.1}$$

For example, suppose the Benson Company is extended $150 of trade credit on terms of "2/10, net 30." As shown is Figure 22–1, the firm either can pay the discounted amount ($147) by the end of the discount period (day 10) or the full amount of the invoice ($150) by the end of the credit period (day 30).

By *not* paying on the 10th day—that is, by forgoing the cash discount—the firm has the use of $147 (98 percent of the invoice amount) for an additional

666

FIGURE 22–1   **Benson Company's Cost of Forgoing the Cash Discount**

FIGURE 22–1   **Benson Company's Cost of Forgoing the Cash Discount**

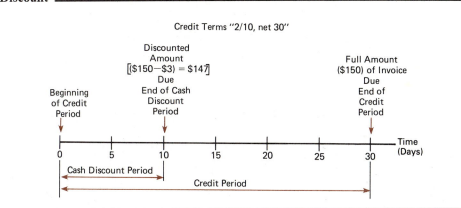

Credit Terms "2/10, net 30"

20 days and effectively pays $3 in interest. Substituting this information into Equation 22.1 yields the following:

$$\text{Effective annual percentage cost} = \frac{2}{100 - 2} \times \frac{360}{30 - 10}$$

$$= \frac{2}{98} \times \frac{360}{20}$$

$$= 36.7\% \; .$$

As this example shows, the annual cost of forgoing cash discounts can be quite high. Therefore, when making financing decisions, a firm should compare this cost to the costs of other sources of credit.

STRETCHING ACCOUNTS PAYABLE

Rather than pay suppliers within the credit period specified in the terms of sale, a firm can postpone payment of the amount due to beyond the end of the credit period. *Stretching* payments in this manner generates additional short-term financing for the firm, but this credit is not cost-free. Not only does the firm incur the costs of forgoing any cash discounts, but its credit rating may also deteriorate, along with its ability to obtain future credit. Late payment penalties or interest charges also may be added to these costs. Although occasional stretching of payables—for example, to meet a seasonal need for funds—might be tolerated by suppliers and involve little or no cost to the firm, a firm that persistently stretches accounts payable well beyond their due dates may find its trade credit cut off by suppliers, who may adopt a cash before delivery (CBD) or a cash on delivery (COD) policy when dealing with the firm in the future. Finally, when a firm develops a reputation for being consistently slow in meeting financial obligations, banks and other lenders may refuse to loan funds on reasonable terms.

ACCRUED EXPENSES AND DEFERRED INCOME

Accrued expenses and deferred income are additional spontaneous sources of unsecured short-term credit.

ACCRUED EXPENSES

Accrued expenses—such as *accrued wages, taxes,* and *interest*—represent liabilities for services rendered to the firm that have not yet been paid for by the firm. As such, they constitute an interest-free source of financing.

Accrued wages represent the money the firm owes to its employees. Accrued wages build up between paydays and fall to zero again at the end of the pay period, when the employees receive their paychecks. A firm can increase the average amount of accrued wages by lengthening the period between paydays. For example, changing from a 2-week pay cycle to a 4-week pay cycle would effectively double a firm's average level of accrued wages. Legal and practical considerations, however, limit the extent to which a firm can increase accrued wages in this manner.

The amounts of *accrued taxes and interest* a firm may accumulate also is determined by the frequency with which these expenses must be paid. For example, corporate income tax payments are normally due quarterly, and a firm can use accrued taxes as a source of funds between these payment dates. Similarly, accrued interest on a bank loan or bond issue requiring semiannual interest payments can be used as a source of financing for periods as long as 6 months. Of course, a firm has no control over the frequency of these tax and interest payments, so the amount of financing provided by these sources depends solely on the amounts of the payments themselves.

DEFERRED INCOME

Deferred income consists of payments received for goods and services that the firm has agreed to deliver at some future date. Since these payments increase the firm's liquidity and assets—namely, cash—they constitute a source of funds.

Advance payments made by customers are the primary sources of deferred income. These payments are common on large, expensive products, such as jet aircraft. Since these payments are not "earned" by the firm until delivery of the goods or services to the customers, they are recognized on the firm's balance sheet as a liability called *deferred income.*

SHORT-TERM BANK CREDIT

Commercial banks are an important source of both secured and unsecured short-term credit. In terms of the aggregate amount of short-term financing they provide to business firms, they rank second behind trade credit. While trade credit is a primary source of *spontaneous* short-term financing, bank loans represent the major source of *negotiated* short-term funds.

A major purpose of short-term bank loans is to meet the firm's seasonal needs for funds—such as financing the buildup of inventories and receivables. Bank loans used for this purpose are regarded as self-liquidating, since sale of the inventories and collection of the receivables are expected to generate sufficient cash flows to permit the firm to repay the loan prior to the next seasonal buildup.

When a firm obtains a short-term bank loan, it normally signs a promissory note specifying the amount of the loan, the interest rate being charged, and the due date. The loan agreement also may contain various protective covenants.[7] Short-term bank loans appear on the firm's balance sheet under *notes payable.*

Short-term bank financing is available under three different arrangements:

- Single loans (notes).
- Lines of credit.
- Revolving credit agreements.

SINGLE LOANS (NOTES)

Firms often need funds for short time periods to finance a particular undertaking. In such a case they may request a bank loan. This type of loan is sometimes referred to as a *note.* The length of this type of loan can range from 30 days to 1 year, with most being for 30 to 90 days.

The interest rate charged on a bank loan usually is related to the *prime rate,* which is the lowest rate banks normally charge on loans made to their most credit-worthy, or *prime,* business customers. The prime rate fluctuates over time with changes in the supply of and demand for loanable funds. During the 1970s and early 1980s, for instance, the prime rate ranged from as low as 4½ percent to as high as 21.5 percent.

The interest rate a bank charges on an individual loan at a given point in time depends on a number of factors, including the borrower's credit-worthiness relative to prime (lowest) credit risks. The interest rate often includes a premium of 1 to 2 or more percentage points higher than the prime rate, depending on how the bank loan officer perceives the borrower's overall business and financial risk. If the borrower is in a weak financial position and has overall risk that is thought to be too high, the bank may refuse to make an unsecured loan, regardless of the interest rate. When making the loan decision, the loan officer also considers the size of the checking account balance the firm maintains at the bank, the amount of other business the firm does with the bank, and the rates that competitive banks are charging on similar loans.

The effective annual percentage cost of a bank loan is also a function of when the borrower must pay the interest and whether the bank requires the borrower to maintain a compensating balance.[8]

---

[7]The section on term loans in Chapter 15 discusses these protective covenants.

[8]The effective annual percentage cost of a bank loan also can depend on the loan payment schedule. Throughout this analysis it is assumed that the firm repays the entire amount of the loan on the maturity date. Some loan agreements, however, call for repayment of the loan in monthly or quarterly *installments* over the year. Calculating the effective annual percentage cost of this type of loan requires the use of slightly different formulas from the ones described here.

Interest payments   If the interest on a loan is paid at *maturity*, the effective annual percentage cost is equal to the stated interest rate. In the case of a *discounted loan*, however, the bank deducts the interest at the time the loan is made, and thus the firm does not receive the full loan amount. In other words, the firm pays interest on funds it does not receive, and the effective annual percentage cost of the loan is greater than the stated interest rate. It can be calculated as follows:

$$\text{Effective annual percentage cost} = \frac{\text{Annual interest charges}}{\text{Funds received}} \times 100 . \quad \textbf{(22.2)}$$

For example, suppose the Wixom Company receives a 1-year, $5,000 discounted loan at an interest rate of 8 percent. The firm pays $400 interest in advance (0.08 × $5,000) and receives only $4,600 ($5,000 − $400). According to Equation 22.2, the effective annual percentage cost of the loan Wixom receives is as follows:

$$\text{Effective annual percentage cost} = \frac{\$400}{\$4,600} \times 100$$
$$= 8.7\% .$$

Compensating balances   If a loan agreement contains a covenant requiring the firm to maintain a compensating balance, the firm must keep a certain percentage of the loan amount—usually in the range of 10 to 20 percent—in its checking account with the bank. The compensating balance requirement is stated either in terms of an *absolute minimum* balance or an *average* balance over some stipulated period; borrowers prefer average balances to minimum balances. A compensating balance increases the return the bank earns on the loan and also provides the bank with a small measure of protection ("right of offset") in the event that the borrower defaults.

If the required compensating balance is *in excess* of the amount of funds that normally would be maintained in the checking account, the effective annual percentage cost of the loan is greater than the stated interest rate. It can be calculated as follows:

$$\text{Effective annual percentage cost} = \frac{\text{Annual interest charges}}{\text{Usable funds}} \times 100 , \quad \textbf{(22.3)}$$

where *usable funds* represent the net amount of the loan that the firm can spend after taking into account the amount borrowed, any required compensating balance, and the balance normally maintained in the bank account.

For example, suppose the Cutler Company obtains a $200,000 bank loan at 9 percent interest but is required to maintain a 20 percent average compensating balance. In other words, the company must maintain a $40,000 (0.20 × $200,000) average compensating balance to obtain the loan. If Cutler currently maintains a $30,000 average balance that can be used to meet the compensating balance requirement, it needs to keep an additional $10,000 in the account, and thus the loan generates $190,000 in usable funds. The interest charges on the loan are $18,000 ($200,000 × 0.09). Substituting these values into Equation 22.3 yields the following:

$$\text{Effective annual percentage cost} = \frac{\$18,000}{\$190,000} \times 100$$
$$= 9.5\% \ .$$

However, if Cutler currently has no balances in its bank account that can be used to meet the average compensating balance requirement, it has to keep $40,000 of the $200,000 loan in the checking account, and the amount of usable funds is reduced to $160,000. In this case, the effective annual percentage cost becomes significantly higher:

$$\text{Effective annual percentage cost} = \frac{\$18,000}{\$160,000} \times 100$$
$$= 11.3\% \ .$$

LINES OF CREDIT

A firm that needs funds periodically throughout the year for a variety of purposes may find it useful to negotiate a line of credit with its bank. A line of credit is an agreement that permits the firm to borrow funds up to a predetermined limit at any time during the life of the agreement. The major advantage of this type of borrowing agreement, as compared with single loans, is that the firm does not have to renegotiate with the bank every time funds are required. Instead, it can obtain funds on short notice with little or no additional justification. Another advantage to establishing a line of credit is that the firm can plan for its future short-term financing requirements without having to anticipate exactly how much it will have to borrow each month.

A line of credit usually is negotiated for a 1-year period, with renewals being subject to renegotiation each year. In determining the size of a credit line, a bank will consider a firm's credit-worthiness, along with its projected financing needs. As part of the application for a line of credit, the firm is normally required to provide the bank with a cash budget for the next year, along with current and projected income statements and balance sheets. The interest rate on a line of credit usually is determined by adding to the prime rate a premium based on the borrower's credit-worthiness. Since the prime rate normally fluctuates over time, the interest rate charged varies during the life of the agreement.

A line of credit agreement normally includes certain protective covenants. In addition to possibly including a compensating balance requirement, the loan agreement usually contains an annual "clean-up" provision requiring that the firm have no loans outstanding under the line of credit for a certain period of time each year, usually 30 to 90 days. This type of policy helps reassure the bank that the firm is using the line of credit to finance seasonal needs for funds, and not to finance permanent capital requirements. Finally, a line of credit agreement may also contain provisions (similar to those in a term loan agreement) that require the firm to maintain a minimum working capital position, limit total debt and lease financing, and restrict dividend payments.

REVOLVING CREDIT AGREEMENTS

Although a line of credit agreement does not legally commit the bank to making loans to the firm under any and all conditions, the bank normally will feel morally obligated to honor the line of credit. Some banks, however, have chosen not to provide financing to a firm when the firm's financial position has deteriorated significantly or when the bank lacks sufficient loanable funds to satisfy all its commitments. If the firm desires a guaranteed line of credit, it must negotiate a revolving credit agreement.

Under a revolving credit agreement the bank is *legally committed* to making loans to the firm up to the predetermined credit limit specified in the agreement. Revolving credit agreements differ from line of credit agreements in that they require the firm to pay a commitment fee on the unused portion of the funds. This fee is typically in the range of 0.25 to 0.50 percent. Revolving credit agreements are frequently made for a period of 2 to 3 years.

Calculating the effective annual percentage cost of funds borrowed under a revolving credit agreement is slightly more complex than with either a single loan or a line of credit. In addition to the interest rate, commitment fee, compensating balance, and the firm's normal account balance, the effective cost of a revolving credit loan also depends on the amount borrowed and the credit limit of the agreement. The effective annual percentage cost can be obtained by means of the following equation:

Effective annual percentage cost

$$= \frac{\text{Annual interest charges} + \text{Annual commitment fee}}{\text{Usable funds}} \times 100 \, . \quad \textbf{(22.4)}$$

For example, suppose the Kalamazoo Company has a $4 million revolving credit agreement with its bank. The agreement requires the company to maintain a 20 percent average compensating balance on any funds borrowed under the agreement, as well as to pay a 0.5 percent commitment fee on the unused portion of the credit line. The interest rate on borrowed funds is 8 percent. Kalamazoo's average borrowing under the agreement during the current year is expected to be $2 million. The company maintains an average of $100,000 in its account at the bank, which can be used to meet the compensating balance requirement.

To calculate the effective annual percentage cost of the revolving credit agreement, Kalamazoo must determine the amount of usable funds generated by the loan, the total interest charges, and the commitment fees. Given average borrowing of $2 million during the year, Kalamazoo is required to maintain an average compensating balance of $400,000 (0.20 × $2 million). Since the company currently maintains an average balance of $100,000, $300,000 of the loan is needed to meet the compensating balance requirement. Therefore, the amount of usable funds is $1.7 million. Interest charges on the average amount borrowed are $160,000 (0.08 × $2 million), and the commitment fee on the unused portion of the credit line is $10,000 [0.005 × ($4 million − $2 million)]. Substituting these figures into Equation 22.4 yields the following effective annual percentage cost of the loan:

$$
\begin{aligned}
\text{Effective annual percentage cost} &= \frac{\$160{,}000 + \$10{,}000}{\$1{,}700{,}000} \times 100 \\
&= \frac{\$170{,}000}{\$1{,}700{,}000} \times 100 \\
&= 10\% \ .
\end{aligned}
$$

Thus, the effective cost of the revolving credit agreement can be significantly higher than the stated interest rate.

COMMERCIAL PAPER

Commercial paper consists of short-term unsecured promissory notes issued by large, well-known corporations. Only firms with high-quality credit ratings are able to borrow funds through the sale of commercial paper. Purchasers of commercial paper include corporations with excess funds to invest, banks, insurance companies, pension funds, and other types of financial institutions.

Large finance companies, such as General Motors Acceptance Corporation (GMAC) and CIT Financial Corporation, issue sizable amounts of commercial paper on a regular basis, selling it directly to investors like those just mentioned. Large industrial, utility, and transportation firms, as well as smaller finance companies, issue commercial paper less frequently and in smaller amounts; they sell it to dealers who, in turn, sell the commercial paper to investors.

Maturities on commercial paper at the time of issue range from several days to a maximum of 9 months. Firms usually do not issue commercial paper with maturities beyond 9 months, since these issues must be registered with the Securities and Exchange Commission. The size of an issue of commercial paper can range up to several million dollars. It is usually sold to investors in multiples of $100,000 or more. Large issuers of commercial paper normally attempt to tailor the maturity and amount of an issue to the needs of investors.

Commercial paper represents an attractive financing source for large, financially sound firms, since interest rates on commercial paper issues tend to be below the prime lending rate. To successfully market commercial paper (and get an acceptable rating from Moody's, Standard and Poor's, or both), however, the firm must normally have unused bank lines of credit equal to the amount of the issue.

The primary disadvantage of this type of financing is that it is not always a reliable source of funds. The commercial paper market is impersonal. A firm that is suddenly faced with temporary financial difficulties may find that investors are unwilling to purchase new issues of commercial paper to re-place maturing issues. (This happened to Penn Central just prior to its bankruptcy.) In addition, the amount of loanable funds available in the commercial paper market is limited to the amount of excess liquidity of the various purchasers of commercial paper. During tight money periods there may not be enough funds available to meet the aggregate needs of corporate issuers of commercial paper at reasonable rates. As a result, a firm should maintain adequate lines of bank credit and recognize the risks of relying too heavily on commercial paper. Finally, a commercial paper issue usually cannot be paid off until maturity. Even if a firm no longer needs the funds from a commercial paper issue, it still must pay the interest costs.

Commercial paper is sold on a discount basis. This means that the firm receives less than the stated amount of the note at issue and then pays the investor the full face amount at maturity. The effective annual percentage cost of commercial paper depends on the maturity date of the issue and the prevailing short-term interest rates. In addition to the interest charges, borrowers also must pay a *placement fee* to the commercial paper dealer for arranging the sale of the issue. The effective annual percentage cost can be computed as follows:

$$\text{Effective annual percentage cost} = \frac{\text{Interest charges} + \text{Placement fee}}{\text{Funds received}} \times \frac{360}{\text{Maturity length (days)}} \times 100 . \quad \text{(22.5)}$$

The funds received are equal to the face amount of the issue less the interest charges and placement fee. The second term on the right-hand side of Equation 22.5—360/maturity length (days)—is used to convert the stated interest charges and placement fee to an annual rate.

For example, suppose Mammouth Steel Company is considering issuing $10 million in commercial paper. A commercial paper dealer has indicated that Mammouth could sell a 90-day issue at an interest rate of 9.5 percent. The placement fee would be $25,000. Using Equation 22.5, the effective annual percentage cost of this commercial paper issue is as follows:

$$
\begin{aligned}
\text{Effective annual percentage cost} &= \frac{(0.095/4)\$10,000,000 + \$25,000}{\$10,000,000 - (0.095/4)\$10,000,000 - \$25,000} \\
&\quad \times \frac{360}{90} \times 100 \\
&= \frac{\$262,500}{\$9,737,500} \times 4 \times 100 \\
&= 10.78\% .
\end{aligned}
$$

The interest rate (9.5 percent, or 0.095) in this calculation is divided by 4, since the interest is to be paid for only one-fourth (90 days) of the year.

ACCOUNTS RECEIVABLE LOANS

Accounts receivable are one of the most commonly used forms of collateral for *secured* short-term borrowing. From the lender's standpoint, accounts receivable represent a desirable form of collateral, since they are relatively liquid and their value is relatively easy to recover if the borrower becomes insolvent. In addition, accounts receivable involve documents representing customer obligations rather than cumbersome physical assets. Offsetting these advantages, however, are potential difficulties. One disadvantage is that the borrower may attempt to defraud the lender by pledging nonexistent accounts. Also, the recovery process in the event of insolvency may be hampered if the customer who owes the receivables returns the merchandise or files a claim alleging that the merchandise is defective. Finally, the administrative costs of processing the receivables can be high, particularly when there is a large number of invoices involving small dollar amounts.

Nevertheless, many firms use accounts receivable as collateral for short-term financing by either *pledging* their receivables or *factoring* them.

PLEDGING ACCOUNTS RECEIVABLE

The pledging process begins with a loan agreement specifying the procedures and terms under which the lender will advance funds to the firm. When accounts receivable are pledged, the firm retains title to the receivables and continues to carry them on its balance sheet. However, the pledged status of the firm's receivables should be disclosed in a footnote to the balance sheet. A firm that has pledged receivables as collateral is required to repay the loan, even if it is unable to collect the pledged receivables. In other words, the firm assumes the default risk. Both commercial banks and finance companies make loans secured by accounts receivable.

Once the pledging agreement has been established, the firm periodically sends the lender a group of invoices along with the loan request. Upon receipt of the customer invoices, the lender investigates the credit-worthiness of the accounts to determine which are acceptable as collateral. The percentage of funds that the lender will advance against the collateral depends on the quality of the receivables and the financial position of the firm. The percentage normally ranges from 50 to 90 percent of the face amount of the receivables pledged. The firm then is required to sign a promissory note and a security agreement, after which it receives the funds from the lender.

Most receivables loans are made on a *nonnotification basis*, which means the customer is not notified that the receivable has been pledged by the firm. The customer continues to make payments directly to the firm. To protect itself against possible fraud, the lender usually requires the firm to forward all customer payments in the form in which they are received. In addition, the borrower is usually subject to a periodic audit to insure the integrity of its receivables and payments. Receivables that remain unpaid for 60 days or so usually must be replaced by the borrower.

When loans are made on a *notification basis*, the customer is instructed to make payments directly to the lender. Whereas firms obviously prefer to borrow on a nonnotification basis, this latter arrangement provides the lender with more protection against possible fraud.

The customer payments received by the lender are used to reduce the firm's loan balance and eventually repay the loan. Receivables loans can be a continuous source of financing for the firm, however, provided that new receivables are pledged to the lender as existing accounts are collected. By periodically sending the lender new receivables, the company can maintain its collateral base and obtain a relatively constant amount of financing.

Receivables loans can be an attractive source of financing for a company that does not have access to unsecured credit. As the company grows and its level of receivables increases, it can normally obtain larger receivables loans fairly easily. And, unlike line of credit agreements, receivables loans usually do not have compensating balance or "clean-up" provisions.

The effective annual percentage cost of a loan in which receivables are pledged as collateral includes both the interest expense on the unpaid balance of the loan and the service fees charged for processing the receivables. Typically, the interest rate ranges from 2 to 5 percent above the prime rate, and service fees are approximately 1 to 2 percent of the amount of the pledged receivables. The services performed by the lender under a pledging agreement can include credit checking, keeping records of the pledged accounts and collections, and monitoring the agreement. This type of financing can be quite expensive for the firm.

FACTORING ACCOUNTS RECEIVABLE

Factoring receivables involves the outright sale of the firm's receivables to a financial institution known as a *factor*. A number of so-called old-line factors, in addition to some commercial banks and finance companies, are engaged in factoring receivables. When receivables are factored, title to them is transferred to the factor, and the receivables no longer appear on the firm's balance sheet.

The factoring process begins with an agreement that specifies the procedures for factoring the receivables and the terms under which the factor will advance funds to the firm. Under the normal factoring arrangement, the firm sends the customer order to the factor for credit checking and approval *before* filling it. The factor maintains a credit department to perform the credit checking and collection functions. Once the factor decides that the customer is an acceptable risk and agrees to purchase the receivable, the firm ships the order to the customer. The customer usually is notified that its account has been sold and is instructed to make payments directly to the factor.

Most factoring of receivables is done on a *nonrecourse* basis; in other words, the factor assumes the risk of default.[9] If the factor refuses to purchase a given receivable, the firm still can ship the order to the customer and as-

---

[9]If the receivables are sold to the factor on a *recourse* basis, the firm is liable for losses on any receivables that are not collected by the factor.

sume the default risk itself, but this receivable does not provide any collateral for additional credit.

In the typical factoring agreement, the firm receives payment from the factor after the normal collection or due date of the factored accounts. If the firm wants to receive the funds prior to this date, it usually can obtain an advance from the factor. Therefore, in addition to credit checking, collecting receivables, and bearing default risk , the factor also performs a lending function and assesses specific charges for each service provided. The maximum advance the firm can obtain from the factor is limited to the amount of factored receivables *less* the factoring commission, interest expense, and reserve that the factor withholds to cover any returns or allowances by customers. The reserve is usually 5 to 10 percent of the factored receivables and is paid to the firm after the factor collects the receivables.

The factor charges a factoring commission, or service fee, of 1 to 3 percent of the factored receivables to cover the costs of credit checking, collection, and bad-debt losses. The rate charged depends on the total volume of the receivables, the size of the individual receivables, and the default risk involved. The factor charges an interest rate of 2 to 5 percent above the prime rate on advances to the firm. These costs are somewhat offset by a number of internal savings that a firm can realize through factoring its receivables. A firm that factors all its receivables does not need a credit department and does not have to incur the administrative and clerical costs of credit investigation and collection or the losses on uncollected accounts. In addition, the factor may be better able to control losses than a credit department in a small or medium-sized firm due to its greater experience in credit evaluation. Thus, although factoring receivables may be a more costly form of credit than unsecured borrowing, the net cost usually will be below the stated factoring commission and interest rates because of credit department and bad-debt loss savings.

For example, the Masterson Lock Company is considering factoring its receivables. The factor requires a 5 percent reserve for returns and allowances, charges a 2 percent factoring commission, and will advance Masterson funds at an annual interest rate of 12 percent. Factoring receivables will allow the company to eliminate its credit department and save $50,000 per year in administrative and clerical costs. Factoring also will eliminate bad-debt losses, which average 0.5 percent of credit sales of $6 million per year. The company's receivables turn over 6 times per year.

Table 22–1 calculates the amount of funds Masterson can borrow from the factor and the effective annual percentage cost of these funds.[10] As can be seen in the table, Masterson can obtain an advance of $911,400 from the factor. *Net* annual costs of these funds are $151,600 for an effective annual percentage cost of 16.6 percent. Masterson can compare the cost of this factoring arrangement with the cost of other sources of funds in deciding whether or not to factor its receivables.

---

[10]Although the reserve for returns is deducted when figuring the amount of funds advanced by the factor, it is not part of the cost of factoring, since the factor will return it to Masterson provided that the company's customers make no returns or adjustments.

TABLE 22–1   Cost of Factoring Receivables for the Masterson Lock Company

Annual credit sales	$6,000,000	
Receivables turnover	6 times (evey 60 days)	
Average level of receivables	$6,000,000 ÷ 6	$1,000,000
Less: Factoring commission	0.02 × $1,000,000	− 20,000
Less: Reserve for returns	0.05 × $1,000,000	− 50,000
Amount available for advance before interest is deducted		$ 930,000
Less: Interest on advance	(0.12 × 60/360) × $930,000	− 18,600
Amount of funds advanced by factor		$ 911,400
Factoring commission per 60 days	$20,000	
Interest expense per 60 days	18,600	
Gross factoring cost per 60 days	$38,600	
Gross factoring cost per year ($38,600 × 6)		$ 231,600
Less: Annual credit department savings		− 50,000
Less: Annual bad-debt losses (0.005 × $6,000,000)		− 30,000
Net annual cost of factoring receivables		$ 151,600

$$\text{Effective annual percentage cost} = \frac{\text{Net annual cost of factoring receivables}}{\text{Amount of funds advanced by factor}} \times 100$$

$$= \frac{\$151,600}{\$911,400} \times 100$$

$$= 16.6\%$$

INVENTORY LOANS

Inventories are another commonly used form of collateral for secured short-term loans. Like receivables, many types of inventories are fairly liquid. Thus, lenders consider them to be a desirable form of collateral. When judging whether a firm's inventory would be suitable collateral for a loan, the primary considerations of the lender are the type, physical characteristics, identifiability, liquidity, and marketability of the inventory.

Firms hold three types of inventories—*raw materials, work-in-process,* and *finished goods.* Normally, only raw materials and finished goods are considered acceptable as security for a loan. The physical characteristic with which lenders are most concerned is the item's *perishability.* Inventory that is subject to significant physical deterioration over time is usually not suitable as collateral.

Inventory items also should be *readily identifiable* by means of serial numbers or inventory control numbers. This helps protect the lender against possible fraud and also aids the lender in establishing a valid title claim to the collateral if the borrower becomes insolvent and defaults on the loan. The ease with which the inventory can be *liquidated* and the stability of its *market price* are other important considerations. In the event that the borrower defaults, the lender wants to be able to take possession, sell the collateral, and recover the full amount owed with minimal expense and difficulty.

Both commercial banks and finance companies make inventory loans. The percentage of funds that the lender will advance against the inventory's book value ranges from about 50 to 90 percent and depends on the inventory's characteristics. Advances near the upper end of this range normally are made only for inventories that are standardized, nonperishable, easily identified, and readily marketable. To receive an inventory loan, the firm must sign both a promissory note and a security agreement describing the inventory that will serve as collateral.

In making a loan secured with inventories, the lender can either allow the borrower to hold the collateral or require that it be held by a third party. If the borrower holds the collateral, the loan may be made under a *floating lien* or *trust receipt* arrangement. If a third party is employed to hold the collateral, either a *terminal warehouse* or a *field warehouse* financing arrangement can be used.

FLOATING LIENS

Under a floating lien arrangement, the lender receives a security interest or general claim on *all* of the firm's inventory; this may include both present and future inventory. This type of agreement often is employed when the average value of the inventory items is small, the inventory turns over frequently, or both. Specific items are not identified. Thus, a floating lien does not offer the lender much protection against losses from fraud or bankruptcy. As a result, most lenders will not advance a very high percentage of funds against the book value of the borrower's inventory.

TRUST RECEIPTS

A trust receipt is a security agreement under which the firm holds the inventory and proceeds from the sale in trust for the lender. Whenever a portion of the inventory is sold, the firm is required to immediately forward the proceeds to the lender; these then are used to reduce the loan balance.

Some firms engage in inventory financing on a continuing basis. In these cases, a new security agreement is drawn up periodically, and the lender advances the firm additional funds using recently purchased inventories as collateral.

All inventory items under a trust receipt arrangement must be readily identified by serial number or inventory code number. The lender makes periodic, unannounced inspections of the inventory to make sure that the firm has the collateral and has not withheld payment for inventory that has been sold.

Firms who must have their inventories available for sale on their premises, such as automobile and appliance dealers, frequently engage in trust receipt financing. This is also known as *floor planning*. Many "captive" finance companies that are subsidiaries of manufacturers, such as General Motors Acceptance Corporation (GMAC), engage in floor planning for their dealers. Figure 22–2 is a sample of a GMAC security agreement.

FIGURE 22–2   Sample GMAC Trust Receipt ⎯⎯⎯⎯⎯⎯⎯⎯⎯⎯⎯⎯⎯⎯⎯⎯⎯

WHOLESALE SECURITY AGREEMENT

To: General Motors Acceptance Corporation (GMAC)

In the course of our business, we acquire new and used cars, trucks and chassis ("Vehicles") from manufacturers or distributors. We desire you to finance the acquisition of such vehicles and to pay the manufacturers or distributors therefor.

We agree upon demand to pay to GMAC the amount it advances or is obligated to advance to the manufacturer or distributor for each vehicle with interest at the rate per annum designated by GMAC from time to time and then in force under the GMAC Wholesale Plan.

We also agree that to secure collectively the payment by us of the amounts of all advances and obligations to advance made by GMAC to the manufacturer, distributor or other sellers, and the interest due thereon, GMAC is hereby granted a security interest in the vehicles and the proceeds of sale thereof ("Collateral") as more fully described herein.

The collateral subject to this Wholesale Security Agreement is new vehicles held for sale or lease and used vehicles acquired from manufacturers or distributors and held for sale or lease, and all vehicles of like kinds or types now owned or hereafter acquired from manufacturers, distributors or sellers by way of replacement, substitution, addition or otherwise, and all additions and accessions thereto and all proceeds of such vehicles, including insurance proceeds.

Our possession of the vehicles shall be for the purpose of storing and exhibiting same for retail sale in the regular course of business. We shall keep the vehicles brand new and we shall not use them illegally, improperly or for hire. GMAC shall at all times have the right of access to and inspection of the vehicles and the right to examine our books and records pertaining to the vehicles.

We agree to keep the vehicles free of all taxes, liens and encumbrances, and any sum of money that may be paid by GMAC in release or discharge thereof shall be paid to GMAC on demand as an additional part of the obligation secured hereunder. We shall not mortgage, pledge or loan the vehicles and shall not transfer or otherwise dispose of them except as next hereinafter more particularly provided. We shall execute in favor of GMAC any form of document which may be required for the amounts advanced to the manufacturer, distributor or seller, and shall execute such additional documents as GMAC may at any time request in order to confirm or perfect title or security in the vehicles. Execution by us of any instrument for the amount advanced shall be deemed evidence of our obligation and not payment therefor. We authorize GMAC or any of its officers or employees or agents to execute such documents in our behalf and to supply any omitted information and correct patent errors in any document executed by us.

We understand that we may sell and lease the vehicles at retail in the ordinary course of business. We further agree that as each vehicle is sold, or leased, we will, faithfully and promptly remit to you the amount you advanced or have become obligated to advance on our behalf to the manufacturer, distributor or seller, with interest at the designated rate per annum then in effect under the GMAC Wholesale Plan. The GMAC Wholesale Plan is hereby incorporated by reference.

GMAC's security interest in the vehicles shall attach to the full extent provided or permitted by law to the proceeds, in whatever form, of any retail sale or lease thereof by us until such proceeds are accounted for as aforesaid, and to the proceeds of any other disposition of said vehicles or any part thereof.

In the event we default in payment under and according to this agreement, or in due performance or compliance with any of the terms and conditions hereof, or in the event of a proceeding in bankruptcy, insolvency or receivership instituted by or against us or our property, or in the event that GMAC deems itself insecure or said vehicles are in danger of misuse, loss, seizure or confiscation, GMAC may take immediate possession of said vehicles, without demand or further notice and without legal process; for the purpose and in furtherance thereof, we shall, if GMAC so requests, assemble said vehicles and make them available to GMAC at a reasonable convenient place designated by it, and GMAC shall have the right, and we hereby authorize and empower GMAC, to enter upon the premises wherever said vehicles may be and remove same. We shall pay all expenses and reimburse GMAC for any expenditures, including reasonable attorney's fees and legal expenses, in connection with GMAC's exercise of any of its rights and remedies under this agreement.

(continued)

In the event of repossession of the vehicles by GMAC, then the rights and remedies applicable under the Uniform Commercial Code shall apply.

Any provision hereof prohibited by law shall be ineffective to the extent of such prohibition without invalidating the remaining provisions hereof.

IN WITNESS WHEREOF, each of the parties has caused this Agreement to be executed by its duly authorized representative this _____ day of _____ 19_____.

Witness and Attest:

_____

Accepted
GENERAL MOTORS ACCEPTANCE CORPORATION

By: _____
             Its Authorized Agent

_____
                    Address

_____
               Dealer's Name

By: _____

Its: _____

_____
             Address of Dealer

Terminal warehouse and field warehouse financing arrangements

Under a *terminal warehouse* financing arrangement, the inventory being used as loan collateral is stored in a bonded warehouse operated by a public warehousing company. When the inventory is delivered to the warehouse, the warehouse company issues a warehouse receipt listing the specific items received by serial or lot number. The warehouse receipt is forwarded to the lender, who then advances funds to the firm.

Holding the warehouse receipt gives the lender a security interest in the inventory. Since the warehouse company will release the stored inventory to the firm only when authorized to do so by the holder of the warehouse receipt, the lender is able to exercise control over the collateral. As the firm repays the loan, the lender authorizes the warehouse company to release appropriate amounts of the inventory to the firm.

Under a *field warehouse* financing agreement, the inventory that serves as collateral for a loan is segregated from the firm's other inventory and stored on its premises under the control of a field warehouse company. The field warehouse company issues a warehouse receipt, and the lender advances funds to the firm. The field warehouse releases inventory to the firm only when authorized to do so by the lender.

Although terminal warehouse and field warehouse financing arrangements provide the lender with more control over the collateral than it has when the borrower holds the inventory, fraud and/or negligence on the part of the warehouse company can result in losses for the lender. The fees charged by the warehouse company make this type of financing more expensive than floating lien or trust receipt loans. In a terminal warehouse arrangement, the firm incurs storage charges, in addition to fees for transporting the inventory to and from the public warehouse. In a field warehouse arrangement, the firm normally has to pay an installation charge, a fixed operating charge based on the overall size of the warehousing operation, and a monthly storage charge based on the value of the inventory in the field warehouse.

Overall warehousing fees are generally 1 to 3 percent of the inventory value. The total cost of an inventory loan includes the service fee charged by the lender and the warehousing fee charged by the warehousing company, plus the interest on the funds advanced by the lender. Any internal savings in inventory handling and storage costs that result when the inventory is held by a warehouse company are deducted in computing the cost of the loan.

SUMMARY

- Short-term credit may be either *secured* or *unsecured*. In the case of secured credit, the borrower pledges certain assets (such as inventory, receivables, or fixed assets) as collateral for the loan. In general, firms prefer to borrow on an unsecured basis, since pledging assets as security generally raises the overall cost of the loan and also can reduce the firm's flexibility by restricting future borrowing.

- *Trade credit, accrued expenses,* and *deferred income* are the primary sources of spontaneous short-term credit. *Bank loans, commercial paper, receivables loans,* and *inventory loans* represent the major sources of *negotiated* short-term credit.

- Trade credit is extended to a firm when it makes purchases from a supplier and is permitted to wait a specified period of time before paying for them. It is normally extended on an *open-account* basis, which means that once a firm accepts merchandise from a supplier, it agrees to pay the amount due as specified by the terms of sale on the invoice.

- *Stretching accounts payable,* or postponing payment beyond the end of the credit period, can be used to obtain additional short-term financing. The costs of stretching accounts payable include forgone cash discounts, penalties, and interest, as well as possible deterioration of the firm's credit rating and ability to obtain future credit.

- *Accrued expenses,* such as accrued wages, taxes, and interest, are liabilities for services provided to the firm that have not yet been paid for by the firm.

- *Deferred income* consists of payments received for goods and services the firm will deliver at a future date.

- Short-term *bank credit* can be extended to the firm under a *single loan,* a *line of credit,* or a *revolving credit agreement.* A line of credit permits the firm to borrow funds up to a predetermined limit at any time during the life of the agreement. A revolving credit agreement legally commits the bank to provide the funds when the firm requests them.

- *Commercial paper* consists of short-term unsecured promissory notes issued by large, well-known corporations with excellent credit ratings.

- *Accounts receivable* loans can be obtained by either *pledging* or *factoring* receivables. In the case of a pledging arrangement, the firm retains title to the receivables, and the lender advances funds to the firm based on the amount and quality of the receivables. With factoring, receivables are sold to a factor, who takes the responsibility for credit checking and collection of the accounts.

- Several types of *inventory loans* are available. In a *floating lien* or *trust receipt* arrangement, the borrower holds the collateral. In a floating lien arrangement, the lender has a general claim on all of the firm's inventory. In a trust receipt arrangement, the inventory being used as collateral is specifically identified by serial or inventory code numbers. In a *terminal warehouse* and a *field warehouse* arrangement, a third party holds the collateral; in the case of a terminal warehouse arrangement, collateral is stored in a public warehouse, whereas in a field warehouse arrangement, collateral is stored in a field warehouse located on the borrower's premises.

- No one source (or combination of sources) of short-term financing is necessarily optimal for all firms. Many other factors, in addition to effective annual percentage cost, need to be considered when choosing the optimal source or sources of short-term financing. Some of these factors include the availability of funds during periods of financial crisis or tight money, restrictive covenants imposed on the firm, and the nature of the firm's operations and funds requirements.

Corporate Credit Analysis

Richard H. Brock
Vice-President
InterFirst Bank Dallas, N.A.

The purpose of corporate credit analysis is to identify risks inherent in a loan transaction through assessing complete and accurate financial and business information about the prospective borrower. Whether a lender is extending credit to a privately held middle market company or one ranked in the Fortune 500, fundamental factors of sound credit analysis remain principally the same. Emphasis is on the borrower's ability to meet the terms of repayment as agreed upon with the lender. Key areas of focus in the credit process include an evaluation of (1) the loan purpose; (2) company background and management review; (3) growth and profitability; (4) financial, ratio, and cash flow analysis; and (5) industry analysis.

Underlying these factors is an assessment of the borrower's integrity, reliability, and character. Technical or analytical analysis is only complete when viewed in the context of past track record and performance. The verification of information obtained from the customer through credit investigations; audited financial statements (3 years' minimum); on-site plant or office visits; industry sources; and data from Standard and Poors, Moody's or SEC reports (if the firm is publicly held) represent an important step in the analysis.

Furthermore, a credible analysis relies heavily on the bank officer's ability to judge various credit strengths and weaknesses. The importance of judgment cannot be overemphasized, as few lending decisions are considered absolutely risk-free. Properly assessing critical factors and structuring the credit to address these risks facilitate many transactions that otherwise would be considered unbankable. For example, during the early years of exploration and production, the oil and gas industry found obtaining credit based on oil reserves in the ground to be extremely difficult. Today, bankers (and other institutional and equity partners) use petroleum engineering expertise to evaluate the net present value of future net income of the producing properties used as collateral. This method, referred to as *production payment financing*, is now commonplace and represents an important vehicle for providing capital to the energy industry.

LOAN PURPOSE ANALYSIS

A primary consideration in credit analysis is the specific purpose for which the loan proceeds are to be used. It is also important to identify the source of funds to liquidate the credit (that is, working capital, cash flow, debt refinancing, or equity placement). The use of funds generally falls into two broad categories: working capital (short term) and capital/

asset financing (long term). A fertilizer manufactuer's seasonal credit needs (primarily receivables and inventory financing) stand in stark contrast to a forest products firm's capital expansion need to increase paper mill capacity. The sale of the current assets serves as the primary repayment source in the case of the fertilizer manufacturer. In contrast, the profitable operation of the new paper mill over a prolonged period of time is the primary repayment source in the case of the forest products firm. Other special financing requirements include acquisitions, recapitalization, project financing, and off balance sheet activities, all of which can require unique and innovative structures. Conformity with bank policy and regulatory statutes (such as usury laws) must be considered in the initial stages of the loan, in addition to evaluating sources of collateral or other credit support.

COMPANY BACKGROUND AND MANAGEMENT REVIEW

Obtaining a detailed knowledge of the borrower's business is absolutely essential to a comprehensive analysis. Ownership and corporate structure, production and distribution facilities, raw material supply, major trade creditors, major customers, customer concentration, and product/service quality are major elements. Determining the scope of operations, such as domestic and/or international activities, facilitates the assessment of political, economic, and social risks. In recent years, employee and labor relations have increased in importance and must be considered. In industries such as high technology, product obsolescence represents a major risk, whereas in other companies, price, quality, and service may be of primary importance.

A complete review of management depth, reputation, stability, and experience is a critical element of the analysis. Quality management can be considered one of the most important advantages in operating a business during economic declines or in capitalizing on an opportunity in the marketplace. Information outlining management history and employment generally is required to be submitted with the credit request.

GROWTH AND PROFITABILITY

Sales and profit growth over a period of years reflects consistency, a highly desirable factor in the extension of credit. Of primary interest is performance during adverse economic conditions or events such as the 1973 Arab oil embargo. Ability to repay debts generally is agreed to be a function of the quality and consistency of earnings and cash flow. The source of earnings and sales growth (that is, by line of business and by price or volume), as well as profit margin and income statement trend analysis, are of primary interest. Much of this information can be obtained based on a review of the most recent fiscal and quarterly (or monthly) financial statements. Return on sales, assets and equity and ratios reflecting efficiency are useful analytical tools. Revenue recognition methods also must be examined to determine the quality of sales and earnings. Other accounting policies affecting the income statement (such as amortization of investment tax credits and inventory valuation) require complete review. Actual debt service ability can be determined only after examining the method of financial presentation.

FINANCIAL, RATIO, AND CASH FLOW ANALYSIS

An analysis of the balance sheet indicates the quality and liquidity of the assets, the nature of the liabilities, and the relationship between assets and liabilities. A complete dissection of each major category must be accompanied by analytical information—such as an analysis of the working capital cycle, accounts receivable aging and credit policies, inventory controls, and valuation method (LIFO or FIFO). Fixed assets that have *actually* depreciated faster than represented on the financial statements can overstate net worth. Conversely, assets whose market value exceeds cost or book value can be sources of hidden equity or possibly values for collateral. Capitalization of the firm reflects the relative level of debt (senior or subordinated) and equity (common or preferred stock and retained earnings) used to finance the entity and reflects the additional borrowing capacity of the firm. Access to long-term debt and equity capital markets provides sources of additional financial flexibility.

Accounting policies also must be analyzed in light of a conservative or liberal presentation. This can have a considerable impact on the quality of reported earnings and net worth. Items such as contingent liabilities, unfunded pension liabilities or pending litigation represent additional risk factors. Measures of various balance sheet items include the current and quick ratio (liquidity), total debt to tangible worth (leverage), and debt as a percentage of total capital (capitalization). Many other analytical ratios also are used, depending on the specific firm or industry being evaluated.

The generation of cash flow sufficient to meet demands for the repayment of current maturities of term debt, capital expenditures, dividends, and growing working capital requirements is required. A strong and stable cash flow that provides excellent coverage for both debt service and internal financing of growth generally characterizes high quality credits. In certain instances, such as for a radio or cable television operation, leverage could be fairly high, but excellent cash flows may reduce risk significantly.

Considering that loan repayments are scheduled for future periods, cash flow projections should be provided for at least the term of the credit. These projections, combined with various assumptions for factors such as sales growth, operating and gross profit margins, and interest rate levels, typically are presented under a worst case, best case, and most likely scenario. Cash flow projections also are useful in analyzing the proposed amortization of the loan and in structuring financial covenants in the loan agreement in order to maintain a degree of control over this source of repayment.

INDUSTRY ANALYSIS

In addition to analyzing the company seeking credit, the credit analyst also must make a thorough and long-range analysis of the industry in which the borrower operates. Factors unique to each industry must be viewed in the context of the impact on the credit applicant. Comparisions with other companies are useful in determining relative strength. The overall industry condition also must be viewed from an economic perspective. For example, is the industry in the growth or mature phase of development? Not only must the lender feel assured that the borrower will remain in business, but also that the overall industry outlook itself is fundamentally sound.

SUMMARY

This "Focus on Corporate Practice" example has discussed the factors a commercial loan officer considers when evaluating a credit applicant. A good financial manager will be equally aware of the lender's decision process, so it will be possible to present a strong loan application to the lending institution.

QUESTIONS AND TOPICS FOR DISCUSSION

1. Define and discuss the function of *collateral* in short-term credit arrangements.

2. Explain the difference between *spontaneous* and *negotiated* sources of short-term credit.

3. Under what condition or conditions is trade credit *not* a "cost-free" source of funds to the firm?

4. Define the following:
   a. Accrued expenses.
   b. Deferred income.

5. Explain the differences between a line of credit and a revolving credit agreement.

6. What are some of the disadvantages of relying too heavily on commercial paper as a source of short-term credit?

7. Explain the difference between pledging and factoring receivables.

8. Explain the difference between a floating lien and a trust receipts arrangement.

9. Explain why the effective annual percentage cost of secured credit is frequently higher than that of unsecured credit.

10. Explain why banks normally include a "clean-up" provision in a line of credit agreement.

11. Define the following terms:
    a. Prime rate.
    b. Compensating balance.
    c. Discounted loan.
    d. Commitment fee.

12. What savings are realized when accounts receivable are factored rather than pledged?

13. Determine the effect of each of the following conditions on the costs of borrowing under a line of credit arrangement (assuming that all other factors remain constant):
    a. The bank raises the prime rate.
    b. The bank lowers its compensating balance requirements.
    c. The firm's average bank balance increases as the result of its instituting more stringent credit and collection policies.

14. Under what condition or conditions, if any, might a firm find it desirable to borrow funds from a bank or other lending institution in order to take a cash discount?

PROBLEMS*

(NOTE: Assume that there are 360 days per year when converting from annual to daily amounts or vice versa.)

1. The Wilcox Company currently purchases an average of $10,000 per day in raw materials on credit terms of "net 30." The firm expects sales to increase substantially next year and anticipates that its raw material purchases will increase to an average of $12,000 per day. Wilcox feels that it will need to finance part of this sales expansion by *stretching* accounts payable.
    a. Assuming that Wilcox currently waits until the end of the credit period to pay its raw material suppliers, what is its current level of trade credit?
    b. If Wilcox stretches its accounts payable an extra 15 days beyond the due date next year, how much *additional* short-term funds (that is, trade credit) will be generated?

2. Determine the annual percentage cost of forgoing the cash discount under each of the following credit terms:
    a. 2/10, net 60.
    b. 1½/10, net 60.
    c. 2/30, net 60.
    d. 5/30, net 4 months (assume 30 days per month).
    e. 1/10, net 30.
    f. 3/10, net 4 months.
    g. 2/10, net 120.

3. Determine the effective annual percentage cost of a 1-year, $10,000 discounted bank loan at an interest rate of 8.5 percent. Assume that no compensating balance is required.

4. The Wilson Company has a line of credit with a bank under which it can borrow funds at an 8 percent interest rate. The firm plans to borrow $100,000 and is required by the bank to maintain a 20 percent compensating balance. Determine the effective annual percentage cost of the loan under each of the following conditions:
    a. The firm currently maintains $10,000 in its account at the bank that can be used to meet the compensating balance requirement.
    b. The firm currently has no funds in its account at the bank that can be used to meet the compensating balance requirement.

5. Hastings Company has a revolving credit agreement with its bank. The firm can borrow up to $2 million under the agreement at an annual interest rate of 9 per-

*Problems in color have check answers provided at the end of the book.

cent. Hastings is required to maintain a 15 percent compensating balance on any funds borrowed under the agreement and to pay a 0.5 percent commitment fee on the unused portion of the credit line. Determine the effective annual percentage cost of borrowing each of the following amounts under the credit agreement:

a. $250,000.
b. $500,000.
c. $1,000,000.
d. $2,000,000.

6. Wellsley Manufacturing Company has been approached by a commercial paper dealer offering to sell an issue of commercial paper for the firm. The dealer indicates that Wellsley could sell a $5 million issue maturing in 180 days at an interest rate of 7.5 percent per annum (deducted in advance). The fee to the dealer for selling the issue would be $7,500. Determine Wellsley's effective annual percentage cost of this commercial paper financing.

7. Alberta Oil Company has been approached by two different commercial paper dealers offering to sell an issue of commercial paper for the firm. Dealer A offered to market an $8 million issue maturing in 90 days at an interest cost of 9.50 percent per annum (deducted in advance). The fee to Dealer A would be $12,000. Dealer B has offered to sell a $10 million issue maturing in 120 days at an interest rate of 9.75 percent per annum (deducted in advance). The fee to Dealer B would be $15,000. Assuming that Alberta Oil wishes to minimize the effective annual percentage cost of issuing commercial paper, which dealer should the firm choose?

8. Gibson Sporting Goods Company needs to raise $1,500,000 during the next year. One option under consideration is to pledge a portion of its receivables as collateral for a loan from the Business Finance Corporation (BFC). BFC has agreed to advance Gibson 75 percent of the face value of the receivables at 3 percent above the prime lending rate, which is currently 8 percent. The service fee will be 1.5 percent of the amount of the pledged receivables. Gibson's average collection period for receivables is 45 days. Assume that the interest and service fees are *not* deducted in advance. Determine the following:

a. The amount of receivables Gibson must pledge during the coming year to obtain the needed funds.
b. The *annual* cost of pledging its receivables and borrowing under this arrangement.
c. The effective annual percentage cost of this source of financing.

9. Rework Problem 8 assuming Gibson's average collection period is 60 days.

10. Westex Company is considering factoring its receivables. The firm has annual credit sales of $2,400,000, with a 90-day average collection period. Bad-debt losses average 1 percent of sales, and credit department costs are $2,000 per month. Both of these costs will be eliminated if Westex factors its receivables. The factor charges a fee of 3 percent on all receivables and requires a 10 percent reserve for returns and allowances. It will advance funds to Westex at an annual interest rate of 12 percent (interest is deducted from the amount of the advance). Determine the following:

a. The amount of funds Westex can obtain by factoring its receivables.
b. The *net* annual cost of factoring its receivables and borrowing under this arrangement.
c. The effective annual percentage cost of this factoring arrangement.

11. Rework Problem 10 assuming that Westex has a 60-day average collection period.

12. The Eaton Company needs to raise $250,000 to expand its working capital and

has been unsuccessful in attempting to obtain an unsecured line of credit with its bank. The firm is considering *stretching* its accounts payable. Eaton's suppliers extend credit on terms of "2/10, net 30." Payments beyond the credit period are subject to a 1½ percent per month penalty. Eaton purchases $100,000 per month from its suppliers and currently takes cash discounts. Assuming that Eaton is able to raise the $250,000 it needs by stretching its accounts payable, determine the following:

a. The firm's annual lost cash discounts.
b. Annual penalties.
c. The effective annual percentage cost of this source of financing.

13. The Eaton Company (see Problem 12) decides that the cost of stretching accounts payable is too high and is considering obtaining a loan from a sales finance company secured by inventories under a field warehousing arrangement. Eaton would be permitted to borrow up to $300,000 under such an arrangement at an annual interest rate of 12 percent. The additional cost of maintaining a field warehouse is $15,000 per year. Determine the effective annual percentage cost of a loan under this arrangement if Eaton borrows the following amounts:

a. $300,000.
b. $250,000.

AN INTEGRATIVE CASE PROBLEM

Working Capital Management

Anderson Furniture Company manufactures furniture and sells its products to department stores, retail furniture stores, hotels, and motels throughout the United States and Canada. The firm has nine manufacturing plants located in Virginia, North Carolina, and Georgia. The company was founded by Edward G. Anderson in 1906 and has been managed by members of the Anderson family since that time. E. G. Anderson III is currently chairman and president of the company. The treasurer and controller of the company is Claire White, who was hired away from a competing furniture company a few years ago. Anderson owns 35 percent of the common stock of the company and (along with the shares of the firm owned by relatives and employees) has effective control over all of the firm's decisions.

Financial data relating to last year's (19X1) operations, along with relevant industry comparisons, are shown in Table 1. The firm's overall rates of return on equity and total assets have been around the industry average over the past several years—sometimes slightly above average and sometimes slightly below average. The company currently is operating its plants near full capacity and would like to build a new plant in Georgia at a cost of approximately $7.5 million. White has been exploring various alternative methods of financing this expansion and has been unsuccessful thus far in developing an acceptable plan. The sale of new common stock is not feasible at this time because of depressed stock market prices. Likewise, Anderson's banker has advised the firm

TABLE 1 Anderson Furniture Company's Financial Data (in Thousands of Dollars)

DECEMBER 31, 19X1

Balance Sheet			Industry Average
Assets			
Cash	$ 3,690	6.5%	5.0%
Receivables, net	15,000	26.3	21.6
Inventories	20,250	35.5	33.4
Total current assets	$38,940	68.3%	60.0%
Net fixed assets	18,060	31.7	40.0
Total assets	$57,000	100.0%	100.0%
Liabilities and owners' equity			
Accounts payable	$ 3,000	5.3%	7.0%
Notes payable (8%)	3,750	6.6	10.0
Total current liabilities	$ 6,750	11.8%	17.0%
Long-term debt (10%)	18,000	31.6	28.0
Owners' equity	32,250	56.6	55.0
Total liabilities and owners' equity	$57,000	100.0%	100.0%

INCOME STATEMENT FOR THE YEAR ENDED DECEMBER 31, 19X1

Net sales (all on credit)	$75,000	100.0%
Cost of goods sold	60,750	81.0
Gross profit	$14,250	19.0
Selling and administrative expenses	7,500	10.0
Earnings before interest and taxes	$ 6,750	9.0
Interest expense	2,100	2.8
Net income before taxes	$ 4,650	6.2
Income taxes (45.16%)	2,100	2.8
Net income after taxes	$ 2,550	3.4%

Significant Ratios	Anderson	Industry Average
Current	5.76	3.5
Quick	2.77	1.6
Average collection period (days)	72	58
Inventory turnover (Cost of goods sold/inventory)	3.0	3.5
Sales to total assets	1.3	1.6
Debt to equity	0.8	0.9
Times interest earned	3.2	4.7
Net income after tax/sales	3.4%	2.4%
Net income after tax/equity	7.9%	7.9%

that the use of additional long-term debt or lease financing is not possible at this time, given the firm's large amount of long-term debt currently outstanding and its relatively low times interest earned ratio. Anderson has ruled out a cut in the firm's dividend as a means of accumulating the required financing. The only other possible sources of financing available to the firm at this time, according to White, appear to be a reduction in working capital (current assets), an increase in short-term liabilities, or both.

Upon learning of these proposed financing methods, Anderson expressed concern about the effect these plans might have on the liquidity and risk of the firm. White replied that the firm currently follows a very conservative working capital policy and that these financing methods would not increase shareholder risk significantly. As evidence, she cited the firm's relatively high current and quick ratios. Anderson was unconvinced and asked White to provide additional information on the effects of these financing plans on the firm's financial status.

1. Anderson's bank requires a compensating balance of $3 million. How much additional funds can be freed up for investment in fixed assets if the firm reduces its cash balance to the minimum required by the bank?

2. How much additional financing can be obtained from receivables if Anderson institutes more stringent credit and collection policies and is able to reduce its average collection period to the industry average? (Assume that credit sales remain constant at $75 million.)

3. How much additional financing can be obtained for fixed-asset expansion if Anderson is able to increase its inventory turnover ratio to the industry average through tighter control of its raw materials, work-in-process, and finished goods inventories? (Assume that the cost of goods sold remains constant at $60.75 million.)

4. Anderson's suppliers extend credit to the firm on terms of "net 30." Anderson normally pays its bills on the last day of the credit period. How much additional financing could be generated if Anderson were to *stretch* its payables 10 days beyond the due date?

5. Prepare a pro forma balance sheet (dollars and percentages) as of December 31, 19X2, assuming that Anderson has instituted *all* actions described in Questions 1, 2, 3, and 4, and that the funds generated have been used to build a new plant. (Assume that long-term debt and owners' equity at the end of 19X2 remain the same as at the end of 19X1. In other words, no new long-term debt is issued or old long-term debt is retired, and all net income after taxes is paid out in common stock dividends. Also assume that net fixed assets, *except for the new plant*, remain unchanged during 19X2. Finally assume that notes payable remain unchanged during 19X2.) HINT: The *total* amount of funds generated from the reduction of current assets and the increase in current liabilities determined in Questions 1, 2, 3, and 4 is $7.5 million (rounded to the nearest $1,000). Round all figures to the nearest $1,000.

6. Prepare a pro forma income statement for 19X2. Assume that sales increase to $87 million as a result of the plant expansion. Also assume that the cost of goods sold and selling and administrative expense ratios (as a percentage of sales) remain constant. Finally, assume that interest expense and the firm's tax rate remain the same in 19X2.

7. Calculate the firm's current, quick, times interest earned, and rate of return on equity ratios based on the pro forma statements determined in Questions 5 and 6. How do these ratios compare with the actual values for 19X1 and the industry averages?

8. What considerations might lead Anderson and White to disagree about the desirability of using short-term sources of funds to finance the plant expansion?

9. What other sources of short-term funds might the firm consider using to finance the plant expansion?

ADDITIONAL READINGS AND REFERENCES

Abraham, Alfred B. "Factoring: The New Frontier for Commercial Banks." *Journal of Commercial Bank Lending* (April 1971): 32–43.

Adler, M. "Administration of Inventory Loans under the Uniform Commercial Code." *Journal of Commercial Bank Lending* 52 (April 1970): 55–60.

Baxter, Nevins D. "Marketability, Default Risk, and Yields on Money-Market Instruments." *Journal of Financial and Quantitative Analysis* 3 (March 1968): 75–85.

Baxter, Nevins D. *The Commercial Paper Market.* Princeton, N.J.: Princeton University Press, 1964.

Berger, Paul D., and Harper, William K. "Determination of an Optimal Revolving Credit Agreement." *Journal of Financial and Quantitative Analysis* 8 (June 1973): 491–498.

Cook, Timothy Q. ed. *Instruments of the Money Market*, 4th ed. Richmond, Va.: Federal Reserve Bank of Richmond, 1976.

Daniels, Frank, Legg, Sidney, and Yueille, E. C. "Accounts Receivable and Related Inventory Financing." *Journal of Commercial Bank Lending* 53 (July 1970): 38–53.

Dennon, Lester E. "The Security Agreement." *Journal of Commercial Bank Lending* 50 (February 1968): 32–40.

Nadler, Paul S. "Compensating Balances and the Prime at Twilight." *Harvard Business Review* 50 (Jan–Feb. 1972): 112–120.

Quarles, J. Carson. "The Floating Lien." *Journal of Commercial Bank Lending* 53 (November 1970): 51–58.

Quill, Gerald D., Cresci, John C., and Shuter, Bruce D. "Some Considerations about Secured Lending." *Journal of Commercial Bank Lending* 59 (April 1977): 41–56.

Rogers, R. W. "Warehouse Receipts and Their Use in Financing." *Bulletin of the Robert Morris Associates* (April 1964): 317–327.

Shadrack, Frederick C., Jr. "Demand and Supply in the Commercial Paper Market." *Journal of Finance* 25 (Sept. 1970): 837–852.

Stone, Bernell K. "Allocating Credit Lines, Planned Borrowing and Tangible Services over a Company's Banking System." *Financial Management* (Summer 1975): 65–83.

Stone, Bernell K. "The Cost of Bank Loans." *Journal of Financial and Quantitative Analysis* 7 (Dec. 1972): 2077–2086.

PART EIGHT

Selected Topics in Contemporary Financial Management

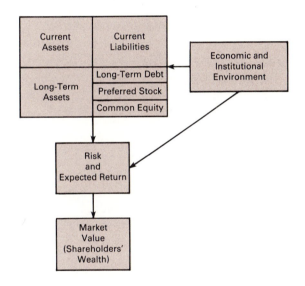

Part Eight looks at a number of additional topics that are important for the financial manager. Chapter 23 considers the merger and acquisition alternative to internal investment growth. Chapter 24 discusses alternatives that are open to the failing firm. Finally, Chapter 25 discusses some key aspects of international financial management and financial management in public and not-for-profit enterprises. The financial manager who wishes to maximize the value of the firm for its investors needs to have a solid working knowledge of decision-making techniques in each of these areas.

CHAPTER 23

Mergers and Acquisitions

A FINANCIAL DILEMMA

The Bendix–Martin Marietta–
Allied–United Technologies Affair

In August 1982, Bendix offered to buy Martin Marietta for $43 a share. Just prior to that time, the Martin Marietta stock was trading in the range of $33 to $39 a share. The Bendix shares were trading in the range of $50 a share, and Bendix was offering to swap 0.82 shares of Bendix for each share of Martin Marietta.

In late August, Martin Marietta called the Bendix offer inadequate and countered with a $75 a share offer for Bendix. The financial press referred to this strategy as a "Pac Man strategy": my company eats yours before yours eats mine. Martin Marietta was apparently serious in its offer, since it had secured credit lines with banks of up to $1 billion.

In early September, both boards of directors rejected the offers. Then United Technologies got into the act and offered $75 a share for Bendix. It was acting as an ally to Martin Marietta, agreeing to divide up Bendix. Bendix then raised its Martin Marietta offer to $48 a share. Shortly after that, United Technologies raised its Bendix offer to $85 a share.

The next act featured Allied Corporation's agreeing to merge with Bendix. Martin Marietta agreed to swap its Bendix shares with Allied in return for some of the Martin Marietta shares held by Bendix.

Allied, the late entrant in this unusual merger plot, appears to have emerged a winner. It took over the aggressor, Bendix, and acquired 39 percent of Martin Marietta. Martin Marietta did walk away a "free" company, but one with a large amount of debt on its books due to its having to buy its stock back.

In examining this merger, it is apparent that a number of valuation determinations had to be made. This chapter presents an overview of mergers and discusses the methods used to value merger candidates.

GLOSSARY OF NEW TERMS

Conglomerate merger   a combination of two or more companies in which neither competes directly with the other and no buyer-seller relationship exists.

Exchange ratio   the number of shares an acquiring firm must give, or *exchange,* for each share of an acquired firm in a merger.

Goodwill   an intangible asset equal to the premium over fair market value of the acquired assets that is paid for a company in a merger.

Holding company   a corporation that controls the voting power of one or more other companies.

Horizontal merger   a combination of two or more companies that compete directly with each other.

Merger   a combination of two or more companies into one surviving company. Mergers are also called *acquisitions* or *consolidations.*

Pooling of interests method   a method of accounting for mergers in which the acquired company's assets are recorded on the acquiring company's books at their cost when originally acquired. No goodwill account is created under the pooling method.

Purchase method   a method of accounting for mergers in which the total value paid or exchanged for the acquired firm's assets is recorded on the acquiring firm's books. Any difference between the acquired assets' fair market value and their purchase price is recorded as goodwill.

Tender offer   a public announcement by a firm or individual indicating that it will pay a price above the current market price for the shares "tendered" of a company it wishes to acquire.

Vertical merger   a combination of two or more companies that have a buyer-seller relationship with one another.

INTRODUCTION

Whereas mergers and acquisitions encompass a wider area of a firm's activities than the financial area alone, they nevertheless have significant implications for the financial management function. This chapter discusses various features of mergers and acquisitions, emphasizing their financial aspects.

MERGER TERMINOLOGY

Businesses grow *externally* by acquiring, or combining with, other ongoing businesses. This is in contrast to *internal* growth, which is achieved by purchasing individual assets, such as those evaluated in the discussion of capital expenditures in Chapters 9 through 11. When two companies combine, generally the acquiring company pays for the acquired business either with cash or with its own securities, and the acquired company's liabilities and assets are transferred to the acquiring company.

A *merger* is technically a combination of two or more companies in which all but one of the combining companies legally cease to exist and the surviving company continues in operation under its original name. A *consolidation* is a combination in which all of the combining companies are dissolved and a new firm is formed. The term *merger* generally is used to describe both of these types of business combinations. *Acquisition* also is used interchangeably with *merger* to describe a business combination. In the following discussion, the term *merger* is used, and it is assumed that only two companies are involved—the acquiring company and the merger candidate.[1]

Tender offers   Although many mergers are the result of a friendly agreement between the two companies, a company may wish to acquire another company even when the combination is opposed by the management (or board of directors) of the merger candidate company. In such a case, the acquiring company makes a *tender offer* for common shares of the merger candidate. In a tender offer, the acquiring company effectively announces that it will pay a certain price above the then existing market price for any of the merger candidate's shares that are "tendered" (that is, offered to it) before a particular date.

After an unfriendly takeover attempt has been initiated, the merger candidate's management frequently trys to find another, more friendly acquiring company (called a "white knight") that would be willing to enter into a bidding war with the first acquiring company.

In recent years many companies have taken various measures designed to discourage unfriendly takeover attempts.[2] One such measure involves staggering the terms of the board of directors over several years instead of having the entire board come up for election at one time. Thus, the acquiring firm will have difficulty electing its own board of directors in order to gain control. Another measure is to give key executives "golden parachute" contracts, under which the executives would receive large benefits if they were terminated without sufficient cause after a merger.

Holding companies   Another form of business combination is the *holding company*, in which the acquiring company simply purchases all or a controlling block of another company's common shares. The two companies then become *affiliated*, and the acquiring company becomes the holding company in this *parent-subsidiary* relationship. For example, Central and South West Corporation is an electric utility holding company. Its principal subsidiaries are Central Power and Light Company, Public Service Company of Oklahoma, Southwestern Electric Power Company, and West Texas Utilities Company.

---

[1]In some instances, merger candidates may be referred to as *takeover candidates, to-be-acquired companies, acquired companies,* or *target companies.*

[2]The financial press has described these antitakeover measures as "shark repellents."

Stock purchases and asset purchases   A merger transaction may be a stock purchase or an asset purchase. In a *stock purchase,* the acquiring company buys the stock of the to-be-acquired company and assumes its liabilities. In an *asset purchase,* the acquiring company buys only the assets (some or all) of the to-be-acquired company and does not assume any of its liabilities.

Normally, the buyer of a business prefers an asset purchase rather than a stock purchase, because unknown liabilities, such as any future lawsuits against the company, are not incurred. In addition, an asset purchase frequently allows the acquiring company to depreciate its new assets from a higher basis than is possible in a stock purchase. As a result of the unknown liability question, many large companies that acquire small companies refuse to negotiate on any terms other than an asset purchase.

Divestitures   *Divestitures* are an important part of a company's merger and acquisition strategy. After an acquiring company completes an acquisition, it frequently examines the various assets and divisions of the recently acquired company to determine whether or not all the acquired company's pieces "fit" into the acquiring company's future plans. For example, after Du Pont acquired Conoco in 1981, it began selling off various Conoco assets in an attempt to restructure Conoco and also reduce the debt it used to finance the acquisition.

Leveraged buyouts   Divestitures also can be an important strategy even for companies that are not involved in mergers. One frequently used method to buy a division of a large company is a leveraged buyout. In a *leveraged buyout,* the buyer borrows a large amount of the purchase price, using the purchased assets as collateral for the loan. The buyers are usually the managers of the division that is being sold. It is hoped that the earnings of the new company will be sufficient to service the debt and permit the new owners to earn a reasonable return on their investment.

TYPES OF MERGERS

Mergers generally are classified according to whether they are *horizontal, vertical,* or *conglomerate.* A *horizontal merger* is a combination of two or more companies that compete directly with one another; the merger of Connecticut Corporation and INA Corporation, two large insurance companies, to form CIGNA Corporation in 1982, for example, was a horizontal merger. The U.S. government has vigorously enforced antitrust legislation in an attempt to stop large horizontal combinations, and this effort has been effective. However, horizontal combinations in which one of the firms is failing often are viewed more favorably.

A *vertical merger* is a combination of companies that may have a buyer-seller relationship with one another. For example, if Sears were to acquire one of its appliance suppliers, this would constitute a vertical merger. This type of business combination has gradually declined in importance since World War II.

A *conglomerate merger* is a combinatin of two or more companies in which neither competes directly with the other and no buyer-seller relationship exists. For example, the U.S. Steel acquisition of Marathon Oil Company in 1982 for $6.6 billion in cash and notes was a conglomerate merger. Another conglomerate merger example was the 1982 Xerox acquisition of Crum & Foster, a major property and casualty insurance company.

REASONS FOR MERGERS

The following are some of the reasons why a firm might consider acquiring another firm rather than choosing to grow internally:

- A firm may be able to acquire certain desirable assets at a lower cost by combining with another firm than it could if it purchased the assets directly.[3]

- A firm may be able to achieve greater economies of scale by merging with another firm; this is particularly true in the case of a horizontal merger. When the net income for the combined companies after merger exceeds the sum of the net incomes prior to the merger, *synergy* is said to exist.

- A firm that is concerned about its sources of raw materials or end-product markets might acquire other firms at different stages of its production or distribution processes. These are vertical mergers. For example, in 1966 the Atlantic Refining Company, considered strong in refining and marketing but "crude poor," merged with the Richfield Oil Corporation, which was considered strong in the production-exploration end of the business. The merger created a stronger, more fully integrated oil company, Atlantic-Richfield.

- A firm may wish to grow more rapidly than is possible through internal expansion. Acquiring another company may allow a growing firm to move more rapidly into a geographic or product area in which the acquired firm already has established markets, sales personnel, management capability, warehouse facilities, and so on, than would be possible by starting from scratch. For example, Schlumberger, in an attempt to partially diversify out of the oil field services business into electronics and computer technology, acquired Fairchild (a semiconductor producer) and Applicon (a manufacturer of computer-related systems), among other companies. These companies had established products and markets.

- A firm may desire to diversify its product lines and businesses in an attempt to reduce its business risk by smoothing out cyclical movements in its earnings. For example, a capital equipment manufacturer might achieve steadier earnings by expanding into the replacement parts business. During a recession, expenditures for capital equipment may slow down, but expenditures on maintenance and replacement parts may increase.

This list, while not exhaustive, does indicate the principal reasons why a firm may choose external expansion over internal growth.

---

[3]In this context, when the *market* value of a company's common stock is below its *book* value (or, more importantly, below the replacement value of the firm's net assets), this company frequently is referred to as a possible "takeover candidate."

VALUATION OF MERGER CANDIDATES

The most important factors considered in determining the value placed on an acquisition candidate for an acquiring firm normally are the *market value*, the *current net income*, and *future growth prospects* of the candidate.

In the case of an acquisition candidate whose common stock is actively traded, the market value of the stock is a key factor in the valuation process. To induce the stockholders of the acquisition candidate to give up their shares for the cash and/or securities of the acquiring firm, they have to be offered a premium over the market value of the stock (prior to the merger announcement). Generally, a 10 to 20 percent premium is considered a minimum offer. Even then, in many situations, stockholders may hold out for better offers—either from the company making the initial offer or from other interested companies.

Three major methods typically are used to value merger candidates: the comparative price-earnings ratio method, the adjusted book value method, and the discounted cash flow method.

The *comparative price-earnings ratio method* examines the recent prices and price-earnings (P/E) ratios paid for other merger candidates that are comparable to the company being valued. For example, if two companies in a specific industry recently were acquired at P/E ratios of 10, the comparative P/E ratio method suggests that a P/E ratio of 10 may be reasonable for other, similar companies. Financial analysts who use this method should exercise caution and determine whether the companies being compared are really similar. This method, which focuses on the current income statement, may not be useful if the P/E ratios of recent, similar mergers vary widely.

The *adjusted book value method* involves determining the market value of the company's underlying assets. For example, suppose a company has equipment on its books that is fully depreciated but still in use. The market value of this equipment is determined, and the company's shareholders' equity (book value) is adjusted by the difference between the asset's book value and its market value. Financial analysts who use this method should exercise caution, because the determination of the market value of the merger candidate's assets may be difficult.

The *discounted cash flow method* for valuing merger candidates calculates the present value of the company's expected future cash flows and compares this figure to the proposed purchase price to determine the proposed acquisition's net present value. Thus, this method is an application of the capital budgeting techniques described in Chapters 9 through 11. Consider the following example. Suppose the annual after-tax cash flow from a merger is calculated to be $2 million and is expected to continue for 15 years. If the appropriate risk-adjusted discount rate is 14 percent, for example, the present value of the expected cash inflows is as follows:

Present value of an annuity of $2 million for 15 years at 14%

$$= \$2,000,000 \ (\text{PVIFA}_{0.14,15})$$
$$= \$2,000,000 \ (6.142)$$
$$= \$12,284,000 \ .$$

Therefore, if the merger candidate's purchase price is less than $12,284,000, the proposed merger has a positive net present value and is an acceptable "project."

In principle, the discounted cash flow method is the most correct of the three methods discussed in this section, because this method compares the present value of the cash flow benefits from the merger with the present value of the merger costs. However, in practice, the future cash inflows from a merger can be quite difficult to estimate.

Most financial analysts who work on proposed mergers use all of these methods to attempt to value merger candidates. In addition, they consider a large number of other factors in valuing merger candidates. These factors include the merger candidate's management, products, markets, distribution channels, production costs, expected growth rate, debt capacity, and reputation.

ANALYSIS OF A MERGER

The following merger examples illustrate some the steps and considerations involved in typical mergers. Diversified Industries, Inc., is considering acquiring either High-Tech Products, Inc., or Stable Products, Inc. High-Tech Products has a high expected growth rate and sells at a higher P/E ratio than Diversified. Stable Products, on the other hand, has a low expected growth rate and sells at a lower P/E ratio than Diversified. Table 23–1 contains financial statistics on Diversified and the two merger candidates.

The possible merger of Diversified with Stable Products is considered first. To entice Stable Products' present stockholders to tender their shares, Diversified probably would have to offer them a premium of at least 10 to 20 percent above Stable Products' present stock price. Suppose Diversified decides to offer a price of $24 per share, and Stable Products accepts. The exchange is on a stock-for-stock basis. As a result, Stable Products' shareholders receive 1 share of Diversified common stock for every 1.25 shares of Stable Products stock they hold; in other words, the *exchange ratio* is 1:1.25.

Next, the possible merger of Diversified with High-Tech Products is considered. If Diversified decides to offer $60 a share and High-Tech Products

TABLE 23–1   Selected Financial Data: Diversified Industries and Two Merger Candidates

	Diversified Industries	Stable Products	High-Tech Products
Sales	$1,200 million	$130 million	$100 million
Net income	$ 120 million	$ 12 million	$ 16 million
Common shares outstanding	40 million	4 million	4 million
Earnings per share	$3.00	$3.00	$4.00
Dividends per share, D_0	$1.65	$1.50	$0.80
Common stock market price	$30.00	$21.00	$52.00
Price-earnings ratio	10.0	7.0	13.0
Expected growth rate, g	7%	5%	12%

TABLE 23-2   Diversified Industries: Pro Forma Financial Statement Summary Assuming Separate Mergers*

	Before Merger	After Merger With Stable Products	After Merger With High-Tech Products
Sales	$1,200 million	$1,330 million	$1,300 million
Net income	$120 million	$132 million	$136 million
Common shares outstanding	40 million	43.2 million	48 million
Earnings per share	$3.00	$3.06	$2.83

*The exchange ratio is 1 share of Diversified common stock for each 1.25 shares of Stable Products and 2.0 shares of Diversified for each 1.0 share of High-Tech Products. The net income figure for Diversified Industries (after merger) assumes that no economies of scale or synergistic benefits are realized as a result of either proposed merger.

accepts, the High-Tech Products' shareholders would receive 2 shares of Diversified common stock for every share of High-Tech Products stock they hold; in other words, the exchange ratio would be 2:1.

The pro forma financial statement summary is shown in Table 23-2 for Diversified, assuming separate mergers with each of the merger candidates. Assuming a merger with Stable Products, Diversified's pro forma net income is $132 million, with 43.2 million shares outstanding (the original 40 million plus 3.2 million shares issued in exchange for Stable Products' 4 million). As a result, Diversified has earnings per share of $3.06, as compared with $3.00 without the merger. In other words, the merger transaction can cause Diversified's earnings to change due to the P/E differences between merging companies. Specifically, if the exchange ratio is based on current stock market prices and no synergy exists, *the acquisition of a company with a lower P/E ratio causes the earnings per share figure of the acquiring company to increase.* Similarly, *the acquisition of a company with a higher P/E ratio causes the earnings per share figure to decrease.* This short-term earnings per share change is caused solely by the merger transaction, and a rational stock market does not perceive this change to be *real* growth or *real* decline.

A more important question remains: What will happen to the price and the P/E ratio of Diversified's stock after a merger has been accomplished? Obviously, it can either go up, stay the same, or go down. In recent years, the stock market seems to view mergers rationally, recognizing that the postmerger P/E ratio is a weighted average of the two premerger P/E ratios. As a result, the postmerger share price of the acquiring company is normally in the same range as it was prior to the merger, unless significant economies of scale or synergistic benefits are achieved in the merger.

It is interesting to observe what happened during the 1960s merger period. During the 1960s many investors acted as if they believed that the growth in merging firms' earnings was *real* (instead of being generated by accounting transactions) and bid up the conglomerates' stock prices. This simply helped the conglomerates to achieve further increases in their reported earnings through subsequent acquisitions. In the mid and late 1960s it appeared to many investors that the cycle of earnings per share increases and price increases for conglomerates would continue forever. Indeed, it was something of a self-fulfilling prophecy. Finally, however, the supply of good acquisition candidates decreased, and, at the same time, their prices were bid up by merger-oriented companies. Thus, the rate of increase in accounting-generated earnings could not be maintained. Also, a number of major conglomerate firms began to experience difficulties in managing and controlling their diverse interests. As a result, the investment community began to look with disfavor on conglomerates. In addition, during this time the government increased its enforcement of antitrust laws.

ACCOUNTING ASPECTS OF MERGERS

Two basic methods can be used to account for mergers: the *purchase method* or the *pooling of interests method.* In the purchase method, the total value paid or exchanged for the acquired firm's assets is recorded on the acquiring company's books. The tangible assets acquired are recorded at their fair market values, which may or may not be more than the amount at which they were carried on the acquired firm's balance sheet prior to the merger. Any difference between the total value paid and the fair market value of the acquired assets is termed *goodwill.*[4]

In the pooling of interests method, the acquired company's assets are recorded on the acquiring company's books at their cost (net of depreciation) when originally acquired. Thus, any difference between the purchase price and the book value is not recorded on the acquiring company's books, and no goodwill account is created.

The pooling of interests method has certain advantages over the purchase method. All other things being equal, reported earnings will be higher under the pooling method, primarily because depreciation will not be more than the sum of the depreciation charges prior to the merger. In addition, since goodwill is not created on the balance sheet in a pooling, it cannot appear as an amortization charge on the acquiring firm's income statement. Finally, since goodwill is not recognized as a deduction for income tax purposes, it has to be deducted from net income *after taxes.*

For example, suppose that Company B acquires Company A's outstanding common stock for $10 million. The book value of the acquired shares is $7 million. Table 23–3 shows the results of this merger, according to both the purchase and pooling of interests methods.

In the pooling of interests method, the two balance sheets are combined, and the $3 million difference between the purchase price and the book value of Company A's stock is not considered. In the purchase method, in contrast, the $3 million difference between the purchase price and the book value is recorded on both sides of Company B's postmerger balance sheet as an increase in total assets and as shareholders' equity.

---

[4]The expression *goodwill* rarely appears on the balance sheet; instead, one often finds "investment in consolidated subsidiaries in excess of net assets at date of acquisition, less amortization."

TABLE 23–3   Comparison of the Purchase and the Pooling of Interests Methods of Accounting for Mergers*

| | BEFORE ACQUISITION | | COMPANY B (AFTER ACQUISITION OF COMPANY A) | |
	Company A	Company B	Purchase Method	Pooling of Interests Method
Total assets, book value	$10	$50	$63	$60
Liabilities, book value	3	15	18	18
Shareholders' equity, book value	7	35	45	42

*Terms of merger: Company B acquires common stock of Company A for $10 million.

The book value of Company A's *assets* is $10 million. Suppose that the market value of Company A's assets at the date of acquisition is $11 million. Company B paid $3 million above the book value of *shareholders' equity*. Of this $3 million, the $1 million difference between the assets' market value and book value is recorded on the balance sheet in the appropriate tangible assets accounts. The other $2 million is recorded as goodwill.

When the pooling of interests concept originally was conceived, it was generally intended to be used for combinations of companies of more or less the same size. The purchase method was intended for use when a "large" company acquired a "small" company. During the 1960s, the popularity of the pooling of interests method increased to a point where many accountants felt it was being abused. As a result, the Accounting Principles Board (APB), which at that time governed the public accounting profession, issued its *Opinion 16* in August 1970. The basic intention of this opinion is to insure that the pooling of interests method will only be used for mergers that combine the entire existing interests of *common* stockholders in independent companies. *APB Opinion 16* sets forth twelve conditions that must be met before the pooling of interests method can be applied. These include the following:

- The transaction must consist of voting common stock of the acquiring company that is exchanged for voting common stock of the acquired company.

- Each of the combining companies must be autonomous and must not have been a subsidiary or division of another corporation within 2 years before the initiation of the plan of combination.

- The entire combination must be completed within 1 year of the plan's initiation.

- No future transactions involving the exchanged shares (such as retirement) may be planned or intended at the time of the combination.

APB Opinion 17, which was issued concurrently with *APB Opinion 16*, deals with the purchase method and requires that goodwill be written off against income over a period not to exceed 40 years. For a company with large amounts of goodwill, the required 2.5 percent amortization can decrease reported earnings materially. Prior to *APB Opinion 17,* many companies were not amortizing the goodwill on their balance sheets.

TAX ASPECTS OF MERGERS

Taxes can play an important role in determining how an acquired company's shareholders receive compensation for their shares. For example, merger transactions that are effected through the use of voting equity securities (either common stock or *voting* preferred stock) are tax-free. For example, if an acquired company's stockholders have a gain on the value of their shares at the time of the merger, the gain is not recognized for tax purposes if these shareholders receive voting equity securities of the acquiring company; any gains are not recognized until the newly acquired shares are sold.

In contrast, if the acquired company's shareholders receive cash or *nonvoting* securities (such as debt securities, *nonvoting* preferred stock, or warrants) in exchange for their shares, any gains are taxable at the time of the merger. When a partial cash down payment is made, however, the exchange can be treated as an installment purchase, and the seller can spread the capital gains tax over the payment period.

The majority of mergers are stock-for-stock exchanges and thus are taxfree.

SUMMARY

- Business combinations include *mergers, consolidations,* and *holding companies.* Technically, a merger is a business combination in which all but one of the companies legally cease to exist, and the surviving company continues in operation under its original name. A consolidation is a business combination in which all the combining companies are dissolved and a new firm is formed. A holding company owns controlling interest in another legally separate company, and the relationship between these *affiliated* companies is called a *parent-subsidiary relationship.*

- *Mergers are classified according to whether they are horizontal, vertical,* or *conglomerate.* In a horizontal merger, the combining companies are direct competitors. In a vertical merger, the companies have a buyer-seller relationship. In a conglomerate merger, neither company competes directly with the other, and no buyer-seller relationship exists.

- There are a number of reasons why companies choose external growth over internal growth, including the following:

1. The availability of lower cost assets.

2. Greater economies of scale.

3. The availability of more secure raw material supplies and additional end-product markets.

4. The possibility of more rapid growth.

5. Greater diversification.

- Three major methods are used to value merger candidates: the *comparative price-earnings ratio method, the adjusted book value method, and the discounted cash flow method.* The discounted cash flow method, which is an application of capital budgeting techniques, is the most theoretically correct valuation method.

- In the *pooling of interests* method of accounting for mergers, the acquired assets are recorded at their cost when acquired. In the *purchase* method, acquired assets are recorded at their fair market values, and any additional amount paid is listed as *goodwill*, which then must be amortized.

QUESTIONS AND TOPICS FOR DISCUSSION

1. Define the following terms:
   a. Merger.
   b. Consolidation.
   c. Holding company.
2. Discuss the differences between the following types of mergers:
   a. Horizontal mergers.
   b. Vertical mergers.
   c. Conglomerate mergers.
3. What are some of the reasons why firms merge with other firms?
4. What methods do financial analysts use to value merger candidates? What are the limitations of each method?
5. What are the differences between the *purchase* method and the *pooling of interests* method of accounting for mergers?
6. How have *APB Opinion 16* and *APB Opinion 17* affected mergers?
7. What is a "tax-free merger?"

PROBLEMS*

1. The Anniston Oil Corporation and the Valley Plastics Company have agreed to a merger. The Valley Plastics stockholders will receive 0.75 shares of Anniston for each share of Valley Plastics held. Assume that no synergistic benefits are expected.
   a. Complete the following table:

	Anniston Oil	Valley Plastics	Combined Companies
Sales (millions)	$425	$125	_____
Net income (millions)	$60	$13	_____
Common shares outstanding (millions)	15	4	_____
Earnings per share	$4.00	$3.25	_____
Common stock (price per share)	$40	$26	_____
Price-earnings ratio	_____	_____	9.5

   b. Calculate the premium percentage received by the Valley Plastics stockholders.

*Problems in color have check answers provided at the end of the book.

2. The McPherson Company is considering acquiring the McAlester Company. Selected financial data for the two companies are shown here:

	McPherson	McAlester
Sales (millions)	$250	$30
Net income (millions)	$20	$2.25
Common shares outstanding (millions)	5	1
Earning per share	$4.00	$2.25
Dividends per share	$1.20	$0.40
Common stock (price per share)	$40.00	$18.00

Both companies have 40 percent marginal tax rates. Assume that no synergistic benefits are expected.

a. Calculate the McPherson Company's postmerger earnings per share if the McAlester stockholders accept an offer of $20 a share in a stock-for-stock exchange. (The expression *stock-for-stock exchange* means that the common stock of one company is exchanged for the common stock of another company.)

b. Recalculate Part a, assuming that the McPherson common stock price is $42 a share. (All other figures remain constant.)

c. Calculate McPherson's earnings per share if the McAlester stockholders accept one $6 convertible preferred share (stated value, $100) for each 5 shares of McAlester stock held.

d. Calculate McPherson's earnings per share if each group of 50 shares of McAlester stock is exchanged for one 8 percent, $1,000 debenture.

e. Compare the premerger expected dividend return on the McAlester stock with the expected postmerger dividends or interest available with the exchanges described in Parts a, c, and d. (Undoubtedly, at the time of acquisition, McPherson would have pointed out these expected increases in yield to the McAlester stockholders.) Assume that an investor initially holds 100 shares of McAlester stock.

f. What can be said about comparing the expected total premerger return (dividends plus price appreciation) on the McAlester stock versus the expected total postmerger return on the McPherson securities?

3. Grinnell Industries is considering acquiring the Natrium Corporation in a stock-for-stock exchange. Selected financial data on the two companies follow:

	Grinnell	Natrium
Sales (millions)	$600	$75
Net income (millions)	$30	$10
Common shares outstanding (millions)	6	4
Earnings per share	$5.00	$2.50
Common stock (price per share)	$50	$20

Assume that no synergistic benefits are expected.

a. What is the maximum exchange ratio Grinnell should agree to if one of its acquisition criteria is no initial dilution in earnings per share?

b. Suppose an investor had purchased 100 shares of Natrium common stock 5 years ago at $12 a share. If the Natrium stockholders accept an offer of $24 a share in a stock-for-stock exchange, how much capital gains tax would this investor have to pay at the time the Natrium shares are exchanged for the Grinnell shares? (Assume a capital gains tax rate of 20 percent for this investor.)

708

Mergers and Acquisitions

Admiral Foods Corporation is a diversified food processing and distributing company that has shown excellent growth over the past 10 years as a result of a balanced program of acquisitions and internal growth.

One segment of the food business in which Admiral has only recently begun to compete, however, is the fast-food business. The present top management of Admiral Foods feels that good future growth in the fast-food business is still possible, regardless of the rapid expansion of the 1970s. During the past year, members of the Admiral staff have examined and analyzed a number of independent fast-food firms.* One company that the analysis indicated was potentially suitable for acquisition by Admiral is Favorite Food Systems, Inc.

Favorite Food Systems, Inc., which was founded by John Favorite in 1961, is a West Coast chain with current annual sales of approximately $75 million. Favorite's history can best be described as up and down, with the general trend up. The company survived several brief shaky periods during the early and mid-1960s. In 1969 the company went public. (The Favorite family now controls about 57 percent of the common stock.) By 1972 Favorite Foods was recommended by two brokerage firms and was touted by one investment service as "another potential McDonald's." This and other predictions never came true. In fact, Favorite Food Systems' growth rate has slowed appreciably during the past 5 years. One reason frequently given in the trade for Favorite's growth slowdown is Mr. Favorite's apparent indecision regarding expansion. As a result, the competition has increasingly gotten the jump on Favorite with the best locations in new residential growth areas.

The following table shows last year's balance sheets and income statements for both Admiral and Favorite.

Admiral Foods Corporation Balance Sheet (in Millions of Dollars)

Current assets	$225.0	Current liabilities	$101.0
Fixed assets, net	307.0	Long-term debt	106.0
		Common equity (10,000,000 shares issued and outstanding)	325.0
		Total liabilities	
Total assets	$532.0	and equity	$532.0

---

*Many of the fast-food chains are divisions of larger firms. For example, Burger King and Steak and Ale are part of Pillsbury, and Red Lobster is part of General Mills.

Admiral Foods Corporation Income Statement (in Millions of Dollars)

Sales	$1261.0
Expenses, excluding depreciation	1118.2
Depreciation	36.0
Earnings before interest and taxes	$ 106.8
Interest	12.8
Earnings before taxes	$ 94.0
Taxes (40%)	37.6
Net income	$ 56.4

Favorite Food Systems, Inc. Balance Sheet (in Millions of Dollars)

Current assets	$10.6	Current liabilities	$ 6.5
Fixed assets, net	12.1	Long-term debt	2.2
		Common equity (2,000,000 shares issued and outstanding)	14.0
Total assets	$22.7	Total liabilities and equity	$22.7

Favorite Food Systems, Inc. Income Statement (in Millions of Dollars)

Sales	$75.2
Expenses, excluding depreciation	65.4
Depreciation	1.4
Earnings before interest and taxes	$ 8.4
Interest	0.4
Earnings before taxes	$ 8.0
Taxes (40%)	3.2
Net income	$ 4.8

Additional Information

	Admiral Foods Corporation	Favorite Food Systems
Dividends per share	$2.50	$0.60
Common stock (price per share)	$50.00	$15.00

Marie Harrington received her B.B.A. degree in finance 3 years ago and went to work for Admiral Foods as a financial analyst in the corporate budget department. Recently she became a senior financial analyst responsible for analyzing mergers and major capital expenditures. One of her first assignments is to prepare a financial analysis of the proposed Favorite acquisition. It is the conservative policy of Admiral Foods to analyze acquisitions assuming that no synergistic benefits will occur. Admiral Foods has found that the amount of synergy in a merger is relatively difficult to forecast. During Ms. Harrington's discussions with her supervisor, the following questions came up. Answer these questions.

1. Calculate the exchange ratios, based on the common stock market value and earnings per share.

2. Mr. Favorite has suggested an exchange ratio based on a 25 percent increase over Favorite's current market price. Calculate this exchange ratio.

3. What is the maximum exchange ratio Admiral Foods should agree to if one of its acquisition criteria specifies no initial dilution in earnings per share? What per-share price for Favorite Food Systems does this exchange ratio represent?

4. Even though Ms. Harrington's assignment is primarily financial in nature, what other considerations are important in a merger such as this?

5. Calculate the Admiral Foods postmerger earnings per share based on the following exchanges:
   a. Each share of Favorite stock is exchanged for 0.40 shares of Admiral stock.
   b. Each group of 5 shares of Favorite stock is exchanged for one $5.50 convertible preferred share (stated value, $100) of Admiral.
   c. Each group of 50 shares of Favorite stock is exchanged for one 8 percent, $1,000 debenture.

6. In discussions with Admiral, Mr. Favorite has stated that he would prefer to exchange his Favorite shares for either Admiral common stock or a convertible preferred rather than cash or debentures. Why?

7. If Admiral Foods is concerned about the possibility that Mr. Favorite will sell his new Admiral shares relatively soon after the merger (and thereby put downward pressure on the price of Admiral's stock), what can Admiral do to effectively prevent such a sale?

8. Based on the information given in the case and your analysis, what do you feel is a fair exchange ratio?

ADDITIONAL READINGS AND REFERENCES

Appleyard, A. R., and Yarrow, G. K. "The Relationship between Take-Over Activity and Share Valuation." *Journal of Finance* 30 (Dec. 1975): 1239–1249.

Austin, Douglas V. "The Financial Management of Tender Offer Takeovers." *Financial Management* 3 (Spring 1974): 37–43.

Briloff, Abraham L. "The Funny-Money Game." *Financial Analysts Journal* 25 (May–June 1969): 73–79.

Desmond, Glenn M., and Kelley, Richard E. *Business Valuation Handbook*. Llano, Calif.: Valuation Press, 1977.

Elgers, Pieter T., and Clark, John J. "Merger Types and Shareholder Returns: Additional Evidence." *Financial Management* 9 (Summer 1980): 66–72.

Heath, John, Jr. "Valuation Factors and Techniques in Mergers and Acquisitions." *Financial Executive* 40 (April 1972): 34–44.

Higgins, Robert, and Schall, Lawrence. "Corporate Bankruptcy and Conglomerate Merger." *Journal of Finance* (March 1975): 93–113.

Hogarty, Thomas F. "The Profitability of Corporate Mergers." *Journal of Business* 44 (July 1970): 317–327.

Kelly, Emmon M. *The Profitability of Growth through Mergers.* University Park, Pa.: Pennsylvania State University, 1967.

Lewellen, Wilbur G. "A Pure Financial Rationale for the Conglomerate Merger." *Journal of Finance* 26 (May 1971): 521–537.

Mandelker, G. "Risk and Return: The Case of Merging Firms." *Journal of Financial Economics* 1 (Dec. 1974): 303–336.

Melicher, Ronald W., and Rush, David F. "Evidence on the Acquisition-related Performance of Conglomerate Firms." *Journal of Finance* 29 (March 1974): 141–149.

Nielson, J. F., and Melicher, R. W. "A Financial Analysis of Acquisition and Merger Premiums." *Journal of Financial and Quantitative Analysis* (March 1973): 139–148.

Rappaport, Alfred. "Strategic Analysis for More Profitable Acquisitions." *Harvard Business Review* (July–August 1979): 99–110.

Reilly, Frank K. "What Determines the Ratio of Exchange in Corporate Mergers?" *Financial Analysts Journal* 18 (Nov.–Dec. 1962): 47–50.

Scott, James H. "On the Theory of Conglomerate Mergers." *Journal of Finance* (Sept. 1977): 1235–1250.

Shick, Richard A., and Jen, Frank C. "Merger Benefits to Shareholders of Acquiring Firms." *Financial Management* (Winter 1974): 45–53.

Smith, Keith V., and Weston, J. Fred. "Further Evaluation of Conglomerate Performance." *Journal of Business Research* 5 (1977): 5–14.

Weston, J. Fred, Smith, Keith V., and Shrieves, Ronald E. "Conglomerate Performance Using the Capital Asset Pricing Model." *Review of Economics and Statistics* (Nov. 1972): 357–363.

CHAPTER 24

Business Failure

A FINANCIAL DILEMMA

Manville's Bankruptcy

In August 1982 Manville Corporation, an asbestos producer and a conglomerate with over $2.2 billion in assets, became the largest industrial company ever to declare bankruptcy in the United States. Specifically, Manville filed under Chapter 11 of the Bankruptcy Reform Act for protection from individuals suing the company because of asbestos-related health problems.

The company had estimated that its potential liabilities from the lawsuits could exceed its future assets. Therefore, the company decided to use the bankruptcy laws to attempt to work out a reorganization plan. The company is negotiating with its creditors over how it will pay its obligations. If Manville cannot pay the creditors all their claims, they may become stockholders of a reorganized company. The company also is negotiating with asbestos victims and insurance companies in the hopes of keeping the company going and avoiding ultimate liquidation.

Everyone in a situation such as Manville's is involved in the dilemma of what is feasible and fair for all parties. This chapter discusses the alternatives available to failing businesses like Manville Corporation.

GLOSSARY OF NEW TERMS

Assignment the process of informally liquidating a business. Assignment occurs outside the jurisdiction of the bankruptcy courts.

Bankruptcy a situation in which a firm is unable to pay its debts, and its assets are turned over to the court for administration.

Bankruptcy Reform Act of 1978 a new U.S. bankruptcy act that significantly changed certain aspects of the Federal bankruptcy laws.

Chapter 11 the reorganization chapter of the Bankruptcy Reform Act. Under Chapter 11, a company continues to operate while it attempts to work out a reorganization plan.

Chapter 7   the liquidation chapter of the Bankruptcy Reform Act. Under Chapter 7, a company's assets are sold off, and the proceeds are distributed to creditors.

Composition   a situation in which a failing business is permitted to discharge its debt obligations by paying less than the full amounts owed to creditors.

Extension   a situation in which a failing business is permitted to lengthen the amount of time it has to meet its obligations with creditors.

Legal insolvency   a situation in which the recorded value of a firm's assets is less than its liabilities.

Technical insolvency   a situation in which a firm is unable to meet its current obligations as they come due, even though the value of its assets may exceed its liabilities.

INTRODUCTION

This chapter considers what happens when businesses experience severe and extended problems that might cause failure. The purpose is to present an overview of business failure and the alternatives available to the failing firm. The chapter first defines business failure and then discusses its frequency and causes. Next, the various alternatives available to failing firms are discussed, including the procedures involving the Federal bankruptcy laws.

DEFINITIONS OF BUSINESS FAILURE

Business failure can be considered from both an *economic* and a *financial* viewpoint. In an economic sense, *business success* is associated with firms that earn an adequate return (equal to or greater than the cost of capital) on their investments. Similarly, *business failure* is associated with firms that earn an inadequate return on their investments. An important aspect of business failure involves the question of whether the failure is *permanent* or *temporary*. For example, suppose a company has $1,000,000 invested in assets and only generates operating earnings of $10,000. Obviously, this 1 percent return on investment is inadequate. However, the appropriate course of action depends to some extent on whether this business failure is judged to be permanent or temporary. If it is permanent, the company probably should be liquidated. If failure is temporary, the company probably should attempt "to ride out the storm," especially if steps can be taken to speed the company's return to business success. From an economic standpoint, business failure also is said to exist when a firm's revenues are not sufficient to cover the costs of doing business.

It is more common, however, for business failure to be viewed in a *financial context*, either as a *technical insolvency*, a *legal insolvency*, or a *bankruptcy*. A firm is said to be *technically insolvent* if it is unable to meet its

714

current obligations as they come due, even though the value of its assets exceeds its liabilities.[1] A firm is *legally insolvent* if the recorded value of its assets is less than the recorded value of its liabilities. A firm is *bankrupt* if it is unable to pay its debts and it files a bankruptcy petition in accordance with the Federal bankruptcy laws.

BUSINESS FAILURE TRENDS

Table 24–1 shows several kinds of statistics dealing with business failures over time. Between 1968 and 1979, the number of failures in the United States averaged about 10,000 per year. With the deep 1981–1982 recession, the failure figure increased to about 17,000 in 1981 and to over 25,000 in 1982.

Typically, less than 5 percent of the business failures involve companies with liabilities over $1 million. However, the 1981–1982 recession claimed

TABLE 24–1 Failure Trends since 1925

Year	Number of Failures	Total Failure Liabilities	Failure Rate Per 10,000 Listed Concerns	Average Liability Per Failure
1925	21,214	$ 443,744,000	100	$ 20,918
1930	26,355	668,282,000	122	25,357
1935	12,244	310,580,000	62	25,366
1940	13,619	166,684,000	63	12,239
1945	809	30,225,000	4	37,361
1950	9,162	248,283,000	34	27,099
1955	10,969	449,380,000	42	40,968
1960	15,445	938,630,000	57	60,772
1965	13,514	1,321,666,000	53	97,800
1966	13,061	1,385,659,000	52	106,091
1967	12,364	1,265,227,000	49	102,332
1968	9,636	940,996,000	39	97,654
1969	9,154	1,142,113,000	37	124,767
1970	10,748	1,887,754,000	44	175,638
1971	10,326	1,916,929,000	42	185,641
1972	9,566	2,000,244,000	38	209,099
1973	9,345	2,298,606,000	36	245,972
1974	9,915	3,053,137,000	38	307,931
1975	11,432	4,380,170,000	43	383,150
1976	9,628	3,011,271,000	35	312,762
1977	7,919	3,095,317,000	28	390,872
1978	6,619	2,656,006,000	24	401,270
1979	7,564	2,667,362,000	28	352,639
1980	11,742	4,635,080,000	42	394,744
1981	16,794	6,955,180,000	61	414,147
1982	25,346*	—	89*	—

*Preliminary.
SOURCE: *The Business Failure Record.* New York: Dun and Bradstreet, 1983. Reprinted by permission.

[1] A firm that is *technically insolvent* can also be said to be *illiquid.*

TABLE 24–2   Large NYSE Companies Filing Bankruptcy Petitions during the 1981–1982 Recession

Company	Type of Business
AM International	Office equipment manufacturer
Braniff International	Airline
H.R.T. Industries	Retailer
Lionel	Toy manufacturer
Manville	Diversified manufacturing and mining company
Revere Copper	Copper, brass, and aluminum producer
Saxon Industries	Copier manufacturer and distributor of paper products
Wickes	Diversified retailing and manufacturing company

an unusually high number of large companies, as is shown in Table 24–2. Some of these companies may successfully reorganize while in bankruptcy and emerge to become profitable companies again. Some of them, however, may be liquidated and cease to exist.

Another interesting business failure trend involves the ages of failed businesses. Of the 16,794 businesses that failed in 1981, approximately 23 percent had been in business 3 years or less, and approximately 49 percent had been in business 5 years or less. Only 20 percent had been in business more than 10 years.[2]

CAUSES OF BUSINESS FAILURE

Although there are a number of reasons why businesses fail, most failures seem to be due at least in part to incompetent and inexperienced management. Dun and Bradstreet compiles a large amount of bankruptcy data, including causes of business failure. Table 24-3 shows the *underlying* causes of the business failures that occurred in 1981. The results show that almost 90 percent of these businesses failed because of management inexperience or incompetence. The Dun and Bradstreet analysis includes a classification of *apparent* causes, as well as *underlying* causes. In 1981, of the businesses that failed due to inexperience and incompetence (that is, the first four items shown in Table 24–3), about two-thirds were "evidenced by the inability to avoid conditions which resulted in inadequate sales." The next most frequent apparent cause was heavy operating expenses.[3]

When businesses experience problems such as inadequate sales and heavy operating expenses, they frequently encounter cash flow problems as well. As a result of the cash flow problems, these businesses often increase their short-term borrowings. If the problems persist, the cash flow difficulties can become more acute, and the business may not be able to meet its obligations

---

[2]*The Business Failure Record*, New York: Dun and Bradstreet, 1983, p. 10.
[3]*Ibid.*, p. 13.

TABLE 24–3   Causes of 16,794 Business Failures in 1981 (Classification of Failures Based on Opinion of Informed Creditors and Information in Dun and Bradstreet Reports)

Underlying Causes	Percentage
Lack of experience in the line	11.1
Lack of managerial experience	12.5
Unbalanced experience*	19.2
Incompetence	45.6
Neglect	0.7
Fraud	0.3
Disaster	0.5
Reason unknown	10.1
Total	100.0
Number of failures	16,794
Average liabilities per failure	$414,147

*Experience not well rounded in sales, finance, purchasing, and production on the part of the individual in the case of a proprietorship, on the part of two or more partners or officers constituting a management unit.
SOURCE: *The Business Failure Record.* New York: Dun and Bradstreet, 1983, p. 12. Adapted by permission.

to its creditors on a timely basis. At this point, the firm's owners and management have to ask about the alternatives that are available to failing businesses.

ALTERNATIVES FOR FAILING BUSINESSES

In general, a failing company has two alternatives:

- It can attempt to resolve its difficulties with its creditors on a *voluntary*, or *informal*, basis.
- It can petition the courts for assistance and *formally* declare *bankruptcy*.

A company's creditors also may petition the courts, and this may result in the company's being involuntarily declared bankrupt.

Regardless of whether a business chooses informal or formal methods to deal with its difficulties, eventually the decision has to be made whether to *reorganize* or *liquidate* the business. Before this decision can be made, both the business's liquidation value and its going-concern value have to be determined. *Liquidation value* equals the proceeds that would be received from the sale of the business assets minus its liabilities. *Going-concern value* equals the capitalized value of the company's operating earnings minus its liabilities. Basically, if the going-concern value exceeds the liquidation value, the business should be reorganized; otherwise, it should be liquidated. However, in practice, the determination of the going-concern and liquidation values is not an easy matter. For example, problems may exist in estimating the price the company's assets will bring at auction. In addition, the company's future operating earnings and the appropriate discount rate at which to capitalize the earnings may be difficult to determine. Also, management is understandably not in a position to be completely objective about these values.

INFORMAL ALTERNATIVES FOR FAILING BUSINESSES

Regardless of the exact reasons why a business begins to experience difficulties, the result is often the same—namely, cash flow problems.

Frequently, the first steps taken by the troubled company involve stretching its payables. In some cases, this action can buy the troubled company up to several weeks of needed time before creditors take action.

If the difficulties are more than just minor and very temporary, the company may next turn to its bankers and request additional working capital loans. In some situations, the bankers may make the additional loans, especially if they perceive the situation to be temporary. Another possible action the company's bankers and creditors may take is to restructure the company's debt.

Debt restructuring by bankers and other creditors can be quite complex. However, debt restructuring basically involves either *extension, composition,* or a combination of the two. In an *extension,* the failing company tries to reach an agreement with its creditors that will permit it to lengthen the time it has to meet its obligations. In a *composition,* the firm's creditors accept some percentage amount less than their actual original claims, and the company is permitted to discharge its debt obligations by paying less than the full amounts owed. The percentage a company's creditors will agree to in the event of a composition is usually greater than the percentage they could net if the company had to sell its assets to satisfy their claims. If a company's creditors feel that the company can overcome its financial difficulties and become a valuable customer over the long run, they may be willing to accept some form of composition.

Debt restructuring by lenders can involve deferment of both interest and principal payments for a time. Before lenders will agree to these deferments, they often require the troubled company's suppliers to also make various concessions. In addition, the lenders frequently demand and receive *warrants* in return for making their deferment concessions.

Large companies that experience cash flow difficulties often sell off real estate, various operating divisions, or both to raise needed cash. For example, Chrysler, in the midst of its 1980–1982 problems, sold its profitable tank-manufacturing division, as well as certain real estate assets. Also, International Harvester sold its construction equipment division in 1982 to raise the cash needed to stay in business.

Another method often used by failing companies to raise needed cash involves the sale and leaseback of its land and buildings. Some companies also resort to more unusual methods of conserving cash, such as offering preferred stock to certain employees in exchange for a portion of their salary.

Frequently, failing companies voluntarily form a *creditors' committee,* which meets regularly and attempts to help the company out of its predicament. The creditors usually are requested to accept deferred payments, and in return the creditors usually request that the company cut various expenditures. If the company and its creditors are able to reach an agreement on the appropriate actions to take, the legal and administrative expenses associated with formal bankruptcy procedures are not incurred. Accordingly, both the company and creditors may be better off as a result.

Liquidation also can occur outside the bankruptcy courts. The process is called an *assignment*. Usually a trustee, who is probably one of the major creditors, is assigned the assets. The trustee then has the responsibility of selling the assets and distributing the proceeds in the best interests of the creditors.

FORMAL ALTERNATIVES FOR FAILING BUSINESSES UNDER THE BANKRUPTCY LAWS

If a failing company is unable to reach a voluntary agreement with its creditors, it can seek assistance and protection in the bankruptcy courts. The Bankruptcy Reform Act of 1978 states the basic mechanics of the bankruptcy procedure.[4]

Either the debtor company or its unsecured creditors may initiate bankruptcy procedures. After the initial *bankruptcy petition* has been filed, both the failing company and its creditors receive protection from the courts. The company itself is protected from any further actions on the part of the creditors while it attempts to work out a *plan of reorganization*.[5] Normally, the troubled company is allowed to continue operations. If there is reason to believe that continuing operations will result in further deterioration of the creditors' position, however, the court can order the firm to cease operating.

An important aspect of the bankruptcy procedures involves what to do with the failing firm. Just as in the case of the informal alternatives, a decision has to be made about whether a firm's value as a *going concern* is greater than its *liquidation* value. Generally, if this is the case and a suitable plan of reorganization can be formulated, the firm is reorganized; otherwise, it is liquidated.

Reorganization Chapter 11 of the Bankruptcy Reform Act outlines different bankruptcy procedures. In a Chapter 11 proceeding, the failing company basically seeks court protection from its creditors while it attempts to work out a *plan of reorganization*.

During Chapter 11 proceedings, the failing company presents its current financial status and its proposed plan of reorganization. This plan of reorganization is normally similar to either composition or extension. The reorganization plan then must be approved by a majority of each class of creditors (who are classified by number and the dollar amount owed them). If the plan is approved, any dissenters are bound to it under the law. The court has con-

---

[4]The Bankruptcy Reform Act of 1978, in general, streamlined the U.S. bankruptcy procedures and increased the number of bankruptcy courts. The Reform Act contains eight odd-numbered chapters, 1 through 15, which are labeled with arabic numerals instead of the roman numerals used in the old Bankruptcy Act.

[5]The debtor company has 120 days to work out a plan of reorganization. After that, the creditors may file a plan of their own.

siderable latitude in a Chapter 11 bankruptcy. For example, depending on the nature of the case, it may decide to appoint a *trustee,* who will be responsible for running the business and protecting the creditors' interests.

Chapter 11 bankruptcy proceedings may be initiated either voluntarily by the failing company or by a group of three or more of its unsecured creditors that have aggregate claims of at least $500. The only requirement the three or more unsecured creditors have for filing the bankruptcy petition is to assert that the debtor company is not paying its present debts as they come due.

After the plan of reorganization has been worked out and submitted to the bankruptcy court for its approval, it is also presented to the creditors for their approval. If the bankrupt company is able to obtain approval from the bankruptcy court and its creditors, it can leave Chapter 11. As an example of a reorganization plan, consider Lionel Corporation, one of the companies listed in Table 24–2, which filed for bankruptcy under Chapter 11 in February 1982.[6] Lionel has unsecured creditors whose claims totaled $139 million. The company proposed paying the creditors $70 million in cash initially and another $45.5 million in cash over 11 years, beginning in 1984. In addition, the creditors would receive $10 million par value of a new 8 percent convertible preferred stock and about 3.8 million newly issued common shares. The creditors would then own 35 percent of the company's outstanding common shares.

The bankruptcy court and the Securities and Exchange Commission (SEC) review the plan of reorganization for *fairness* and *feasibility.* The term *fairness* means that the claims are to be settled in the order of their priority. The priority of claims is discussed in detail in the next section on liquidation. A *feasible* plan of reorganization is one that gives the business a good chance of reestablishing successful operations. For example, the plan must provide an adequate level of working capital, a reasonable capital structure and debt-to-equity ratio, and an earning power sufficient to reasonably cover interest and dividend requirements.

The following example illustrates the procedures involved in formulating a reorganization plan. Suppose that the capital structure listed on the books of Troubled Times, Inc., a company undergoing reorganization, is as follows:

Mortgage bonds	$ 6,000,000
Debentures	5,000,000
Preferred stock	1,000,000
Common stock	8,000,000
	$20,000,000

The trustee estimates the company's liquidation value to be $10 million and its going-concern value to be $12 million. Thus, the company is "worth more alive than dead," and a reorganization rather than a liquidation is attempted. The following is one possible recapitalization that the trustee might submit to the bankruptcy court:

[6]*Wall Street Journal* (March 23, 1983):1.

Debentures	$ 3,000,000
Income bonds	2,000,000
Preferred stock	1,000,000
Common stock	6,000,000
	$12,000,000

This recapitalization would result in fewer fixed charges for the reorganized company and thereby afford it a better chance of succeeding. The reorganization also might involve an extension of the debt maturities, which would help the company's funds flow by causing the debt's principal retirement to occur at later dates.

The trustee's next task is to allocate these new securities to the old security holders according to the priority of claims. The claims of senior security holders must be settled before those of junior security holders. In this example, the original mortgage bonds are exchanged for the new debentures, income bonds, and new preferred stock. The original debenture holders receive five-sixths of the new common stock, and the original preferred stockholders receive one-sixth of the new common stock. The original common stockholders receive nothing.

Following the SEC review for fairness and feasibility, the bankruptcy court approves the plan for submission to the firm's security holders. The holders who are affected by the reorganization plan then vote by group. Before the court can finally approve the plan, a two-thirds majority of each group of affected debtholders and a simple majority of the firm's stockholders must vote in its favor. Dissenters may appeal the decision to a higher court.

For example, Penn Central, the largest U.S. railroad, declared bankruptcy in 1970. Following 8 years of bankruptcy proceedings, a court-approved plan of reorganization became effective in October 1978. Under the terms of this plan, the holders of Penn Central's secured bonds received 10 percent of their claims in cash (generated from the sale of various assets), 30 percent in new mortgage bonds, 30 percent in new preference (preferred) stock, and 30 percent in new common stock. Thus, the reorganization plan effectively established a *new* capital structure for the firm that consists of less debt and more equity. Penn Central's common stockholders also participated in the reorganization, although they received only $\frac{1}{25}$ share of the new common stock for each Penn Central share they held at that time.

Liquidation   If for some reason reorganization is judged unfeasible, a legally declared bankrupt company may be liquidated. The liquidation procedures are described in Chapter 7 of the Bankruptcy Reform Act. In the liquidation procedure, a *referee* normally is appointed to handle the administrative aspects of the bankruptcy procedure. The referee then arranges for a meeting of the creditors, and they in turn select a *trustee,* who liquidates the business and pays the creditors' claims according to the priority of claims set forth in Chapter 7.

The priority of claims states that in general, secured debts are satisfied first, from the sale of the secured assets. Then the following list specifies the order of priority in which unsecured debts must be paid:

1. The expenses involved in the administration of the bankruptcy.

2. Business expenses incurred after an involuntary petition has been filed, but before a trustee has been appointed.

3. Wages owed for services performed during the 3 months prior to the bankruptcy proceedings, not to exceed $2,000 per employee.

4. Certain unpaid contributions to employee benefit plans (limited to $2,000).

5. Certain customer layaway deposits, not to exceed $900 per individual.

6. Taxes owed to Federal, state, and local governments.

7. Claims of general and unsecured creditors.

8. Preferred stockholders; they receive an amount up to the par value or stated value of the preferred stock.

9. Common stockholders; they share any remaining funds equally on a per-share basis.

To illustrate the priority of claims in a liquidation, consider the balance sheet prior to liquidation of Failures Galore, Inc., shown in Table 24–4.[7]

Suppose that the total proceeds of the liquidation are $6.8 million. The distribution of these proceeds is shown in Table 24–5. The proceeds have been distributed in accordance with the priority of claims. Each general and unsecured creditor receives a settlement percentage of the funds owed after priority claims have been settled. As shown in Table 24–5, these priority claims are bankruptcy administration expenses, wages, and taxes owed. In addition, mortgage bondholders receive $1.5 million from the sale of secured assets; this leaves the mortgage bondholders as general creditors for the balance of their claim ($500,000). After these priority claims have been met, there is $4.25 million in assets remaining to meet the remaining creditor

TABLE 24–4   Balance Sheet, Failures Galore, Inc.*

Assets		Liabilities and Capital	
Current assets	$ 6,000,000	Accounts payable	$ 2,000,000
Fixed assets, net	6,500,000	Bank notes payable	2,000,000
		Accrued wages	200,000
		Accrued taxes	300,000
		Mortgage bonds	2,000,000
		Debentures	2,000,000
		Subordinated debentures	2,000,000
		Preferred stock	1,000,000
		Common equity	1,000,000
Total assets	$12,500,000	Liabilities and equity	$12,500,000

*The subordinated debentures are subordinate to the bank notes payable. Assume that all the accrued wages can be paid out of the liquidation proceeds.

[7]Assume that this liquidation is a voluntary petition, that no unpaid contributions to employee benefit plans exist, and that no customer layaway deposits are involved. In other words, Items 2, 4, and 5 in the priority of claims do not apply to this example.

TABLE 24–5   Distribution of the Proceeds from the Liquidation of Failures Galore, Inc.

Total liquidation proceeds	$6,800,000
1. Bankruptcy administration expenses	$ 550,000
2. Wages owed to employees	200,000
3. Taxes owed to governments	300,000
Total priority claims	$1,050,000
Funds available for claims of creditors	$5,750,000
4. Payment to mortgage bondholders (proceeds from sale of secured assets)	1,500,000
Funds available for claims of general and unsecured creditors	$4,250,000

$$\text{Settlement percentage for general and unsecured creditors} = \frac{\text{Funds available for general and unsecured creditors}}{\text{Total claims of general and unsecured creditors}}$$

$$= \frac{\$4,250,000}{\$8,500,000}$$

$$= 50\% \ .$$

	Total Claim	Settlement, 50% of Claim (Before Subordination Adjustment)	Settlement, 50% of Claim (After Subordination Adjustment)
Accounts payable	$2,000,000	$1,000,000	$1,000,000
Bank notes payable	2,000,000	1,000,000	2,000,000
Mortgage bonds	500,000	250,000	250,000
Debentures	2,000,000	1,000,000	1,000,000
Subordinated debentures	2,000,000	1,000,000	0
	$8,500,000	$4,250,000	$4,250,000

Funds available for preferred and common stockholders $0

claims of $8.5 million. Each general creditor receives 50 percent of the claim, except bank notes. Because the subordinated debentures are subordinate to bank notes, the bank notes receive the proportionate claim of the subordinated holders ($1 million in this case), in addition to the $1 million directly due the bank notes. Hence, because of the subordination provision in the debentures, the bank notes are paid off in full.

SUMMARY

- A firm is *bankrupt* if its total liabilities exceed the value of its total assets. A firm is *technically insolvent* if it cannot meet its current obligations as they come due, even though the value of its assets exceeds its liabilities.

- *Incompetent and inexperienced management* are generally considered to be the primary causes of most business failures.

- Failing firms have two basic alternatives:

1. They can attempt to resolve the difficulties with their creditors on an *informal*, voluntary basis.

2. They can petition the courts for assistance and *formally* declare *bank-ruptcy.*

In addition, the creditors may petition the courts, and the firm may involuntarily be declared bankrupt.

- Legal bankruptcy proceedings focus on the decision of whether the failing firm should be *reorganized* or *liquidated.* If its going-concern value is greater than its liquidation value, the business will usually be reorganized; otherwise, it will be liquidated.

- The Bankruptcy Reform Act contains two chapters that outline different bankruptcy procedures. In a Chapter 11 proceeding, the troubled company seeks court protection from its creditors while it works out a *reorganization plan.* If reorganization is judged not feasible, the bankrupt company is liquidated. The liquidation procedures are set forth in Chapter 7 of the Bankruptcy Reform Act.

Bankers Who Step in
If Loans Go Bad Reveal
Lenders' Other Face*

Julie Salamon
Staff Reporter of The Wall Street Journal

They are variously known as undertakers, morticians, black hats, or goons. But members of this banking fraternity prefer to think of themselves as surgeons.

They are workout specialists, the bankers who take over when a business loan goes bad. Most companies don't know these specialists exist. Those companies that do wish they didn't.

"You come to dread them," says the treasurer of a Midwestern leisure-products maker. Back when its prospects were bright, this company had been wooed and won by an eager loan officer from Continental Illinois Bank & Trust Co. "He brought me to Chicago to meet the president of the bank, to eat lunch in the executive dining room," the treasurer recalls. "He knocked himself out coming to the company and telling me what the bank could do for us. It was nice."

But when business soured, the solicitous loan officer disappeared. Then "this new banker shows up. And he keeps coming back every day, wanting to know why this or that employee is needed, why we had to have those airline tickets," says the treasurer. "Suddenly you've lost control. The bank has become your boss."

PLENTY TO DO

Such trauma is becoming more common. Business failures rose nearly 50% in 1981, and what bankers refer to as "nonperforming loans" doubled and tripled at many institutions. Banks' intensive-care wards, or workout areas (literally, where problems are "worked out"), are already crowded and likely to become more so if the economy doesn't improve.

Neither companies nor banks trumpet the arrival of the special forces, but an announcement of "debt restructuring" is a signal that the workout crew has taken charge. Other signs: news reports that "lenders" forced a "troubled company" to dismiss its president, sell a division or forgo new products. Those mysterious and pushy "lenders" are usually workout people.

Thus, when the chairman and six other officers or directors of Wickes Co., quit this week, holders of the company's heavy debt insisted they were just bystanders. But the chief workout officer at one bank, Richard Daniel of Security Pacific, did comment that "we've long been dissatisfied with what was going on at Wickes and let our feelings be known."

Despite these suggestions of omnipotence, a bank can't actually take control of a customer's business when a loan looks shaky. By law, if a bank starts running a business, the lender risks losing its status as a creditor should the company go bankrupt. So workout officers don't tell a company what to do. They simply say no to so many things that only one course of action is left.

BIG STICK

Or, they hint. Strongly. "We don't say you've got to hire Joe Smith to be your top financial guy or we're finished with you," says Paul T. Walker, Chase Manhattan Bank's chief workout officer. "We can say, 'You have a void in your present management.' Then we may offer some suggestions, give them a list of 10 people." Continental Illinois' workout man rejected the Midwestern leisure-products company's plans to expand its business and then told the company a 15% sales-force reduction would be "prudent."

Companies listen for one reason: Knuckling under beats bankruptcy, the likely consequence of a loan default. When asked about his worst times since International Harvester began rescheduling its $4.7 billion debt last year, Archie R. McCardell, its chairman, recalls "the many nights when several of us would go home knowing we'd have to get up at 2 a.m. or 3 a.m." to answer a phone call from an anxious European banker. He never knew, he adds, "whether someone would take that final step" and force the company into bankruptcy.

Big workouts, such as Chrysler and International Harvester, attract lots of attention. But mostly workout units move quietly, much to the relief of their patients. Like people who undergo radical surgery, companies often find workout so painful and embarrassing they don't want to discuss it, even after they are back on their feet. Says Harris Levin, a New York bankruptcy lawyer: "It's a humiliation and a nightmare."

A bank, too, usually is content to keep the spotlight off its workout people; after all, the busier they are, the more mistakes the loan department has made. Thus, workout people operate in relative obscurity in less glorious parts of banks. Plush carpets and original paintings may be needed to attract new customers, but potential deadbeats don't require such niceties. At Security Pacific Bank in Los Angeles, the workout department is on the 13th floor. A long, bleak corridor leads to Citibank's workout staff in New York. Visitors to Chase's problem loan section in New York step off the elevator onto linoleum.

Workout departments aren't usually listed in bank directories. But a company can guess it has troubles if it is asked to report to Institutional Recovery Management (Citibank), to Special Assets (Security Pacific in Los Angeles), to Central Loan Department (Irving Trust Co. in New York), or to other departments beginning with "special."

The euphemisms serve a practical purpose. Sometimes ailing companies extricate themselves from workout at one bank by borrowing from another institution. If the new banker, unaware of the customer's less-than-perfect status, calls the old one for information and hears "workout," he will run the other way.

A company's change in status from master to slave often comes abruptly. At Citibank, customers are simply told one day to arrive at the 19th floor of the bank's Park Avenue office. "It's always interesting to watch them walk down that corridor, look at that sign (Institutional Recovery Management) and watch their faces change as it dawns on them they might be in trouble," chuckles Peter Fitts, Citibank's top workout officer.

Some banks make the transfer more gently. At Chase, workout officers start showing up at meetings along with the company's regular banker. After a couple of meetings, the account officer disappears.

Workouts usually last at least a year, sometimes much longer. The Midwestern leisure-products company was in workout for five years before it could get loans again. International Harvester has been struggling with its lenders for more than a year and is far from free of them.

The process is tedious. Bankers negotiate fine points in meeting after meeting with companies and, in big workouts, with other bankers. Sometimes they have to go to great lengths to win allies among other bankers whose stake in a company might not be as great but who can still veto decisions. To keep other lenders informed of the progress of Chrysler's K-cars, Scott Taylor, a former Chase workout officer, produced a film on how the cars were assembled. "If you keep people out in the cold, they're likely to say no," he explains.

In dealing with borrowers, however, workout specialists can be a bit more forceful. Citibank's Mr. Fitts, a big, tall man, has his own technique: He states his views, then puffs quietly on his cigar until everyone else agrees.

WHAT IT TAKES

The list of qualities distinguishing a good workout officer varies with who is asked. Practitioners assess themselves as analytical, patient, perceptive, decisive and humorous. Other bankers offer such adjectives as churlish, sadistic, thick-skinned, single-minded, obnoxious and insensitive.

The S.W.A.T. teams naturally have developed their own lingo. Troubled companies are rarely called customers; workout people refer to them as "clients" or "turkeys" or, most frequently, simply as "names." As Mr. Taylor, who dealt with Chrysler, explains, "When you spend two weeks locked in a hotel and at the Treasury in Washington and you don't get to see your family because of some company, you don't think of that company as a customer anymore."

Linked by work that is often grueling and sometimes thankless, the specialists tend to stick together. An example came at International Harvester's first meeting with creditors to discuss delaying debt repayment. Workout officers weren't invited. But those from three banks, who knew one another from the Chrysler case, conspired to get themselves invited, figuring they would end up handling the matter anyway. Each told his superiors the other workout people were going, and soon all had invitations from their own banks.

NEED FOR SPECIALISTS

There once was a time when workout was a banking backwater, where bankruptcy specialists kicked the bones of dead customers. It was thought easier to let sick companies go under and bear the loss than to try to find a way to keep them alive. But the bankruptcy actions arose at such giants as Penn Central and W.T. Grant; their debts were scattered among many banks, which had to squabble over the remains. There were huge, embarrassing write-offs.

Next, Chrysler and other big borrowers got in trouble with the changing markets and difficult economy. Banks realized they would have to start restructuring debts en masse or face numerous multimillion-dollar write-offs. Most chose to create squads of officers who did nothing but work with customers to change business habits and try to restore profitability. Even smaller banks began adding full-time trouble-shooters.

But not all troubled companies are ready to accept a bank as Big Brother. William F. (Willie) Farah recently took some lenders to court on a complaint that they brought his company close to bankruptcy. He had quit as president of Farah Manufacturing Co. when it went through hard times in the mid-1970s. As a condition of a loan from State National Bank of El Paso, Continental Illinois and Republic Bank of Dallas, Mr. Farah had to stay on the sidelines while a turnaround specialist the banks brought in sold millions of dollars of the Texas clothing company's assets to repay loans. In a judgment the banks plan to appeal, a Texas court awarded Mr. Farah $19 million in damages.

Bankers say they have only one concern in these spats: getting their money back. "We have the right to get paid and they have an obligation to pay us," says Mr. Walker, the chief workout officer at Chase. "The bank didn't cause the company to make bad investments or whatever it was that caused them to lose money."

PLAYING CLEANUP

Workout specialists often feel they are looking at the error of others' ways: unwillingness by companies to admit that their projections were off, or bad judgment by a bank loan officer who acted out of friendship, pressure to make loans, or simply ineptitude. "Loan officers are supposed to get a detailed forecast of where a company's going before they make a loan," says Richard Daniel, the head of Security Pacific's Special Assets division. "But most officers don't watch whether sales are what were projected or whether receivables are turning over like they were supposed to."

Such remarks don't endear workout people to their banker colleagues, who resent being depicted as financial Santa Clauses. Winning a single big account, loan officers note, can take two or three years of work. First, they must come up with a financial package somehow distinguishable from competitors. Then there are the endless lunches, dinners, and other mandatory social contacts. "Your personal relationship with the treasurer can make or break a deal," says a Citibank loan officer. "He isn't just looking at the institution—the big banks look alike to him. He's wondering, 'Is this guy like me?' "

Once the deal is made, the loan officer has to turn to new conquests and thus is often juggling 25 or more big accounts at once. So when one of those loans looks shaky (most banks have regular reviews), the special team is called for what may be a seven-day-a-week job working out the company's problems in repaying.

GETTING THE NEWS

This can be a dreadful moment for the officer who arranged the loan. The workout people "just march in and say to the company, 'Your business plan looks crummy; this and this will have to go,' " says the Citibank loan officer. "You say to yourself, 'My God, I don't want to give my company up to these goons.' "

The dread is also more personal, he adds: "You also start agonizing about your own reputation. You feel like you've totally lost face." In fact, losing an account to workout usually doesn't mean the end of a promising career, unless the loan officer essentially hoodwinked superiors into accepting the loan—or unless it is the officer's second or third loser.

Partly to keep such officers on their toes, some banks shun the workout system. Explains John Greathouse, the top credit officer at Chicago's Amalgamated Bank & Trust Co., "If a loan officer knows he's going to have to live with those loans, day and night, good or bad, he'll learn to stay away from problems."

Most workout specialists once were loan officers themselves. They didn't necessarily bring in the most business—they often lacked the slap and tickle a good salesman needs—but they were quickest to spot trouble and fix it. They understand balance sheets and business plans. What they don't understand is why anyone should be so eager for new business as to skim over such details.

"It doesn't take a whole lot of skill to lend people money," says one workout officer. "Getting money back—that makes you feel like a banker."

QUESTIONS AND TOPICS FOR DISCUSSION

1. Discuss the differences between *technical insolvency* and *bankruptcy*.
2. What are the alternatives available to the failing firm?
3. What are the differences between Chapter 7 and Chapter 11 of the Bankruptcy Reform Act?

4. In connection with reorganization plans, what do *fairness* and *feasibility* mean?

5. Basically, what determines whether a bankrupt company is reorganized or liquidated?

PROBLEMS*

1. Calculate the distribution of the proceeds from the liquidation of Failures Galore, Inc. (Tables 24–4 and 24–5), if total liquidation proceeds are as follows:
   a. $5,950,000.
   b. $7,650,000.

ADDITIONAL READINGS AND REFERENCES

Aharony, Joseph, Jones, Charles P., and Swary, I. "Analysis of Risk and Return Characteristics of Corporate Bankruptcy Using Capital Market Data." *Journal of Finance* 35 (Sept. 1980): 1001–1016.

Altman, Edward I. *Corporate Bankruptcy in America.* Lexington, Mass.: Heath Lexington Books, 1971.

————. "Financial Ratios, Discriminant Analysis and the Prediction of Corporate Bankruptcy." *Journal of Finance* 23 (Sept. 1968): 589–609.

Altman, Edward I., Haldeman, R. G., and Narayanan, P. "ZETA Analysis: A New Model to Identify Bankruptcy Risk of Corporations." *Journal of Banking and Finance* 1 (June 1977): 29–54.

Beaver, William H. "Financial Ratios as Predictors of Failure." *Empirical Research in Accounting: Selected Studies.* Supplement to *Journal of Accounting Research* (1966): 71–111.

Gordon, Myron J. "Towards a Theory of Financial Distress." *Journal of Finance* 26 (May 1971): 347–356.

Higgins, Robert, and Schall, Lawrence. "Corporate Bankruptcy and Conglomerate Merger." *Journal of Finance* (March 1975): 93–113.

Murray, Roger F. "The Penn Central Debacle: Lessons for Financial Analysis." *Journal of Finance* 26 (May 1971): 327–332.

Scott, James H., Jr. "Bankruptcy, Secured Debt and Optimal Capital Structure." *Journal of Finance* 32 (March 1977): 1–20.

*Problems in color have check answers provided at the end of the book.

CHAPTER 25

International Financial Management and Financial Decision Making in Not-For-Profit Enterprises

A FINANCIAL DILEMMA

Franklin National Bank

The story of Franklin National Bank, formerly the 20th largest bank in the United States with deposits of nearly $3 billion, is one of incredible misman-agement, culminating in huge foreign exchange losses. In the 1960s Frank-lin's growth strategy led it to make many high-risk loans. As these loans gradually went bad, Franklin turned to bond investments, more than dou-bling the size of its securities portfolio. Many of these bonds were low yield-ing (3 to 4 percent) tax-exempt municipal bonds. Since the bank had little or no taxable income, however, these bonds provided particularly unattractive returns. As interest rates rose, the bonds fell in value, but Franklin was re-luctant to liquidate them and take the losses. It ended up with large amounts of low-yielding assets that were financed with progressively higher cost money.

In 1972 and 1973 Franklin attempted to recover its position by expanding its loans and bond portfolios, and it financed this expansion largely with bor-rowed funds. Loan rates were low, however, and the cost of money was in-creasing rapidly. As a result, the bank made many loans at rates that were *less* than the cost of funds used to finance them.

With profit margins of nearly zero on its domestic loans, the bank turned to its international department to make up the losses. The bank speculated heavily in foreign currencies, hoping that these could be sold for a profit at a later date. Franklin also speculated in the futures market for foreign currencies. During the first half of 1974, the bank lost $45.8 million on these transactions.

In May 1974 Franklin canceled its second-quarter dividend. During the next 4 months the bank faced deposit withdrawals that exceeded $1.5 billion. Finally, the bank failed.

The increased amount of international trade and the internationalization of money and capital markets make it essential for financial managers to understand the basic elements of international financial management. This is the topic of the first half of this chapter. The balance of the chapter examines some key elements of financial decision making in not-for-profit enterprises.

GLOSSARY OF NEW TERMS

Cost-benefit analysis   an analytical tool that requires the measurement of all benefits and costs arising from a particular project or program. It is designed to assist public decision makers in determining their resource allocations.

Eurodollars   U.S. dollars that have been deposited in European banks or European branches of U.S. banks.

Forward rate   the rate of exchange between two currencies being bought and sold for delivery at a *future* date.

Letter of credit   a document issued by a bank guaranteeing payment for a particular shipment of goods.

Multinational corporation   a firm that has direct investments in more than one country.

Social rate of discount   the discount rate used to value costs and benefits in cost-benefit analysis.

Spot rate   the rate of exchange between two currencies that are being bought and sold for *immediate* delivery.

INTRODUCTION

This chapter examines two important topics that encompass several of the broad subject areas of financial management. First, it focuses on *international financial management* and considers how the foreign currencies markets may be effectively used by firms engaged in financing international transactions, emphasizing how exchange risk may be avoided. Second, the chapter considers *financial decision making in public and not-for-profit enterprises.*

INTERNATIONAL FINANCIAL MANAGEMENT

A growing number of firms engage in various types of international financial transactions. These transactions can take many different forms. At one end of the spectrum are firms that *export* finished goods for sale in a foreign country and/or *import* raw materials or products from abroad for use in a domestic operation. In 1981 U.S. exports and imports totaled over $233 billion and $261 billion, respectively. At the other end of the spectrum are the *multinational corporations*, which have direct investments in manufacturing and/or distribution facilities in more than one country. In 1981 direct investment by U.S. firms was over $227 billion. Between these extremes are various other degrees of involvement in international financial transactions, including foreign branch sales offices, licensing arrangements, and joint ventures with foreign firms.

Firms that are engaged in international financial transactions face unique problems and risks not encountered by firms that operate in only one country. First, there are difficulties associated with doing business in different currencies. Financial transactions between U.S. firms and firms (or individuals) in foreign countries normally involve foreign currency, which has to be converted into U.S. dollars at some stage. Thus, firms that do business on an international basis are concerned with the *exchange rate* between U.S. dollars and foreign currencies. Second, there are problems associated with the different governmental regulations, tax laws, business practices, and political environments in foreign countries. Some of the more important aspects of these problems are considered in the following sections.[1]

FOREIGN CURRENCIES AND EXCHANGE RATES

Whenever a U.S. firm purchases goods or services from a firm in another country, two currencies normally are involved. For example, when a U.S. company purchases materials from a British supplier, the British firm usually prefers payment in British pounds, whereas the U.S. company prefers to make payment in U.S. dollars. If the sales agreement requires that payment be made in pounds, the U.S. company will have to exchange (that is, *sell*) dollars to obtain the required number of pounds. The exact amount of dollars the U.S. company will have to sell depends on the *exchange rate* between the two currencies.

---

[1]Space limitations make it impossible to consider the entire scope of these problems in this text. For a more complete discussion of these issues, see the following references: J. Fred Weston and Bart W. Sorge. *International Managerial Finance.* Homewood, Ill.: Irwin, 1972; J. Fred Weston and Bart W. Sorge. *Guide to International Financial Management.* New York: McGraw-Hill, 1977; David K. Eiteman and Arthur T. Stonehill, *Multinational Business Finance,* Reading, Mass.: Addison-Wesley, 1979; Charles N. Henning, William Pigott, and Robert H. Scott, *International Financial Management.* New York: McGraw-Hill, 1978; and Rita N. Rodriguez and E. Eugene Carter, *International Financial Management,* 2nd ed. Englewood Cliffs, N.J.: Prentice-Hall, 1979.

Suppose, for example, that the exchange rate at the time of the transaction is $1.50 per pound.[2] Furthermore, assume that the British supplier and the U.S. firm have agreed on a price of £2,000,000 for the materials. Therefore, the U.S. firm will have to exchange $3,000,000 (that is, £2,000,000 × $1.50/ pound) to obtain the British currency to pay for the purchase.

The exchange rate can be expressed either in terms of dollars per pound or in terms of pounds per dollar. If the exchange rate from dollars to pounds is $1.50/pound, the exchange rate from pounds to dollars is £0.6667/dollar (that is, 1 ÷ $1.50/pound). Thus, a *reciprocal* relationship exists between the two exchange rates.

Foreign currency that is needed for international financial transactions usually can be exchanged for domestic currency in most countries either at large commercial banks or at a central bank operated by the government. Banks normally charge a small fee for this service. Exchange rates between U.S. dollars and the currencies of most countries are reported daily in the *Wall Street Journal*. Table 25–1 lists the exchange rates between U.S. dollars and various currencies as of March 1, 1983, and March 1, 1982. These are known as *spot rates*. Spot rates represent the rate of exchange for currencies being bought and sold for *immediate delivery* today.

Currencies also can be bought and sold today for delivery at some *future time*, usually 30, 90, or 180 days from today. In these cases, *forward rates* are used rather than spot rates. Forward exchange rates between U.S. dollars and the currencies of several of the major industrial countries also are reported daily in the *Wall Street Journal*. Table 25–2 lists some forward exchange rates as of March 1, 1983.

Forward exchange rates can be either higher or lower than the spot rates; higher rates are termed *premiums*, and lower rates are termed *discounts*. A comparison of the spot and forward rates in Table 25–1 and 25–2 shows that

TABLE 25–1   Sampling of Spot Foreign Exchange Rates

COUNTRY	CURRENCY	EXCHANGE RATE (U.S. DOLLARS)	
		March 1, 1983	March 1, 1982
Australia	Dollar	0.9510	1.0698
Brazil	Cruzeiro	0.00263	0.00709
Britain	Pound	1.5050	1.8185
Canada	Dollar	0.8148	0.8142
China-Taiwan	Dollar	0.0250	0.0264
France	Franc	0.1447	0.1639
India	Rupee	0.1004	0.1079
Italy	Lira	0.0007097	0.000781
Japan	Yen	0.004189	0.00410
Mexico	Peso	0.00625	0.0227
South Africa	Rand	0.9160	1.0160
Sweden	Krona	0.1336	0.1716
Switzerland	Franc	0.4845	0.5263
West Germany	Mark	0.4103	0.4182

SOURCE: *Wall Street Journal* (March 2, 1983, and March 2, 1982).

[2]This was the approximate exchange rate on March 1, 1983.

TABLE 25–2 Sampling of Forward Foreign Exchange Rates

EXCHANGE RATE
(U.S. DOLLARS)—MARCH 1, 1983

Currency	30-Day Futures	90-Day Futures	180-Day Futures
Pound	1.5017	1.4959	1.4895
Canadian dollar	0.8141	0.8136	0.8130
French franc	0.1425	0.1393	0.1364
Yen	0.004197	0.004213	0.004242
Swiss franc	0.4872	0.4918	0.4983
Mark	0.4116	0.4140	0.4176

SOURCE: *Wall Street Journal* (March 2, 1983).

the forward exchange rates of British pounds, Canadian dollars, and French francs are below their respective spot exchange rates, whereas the forward exchange rates of Japanese yen, Swiss francs, and West German marks are above their respective spot rates. When forward rates are *above* a spot rate, it means that foreign exchange traders expect the spot rate to *increase* in the future. Conversely, when the forward rates are *below* the spot rate, it indicates that foreign exchange traders expect the spot rate to *decrease* in the future. As will be shown later in this chapter, firms engaged in international transactions can use the forward foreign exchange market to protect themselves against adverse fluctuations in exchange rates.

FACTORS THAT AFFECT EXCHANGE RATES

Exchange rates between currencies change over time, reflecting supply and demand considerations for each currency. For example, the demand for British pounds comes from a number of sources, including foreign buyers of British exports who must pay for their purchases in pounds, foreign investors who desire to make investments in physical or financial assets in Britain, and speculators who expect British pounds to increase in value relative to other currencies. The British government also may be a source of demand if it attempts to keep the value of the pound (relative to other currencies) from falling by using its supply of foreign currencies or gold to purchase pounds in the market.

Sources of supply include British importers who need to convert their pounds into foreign currency to pay for purchases, British investors who desire to make investments in foreign countries, and speculators who expect British pounds to decrease in value relative to other currencies.

Exchange rates also are affected by economic and political conditions that influence the supply or demand for a country's currency. Some of these conditions include differential inflation and interest rates among countries, the government's trade policies, and the government's political stability. A high rate of inflation within a country tends to lower the value of its currency with respect to the currencies of other countries that are experiencing lower rates of inflation. The exchange rate will tend to decline as holders sell or exchange the country's currency for other currencies whose purchasing power is not declining at as high a rate. In contrast, relatively high interest rates within a country tend to increase the exchange rate as foreign investors seek to convert their currencies and purchase these higher yielding securities.

Government trade policies that limit imports—such as the imposition of tariffs, import quotas, and restrictions on foreign exchange transactions—reduce the supply of the country's currency in the foreign exchange market. This, in turn, tends to increase the value of the country's currency with respect to other currencies and thus increase exchange rates.

Finally, the political stability of the government will affect the risks perceived by foreign investors and companies doing business in the country. These risks include the possible expropriation of investments or restrictions on the amount of funds (such as returns from investments) that may be taken out of the country.

EXCHANGE RATE RISK

Since exchange rates between currencies can and do fluctuate over time, firms engaged in international transactions are subject to *exchange rate risk*.

Foreign trade   Consider again the situation described earlier in which a U.S. company purchases materials from a British supplier. Since the amount of the transaction (£2,000,000) is stated in pounds, the U.S. company bears the exchange risk. This is illustrated in Table 25–3. Assume that the British supplier extends 90-day trade credit to the U.S. company and that the value of the pound increases from $1.50/pound on the purchase date to $1.55/pound on the payment date. If the U.S. firm takes the trade credit extended to it, the cost of the purchase effectively increases from $3,000,000 to $3,100,000 (that is, £2,000,000 × $1.55/pound).[3]

There are three methods that the U.S. firm can use to protect itself against this exchange rate risk:

- Making full payment at the time of purchase.
- Executing a contract in the forward exchange market.
- Borrowing U.S. funds and investing in interest-bearing British securities.

Each of these methods is examined in the paragraphs that follow.

The U.S. firm could convert $3,000,000 into £2,000,000 and pay for the materials at the time of purchase. With this method, it would have to forgo

TABLE 25–3   Example of Exchange Rate Risk

DATE	EXCHANGE RATE	AMOUNT OF TRANSACTION	
		U.S. dollars	British pounds
Purchase date	$1.50/pound	$3,000,000	£2,000,000
Payment date	$1.55/pound	$3,100,000	£2,000,000

[3]In this and the following discussion of exchange rate risk, we are ignoring the brokerage fees involved in executing foreign exchange contracts. Due to these costs, some firms choose not to protect themselves against exchange rate risk.

the 90 days of "free" trade credit extended to it by the British supplier. This obviously would not be advantageous to the U.S. firm.

Alternatively, the U.S. firm could execute a contract in the forward exchange market to buy £2,000,000 at the *known* 90-day forward rate rather than at the *uncertain* spot rate prevailing on the payment date. Assume, for example, that the 90-day forward rate is $1.505/pound. Based on this rate, the U.S. firm would be able to exchange $3,010,000 (that is, £2,000,000 × $1.505/pound) 90 days later on the payment date when it is required to pay for the materials. Thus, the U.S. firm would be able to take advantage of the trade credit and, at the same time, avoid any exchange rate risk.

A third method for avoiding the risk would be for the U.S. firm to borrow the funds from its bank, exchange them for pounds at the spot rate, and invest them in interest-bearing British securities. By investing in securities that mature on the same date as the payment is due to the British supplier (that is, 90 days after the purchase date), the U.S. firm will have the necessary amount of pounds available to pay for the materials . The net cost of this method to the U.S. firm will depend on the interest rate on the funds it borrows from its bank relative to the interest rate on the funds it invests in securities. For example, if the bank charges 10 percent per annum and the securities yield 8 percent per annum, the net cost to the U.S. firm would be approximately $15,000, that is, $(0.10 - 0.08) \times (90/360) \times \$3,000,000$.

Foreign investment   Firms with direct investments in foreign subsidiaries also face exchange rate risk. Changes in the exchange rate affect the value of the subsidiary's assets and liabilities and, ultimately, the income of the multinational parent company. Under current accounting procedures, the following general rules apply when the balance sheets of foreign subsidiaries are consolidated into the parent company's balance sheet:[4]

- Current assets, unless covered by forward exchange contracts, should be translated into dollars at the rate of exchange prevailing on the date of the balance sheet.

- Fixed assets should be translated into dollars at the rates of exchange prevailing when the assets were acquired or constructed.

- Current liabilities payable in foreign currency should be translated into dollars at the rate of exchange prevailing on the date of the balance sheet.

- Long-term liabilities and capital stock should be translated at the rates of exchange prevailing when they were originally incurred or issued.

A decline in the value of a foreign currency relative to the U.S. dollar reduces the conversion value of the foreign subsidiary's current liabilities, as well as its current assets. Therefore, the parent company's risk exposure depends on the foreign subsidiary's net current position (that is, current assets minus current liabilities). Thus, on the books of the parent company, the subsidiary's creditors in effect bear part of the decline in the value of the subsidiary's current assets. Current accounting practice requires that these

---

[4]See Financial Accounting Standards Board. *Current Text* Stamford, Conn.: FASB, August 1982, sections F59: 19151–19174 and F60: 19251–19273.

TABLE 25-4   Effect of a Decrease in the Exchange Rate on American Products' Balance Sheet

	EXCHANGE RATE			
	$0.80 (Canadian) = $1.00 (U.S.)		$0.75 (Canadian) = $1.00 (U.S.)	
	$(Canadian)	$(U.S.)	$(Canadian)	$(U.S.)
Current assets	$12,000,000	$9,600,000	$12,000,000	$9,000,000
Current liabilities	8,000,000	6,400,000	8,000,000	6,000,000
Net current position	$4,000,000	$3,200,000	$4,000,000	$3,000,000

losses (as well as gains) be reported on the income statement of the parent company. The parent company's losses are limited to its equity investment in the foreign subsidiary.[5]

The impact of a decrease in the exchange rate on the firm's balance sheet can be illustrated with the following example. American Products has a subsidiary, Canadian Products, with current assets of $12,000,000 (Canadian) and current liabilities of $8,000,000 (Canadian). Based on an exchange rate of $0.80 (Canadian) per dollar (U.S.), the net current position of the Canadian subsidiary on American Products' balance sheet as shown in Table 25-4 is $3,200,000 (U.S.). Suppose now that the exchange rate declines to $0.75 (Canadian) per dollar (U.S.) and all other things remain the same. As can be seen in the table, the net current position of the Canadian subsidiary on American Products' balance sheet declines to $3,000,000 (U.S.), resulting in a $200,000 currency exchange loss.

In general, when a foreign subsidiary's current assets are greater than (less than) its current liabilities, currency exchange losses (gains) will occur when the exchange rate decreases. The opposite effects are true for increases in the exchange rate.

The multinational company can also minimize its exchange rate risk, as well as the risk of expropriation and/or nationalization of its assets by a foreign government, by developing a *portfolio* of foreign investments. Rather than making all its direct investments in foreign subsidiaries that are located in one particular country, the firm can spread its foreign investments among a number of different countries, thus limiting the risk of incurring large losses within any one country.

FINANCING FOREIGN TRANSACTIONS

Firms engaged in foreign trade and investment have a variety of sources of financing that may not be available to domestic firms. This section examines some of these sources.

---

[5]The parent company also incurs losses as the result of a decline in the exchange rate on any debt capital (that is, loans) the parent has supplied to the subsidiary.

FOREIGN TRADE

Firms that import goods into their countries often can arrange an import *letter of credit* to finance the transaction. Basically, a letter of credit is a document issued by a bank guaranteeing payment for a particular shipment of goods. A letter of credit substitutes the credit-worthiness of the bank for that of the importer, thereby greatly reducing the credit risk to the seller.

To illustrate the use of a letter of credit, consider again the example discussed earlier in the chapter of the U.S. company that is purchasing materials from a British supplier. Suppose the British supplier agrees to ship the materials upon receipt of an irrevocable letter of credit from the U.S. firm's bank, with payment to be made in 90 days. The U.S. firm then would arrange with its bank for the letter of credit. By issuing a letter of credit, the bank agrees to pay drafts drawn on the firm's account when they are presented by the British supplier's bank. Upon shipment of the materials, the British firm presents a draft to its bank for payment in 90 days. The draft then is sent to the U.S. firm's bank for acceptance. Once the draft has been accepted by the U.S. bank, it becomes a *bankers' acceptance*—a form of marketable security. If the British firm does not wish to wait 90 days for payment, it can sell the draft at a discount from the face amount to the bank or another investor.

FOREIGN INVESTMENT

For a number of reasons, U.S. firms frequently find it desirable to finance a substantial portion of their foreign investments with funds raised abroad. First, the U.S. government has at various times imposed restrictions, or *quotas*, on the amount of funds U.S. firms can invest abroad. As a result, non–U.S. sources of financing must be used in part to finance foreign investments. Second, firms often find it desirable to obtain part of their financing in the foreign countries in which they are making their investments. This helps minimize any losses the firms might incur if the foreign currencies were devalued or if the foreign governments imposed restrictions on the outflow of funds from their countries. Finally, by borrowing funds abroad, U.S. firms can avoid the disclosure requirements (and associated costs) imposed by the SEC on debt securities that are issued in the United States.

As an alternative to borrowing funds in the United States, large, well-established firms can borrow funds in the *Eurodollar* markets. Eurodollars are U.S. dollars that have been deposited in foreign (primarily "European") banks or foreign branches of U.S. banks. They are created, for example, when a U.S. firm transfers funds (that is, dollars) from its U.S. bank to a foreign bank where it has an account. The foreign bank then can lend these dollar deposits in the form of *Eurodollar loans* or *Eurobonds* to other firms (such as foreign subsidiaries of U.S. firms). A foreign subsidiary also may be able to obtain loans from international agencies, such as the World Bank and the Inter-American Development Bank. In addition, a number of governments have established national banks that provide financing for projects that promote economic development within their countries.

Thus, a wide variety of sources of funds is available for financing foreign investments. In determining the most appropriate mix of financing for a given overseas investment, the firm should consider many other factors besides interest rates.

FINANCIAL DECISION MAKING IN NOT-FOR-PROFIT ENTERPRISES

Financial managers in government agencies and not-for-profit (NFP) enterprises are faced with many of the same types of financial decisions as their counterparts in private, profit-oriented firms. The responsibilities of the financial officer in these types of organizations frequently include the following:

- Managing working capital.
- Analyzing long-term investment proposals.
- Obtaining funds from banks and other financing sources.

Effective financial planning is essential if public and NFP organizations are going to be successful in achieving their objectives.

GOALS IN THE PUBLIC SECTOR AND NOT-FOR-PROFIT ORGANIZATION[6]

Although there are substantial similarities in the financial decisions that face managers in both the public and the private sectors of the economy, there are also some significant differences that require specific attention. The shareholder wealth maximization objective developed for private sector firms is not an appropriate objective in the public sector or in NFP organizations. These organizations pursue a different set of objectives because of the nature of the good or service they supply and because of the manner in which they are funded.

Public sector (government) agencies tend to provide services with a significant *public good* character. Public goods may be consumed by more than one person at the same time, and the transaction cost of charging a market price for a public good exceeds the benefits that are derived from charging the price. Examples of public goods include national defense, the services of a lighthouse beacon, and flood control protection. Many goods, such as the performing arts, have both public and private good characteristics.[7] In addition to providing direct (private) benefits to the audience, a quality performing arts group also benefits the local community and local business through prestige and a perceived high quality of life. The closer a good or service is to being a public good, the more likely it is to be provided by the government sector.

---

[6]This section draws heavily on Thomas E. Copeland and Keith V. Smith, "An Overview of Nonprofit Organizations," *Journal of Economics and Business* 30 (2, 1978).

[7]William J. Baumol and W. G. Bowen, *Performing Arts: The Economic Dilemma.* Cambridge, Mass.: MIT Press, 1966.

Not-for-profit organizations include performing arts groups, museums, libraries, hospitals, churches, volunteer organizations, cooperatives, credit unions, labor unions, professional societies, foundations, and fraternal organizations. Some of these organizations provide services to a group of clients, such as the patients of a hospital. Others provide services primarily to members, such as the members of a country club or credit union. Finally, some NFP organizations produce public benefits, as is the case with a local symphony or theater company.[8]

The most important feature that distinguishes NFP organizations from private sector and public (government) sector organizations is their sources of financial support. NFP organizations receive a large percentage of their externally generated funds from voluntary contributions. The greater the proportion of external funds from contributions as a percentage of total revenue, the closer the organization is to being a pure NFP organization. In contrast, the lower the percentage of contributions to total revenue, the closer the organization is to being a business firm or government agency. For example, by this criterion a credit union would be expected to have organizational objectives that are very near to those of banks, whereas the American Economic Association, a professional association of economists, is more nearly like an NFP organization. For those NFP organizations with a heavy reliance on external contributions, the overriding objective is to satisfy current and prospective contributors.

Although both the public sector agency and the NFP organization may pursue many objectives, one of the major focuses of economists is on the efficiency dimension of organizational objectives. Whatever set of objectives the organization decides to pursue, these objectives should be pursued in the most resource-efficient fashion.

The model that has been developed to provide a framework for the allocation of public and NFP resources among competing uses has primarily been the cost–benefit analysis model.[9] This model is the analogue to the capital-budgeting model in the private sector. Benefits and costs associated with investments are estimated and discounted by an appropriate discount rate, and projects are evaluated on the basis of the magnitude of the discounted benefits in relation to the costs. Because government and NFP organization spending normally is constrained by a budget ceiling, the criteria actually used in evaluating expenditures for any public purpose may be the following:

- Maximize benefits for given costs.

- Minimize costs while achieving a fixed level of benefits.

- Maximize net benefits (benefits minus costs).

---

[8]R. M. Anthony and R. Herzlinger, *Management Control in Non-Profit Organizations*, Homewood, Ill.: Irwin, 1975, chap. 1.

[9]Space limitations prevent a thorough treatment here of the issues involved in performing cost-benefit studies. The following references provide a more comprehensive treatment of this topic: Jesse Burkhead and Jerry Miner, *Public Expenditure*. Chicago: Aldine-Atherton, 1971; Harvey Hinrichs and Graeme M. Taylor, *Program Budgeting and Benefit-Cost Analysis*. Pacific Palisades, Calif: Goodyear, 1969; Ezra J. Mishan, *"Cost-Benefit Analysis: An Introduction*. New York: Praeger, 1971; and A. R. Prest and R. Turvey, "Cost-Benefit Analysis: A Survey." *Economic Journal* (Dec. 1965).

It must be cautioned that cost-benefit analysis (or benefit-cost analysis), as a guide to a more efficient allocation of resources by a public agency or an NFP institution, provides only one input necessary to the final decision. It *does* provide decision makers with the results of a careful analysis of the costs and returns associated with alternative actions. It *does not*, however, incorporate some of the more subjective considerations or less easily quantifiable objectives into the analysis. For example, a benefit-cost analysis typically does not consider the effect of a proposed project on income distribution. Concern for these matters must be introduced at a later stage in the analysis, generally through the political process.

STEPS IN COST-BENEFIT ANALYSIS

The general principles of cost-benefit analysis are contained in the answers to the following questions:

- What is the objective function that is to be maximized?
- What are the constraints placed on the analysis?
- Which costs and benefits are to be included, and how should they be valued?
- What investment evaluation criterion should be used?
- What is the appropriate discount rate?

Figure 25–1 traces the decision-making process in cost-benefit analysis. First, program objectives are set by the decision makers; the primary objective is usually the maximization of society's wealth. Next, alternatives are enumerated, explored, and revised in light of constraints that may be operating in the system; these include physical (technological), legal, administrative, financial, political, social, and religious constraints. The alternatives then are compared by enumerating and evaluating program benefits and costs in a present value framework. Finally, discounted benefits are compared with discounted costs, and intangibles are considered in order to make recommendations about the merits of one or more alternative programs.

MEASURING BENEFITS AND COSTS

Cost-benefit analysis is very similar to traditional private sector profit-and-loss accounting. In the private sector, the firm is guided by the criterion that private revenues must be equal to or exceed private costs over the long run in order for the firm to survive. In cost-benefit analysis, the analyst asks whether society as a whole will be better off by the adoption of a specific project or by the acceptance of one project to the exclusion of other alternatives.

Benefits and costs can be categorized in a number of ways. A project's *primary*, or *direct, benefits* consist of the value of goods or services it yields. For instance, the primary benefit of an irrigation project is the value of the additional crops produced on the irrigated land, less the costs of seeds, labor, and the equipment required to produce the crops. The primary benefits attributable to a college education might be considered as the increase in the

FIGURE 25–1   Cost-Benefit Analysis Process

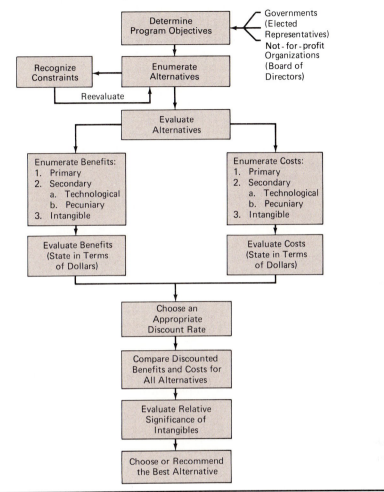

graduate's gross earnings over what would have been earned without a college degree. The value of the primary, or direct, benefits of a project is the total amount users pay for them (assuming pure competition) or would be willing to pay (in the case where pure competition does not exist). Although this principle of evaluating direct benefits may be reasonably straightforward for irrigation projects and the like, estimating direct benefits in the case of recreational resources or placing a value on human life in health care or accident prevention programs poses serious conceptual problems.

Primary, or *direct, costs* generally are easier to measure than direct benefits. They include the capital costs necessary to undertake the project, operating and maintenance costs incurred over the life of the project, and personnel expenses required in the administration of the project. Once again, however, estimating these costs is generally much easier for investments in physical assets, such as dams and canals, than for human resource investments.

The costs being measured are essentially *opportunity costs*, that is, the social value forgone elsewhere as a result of moving factors of production into the project. If, for example, a proposed project draws 20 percent of its required labor from the ranks of the unemployed, the market cost (wage payments) of these workers' services will overstate the true social cost. In the case of idle land, the opportunity cost of its use is zero (for as long as no productive alternative uses exist), no matter what the government happens to actually pay the owner in compensation, since such compensation only affects the *distribution* of the benefits derived from the land usage.

In addition to the primary impacts of a project, government investment invariably also creates *secondary*, or *indirect*, *costs* and *benefits*. These may be of two types: *real*, or *technological*, and *pecuniary*. Real secondary *benefits* include reductions in the necessary outlays for other government projects. For example, a glaucoma detection program that reduces the number of people who go blind also will reduce the need for job retraining, as well as the need for future government disability transfer payments. Similarly, an irrigation dam may reduce flooding, create a recreational area, or both. Meaningful cost-benefit studies should attempt to measure these secondary benefits. The same principle applies to *secondary costs*. For example, the Wallisville Dam Project in Texas was alleged to cause in excess of $500,000 in damages annually to saltwater fishing because of its impact on the tidal marshlands. This real secondary cost should have been included in the cost-benefit analysis of the project.

Pecuniary benefits generally should *not* be included in a study's "countable" benefits. They generally arise in the form of lower input costs, increased volumes of business, or changes in land values resulting from a project. For example, an improved highway may lead to greater business volume and increased profitability of gas stations, souvenir shops, and restaurants along it, as well as higher land values and consequently higher rents to landowners. Many of these benefits are purely *distributional* in nature, because some business also will be drawn away from firms along other roads once the new road has been completed.

If the economy is operating under conditions of full employment, the secondary impacts of the multiplier effect and induced investment—which may occur as a result of the particular government investment—should not be counted. Instead, these benefits must be presumed to occur whether the expenditure of funds is public or private. In contrast, the objective of a regional project may be to induce local investment, generate multiplier effects, and reduce regional unemployment. Under these special circumstances, it may be appropriate to include some of these secondary effects in the analysis.

Intangibles make up a final group of program benefits and costs. They are defined as the recognizable impacts of a project for which it is either extremely difficult or impossible to calculate dollar values, and they may include such notions as the quality of life, aesthetic contributions (or detriments), and balance of payments impacts. If it proves impossible to translate intangibles into reasonable estimates of dollar benefits and costs, they may be merely listed in the analysis. Alternatively, they may be analyzed by making tradeoffs against tangibles in such a way that the cost of additional increments of intangible improvement may, for example, be compared with the forgone tangible benefits of a project.

INVESTMENT DECISION CRITERIA

In choosing an appropriate model to use in evaluating a public program's economic worth, the public or NFP organization is faced with problems very similar to those the private firm faces in its capital expenditure analysis. As discussed in Chapter 10, the model must be able to provide guidance in answering three types of investment questions. First, it must give some indication of whether a particular project should be adopted or not, assuming that adequate funds are available for all economically justifiable programs. Second, if two or more alternatives are being compared that will accomplish the same purpose—that is, if the investments are *mutually exclusive*—the model must answer the question of which should be accepted. For example, when Pittsburgh was deciding whether it should construct a rapid transit system, it had to choose between two competing systems—a steel wheel on rails system and a rubber-tired Skybus system. Since the city needed and could afford only one system, only one of these alternatives could be selected. Finally, if adequate resources are not available to fund all economically acceptable projects, the investment model must aid in the ordering and selection of projects in such a way that net social benefits are maximized (subject to the available funds constraint).

Whereas a number of alternative investment evaluation models are discussed at some length in Chapter 10, this discussion is limited to merely restating some of these models in terms of program benefits and costs rather than private cash inflows and outflows.

Internal rate of return method When this method is used, a discount rate is calculated that equates the net benefits of a project over its life with the original cost. This method has been used rather extensively in evaluating human resource programs, such as investments in education. One advantage of this approach is that it avoids making an appropriate social discount rate explicit in the calculation procedure. The internal rate of return method does not completely avoid the social discount rate problem, however; it merely puts it off until the end of the analysis. Ultimately, a decision about a program's economic worth must be made by comparing the calculated internal rate of return with the social discount rate. If the internal rate of return exceeds the social discount rate, the program is an acceptable investment; if not, it is unacceptable.

Net present value method In this approach, the program benefits and program costs for each year during the project are discounted back to the present, using the social rate of discount. If the present value of benefits exceeds the present value of costs, the project is acceptable.

Benefit-cost ratio method This approach is really only a variation of the net present value method. Using this criterion, a project is acceptable if the ratio of the present value of benefits (discounted at the social rate of discount) to the present value of costs (also discounted at the social rate of discount) exceeds 1.0. Obviously, this solution is logically equivalent to the net present value method, since the benefit-cost ratio will exceed 1.0 only when benefits exceed costs. This method has an advantage over the net present value method, however. The benefit-cost ratio in a capital rationing situation places all projects on an equal basis by indicating how much benefit can be achieved for *each dollar of program outlay*, whereas the net present value method has an inherent bias in favor of large projects.

SOCIAL RATE OF DISCOUNT

When the benefits and/or costs of a program extend beyond a 1-year time limit, they must be discounted back to some common point in time for purposes of comparison. This is an essential step, due to the fact that most people prefer current consumption to future consumption. The discount rate adjusts for this preference.

The choice of an appropriate discount rate to use in evaluating public investments is critical to the conclusions of any cost-benefit analysis. For example, projects that appear to be justified at a low discount rate, such as 2 percent, may seem to be a gross misallocation of resources at a higher rate, such as 10 percent. The choice of a discount rate is likely to have a profound impact on the types of projects accepted. Specifically, whereas a low rate favors investments with long lives, most of which will probably be of the durable "bricks-and-mortar" variety, a high rate favors those projects whose benefits become available soon after the initial investment is made.

The literature on the social discount rate is extensive and, in many cases, contradictory. Rather than attempt to synthesize and summarize the many points of view that have been expressed in the literature, the focus here is on the opportunity cost criterion for estimating the social discount rate.[10]

Resources invested in a particular manner in one sector often are withdrawn from that sector and invested in another, where they may yield either a higher or a lower return. Once it has been recognized that the discount rate performs the function of allocating resources between the public and private sectors, a discount rate should be chosen that will properly indicate when resources should be transferred from one sector to another. This simply means that if resources can earn 12 percent in the *private* sector, they should not be transferred to the *public* sector unless they can earn more than 12 percent there.

The social discount rate is analogous to the calculation of the weighted cost of capital in private sector capital budgeting, since it is computed by

[10]For a more thorough discussion of this topic, see the following works of William J. Baumol. "On the Social Rate of Discount." *American Economic Review* (Sept. 1968): 778–802; "On the Discount Rate for Public Projects," in Robert Haveman and Julius Margolis, eds. *Public Expenditures and Policy Analysis.* Chicago: Markham, 1970, pp. 273–290; and "On the Appropriate Discount Rate for Evaluation of Public Projects." Statement in *The Planning-Programming-Budgeting System: Progress and Potentials.* Subcommittee on Economy in Goverment, Joint Economic Committee, 90th Congress, 1st Session. Washington, D.C.: U.S. Government Printing Office, 1967.

weighting the opportunity cost rates for the various sectors from which a project will draw its resources. The weights are equal to the proportion of total resources that come from each sector. In 1970 a Bureau of the Budget (now the Office of Management and Budget) study of the opportunity costs of public investment led to a conclusion that a rate of 7.5 percent was appropriate. In the inflationary environment of the 1970s, however, all Federal government agencies were ordered to use at least a 10 percent rate in discounting program costs and benefits.

EXAMPLES OF COST-BENEFIT ANALYSIS

Higher education In a study entitled "Private and Social Rates of Return for the Education of Academicians," Duncan Bailey and Charles Schotta calculated the private rates of return accruing to the individual from an investment in a doctoral degree by comparing lifetime income patterns of persons with Ph.D.s to incomes of persons with bachelor's degrees.[11] The costs included opportunity costs of earnings forgone while the individual was in graduate school, as well as any direct outlays that would not have been incurred if the individual had not been in graduate school (for example, tuition and books). The social rates of return included the cost of social resources provided in most graduate education programs, in addition to private costs and benefits, since tuition in most state-supported universities covers only a small part of the cost of providing instructional and research resources.

Using a series of reasonable assumptions relating to the average length of time spent in a doctoral program, as well as to dropout rates, the study found a *private* real rate of return to graduate education of 0 to 1 percent. The *social* rate of return was also found to be 0 to 1 percent. When compared with other findings of rates of return to undergraduate education in excess of 10 percent,[12] it seems reasonable to conclude that some resources should be shifted from graduate to undergraduate education. This is especially true in such areas as the humanities, education, and certain social sciences, where returns to advanced degree holders are extremely low in comparison to returns to bachelor's degree holders. The study also suggests that because of the high social costs of dropouts from graduate degree programs, more attention should be devoted to preselection and early quality control measures. One limitation of the study is that it merely examines the future monetary benefits to be gained from graduate education and does not consider the "intangible" psychological benefits achieved by acquiring an advanced degree.

Medical research The second cost-benefit analysis is a case study completed by Burton A. Weisbrod of the costs and benefits of polio research.[13] The major contribution of this study is that it provides a checklist of items to be con-

[11]Duncan Bailey and Charles Schotta. *American Economic Review* (March 1972): 19–31.

[12]Gary Becker, *Human Capital.* New York: Columbia University Press, 1964 and Bruce Wilkinson, "Present Values of Lifetime Earnings for Different Occupations." *Journal of Political Economy* (Dec. 1966): 556–573.

[13]Burton A. Weisbrod, "Costs and Benefits of Medical Research: A Case Study of Poliomyelitis," *Journal of Political Economy* (May–June 1971): 527–544.

sidered when a public decision maker is seeking information prior to allocating funds to competing research programs. The approach used involved estimating the following:

- The time stream of research expenditures directed toward poliomyelitis.
- The time stream of benefits resulting from (or predicted to result from) the application of the knowledge gained by the research.
- The cost of applying that knowledge.

The benefits from the prevention of polio were taken to include the following:

- The market value of production lost because of premature death due to polio.
- The market value of production lost due to illness and disability from polio.
- The resource costs devoted to treatment and rehabilitation of victims.

This excludes estimates of the costs of pain and suffering that those with the disease had to bear. Thus, the rates of return generated probably underestimate the true rates of return.

The internal rate of return on medical (in this case, polio) research is the discount rate that equates the time stream of research costs with the stream of benefits. It is calculated by solving the following equation for r:

$$\sum_{t=0}^{T} \frac{R_t - [B_t(N_t - W_t) - V_t]}{(1 + r)^t} = 0 \, ,$$

where R = Research costs

B = Benefit per case of disease prevented (or the loss per case occurring).

N = Number of cases occurring in the absence of a successful research and application program.

W = Number of cases occurring after a successful program.

V = Cost of applying research findings (for example, the cost of a vaccination program).

t = A particular year.

T = The time horizon of benefits and costs, beyond which the time value of these benefits and costs are insignificant due to discounting.

Weisbrod concludes that, on the basis of his analyses, the resources devoted to polio research and the application of this research are generating returns in the form of increased output and reduced treatment expenditures of about 11 to 12 percent. Because no figures are imputed for the value to the individual of reduced illness and increased longevity, the real value of this medical research program is undoubtedly higher than the 11 to 12 percent estimate.

SUMMARY

This chapter discusses two topics: international financial management and financial decision making in not-for-profit enterprises. Each of these topics is summarized separately here.

INTERNATIONAL FINANCIAL MANAGEMENT

- Firms engaged in international financial transactions face risks and problems that are not faced in domestic transactions, including difficulties encountered in doing business in different currencies and problems associated with different governmental regulations, tax laws, business practices, and political environments.

- The *exchange rate* is the rate at which one currency can be converted into another. The *spot rate* is the rate of exchange for currencies being bought and sold for *immediate delivery today*. The *forward rate* is the rate of exchange between currencies to be delivered at a future point in time—usually 30, 90, and 180 days from today.

- Firms engaged in international transactions incur *exchange rate risk* because of fluctuations over time in the exchange rates between currencies. *Forward exchange contracts* can be used to minimize some of the effects of unfavorable changes in exchange rates.

- A wide variety of sources of funds is available for financing foreign trade and investments, including letters of credit, the Eurodollar market, and both national and international development banks.

FINANCIAL DECISION MAKING IN NOT-FOR-PROFIT ENTERPRISES

- Managers of NFP enterprises and government organizations face many of the same types of financial decisions as managers in private, profit-oriented enterprises. One primary difference between financial decision making in these types of enterprises concerns their *normative goals*. Whereas private firms usually are concerned with maximizing shareholder wealth, NFP enterprises and government organizations typically pursue much different normative goals, such as redistributing income, promoting economic stability and full employment, and providing various services at a reasonable cost.

- NFP enterprises and government organizations normally are concerned with the efficient utilization of the resources available to them (such as private donations and tax revenues). *Cost-benefit analysis* is a useful technique in pursuing this efficiency objective. It is used to evaluate public investment decisions by measuring and comparing the *social benefits* and *social costs* of individual projects. Projects usually are judged economically justifiable only when their discounted social benefits exceed their discounted social costs.

- The discount rate for public investment projects, known as the *social discount* rate, is equal to a weighting of the opportunity cost rates for the various sectors from which the project will draw its resources.

QUESTIONS AND TOPICS FOR DISCUSSION

1. Define the following terms:
    a. Multinational corporation.
    b. Spot exchange rate.
    c. Forward exchange rate.
    d. Letter of credit.

2. Describe the factors that cause exchange rates to change over time.

3. Describe three methods an importer can use to protect itself against exchange rate risk.

4. How can a firm with direct investments in foreign subsidiaries minimize its exchange rate risk?

5. What are the advantages to a U.S. firm of financing its foreign investments with funds raised abroad?

6. Define the following terms:
    a. Social benefits.
    b. Social costs.
    c. Direct benefits.
    d. Direct costs.
    e. Secondary effects.
    f. Intangibles.
    g. Benefit-cost ratio.
    h. Net present value.
    i. Social discount rate.

7. How does the normative goal of private, profit-oriented firms differ from the goals pursued by public and NFP institutions?

8. What are the functions of the social discount rate in cost-benefit analysis?

9. Describe the major steps involved in performing a cost-benefit study.

PROBLEMS*

1. Japanese Motors exports cars and trucks to the U.S. market. On March 1, 1982, its most popular model was selling (wholesale) to U.S. dealers for $5,550. What price must Japanese Motors charge for the same model on March 1, 1983, to realize the same amount (of Japanese yen) as it did a year earlier? Refer to Table 25–1.

2. Discount Stores, Inc., a U.S. nationwide department store chain, annually negotiates a contract with Alpine Watch Company, located in Switzerland, to purchase a large shipment of watches. On March 1, 1982, Discount Stores purchased 50,000 watches for 3,074,274.47 Swiss francs. Refer to Table 25–1 and determine the following:
    a. The total cost and cost per watch in U.S. dollars.
    b. The total cost and cost per watch in U.S. dollars of 60,000 watches on March 1, 1983, assuming that Alpine's price per watch (in Swiss francs) remains unchanged.

3. Discount Stores, Inc. (see Problem 2), decided to purchase 60,000 watches from Alpine on March 1, 1983. Alpine offered Discount Stores credit terms of "net 90 days," payable in Swiss francs. However, Discount Stores is concerned about a possible decline in the value of the U.S. dollar (relative to the Swiss franc) over

*Problems in color have check answers at the end of the book.

this period and wishes to protect itself against any unfavorable changes in the exchange rate. One possible method for avoiding the exchange rate risk would be to purchase a 90-day futures contract to buy the required amount of Swiss francs in the forward exchange market. Another method would be to forgo the trade credit by purchasing the required amount of Swiss francs at the current (March 1, 1983) spot rate and paying Alpine immediately. Under this latter method, Discount Stores would have to sell securities from its marketable securities portfolio to pay for the purchase. These marketable securities are currently yielding 8 percent per annum. Refer to Tables 25–1 and 25–2 to answer the following questions:

a. Determine the total cost of the watches under each method. (Ignore any transaction costs associated with exchanging currencies or selling marketable securities.) Which method would you recommend that Discount Stores use in protecting itself against exchange rate risk in this transaction?

b. How would your answers to Part a be affected if Alpine offered Discount Stores a 1 percent *discount* for immediate payment?

4. Determine the percentage change in the value of the U.S. dollar between March 1, 1982, and March 1, 1983, relative to the value of the currencies of the following countries (refer to Table 25–1):

  a. Brazil.

  b. Britain.

  c. Japan.

  d. Sweden.

  e. West Germany.

5. Mammouth Mutual Fund of New York has $5 million to invest in certificates of deposit (CDs) for the next 6 months (180 days). It can buy either a Philadelphia National Bank (PNB) CD with an annual yield of 10 percent or a Cologne (West Germany) Bank CD with a yield of 12.5 percent. Assume that the CDs are of comparable default risk. The analysts of the mutual fund are concerned about exchange rate risk. They were quoted the following exchange rates by the international department of a New York City bank:

West Germany (Deutsche Marks)	
Spot	$0.4200
30-day futures	0.4190
90-day futures	0.4170
180-day futures	0.4155

  a. If the Cologne Bank CD is purchased and held to maturity, determine the net gain (loss) in U.S. dollars relative to the PNB CD assuming that the exchange rate in 180 days equals today's spot rate.

  b. Suppose the West German mark declines in value by 5 percent relative to the U.S. dollar over the next 180 days. Determine the net gain (loss) of the Cologne Bank CD in U.S. dollars relative to the PNB CD for an uncovered position.

  c. Determine the net gain (loss) from a covered position.

  d. What other factor or factors should be considered in the decision to purchase the Cologne Bank CD?

6. The United States Motor Company (USMC) has a Japanese subsidiary, Japan Motor Company (JMC). JMC has current assets of 12,500,000,000 yen and current liabilities of 8,800,000,000 yen. The current exchange rate is $0.0040/yen.

  a. Determine JMC's net current position in Japanese yen and U.S. dollars.

b. Detemine the effect on USMC's balance sheet (that is, the net current position) if the exchange rate changed to $0.00425/yen.

c. Determine the effect on USMC's balance sheet (that is, the net current position) if the exchange rate changed to $0.0035/yen.

7. Rework Problem 6 assuming that JMC has current assets of 12,500,000,000 yen and current liabilities of 16,000,000,000 yen.

8. The state of Glottamora has a $150 million surplus remaining in its budget for the current year. One alternative is to give Glottamorans a one-time tax rebate. Two proposals also have been made for the expenditure of these funds. The first proposed project is to invest in a new power plant, costing $150 million and having an expected useful life of 20 years. Projected benefits accruing from this project are as follows:

Years	Benefits Per Year (In Millions of Dollars)
1–5	$ 0
6–20	30

The second alternative is to undertake a job-retraining program, also costing $150 million and generating the following benefits:

Years	Benefits Per Year (In Millions of Dollars)
1–5	$30
6–10	20
11–20	5

The State Power Department argues that a 5 percent discount rate should be used in evaluating the projects, since this is the government's borrowing rate. The Human Resources Department suggests using a 12 percent rate, since this more nearly equals society's true opportunity rate.

a. What is implied by the various departments' desires to use different discount rates?

b. Determine the net present values of the two projects, using both the 5 and 12 percent rates.

c. What rate do you believe is more appropriate?

d. Which of the three alternatives (tax rebate, power plant, or job-retraining program) would you recommend the state select? Why?

Cost-Benefit Analysis

The Michigan State Fairgrounds is centrally located in the Detroit Standard Metropolitan Statistical Area (SMSA), which consists of Wayne, Oakland, and Macomb counties. The population within the SMSA numbered 4,197,931 persons in 1970—over 47 percent of the state's total population. More than 59 and 75 percent of the state's population reside within 60 and 100 miles, respectively, of the fairground site. The site is located near an efficient freeway system that connects many areas of the state. The State Fairgrounds is operated by the Agriculture Department and is currently in a deplorable state of disrepair. Costs have exceeded revenues by a substantial margin every year in the recent past. A redevelopment program has been proposed for the fairgounds that would serve several purposes:

- Revitalization of the fairgrounds would prevent further economic deterioration of the existing facilities; increase attendance, and consequently revenues; and, it is hoped, make the fairgrounds an economically viable entity.

- A further benefit to be realized would be an economic stimulus to the area resulting from increased employment from the initial construction program, as well as increased revenues realized from the additional business that the proposed new facilities would generate.

- Finally, there is also the aesthetic value that can be realized from the upgrading and redevelopment of what is currently a marginal area of the city.

The redevelopment program would consist of the overall rehabilitation of the grounds and buildings, as well as the construction of several income-producing buildings, including a hotel and convention facility and a dog track (provided dog racing is legalized in Michigan and the fairgrounds can obtain the necessary license). Either a new coliseum would be constructed or the present one redesigned and refurbished. The cost of the redevelopment program would be $30 million. Construction would take 3 years, with 50 percent of the cost incurred in year 0, 30 percent in year 1 and 20 percent in year 2. The redevelopment program would require funding by the state government, Federal government, or both. The following estimated benefits would be derived from the project:

- *Initial construction benefits.* Previous studies showed that 38 labor years of employment are derived from each $1 million in construction. Assuming an hourly rate of $6.00, 40 hours per week, and 50 weeks per year, and relating this to the $30 million cost of the redevelment program, results in $13,680,000 of economic benefit to be derived through increased employment. Like the construction costs, these benefits

*Adapted from an unpublished paper by Eric Hartshorn, "Cost-Benefit Analysis Concerning the Proposed Redevelopment Program for the Michigan State Fairgrounds."

would be spread over 3 years ($6.840 million in year 0, $4.104 million in year 1, and $2.736 million in year 2).

- *Coliseum.* An appropriate coliseum facility could generate, in excess of current levels, an additional $750,000 annually (years 3 through 20) from shows and events not currently available in the Detroit area.

- *Increased state fair attendance.* With improved facilities (such as those planned in the redevelopment program), attendance at the state fair is expected to increase from the current 700,000 to 1 million people annually. Assuming present per-capita expenditures ($5.00) at the Michigan State Fair, the increased attendance would result in an additional $1.5 million in revenue annually (years 3 through 20).

- *Convention and hotel facility.* It is estimated that a 200-room hotel, convention, and dining facility located at the fairgrounds would generate nearly $2.25 million in additional revenue annually (years 3 through 20).

- *Dog racing track.* It is estimated that an average dog racing facility would produce $2.25 million in revenue annually. However, it must be realized that dog racing is similar to horse racing, and it is expected that a portion of the revenues generated by a dog track would be realized due to a transfer of funds from local horse racing facilities. Since this transfer of funds should not be considered in the analysis, it will be assumed that one-third of the dog racing revenues would result from the redistribution of funds from local horse racing tracks. Consequently, only $1.5 million in annual revenues (years 3 through 20) will be attributed to the proposed dog racing track.

The costs and benefits of the proposed redevelopment program are summarized in the following table. Assume that a 10 percent interest rate is appropriate for discounting the costs and benefits of the proposed project.

Type of Cost or Benefit	Year(s)	Annual Benefit (+) or Cost (−) (In Millions of Dollars)
Construction outlay	0	$ − 15.000
Construction outlay	1	− 9.000
Construction outlay	2	− 6.000
Increased employment	0	+ 6.840
Increased employment	1	+ 4.104
Increased employment	2	+ 2.736
Coliseum	3–20	+ 0.750
State Fair attendance	3–20	+ 1.500
Convention and hotel facility	3–20	+ 2.250
Dog racing track	3–20	+ 1.500

1. Determine the benefit-cost ratio for the proposed fairground redevelopment.

2. Based on this analysis, should the redevelopment program be undertaken?

3. List some of the secondary benefits and costs, as well as intangibles, associated with the project.

In calculating the benefits of the fairground redevelopment program, increased employment opportunities were included.

4. What assumption about employment in the Detroit area must be made in associating these benefits with the project?

5. Recalculate the benefit-cost ratio, assuming that these benefits are not included in the analysis. How does this affect the desirability of the project?

In calculating the benefits of the fairground redevelopment project, it was assumed that $2.25 million in additional annual revenue would be generated from the convention and hotel facility.

6. What assumption is being made about the effects of this facility on other hotel and convention facilities? Is this a realistic assumption?

7. Suppose that only $750,000 of the facility's annual revenues can be attributed to "new" convention and hotel business. Recalculate the benefit-cost ratio under this assumption (also exclude employment benefits). How does this affect the desirability of the project?

8. Suppose the fairground is unable to obtain a license to operate a dog racing track. Assume that construction costs are reduced by 15 percent if a dog racing track is not built. Recompute the benefit-cost ratio under this assumption (also exclude employment and $1.5 million in convention facility benefits). How does this affect the desirability of the proposed redevelopment project?

ADDITIONAL READINGS AND REFERENCES

Anderson, Gerald L. "International Project Financing." *Financial Executive* 45 (May 1977): 40–45.

Baumol, William J. "On the Social Rate of Discount," *American Economic Review* (Sept. 1968): 788–802.

Bowditch, Richard L., and Burtle, James L. "The Corporate Treasurer in a World of Floating Exchange Rates," in *The Treasurer's Handbook*. J. Fred Weston and Maurice B. Goudzwaard, eds. Homewood, Ill.: Dow Jones-Irwin, 1976, pp. 84–112.

Buchanan, J. M., ed. *Public Finances: Needs, Sources and Utilization.* Princeton, N.J.: Princeton University Press, 1961.

Burkhead, Jesse, and Miner, Jerry. *Public Expenditure.* Chicago: Aldine-Atherton, 1971.

Denis, Jack, Jr. "How to Hedge Foreign Currency Risk." *Financial Analysts Journal* 32 (Jan.–Feb. 1976): 50–54.

Due, John F., and Friedlander, Ann F. *Government Finance: Economics of the Public Sector,* 6th ed. Homewood, Ill.: Irwin, 1977.

Dufey, Gunter. "Corporate Finance and Exchange Rate Variations." *Financial Management* 1 (Summer 1972): 51–57.

Folks, William R., Jr., and Ramesh, Advani. "Raising Funds with Foreign Currency." *Financial Executive* 48 (February 1980): 44–49.

Gordon, Myron J. "A Portfolio Theory of the Social Discount Rate and the Public Debt." *Journal of Finance* 31 (May 1976): 199–214.

Hanson, W. L., and Weisbrod, B. A. *Benefits, Costs and Finance of Public Higher Education.* Chicago: Markham, 1969.

Heckerman, Donald. "The Exchange Risks of Foreign Operations." *Journal of Business* 46 (Jan. 1972): 42–48.

Imai, Yutaka. "Exchange Rate Risk Protection in International Business." *Journal of Financial and Quantitative Analysis* 10 (Sept. 1975): 447–456.

Lietaer, Bernard A. "Managing Risks on Foreign Exchange." *Harvard Business Review* 48 (March–April 1970): 127–138.

Mishan, Ezra J. *Cost-Benefit Analysis: An Introduction,* rev. ed. New York: Praeger, 1977.

Musgrave, R. A., and Musgrave, Peggy B. *Public Finance in Theory and Practice,* 2nd ed. New York: McGraw-Hill, 1975.

Robbins, Sidney M., and Stobaugh, Robert B. "Financing Foreign Affiliates." *Financial Management* 1 (Winter 1972): 56–65.

Rodriguez, Rita M., and Carter, E. Eugene. *International Financial Management,* 2nd ed. Englewood Cliffs, N.J.: Prentice-Hall, 1979.

Shapiro, Alan C. "Capital Budgeting for the Multinational Corporation." *Financial Management* 7 (Spring 1978): 7–16.

Shapiro, Alan C., and Rutenbert, David P. "Managing Exchange Risks in a Floating World." *Financial Management* 5 (Summer 1976): 48–58.

Weston, J. Fred, and Sorge, Bart W. *International Managerial Finance.* Homewood, Ill.: Irwin, 1972.

■ Reference Materials ■

TABLE I Compound Value Interest Factor (CVIF)

($1 at i% for n years)

$CVIF = (1 + i)^n$

$FV_n = PV_0(CVIF_{i,n})$

PERIOD, n	1%	2%	3%	4%	5%	6%	7%	8%	9%	10%	11%	12%	13%
0	1.000	1.000	1.000	1.000	1.000	1.000	1.000	1.000	1.000	1.000	1.000	1.000	1.000
1	1.010	1.020	1.030	1.040	1.050	1.060	1.070	1.080	1.090	1.100	1.110	1.120	1.130
2	1.020	1.040	1.061	1.082	1.102	1.124	1.145	1.166	1.186	1.210	1.232	1.254	1.277
3	1.030	1.061	1.093	1.125	1.158	1.191	1.225	1.260	1.295	1.331	1.368	1.405	1.443
4	1.041	1.082	1.126	1.170	1.216	1.262	1.311	1.360	1.412	1.464	1.518	1.574	1.630
5	1.051	1.104	1.159	1.217	1.276	1.338	1.403	1.469	1.539	1.611	1.685	1.762	1.842
6	1.062	1.126	1.194	1.265	1.340	1.419	1.501	1.587	1.677	1.772	1.870	1.974	2.082
7	1.072	1.149	1.230	1.316	1.407	1.504	1.606	1.714	1.828	1.949	2.076	2.211	2.353
8	1.083	1.172	1.267	1.369	1.477	1.594	1.718	1.851	1.993	2.144	2.305	2.476	2.658
9	1.094	1.195	1.305	1.423	1.551	1.689	1.838	1.999	2.172	2.358	2.558	2.773	3.004
10	1.105	1.219	1.344	1.480	1.629	1.791	1.967	2.159	2.367	2.594	2.839	3.106	3.395
11	1.116	1.243	1.384	1.539	1.710	1.898	2.105	2.332	2.580	2.853	3.152	3.479	3.836
12	1.127	1.268	1.426	1.601	1.796	2.012	2.252	2.518	2.813	3.138	3.498	3.896	4.335
13	1.138	1.294	1.469	1.665	1.886	2.133	2.410	2.720	3.066	3.452	3.883	4.363	4.898
14	1.149	1.319	1.513	1.732	1.980	2.261	2.579	2.937	3.342	3.797	4.310	4.887	5.535
15	1.161	1.346	1.558	1.801	2.079	2.397	2.759	3.172	3.642	4.177	4.785	5.474	6.254
16	1.173	1.373	1.605	1.873	2.183	2.540	2.952	3.426	3.970	4.595	5.311	6.130	7.067
17	1.184	1.400	1.653	1.948	2.292	2.693	3.159	3.700	4.328	5.054	5.895	6.866	7.986
18	1.196	1.428	1.702	2.026	2.407	2.854	3.380	3.996	4.717	5.560	6.544	7.690	9.024
19	1.208	1.457	1.754	2.107	2.527	3.026	3.617	4.316	5.142	6.116	7.263	8.613	10.197
20	1.220	1.486	1.806	2.191	2.653	3.207	3.870	4.661	5.604	6.728	8.062	9.646	11.523
24	1.270	1.608	2.033	2.563	3.225	4.049	5.072	6.341	7.911	9.850	12.239	15.179	18.790
25	1.282	1.641	2.094	2.666	3.386	4.292	5.427	6.848	8.623	10.835	13.585	17.000	21.231
30	1.348	1.811	2.427	3.243	4.322	5.743	7.612	10.063	13.268	17.449	22.892	29.960	39.116
40	1.489	2.208	3.262	4.801	7.040	10.286	14.974	21.725	31.409	45.259	65.001	93.051	132.782
50	1.645	2.692	4.384	7.107	11.467	18.420	29.457	46.902	74.358	117.391	184.565	289.002	450.736
60	1.817	3.281	5.892	10.520	18.679	32.988	57.946	101.257	176.031	304.482	524.057	897.597	1,530.05

PERIOD, n	14%	15%	16%	17%	18%	19%	20%	24%	28%	32%	36%	40%
0	1.000	1.000	1.000	1.000	1.000	1.000	1.000	1.000	1.000	1.000	1.000	1.000
1	1.140	1.150	1.160	1.170	1.180	1.190	1.200	1.240	1.280	1.320	1.360	1.400
2	1.300	1.322	1.346	1.369	1.392	1.416	1.440	1.538	1.638	1.742	1.850	1.960
3	1.482	1.521	1.561	1.602	1.643	1.685	1.728	1.907	2.067	2.300	2.515	2.744
4	1.689	1.749	1.811	1.874	1.939	2.005	2.074	2.364	2.684	3.036	3.421	3.842
5	1.925	2.011	2.100	2.192	2.288	2.386	2.488	2.932	3.436	4.007	4.653	5.378
6	2.195	2.313	2.436	2.565	2.700	2.840	2.986	3.635	4.398	5.290	6.328	7.530
7	2.502	2.660	2.826	3.001	3.185	3.379	3.583	4.508	5.629	6.983	8.605	10.541
8	2.853	3.059	3.278	3.511	3.759	4.021	4.300	5.590	7.206	9.217	11.703	14.758
9	3.252	3.518	3.803	4.108	4.435	4.785	5.160	6.931	9.223	12.166	15.917	20.661
10	3.707	4.046	4.411	4.807	5.234	5.695	6.192	8.594	11.806	16.060	21.647	28.925
11	4.226	4.652	5.117	5.624	6.176	6.777	7.430	10.657	15.112	21.199	29.439	40.496
12	4.818	5.350	5.926	6.580	7.288	8.064	8.916	13.215	19.343	27.983	40.037	56.694
13	5.492	6.153	6.886	7.699	8.599	9.596	10.699	16.386	24.759	36.937	54.451	79.372
14	6.261	7.076	7.988	9.007	10.147	11.420	12.839	20.319	31.961	48.757	74.053	111.120
15	7.138	8.137	9.266	10.539	11.974	13.590	15.407	25.196	40.565	64.359	100.712	155.568
16	8.137	9.358	10.748	12.330	14.129	16.172	18.488	31.243	51.923	84.954	136.969	217.795
17	9.276	10.761	12.468	14.426	16.672	19.244	22.186	38.741	66.461	112.139	186.278	304.914
18	10.575	12.375	14.463	16.879	19.673	22.901	26.623	48.039	85.071	148.023	253.338	426.879
19	12.056	14.232	16.777	19.748	23.214	27.252	31.948	59.568	108.890	195.391	344.540	597.630
20	13.743	16.367	19.461	23.106	27.393	32.429	38.338	73.864	139.380	257.916	468.574	836.683
24	23.212	28.625	35.236	43.297	53.109	65.032	79.497	174.631	374.144	783.023	1,603.00	3,214.20
25	26.462	32.919	40.874	50.658	62.669	77.388	95.396	216.542	478.905	1,033.59	2,180.08	4,499.88
30	50.950	66.212	85.850	111.065	143.371	184.675	237.376	634.820	1,645.50	4,142.07	10,143.0	24,201.4
40	188.884	267.864	378.721	533.869	750.378	1,051.67	1,469.77	5,455.91	19,426.7	66,520.8	219,562	700,038
50	700.233	1,083.66	1,670.70	2,566.22	3,927.36	5,988.91	9,100.44	46,890.4	229,350	*	*	*
60	2,595.92	4,384.00	7,370.20	12,335.4	20,555.1	34,105.0	56,347.5	402,996	*	*	*	*

*These interest factors exceed 1,000,000.

R–3

TABLE II Present Value Interest Factor (PVIF)
($1 at i% for n years)

$$PVIF = \frac{1}{(1 + i)^n}$$

$$PV_0 = FV_n(PVIF_{i,n})$$

PERIOD, n	1%	2%	3%	4%	5%	6%	7%	8%	9%	10%	11%	12%	13%
0	1.000	1.000	1.000	1.000	1.000	1.000	1.000	1.000	1.000	1.000	1.000	1.000	1.000
1	0.990	0.980	0.971	0.962	0.952	0.943	0.935	0.926	0.917	0.909	0.901	0.893	0.885
2	0.980	0.961	0.943	0.925	0.907	0.890	0.873	0.857	0.842	0.826	0.812	0.797	0.783
3	0.971	0.942	0.915	0.889	0.864	0.840	0.816	0.794	0.772	0.751	0.731	0.712	0.693
4	0.961	0.924	0.889	0.855	0.823	0.792	0.763	0.735	6.708	0.683	0.659	0.636	0.613
5	0.951	0.906	0.863	0.822	0.784	0.747	0.713	0.681	0.650	0.621	0.593	0.567	0.543
6	0.942	0.888	0.838	0.790	0.746	0.705	0.666	0.630	0.596	0.564	0.535	0.507	0.480
7	0.933	0.871	0.813	0.760	0.711	0.665	0.623	0.583	0.547	0.513	0.482	0.452	0.425
8	0.923	0.853	0.789	0.731	0.677	0.627	0.582	0.540	0.502	0.467	0.434	0.404	0.376
9	0.914	0.837	0.766	0.703	0.645	0.592	0.544	0.500	0.460	0.424	0.391	0.361	0.333
10	0.905	0.820	0.744	0.676	0.614	0.558	0.508	0.463	0.422	0.386	0.352	0.322	0.295
11	0.896	0.804	0.722	0.650	0.585	0.527	0.475	0.429	0.388	0.350	0.317	0.287	0.261
12	0.887	0.788	0.701	0.625	0.557	0.497	0.444	0.397	0.356	0.319	0.286	0.257	0.231
13	0.879	0.773	0.681	0.601	0.530	0.469	0.415	0.368	0.326	0.290	0.258	0.229	0.204
14	0.870	0.758	0.661	0.577	0.505	0.442	0.388	0.340	0.299	0.263	0.232	0.205	0.181
15	0.861	0.743	0.642	0.555	0.481	0.417	0.362	0.315	0.275	0.239	0.209	0.183	0.160
16	0.853	0.728	0.623	0.534	0.458	0.394	0.339	0.292	0.252	0.218	0.188	0.163	0.141
17	0.844	0.714	0.605	0.513	0.436	0.371	0.317	0.270	0.231	0.198	0.170	0.146	0.125
18	0.836	0.700	0.587	0.494	0.416	0.350	0.296	0.250	0.212	0.180	0.153	0.130	0.111
19	0.828	0.686	0.570	0.475	0.396	0.331	0.276	0.232	0.194	0.164	0.138	0.116	0.098
20	0.820	0.673	0.554	0.456	0.377	0.312	0.258	0.215	0.178	0.149	0.124	0.104	0.087
24	0.788	0.622	0.492	0.390	0.310	0.247	0.197	0.158	0.126	0.102	0.082	0.066	0.053
25	0.780	0.610	0.478	0.375	0.295	0.233	0.184	0.146	0.116	0.092	0.074	0.059	0.047
30	0.742	0.552	0.412	0.308	0.231	0.174	0.131	0.099	0.075	0.057	0.044	0.033	0.026
40	0.672	0.453	0.307	0.208	0.142	0.097	0.067	0.046	0.032	0.022	0.015	0.011	0.008
50	0.608	0.372	0.228	0.141	0.087	0.054	0.034	0.021	0.013	0.009	0.005	0.003	0.002
60	0.550	0.305	0.170	0.095	0.054	0.030	0.017	0.010	0.006	0.003	0.002	0.001	0.001

PERIOD, n	14%	15%	16%	17%	18%	19%	20%	24%	28%	32%	36%	40%
0	1.000	1.000	1.000	1.000	1.000	1.000	1.000	1.000	1.000	1.000	1.000	1.000
1	0.877	0.870	0.862	0.855	0.847	0.840	0.833	0.806	0.781	0.758	0.735	0.714
2	0.769	0.756	0.743	0.731	0.718	0.706	0.694	0.650	0.610	0.574	0.541	0.510
3	0.675	0.658	0.641	0.624	0.609	0.593	0.579	0.524	0.477	0.435	0.398	0.364
4	0.592	0.572	0.552	0.534	0.516	0.499	0.482	0.423	0.373	0.329	0.292	0.260
5	0.519	0.497	0.476	0.456	0.437	0.419	0.402	0.341	0.291	0.250	0.215	0.186
6	0.456	0.432	0.410	0.390	0.370	0.352	0.335	0.275	0.227	0.189	0.158	0.133
7	0.400	0.376	0.354	0.333	0.314	0.296	0.279	0.222	0.178	0.143	0.116	0.095
8	0.351	0.327	0.305	0.285	0.266	0.249	0.233	0.179	0.139	0.108	0.085	0.068
9	0.308	0.284	0.263	0.243	0.225	0.209	0.194	0.144	0.108	0.082	0.063	0.048
10	0.270	0.247	0.227	0.208	0.191	0.176	0.162	0.116	0.085	0.062	0.046	0.035
11	0.237	0.215	0.195	0.178	0.162	0.148	0.135	0.094	0.066	0.047	0.034	0.025
12	0.208	0.187	0.168	0.152	0.137	0.124	0.112	0.076	0.052	0.036	0.025	0.018
13	0.182	0.163	0.145	0.130	0.116	0.104	0.093	0.061	0.040	0.027	0.018	0.013
14	0.160	0.141	0.125	0.111	0.099	0.088	0.078	0.049	0.032	0.021	0.014	0.009
15	0.140	0.123	0.108	0.095	0.084	0.074	0.065	0.040	0.025	0.016	0.010	0.006
16	0.123	0.107	0.093	0.081	0.071	0.062	0.054	0.032	0.019	0.012	0.007	0.005
17	0.108	0.093	0.080	0.069	0.060	0.052	0.045	0.026	0.015	0.009	0.005	0.003
18	0.095	0.081	0.069	0.059	0.051	0.044	0.038	0.021	0.012	0.007	0.004	0.002
19	0.083	0.070	0.060	0.051	0.043	0.037	0.031	0.017	0.009	0.005	0.003	0.002
20	0.073	0.061	0.051	0.043	0.037	0.031	0.026	0.014	0.007	0.004	0.002	0.001
24	0.043	0.035	0.028	0.023	0.019	0.015	0.013	0.006	0.003	0.001	0.001	0.000
25	0.038	0.030	0.024	0.020	0.016	0.013	0.010	0.005	0.002	0.001	0.000	0.000
30	0.020	0.015	0.012	0.009	0.007	0.005	0.004	0.002	0.001	0.000	0.000	0.000
40	0.005	0.004	0.003	0.002	0.001	0.001	0.001	0.000	0.000	0.000	0.000	0.000
50	0.001	0.001	0.001	0.000	0.000	0.000	0.000	0.000	0.000	0.000	0.000	0.000
60	0.000	0.000	0.000	0.000	0.000	0.000	0.000	0.000	0.000	0.000	0.000	0.000

TABLE III Compound Sum of an Annuity Interest Factor
(CVIFA)
($1 per year at i% for n years)

$$\text{CVIFA} = \frac{(1+i)^n - 1}{i}$$

$$\text{CSAN} = R(\text{CVIFA}_{i,n})$$

PERIOD, n	1%	2%	3%	4%	5%	6%	7%	8%	9%	10%	11%	12%	13%
1	1.000	1.000	1.000	1.000	1.000	1.000	1.000	1.000	1.000	1.000	1.000	1.000	1.000
2	2.010	2.020	2.030	2.040	2.050	2.060	2.070	2.080	2.090	2.100	2.110	2.120	2.130
3	3.030	3.060	3.091	3.122	3.152	3.184	3.215	3.246	3.278	3.310	3.342	3.374	3.407
4	4.060	4.122	4.184	4.246	4.310	4.375	4.440	4.506	4.573	4.641	4.710	4.770	4.850
5	5.101	5.204	5.309	5.416	5.526	5.637	5.751	5.867	5.985	6.105	6.228	6.353	6.480
6	6.152	6.308	6.468	6.633	6.802	6.975	7.153	7.336	7.523	7.716	7.913	8.115	8.323
7	7.214	7.434	7.662	7.898	8.142	8.394	8.654	8.923	9.200	9.487	9.783	10.089	10.405
8	8.286	8.583	8.892	9.214	9.549	9.897	10.260	10.637	11.028	11.436	11.859	12.300	12.757
9	9.369	9.755	10.159	10.583	11.027	11.491	11.978	12.488	13.021	13.579	14.164	14.776	15.416
10	10.462	10.950	11.464	12.006	12.578	13.181	13.816	14.487	15.193	15.937	16.722	17.549	18.420
11	11.567	12.169	12.808	13.486	14.207	14.972	15.784	16.645	17.560	18.531	19.561	20.655	21.814
12	12.683	13.412	14.192	15.026	15.917	16.870	17.888	18.977	20.141	21.384	22.713	24.133	25.650
13	13.809	14.680	15.618	16.627	17.713	18.882	20.141	21.495	22.953	24.523	26.212	28.029	29.985
14	14.947	15.974	17.086	18.292	19.599	21.051	22.550	24.215	26.019	27.975	30.095	32.393	34.883
15	16.097	17.293	18.599	20.024	21.579	23.276	25.129	27.152	29.361	31.772	34.405	37.280	40.417
16	17.258	18.639	20.157	21.825	23.657	25.673	27.888	30.324	33.003	35.950	39.190	42.753	46.672
17	18.430	20.012	21.762	23.698	25.840	28.213	30.840	33.750	36.974	40.545	44.501	48.884	53.739
18	19.615	21.412	23.414	25.645	28.132	30.906	33.999	37.450	41.301	45.599	50.396	55.750	61.725
19	20.811	22.841	25.117	27.671	30.539	33.760	37.379	41.446	46.018	51.159	56.939	63.440	70.749
20	22.019	24.297	26.870	29.778	33.066	36.786	40.995	45.762	51.160	57.275	64.203	72.052	80.947
24	26.973	30.422	34.426	39.083	44.502	50.816	58.117	66.765	76.790	88.497	102.174	118.155	136.831
25	28.243	32.030	36.459	41.646	47.727	54.865	63.249	73.106	84.701	98.347	114.413	133.334	155.620
30	34.785	40.568	47.575	56.805	66.439	79.058	94.461	113.283	136.308	164.494	199.021	241.333	293.199
40	48.886	60.402	75.401	95.026	120.080	154.762	199.635	259.057	337.882	442.593	581.826	767.091	1,013.70
50	64.463	84.572	112.797	152.667	209.348	290.336	406.529	573.770	815.084	1,163.91	1,668.77	2,400.02	3,459.51
60	81.670	114.052	163.053	237.991	353.584	533.128	813.520	1,253.21	1,944.79	3,034.82	4,755.07	7,471.64	11,761.9

PERIOD, n	14%	15%	16%	17%	18%	19%	20%	24%	28%	32%	36%	40%
1	1.000	1.000	1.000	1.000	1.000	1.000	1.000	1.000	1.000	1.000	1.000	1.000
2	2.140	2.150	2.160	2.170	2.180	2.190	2.200	2.240	2.280	2.320	2.360	2.400
3	3.440	3.473	3.506	3.539	3.572	3.606	3.640	3.778	3.918	4.062	4.210	4.360
4	4.921	4.993	5.066	5.141	5.215	5.291	5.368	5.684	6.016	6.362	6.725	7.104
5	6.610	6.742	6.877	7.014	7.154	7.297	7.442	8.048	8.700	9.398	10.146	10.846
6	8.536	8.754	8.977	9.207	9.442	9.683	9.930	10.980	12.136	13.406	14.799	16.324
7	10.730	11.067	11.414	11.772	12.142	12.523	12.916	14.615	16.534	18.696	21.126	23.853
8	13.233	13.727	14.240	14.773	15.327	15.902	16.499	19.123	22.163	25.678	29.732	34.395
9	16.085	16.786	17.518	18.285	19.086	19.923	20.799	24.712	29.369	34.895	41.435	49.153
10	19.337	20.304	21.321	22.393	23.521	24.709	25.959	31.643	38.592	47.062	57.352	69.814
11	23.044	24.349	25.733	27.200	28.755	30.404	32.150	40.238	50.399	63.122	78.998	98.739
12	27.271	29.002	30.850	32.824	34.931	37.180	39.580	50.985	65.510	84.320	108.437	139.235
13	32.089	34.352	36.786	39.404	42.219	45.244	48.497	64.110	84.853	112.303	148.475	195.929
14	37.581	40.505	43.672	47.103	50.818	54.841	59.196	80.496	109.612	149.240	202.926	275.300
15	43.842	47.580	51.660	56.110	60.965	66.261	72.035	100.815	141.303	197.997	276.979	386.420
16	50.980	55.717	60.925	66.649	72.939	79.850	87.442	126.011	181.868	262.356	377.692	541.988
17	59.118	65.075	71.673	78.979	87.068	96.022	105.931	157.253	233.791	347.310	514.661	759.784
18	68.394	75.836	84.141	93.406	103.740	115.266	128.117	195.994	300.252	459.449	700.939	1,064.70
19	78.969	88.212	98.603	110.285	123.414	138.166	154.740	244.033	385.323	607.472	954.277	1,491.58
20	91.025	102.444	115.380	130.033	146.628	165.418	186.688	303.601	494.213	802.863	1,298.82	2,089.21
24	158.659	184.168	213.978	248.808	289.494	337.010	392.484	723.461	1,332.66	2,443.82	4,450.00	8,033.00
25	181.871	212.793	249.214	292.105	342.603	402.042	471.981	898.092	1,706.80	3,226.84	6,053.00	11,247.2
30	356.787	434.745	530.321	647.439	790.948	966.712	1,181.88	2640.92	5,873.23	12,940.9	28,172.3	60,501.1
40	1,342.03	1,779.09	2,360.76	3,134.52	4,163.21	5,529.83	7,343.86	22,728.8	69,377.5	207,874	609,890	*
50	4,994.52	7,217.72	10,435.6	15,089.5	21,813.1	31,515.3	45,497.2	195,373	819,103	*	*	*
60	18,535.1	29,220.0	46,057.5	72,555.0	114,190	179,495	281,733	*	*	*	*	*

*These interest factors exceed 1,000,000.

R–7

TABLE IV Present Value of an Annuity Interest Factor
(PVIFA)
($1 per year at i% for n years)

$$PVIFA = \frac{1 - \dfrac{1}{(1 + i)^n}}{i}$$

$$PVAN = R(PVIFA_{i,n})$$

Period, n	1%	2%	3%	4%	5%	6%	7%	8%	9%	10%	11%	12%	13%
1	0.990	0.980	0.971	0.962	0.952	0.943	0.935	0.926	0.917	0.909	0.901	0.893	0.885
2	1.970	1.942	1.913	1.886	1.859	1.833	1.808	1.783	1.759	1.736	1.713	1.690	1.668
3	2.941	2.884	2.829	2.775	2.723	2.673	2.624	2.577	2.531	2.487	2.444	2.402	2.361
4	3.902	3.808	3.717	3.630	3.546	3.465	3.387	3.312	3.240	3.170	3.102	3.037	2.974
5	4.853	4.713	4.580	4.452	4.329	4.212	4.100	3.993	3.890	3.791	3.696	3.605	3.517
6	5.795	5.601	5.417	5.242	5.076	4.917	4.766	4.623	4.486	4.355	4.231	4.111	3.998
7	6.728	6.472	6.230	6.002	5.786	5.582	5.389	5.206	5.033	4.868	4.712	4.564	4.423
8	7.652	7.325	7.020	6.733	6.463	6.210	5.971	5.747	5.535	5.335	5.146	4.968	4.799
9	8.566	8.162	7.786	7.435	7.108	6.802	6.515	6.247	5.995	5.759	5.537	5.328	5.132
10	9.471	8.983	8.530	8.111	7.722	7.360	7.024	6.710	6.418	6.145	5.889	5.650	5.426
11	10.368	9.787	9.253	8.760	8.306	7.887	7.499	7.139	6.805	6.495	6.207	5.938	5.687
12	11.255	10.575	9.954	9.385	8.863	8.384	7.943	7.536	7.161	6.814	6.492	6.194	5.918
13	12.134	11.348	10.635	9.986	9.394	8.853	8.358	7.904	7.487	7.103	6.750	6.424	6.122
14	13.004	12.106	11.296	10.563	9.899	9.295	8.745	8.244	7.786	7.367	6.982	6.628	6.302
15	13.865	12.849	11.938	11.118	10.380	9.712	9.108	8.559	8.060	7.606	7.191	6.811	6.462
16	14.718	13.578	12.561	11.652	10.838	10.106	9.447	8.851	8.312	7.824	7.379	6.974	6.604
17	15.562	14.292	13.166	12.166	11.274	10.477	9.763	9.122	8.544	8.022	7.549	7.120	6.729
18	16.398	14.992	13.754	12.659	11.690	10.828	10.059	9.372	8.756	8.201	7.702	7.250	6.840
19	17.226	15.678	14.324	13.134	12.085	11.158	10.336	9.604	8.950	8.365	7.839	7.366	6.938
20	18.046	16.351	14.877	13.590	12.462	11.470	10.594	9.818	9.128	8.514	7.963	7.469	7.025
24	21.243	18.914	16.936	15.247	13.799	12.550	11.469	10.529	9.707	8.985	8.348	7.784	7.283
25	22.023	19.523	17.413	15.622	14.094	12.783	11.654	10.675	9.823	9.077	8.422	7.843	7.330
30	25.808	22.397	19.600	17.292	15.373	13.765	12.409	11.258	10.274	9.427	8.694	8.055	7.496
40	32.835	27.355	23.115	19.793	17.159	15.046	13.332	11.925	10.757	9.779	8.951	8.244	7.634
50	39.196	31.424	25.730	21.482	18.256	15.762	13.801	12.233	10.962	9.915	9.042	8.304	7.675
60	44.955	34.761	27.676	22.623	18.929	16.161	14.039	12.377	11.048	9.967	9.074	8.324	7.687

PERIOD, n	14%	15%	16%	17%	18%	19%	20%	24%	28%	32%	36%	40%
1	0.877	0.870	0.862	0.855	0.847	0.840	0.833	0.806	0.781	0.758	0.735	0.714
2	1.647	1.626	1.605	1.585	1.566	1.547	1.528	1.457	1.392	1.332	1.276	1.224
3	2.322	2.283	2.246	2.210	2.174	2.140	2.106	1.981	1.868	1.766	1.674	1.589
4	2.914	2.855	2.798	2.743	2.690	2.639	2.589	2.404	2.241	2.096	1.966	1.849
5	3.433	3.352	3.274	3.199	3.127	3.058	2.991	2.745	2.532	2.345	2.181	2.035
6	3.889	3.784	3.685	3.589	3.498	3.410	3.326	3.020	2.759	2.534	2.399	2.168
7	4.288	4.160	4.039	3.922	3.812	3.706	3.605	3.242	2.937	2.678	2.455	2.263
8	4.639	4.487	4.344	4.207	4.078	3.954	3.837	3.421	3.076	2.786	2.540	2.331
9	4.946	4.772	4.607	4.451	4.303	4.163	4.031	3.566	3.184	2.868	2.603	2.379
10	5.216	5.019	4.833	4.659	4.494	4.339	4.193	3.682	3.269	2.930	2.650	2.414
11	5.453	5.234	5.029	4.836	4.656	4.486	4.327	3.776	3.335	2.978	2.683	2.438
12	5.660	5.421	5.197	4.988	4.793	4.611	4.439	3.851	3.387	3.013	2.708	2.456
13	5.842	5.583	5.342	5.118	4.910	4.715	4.533	3.912	3.427	3.040	2.727	2.469
14	6.002	5.724	5.468	5.229	5.008	4.802	4.611	3.962	3.459	3.061	2.740	2.478
15	6.142	5.847	5.575	5.324	5.092	4.876	4.675	4.001	3.483	3.076	2.750	2.484
16	6.265	5.954	5.669	5.405	5.162	4.938	4.730	4.033	3.503	3.088	2.758	2.489
17	5.373	6.047	5.749	5.475	5.222	4.990	4.775	4.059	3.518	3.097	2.763	2.492
18	6.467	6.128	5.818	5.534	5.273	5.033	4.812	4.080	3.529	3.104	2.767	2.494
19	6.550	6.198	5.877	5.584	5.316	5.070	4.844	4.097	3.539	3.109	2.770	2.496
20	6.623	6.259	5.929	5.628	5.353	5.101	4.870	4.110	3.546	3.113	2.772	2.497
24	6.835	6.434	6.073	5.746	5.451	5.182	4.937	4.143	3.562	3.121	2.776	2.499
25	6.873	6.464	6.097	5.766	5.467	5.195	4.948	4.147	3.564	3.122	2.776	2.499
30	7.003	6.566	6.177	5.829	5.517	5.235	4.979	4.160	3.569	3.124	2.778	2.500
40	7.105	6.642	6.233	5.871	5.548	5.258	4.997	4.166	3.571	3.125	2.778	2.500
50	7.133	6.661	6.246	5.880	5.554	5.262	4.999	4.167	3.571	3.125	2.778	2.500
60	7.140	6.665	6.249	5.882	5.555	5.263	5.000	4.167	3.571	3.125	2.778	2.500

TABLE V   Normal Distribution (Area of the Normal Distribution That is z Standard Deviations to the Left or Right of the Mean)

NUMBER OF STANDARD DEVIATIONS FROM MEAN (z)	AREA TO THE LEFT OR RIGHT (ONE TAIL)	NUMBER OF STANDARD DEVIATIONS FROM MEAN (z)	AREA TO THE LEFT OR RIGHT (ONE TAIL)
0.00	0.5000	1.55	0.0606
0.05	0.4801	1.60	0.0548
0.10	0.4602	1.65	0.0495
0.15	0.4404	1.70	0.0446
0.20	0.4207	1.75	0.0401
0.25	0.4013	1.80	0.0359
0.30	0.3821	1.85	0.0322
0.35	0.3632	1.90	0.0287
0.40	0.3446	1.95	0.0256
0.45	0.3264	2.00	0.0228
0.50	0.3085	2.05	0.0202
0.55	0.2912	2.10	0.0179
0.60	0.2743	2.15	0.0158
0.65	0.2578	2.20	0.0139
0.70	0.2420	2.25	0.0122
0.75	0.2264	2.30	0.0107
0.80	0.2119	2.35	0.0094
0.85	0.1977	2.40	0.0082
0.90	0.1841	2.45	0.0071
0.95	0.1711	2.50	0.0062
1.00	0.1587	2.55	0.0054
1.05	0.1469	2.60	0.0047
1.10	0.1357	2.65	0.0040
1.15	0.1251	2.70	0.0035
1.20	0.1151	2.75	0.0030
1.25	0.1056	2.80	0.0026
1.30	0.0968	2.85	0.0022
1.35	0.0885	2.90	0.0019
1.40	0.0808	2.95	0.0016
1.45	0.0735	3.00	0.0013
1.50	0.0668	3.05	0.0011
		3.10	0.0010
		3.25	0.0006
		3.50	0.00023
		4.00	0.00003
		4.99	0.0000003

INDEX TO GLOSSARY TERMS*

*The number in parentheses indicates the chapter or appendix in which the term is discussed.

SUBJECT INDEX

CHECK ANSWERS TO SELECTED PROBLEMS

Chapter 2
1. 14.7%
3a. −20%

Chapter 2, Appendix A
1. $1,063,450

Chapter 3
1a. $1,191
3. 13%
4a. 14.4 years
6a. $438.60
8. 20%
11a. $1,422.52
12. $4,993.35
14. $10,906.82
17a. $28,372
19. $1,333
21. P.V. of annuity = $45,540
23. $19,440
24. $658,198
26. $3,120
28a. $23,932

Chapter 3, Appendix A
1. $192,736.80

Chapter 4
1b. $800
3a. $1,069
4. 11%
8a. $22.22
9a. $44.17
11. $7.11
13. $45.88
16. $5.40
17. $964

Chapter 5
1a. Stock x: $\hat{R}$ = 15%
1b. Stock x: σ = 11.62%
2. 15.87% chance of returns > 33%
4a. $39.75
5a. 10.4%
6a. $\hat{R}$ = 0.082
σ_p = 0.0487
9a. 1.4
10a. $11.11
14a. W_A = 61.54%
15. $\hat{R}_p$ = 14.93%
σ_p = 2.07%

Chapter 6
1a. $194,444
2a. Firm A: TA turnover = 1.33x
NPM = .15
EM = 1.5x
ROE = .30
3a. 15%
10. Cash = $222,000
12b. Current ratio = 2.2x
Quick ratio = 1.4x
13. $3,000,000
15. Old return on equity = 12.5%
New return on equity = 14.3%

Chapter 7
1. New EPS = $2.70
4a. 5.0
7ai. 5000 copies
10bi. DOL = 1.875
10bii. DFL = 1.67
10biii. DCL = 3.13
11a. $3,000,000
14a. DOL = 10.67
14b. DFL = 1.765

Chapter 8
1a. $1,000,000
3. $500,000
6. Loans needed in February—
135,500
8. $85 million

Chapter 9
1a. Year 1 depreciation = $2,850
2. Total tax owed = $14,060
4. 1984 depreciation = $20,000
6. $1533
9. NCF_1 = $188,400
NCF_6 = $120,000
10. $340,500
14. NCF_1 = $4,194

Chapter 10
1b. NPV = $455
2. 11.6%
4. $235 per acre
7. $16,077
9. 8%
11. NPV = $5,431
13a. NPV = $24,266

Chapter 10, Appendix A
1a. NPV_A = $1,888.50
NPV_B = $2,292

Chapter 11
1b. $125
1c. $43.30
3a. 5.48%
7a. $629,500
8a. $55,141
9b. $−0.179 million
11a. $255,250

Chapter 12
2. 6.6%
4b. 13%
5a. 12.9%
8a. 14.5%
9. 17.3%
12. First break point at $33.33 million. Marginal cost of capital in first block = 13.1%

Chapter 13
1a. $15 million
3a. $2.4 million
6a. 45% debt + 55% equity
7a. $170,000

Chapter 14
1b. 50¢
3. 16.7%
4. $1,425,000
7b. $0.80

Chapter 15
1a. $1,558,118
4a. $1,944,745
6. 9%
7a. $25,083
9a. 6.24%
10a. $136,008
10b. $114,404
14. $38,415
15. Year 1 = $3.6 million

Chapter 16
1b. 2.1%
2c. $673.75
3. 13.88% or 14%
4b. 14.3%

5b. $21.4 million
8a. Common stock = 96.8%
Preferred stock = 52.1%
10. Total assets = $168 million

Chapter 16, Appendix A
1. $7,813,895
3a. $0.45 for both cases

Chapter 17
1a. $800
1b. $726
2a. 9.78 shares
4a. $1.50
4b. $4.50
5c. No additional funds
6c. $131.25 million
8a. $1,950

Chapter 18
1. Aggressive = 12.13%
3ai. Aggressive = 12.29%
4aiii. Aggressive = 1.25
5ai. Aggressive = 9.54%
7b. $7.79 million
10a. $886,667

Chapter 19
1a. $7,500,000
3bi. $1,050,000

4d. −$25,000
6. $351,250
7c. $92,500
9a. $10,617.10

Chapter 19, Appendix A
1a. $200,000
2a. $5,241

Chapter 20
1b. 38 days
3. Net change in pre-tax profits = $7,000
5. Net change in pre-tax profits = $20,000
7c. $−5,250
9. $122,417
11. $23,889

Chapter 21
1a. 80,000
3. Total cost at 2000 = $2,568.75
4. $1911.25
6a. 17,678 and 10,607
8a. 30,000
10a. Q* = 5500

Chapter 22
1b. $240,000
2a. 14,69%

4a. 8.88%
5a. 14.71%
7. Dealer A cost = 10.36%
8a. $16,000,000
8c. 27.0%
10c. 17.1%
12c. 20.4%

Chapter 23
1b. 15.4%
2a. $4,045
2d. $4,258
3a. 0.50 shares Grinnell for each Natrium share

Chapter 24
1a. Settlement percentage for general and unsecured creditors = 40%

Chapter 25
1. $5,670
2a. $32.36
4a. +62.9%
5a. Net gain = $62,500
6a. $18 million U.S. dollars
8b. Power Plant:
NPV @ 5% = $93.99 million
NPV @ 12% = $34.08 million

The Texas Instruments
Professional Business Analyst (BA-55) Rebate

In order to receive a rebate of $5.00 on the purchase of a Texas Instruments Professional Business Analyst (BA-55) calculator, complete the form below and follow the instructions for eligibility. The use of this calculator is illustrated throughout the text. (Note: Clip this coupon from your book since Texas Instruments will not accept copies of this form.)

THE PROFESSIONAL BUSINESS ANALYST REBATE

(Complete the following)

Name _____

Address _____

City _____ State _____ Zip _____

Date of purchase _____

Telephone (_____) _____

Store where purchased _____

Serial number on back of calculator _____

University attended _____

(See reverse side for rebate terms)

THE TEXAS INSTRUMENTS PROFESSIONAL BUSINESS ANALYST
REBATE OFFER GOOD THROUGH DECEMBER 30, 1986

To Be Eligible For Rebate You Must:

A. Fill out the reverse side COMPLETELY.

B. Fill out CUSTOMER REGISTRATION CARD COMPLETELY and MAIL IT WITH THIS REBATE FORM.

C. Cut out the bar code from the lower right hand corner of the back of the box and MAIL IT WITH THIS REBATE FORM.

D. Mail ORIGINAL sales receipt (no copies will be accepted) with this rebate form. Sales slip will NOT be returned, so save a copy for your future needs.

E. Mail REBATE FORM, CUSTOMER REGISTRATION CARD, PROOF OF PURCHASE, and ORIGINAL SALES RECEIPT to:
TI Professional Business Analyst Rebate
P.O. Box 10559
Lubbock, Texas 79408
Postmark must be no later than January 31, 1987.

F. This $5 rebate offer applies only to TI Professional Business Analyst calculator purchases made in the U.S. between Jan. 1, 1984 and Dec. 30, 1986.

G. This $5 rebate is exclusive and replaces any other TI rebate on the BA-55.

H. Retail customers only.

I. During the period of this rebate offer only, any defective calculators must be returned to a Texas Instruments Exchange/Service Center, or to the Lubbock address specified in your owner's manual.

Over-the-counter returns to your retailer can be made only if you have not applied for the rebate listed above.

J. Offer void where prohibited by law.

K. Allow 6–8 weeks for rebate to arrive.

L. If you purchase more than one calculator you must submit s separate rebate form (and other documentation) for each calculator purchased.

†